Annotated Bibliography:

World's Columbian Exposition, Chicago 1893

SUPPLEMENT

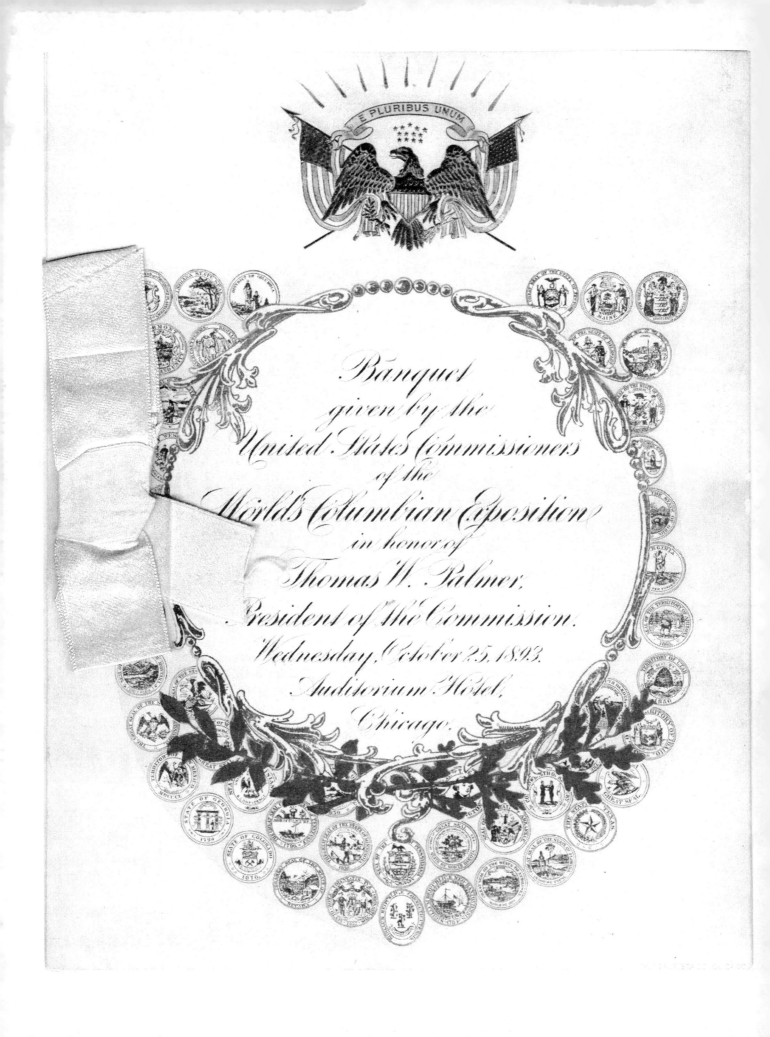

E PLURIBUS UNUM

Banquet
given by the
United States Commissioners
of the
World's Columbian Exposition
in honor of
Thomas W. Palmer,
President of the Commission.
Wednesday, October 25, 1893.
Auditorium Hotel,
Chicago.

Annotated Bibliography:

World's Columbian Exposition, Chicago 1893

SUPPLEMENT

WITH:

440 ILLUSTRATIONS AND PRICE GUIDE

MASTER INDEX FOR BOTH VOLUMES INCLUDING SUBJECTS

MASTER SOURCE LIST WITH 140 NEW ENTRIES

OVER 3500 NEW CITATIONS AND ANNOTATIONS

by

G. L. Dybwad, Ph.D.

Joy V. Bliss, M.D., J.D.

Edition Limited to 500 copies: #*174*

The Book Stops Here
Albuquerque, New Mexico
1999

Other books by Dybwad and Bliss:

Annotated Bibliography: World's Columbian Exposition, Chicago 1893
James A. Michener, The Beginning Teacher and His Textbooks
Chicago Day at the World's Columbian Exposition: Illustrated With Candid Photographs

Dybwad, G. L., and Joy V. Bliss
*Annotated Bibliography: World's Columbian Exposition, Chicago 1893. SUPPLEMENT. With Illustrations and
Price Guide*

Includes index.
1. World's Columbian Exposition, 1893.

ISBN 0-9631612-4-5 (Paper).
Library of Congress Catalog Card Number: 99-72573.

Front cover illustration: Photograph used by the Ferris Wheel Company, 1893, on a 16½x11 advertising card.

Frontispiece illustration: *Banquet given by the United States Commissioners of the World's Columbian Exposition in
honor of Thomas W. Palmer, President of the Commission.* Front cover of citation #54.1.

Back cover illustrations: Three of the 50 Chase & Sanborn Coffee Company coasters issued for the Fair, citation
#787.11.

Citation illustrations: 1200 dpi scanned laser half-tones.

Pre-press by Southwest Electronic Pre-press Services, Inc., Albuquerque, New Mexico

Printing by Network Printers, Milwaukee, Wisconsin

TABLE OF CONTENTS

SUPPLEMENT EXPLANATIONS

COMMENTS

This *Supplement* to our 1992 *Annotated Bibliography: World's Columbian Exposition, Chicago 1893*, includes new Columbian Exposition material and sources, completes unfinished citations, and corrects errors.

The sixteen subject chapters are the same as those in the original *Annotated Bibliography*. With a few exceptions, this *Supplement* contains publications with four or more pages. Thus, the vast variety of single cards, sheet ads, flyers, invitations, and official letters from the Fair have been omitted. Consult the first page of the index for guidance on material printed at head of title, definite articles, and alphabetization.

The Index in this volume is a complete Master Index. Use it to locate all citations in both volumes. If a listing is an integer, consult both volumes for the complete citation; if a listing has a decimal extension, the *Supplement* volume alone has the complete citation. That is, citation numbers assigned to entries in the original book are purposely retained. In alphabetical order, new citations are entered in one tenth (0.1) increments. For reference, the citation format is reproduced on page x. However, the format for Chapter 15, Unpublished Unique Works, has been simplified by dropping the alphabetic notation and identifying an item by citation number plus source abbreviation, for example, Winterthur Museum's miscellaneous collection was "2446. ar. WM" and becomes "2446.WM" in this supplement.

We are particularly pleased with the large expansion of Chapter 14, "Recent Books." These numerous publications demonstrate that the Fair has had a continuing impact and interest for over one hundred years. The Columbian Exposition was an international historical event in its own right and continues to be worthy of teaching us new lessons. We are also happy with the vast increase in the size of Chapter 5, "General." Included here are many more company advertising items, such as railroad, hotel, excursion trips, and commercial exhibitors. The new citations in Chapter 3, "Federal Publications," are numerous too. They are important since they define the legal and administrative activities at the Fair. In Chapters 2 and 4, "Exposition Publications" and "Foreign Country Publications," we have included a number of invitations to ceremonies and dinners to give a flavor of the gala events which took place behind the scenes of the Fair.

The additional material is from newly visited libraries, written requests from new library sources, and purchases. Generally, the original sources from 1992 were not updated for their new acquisitions. The complete list of source locators for both the *Bibliography* and *Supplement* are given below.

COMPLETE LIST OF SOURCE ABBREVIATIONS

*A	Amato, Dan, Columbus Museum, Columbus, WI		*Berk	Berkeley Public Library, Berkeley, CA
AA	Australian Archives, Dickson, Australia		bgsu	Bowling Green State U, Bowling Green, OH
AIC	The Art Institute of Chicago		BM	British Museum, London
AKLRL	Alaska Legislative Reference Library, Juneau		*BMF	Biblioteca Marucelliana, Florence, Italy
AkSt	Alaska State Library, Juneau		*BNCF	Biblioteca Nazionale Centrale, Florence, Italy
ALB	State U of New York - Albany		BNCR	Biblioteca Nazionale Centrale, Rome, Italy
*Amh	Amherst College Library, Amherst, MA		*BPL	Boston Public Library, Boston, MA
ANQ	Assemblée Nationale, Québec, PQ		BRA	Bibliotheque Royale Albert Ier, Brussels, Belgium
*APL	Austin Public Library, Austin, TX		*BrU	Bradley University, Peoria, IL
ArkHx	Arkansas Historical Society		*BU	Boston University, Boston, MA
ASL	Archives of the State of Illinois, Springfield			
AzHx	Arizona Historical Society, Phoenix and Tucson		cat	Auction or sales catalog
			CC	Colby College, Waterville, ME
B	Beck, Paul, private collection, IN		CCA	Centre Canadien d'Architecture, Montreal, Canada
BBM	Buffalo Bill Museum, Golden, CO		*CHx	Chicago Historical Society Library
*BC	Beloit College, Beloit, WI		*CLM	Camden Public Library, Camden, ME
*BCHx	Bucks County Historical Society, Doylestown, PA		CLP	Carnegie Library of Pittsburgh, PA
*BCM	Bowdoin College, Brunswick, ME		Col	Columbia U, New York City
*BCPL	Bucks County Public Library, Doylestown, PA		CoU	Colorado U, Boulder
BD	Brian Day, private collection, MI		*CPL	Chicago Public Library

CSA	California State Archives, Sacramento
CSL	Connecticut State Library, Hartford
*csuf	California State U - Fresno
CtHx	Connecticut Historical Society, Hartford
*CU	Cornell U, Ithaca, NY
*CUA	Catholic U of America, Washington, DC
CUE	Cambridge U Library, Cambridge, England
cul	Clemson U Libraries, Clemson, SC
CVHx	Carson Valley Historical Society, Minden, NV
CWM	College of William & Mary, Williamsburg, VA
*D	Drachler, Carole, private collection, AZ
DAR	Daughters of American Rev Archives, Washington, DC
*DC	Dartmouth College, Hanover, NH
DelHx	Historical Society of Delaware, Wilmington
DU	Duke U, Durham, NC
*E	Emple, Jim, private collection, ME
ENM	Elisabet Ney Museum, Austin, TX
EPL	Enoch Pratt Free Library, Baltimore, MD
*ESU	Emporia State U, Emporia, KS
*EvP	Evanston Public Library, Evanston, IL
*F	Frank, Russ, private collection, NC
*Fess	Fess, Art and Linda, private collection, IL
FLP	Free Library of Philadelphia, Philadelphia, PA
*FM	Field Museum, Chicago
*FPL	Forbes Public Library, Northampton, MA
FSA	Florida State Archives, Tallahassee
FU	Fordham U, Bronx, NY
*GBP	Gail Borden Public Library, Elgin, IL
GDF	Grace Dangberg Foundation, Inc., Carson City, NV
*GLD	Gay Leon Dybwad, private collection, NM
*GMU	George Mason U, Washington, DC
*GPL	Galesburg Public Library, Galesburg, IL
*GU	Georgetown U, Washington, DC
*H	Harris, L. John, private collection, MN
*Heb	Hebrew University, Jerusalem, Israel
*HL	The Huntington Library, San Marino, CA
*HML	Hagley Museum and Library, Wilmington, DE
HNO	The Historic New Orleans Collection, New Orleans, LA
*HPL	Hartford Public Library, Hartford, CT
*HU	Harvard U, Cambridge, MA
*HxDC	The Historical Society of Washington, DC
*IaHx	State Historical Society of Iowa, Des Moines/Iowa City
IBN	Instituto da Biblioteca Nacional, Lisbon, Portugal
*ICRL	(Illinois) Center for Research Libraries, Chicago
IdHx	Idaho State Historical Society, Boise
*IHi	Illinois State Library, Springfield
InHx	Indiana Historical Society, Indianapolis
*IStU	Illinois State U, Normal
ISU	Indiana State U, Terre Haute
*IWU	Illinois Wesleyan U, Bloomington
JHU	Johns Hopkins U, Baltimore, MD
KBS	Kungliza Biblioteket, Stockholm, Sweden
*KCPL	Kansas City Public Library (Main), Kansas City, MO
KNM	Knihovna Národní Muzeum, Prague, Czechoslovakia
*Knox	Knox College Library, Galesburg, IL
KS	Kenneth B. Srail, private collection, IN
KsHx	Kansas Historical Society, Topeka
*KSU	Kansas State U, Manhattan
*KU	Kansas U Libraries, Lawrence
KyU	U of Kentucky
L	L'Heureux, Richard, private collection, ME

*LACL	Los Angeles County Library System, Los Angeles, CA
LaMus	State of Louisiana Office of State Museum, New Orleans
*LBA	Library of the Boston Athenæum, Boston, MA
*LC	Library of Congress
*LHL	Linda Hall Library, Kansas City, MO
*LL	Lincoln Library, Springfield, IL
llpl	Libertyville and Lake County Public Library, IL
LM	Lightner Museum, St. Augustine, FL
LMi	Library of Michigan, Lansing
*LPL	Leeds Public Library, Leeds, ND
LSU	Louisiana State U, Baton Rouge
*LU	Lehigh U, Bethlehem, PA
MA	Mellette Association, Watertown, SD
MaHx	Massachusetts Historical Society, Boston
*MarL	Marshall Law School, Chicago
mcg	McGill U, McLennan Library, Montreal, PQ.
*MCHx	McLean County Historical Society, Bloomington, IL
Merc	Mercantile Library, St. Louis, MO
MH	Mount Holyoke, Mt. Holyoke, MA
*MIT	Massachusetts Institute of Technology, Boston
*MnSA	Minnesota State Archives, St. Paul
MnStL	Minnesota State Law Library, St. Paul
*MOHx	State Historical Society of Missouri, Columbia
MPA	Manitoba Provincial Archives, Winnipeg, MB
MPL	Milwaukee Public Library, Milwaukee, WI
MsA	Mississippi Department of Archives and History, Jackson
*MSI	Museum of Science and Industry, Chicago
MSL	Massachusetts State Library, Boston
MSU	Montana State U, Boseman
*MU	Marquette U, Milwaukee, WI
*NA	National Archives, Washington, DC
NAC	National Archives of Canada, Ottawa, ON
*NAG	Nelson Art Gallery Library, Kansas City, MO
*NAL	U.S. National Agriculture Library, Washington, DC and Beltsville, MD
ncsu	North Carolina State U, Raleigh
NDU	Notre Dame U, Notre Dame, IN
NeHx	Nebraska State Historical Society, Lincoln
NHHx	New Hampshire Historical Society, Concord
NHL	Nahum H. Lewis, private collection, NY
NHSt	New Hampshire State Library, Concord
NJHx	New Jersey Historical Society, Newark
NJSt	New Jersey Dept. of Education, State Library, Trenton
*NL	Newberry Library, Chicago
NLA	National Library of Australia (Canberra libraries), Canberra, ACT
NLC	National Library of Canada, Ottawa, ON
NLI	National Library of Ireland, Dublin
nmsu	New Mexico State U, Las Cruces
*NPG	National Portrait Gallery and National Museum of American Art, Washington, DC (Branches of the Smithsonian Institute)
NSW	State Library of New South Wales, Sydney, NSW, Australia
*NUL	Norwich University Library, Northfield, VT
NvSt	Nevada State Library and Archives, Carson City
nwu	Northwestern U, Evanston, IL
*NYPL	New York City Public Library
NYSt	New York State Library, Albany
OC	Oberlin College, Oberlin, OH
*ODL	Oklahoma Department of Libraries, Oklahoma City
OhHx	Ohio Historical Society, Columbus
*OHxS	Oklahoma Historical Society, Oklahoma City
ONB	Österreichische Nationalbibliothek, Vienna, Austria
OrHx	Oregon Historical Society, Portland
OSL	Oregon State Library, Salem
OSU	Ohio State U, Columbus
*OTM	Oklahoma Territorial Museum, Guthrie
*OU	U of Oklahoma, Norman

PI	Pratt Institute, Brooklyn, NY
*PPL	Peoria Public Library, Peoria, IL
PSU	Pennsylvania State U, University Park
PU	Princeton U, Princeton, NJ
R	Raymond, Al, Raymond's Antiques, NY
*RCHx	Rock County Historical Society, Janesville, WI
ref	Shop copy, sale copy, one item fixed price source
RILaw	Rhode Island State Law Library, Providence
RML	Rand, McNally Library, Skokie, IL
RPB	Brown U, Providence, RI
*RPL	Rockford Public Library, Rockford, IL
RRD	R.R. Donnelley & Sons Co., Chicago
RSA	Royal Society of Arts, London, England
*RU	Roosevelt U, Chicago
*S	Sheppard, Dr. Stephen, private collection, NY
*SAL	Spencer Art Reference Library, Nelson-Atkins Art Gallery, Kansas City, MO
SamL	Samford U Law Library, Birmingham, AL
*sapl	San Antonio Public Library, San Antonio, TX
SCAG	South Carolina Attorney General's Office Library, Clinton
SCSt	South Carolina State Library, Columbia
*SDHx	San Diego Historical Society, San Diego, CA
SDSHx	South Dakota State Historical Society, Pierre
*SFe	New Mexico State Records Center & Archives, Santa Fe
*sfpl	San Francisco Public Library, San Francisco, CA
*sfsu	San Francisco State University, San Francisco, CA
*SHB	Swarthmore/Haverford/Bryn Mawr: Tri-Col. Lib., PA
*SHM	Spanish History Museum, Albuquerque, NM
*SI	Smithsonian Institution - American History Library
slcl	St. Louis County Library, St. Louis, MO
SLP	State Library of Pennsylvania, Harrisburg
slpl	St. Louis Public Library, St. Louis, MO
slu	St. Louis University, St. Louis, MO
*SML	Science Museum Library, London, England
*Smth	Smith College, Northampton, MA
SMU	Southern Methodist U, Dallas, TX
SPL	Seattle Public Library, Seattle, WA
SSLa	State of Louisiana, Secretary of State, Baton Rouge
SStu	U of Illinois at Springfield [formerly Sangamon State U]
*Stfd	Stanford University, Stanford, CA
StLa	State Library of Louisiana, Baton Rouge
SU	Syracuse U, Syracuse, NY
SUL	Syracuse U College of Law, Syracuse, NY
SZB	Staatsbibliothek zu Berlin, Germany
*TD	Thomas J. Diddle, private collection, FL
TnSt	Tennessee State Library & Archives, Nashville
TU	Tulane U, New Orleans, LA
*U	Lloyd Unger, private collection, NV
*UAB	U of Alabama, Birmingham
*UAH	U of Alabama, Huntsville
UAT	U of Alabama, Tuscaloosa
*UBO	Universitetsbiblioteket i Oslo, Norway
UBW	Universitätsbibliothek Wien, Austria
UC	National Union Catalog
*UCB	U of California, Berkeley
UCD	U of California, Davis
*UCI	U of California, Irvine
*UCLA	U of California, Los Angeles
UDe	U of Delaware, Newark
UdM	Université de Montréal, Montréal, Québec; (Bibliotèque des lettres et sciences humaines)
UFl	U of Florida, Gainsville
UGa	U of Georgia, Athens
UH	U of Houston, Houston, TX
UI	U of Idaho, Moscow
*UIC	U of Illinois–Chicago

*ULC	Union League Club, Chicago
uiuc	U of Illinois–Urbana Champaign
*UMA	U of Massachusetts, Amherst
*UMC	U of Missouri–Columbia
*UMD	U of Maryland, College Park
UMe	U of Maine, Orono
UMi	U of Michigan, Ann Arbor
*UMKC	U of Missouri–Kansas City
*UMN	U of Minnesota, Minneapolis
UMSL	U of Missouri–St. Louis
UNC	U of North Carolina at Chapel Hill
*UND	U of North Dakota, Chester Fritz Library, Grand Forks
UNe	U of Nebraska, Lincoln
*UNLV	U of Nevada–Las Vegas
*UNM	U of New Mexico Libraries, Albuquerque
UNO	U of New Orleans, New Orleans, LA
UNR	U of Nevada–Reno
UoA	U of Arkansas, Fayetteville
*UoC	U of Chicago, Chicago
uofs	U of the Orange Free State, Bloemfontein, S. Africa
UOL	U of Oklahoma Law Library, Norman
*UPa	U of Pennsylvania, Philadelphia
UR	U of Rochester, Rochester, NY
URI	U of Rhode Island, Kingston
USD	U of South Dakota, Vermillion
*USF	U of South Florida, Tampa
*USFr	U of San Francisco, San Francisco, CA
*UTA	U of Texas at Austin
UTn	U of Tennessee, Knoxville
UVa	U of Virginia, Charlottesville
*UVM	U of Vermont, Burlington
UWa	U of Washington, Seattle
*UWM	U of Wisconsin, Milwaukee
UWy	U of Wyoming, Laramie
VaHx	Virginia Historical Society, Richmond
*VAM	National Art Library, Victoria & Albert Museum, London
VCU	Virginia Commonwealth U, Richmond
*VSA	Vermont State Archives, Montpelier
VT	Virginia Polytechnic Institute and State U, Blacksburg
*VtHx	Vermont Historical Society, Montpelier
*VtSSt	Vermont Secretary of State (VT State Library), Montpelier
WaSt	Washington State Library, Olympia
*whmc	Western History Manuscript Collection, Columbia, MO
WiHx	The State Historical Society of Wisconsin, Madison
*WM	Winterthur Museum Library, Winterthur, DE
*WML	Francis E. Willard Library, W.C.T.U. Headquarters, Evanston, IL
wslb	Wiener Stadt- und Landesbibliothek, Vienna, Austria
wsu	Wayne State U, Detroit, MI
wusl	Washington U - St. Louis, St. Louis, MO
WYLaw	Wyoming State Law Library, Cheyenne
WYMus	Wyoming State Museum, Cheyenne
Yale	Yale U, New Haven, CT
*	WCE Maine Building, Poland Spring, ME

* = Personal Visits

SOURCE ABBREVIATIONS
(Arranged alphabetically by State and Foreign Country)

STATES:

Alabama: SamL, UAB, UAH, UAT
Alaska: AKLRL, AkSt
Arizona: AzHx, D
Arkansas: ArkHx, UoA
California: Berk, CSA, csuf, HL, LACL, SDHx, sfpl, sfsu, Stfd, UCB, UCD, UCI, UCLA, USFr
Colorado: BBM, CoU
Connecticut: CSL, CtHx, HPL, Yale
Delaware: DelHx, HML, UDe, WM
District of Columbia: CUA, DAR, GMU, GU, HxDC, LC, NA, NAL, NPG, SI
Florida: FSA, LM, TD, UFl, USF
Georgia: UGa
Idaho: IdHx, UI
Illinois: AIC, ASL, BrU, CHx, CPL, EvP, Fess, FM, GBP, GPL, ICRL, IHi, IStU, IWU, Knox, LL, llpl, MarL, MCHx, MSI, NL, nwu, PPL, RML, RPL, RRD, RU, SStu, UIC, ULC, uiuc, UoC, WML
Indiana: B, InHx, ISU, KS, NDU
Iowa: IaHx
Kansas: ESU, KsHx, KSU, KU
Kentucky: KyU
Louisiana: HNO, LaMus, LSU, SSLa, StLa, TU, UNO
Maine: BCM, CC, CLM, E, L, UMe
Maryland: EPL, JHU, UMD
Massachusetts: Amh, BPL, BU, FPL, HU, LBA, MaHx, MH, MIT, MSL, Smth, UMA
Michigan: BD, LMi, Umi, wsu
Minnesota: H, MnSA, MnStL, UMN
Mississippi: MsA
Missouri: KCPL, LHL, Merc, MOHx, NAG, SAL, slcl, slpl, slu, UMC, UMKC, UMSL, whmc, wusl
Montana: MSU

Nebraska: NeHx, UNe
Nevada: CVHx, GDF, NvSt, U, UNLV, UNR
New Hampshire: DC, NHHx, NHSt
New Jersey: NJHx, NJSt, PU
New Mexico: GLD, nmsu, SFe, SHM, UNM
New York: ALB, Col, CU, FU, NHL, NYPL, NYSt, PI, R, S, SU, SUL, UR
North Carolina: DU, F, ncsu, UNC
North Dakota: LPL, UND
Ohio: bgsu, OC, OhHx, OSU
Oklahoma: ODL, OHxS, OTM, OU, UOL
Oregon: OrHx, OSL
Pennsylvania: BCHx, BCPL, CLP, FLP, LU, PSU, SHB, SLP, UPa
Rhode Island: RILaw, RPB, URI
South Carolina: cul, SCAG, SCSt
South Dakota: MA, SDSHx, USD
Tennessee: TnS, UTn
Texas: APL, ENM, sapl, SMU, UH, UTA
Vermont: NUL, UVM, VSA, VtHx, VtSSt
Virginia: CWM, UVa, VaHx, VCU, VT
Washington: SPL, UWa, WaSt
Wisconsin: A, BC, MPL, MU, RCHx, UWM, WiHx
Wyoming: UWy, WYLaw, WYMus

FOREIGN COUNTRIES:

Africa: uofs
Australia: AA, NLA, NSW
Austria: ONB, UBW, wslb
Belgium: BRA
Canada: ANQ, CCA, mcg, MPA, NAC, NLC, UdM
Czechoslovakia: KNM
England: BM, CUE, RSA, SML, VAM
Germany: SZB
Ireland: NLI
Israel: Heb
Italy: BMF, BNCF, BNCR
Norway: UBO
Portugal: IBN
Sweden: KBS

COMBINED ABBREVIATION KEY AND CONVENTIONS

Generic Citation Example

#. Primary Author. Secondary Author. Tertiary Author. *Title*. Place of Publication: Publisher (Printer), Date of Publication, © Date by whom; Another Place of Publication: Publisher, Date of Publication © Date.

Size. Paging. Cover description. Further annotation. [Short notes about author or entry which are not found in the text.]
---- Also found: (found variant)
---- Also listed: (listed variant)
   * P   . (sources) $ Price range

☞ Notes about the author or entry that are not in the text of the entry, but are related.

Explanation of the above chart:

Citation *#*. Unique to the item; used in the index and for cross-reference.

Author. Multiple authors are listed in descending order. Titles and degrees, such as Rev., Capt., D.D., are omitted. Author names which appear in brackets are not found on the title page. These authors were obtained from Library of Congress copyright information or elsewhere in the item.

Title. The title page title is always used unless otherwise noted. If the cover title is used, the notation is "C.t." When the wording of the cover title is the same as the title page, this is noted "C.t. = t.p." Capitalization may vary. If the cover title is used but it is not certain whether there is a title page (e.g., missing), the notation is "title given is from cover." When the item has neither cover title nor title page, the title found above the text on the first page is used and the notation is "caption title."

Capitals are used when the book title has the word's first letter capitalized, the word follows a period, or the noun is known to be capitalized, e.g., "New Mexico." Lower-case is used everywhere else even though the printed title uses capital letters for entire words. "World's" and "Columbian" are always capitalized; "exposition" is capitalized when capitalized in the title used. A colon preceded and followed by a space denotes a line break; not all line breaks are shown.

Publication information. Location(s): publisher(s), and date(s) follow the title. Brackets denote the information is not on the title page. "Company" is consistently abbreviated in the publication data.

Size. In centimeters, height followed by width. Both are given when known. Expect ½ centimeter variations.

Pagination. Includes Roman numerals, unpaged pages, leaves, and Arabic paging.

Cover description. Given when known. Expect color variations due to aging.

Annotation. Content annotation is brief since the combination of the chapter heading and full title generally give an excellent idea of the content and intent of the item. Short annotation not found in the item is placed in brackets.

---- Also found: denotes a variant seen and verified.

---- Also listed: is a variant card catalog or source listing of the item. When the source information differs significantly from verified information, a "?" is appended.

The last line is reserved for * (importance symbol), source locations, and price range;. A ☺ means we give the title and publication information our highest accuracy rating. A period (.) following a source list means we have a copy of the title page (or cover) in our files. The number of sources listed is a rough measure of the availability of the item. P (picture) means the item is illustrated.

☞ Annotation which is not found in the citation but related to it.

ABBREVIATION KEY

b/w	Black and white
bldg	Building
BLM	The Board of Lady Managers
ca	Circa, about
chap	Chapter
CIHM	Canadian Institute for Historical Microreproductions, Ottawa, Canada.
co	Company
c.t.	Cover title
c.t. = t.p.	Cover title same as that given on title page
chromolith	Color lithograph, i.e., a chromolithograph
dept	Department
dj	Dust jacket
ed	Edition or editor
frontis	Frontispiece
GPO	Government Printing Office, Washington, D.C.
hc	Hardcover
HULMS	Harvard University Library Microreproduction Service (microfilm): Cambridge, MA
illus	Illustration(s), illustrated
introd	Introduction
l	Leaf, leaves. Unpaged paper with print or illustration on one side
LAC	Library Resources Inc. (microfiche), Chicago, Library of American Civilization
laid in	Inserted and loose
litho	Lithographic engraved illustration
n.d.	No date of publication given
no(s)	Number(s)
N.p.	No place of publication given
n.p.	No publishing agency given
n.s.	New series
o.s.	Old series
P	Press
(__) p	Unpaginated counted pages of quantity __
__ p	Paginated with __ pages
pp	Pages
port(s)	Portrait(s)
pt(s)	Part(s)
pub info	Publication information
ref	Reference(s)
RPI	Research Publications, Inc. (microfilm), Woodbridge, CT, and Reading, England
rpt	Reprint
self-wraps	Covers of the same paper as text stock
tipped-in	Glued into place
t.p.	Title page
trans	Translation
UMI	University Microfilm International: Ann Arbor, MI
U	University
UP	University Press
vol(s)	Volume(s)
wraps	Soft paper cover, wrappers
WCA	World's Congress Auxiliary
WCC	World's Columbian Commission
WCE	World's Columbian Exposition
WCR	World's Congress of Religions
WCRW	World's Congress of Representative Women
WF	World's Fair
WPR	World's Parliament of Religions
23x12½	Height in centimeters by width in centimeters (HxW)
*	Excellent book with much information about WCE
__: __, __	Publication information unknown to authors (e.g., t.p. missing, torn, etc.)
[ ]: [ ], [ ]	Information from a source other than the title page (or cover, if c.t. is used)

---.	Same author as cited directly above
---. ---.	Same author(s) or same author and title as cited directly above
----	Variant item with listed exceptions
▶	Clarification of changes: corrections or additions
◆	Magazine article when more than one is listed
(printer)	The printer is in parentheses following the publisher. If a printer but no publisher is on the document, printer information is given in lieu of publisher.
Bradley, Milton, Co.	Authors' sir names are alphabetized for citation location and indexing. Companies starting with a person's name, such as the Milton Bradley Company, are treated the same.

State Abbreviations

AK	Alaska
AL	Alabama
AR	Arkansas
AZ	Arizona
CA	California
CO	Colorado
CT	Connecticut
DC	District of Columbia
DE	Delaware
FL	Florida
GA	Georgia
HI	Hawaii
IA	Iowa
ID	Idaho
IL	Illinois
IN	Indiana
KS	Kansas
KY	Kentucky
LA	Louisiana
MA	Massachusetts
MD	Maryland
ME	Maine
MI	Michigan
MN	Minnesota
MO	Missouri
MS	Mississippi
MT	Montana
NC	North Carolina
ND	North Dakota
NE	Nebraska
NH	New Hampshire
NJ	New Jersey
NM	New Mexico
NV	Nevada
NY	New York
OH	Ohio
OK	Oklahoma
OR	Oregon
PA	Pennsylvania
RI	Rhode Island
SC	South Carolina
SD	South Dakota
TN	Tennessee
TX	Texas
UT	Utah
VA	Virginia
VT	Vermont
WA	Washington
WI	Wisconsin
WV	West Virginia
WY	Wyoming

ADDITIONAL RESOURCE MATERIALS

Libraries are a great source of World's Columbian Exposition material. The following references containing addresses, holdings, and personnel of domestic and foreign libraries, archives, and special collections were especially helpful.

American Library Directory : 1998–1999 : 51st Edition. 2 Vol. New York: Bowker, [ᶜ1998].

CIS US Serial Set Index. Washington, DC: Congressional Information Service, [ᶜ1977]. The Serial Set is a bound compilation of *House Documents, Senate Documents, House Reports*, and *Senate Reports*. They are arranged in numerical sequence and refer to the relevant bound volume of Congressional documents.

Dictionary Catalog of the National Agricultural Library : 1862-1965. Vol. 13. New York: Rowman and Littlefield, 1967 [ᶜ1967]. 73 volume set. Subject: "Chicago. World's Columbian Exposition, 1893."

Stanford University. Four bound volumes of pamphlets from the Transportation Department exhibits. Bound and presented to Stanford after the World's Columbian Exposition by Timothy Hopkins.

Stock Montage. 104 N. Halsted Street – Suite 200. Chicago, IL 60661-2102. Phone (312) 733-3239. Shirley Neiman, Business Manager. Archival photographs of Chicago and the WCE for loan.

Winterthur Museum and Library. McKinstry, E. Richard. *Personal Accounts of Events, Travels, and Everyday Life in America : An Annotated Bibliography.* [Winterthur, DE]: Winterthur, 1997. A catalog of holdings in the Archives.

Winterthur Museum and Library. McKinstry, E. Richard. *Trade Catalogues at Winterthur : A Guide to the Literature of Merchandising : 1750 to 1980.* New York & London: Garland, 1984. xv, 438 p.

WorldCat. On-line computer library catalog for subscribers. Contains over 1900 items under the subject World's Columbian Exposition with source locations.

The World of Learning : 1992 : Forty-second edition. [London]: Europa, [1992]. A listing of libraries in foreign countries.

ABOUT PRICES

In the course of compiling this supplement from 1992 to the present, we have watched sales prices for Columbian paper items. For about five years, prices were basically the same as listed in our original bibliography except for a few rare or unusual items. Around late 1996, prices started rising rapidly. A general rule-of-thumb is that the price ranges given in the 1992 book should be times 1.5 and scarce or unusual items times 2 or 3; known prices for new items are given in this volume. Publications with chromolithographs are particularly prized; excellent condition commands a premium price. The reasons for this dramatic change may be due to several factors: internet on-line auctions and electronic antique malls, which reach a rapidly increasing worldwide audience; museums and libraries that are actively buying World's Fair Americana; and an increasing interest in the impact of the Columbian Exposition, as judged from continuing publication of books, magazines, and newspaper articles on the subject.

INTACT WORLD'S COLUMBIAN EXPOSITION COLLECTIONS

This supplement contains entries that do not specifically mention the World's Fair. They are included because they have provenance of having come from collections assembled during the Fair. Unmarked items of the time period without such credentials have been excluded. We are especially indebted to LBA, SML, WM, S, GLD, FM, and Stfd for saving these collections; without them, we could not get a true sense of all the materials distributed during the six-month run of the Exposition. Although companies, states, and foreign countries issued items specifically for the Fair (printed with words indicating an Exposition handout), they also handed out unmarked literature that was intended for general distribution too. We have been gratified to observe that a number of these unmarked items were found in two or more intact collections thus further substantiating their validity as handouts at the Columbian Exposition, 1893.

ACKNOWLEDGEMENTS

We are especially grateful to Ben Williams and his staff at the Field Museum Library for four years of dedicated help during our visits. The result is inclusion of the extensive collections that have been held by the Museum for over 100 years and which were acquired either directly or indirectly from the World's Columbian Exposition. We thank Dr. Stephen Sheppard for his warm hospitality and for sharing his amazing collection, which defines the full extent of the Fair; his enthusiasm for the Columbian Exposition is infectious. We are indebted to Neville Thompson and her library staff at the Winterthur Museum and Library who cheerfully helped us locate thousands of Columbian items in the library's huge, impressive, and well preserved collection. Collector Jim Emple is thanked for his hospitality and for apprising us of new Columbian acquisitions as he has obtained them over the past seven years. We appreciated the informative tour of Columbian books and artifacts by Laura Graedel and the staff in Archives at the Museum of Science and Industry (formerly Columbian Fine Arts Building). We thank all librarians who gave us personal help during our visits and answered detailed follow-up questions. We thank collectors Art and Linda Fess for their hospitality and for sharing their impressive collection of Columbian books and beautifully displayed 3-D souvenirs; unfortunately, we were only able to catalog a sample of their Columbian paper items. Friends helped as well and we thank them: Bob Duphorne, Albuquerque, for locating New Mexico newspaper articles; Claes Ekman, Hallstahammer, Sweden, for translations; and Dan Dybwad for patiently giving us computer help. And we thank John Tandarich, Department of Agronomy, University of Illinois, for directing us to specialized Russian soil publications written for the Columbian Exposition.

ILLUSTRATION CREDITS

Unless otherwise noted, illustrations are from the collection of The Book Stops Here (GLD). We heartily thank the following libraries and collectors for granting us permission to use images at the citations listed below:

Biblioteca Nazionale Central, Florence: 543.1
California State University-Fresno: 1076.1, 1800.3
Catholic University of America: 1022
Center for Research Libraries, Chicago: 227.1, 351.1, 853.1, 950.2, 1961.2, 1971.1, 2284.
Centre Canadien d'Architecture, Montreal: 2372.4, 2446.CCA
Columbia University: 498.2, 867
Emple, Jim: 51.1, 721.10, 767.7, 814.2, 859.5, 884, 932.3, 945.3, 989.2, 1005.5, 1042.3, 1045.4, 1163.1, 1643.1, 1668.1, 1730.2, 1915.2
Field Museum: 228.3, 352.1, 529.1, 558, 572., 580, 620.2, 722.2, 732.2, 741.1, 909.2, 984.2, 1038, 1360.2, 1833.1, 1900.1, 1978.2, 2446.FM
Hagley Museum and Library: 385.2, 457.5, 757.2, 911.3, 926.2, 948.9, 2037.1, 2049.1
Harvard University: 506.3
Hunter, Stanley: 2372.2
Illinois Historical State Library: 475.1, 787.19, 791.1, 1134.1, 1534.1, 1961.2
Kansas Historical Society: 251.2, 1890.1
Lewis, Nahum H.: 995.6, 2264.1
Library of the Boston Athenaeum: 624.1, 812.1, 996.1, 1305.1, 1825.1
Mass. Institute of Technology Library: 648.1
McShane, Linda: 2395.2
Museum of Science and Industry: 52.2, 462., 2446.MSI
New South Wales Library: 594.2
Oklahoma Dept. of Libraries: 2034.
Österreichische Nationalbibliothek: 318.1, 1375.2
Pogo Press: 2402.3, 2424., 2457.1
Robinson, Ted: 155.1
Science Museum Library, London: 2092.2
Sheppard, Stephen: 44, 54.2, 151.6, 300, 523, 543.3, 570.1, 624, 658, 669.1, 697, 715.1, 720.1, 776.4, 791, 795.2, 834.3, 843.1, 892.2, 1003.21, 1050.14, 1079, 1179, 1185, 1189, 1200, 1259, 1280.1, 1383.1, 1635, 1836, 1837.1, 1908.1, 2050.2, 2080.2
Shipley, Mike: 1423.1

Stanford University Library: 631, 762.1, 767.5, 814.3, 814.14, 822.2, 842.7, 896.7, 961.2, 1034.2, 1053.9, 1321.2, 1901.4
State Historical Society of Missouri, Columbia, MO: 1957.2
Union League Club, Chicago: 2360.3
United Federation of Doll Clubs: 2437.4
Universitetsbiblioteket I Oslo: 346.2, 1301.1
University of CA Los Angeles: 1792.1
University of IL-Chicago: 767.1
University of Maryland: 122.1, 188, 232, 851.2, 1208.1, 2164.2, 2213.1, 2225
University of Minnesota. Tell G. Dahllöf Collection; Special Collections and Rare Books Dept.: 669.4, 672.1
University of New Mexico: 277.2
University of Oklahoma: 1362.2
Victoria and Albert Museum Library, London: 372.1
Winterthur Library – Printed Book and Periodical Collection: 377.1, 457.4, 460.1, 465, 480.1, 485.1, 490, 523, 537.1, 537.2, 566, 571, 576.3, 669.3, 674, 677.1, 714.4, 744.2, 745.4, 746.4, 753.1, 754.1, 761, 764.1, 776.1, 777.1, 833.2, 836.9, 848.1, 850.1, 851.1, 851.8, 859.2, 862.8, 877.2, 921.9, 931.6, 942.9, 950.1, 958.1, 986.2, 988.2, 994.3, 1003.14, 1004.2, 1005.4, 1017.1, 1017.4, 1035.1, 1042.1, 1045.5, 1045.8, 1050.6, 1050.15, 1173, 1180.1, 1212, 1290.1, 1365.4, 1386.3, 1410.1, 1547, 1739, 1787, 1849, 1901.2, 1984.1, 2029.1, 2202.2, 2296
Yale University Library: 1053

Chapter 1

FICTION, POETRY, CHILDREN'S BOOKS

1.1 Bender, Mary W. *Our First Columbian __ four hundred years ago : A Columbian Poem for the Children who were unable to attend the World's Fair.* Ostego, MI: Published by the Author, 1893.

26½x18. __ p. Morocco leather hc, gilt print. Poems about Columbus and his landing. (Title torn). (B)

3. Brooks. *The True Story of Christopher Columbus*: (GLD,A) $22 - 45
▸Correct and add: Brooks, Elbridge S[treeter]. Lothrop, Lee & Shepard Co., [ᶜ1892 by D. Lothrop Co.]. 1 *l* frontis litho of Columbus on stairs, 187, (2) p ads for Brooks' other books.
---- Also found: Boston: D. Lothrop co., 1893 [ᶜ1892 by D. Lothrop Co.]. 1 *l* frontis litho of Columbus on stairs, 187, (2) p ads for Margaret Sidney's "Five Little Peppers" books. Smooth chromolith paper covered boards.   P➔

4. Burnett. *Two Little Pilgrims'*:
(cul,DU,E,ESU,IStU,IWU,KSU,MU,S,sfsu,Stfd,UAT,UCI,UMC,UMN,UPa,WM,wsu)
▸Add Content: The fictional account of Meg and Rob, the two young pilgrims, traveling to and touring the WCE.
---- Also found: *Two little pilgrims' progress : A Story of the City Beautiful.* Tenth thousand. London: Frederick Warne and co., 1895 [copyright entered at Stationers' Hall]. 21x15½. (2) p, 1 *l* frontis (with tissue guard) of 3 children and man in a courtyard, (3)-215 p. Green cloth hc with beautiful gilt and black lettering and a design that includes 2 children (Meg and Rob) in the straw reading a book. All edges gilt. Illus by R.W. Macbeth. British ed. (GLD)   P➔ $30 - 50
---- Also found: 1896. Fifteenth thousand. Same title, publisher, size, and paging as 1895 edition above. Brown cloth hc, beautiful gilt and black lettering. Cover design and gilt edges as above. Illus by R.W. Macbeth. British ed. (GLD) $30 - 50

5. Burnham. *Sweet clover*: (GLD,Col,CU,DU,ESU,HU,S,Smth,SPL,UCB,Yale) $15 - 35
---- Also found: Centennial ed. Caledonia, MI: Bigwater Pub., 1992. 250 p. Series: Great Lakes Romances.
---- Also listed: Microfilm ed. Woodbridge, CT: RPI, ___. Wright American Fiction, v. III, 1876–1900, no 829, reel B-81.

6. Butterworth. *Zigzag Journeys*: (GLD,CCA,E,HU,RU,UIC,UMN,UTA) $40 - 75
▸Add: Red and white cloth hc: viii, 1 *l* (contents), (11)-320 p.
▸Correction: All start with viii pp, not vii pp.

7.1 *Columbus Panorama. Three Pictures from American History.* New York: The International News Co., n.d.

36x28. Tri-fold making 3 panels for elaborate pop outs. Chromolith paper over red and green cloth boards. Cover bird's-eye of WCE grounds. ☺ (S)

7.2 *Columbus Series : may blessings be upon the head of Cadmus the Phoenicians or whoever it was that invented books : Thos. Carlyle : 1492 1892.* New York: Empire publishing co., [1892]; New York: International book co., [1892]. P➔

19x13. Various paging and titles. C.t. Uniform cloth covers in gray and black (Empire) or red and black (International) show Columbus and the caravels. This was a large series of inexpensive reprinted fiction titles capitalizing on the 400ᵗʰ anniversary but, were not directly related to the WCE. (GLD,S)   each: $7 – 18

7.3 Cox, Palmer. *The brownies at home*. New York: The Century co., [ᶜ1891, 1892 by The Curtis Publishing Co.; ᶜ1893 by The Century Co. (The De Vinne Press)]. **P➜**

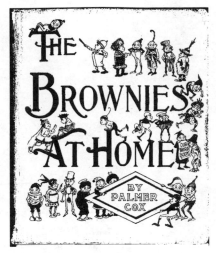

26x21½. 1 *l* (presentation), (2) p (t.p./copyright), 1 *l*, ix-xi, (1)-144. *l* following copyright page has description of the helpful Brownie. Yellow-tan shiny paper covered boards, chocolate print, multicolored brownie figures. C.t. = t.p. Twelve chap—one for each month of 1892. September's poem (p 104-14) describes Brownie help in completing the yet unfinished WCE grounds and bldgs. Bird's-eye b/w illus of WCE by Palmer Cox p 105. ©(GLD,WM) $125 - 200

8.   Crowley. *The city of wonders*: (GLD) $30 - 60

8.1 *Dewdrops and diamonds : of poetry and prose*. Chicago and Philadelphia: H.J. Smith & co., [ᶜ1892 by E.E. Fowler]. **P↘**

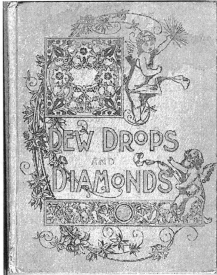

26½x21. 2 *l*, iv, 5-304 p. Bright red cloth hc, gilt print, embossed design of cherubs and flowers in black ink. Color litho plates of the WCE bldgs (2 bldgs on each of 4 plates) are not included in paging; one is the frontis. Early description of WCE pages 5-11; WCE lithos distributed throughout book. An illustrated pulp reader of the type popular in its day. ©(GLD) $25 - 45

12.   Ferris Wheel Co. *Car No*: (GLD)   **P↘** $60 - 130
13.   Finley. *Elsie at the World's fair*: (GLD,S,UMN,UTA)

15.   Fuller. *The Cliff-Dwellers*:
       ☞ Issued in installments in *Harper's Weekly*, 1893.

17.1 Hayes, Harold Vincent. *...Columbus and The Fair. 1892*. N.p.: George Mills Rogers and Harold Vincent Hayes, [ᶜ1893 Harold Vincent Hayes].

25½x17½. 1 *l* frontis, 23 p on glossy stock. Tan stiff wraps, gilt print and gilt bust of Columbus design, black cloth spine. C.t. At head of title, "1492." Ode to Columbus and upcoming WCE. LC stamp; unique? ©(S)

18.   Holley. *Samantha at the World's fair*: (B,CCA,D,HU,UIC)
19.   Ingham. *Pompeii of the west*: (Stfd,Yale)

20.   Jenks. *The Century*: (bgsu,CCA,CWM,D,DU,E,FM,HU,IHi,IStU,KSU,NDU,NSW,PSU,S,SHB, slpl,Smth,UIC,uiuc,UMD,UTA,WM,Yale)
       ▶Add annotation: This book was originally issued with a dj: yellow-tan paper, red print, illus of part of the Ferris wheel. Jacket title: "The Century World's fair book for boys and girls : Harry and Philip at the fair."

20.1 *Little Ones Annual : stories and poems : for : little people*. Boston: Estes and Lauriat, [ᶜ1894 By Russel Publishing Co.].

23½x17½. xiv, 1 *l*, (3)-382 p. Brown cloth hc, gilt print and design with girl's port in center circle. The 1 *l* is illus of a girl in a Columbian Rolling Chair "at the World's fair." Same title for illustrated article, pp (3)-6, on the Children's Bldg. ©(S)

22.   Loy. *Poems of the white city*: (DU,ref,S) $45

23.1 Mercur, Anna Hubbard. *Cosmos : and other poems*. Buffalo, NY: Peter Paul and brother, 1893 [ᶜ1893 by Anna Hubbard Mercur].

20x16½. x, 215 p. Light blue cloth spine over chromolith paper covered boards. No poems on WCE but on cover: "Souvenir Columbian exposition 1893." ☺ (S)

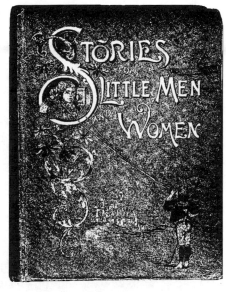

23.2 Milburn, William Henry, ed. ...*Stories for Little Men and Women : Profusely Illustrated by Celebrated American Artists*. N.p.: Prospect? publishing co., 1893 [ᶜ1893 by A.L. Smith].

26½x21. xviii, (11)-336 p. Turquoise cloth hc, silver bold print, silver/black design of two children talking on Bell telephone. Pulp paper text, woodcut illus. At head of title: "Selections from the best Juvenile Authors." A. Zeese & Co. sepia plates of the WCE are interspersed and not included in paging; two bldg illus per plate. World's fairs, pp 313-36, include the WCE. ☺ (GLD) P➔ $25 - 40

24.   Monroe. *The Columbian Ode*: (Col,DU,GU,LBA,ref,Stfd,UCLA,UIC) $300
25.   Monroe. *Commemoration Ode*: (UIC,wusl)

26.   [Neely]. *Looking forward*: (UMN)
      ---- Also found: 1889 Hardcover. 19x13½. (2) p ads, (3)-228, (14) p ads. Red-brown cloth hc, black print and design. Pulp text paper. C.t.: "Looking Forward. Tennyson." (GLD) $22 - 45

      ☞ This book was issued shortly after the 1888 Congressional proposal for an 1892 WF. It is an early imaginative speculation of the grandeur of an international fair and heavily "suggests" (wishes) Chicago as an ideal site. Chicago was officially declared the site on April 25, 1890.

27.   [Neely]. *A tale of the World's fair : Giving the Experience*: (GLD)
      ▶Add: Title given is c.t. T.p. title on p (7): *A tale of the World's fair*. The entire story is a pulp tale of the impending fair; story plus many ads make (128) p. Copyright and publishing info are found on both the cover and t.p. Orange wraps, black print and decorative border. Outside back cover litho and ad for Phoenix Insurance Co of Brooklyn. ☺ (GLD) $22 - 45

28.1 Nye, Edgar Wilson. *Bill Nye's History of the United States*. Chicago: Stanton and Van Vliet Co., [ᶜ1894 By J.B. Lippincott Company : ᶜ1906 By Thompson & Thomas].

      21½x16. 1 *l*, 328 p. Sketch of author on the lecture stage on the 1 *l*. Blue cloth hc, b/w print, illus of Pilgrim in a stock viewed by 2 children. Spoof on US history including the WCE, p 327. ☺ (GLD) $16 - 32

      ☞ Humorist Nye and Mark Twain were friends. Nye died in 1896 at age 46; Twain, also a platform speaker, was 75 when he died in 1910.

33.   [Plautus]. *The Latin play*: (UPa)

33.1 Pollard, Josephine. *The History of the United States; told in one syllable words*. New York: McLoughlin brothers, publishers, n.d. (1898?)

      25x20½. 1 *l* frontis, 136 p+ unpaged chromoliths. Frontis chromolith of Columbus landing. Gray cloth hc, gilt print; black, silver, gilt, and red design. Chap 16, pp 122-23, on the WCE. ☺ (GLD) $15 - 30

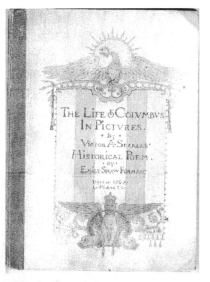

34.   Russell. *The Story of Columbus*: (HU)

34.1 Schorb, George. *Nuts to crack. Try one...A whetstone for dull wits. The World's Fair "Riddle book," Conundrums, Puzzles, Puns and Repartee,...* Chicago: n.p., 1892.

      20x14. 46 p. Self-wraps, black print. 400 riddles, etc., with answers in the back. ☺ (GLD) $20 - 44

35.   Searles. *The Life of Columbus*: (GLD,S)   P➔ $60 - 120

38.   Stead. *From the Old World*: (GLD,Fess,Yale) $20 - 40
        ---- Also found: Red cloth hc, black print and blind stamped.

        ☞ Stead, an English journalist, founded the *Review of Reviews* magazine. He drowned when the Titanic
        sank in April 1912.

39.   [Stevens]. *The Adventures of Uncle Jeremiah*: (bgsu,Col,DU,FM,FU,HML,HU,ICRL,NDU,PSU,S,sfpl,UAB,UAT,UCB,UMD,WM,Yale)
        ---- Wraps: All listed below are published by Laird & Lee. All have Pastime Series, no 108 at bottom of
        cover. All are 19½x13½. All are illus by H. Mayer. Date of pub, cover description, frontis, and paging
        vary as follows:

        1893: Light green glossy wraps, red and black print, illus of The Family
        viewing the Agriculture Bldg [illus in original bibliography]. Mayer's name
        is not on cover but appears on several illus (see p 181). Frontis illus of
        passengers on train is captioned: "Apples, pears, bananas, sweet oranges."
        1 *l* frontis, (1) t.p., (1) copyright, (1) dedication, 6-229, (3) p ads, cocoa ad
        on back cover. (GLD)
        1893: "Century Edition : 100ᵗʰ Thousand" at top of cover. Maize glossy
        wraps, red and black print, illus of The Family viewing the Admin Bldg.
        Mayer's name on cover. Frontis illus of Uncle and family viewing the
        Ferris wheel and Midway. 1 *l* frontis, (1) t.p., (1) copyright and dedication,
        (4) b/w photo illus on glossy stock of Cold Storage fire, (1) preface, 6-237,
        (3) p ads, cocoa ad on back cover. Pages 6-204 are identical to green wraps
        version above. Century ed has an extra chap: "The horrible exposition fire,
        p 205. Final chap same. (GLD)   P➔
        1894: "Historic Edition : 400ᵗʰ Thousand" at top of cover. Gray glossy
        wraps. Illus of The Family viewing the Admin Bldg. Mayer's name on
        cover.
        ---- Hardcover: Red (or rust) cloth hc, gilt print, black spine print. (1) ad, (1) Ferris wheel and Midway
        frontis, (1) t.p., (1) copyright, (4) b/w photo illus of Cold Storage fire, (5)-237, (3) p ads. (FM)
        ---- Microfilm: Woodbridge, CT: RPI, ___ . Wright American Fiction, v III, 1876–1900, no 5188, reel S-59.

41.   Taylor. *Halcyon days*: © (GLD,UIC)   P↙ $25 - 50
        ▶Add and correct: *Halcyon days in the dream city*. [Kankakee, IL: n.p., ᶜ1894 by Mrs. D.C. Taylor].

44.   Western. *Adventures of Reuben and Cynthy*: (S)   P↓
45.   White. *The Story of*: (CCA)
47.   Yandell. *Three girls in a flat*: (GLD,WM)   P↘   35 - 70

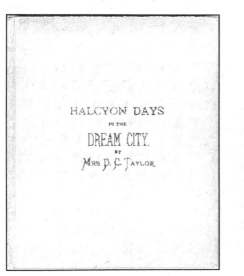

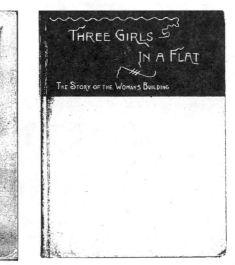

Chapter 2

EXPOSITION PUBLICATIONS

48.   *Brief of W.P. Black*: (Col,HU,SHB,slpl,Smth,Stfd,UMN,UVM)
▶Caption Title: "Brief of points, and suggestions for consideration before the government officials, in the matter of Miss Phoebe Couzins, …"

48.1 City Council of Chicago. *Memorial to Congress : adopted by the : city council of the City of Chicago : on December 5th, 1892.* Chicago: John F. Higgins, Printer, 1893.

> 25x17. 24 p. Tan wraps, black print. C.t. Mayor Hempstead Washburne led the committee, listed on p 24, proposing repeal of all Federal legislation forbidding Sunday opening of the WCE. Chicago put forth many reasons for keeping the Fair open, for example, to off-set reduced Congressional appropriations, a benefit to foreign visitors, and ameliorate costs of construction. The city also proposed that elaborate Sunday religious services be held in the WCE buildings so that the Sabbath would be kept. ☺ (GLD) $30 - 60

49.   Goode. *First draft of A System of Classification*: (HU,KSU,NAL,S,sfpl,UPa,VAM)

49.1 Goode, G[eorge] Brown. *…First draft of a system of classification for the World's Columbian exposition.* Rpt. Washington: GPO, 1893.

> 24½x14. 1 *l*, 649-735 p. Blue-flecked tan wraps, black print. At head of title: "Smithsonian Institution. United States National Museum." Also on t.p.: "Reprint." This is the reprint of Goode's article from #293; although title matches #49, it is not a reprint of #49. ☺. (HU,SML)

50.   Olmsted. *Olmsted's report on the choice of site*;
---- Rpt: Tager, Jack. (bgsu,BU,CU,HU,MU,NDU,nmsu,OU,SHB,UMA,UMD,USFr,VCU)

50.1 Olmsted, F[rederick] L[aw], & Co. *Report submitted to the Joint Committee on the Site of the World's Columbian Exposition on the comparative advantages and disadvantages of Washington and of Jackson Parks as sites for the exposition.* N.p.: n.p., [1890].

> 25x__. 13 p. Olmsted, John W. Root, and D.H. Burnham submitted the report. [Jackson Park was chosen as described in #50. Olmsted Co contributed the design of the grounds: #201.2, #201.3] (HU)

51.   US. WCC&WCE. Joint Board of Ref. Sub-Committee. *Report*: (ICRL)

51.1 U.S. World's Columbian Commission and World's Columbian Exposition. *Inaugural Reception of the World's Columbian Exposition. Auditorium. Chicago. October nineteenth, 1892.* N.p.: n.p., 1892?

> 12½x9. (6) p not including buff stiff card wraps. Steel engraved print and bust of Columbus. Red ribbon tied with a 30 cm extension to which is attached a 5 cm long pencil wrapped in red silk; very elegant. Lists "Patronesses" and "Managers"; 16 lines for signatures of dance partners. (MCHx Fifer-Bohrer Box 1). ☺. (E,IHi,MCHx,S)   **P➔**

52.   US. WCC&WCE. Joint Committee on Ceremonies. *Dedicatory and Opening*:
(BrU,CCA,CLP,CSL,CU,CUA,D,GBP,HML,ICRL,IHi,KBS,KCPL,LU,Merc,NLA,NPG,NSW,PSU,RPL,RSA,RU,SML,SStu,UCB,UCD,UCLA,uiuc,UMA,Yale)
---- Stone: ▶Add: 319 p. [c1893 by Stone, Kastler & Painter]. Turquoise cloth hc, gilt edges.
---- Stone, Kastler & Painter (Donohue & Henneberry): ▶Add: Blue cloth hc.

52.1 [U.S. World's Columbian Commission and World's Columbian Exposition. Joint Committee on Ceremonies.] National Guard Officers. *Official minutes of the Convention of National Guard Officers, Held in the City of Chicago. First Session--First Day, Tuesday, October 27, 1891.* [Chicago]: n.p., 1891?

> 23x15½. 30 p. No wraps. Caption title. Second paragraph of first page: "The object of holding the Convention is to canvass the military features contemplated at the dedication ceremonies to begin October

11, 1892, and incidentally take up the subject of an encampment of the National Guard to be held in Chicago in the summer of 1893." Meeting held in the Director's Room of the WCE. ☺. (MSL)

52.2 U.S. World's Columbian Commission and World's Columbian Exposition. Joint Committee on Ceremonies. *World's Columbian Exposition, Closing Ceremonies, October 30th 1893.* Chicago: Western Banknote Co., n.d.

20x14. (3) p. Folded stiff card, back blank. Steel engraving of the Administration Building on the front cover. ☺. (MSI,WM)　　**P➜**

52.3 U.S. World's Columbian Commission and World's Columbian Exposition. Joint Committee on Ceremonies. *World's Columbian Exposition, Opening Ceremonies, May 1st 1893.* Chicago: Western Banknote Co., n.d.

18x12. (4) p. Buff heavy stock. C.t. Elaborate steel engraved print throughout. Front cover Columbus profile vignette. Members of the Joint Committee listed on back. Description of the eight opening day events, which took place at the Court of Honor and Admin Bldg. ☺(GLD)　$70 - 120

52.4 U.S. World's Columbian Commission and World's Columbian Exposition. Joint Committee on Transportation. Sub-Committee on Physical Difficulties. ...*Report of the Sub-Committee : to the : Joint Committee on Transportation. October 31, 1891.* Chicago: Rand, McNally & Co., Printers, 1891.

22x15½. 1 *l* (t.p.), 3-18 p. Buff (or gray-green) wraps, black print. C.t. = t.p. At head of title: "World's Columbian exposition." Sums the 1891 transportation capacity to the planned WCE by all methods as 39,000 people per hour and suggests methods of increasing the rate to 136,000 per hour by 1893; gives attendant costs. ☺. (ICRL,S)

☞ The committee was quite accurate. Traffic rates never exceeded 150,000 people/hour except on Chicago Day, October 9, 1893, when attendance exceeded 750,000. See #2348.3.

53.　　US. WCC&WCE. *Minutes of the Proceedings of the joint conference*: (NAL,S,UCB)

54.1 U.S. World's Columbian Commission. *Banquet given by the United States Commissioners of the World's Columbian Exposition in honor of Thomas W. Palmer, President of the Commission. Wednesday, October 25, 1893. Auditorium Hotel, Chicago.* Chicago: Metcalf Sta co., 1893.

23½x18. 2 *l.* Two heavy cards tied with satin bow. Beautiful multicolor cover showing the state emblems in a shield; US flag and eagle symbol at top. C.t. Second card front is the menu. Elegant. **P➜** See the frontis in this *Supplement* for an illustration of the invitation. ☺(GLD,IHi)　　$70 - 150

54.2 U.S. World's Columbian Commission. *Banquet in honor of : The World's Columbian Commission : tendered by : The President. Kinsley's : Oct. 24, 1892.* N.p.: n.p., n.d.

21½x17½. 2 *l.* Two heavy cards tied by a wide satin bow. C.t. Cover has fancy steel engraved litho of Santa Maria captioned "Tierra!" Black print and illus. See #54.1 for a return favor from the Commissioners. ☺(GLD,S)　　**P➜**　　$70 - 150

54.3 U.S. World's Columbian Commission. *Banquet to Don Cristoval Colon de la Cerda : Duke de Veragua : by Thomas Wetherill Palmer...May second, 1893. Auditorium Hotel, Chicago.* Chicago: n.p., 1893.

21x15. 3 cards making 3 *l*; red/white/blue bow-tied. Illus port of the Spanish Infanta and Duke's wife on cover with no print. Caption title on second *l*; menu on third *l*. (S)

54.4 U.S. World's Columbian Commission. *Dedication of the Buildings of the World's Columbian Exposition : Chicago, Friday, October 21st 1892.* Chicago: [Western Bank Note Company], n.d.

25½x20½. (3) p. Folded sheet. C.t. This is the program for #54.5. ☺(GLD,IHi,S,WM)　　$60 - 100

54.5 U.S. World's Columbian Commission. *The World's Columbian Commission invites you to participate in the Ceremonies attending the Dedication of the Buildings of the World's Columbian Exposition at Jackson Park in the city of Chicago...* N.p.: n.p., n.d.

28x21½. (4) p. Folded stiff stock. See the frontis of our original *Annotated Bibliography* for a reproduction of this important souvenir. C.t. There were two printed versions: after the ellipse came "October 11ᵗʰ, 12ᵗʰ and 13ᵗʰ 1892" or "October 19ᵗʰ, 20ᵗʰ and 21ˢᵗ 1892." The first invitation was not used since the event took place on the later dates. ☺ (GLD,B,FM,IHi,MSI,S,WML) $80 - 200

57.   US. WCC. BLM. *Address at the Dedicatory Ceremonies*: (HML)
59.   US. WCC. BLM. *Addresses and Reports of Mrs. Potter Palmer*: (GLD,CLP,Col,HU,IHi,S,Stfd,uiuc,UTA) $100 - 250
60.   US. WCC. BLM. *Addresses delivered at the opening*: (CLP)
61.   US. WCC. BLM. *Approved Official Minutes...third session*: (S)

64.   US. WCC. BLM. *Assembly : In honor of the Judges*: (WM)
▶Completed citation: 25½x20½. (4) p. Folded buff sheet, navy print. C.t. 18-part program "proposed by Mrs. Virginia C. Meredith, Indiana, Chairman Committee on Awards of the Board of Lady Managers." Printing info, p (4): [Chicago: Rand, McNally & Co.], n.d.

64.1 U.S. World's Columbian Commission. Board of Lady Managers. Cantrill, Mary Cecil. "Letter to Members, Committee on the National Flower." 1 Apr. 1893. Georgetown, KY.

28x21½. BLM letterhead sheet with illus of Woman's Bldg. Letter begins: "My friend and colleague:-- The following is a list of flowers adopted..." Listing of 24 states and territories and their chosen flower as reported to the Committee on the National Flower. Cantrill was BLM member-at-large from KY and Committee chairman. No two states could have the same flower. ☺ (S)

69.1 U.S. World's Columbian Commission. Board of Lady Managers. *Dedication of : Children's Building : June 1, 1893, at 3 p.m.* N.p.: n.p., 1893.

20½x12½. Single card, turquoise print one side. Lists 7-part music program. ☺ (WM)

70.   US. WCC. BLM. *Diploma of honorable mention*: (B,MSI)

71.   US. WCC. BLM. Eagle. *The Congress*:
(Amh,bgsu,CLP,CU,DC,E,GBP,HML,HU,IHi,MOHx,MSI,NDU,RPL,RU,SHB,slpl,Smth,Stfd,UCD,UCLA,UIC,UMA,UMD,UMN,UoA,UPa,UWM,WM,WML)
▶Add pub: Boston: Geo. M. Smith & Co., 1894. 824 p. Olive cloth hc, gilt print.
▶Add pub: Chicago: A.B. Kuhlman, 1894.
▶Add pub: Chicago: Beezley publishing co., 1895 [ᶜ1894 by W.B. Conkey co.]. 824 p. Found with black half leather over maroon cloth covered beveled boards; gilt print and design as illustrated; marbled edges, decorative green end papers.   Half leather: $50 - 90
▶Add pub: Chicago: International publishing co., 1895. 824 p.
▶Add pub: Chicago: Wabash Publishing House, 1895 ᶜ1894. 824 p.
▶Add pub: Denver: Charles Westley, 1894 [ᶜ1894 by W.B. Conkey co.].
▶Add pub: Kansas City, MO.: Thompson & Hood, 1894.
▶Add pub: Minneapolis: L.M. Aver Publishing Co., 1894.

---- Rpt. New York: Arno Press, 1974 [ᶜ1894]. Rpt of the edition published by American Publishing House, Chicago. 23½x16. (4) p of new material, 824, (4) p of Arno Press ads: "Women in America." Gray-tan cloth hc. C.t. in blue: "Women in America : from colonial times to the 20th century." ☺ (UMD)

72.1 U.S. World's Columbian Commission. Board of Lady Managers. *Exhibits by women. How They Will be Installed, Etc.* N.p.: n.p., n.d.

23x15½. 8 p. Self-wraps. Caption title. A statement to home and foreign committees regarding the purpose and scope of the exhibits to be placed in general WCE bldgs and Woman's Bldg. ☺ (S)

73.1 U.S. World's Columbian Commission. Board of Lady Managers. *The honor of your presence is requested at the Opening Exercises of the Woman's Building of the World's Columbian Exposition...* N.p.: n.p., n.d.

28x23. Thick buff card, black print, a woman's port at top with "Board of Lady Managers" caption. C.t. Invitation for "May First, Eighteen Hundred and Ninety Three," the WF opening. ☺ (S)

74.   US. WCC. BLM. *List of books sent by home and foreign committees*: (Col,HU,SHB,Smth,Stfd,UMN,UTA,UVM,Yale)
75.   US. WCC. BLM. *List of Officers, Lady Managers*: (UTA)
76.   US. WCC. BLM. *Mrs. Palmer's Address to the Fortnightly Club*: (WM) ▶Add: Self wraps. Caption title.
79.   US. WCC. BLM. *Official manual of the Board of Lady Managers*: (UIC)

99.1 U.S. World's Columbian Commission. Board of Lady Managers. *Rules for Sales in the Woman's Building.* N.p.: n.p., n.d.

23x15½. (3) p. A list of 19 rules. ☺ (UCB)

100.   US. WCC. BLM. Shuman. *Favorite dishes*: (CU,HU,KSU)

101.   US. WCC. BLM. *The Woman's Building*: (S)
▶Add annotation: Description of the intended contents of the bldg. List of ten numbered requests to be submitted to commissions cooperating with the Board of Lady Managers.
---- Also found: Same text issued by New South Wales: [Sydney: Charles Potter, Government Printer, 1892]. 22x14. (3) p. Folded buff sheet. Caption title. (S)

102.1 U.S. World's Columbian Commission. Board of Lady Managers. *The woman's dormitory association of the Columbian exposition.* N.p.: n.p., n.d.

23x15½. (4) p. Proposed place for women to stay while visiting the WCE. ☺ (S)

109.   US. WCC. BRC. *Official minutes of the Board of Reference*: (FM)
112.   US. WCC. Commission to Europe. *Report of the Commission to Europe*: (UMD)

113.   US. WCC. COA. *Final report of executive committee of awards*: (HU)
▶Add cover description: Pale blue glossy wraps, black print.

115.   US. WCC. COA. *Report of the committee on awards*: (GLD,HML,HU,ICRL,MOHx,Merc,slpl,uiuc,UMC,UTA)
117.   US. WCC. COA. Thacher. *Address of John Boyd Thacher*: (HU,WM)
119.   US. WCC. COA. Thacher. *Awards...Together with an appendix*: (FLP)
120.   US. WCC. COC. *Classification...adopted*: (CCA,Col,FLP,FM,ICRL,LU,Merc,MSI,NLA,NSW.S,SHB,SML,UCLA,UMC,UTA)
121.   US. WCC. COC. *Classification...prepared*: (MIT)
122.   US. WCC. COC. *Draft of a System of Classification*: (NAL)

122.1 U.S. World's Columbian Commission. Committee on Permanent Organization. *Appendix to the report of the committee on permanent organization, submitted to the : Meeting of the Commission, September 15, 1890.* Chicago: Rand, McNally & Co., Printers, 1890.   P➔

21½x15. 84 p. Self-wraps. C.t. On p 84: F.W. Putnam. First report, p 3: "Proceedings of the Sub-Committee on Permanent Organization. Report of Meeting in Philadelphia, July 16, 1890, with Mr. Thomas Cochran, late President of the Centennial Board of Finance of the Philadelphia Centennial Exposition of 1876." [WCE organizers solicited input from organizers of the Centennial Exposition of 1876 and the Paris Exposition, 1889.] ☺ . (UMD)

122.2 U.S. World's Columbian Commission. Committee on Permanent Organization. *Report of a Sub-Committee on Permanent Organization to the full Committee in reference to the Exhibit of Mines and Mining at the World's Columbian Exposition. Submitted September 11, 1890.* Chicago: n.p., 1890.

21x15. (2) p. Caption title. Three names at end are headed by Mark L. McDonald. Sub-committee recommended a separate department for Mines and Mining and that it be in a separate bldg. ☺ . (UMD)

122.3 U.S. World's Columbian Commission. Committee on Permanent Organization. *Report of the Committee on*

Permanent Organization through its Chairman, Hon. Jas. A. McKenzie, of Kentucky, containing an Account of the Proceedings of said Committee. Submitted to the Commission September 15, 1890. Chicago: n.p., 1890.

21½x15. 6 p. Caption title. To Thomas W. Palmer, President, WCC. The committee met and gathered information in various cities to determine the best organization for the WCE. ☺. (UMD)

122.4 U.S. World's Columbian Commission. Committee on Rules, By-Laws, and Regulations of the By-Laws. *Report of the Committee on Rules, By-Laws, and Regulations of the By-Laws for the Government of the Commission.* N.p.: n.p., n.d.

22x15. 7 p. Caption title. Report lists the 16 articles of the WCC bylaws. ☺. (UMD)

122.5 U.S. World's Columbian Commission. Judiciary Committee. Lindsay, W[illia]m. *Opinion of Hon. Wm. Lindsay, Chairman Judiciary Committee of the World's Columbian Commission, upon the report of the Congressional sub-committee of the select committee on : Quadro-Centennial of the Discovery of America.* Chicago: n.p., 1891.

23x15½. 10 p. Caption title. Dated Jan 22, 1891, and addressed to Thomas W. Palmer, Pres of the WCC. Lindsay describes the Congressional Committee's report and its inaccuracies. ☺. (HU,ICRL,UMD)

122.6 U.S. World's Columbian Commission. Judiciary Committee. *Report of the Judiciary Committee, Defining the Rights, Duties and Powers of the World's Columbian Commission.* N.p.: n.p., 1890.

21½x15. 4 p. Caption title. Report dated Sept 15, 1890. William Lindsay, Chairman, and four other members are listed on p 4. In July, the Commission empowered this six (actually five) member Judicial committee to consider the legal definition of the rights, duties and powers of the WCC as set up by Congress on April 25, 1890. This is their report. ☺. (UMD)

122.7 U.S. World's Columbian Commission. Office of the Secretary. *Report of the Secretary of the World's Columbian Commission and Accompanying Documents, September 15, 1890.* Chicago: n.p., 1890.

22x15. 10 p. String-tied. Caption title. Name on p 10 is A.C. Matthews, Comptroller. Describes securing office space in downtown Chicago for Commission committee members. The Secretary reports securing suites in the Pullman Bldg for the President, Secretary, and Executive Committee. (UMD)

123. US. WCC. *The Official Directory of the World's Columbian Commission*: (S,UMN)
---- Also found: Green fleck wraps.

124. US. WCC. *The Official directory of the World's Columbian Commission*: (KS) $40
125. US. WCC. *Official manual of the World's Columbian Commission*: (GLD,FM,HU,ICRL,MSL,UCB,UMN,Yale) $30 - 50

125.1 U.S. World's Columbian Commission. *Official manual of the World's Columbian Commission : containing : The Minutes of the Commission from the Date of its Organization, June 26, 1890, to the Close of its Third Session, November 26, 1890, and other Official Data.* Chicago: Knight, Leonard & co., printers, 1892.

22x15. Minutes separately paginated. Contains six sessions from June 26, 1890, to April 6, 1892, plus other official data. 363? p. [Related to, or rpt of, #125.] ☺. (NSW)

127. US. WCC. *Official minutes* (4th): (NSW)
128. US. WCC. *Official minutes* (5th): (NSW)
129. US. WCC. *Official minutes* (6th): (FM,NSW)
130. US. WCC. *Official minutes* (7th): (NSW)
131. US. WCC. *Official minutes* (8th): (NSW)

140. US. WCC. *The World's Columbian Exposition : Memorial for International*: (GLD,Col,CUA,S,Yale) $35 - 70
▸Add info: Issued with a buff dj, which has the same printed words except black ink instead of gilt.

141. US. WCC. *World's Columbian Exposition. Regulations governing awards*: * ☺ (HU,WM)
▸Added annotation: 28½x21½. (4) p. Folded buff sheet, black print. At end: "John Boyd Thacher,

Chairman Executive Committee on Awards...June 8, 1893. George R. Davis, Director-General."
Alternate author: Committee on Awards. A committee for each of the 13 WCE depts received these same
13 rules of judging and committee administration.

142.   US. WCC. *World's Fair Appropriations : Extent of state exhibits*: (CCA,FM,NSW,UCB)
▶Correct pagination: 19, (1) p.

144.1 World's Columbian Exposition. *...Application for space.—Domestic.* N.p.: n.p., n.d.

30½x24½. (4) p. Folded cream high-rag sheet; black print with blue and purple ruled grid for date,
article, and space needed. 24 rules of the WCE pp (2)-(3). Permit form intended for office filing. ☺ (WM)

150.   WCE. *Banquet tendered to the* Foreign: ☺ (GLD,IHi,S) $85 – 170
▶Alternate title: *In Honor of the Foreign Commissioners to the World's Columbian Exposition.* Invitation.

151.   WCE. Bureau de Publicité. *Apres quatre siecles*: (CCA,DU,HU,PSU,S,UCB,UMD)
---- Also found: 16 p [i.e. without the (4) p].

151.1 World's Columbian Exposition. Bureau of Construction. *Official perspective views of the : Buildings Being
Constructed for : The World's Columbian Exposition. Chicago : 1893.* Chicago?: Published by the
Construction Department, n.d.

29½x37. 11 *l* of fine photogravures separated by tissue guards. Published without text or t.p. Manila
envelope. Title is from the envelope. A promotional item. ☺ (UMD)

151.2 World's Columbian Exposition. Bureau of Construction. *Specification : FOR ___ : ON ___ .* Chicago:
Rand, McNally & Co., n.d.

35x22. (3) p of printed instructions for bidding, which are followed by typed pages of specifications for a
specific job. Green wraps with black print. Secured at the top edge by two brass fasteners. C.t. The
blanks in the c.t. are for specific job and specific WCE site. Examples of these typescripts:
1) *Specification : FOR tile floor and marble wainscot in toilet rooms. ON galleries of fine arts.* (2) p.
2) *Specification : FOR marble mosaic and cement floors. ON galleries of fine arts.* (3) p.
☺ (GLD)   Each: $200 - 400

151.3 World's Columbian Exposition. Bureau of Construction. *...Specification : For Machinery and Apparatus for
Generating Electricity for Operation of Motors in Transportation Building.* Chicago: Rand, McNally &
co., printers, 1892.

35½x21½. 3 p+ (1) p map of Jackson Park fairgrounds. Green wraps, black print. C.t. At head of
title: "World's Columbian Exposition. Bureau of Construction, 1143 Rookery B'ld'g. Chicago, January
25, 1892." ☺ (SML)

151.4 [World's Columbian Exposition]. [Bureau of Education]. [Art Institute of Chicago].
Carpenter, Newton H. *World's Columbian exposition. Department of
Zoopraxography. Announcement. By invitation ...* Chicago: Art Institute, 1893.

20½x13½. 2 *l*. Folded high-rag sheet, black print. Announcement of lectures and
demonstrations by E. Muybridge in his Zoopraxographical Hall, WCE Midway from
"May to October, 1893." [Formative for the US film industry. May have been
issued jointly by US Govt, Art Institute, and WCE.] ☺ (WM)

151.5 World's Columbian Exposition. Bureau of Public Comfort. Kasson, W. Marsh.
...Bureau of public comfort—hotel and rooming department. To Prospective Visitors.
Chicago: n.p., 1 Jan. 1893.

37x20½. 1 *l*. Sheet printed in black ink. At head of title: "World's Columbian
Exposition." Caption title. Letter format dated at end under Kasson's name. Illus
of the rental certificate form at bottom. ☺ (WM)

151.6 World's Columbian Exposition. Bureau of Public Comfort. *...Office of : Bureau of Public Comfort : hotel
and rooming department : Rand-McNally building, Chicago, Ill.* Chicago: Poole Bros., [1893]. P↑

20½x9. Fourfold leaf. Peach with red and black print. World globe on the cover showing the Americas with "Chicago" highlighted. Dated Jan 1, 1893. Room info and a sample of visitor's application for a room. © . (S,UCB)

155.1 World's Columbian Exposition. ...*Capital Stock : $10,000,000. This is to certify that (blank) .* Chicago: Western bank note Co., 189_. **P➜**

18x27½. 1 *l*. Printed stock with various face values; one share was $10. Each is numbered, shows the number of shares, and has the subscriber's name written in the blank. Vignette of woman and early bird's-eye of the WCE grounds. These are prized collectibles from the WCE. They are beautifully engraved and colored and represent the financial underpinnings of the company and the resulting fair. Signatures on the certificates are also valuable. See #216.1 for the related debenture bonds . (IHi, ref, S, UIC)

156.   WCE. *Concession Agreements*: © (UCLA)
---- Found in 1st, 2nd, and 3rd editions. C.t.: "World's Columbian Exposition. Concession agreements. Volume I [to VII], numbers __ to __." Each of the 7 vols has its own t.p.
T.p. from 3rd ed, vol III: *World's Columbian Exposition. Concession Agreements. Vol. III. Nos. 41-60. 31st March, 1892, to 12th December, 1892. Third edition.* N.p.: Auditor's office, 1893.
In addition, each agreement is separately paged and each has its own t.p. For example, *C.D. Arnold and Harlow D. Higinbotham. Chicago, Ill. Agreement. 21st April, 1893. Right to establish a bureau of photography and make and sell photographs of the grounds and buildings of the World's Columbian exposition.* Chicago: Printed by the Chicago Legal News Co., 1893.
▶Cover variant: Half black leather over black cloth hc, glued on leather spine label with gilt print.

☞ See #2446.UCLA for a concession accounting item.

156.1 World's Columbian Exposition. *[Concession Agreements].* Individual Issues. Chicago: Legal News Co., 1891–93.

30½x23 (larger than bound versions). Variously paged as described in #156. Example titles:
1) *C.D. Arnold and Harlow D. Higinbotham. Chicago, Ill. : Agreement. 21st April, 1893. Right to establish a bureau of photography and make and sell photographs of the grounds and buildings of the World's Columbian exposition.* 1893. 3 p.   **P➜**
2) *Ulrich Jahn, of Germany, agreement. 31st December, 1891. German Village and German Town of Mediæval Times.* 1892. 8? p.
© (GLD)   Each: $200 - 500

157.   WCE. Council of Ad. *Constitution and by-laws*: (ICRL)

☞ The Council of Administration was a powerful four-man joint committee of the WCC Board of Control and WCE, having authority to define the office of director-general and WCE general administration. H.N. Higinbotham, Chairman. See #158 and #159, as well as #209 to #213.1.

159.   WCE. Council of Ad. *Minutes of the Meeting of the Council of Administration*: (GLD,FM)
▶Add annotation: [The meetings spanned Aug 22, 1892–Nov 6, 1893. These meetings generated a total of 65 volumes of booklets. The Field Museum has all issues bound in 10 vol.]

160.   WCE. Departimento di Pubblicita. *Dopo quattro Secoli*: (UCB)

160.1 World's Columbian Exposition. Department of Admissions. Tucker, Horace. *1st May to 30th Oct. 1893 : The World's Columbian exposition, Chicago.* New York: American Bank Note co., n.d.

12x8½. Unpaged leaves with 6 coupons per leaf dated from May 1 to Oct 30, 1893, each with a serial number. Buff card wraps, red cloth hinge at top, two cherubs, a red serial number under title. Lines for name, "Account," and "Dept." C.t. Port of Columbus on back. Inside front cover is place for photograph of owner; photos were taken by the Dept of Photography. These free pass booklets were made for officials, staff and exhibitors; the appropriate dated coupon would be removed when the owner entered the park. ☺ (GLD,HL,S) P➔ $130 - 250

161. WCE. Dept Agriculture. *Special rules and information*: (HU,MSL,UMD)
163. WCE. Dept Electricity. Barrett. *Electricity*: $150
(Col,CU,cul,EvP,FLP,FM,HU,ICRL,LHL,MIT,MSI,NSW,ref,UTA)
164. WCE. Dept Electricity. *Classification*: $30 - 50
(GLD,CCA,DU,FM,HML,HU,ICRL,IHi,LBA,Merc,MSL,PSU,SML,UCB,UMC,UMD)

164.1 World's Columbian Exposition. Department of Ethnology and Archæology. Putnam, F[rederick] W[ard], and Franz Boas. *World's Columbian Exposition, Chicago, 1893. Department of ethnology and archæology.* N.p.: n.p., n.d.

28x21½. 4 p. Caption title. Instructions for taking required measurements "of the various Native Peoples of the American Continent for the World's Columbian Exposition in Chicago in 1893." Includes anatomical diagrams and measurement points. The data was to be used to make "a series of charts showing physical characteristics." The records were to be sent to Boas. [The same methods were used to determine the model American Caucasian, also exhibited at the WCE.] ☺. (UMD)

165. WCE. Dept Ethnology. *Plan and classification department M*: (GLD,FM,HU,LBA,MIT,MSL,UBW,UCB,UMD,UPa,UTA,WM)
▶Add pub: Cambridge, MA: HULMS, 1983. Film Mas C 978.

166. WCE. Dept Ethnology. Wilson. *Proposed classification of the section of anthropology*: (UPa)
168. WCE. Dept Fine Arts. *Circular no. 3*: (S)
169. WCE. Dept Fine Arts. *Extracts from rules and regulations*: ▶Delete: Globe publisher. See #169.1.

169.1 World's Columbian Exposition. Department of Fine Arts. *Extracts from Rules and Regulations : governing the administration of the department of fine arts. Approved, July 13, 1891.* Chicago: Globe Lithographing & Printing Co., n.d.

22½x15. 1 *l* (t.p.), (6) p. White self-wraps are not included in paging, black print. C.t.: "Circular No. 2. Information for exhibitors and others interested in the department of fine arts of the World's Columbian exposition." Halsey C. Ives is listed as chief, p (6).
---- Also listed: (10) p. which includes wraps, however this info comes from a card noting a bastard t.p.
☺. (Col,UMD)

169.2 World's Columbian Exposition. Department of Fine Arts. Ives, Halsey C. "Department of fine arts, World's Columbian exposition." Letter. 1 Aug. 1891. Chicago.

22x14. (1) p. Printed letter to potential American art exhibitors requesting a list of principal works. References Circular No 2, #169, for guidance. Ives was Chief of the Fine Arts Dept. ☺. (UMD)

171. WCE. Dept Fish Products. *Classification, Rules and General Information.* (FM,HU,SML)

172.1 World's Columbian Exposition. Department of Foreign Affairs. ...*Commissions of Foreign Countries in the United States. Corrected to April 30, 1893.* N.p.: n.p., n.d.

33x20½. 8 p includes front wrap. C.t. At head of title: "World's Columbian Exposition." Department logo on front. List of foreign commissioners, alphabetical by country represented. ☺ (GLD) $25 - 45

174. WCE. Dept Horticulture. *Classification and rules department*: (CCA,DU,HU,ICRL,LBA,Merc,MSL,PSU,SML,UCLA,UMC)
▶Add publisher: Cambridge, MA: HULMS, 1983. Film Mas C 978.

174.1 World's Columbian Exposition. Department of Horticulture. ...*Department of Horticulture : rules, classifications, and information for intending exhibitors.* Chicago: Rand, McNally & Co., Printers, 1893.

23x15½. 31 p. Gray-green wraps, black print. C.t. = t.p. At head of title: "World's Columbian Exposition : Chicago, Ill., U.S.A. : 1893." ☺. (FM,SML)

174.2 World's Columbian Exposition. Department of Horticulture. *The herbarium exhibit : brief instructions for collecting, preserving and exhibiting dried botanical specimens.* Chicago?: n.p., [1893?].

28x21½. (3) p. Folded sheet. At end of text: Geo. R. Davis and J.M. Samuels (Chief of Dept). (HU)

175. WCE. Dept Liberal Arts, Bureau Charities. *Circular no. 6*: (Col,HU,ICRL,LBA,MIT,UTA)
176. WCE. Dept Liberal Arts. Bureau Charities. *Introduction to the English*: (Col,NSW)
178. WCE. Dept Liberal Arts. *Circular No. 4*: (ICRL,NDU,S)
179. WCE. Dept Liberal Arts. *Circular No. 2*: (CCA,DU,HU,ICRL,LBA,NDU,S,UMD,UTA,Yale)
180. WCE. Dept Liberal Arts. *Classification*: (CCA,DU,FM,HU,ICRL,LBA,Merc,MIT,MSL,PSU,S,SML,UCLA,UMD,WM)

181. WCE. Dept Livestock. *Rules, Information, and Premium List*: (ICRL,IHi,NAL)
▶Add: "Revised to June 1, 1893" printed on the cover is the 80 p version.
---- Also listed: 48 p?

182. WCE. Dept Machinery. *Classification and rules*: (CCA,CSL,DU,FM,HU,ICRL,LBA,Merc,MSL,PSU,SML,UMC,UMD)
▶Correct pub info: Chicago: [Donohue & Henneberry Printers], n.d.

182.1 World's Columbian Exposition. Department of Machinery. Hurlbut, F.J., ed. *Souvenir Bulletin : Machinery hall day. World's Fair, Saturday, August 26, 1893.* [Chicago: Machinery Hall (Miehle Press Co. and McIndoe Bros.)], 1893.

23x15½. 4 p. Folded pulp sheet, black print. The *Bulletin* was issued to illustrate modern publishing and printing. Lists attractions and program for this special day, including a parade. ©(GLD,S) $20 - 45

183. WCE. Dept Manufactures. *Classification*: (GLD,CCA,DU,HU,ICRL,LBA,Merc,MSL,PSU,SML,UCB,UMD,UTA) $25 - 55
▶Found with 1 *l* buff sheet laid-in "special notice to exhibitors." 21½x14. Blue print with James Allison, Chief, facsimile signature and dated "March 1, 1892."

184. WCE. Dept Manufactures. Committee on Awards. *Rules : adopted by the : board of judges in department "H," manufactures. July 21, 1893.* N.p.: n.p., 1893.
▶Completed cite: (4) p. Folded sheet, black print. Caption title. Six basic rules of the committee. Printed at end: "Thomas Hanna, Secretary : H.I. Kimball, President." ©(WM)

184.1 World's Columbian Exposition. Department of Manufactures. *To the director general of the World's Columbian Exposition, Chicago, 1893.* N.p.: n.p., n.d.

10½x20½. One large Dennison tag with eyelet. Tan card, black print, red over-stamp: "Leather & shoe trades building." For exhibitor display packages. Has blanks for R.R. siding no, location, section, column, number of application, and weight. See #195.1 for another display tag. ©(GLD) $25 - 45

185. WCE. Dept Mines and Mining. *Classification*: (B,CCA,Col,DU,HU,ICRL,LBA,Merc,MSL,PSU,SML,UCLA,UMC,UMD,UTA)
---- Also found: Issued without folding tipped-in plan.

185.1 World's Columbian Exposition. Department of Mines, Mining, Metallurgy. *...Collection of Metallurgical Specimens. General information.* N.p.: n.p., n.d.

20½x15½. 35 p. Self-wraps. Illus. Caption title. At head of title: "World's Columbian Exposition : department of mines, mining, and metallurgy. Exposition grounds, Chicago, Ill., U.S.A." Early call for exhibits; shows planned showcases and classification list. © . (FM)

186. WCE. Dept Publicity. *After Four Centuries*: (CCA,Col,DU,HU,ICRL,IHi,LBA,MSL,PSU,UCB,UMD,UTA)
▶Add pub: Cambridge, MA: HULMS, 1983. Film Mas C 978.

187. WCE. Dept Publicity. Cook. *The World's fair*: (CCA,ICRL,DU,HML,HU,LBA,Merc,MSL,uiuc,UMD,UTA,WM)
188. WCE. Dept Publicity. *Depois de*: © . (CCA,DU,HU,LBA,PSU,S,UMD)   P▼
189. WCE. Dept Publicity. *Efter fire*: (CCA,DU,HU,LBA,PSU,S,UMD)
190. WCE. Dept Publicity. *Efter fyra*: (CCA,DU,HU,IHi,KBS,LBA,PSU,S,UMD)
191. WCE. Dept Publicity: *Nach vier*: (CCA,HU,LBA,UCB,wslb,PSU,S,UMD)
192. WCE. Dept Publicity. *New York*: (GLD,HU,ICRL,SML,UPa) $30 - 50

192.1 World's Columbian Exposition. Department of Publicity and Promotion. *Sketches and descriptions of the buildings for the World's Columbian Exposition : with a map of Jackson Park.* [Chicago: Bureau of the Publicity and Promotion of the World's Fair, 1891.]

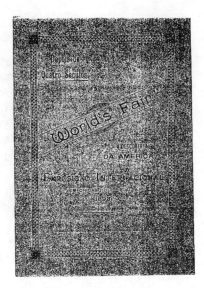

11 sheets. Illus. Map is 48x56. Handwritten title; missing t.p. and cover. (slpl—Central-Stacks: [NonCirc] Folio 907.4)

192.2 World's Columbian Exposition. Department of Publicity and Promotion. *Specimens of Descriptive Matter given by various Exhibitors in different lines of business, for insertion in the Official Catalogue.* N.p.: n.p., n.d.

23x15½. (4) p. Folded sheet, black print. Caption title. Examples as they look in the Official Catalog, #1176, from Dept A to L. Urges submission prior to publication. ☺ (WM)

193. WCE. Dept Publicity. *World's Columbian Exposition : Chicago, Ill., May 1–Oct 30, 1893 : Its scope, present condition:* (GLD,FM,ICRL,S)

194. WCE. Dept Transportation. *Classification:* (CCA,DU,HU,ICRL,LBA,Merc,MIT,MSL,PSU,S,SML,Stfd,UCB,UPa)

194.1 World's Columbian Exposition. Department of Transportation. *...Dept. of transportation exhibits : railways, vessels, vehicles. Permit for Space.* N.p.: n.p., n.d.

30½x24½. (4) p. Folded cream high-rag sheet, black print. Permit form on p (1); 24 Rules of WCE on p (2); "Special rules" on p (3). A directive to enclose all transportation exhibits by railing 2 ft 6 in. high; signs could not be above aisles or "made of muslin, linen, canvas or paper." At head of title: "Worlds' Columbian Exposition : Chicago, Ill." Permit printed in filing format. ☺ (WM)

195.1 World's Columbian Exposition. Department of Transportation. *To the director general of the World's Columbian Exposition, Chicago. 1893.* N.p.: n.p., n.d. **P➔**

10½x20½. One large Dennison tag with eyelet. Tan card stock, black print. Intended for exhibitor display packages. Blanks provided for exhibit location, section, column, number of application, and weight. 8 cm high blue-gray "G" printed on front. [Dept G = Dept of Transportation.] See #184.1 for another tag. ☺ (GLD)

$25 - 50

196.1 World's Columbian Exposition. Department of Transportation. *Transportation exhibits at the World's Columbian Exposition : an address by Willard A. Smith, chief of the department of transportation exhibits, before the American Society of Railroad Superintendents at its twentieth meeting held in NY, October 12, 1891.* N.p.: n.p., n.d.

25x17. 12 p. Caption title (no cover). (UCB)

197. WCE. Departmento de Publicidad. *Despues de cuatro Siglos:* (CCA,HU,IHi,LBA,PSU,S,UMD)

197.1 World's Columbian Exposition. Department of Works. *Map of the buildings and grounds of the World's Columbian Exposition 1893. Chicago, Ills., U.S.A. at Jackson park & midway plaisance.* N.p.: Department of Works (A.L. Swift & co. printers), n.d.

64x68. White sheet with map printed one side in black. "Max Heinze, Del" in lower right corner. (WM)

198. WCE. *Final report of the general manager of the World's Columbian exposition:* (CCA)
---- Also listed: 28½x22. Dark red morocco hc stamped in embossed gilt lettering. ☺ . (CCA)

199. WCE. *First annual report of the president:* (UCB)

200.　WCE. *General regulations for Exhibitors in the United States*:
▶Add: (4) p. Folded sheet, black print. List of Commissioners and basic rules for up-coming WF. Dated at end: "Chicago, June 21, 1891. George R. Davis."

201.　WCE. Grounds. *Committee on grounds and buildings*: (CCA,HU,MSL)
▶Add annotation: Buff self-wraps, black print. Chairman Jeffrey reports substantial building progress but warns that funds are short and the Federal govt should be asked to contribute.

201.1 World's Columbian Exposition. Grounds and Buildings Committee. *The Lake Front and Jackson Park.* N.p.: n.p., n.d.

26½x17½. 15 p. Caption title. Written: "To the President and Directors of the World's Columbian Exposition." Jackson Park had been accepted as the WCE site, but difficulties had arisen, and Washington Park was submitted as a solution. This report lists 10 "facts" in favor of Jackson Park over other Chicago sites. A six person committee, headed by Wm. R. Kerr, is listed on p 15. ☺. (UMD)

☞ Alderman Kerr was instrumental in proposing and chairing the elaborate and record-setting Chicago Day celebration at the WCE on Oct 9, 1893. See #2348.3.

201.2 World's Columbian Exposition. Grounds and Buildings Committee. Olmsted, F.L., & Co. *Instructions for grading and gardening around state and foreign buildings.* Chicago: Rand McNally and Co., 1892.

__x__. 4 p. (HU)

201.3 World's Columbian Exposition. Grounds and Buildings Committee. Olmsted, F.L., & Co. *Planting lists and notes for the World's Columbian Exposition, 1893.* N.p: n.p., [1892?]

__x__. __ p. (HU)

203.　WCE. Grounds. *Report of the grounds and building committee*: (ICRL)

203.1 World's Columbian Exposition. Illinois Central Railroad Co. *World's Columbian exposition and Illinois Central R.R. co. Agreement as to Acceptance of Ordinance for Elevation of Tracks.* N.p.: n.p., 1892.

23½x16. 4 p. Folded sheet, black print. Caption title. Dated "18 June, 1892." WCE corporation would pay ¼ of improvement cost plus 100,000 admission tickets up to $200K total to the railroad. Chicago city ordinance for change passed and approved "May 31, 1892." ☺ (S)

204.　WCE. Latin-American Dept. *Classification*: ☺. (HU,UMD)
Washington: Gibson Bros., Printers and Bookbinders, 1890. 23x15. 1 *l* (cover), 3-24 p includes back cover. Self-wraps, black print. C.t. At head of title: "World's Columbian Exposition, Chicago, U.S.A. : 1893." Classified into five groups. ▶Completed citation.

204.1 World's Columbian Exposition. Latin-American Department. ...*Concessions : granted by steamship and railway companies : in freight and passenger rates for the benefit of the Latin-American department of the World's Columbian exposition.* N.p.: n.p., n.d.

33½x20½. White sheet, black print. Typescript at end lists 3 other companies making the same concessions (price reductions and/or free travel). Agreement with original railroad dated: "May 13, 1891." At head of title: "World's Columbian Exposition. Latin-american department." ☺ (WM)

204.2 World's Columbian Exposition. Latin-American Department. ...*Favores concedido : por las empresas de vapores y de ferro-carril,...* N.p.: n.p., n.d.

33½x20½. (3) p. Folded pale green sheet, black print. Spanish edition of #204.1. At head of title: "Exposición Universal Colombina. Departmento latino-americano." Typescript at end lists 3 other companies making the concession (price reductions and/or free travel). ☺ (WM)

207.　WCE. Mechanical Dept. *Operating report of the Mechanical*: (CU)
208.　WCE. Mechanical Dept. *Report on constructional work of the Mechanical*: (CU)

208.1 World's Columbian Exposition. Medical Bureau. Owens, John E[dwin]. *Sketch of the medical bureau, World's Columbian exposition.* Chicago: American Medical Association Press, 1895.

19x13½. 24 p. Tan-flecked wraps. C.t. Caption title = c.t. Rpt from the *Journal of the American Medical Association*, Mar 16, 1895. Lists all medical and nursing staff and the dates they served the WCE. Dr. Owens was Medical Director from June 1, 1891, to Mar 31, 1894. ☺ . (ICRL)

208.2 World's Columbian Exposition. Medical Bureau. Plummer, S.C. *Punctured wounds of the feet. A report of two hundred and three cases treated at the Medical Bureau, World's Columbian Exposition, during the "construction period", June 1st, 1891, to May 1st, 1893.* Chicago: n.p., 1893.

Octovo. 8 p. (HU)

208.3 World's Columbian Exposition. Office of Director General. *Application for Sewer Connection.* N.p.: n.p., n.d.

16x34½. 1 *l* sheet, black print with attached stub. Numbered application for sewer to an exhibit. ☺ (WM)

208.4 World's Columbian Exposition. Office of Director General. *Application for Water.* N.p.: n.p., n.d.

16x34½. 1 *l* sheet, black print with attached stub. Numbered application for water to an exhibit. ☺ (WM)

208.5 World's Columbian Exposition. Office of Director General. Davis, Geo[rge] R., H.N. Higinbotham, and James W. Scott. *You are hereby cordially invited to attend a meeting to be held Thursday, August 17th,...* Chicago: n.p., 14 Aug. 1893.

22x14. Single sheet printed one side, black ink. Invitation to a meeting to propose a permanent museum of WCE exhibits in Chicago. The meeting was held in Davis's office in the Admin Bldg. The [Field] Columbian Museum resulted. See #2446.FM-B for more about the meeting notes. ☺ . (FM)

209. WCE. Office of Director General. Davis. *Remarks of Director-General Davis, May 17, 1892*: (HU)

210. WCE. Office of Director General. *General regulations for foreign exhibitors*: (HU,UMD)
---- Also found: 54, (1) p. The final (1) p is text on inside back wrap.

211. WCE. Office of Director General. *Information for foreign exhibitors*: (FM,MSL,S,SML,UMD,UMN)

211.1 World's Columbian Exposition. Office of Director General. *...Special notice to exhibitors.* N.p.: n.p., 18 Oct. 1893.

30½x22. 1 *l*. Black print. List of 18 rules for "Re-shipment of Exhibits" back to place of origin after the WF ended. Shipments not to commence before Nov 1, 1893. At bottom, Geo R. Davis and W.H. Holcomb, General Manager of Transportation. Office info at head of title. ☺ (WM)

211.2 World's Columbian Exposition. Office of Director General. *To the : Director General : of the : World's Columbian Exposition : Chicago, 1893. ETHNOLOGY.* Chicago: Pettibone, Wells & co., printers, n.d.

23x40. Tan card label, black print with bold red and blue US flag and huge "M" in blue for the Dept of Ethnology, WCE. Four-part instructions printed on back for use of crate shipping label. Showy. ☺ (WM)

211.3 World's Columbian Exposition. [Office of Director General]. *...Règlements généraux : pour les exposants étrangers, prescrits par le directeur général sous l'autorité de la commission générale, conformément à l'acte du congrés approuvé le 25 avril 1890.* Chicago: Bureau du Directeur Général de l'exposition universelle, 1891.

35x21. 8 p. Self-wraps, black print. C.t. At head of title: "Exposition universelle en commémoration de Christophe Colomb, qui aura lieu à Chicago,..." General regulation for foreign exhibitors from the "Bureau du Director Général" dated Jan 7, 1891. Includes "Circulaire" from William Windom, Secretary of the Treasury on customs regulations. French version of #210. ☺ . (UMD)

213.1 World's Columbian Exposition. Office of Director General. *World's Columbian exposition. 1893. Office of the Director-General, Chicago, May 1, 1891.* N.p.: n.p., n.d.

28x21½. (3) p. Rules and regulations adopted by the Board of Reference and Control (WCC) and Board of Directors (WCE) for the establishment of separate state exhibits. ☺ . (SFe)

216. WCE. *Official manual of the WCE*: (GLD,FM,UMN,Yale)

216.1 World's Columbian Exposition. *...Registered debenture bond. Know all men by these Presents.* Chicago: Western Bank Note Company, n.d. **P➔**

25x35½. 1 *l*. Large ornate bonds printed both sides. Vignette of Columbus landing at top. At head of title: "United States of America. World's Columbian Exposition." These bonds had a guaranteed interest of 6% and were "Due January 1st 1894." The denominations are $100, $500, $1000, and $5000. $4.5M in face value was issued as the first funds raised by the WCE. See #155.1 for the stock. ☺ . (CPL,GLD)

each: $1000+

219. WCE. *Report of the Columbian Guard*: (B)
221. WCE. *Report of the President to the Board of Directors*: (GLD,Amh,Berk,CCA,Col,CU,cul,DC,ESU,FM,GU,HML,HU,IHi,Knox, LU,MH,MOHx,MIT,MSI,MSL,NLA,S,sfpl,slpl,Smth,Stfd,UCB,UGa,UI,UIC,uiuc,UMC,UMN,UTA,VtSSt,Yale)

221.1 World's Columbian Exposition. *...Report of the Special Committee on Federal Legislation to the Board of Directors. Presented May 3, 1892.* Chicago: Rand McNally & co., 1892.

19x13. 15 p. Gray wraps with black print. C.t. = t.p. At head of title: "World's Columbian Exposition." See #230. (HU)

222. WCE. *Rules and regulations of the World's Columbian Exposition*: (HML)

223. World's Columbian Exposition. *...Rules of the director of works for the government of the guard, Chicago, 1893.* [Chicago]: A.R. Barnes & co., printers, [1893?].

14½x10. 1 *l* (t.p.), (1)-26 p, (I)-V p index. Exquisite burgundy leather cover with flap; "COLUMBIAN GUARD" boldly stamped in gilt vertically on the flap. A raised flap reveals holder for a thin pencil inside. At head of title: "World's Columbian Exposition." ☺ . (UCB)
▶Completed and improved citation.

224. WCE. *Rules of the World's Columbian Exposition*: (FM,HML)

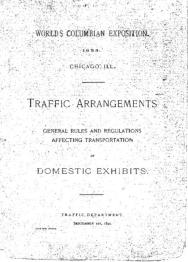

227.1 World's Columbian Exposition. Traffic Department. *...Traffic Arrangements : general rules and regulations affecting transportation of domestic exhibits.* Chicago: Traffic Department (Poole Bro.), 1892. **P➔**

23½x15½. (3)-10 p+ tipped-in folded map before back cover. Buff wraps, black print. At head of title: "World's Columbian exposition. 1893. Chicago, Ill." C.t. is given. Cover dated "September 1st, 1892." Domestic counterpart of #228, foreign rules. See #227 for a related rules supplement. ☺ . (ICRL)

228. WCE. Traffic Dept. *Traffic arrangements...foreign exhibits*: (FM,SML,Stfd)
▶Add: Copyright page: ᶜ1892 by the World's Columbian exposition and Poole Bros. Chicago. C.t. = t.p.

228.1 World's Columbian Exposition. Traffic Department. *...World's Columbian Exposition : Chicago, (Jackson Park), January 4ᵗʰ, 1893.* N.p.: n.p., n.d.

28x22. (4) p. Folded buff sheet, black print. Caption title. At top of p (1): "T.D. 47. Supplement to Traffic Arrangements..." Lists railroad terminal and storage fees for exhibitors. At end: "W.H. Holcomb, General Manager." ☺ (WM)

228.2 World's Columbian Exposition. Traffic Department. ...*World's Columbian Exposition. Rules and regulations governing exhibits consigned to Jackson Park, delivered by wagon, dray or truck.* N.p.: n.p., 5 Jan. 1893.

28x21½. (1) p. At top of p: "T.D. 44. Supplement to Traffic Arrangements..." ☺ (MSI)

228.3 World's Columbian Exposition. Treasurer's Office. Seeberger, A.F. *Final Notice.* N.p: n.p., n.d.

21½x13½. 1 *l.* Black print. Seeberger's warning to capital stock subscribers who were tardy on their payments. ☺ . (FM)   **P➔**

228.4 World's Columbian Exposition. Treasurer's Office. Seeberger, A.F. "To the Subscriber named on the inclosed statement:" Letter. 20 July 1891. Chicago.

22x14½. (1) p. Printed letter on Treasurer's office letterhead. Subject: Call for the third assessment on WCE capital stock. For timely full payment of the outstanding balance, payee to receive a free WCE admission ticket. ☺ . (ICRL)

The following very early stock correspondence from the "Board of Directors of the World's Exposition of 1892" predates the WCE Company and WCC. Entries are arranged chronologically.

229.1 World's Exposition of 1892. Board of Directors. "To the subscriber addressed on the envelope enclosing this notice:" Letter. 22 Mar. 1890. Chicago.

23x14½. 1 *l.* Printed letter. Very early WF fund-raising activity. Notice that all stock to exposition of 1892 had been subscribed; announces shareholders' meeting for Apr 4, 1890. Proxies could be sent to the listed directors, as well as nine members from organized labor representing the "Workingmen's World's Fair Auxiliary Committee." ☺ . (ICRL)

229.2 World's Exposition of 1892. Board of Directors. "To the Stockholders to whom this Notice is Addressed:" Letter. 6 May 1890. Chicago.

28x21½. 1 *l.* Letter printed on buff paper, black print. Subject: Increasing the capital stock to $10 million. The members of the Board of Directors are listed at the bottom of the letter. ☺ . (ICRL)

229.3 World's Exposition of 1892. Board of Directors. Keyes, Rolin A. "To the Stockholder To whom this notice is addressed:" Letter. N.d. [after 6 May and before 1 June 1890]. Chicago.

22x14½. 1 *l.* Letter printed on buff paper, black print. Subject: Report of a Board resolution from their May 6, 1890 meeting. Assessment to be paid to Treasurer Seeberger before June 1, 1890. Keyes was a Board member and Secretary pro tem. ☺ . (ICRL)

229.4 World's Exposition of 1892. Board of Directors. "Important Notice to Stockholders of the World's Exposition of 1892." Letter. N.d. [after 9 May and before 12 July 1890]. Chicago?

21½x14½. 1 *l.* Letter printed on buff paper, black print. Subject: Attention called to the Board's resolution authorizing two free admission tickets for each share of fully paid stock. ☺ . (ICRL)

Chapter 3

FEDERAL PUBLICATIONS

230.   *Address of Special Committee on Federal Legislation*: ☺. (HU)
▶Completed citation: 22x15. 6 p. Light brown wraps with black print. C.t. = t.p. At head of title: "World's Columbian Exposition." The seven signers from Lyman Gage to Benj. Butterworth listed at the end were a special committee of the WCE corp presenting amendments to House Bill 6953.

230.1 American Historical Association. *Annual report of the American Historical Association for the year 1890.* Washington: GPO, 1891.

23½x15½. x, 310 p. Half red morocco leather over maroon cloth hc, marbled edges. On p 140, a list of Frederic Ward Putnam's early publication proposing an ethnology exhibit at the WCE. ☺ (GLD)

230.2 American Historical Association. *Annual report of the American Historical Association for the year 1893.* Washington: GPO, 1894.

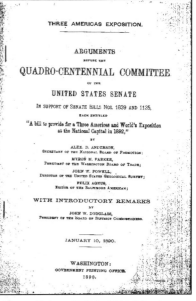

23½x15½. __ p. Contains Frederick Jackson Turner's WCE paper on the impact of closing the American frontier. See #2437.1, #2437.2 for rpts and McClay at #1225 for critique. ☺ (ref)

232.   Anderson. *Arguments before the quadro-centennial*: (HU,MIT,UMD,WM) P➡
▶Annotation for Gibson: Pale green wraps, black print. C.t. = t.p.

233.   Butterworth. *The World's Columbian...Speech*: (HU,ICRL,IHi,MIT,UTA)

233.1 Commissioner of Indian Affairs. *Annual report : of the : commissioner of indian affairs. 1894.* Washington: GPO, 1895.

23x16. viii, 1034 p+ 1 color folded map. Black cloth hc with gilt spine print. Navaho's trip to WCE on p 5 and p 100; WCE awards they obtained, pp 402, 405, 407-08. (ref)

233.2 Commissioner of Indian Affairs. *Sixty-second annual report : of the : commissioner of indian affairs : to the : secretary of the interior. 1893.* Washington: GPO, 1893.

23x16. viii, 5-1016 p+ 1 color fold map. Black cloth hc, gilt spine print. "School exhibit of Indian Bureau at Columbian Exposition," pp 20-22. (ref)

248.   Cregier. *Arguments before a special committee of the United States Senate*: (IHi,MSL)

249.   Depew. *Hearings before the quadro-centennial committee of the United States Senate*: (S)
▶Add reference: See #2011.1 for the NY Committee's issue of the arguments.

249.1 Dockery, A[lexander] M[onroe]. *The World's fair expenditures. Hon. A.M. Dockery, of Missouri, from committee on appropriations, submitted the following report to the house of representatives, Friday, May 20, 1892.* Washington: n.p., 1892.

22½x14. 1 *l* self-wrap cover, 3-15 p. Black print on buff paper. C.t. Caption title: "Report on the World's fair expenditures." Rpt of part of #274.n. concerning national expenditures and income for the WCE including reform and reductions. (MOHx)

249.2 Hawley, J.R., A.H. Colquitt, and Nelson Dingley. *Sunday closing of Columbian exposition. ...Speeches of Senators Hawley and Colquitt...* N.p.: n.p., n.d.

23½x15. 4 p. Self-wraps. Rpt from the *Congressional Record*, July 11, 12, and 18, 1892. Content: Congressmen proposed a compromise to Sunday closing, allowing exhibits to stay open but all machinery and power plants to be stopped. ☺. (HU,ICRL)

249.3 Hitt, Robert Roberts. *...Remarks of Hon. Robert R. Hitt, of Illinois...* Washington: GPO, 1890.

> 23x15. 16 p. At head of title: "Extracts from debates in the House of Representatives." (IHi)

251.   Michael. *The abridgment. Message:* (S)

251.1 Oates, William C. *The Columbian Exposition, or World's fair, at Chicago... Speech of Hon. Wm. C. Oates of Alabama, in the House of Representatives, Monday, July 18, 1892.* Washington: GPO, 1892.

> 22x14. 13 p. Self-wraps. (csuf)

251.2 Pomeroy, S.C. *...The proposed celebration of the discovery of America, within the exclusive jurisdiction of the United States, and solely by national authority. Washington, D.C., December 15th, 1889. Views of the Hon. S.C. Pomeroy, in support of senate bill 613, introduced by Hon. John J. Ingalls, of Kansas, December 5th, 1889.* Washington: Gibson Bros., Printers and Bookbinders, 1889.

> 22½x14½. 10 p. Tan wraps with black print. C.t. given. At head of title: "1492. Columbia. 1992." ☺ . (KsHx)   **P➔**

> ☞ Pomeroy was a former U.S. Senator from Kansas; Ingalls was a Senator in 1889.

253.1 Richardson, James D. *A compilation of the : messages and papers of the presidents : 1789-1897.* Vol. IX. Washington, DC: GPO, 1898 [ᶜ1897 by James D. Richardson].

> 23½x16½. 1 *l* frontis litho of Dept of Justice, (2) p (t.p. and copyright), iii-vi, 3 *l*, 3-801 p. Maroon cloth hc, blind stamped, gilt spine print. Vol IX covers 1889–97: administrations of Harrison and Cleveland. Five presidential ref to the WCE include Harrison's Proclamation of Dec 24, 1890, giving opening and closing dates for the WCE and inviting all nations to participate, p 140. ☺ (GLD) $15 - 35
> ---- Also found: N.p.: Printed by authority of Congress, 1899 [ᶜ1897 by James D. Richardson]. 25x17½.
> 1 *l* frontis litho of Bureau of Engraving, (2) p (t.p. and copyright), iii-iv, 2 *l*, 3-801 p. Brown cloth hc, blind stamped, gilt spine print, gilt top edge. WCE text ref same as 1898 issue. ☺ (GLD) $15 - 35

254.   Smithsonian. *Annual report...to 1890:* (Berk,NPG)
255.   Smithsonian. *Annual report...to 1891:* (NPG)
256.   Smithsonian. *Annual report...to 1892:* (Berk,NPG)
257.   Smithsonian. *Annual report...to 1893:* (Berk,MSL,NPG)

258.   Smithsonian. *Annual report...to 1894:* (Berk,NPG)
> ▸Add paging: xl, 770 p.

260.1 U.S. Army. Adjutant General's Office. *General orders and circulars, adjutant general's office. 1892.* Washington: GPO, 1893.

> 19x13. 4 cm thick. Variously paged general orders. Black half leather over black cloth boards, gilt spine print, red dyed edges. Folding maps. One order, No 58, (pp 6, 7, and 20) is related to appropriations and Sunday closings at WCE. No US Govt officer or employee was to receive additional moneys for work at the WCE. Stipulated that the Govt was not to release appropriated moneys unless the WCE was closed on Sunday. ☺ (GLD) $15 - 30

260.2 U.S. Army. Adjutant General's Office. *General orders and circulars, adjutant general's office. 1893.* Washington: GPO, 1894.

> 19x13. 3 cm thick. Variously paged general orders. Black half leather over black cloth boards, gilt spine print, red speckled edges. Contains three orders related to WCE appropriations and travel: Nos 27, 63, and 89. ☺ (GLD) $15 - 30

260.3 U.S. Army. Corps of Engineers. ...*War department exhibit. Corps of Engineers, U.S. Army. Catalogue.* Washington: GPO, 1893.

21½x15. 104 p. At head of title: "World's Columbian exposition, Chicago, Illinois, 1893." Contents: list and description of models, photographs, maps, surveys shown at the WCE. ☺ . (Col,CU,UBW)

261.   US. Army. Surgeon Gen Office. *Description of microscopes from the Army Medical*: (HU)

262.   US. Army. Surgeon Gen Office. *Description of selected specimens from the Army Medical*: (HU)

262.1 U.S. Army. Surgeon General's Office. *Description of the models of hospital cars from the Army Medical Museum, Washington, D.C.* Chicago: n.p., n.d.

__x__. __ p. (HU)

262.2 U.S. Army. Surgeon General's Office. *Description of the models of hospital steam vessels from the Army Medical Museum, Washington, D.C.* Chicago: n.p., n.d.

__x__. __ p. (HU)

262.3 U.S. Army. Surgeon General's Office. *Description of the models of hospitals.* Chicago: n.p., n.d.

__x__. __ p. (HU)

263.   US. Army. Surgeon Gen Office. Greenleaf. *The personal identity of the soldier*: (HU)

263.1 U.S. Army. Surgeon General's Office. LaGarde, Louis A. ...*War department exhibit. Medical department United States army. No. 4. Description of Ambulance Wagons, Travois, Etc.* Chicago: [US Army Medical Dept.], 1892–'93.

23x15. 11 p. Tan wraps, black print. C.t. = t.p. Diagrams of conveyances. (HU,S)

263.2 U.S. Army. Surgeon General's Office. ...*Standard supply table of the Medical Department, United States Army.* Chicago: n.p., n.d.

__x__. __ p. At head of title: World's Columbian Exposition, Chicago, Illinois." (HU)

263.3 [U.S. Bureau of Education]. American Library Association. ...*World's Columbian Exposition : Library Exhibit. Suggestions of the Committee.* N.p.: n.p., n.d.

13x8. 2-6, (1) p. C.t. At head of title: "American Library Association." On p 2: "This report presents suggestion made, rather that plans adopted." [See A.L.A. in index for related items.] ☺ . (UMD)

264.   US. Bureau of Education. *Catalog of "A.L.A."*:
(GLD,CU,DC,ESU,FM,HU,KCPL,NLI,NSW,OU,SHB,SML,UBW,UCD,UCLA,UTA)
▸Add: C.t. = t.p. [See A.L.A. in index for related items.] P➔ $30 – 65

266.   US. Bureau of Education. *Education at the World's Columbian*: (HU,S)
▸Complete citation: Washington: GPO, 1896. 23½x15. Gray wraps, black print. C.t. = t.p. At top of t.p.: "[Whole Number 223." (No right bracket).

267.   US. Bureau of Education. *Report of the commissioner...1892–93*: (HML,LBA)

268.   US. Commission for Fish. Bean. *Report of the representative*: (Amh,HU,S)
▸Add cover description: Tan wraps with black print.

268.1 U.S. Commission for Fish and Fisheries. Forbes, S.A. *The aquarium of the United States fish commission at the World's Columbian exposition. Report of the director.* Washington: GPO, 1894.

29½x20. 1 *l* (t.p.), 143-90 p. Blue-flecked gray wraps with black print. C.t. = t.p. Rpt of Article 18, Bulletin of the U.S. Fish Commission. [See index under Fish Commission for related reports.] ☺ (S)

269.   US. Commission for Fish. *Report of the commissioner...June 30, 1894*:
---- Also found: Identical except at head of title: "United States commission for fish and fisheries. Part XX." No mention of 54th Congress, etc. [See index under Fish Commission for related reports.]

270.1 U.S. Cong. *The executive documents of the house of representatives for the first session of the fifty-second congress. 1891-'92. In thirty-eight volumes.* Washington: GPO, 1892.

23x14½. Contains WCE Congressional documents which can be found using the index or the *Serial Set*. Individual WCE House Docs from these volumes can be found in the Legislative reports and documents listed from #270.4 to #279.a. (UNM)

270.2 U.S. Cong. *The executive documents of the house of representatives for the second session of the fifty-second congress. 1892-'93. In thirty-four volumes.* Washington: GPO, 1893.

23x14½. Contains WCE Congressional activity which can be found using the index or the *Serial Set*. Individual WCE House Docs from these volumes can be found in the Legislative reports and documents listed in #270.4 to #279.a. (UNM)

270.3 U.S. Cong. *The executive documents of the house of representatives for the second session of the fifty-third congress. 1893-'94. In thirty-one volumes.* Washington: GPO, 1895.

23x14½. Contains WCE Congressional activity which can be found using the index or the *Serial Set*. Individual WCE items from these volumes can be found in the Legislative reports and documents listed in #270.4 to #279.a. (UNM)

The Legislative reports and documents listed below are in chronological order under the Congress and Session that created them. All are 23x14½ unless otherwise noted. SS denotes Serial Set.

49th Cong. 2d Sess.: 1887-88

270.4. U.S. Cong. Senate. Mis. Doc. 47. *Resolutions adopted by the National Board of Trade in favor of a World's Exposition in 1892 in honor of the four-hundredth anniversary of the discovery of America.* 20 Jan. 1887. (SS 2451).

(1) p. Senate resolution based upon the Board of Trade resolutions of Jan 20, 1887. Early indication that what was to become the WCE was grounded in fostering international commerce. ☺. (UNM)

50th Cong. 1st Sess.: 1888-89

271.a.   US. Cong. House. Foreign. H Rept 2601: ☺. (HML,ICRL,UPa,WM)
▶Add date: June 16, 1888. Add at head of title: "Permanent exposition of the three Americas."

51st Cong. 1st Sess.: 1889-90

272.b.1 US. Cong. House. H. R. 8393. *...AN ACT : To provide for celebrating the four hundredth anniversary of the discovery of America by Christopher Columbus by holding an international...* 11 Apr. 1890.

27x17½. 12 p. Printed in large type, each line numbered. This is the act, under revision in the senate, that enabled the Columbian Exposition to be held in Chicago. At head of title: "[Calendar No., 898. ..." [Subsequently passed by both houses, it was signed into law on April 25, 1890]. * ☺. (IHi)

51st Cong. 2d Sess.: 1890-91

273.a.   US. Cong. House. Ex Doc 175: (HML,HU)

273.d. U.S. Cong. House. H. Rept. 3500. *Investigation into the condition of the capitol World's fair.* 17 Jan. 1891.

23x14½. 26 p+ 1 *l* map of Chicago + 1 *l* plat of Jackson Park between p 2 and p 3. 5 *l* illus at end include 4 *l* of proposed Government Building [not realized], and 1 *l* of Navy Dept battleship exhibit. Report of Mr. Chandler of Massachusetts. (HML,S) $15 - 35

52d Cong. 1st Sess.: 1891-92

274.1 U.S. Cong. Senate. Mis. Doc. 24. *Resolution:* [Foreign Relations]. 17 Dec. 1891. (SS 2904).

(1) p. Committee on Foreign Relations instructed to inquire about holding an International Congress on Arbitration at the WCE. ☺ . (UNM)

274.g.   US. Cong. House. Ex Doc 142: (HU)
274.h.   US. Cong. House. Ex Doc 153: (S)

274.k.1 U.S. Cong. Senate. S. Rept. 370. *Report: [To accompany S. R. 42.].* 14 Mar. 1892. (SS 2912).

1 p. The Select Committee on the Quadro-Centennial modified joint resolution S. R. 42 inviting the King and Queen of Spain and the descendants of Columbus to the WCE. ☺ . (UNM)

274.k.2 U.S. Cong. Senate. S. Rept. 371. *Report: [To accompany S. R. 43.].* 14 Mar. 1892. (SS 2912).

(1) p. Select Committee on the Quadro-Centennial modified joint resolution S. R. 43 requesting loan of items for the WCE. ☺ . (UNM)

274.k.3 U.S. Cong. Senate. S. Rept. 372. *Report: [To accompany S. R. 41.].* 14 Mar. 1892. (SS 2912).

(1) p. The Select Committee on the Quadro-Centennial modified S. Rept. 41 which invited the presidents of American Republics to participate in the WCE. ☺ . (UNM)

274.k.4 U.S. Cong. Senate. S. Rept. 388. *Report: [To accompany H. R. 3980.].* 16 Mar. 1892. (SS 2912).

(1) p. Report from the Committee on Territories requesting a one-time grant of Arizona Territory indebtedness ($30,000 for WCE exhibit) which would exceed the "Harrison act" maximum. ☺ . (UNM)

274.k.5 U.S. Cong. House. H. Rept. 923. *Columbian historical exposition at Madrid.* 30 Mar. 1892. (SS 3044).

(1) p. The original request for an appropriation of $25,000 was lowered to $10,000. ☺ (UNM)

274.l.1 U.S. Cong. Senate. S. Rept. 532. *Report: [To accompany S. 866.].* 11 Apr. 1892. (SS 2913).

(1) p. Report from Committee on Military Affairs that the Army would discharge its duty at the WCE and wished to amend S. 866 to have officers report to the Commander, Dept of the Lakes. ☺ . (UNM)

274.l.2 U.S. Cong. Senate. Mis. Doc. 128. *Letter from James G. Blaine, Secretary of State, asking an appropriation to pay the expenses of the commissioners to the Madrid exposition...* 13 Apr. 1892. (SS 2907).

(1) p. Blaine requested increased appropriation from $10,000 to $25,000. ☺ . (UNM)

274.m.1 U.S. Cong. Senate. Mis. Doc. 149. *Resolution:* [Quadro-Centennial]. 10 May 1892. (SS 2907).

(1) p. Select Committee on Quadro-Centennial instructed to inquire into National Guard encamping at WCE with full pay. ☺ . (GLD,UNM) $7 - 15

274.n.   U.S. Cong. House. Committee on Appropriations. *World's fair expenditures*: (HML,HU,IHi,MSL,NPG,NSW,S)
---- Also found: . *The reports of committees of the house of representatives for the first session of the fifty-second congress. 1891-'92.* 12 vol. Washington: GPO, 1892.

Vol. 6 is H Rept 1454: "World's fair expenditures." Paging: clii, index to House Reports, 698 p. Full calf with red and black spine labels. * ☺ (GLD,CU) $40 - 80

274.o.1 U.S. Cong. Senate. Mis. Doc. 163. *Letter from the Secretary of State relative to a peace conference of the governments of the World, to sit in Chicago during and in connection with the Columbian exposition, for the purpose of considering the questions of the settlement of all international differences by arbitration.* 25 May 1892. (SS 2907).

11 p. From the Committee on Foreign Relations which was headed by James G. Blaine. Contains the "Original Announcement" (#2229), "The Scope of this [Government] Department" (#2139), and "Objects [of the Auxiliary]" (#2228.2) from the World's Congress Auxiliary. ©.(UNM)

274.v.1 U.S. Cong. House. Ex. Doc. 260. *Four hundredth anniversary of the discovery of America. Letter from the Secretary of the Treasury, requesting...* 13 June 1892.

(1) p. Request for $250,000 for customs. Secretary of the Treasury: Charles Foster. ©(UNM)

274.w. US. Cong. House. H Rept 1660. *Four hundredth anniversary*: (HU)
▶Paging correction: 7 p. Report of A.C. Durborow.

274.y. US. Cong. House. H Rept 2091. *Dedication of buildings at the World's Columbian exposition*: (ref,S) $10

274.y.1 U.S. Cong. Senate. Mis. Doc. 223. *Resolution:* [Quadro-Centennial]. 1 Aug. 1892. (SS 2907).

(1) p. Authorized the Select Committee on the Quatro-Centennial to visit, with expenses paid, the WCE grounds during the Congressional recess. ©.(UNM)

274.z. US. Cong. House. H Rept 2123. *Foreign exhibitors at the World's Columbian exposition*: (S)

52d Cong. 2d Sess.: 1892-93

275.1 U.S. Cong. House. Ex. Doc. 1, Part 9. *...Report of the board of management U.S. government exhibit, World's Columbian exposition.* 6 Dec. 1892. (SS 3097).

3 p. At head of title: "Government exhibit, World's Columbian exposition." US Govt departmental representatives to report to the US President on the Govt Exhibit. Department heads urged Congressional passage of the remainder of appropriations earlier defined as one million dollars. ©.(UNM)

275.c. US. Cong. Senate. Ex Doc 24. *Letter from the secretary of war*: (S)

275.c.1 U.S. Cong. House. Ex. Doc. 166. *Expenses of committee on awards of the World's Columbian commission. Letter from the secretary of the treasury,...* 9 Jan. 1893. (SS 3105).

2 p. The estimate of appropriation needed by the Committee on Awards was $570,880.94. The Secretary of the Treasury gave it a favorable recommendation. ©.(UNM)

275.e.1 U.S. Cong. Senate. S. Rept. 1215. *Report: [To accompany Senate concurrent resolution authorizing the printing...]* 25 Jan. 1893. (SS 3072).

2 p. Committee on Printing recommended printing 5,000 extra copies of the 5-vol report of the US Commission to the Paris Exposition of 1889, to be used to assist in WCE exhibit preparation. ©.(UNM)

275.f. US. Cong. House. Ex Doc 211. *Message from the president of the United States*: (HML,HU,MSL)

275.f.1 U.S. Cong. House. H. Rept. 2394. *Loan of picture for exhibition at the World's Columbian exposition. Report: [To accompany S. R. 134.].* 1 Feb. 1893. (SS 3141).

(1) p. Select Committee on the Columbian Exposition recommended passage of S. R. 134 authorizing loan of the picture "The recall of Columbus." ©.(UNM)

275.f.2 U.S. Cong. House. H. Rept. 2415. *Powers of United States government exhibit board. ...Report: [To accompany H. Res. 169.].* 3 Feb. 1893. (SS 3141).

2 p. Committee on the Library considered H. Res. 169, which would have broadened the Government Exhibit Board to include colored race participation, and recommended passage. ©.(UNM)

275.h. U.S. Cong. Senate. Ex. Doc. 74. *Letter from the acting secretary of the treasury, in response : To Senate resolution of February 14, 1893, relative to the appropriation for the current year to aid the World's Columbian Exposition.* 16 Feb. 1893. (SS 3062).

(1) p.   The WCE Corporation accepted the government appropriation and the condition of Sunday closing upon which the appropriation was contingent.   ☺ . (UNM)

275.i. U.S. Cong. Senate. Mis. Doc. 60. *Memorial of the general committee of thirty appointed by the chamber of commerce of New York, asking for an appropriation by Congress for the entertainment of such guests…who may visit our shores during the World's Columbian exposition.* 25 Feb. 1893. (SS 3064).

(1) p.   The New York committee members made the request for a "liberal appropriation" by letter to Levi P. Morton, US Vice President, on Feb 23, 1893.   ☺ . (UNM)

275.j. U.S. Cong. Senate. Mis. Doc. 70. *Appropriations, new offices, etc. : Statements showing…* [6 statements]. 3 Mar. 1893. Washington: GPO, 1893.

29½x20½. 1 *l*, 343 p. Full calf with gilt print on red and black spine labels. The first leaf is general title for this series of documents of which this is vol. 8: "The miscellaneous documents of the senate of the United States for the second session of the fifty-second congress. 1892–'93." Eight WCE and two WCC appropriations are listed in the index to this vol. ☺ (GLD) $30 - 60

53d Cong. 1st Sess & Special Sess. of Senate: 1893

276.b. U.S. Cong. House. H. Rept. 156. *World's fair prize winners' exposition. Report: [To accompany H. R. 4015.].* 31 Oct. 1893. (SS 3157).

(1) p.   Committee on Ways and Means recommended passage of H. R. 4015 enabling free entry of foreign exhibits transferred from the closed WCE to the "World's Fair Prize Winners' Exposition" to be held at New York City.   ☺ . (UNM)

276.c. U.S. Cong. Senate. S. Rept. 71. *Report: [To accompany H. Res. 22.].* 2 Nov. 1893. (SS 3147).

2 p.   Committee on Finance suggested that H. Res. 22, which lowered import duties 50% for foreign exhibitors at the WCE, was unfair to foreigners not exhibiting at the WCE.   ☺ . (UNM)

53d Cong. 2d & 3d Sess.: 1894-95

277.1 U.S. Cong. House. H. Rept. 5272. *A bill : For the transfer of a portion of the exhibit of the Department of State at the World's Columbian Exposition to the Columbian Museum of Chicago.* 16 Jan. 1894.

(1) p.   Introduced by Rep. Durborow and referred to the Committee on Appropriations.   ☺ . (FM-Archives)

277.2 U.S. Cong. House. Mis. Doc. 103. *World's Columbian exposition. Report of the auditor to the board of directors of the World's Columbian exposition, January 31, 1894.* 2 Mar. 1894. (SS 3229).

12 p.   This report gives a complete list of receipts and expenses for the WCE up to Feb 11, 1894. Submitted by the Acting Auditor, Charles V. Barrington.   ☺ . (MIT,UNM)   **P➜**

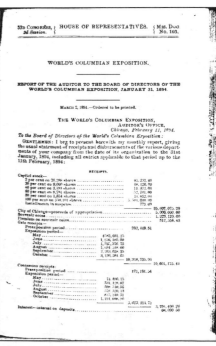

277.3 U.S. Cong. House. H. Rept. 578. *Columbian caravels. Report: [To accompany H. R. 6250.].* 13 Mar. 1894. (SS 3270).

2 p.   Committee on Naval Affairs recommended loaning the caravels to the American National Red Cross for one year so that they could be exhibited along rivers and the US coasts. [See #277.d.] ☺ . (UNM)

277.a.1 U.S. Cong. Senate. S. Rept. 521. *Report: [To accompany S. 1454.].* 12 July 1894. (SS 3192).

(1) p.   Committee on Naval Affairs authorized Secretary of Navy to transfer the Columbus caravels to the Columbian Museum of Chicago, now known as the Field Museum.   ☺ . (UNM)

277.b. US. Cong. House. Ex Doc 100. *Report of the United States Commission to...Madrid*:
▸Add: "order to print" date: Dec 11, 1894.

277.c. U.S. Cong. House. H. Rept. 1497. *Publication of the dairy test made by the Columbian exposition. Report: [To accompany H. Res. 235.].* 13 Dec. 1894. (SS 3345).

4 p. Report details prolonged testing of milk production of three dairy breeds at the WCE. ☺. (UNM)

277.d. U.S. Cong. House. H. Rept. 1716. *Caravels of Columbus. Report: [To accompany S. 1454.].* 29 Jan. 1895. (SS 3345).

(1) p. Committee on Naval Affairs recommended passage of bill transferring caravels to the Columbian Museum in Chicago. [See #277.3.] ☺. (UNM)

277.e. U.S. Cong. House. H. Rept. 1873. *Dairy tests made by the Columbian exposition. Adverse report: [To accompany H. Res. 235.].* 20 Feb. 1895. (SS 3346).

(1) p. Committee on Printing recommended not passing H. Res. 235 because the dairy tests were not conducted by the government. ☺. (UNM)

54th Cong. 2d Sess: 1896-97

277.m. U.S. Cong. House. H. Doc. 259. *Final report World's Columbian commission. Message from the President of the United States, relating to the final report of the World's Columbian commission.* 5 Feb. 1897. (SS 3534).

(1) p. Grover Cleveland's report to Congress. The final report of the Commission consisted of five large boxes of documents which the President submitted to the discretion of Congress. ☺. (UNM)

57 Cong. 1st Sess.: 1901-02

279.a. US. Cong. House. H Doc 510. Committee on Awards. *Report of the committee on awards*:
* (GLD,CCA,CLP,Col,HU,ICRL,LBA,NAL,NLA,OU,sfpl,UCB)

End of Legislative reports and documents.

286.1 U.S. Custom House, Chicago. *Notice of abandonment of World's fair exhibits.* N.p.: n.p., [2 Sept. 1893].

28x21½. Single sheet printed both sides and tri-folded so that title given appears on outside panel. Twenty-five hundred copies were printed. Notice from foreign exhibitor of intention to abandon exhibit materials to the United States at the close of the WCE. ☺. (FM-Archives)

287.   US. Dept Ag. Div of Entomology. *Catalogue of the exhibit of economic*: (GLD,HU,NAL,uiuc) $30 - 65
▸Add alternate author: C.V. Riley, US entomologist.

287.1 U.S. Department of Agriculture. *Report of the secretary of agriculture : 1890.* Washington: GPO, 1890.

23½x15½. 612 p. Black cloth hc, gilt spine print. J.M. Rusk, secretary, in his report to the President, suggests that the Dept not exhibit at the WCE unless sufficient funds are appropriated, pp 52-53. ☺ (GLD)

287.2 U.S. Department of Agriculture. *Report of the secretary of agriculture : 1893.* Washington: GPO, 1894.

23½x15½. 608 p+ interspersed 6 fold maps and 22 plates, some pretty chromoliths. Black cloth hc, gilt spine print. Contains Asst Sec Willits's WCE report (#290), pp 51-86. Nearly all of the other reports of the division chiefs in the book describe their WCE responsibilities. J. Sterling Morton, Secretary of Agriculture. Excellent ref on the extensive role of the Dept at the WF. ☺ (GLD) $16 - 40

288.   US. Dept Ag. Weather Bureau. *Souvenir : Weather Bureau*: (KS,S,WM)
289.   US. Dept Ag. Wiley. *Analysis of cereals collected at the World's Columbian exposition*: (HU)
290.   US. Dept Ag. Willits. "Special report of the assistant secretary of agriculture...1893": (GLD,NAL) $16 - 40

290.1 U.S. Department of the Interior. Bureau of Education. Harris, W[illia]m. L. *[Bulletin No. 1.] Dear Sir:* Washington: Bureau of Education, 5 Feb. 1891.

26x20½. (4) p. Folded sheet. Letter format. First Bulletin in a series issued by Commissioner Harris, this letter to city school superintendents called for formation of state committees with the purpose of unifying educational exhibits in one bldg at the WCE. ☺ . (MSL)

290.2 U.S. Department of the Interior. Bureau of Education. Harris, W[illia]m. L. *Bulletin No. 2. 2d Edition. : Dear Sir:* Washington: Bureau of Education, 10 Sept. 1891.

26x20½. (4) p. Folded sheet. Letter format. Also dated "April 4, 1891," probably for first ed. Caption title: "Education as exhibited at [previous] World's fairs." At upper left of p (1): "World's Columbian exposition : educational exhibit : C. Wellman Parks, Special Agent, Troy, N.Y." ☺ . (MSL)

290.3 U.S. Department of the Interior. Bureau of Education. Harris, W[illia]m. L. *Bulletin No. 3. Dear Sir:* Washington: Bureau of Education, 15 July 1891.

26x20½. (4) p. Folded sheet. Letter format. Harris tells of work and exhibits already completed for the WCE and requests that additional state committees be formed. Upper left of p (1): "World's Columbian exposition : educational exhibit : C. Wellman Parks, Special Agent, Troy, N.Y." ☺ . (MSL)

290.4 U.S. Department of the Interior. Bureau of Education. Harris, W[illia]m. L. *Bulletin No. 7. To Librarians:* Washington: Bureau of Education, 21 Jan. 1893.

26x20½. (4) p. Folded sheet. Letter format. Harris explained that a library would be a special feature of the Bureau's part of the US govt exhibit and that the Bureau would exhibit jointly with the ALA, illustrating means and methods for a village library of 5000 vols to be serviceable to teachers and pupils of the village. Upper left of p (1): "World's Columbian exposition : educational exhibit : C. Wellman Parks, Special Agent, Troy, N.Y." ☺ . (WM)

290.5 U.S. Department of the Interior. U.S. Patent Office. *The official gazette of the United States Patent Office.* [Washington]: GPO?, 1893.

27x19. pp (455)-592. Wraps. Caption title. Issue: "Vol. 62.—No. 4. Tuesday, January 24, 1893." Request on p (455) to inventors and manufacturers to supply models of inventions for the Patent Office exhibit at the WCE. This request was made because fire had destroyed models that had been held at the Patent Office. ☺ (GLD) $15 - 30

290.6 U.S. Light-House Board. Johnson, Arnold Burges. *...Report...upon the exhibit of the light-house board at the World's Columbian exposition held at Chicago, 1893.* [Washington: GPO, 1894].

23x15. pp 221-62. Tan wraps with black print, folded frontis of light-house construction. At head of title: "Report of the light-house board, 1894. Appendix No. III." Ellipse between *Report* and *upon* represents author's name and position as clerk of the board. Rpt from US Light-House Board 1894 annual report. ☺ . (LBA,MIT,MSL)

291.   US. National Archives. Helton. *Preliminary inventory of the records of United States*: (csuf)
293.   US. National Museum. *Annual report...Smithsonian institution...1891*: (NAL,NPG)
294.   US. National Museum. *Annual report...Smithsonian institution...1892*: (NPG)
295.   US. National Museum. *Annual report...Smithsonian institution...1893*: (Amh,NAL,NPG)
296.   US. National Museum. *Annual report...Smithsonian institution...1894*: (NPG)
297.   US. National Museum. *Annual report...Smithsonian Institution...1895*: (NPG)

297.1 U.S. National Museum. *Annual report of the board of regents of the Smithsonian Institution, showing the operations, expenditures, and condition of the institution for the year ending June 30, 1897. Report of the U.S. national museum. Part II.* Washington: GPO, 1901.

23½x16½. 1 *l* frontis, xii, 515 p. Green cloth hc, gilt print spine, gilt logo. Half title: "A memorial of George Brown Goode, together with a selection of his papers on museums and on the history of science in America." Mentions his WCE classification system. ☺ (GLD) $15 - 30

298.   US. National Museum. *Annual report...Smithsonian institution...1901*: (NPG)

299.   US. National Museum. Bureau of Ethnology. *Thirteenth annual report...1891–'92*: (ref)
▶Complete citation: 28x21½. 3 *l*, v-lix, 462 p. Olive cloth hc, gilt print. Tells which Ethnology Bureau staff members collected Native American artifacts for the display at the WCE and where the artifacts were collected.

299.1 U.S. National Museum. Bureau of Ethnology. *Fifteenth annual report of the Bureau of Ethnology to the secretary of the Smithsonian Institution. 1893–'94*. J.W. Powell, director. Washington: GPO, 1897.

28x21½. 2 *l*, iii-cxxi, 366 p+ fold outs. Olive cloth hc with gilt print. Describes collection of Native American displays for the WCE similar to #299. (ref) $60 - 140

300.   US. Navy Dept. Poundstone. *Catalogue of the Exhibit of the U.S. Navy*: (CU,FPL,HML,HU,S)   P↓
302.   US. Treasury Dept. Customs Div. *New regulations governing*: (SML)

302.1 U.S. Treasury Department. Office of Coast and Geodetic Survey. Mendenhall, T.C. *Topography*. [Washington]: n.p., [1 May 1893].

16½x11. 4 p. Buff self-wraps, black print. C.t. Topography, surveying, instruments. Dated at end. Mendenhall was superintendent. No WCE content; probable WCE handout. ☺ (S)

302.2 U.S. Treasury Department. Office of Coast and Geodetic Survey. Mendenhall, T.C. *The U.S. coast and geodetic survey*. [Washington]: n.p., [1 May 1893].

16½x11. 4 p. Buff self-wraps, black print. C.t. Gives the reasons for surveying coasts; description of field and office work. Dated at end. Mendenhall was superintendent. No WCE content; probable handout. ☺ (S)

303.   US. Treasury Dept. OCGS. *The methods and results of the U.S. Coast and Geodetic Survey*: (MSL)

304.   US. Treasury Dept. OCGS. *The Preparation and arrangement*: ☺ . (MSL)
▶Add info: Author: Wainwright, D.B. At head of title: "Appendix No. 10—1893." Contained within Report of the Superintendent of the US Coast and Geodetic Survey for fiscal year 1893.

Chapter 4

FOREIGN COUNTRY PUBLICATIONS

-A-

305.   Argentina. Consejo. *Trabajos escolares*: (NSW,UBW)

306.   Argentina. Decoud. *Les sciences médicales*: (HU,SML,UCB,UMN,UTA)

306.1 Argentina. Departmento Nacional de Minas y Geologia. Hoskold, H.D. *...Informe general : sobre las : colecciones de minerales : productos metalúrgicos : y maquinaria minera : expuestos por las diversas naciones en la exposición internacional Columbiana de Chicago de 1893.* Buenos Aires: Imprenta de Obras, de J.A. Berra, 1894.

    25½x16½. 344 p includes five numbered blank pages headed "para notas." Dept name at head of title. Description of their mineral exhibit (pp 5-61), WCE mineral exhibits (pp 63-102), and minerals found in the US (pp 103-134). In Spanish. Hoskold was commissioner for mines and metallurgy for the Paris and Chicago WFs. ☺. (Stfd)

307.   Argentina. Entre Rios. Comisión. *La provincia de Entre Rios*: (Amh,Col,CU,FM,HU,MIT,SML,Stfd,UCB,UTA,WM,Yale)

309.   Argentina. Ministerio. *Report upon the state of secondary and normal education*: (MSI)

312.   Argentina. Padilla. *Organisation et institutions sanitairies*: (HU,ICRL,LBA,Stfd,UCB)

312.1 Austria. Bayer, A[dolph] H. *Worlds* [sic] *fair zu Chicago. Bericht über innendecoration, möbel, stoffe, tapeten, teppiche und keramische producte...* Wein: Verlag des niederoesterreichischen gewerbevereins (Press of »Reichswehr« G. David & A. Keiss), 1894.

    23x15. 41 p. Rpt from the industrial union's periodical. Bayer was an architect sent to the WCE as an industrial union representative. Trans: World's Fair at Chicago. Report on interior decoration, furniture, fabrics, wall paper, carpets, and ceramic products. ☺. (ONB,UBW)

312.2 Austria. Biberhofer, Franz. *Das kunstgewerbe in Amerika und auf der ausstellung in Chicago : mit besonderer berücksichtigung der metallbranche und der galanterie-artikel. Bericht...* Wein: Verlag des niederoesterreichischen gewerbevereins (Press of »Reichswehr« G. David & A. Keiss), 1894.

    23x15. 46 p. Rpt from the industrial union's periodical. Biberhofer was an architect sent to the WCE as an industrial union representative. Trans: Report on craft work in America and at the World's Fair in Chicago with special emphasis on metal and fancy work. ☺. (ONB)

312.3 Austria. Demuth, Adolf. *Die columbische Welt-Ausstellung. Bericht über eine Studienreise nach Nord-Amerika, erstattet in der ordentl., öffentl. Sitzung der Reichenberger Handels- und Gewerbekammer : am 1. December 1893...* Reichenberg: Verlag der Handel- und Gewerbekammer (Press of "Gebrüder Stiepel), 1893.

    26½x19. 32 p. Demuth was a member of the board. Trans: The Columbian World's Fair. Report on a study trip to North America. Delivered at a public session of the Reichenberg trade and industrial board on Dec 1, 1893. [Reichenberg is the German name of what became Liberec, Czechoslovakia.] ☺. (ONB)

313.   Austria. IR Central Commission. *Official special catalogue of the Austrian*: (MSI,ONB,SML,UBW)
    ---- Also found: Dark green hc, gold lettering, etc. (same as dark tan version).

313.1 Austria. K.K. Central-Commission. *Amtlicher Special-katalog der österreichischen abtheilung auf der weltausstellung in Chicago 1893.* Wien: Druck von Johann N. Vernay, n.d.

    20x13½. 122 p+ 5 interspersed plates. German version of #313. . (ONB,UBW,wslb)

314.   Austria. KK C-C. *Officieller bericht*: (HU,ONB,SML,UBW,wslb,Yale)
    ▸Add: In German. There are 9 official reports in the 4 vols, each with its own author and title. These may be found separately, such as #314.5 (vol 4, part 9.)

314.1 Austria. ...*Official Souvenir of Old Vienna : (Vienna in the seventeenth century) : Midway Plaisance, World's Columbian Exposition, Chicago.* [Chicago: Edward Beeh, Jr., printer, 1893].

> 22½x15. 1 *l*, (3)-43 p. Maize glossy wraps, black print and design. At head of title: "1492 1893." Dual German and English language text. Translated by Sigmund Krausz. Litho on cover is dated 1893. B/w illus. © (GLD)
>
> $25 - 45

314.2 Austria. Palitschek, Anton von. *Ergebnisse der weltausstellung Chicago. Vortrag gehalten am 8. Februar 1894 im K.K. Oesterr. Handels-museum in Wien...* Wien: Verlag von Gerold & C° (Press of Ch. Reisser & M. Werthner), 1894.

> 22½x14½. 24 p. Palitschek was Austrian General Consul at the WCE. Trans: Results of the Chicago World's Fair. A lecture held on Feb 8, 1894, at Handels-Museum in Vienna. © . (ONB,UBW)

314.3 Austria. Palitschek, Anton von. *...Die weltausstellung in Chicago : 1893. Vortrag gehalten im k.k. österr. Handels-Museum am 14. October...* Wien: Verlag des k. k. österr. Handels-museums (Press of Ch. Reisser & M. Werthner), 1891.

> 22x15. 23 p. C.t. = t.p. At head of title: "N$^{R.}$16. K.K. Österr. Handels-Museum." Palitschek was Austrian Consul in New York. Trans: The World's Fair in Chicago. Lecture held in the Handels-Museum on Oct 14, 1891. © . (ONB,UBW)

314.4 Austria. Politzer, Adam. *Bericht über die medizinisch-hygienische Abtheilung der Weltausstellung in Chicago 1893.* Wien: Verlag von Moritz Perles, 1894.

> 21½x14. 30 p. Caption title. Reprint from *Wiener Medizinischen Wochenschrift.* Trans: Report about the medical hygiene division at the World's exposition in Chicago 1893. © . (UBW)

314.5 Austria. Sahulka, Johann. *...Die : elektrotechnik : auf der : weltausstellung in Chicago.* Wien: Verlag der K.K. Central-Commission (druck von Rudolf M. Rohrer in Brünn), 1895.

> 28½x19½. vii, 101 p, 7 folded *l* of plates. Buff wraps, black print. At head of title: "Officieller bericht : der K.K. Österr. : central-commission für die weltausstellung : in : Chicago 1893. Heft IX." Part 9 of vol 4 of #314. In German. © . (CCA,MIT)

315.1 Austria. Schwarz, Adolf. *Die industrie-halle : auf der weltausstellung in Chicago. Vortrag gehalten im niederoesterreichischen gewerbeverein in Wien...* Wein: Verlag des niederoesterreichischen gewerbevereins (Press of »Reichswehr« G. David & A. Keiss), 1893.

> 23x15½. 22 p. Rpt from the Austrian-Hungarian Export Union's periodical. Schwarz was Secretary of the Union. Trans: The Manufactures Building at the World's Fair in Chicago. Lecture held at the Lower Austrian Industrial Union in Vienna. © . (ONB,UBW)

315.2 Austria. Vogel, Karl. *Bericht über die Weltausstellung in Chicago 1893, im Auftrage der Handels- und Gewerbekammer in Pilsen...* Pilsen: Verlag der Handels- und Gewerbekammer (Press of J.R. Port), 1894.

> 26x19. 92 p. Vogel was secretary of the industrial board. Trans: Report about the World's Fair in Chicago 1893, by order of the trade and industrial board in Pilsen. © . (ONB)

-B-

317.   Belgium. *Catalogue général de la section Belge*: (BRA,ICRL,MSI,UBO,Yale)

317.1 Belgium. *...Rapport sur les dentelles and les broderies, adressé à Monsieur A. Vercruysse...président de la Commission belge à l'Exposition de Chicago, par Mademoiselle Jenny Minne-Dausaert...envoyée par le Comité belge, comme délégué-rapporteur à l'Exposition de Chicago. Membre du jury américain.* Bruxelles: Weissenbruch, 1894.

> 22½x__. 30 p. At head of title: "Exposition universelle internationale de 1893 Chicago." French version of #318: Report on the laces and embroideries. (Col)

318.1 [Belgium]. Monthaye, E. *Krupp : l'exposition de Chicago de 1893*.
Bruxelles: Librairie européenne C. Mucquardt, 1894.　　　P➜

22x14.　141 p.　With 31 plates, photography of Krupp Pavilion at
Chicago, and map of the Essen steelworks.　Olive-gray wraps.　C.t.=
t.p.　For other Krupp items see #903.1-906 and #2391.1.
---- Also listed: 138 p.
☺ . (BRA,ONB)

319.　Brazil. Amazon. Bitancourt. *The State of*: (GLD,CLP,Col,CU,FM,HU,LBA,uiuc,Yale)
---- Also found: Pale green wraps.

320.　Brazil. Amazon. *Catalogue of woods*: ☺ . (HU,ICRL,IHi,UBO,UTA)
▶Correct and add: "exposition" in the title should not have been
capitalized.　Pale green wraps, black print, no design.　C.t.= t.p.

321.　Brazil. Bahia. Vianna. *Memoir of the State of Bahia*: (CU,DU,HU,Stfd,UCLA,uiuc)
▶Add: This is the English version of #321.1
---- Also found: Tan wraps with black print.

321.1 Brazil.　Bahia.　Vianna, Francisco Vicente, and José Carlos Ferreira.
Memoria sobre o Estado da Bahia.　Bahia: Typographia e Encadernação do «Diario da Bahia», 1893.

22½x15½.　1 *l*, (3)-647, xxv p+ 6 folded charts.　Tan wraps, black print, speckled edges.　Portuguese
version of #321.　☺ . (CU,DU,HU,UCB,UCLA)

322.　Brazil. Brazilian Commission. *Catalogue of the Brazilian section*: (FM,HU,ICRL,MIT,NAL,SML,Stfd,UPa,UTA,WM,Yale)
---- Also found: Gray-green wraps. (FM)

323.　Brazil. Ceará. *The state of Ceará*: (FM,UMD)
---- Also found: Red cloth hc, gilt print.
---- Also found: 23½x15.　Leaf before t.p. printed for Commissioner's signature.　Blue-green wraps,
black print.

323.1 Brazil.　*A Cidade de Manaus e o pais das seringueiras : recordacao da Exposicao Columbiana, Chicago,
1893*.　Manaus: Assoc. Comercial do Amazonas/Fundo Editorial, 1988.

__x__.　__ p.　Enlarged and revised reproduction of the original 1893 edition.　Trans: The city of Manáos
and the country of rubber tree : souvenir of the Columbian Exposition, Chicago, 1893.　See #324 for the
original publication in English.　(UCLA)

324.　Brazil. *The City of Manáos and the Country of Rubber Tree*: (FM,LBA,WM)

327.　Brazil. Pará. *The state of Pará*: (GLD,Col,CU,FM,IHi,NDU,Stfd,uiuc,UMA,Yale)
---- Also found: Blue-black cloth hc, gilt print.　C.t.: "The State of Pará."
---- Also found: White pebbled-textured paper covered hc, gilt print.
---- Also found: 150 p, 1 *l*.　Contains 5 parts, the 5th being "Industries." (FM)

327.1 Brazil.　Ruge, Sophus.　*Colombo e o quarto centenário do descobrimento de um novo mundo*.　Rio de
Janeiro: Laemmert & C., 1893.

__x__.　107, (1) p.　Trans: Columbus and the fourth centennial of the discovery of the new world. (IBN)

329.　British Guiana. Quelch. *Catalogue of the exhibits of British Guiana*: ☺ . (HU,ICRL,NLI,SML,UCB)
▶Corrected title: ...*Catalogue of the exhibits : of : British Guiana : with notes. By...* At head of title:
"World's Columbian exposition : Chicago, 1893."
---- Also found: Orange wraps, black print.

330.　British Guiana. Rodway. *Hand-book of British Guiana*: (GLD,FM,HU,LBA,UCB,UTA,Yale)
332.　Bulgaria. *Souvenir Bulgaria*: (A,LBA,S)

-C-

333.1 Canada. British Columbia. *British Columbia, its Present Resources and Future Possibilities.* Victoria, BC: "The Colonist" Printing and Publishing Co., 1893.

22½x15. 1 fold map, 1 *l* frontis illus of Victoria, (5)-109 p, (3) p "Appendix C." Buff wraps, red print with lion symbol at top of page. WCE not mentioned; from an intact collection. © (WM)

333.2 Canada. *Canada : An Official Leaflet of Information : Farms for Millions!* Ottawa: Department of the Interior, [1893].

30½x11½. Sheet with colorized map unfolds to 30½x79½. Text on reverse side in dark brown. Prepared for immigration purposes. Title from face of folded map which includes illus of woman sitting on globe flanked by British/Canadian flags and sheaves of grain. Map date is March 1893. No WCE content; from an intact collection. © (WM)

334. Canada. *Canadian Department of Fine Arts*: (NLA)

335. Canada. *Circular to the trustees and teachers*: © . (NLA)
▶Improved annotation. Actual size 29½x21. Response to the invitation from the WCE Education Dept and a call for eight different classes of student exhibits for the WCE. Inspector Dearness of the school would choose the five best in each category.

335.1 [Canada]. Esquimo Village. *...The Esquimaux Village.* [Chicago: Wm. C. Hollister & bro., printers], n.d.

7x11½. White (or blue or salmon) stiff card, black print both sides. Illus of "Prince Pomiuk" on the reverse side. Admission 25ᶜ. At head of title (two versions): "To enjoy The coolest and shadiest retreat inside the World's Fair Grounds visit the..." or "If you must miss seeing ANYTHING in the World's Fair..." © (GLD,E,S,WM)　　　　　　　　　　　　　　　　　　　　　　　　　　$15 - 25

☞ The Eskimo at the village on the Midway Plaisance were from Labrador, Canada.

337. Canada. ECFC. Saunders. *Report of the World's Columbian Exposition*: (NLA,SML)
339. Canada. *Exposition colombienne bureau d'informations*: (NLA)
340. Canada. Geological Survey. Ferrier. *Catalogue of a stratigraphical collection*:
(DC,HU,LBA,LHL,MSL,NSW,Stfd,UCB,UCLA,UIC,UMC,UMN,UPa,UTA,UVM,VT)
341. Canada. *Guide general de la villa de Chicago*: (NLA)

341.1 Canada. *The Mammoth Cheese From Canada : part of the Canadian Exhibit at the World's Columbian Exposition Chicago 1893.* [Chicago: R.R. McCabe & co., printers], n.d.

16x9½. (4) p. Folded glossy sheet, blue-black print and illus. C.t. Illus of 22,000 pound cheese and their exhibit in Ag Bldg on back cover. © (S)

341.2 Canada. Manitoba. Department of Agriculture [of Manitoba]. *The great agricultural : province of Manitoba : General Description and Area, Population, Railway, Government, Soil and Climate, General Resources. With illustrations from photographs.* Winnipeg: Issued under the authority of Hon. Thos. Greenway, minister of agriculture and immigration, n.d.　　**P➔**

15x24. 40 p, map. Buff wraps, purple (or green) print and decorative illus, which includes a sheaf of wheat. WCE exhibit bldg at "5750-60 Stony Island Ave" illus on back wrap; exhibit described on p 27. © . (GLD,LBA)　　　　　　　　　　　　　　　　　　$40 - 85

343. Canada. Nova Scotia. Education Dept. *Education. Nova Scotia (Canada)*: (Yale)
344. Canada. Nova Scotia. Gilpin. *Minerals of Nova Scotia*: (Col,FM,MSL,Yale)

344.1 Canada. Ontario. Canadian Institute. *Seventh annual report of the Canadian institute. Session 1893–4. Being part of appendix to the report of the minister of education, Ontario.* Toronto: Warwick bros. & Rutter, printers, 1894.

24½x16½. 22 p. Rust wraps, black print and border. C.t.= t.p. In "Seventh Archæological Report" by David Boyle (in charge of Ontario's anthropology exhibit), he describes WCE exhibit, pp 6-7. After the close of the Fair, to improve their collection, the Institute traded specimens with other exhibitors. Those WCE items purchased from Mexico are detailed on pp 7-14. ☺ (GLD) $20 - 40

344.2 Canada. Ontario. *...Catalogue of fruit : pomological department, Toronto, Canada.* Toronto: Printed by Warwick & sons, 1893.

24½x16½. 28 p. Orange wraps. Cover style as illus for #347. At head of title: "World's Columbian exposition, 1893." On t.p.: "Published under authority of N. Awrey, Esq., M.P.P., Commissioner for Ontario." History of "fruit culture in Ontario" and a list of their WCE exhibit content. ☺ . (UBO)

344.2 Canada. Ontario. *...Catalogue of Grains & Vegetables : Ontario section.* Toronto: Printed by Warwick & sons, 1893.

24½x16½. 58 p. Pink wraps. Cover style as illus for #347. At head of title: "World's Columbian exposition, 1893." On t.p.: "Published under authority of N. Awrey, Esq., M.P.P., Commissioner for Ontario." Illus of Guelph, Ont. Agricultural College. A detailed list of the overwhelming variety of product exhibited. ☺ . (UBO)

346.   Canada. Ontario. Education Dept. May. *Catalogue of school appliances*: (GLD,Col,NSW,S,WM) $22 - 45

346.1 Canada. Ontario. Education Department. Miller, John. *The educational system of the province of Ontario, Canada.* Toronto: Warwick & Sons, 1893.

25x16½. 2 *l*, (2) p, 1 *l*, 114 p+ unpaged plates. Gray-green wraps, black print. C.t.= t.p. No mention of WCE; from an intact collection. ☺ (WM)

346.2 Canada. Ontario. *...Floricultural Exhibit : Ontario section.* Toronto: Printed by Warwick & sons, 1893; Cambridge, MA: HULMS, [1983]. Film Mas C 978.   **P→**

24½x16½. 5 p. Pink wraps. Cover style same as illus for #347. At head of title: "World's Columbian exposition, 1893." C.t.: "Catalogue of Floricultural Exhibit" On t.p.: "Published under authority of N. Awrey, Esq., M.P.P., Commissioner for Ontario." Lists 12 exhibitors. ☺ . (HU,UBO)

347.   Canada. Ontario. *Mineral Exhibit of the Province*: (Col,FM,NSW,uiuc,WM)

347.1 Canada. Ontario. *The New House of Parliament for the Legislature of the Province of Ontario.* N.p.: n.p., n.d.

45½x62. 1 *l*. Brown print. Center illus of "New Parliament Building" surrounded by 9 ports including N. Awrey, Ontario WCE Commissioner. Handout or poster gift. (WM)

347.2 Canada. *Origin, history and progress of Chicago : guide book to the exhibition : illustrations of the principal buildings : advantages to Canada.* Montreal: n.p., 1893.

__x__. __ p. (HU)

351.1 Canada. Quebec. *...Horse and cattle exhibit. Hon. John MacIntosh, Executive Commissioner. R. Auzias-Turenne, Honorary Commissioner. Columbian Exposition and World's Fair. Chicago 1893.* N.p.: n,p, n.d.

19½x13. 29, (3) p. White wraps, black and red print; red/white/blue crossed flag design. At head of title: "Province of Quebec, Canada." C.t.= t.p. The last (3) p list exhibited breeds, how many of each were exhibited, and the Quebec WCE commissioners. ☺ . (ICRL,UBO)   **P↓**

352.1 Canada. Quebec. MacIntosh, W[illia]m. ...*Minerals. Columbian Exposition and World's Fair. Chicago. 1893.* [Montreal: The Sabiston Litho & Pub'g Co., n.d.].

19½x12½. 16, (3) p. Chromolith wraps; red, black, and blue print. At head of title: "Province of Quebec : Canada." Listing of mineral mines and their output. Wm. MacIntosh was "Supt. Mineral Exhibit, Province of Quebec, World's Columbian Exposition"; John MacIntosh was Executive Commissioner for Quebec. ©. (FM)   **P**↘

352.2 Canada. Quebec. [MacIntosh, John]. ...*Mineraux : Exposition Colombienne et Foire du Monde : Chicago. 1893.* ___: ___, ___.

19½x12½. 16, (3) p. Same wraps as English ed, #352.1, except title is in French. C.t. = t.p. At head of title: "Province de Quebec : Canada." Text in French. McIntosh's name is on last page. (S)

355.1 [Canada]. Quebec. Montreal. ...*Institution des jeunes aveugles : Nazareth : sous la direction des soeurs grises : a Montréal : province de Quebec : Exposition colombienne a Chicago : 1893.* N.p.: n.p., n.d.

22½x15. (4) p. Folded buff sheet. List of the 10 prep school semesters expected: "Travaux Scolaires." WCE ad for the Nazareth school for the blind in Montreal, which was directed by the Gray nuns. (WM)

357.   Canada. Quebec. *Report of the commissioner from the province*: (NLA)

360.   [Canada]. Smith. *Notes on Eskimo tradition*: (NLA)
▶Add: Smith, Harlan I[ngersoll]. N.p.: n.p., 1893? Pp 347-54.

360.1 Canada. Smith, William. *Paper on the fisheries of Canada, read on the 19ᵗʰ September, 1893, before the Fishermen's convention, at the World's fair.* [Chicago?]: n.p., [1893?].

26x___. 7 p. One of the Congress papers. (HU)

363.1 Canada. *Western Canada : Manitoba, Assiniboia, Alberta, Saskatchewan : How to Get There. How to Select Lands. How to Begin. How to Make Money.* N.p.: n.p., n.d.

21½x14½. 40 p. Red wraps with black print. Bold c.t.: "Farming and Ranching in Western Canada : Manitoba, Assiniboia, Alberta, Saskatchewan." WCE handout to encourage immigration. ©. (LBA)

364.   Cape of Good Hope. *Catalogue of exhibits of the Cape of Good Hope*: (Col,ICRL,NAL,SML,UBO)
▶Add: Light green wraps with black print. C.t. = t.p.

366.   Ceylon. *Official handbook & catalogue of the Ceylon*: (CLP,FM,ICRL,Merc,NAL,SML,Stfd,UIC,UTA,Yale)
---- Also found: 22x14. 1 *l* frontis of WCE bldg, viii, 110 p+ unpaged illus and fold maps. Cover variant in b/w only; border design different also. An abbreviated pre-issue of Apr 10, 1892, as written on the cover in red ink and signed by Commissioner Grinlinton. (FM)
---- Also found: A presentation copy to the Library of the South Kensington Museum, given Sept 9, 1893 and signed by J.J. Grinlinton, "Special Commissioner." (SML)

366.1 Colombia. Calderón, Clímaco and Edward E. Britton. *Colombia. 1893.* [New York: Robert Sneider, Grabador y Impresor, 1893].

22x14½. 2 *l* ports, (4) p, 1 *l* ad, 122 p, 1 folded color map + unpaged plates on glossy stock. Rebound. The first 2 *l* are ports of Colombia's Pres and VP. Britton was "Special Commissioner...to the World's Columbian Exposition." Describes and illustrates many aspects of the country. © (FM)

367.   Costa Rica. Calvo. *The Republic of Costa Rica*: (GLD,CU,FM,HU,NDU,NLI,UMC,UMN) $30 - 60

▸Add cover description 2nd ed: Coated linen wraps with bold red, white, and blue bands; black print. Folding map bound in before p 13.

369. Costa Rica. Guzmán. *Catálogo general de los objectos*: (Col,CU,FM,HU,ICRL,NLI,SML,UBO,UCLA,WM,Yale)
370. Cuba. Cabrera. *Cartas a Govin sobra*: (HU)
371. Cuba. Pichardo. *La ciudad blanca*: (HU,LU)

-D-

372.1 [Denmark.] Christesen, V[ilhelm]. ...*V. Christesen, manufacturer of gold and silver ware : jeweler : Copenhagen.* Copenhagen: [Vilhelm Christesen] (Nielsen and Lydiche printers), 1893. **P➔**

20½x13. 8 p, 13 *l* of plates (no color illus). Wraps of light orange-brown with red-brown ornate arabesque design. At head of title: "The World's Columbian Exposition : Chicago. U.S.A. 1893 : Denmark." C.t.: "V. Christesen : Copenhagen : 1893 : Chicago." Ad. ☺ . (VAM)

372.2 [Denmark]. Copenhagen Free Port Co. (Limited). *The Copenhagen Free Port : to be opened for traffic in the course of the year 1894.* N.p.: n.p., n.d.

32½x22. White sheet printed 1 side in blue and red. Color map of routes to the new port from Western Europe and Americas. Benefits included no tides. No WCE content; from intact collection. ☺ (WM)

373. Denmark. Danish Sloyd. *The Danish sloyd*: (MSI)
375. Denmark. *Hans Christian Andersen the celebrated writer*: (S)
376. Denmark. Industriforeningen. RDC. *The World's Columbian Exposition 1893*: (LBA,NSW,S,SML,UBO,Yale)

377.1 [Denmark]. Royal Porcelain Co. *Royal Copenhagen Porcelain.* [Copenhagen: H.H. Thiele, 1893?]. **P➔**

17x13½. (19) p. Tan wraps, brick-red print with blue design and gilt crown; back cover has embossed logo in red. C.t. Illus of items from their WCE exhibit in the center of the Danish Pavilion, p (15). ☺ . (WM)

378. Denmark. Udstillingskomitéen. *Officiel Beretning*: (KBS)

378.1 Dutch West Indies. Higgins, Milton O. *Curaçoa, Aruba, Bonaire : at the : World's Columbian Exposition, Chicago, 1893.* Chicago: Chicago Legal News co., printers, 1893.

23½x15½. 7 p. Salmon wraps with black print and border. C.t. Caption title on p (1): "Information for visitors : and : Official Catalogue of the Curaçoa section." ☺ . (SML)

-E-

379. Ecuador. Diario de Avisos. *El Ecuador en Chicago*: (ICRL,Yale)
381. Egypt. De Potter. *The Egyptian Pantheon*: (PSU)
382. Egypt. Egypt-Chicago Exposition Co. *Street in Cairo*: (LBA,S,UIC,uiuc)

382.1 Egypt. *Egyptological Exhibit : Midway plaisance...Egyptian Temple.* Chicago: Thayer & Jackson stationery co., n.d.

30½x22½. 1 *l* broadside. Green paper, black print. Admittance 25 cents. Nothing printed at head of title. ☺ (GLD)

$20 - 45

---- Also found: 22½x15. 1 *l* broadside. Purple pulp, black print. At head of title: "Don't fail to Visit the..." (S,WM)

383. Egypt. *Guide to the Egyptian temple of Luksor*: (S)

383.1 Egypt. ...*Guide to the Tombs of "Thi" and Apis. (At Sakkarah, Cairo.)* Chicago: Thayer & Jackson Stationery co. Printers and Publishers, 1893.

> 20x14. (4) p. Buff folded sheet, black print and illus of Egyptian fishermen in boat. At head of title: "Chicago World's Fair." Illus of tombs pp (2)-(3). Same format as #383. ☺ (S)

385.   Egypt. *Souvenir of "Street Scene" in Cairo:* (NLA)

-F-

385.1 [France]. ...*Adoption d'un project de loi portant ouverture d'un crédit pour la section française a l'exposition de Chicago : Seances des 12 et 13 Juillet 1892.* N.p.: n.p., 1892?

> 30½x24. 6 p. At head of t.p.: "Extrait du *Journal Officiel* des 13 et 14 Juillet 1892..." Conversational format. Trans: Adoption of a bill concerning opening of a trust for the French section at the WCE. (UMD)

385.2 France. Angers. ...*Orphelinat de Garçons : municipal & professionnel.* Angers: Imprimerie Typographiequeue L. Hudson, 1892.   P➔

> 27½x20½. 18 p. Buff wraps. C.t. = t.p. At head of title: "Ville d'Angers : 1893 1893 : Exposition internationale de Chicago : (États-Unis d'Amérique) : France - Ville d'Angers : (Département de Maine-et-Loire) : Économie sociale." Title trans: Boy's orphanage. ☺. (HML)

385.3 [France]. *Les associations ouvrières de production et la chambre consultative.* Paris: Imprimerie nouvelle, 1893.

> 27½x22. 90 p, 1 *l* printer info. Blue-flecked tan wraps. C.t. = t.p. Describes production workers' assn which started for the 1889 Paris expo; they had a workers' expo in 1891 (Exposition du trevail). No WCE content; from an intact collection. ☺ (WM)

386.1 [France]. *La Banque Populaire de Menton : a L'Exposition Internationale de Chicago : 1883-1893.* N.p.: Imprimerie Coopérative Mentonnaise], n.d.

> 24x17½. 28 p+ 7 tipped-in and folded statistical charts. Wraps. C.t. = t.p. Text in French language. Trans: Popular Bank of Menton at the WCE. ☺. (UMD)

387. France. Bertin. *La marine des États-Unis:* ☺. (BRA,Col,MIT)
> ▶Replace entry with the following:
> Text: Part 7 of 10 part set. No part 8; two parts 9. See #406-411.1 for other volumes in this set.
> ---- Wraps: 27½x18. 2 *l*, 130 p. Variants include green (or tan-gray) wraps with black print. C.t. may or may not = t.p. T.p. may or may not list authors: Grille and H. Falconnet. The t.p. may or may not have: "Review technique : exposition universelle de Chicago en 1893 : Septième Partie:..." in bold print at head of title.
> ---- Hc: 27x18. 2 *l*, 1-130 p. C.t.: "Review technique de l'exposition universelle : de Chicago : 1893" (this is not printed on t.p.). Brown cloth hc, black print and design. On spine: "7ME partie."
> Atlas: Bertin, L. *La marine des États-Unis.* Paris: E. Bernard & Cie, imprimeurs-éditeurs, 1896.
> 37x29½. 2 *l*, 30 plates (some folded). Brown cloth hc, black print and design. C.t.: "Revue technique de l'exposition universelle de Chicago : 1893 : Atlas : 7ÈME Partie." Companion to hc text. Grille and Falconnet are not listed on t.p.

387.1 France. Boileau, H. ...*Touage : par : adhérence magnétique : système de Bovet.* Paris: Publications du journal le génie civil [Imprimie Chaix], 1893.

> 24x15½. 16 p. Blue-green wraps, black print. C.t. = t.p. At head of title: "Extrait du Journal le génie civil." Boileau was an arts and manufacturing engineer. Bovet had presented his system navigation on rivers and canals using magnets at the Congress of Navigation. In French. ☺ (WM)

388.   France. Bonet-Maury. *Le congrès des religions:* (CU,HU,LBA,NPG,UoC)
389.   France. Buisson. *L'enseignement Primaire:* (CU)

391. France. Cercle. Terquem. *Exposition de la librairie*: [separately paged] (Col,CU,HU,MIT,NLA,UPa)
392. France. Cercle. Terquem. *Exposition de la librairie*: [121 *l*] (Col,HU,ICRL,LBA,NSW,UTA,WM)
394. France. Chagot. *Branch of social economy : the Blanzy Colliery company*: (HU,UMD)

394.1 [France]. Chambre de Commerce de Dunkerque. ...*Notice: sur le : port de Dunkerque*. Dunkerque: Imprimerie Paul Michel, n.d.

> 25x16. 28, (5) p tables, 1 *l* folded color map. Blue-flecked tan wraps, black print. C.t. = t.p. At head of title: "Chambre de Commerce de Dunkerque." English and French language on alternate pages. Properties and advantages of Dunkirk as a commercial port. ☺ . (Stfd-bound WCE Trans Dept Collection)

394.2 France. Chambre de Commerce de Paris. *Commercial Instruction organized by the Paris Chamber of Commerce : plates : The Chicago World's fair : 1893*. [Paris: Impr. de Ch. Gillot], n.d.

> 27x19½. 9 *l* of loose plates, one folded. Tan paper covered boards, pale blue print and design, gray cloth spine. C.t. Issued with #396. ☺ . (FM,Stfd)

395. France. Chambre de Commerce de Paris. Lourdelet. *Rapport, novembre, 1893*: (UMD)
     ---- Also found: A Presentation copy to Léon Gruel, author of #412. (UMD)

396. France. Chambre de Commerce de Paris. *Notice on the commercial instruction*: (Col,FM)
     ---- Also found: Issued with a separate hc folder with 9 *l* of plates; same cover design. See #394.2. (FM)

397. France. Chambre de Commerce de Paris. *Notice sur l'enseignement*: (UMN)

397.1 [France]. Chasseloup-Laubat, Marquis de. ...*Voyage en Amérique : et principalement a Chicago*. Paris: Société des ingénieurs civils de France, 1892.

> 24x14½. 90 p+ 3 folded plates. At head of title: "Société des ingénieurs civils : de France...Paris." Trans: Trip to America chiefly at Chicago. Below title: "Extrait des memories de la société des ingénieurs civils de France (Octobre 1892)," which translates: Excerpt from memoranda of the society of civil engineers of France. ☺ . (ICRL,IHI)

398. France. Chiousse. *Historique de la fédération des Sociétés Coopératives*:
     ▶Completed citation: 16 p. Blue-flecked blue wraps. No mention of WCE; from intact collection.

398.1 [France]. Comité Central de l'Union Coopérative. *Almanach : de la : coopérative française : 1893*. Paris: Imprimerie nouvelle, 1892.

> 16x11. 123 p, 1 *l* index, (2) p ads. Lime-green wraps, black print. C.t. = t.p. Illus directory of French co-ops and their condition. No WCE content; from intact collection. ☺ (WM)

399. France. Comité protestant français. *Les oeuvres du protestantisme*: (HU,ref,Yale) $200

400. France. Commissariat. *Instructions pour la réexpédition*: (ICRL)
     ▶Add: French language. ▶Correction: The "g" in General at head of title should be lower case.

401. France. Commission. *Syndicat de la boulangerie*:
     ▶Completed citation: 27 p, 2 *l*. French and English on alternating pages.

401.1 [France]. Compagnie Generale des Asphaltes de France. ...*Exhibit of the Compagnie...* Paris: n.p., n.d.

> 28x21½. 1 *l*. Buff sheet, black print. At head of title: "World's Fair, Chicago, 1893 : French Mining Section : Class 12." Illus of Seyssel block and trade mark at bottom. Asphalt mine of Seyssel. (WM)

401.2 [France]. Compagnie Generale des Asphaltes de France. ...*List of samples and exhibits of the Compagnie...* Paris: n.p., n.d.

> 22x14. 1 *l*. Buff sheet, black print. At head of title: "World's Fair, Chicago, 1893 : French Mining Section : Class 12." No illus. (WM)

402. France. Compayré. *L'enseignement secondaire*: (CU)
403. France. Compayré. *L'enseignement supérieur*: (CU)

404.1 France. Dehérain, D.-P. ...*Station agronomique de Grignon (Seine-et-Oise)*. Paris: Imprimerie de la Cour d'Appel, 1893.

27x18. 1 *l* t.p., (3)-35 p. Blue-flecked tan wraps, black print. C.t.= t.p. At head of title: "République Française." Farming and experimenting activities at the Grignon state facility. Dehérain had title of director. No WCE content; from an intact collection. © (WM)

404.2 [France]. Drouet, Paul L.-M. *Les institutions artistiques et les beaux-arts en général Aux États-Unis, au Canada et à l'Exposition de Chicago en 1893 : Avec une notice complémentaire sur la ville de Boston et diverses Associations américaines*. Caen: Imprimerie Ch. Valin, 1896.

26½x16½. 210 p. From *Bulletin de la Société des Beaux-Arts de Caen*, vol 9, pt 4. Trans: Art institutions and fine arts in general of the United States and Canada at the WCE. An appended section on Boston and diverse American associations. © . (Col,HU)

405.1 France. Gatellier, M. ...*La culture du blé*. Paris: Imprimerie de la bourse de commerce, 1891.

21½x13½. (3) p, 1-27 p. Pink wraps, black print, string-tied. At head of title: "Société nationale d'agriculture de france." C.t.= t.p. Wheat growth with tables of gluten content. In French. A paper presented in Paris, 1890. See #412.4 for more on grains. No WCE content; intact collection. © (WM)

405.2 France. Gautrelet, M. E. *Nouvelles Recherches : chimiques, physiques et physiologiques: sur les : laits alimentaires*. Vichy: Imprimerie A. Wallon, 1892.

24x16. 46, (1) p addenda. Light green wraps, black print and border. C.t.= t.p. Title trans: New research in the chemical, physical, and psychological milk complaints. Gautrelet was a biochemist. In French. Many tables of patient data. No WCE content; from intact collection. (WM)

> Start of *Revue Technique de l'exposition universelle de Chicago en 1893*

☞ Items #387 and #406 to #411.1 are found individually or as a 10 part set with wraps or hc. Each of the 10 parts has a companion atlas; the total is 20 vol. There is no part 8; there are two distinct parts 9. Some binders bound more than one part in a vol. There are t.p. variants. MIT has a complete set bound in brown cloth with black print and design; all 20 text and atlas volumes of their set have the c.t.: "Revue technique de l'exposition universelle : de Chicago : 1893" and the parts are numbered either on the cover (atlas) or spine (text and atlas).

406. France. Grille. *L'Agricultural*: (BRA,CCA,Col,CU,MIT,NAL)
▶Replace entry with the following:
Text: Part 6 of 10 part set. No part 8; two parts 9. See #411.
---- Wraps: 26½x17½. 177 p. Green wraps. Variants found with and without "Revue technique de l'exposition universelle de Chicago en 1893" in bold print at head of t.p. title. Found with and without Falconnet's name on the t.p.
---- Hc: 27x18. 2 *l*, 1-177, (2) p. Brown cloth hc with black print and design. C.t.: "Revue technique de l'exposition universelle : de Chicago : 1893." On spine: 6ME partie." T.p. does not have "Revue technique..."; rather, title is at top of page in bold print.
Atlas: *L'agriculture et les machines agricoles aux États-Unis*. Paris: Bernard & Cie, imprimeurs-éditeurs, 1896. 37x29½. 2 *l*, 64 plates of diagrams and illus. Brown cloth hc, black print and design. C.t.: "Revue technique de l'exposition universelle de Chicago : 1893 : Atlas : 6ÈME Partie." Companion to hc text.

407. France. Grille. *Les Arts militaires*: © . (BRA,CCA,Col,CU,MIT)
▶Replace entry with the following:
Text: Part 5 of 10 part set. No part 8; two parts 9. See #411.
---- Wraps: 26½x17½. 278 p. Variants include green (or tan-gray) wraps with black print. C.t. may or may not = t.p. The t.p. may or may not have at head of title in bold print: "Revue technique de l' exposition universelle de Chicago en 1893." "Cinquième Partie" may or may not be found on t.p.

---- Hc: 27x18. 1 pink *l* ads, 2 *l*, 1-278 p, 1 pink *l* ads. Brown cloth hc with black print and design. C.t.: "Revue technique de l'exposition universelle : de Chicago : 1893." On spine: "5ME partie." T.p. does not have "Revue technique..."; rather, title is at top of page in bold print.
Atlas: *Les Arts Militaires aux États-Unis et a l'exposition de Chicago.* Paris: Bernard & Cie, imprimeurs-éditeurs, 1894. 37x29½. 2 *l*, 104 plates of diagrams and photo reproductions printed one side. Brown cloth hc, black print and design. C.t.: "Revue technique de l'exposition universelle de Chicago : 1893 : Atlas : 5ÈME Partie." Companion to hc text.

408.   France. Grille, [Antoine], and H. Falconnet. *Les chemins de fer a l'exposition de Chicago : les locomotives.* Paris: E. Bernard et Cie, Imprimeurs-Editeurs, 1894.
▶Replace entry with the following:
Text: First part 9 of a 10 part set. No part 8; two parts 9. See #411.
Trans: Railways at the Chicago exposition : The locomotives.
---- Wraps: 26½x17½. 148 p. Green wraps. Found with and without "Revue technique de l'exposition universelle de Chicago en 1893" in bold print at head of t.p. title. Also, found with and without "Neuvième Partie. ...Premier volume" printed on t.p.
---- Hc (original entry): #408 and #408.1 were bound together.
---- Hc: 27x18. 2 *l*, 1-148 p, 4 folding diagrams/tables, 1 pink *l* ads. Brown cloth hc with black print and design. C.t.: "Revue technique de l'exposition universelle : de Chicago : 1893." On spine: "9ME partie." At top of t.p. in bold print: "Les Chemins de fer..."
Atlas: Grille, [Antoine], and H. Falconnet. *Les chemins de fer a l'exposition de Chicago : les locomotives.* Paris: E. Bernard et Cie, imprimeurs-éditeurs, 1894. 37x29½. 2 *l*, 95 plates. Brown cloth hc, black print and design. C.t.: "Revue technique de l'exposition universelle de Chicago : 1893 : Atlas : 9ÈME Partie." Companion to hc text.
☺ . (BRA,CCA,Col,CU,Stfd,MIT)

408.1 France. Grille, [Antoine], and H. Falconnet. *Les chemins de fer a l'exposition de Chicago : Deuxième volume : voies, signaux, matériel roulant et tramways.* Paris: E. Bernard et Cie, Imprimeurs-Editeurs, 1895.

Text: Second part 9 of a 10 part set. No part 8; two parts 9. See #411.
Trans: Railways at the Chicago exposition : Tracks, signals, rolling stock cars and street cars.
---- Wraps: 26½x17½. 188 p. Green wraps. Found with and without "Revue technique de l'exposition universelle de Chicago en 1893" in bold print at head of t.p. title. Also, found with and without "Neuvième Partie. ...Deuxième volume" printed on t.p.
---- Hc: 27x18. 1 pink *l* ads, 2 *l*, 1-188 p, 13 *l* of numbered illus (several to a page) in dark green ink. Brown cloth hc with black print and design. C.t.: "Revue technique de l'exposition universelle : de Chicago : 1893." On spine: "9ME partie." At top of t.p. in bold print: "Les Chemins de fer..."
Atlas: Grille, [Antoine], and H. Falconnet. *Les chemins de fer a l'exposition de Chicago : deuxième volume: voies, signaux, matériel roulant et tramways : par M. Grille.* Paris: E. Bernard et Cie, imprimeurs-éditeurs, 1895. 37x29½. 2 *l*, 142 plates. Brown cloth hc, black print and design. C.t.: "Revue technique de l'exposition universelle de Chicago : 1893 : Atlas : 9ÈME Partie." Companion to hc text. ☺ . (CCA,CU,MIT)

409.   France. Grille. *Électricité*: ☺ . (BRA,CCA,Col,CU,MIT)
▶Replace entry with the following:
Text: Part 3 of 10 part set. No part 8; two parts 9. See #411.
---- Wraps: 26½x17½. 250 p. Green wraps. Found with and without "Revue technique de l'exposition universelle de Chicago en 1893" at head of t.p. title.
---- Hc: 27x18. 1 pink *l* ads, 2 *l*, 1-250 p, 1 pink *l* ads. Brown cloth hc with black print and design. C.t.: "Revue technique de l'exposition universelle : de Chicago : 1893." On spine: "3ME partie." At top of t.p. in bold print: "L'électricité industrielle a l'exposition de Chicago en 1893."
Atlas: Grille, [Antoine], and H. Falconnet. *L'électricité industrielle a l'exposition de Chicago en 1893 : Troisième Partie.-- électricité industrielle.* Paris: Bernard & Cie, imprimeurs-éditeurs, 1894. 37x29½. 2 *l*, 78 plates of diagrams printed one side. Brown cloth hc, black print and design. C.t.: "Revue technique de l'exposition universelle de Chicago : 1893 : Atlas : 3ÈME Partie." Companion to hc text.

410.   France. Grille. *La Méchanique*: ☺ . (BRA,CCA,Col,CU,MIT)

▶Replace entry with the following:

Text: Part 4 of a 10 part set. No part 8; two parts 9.

---- Wraps: 26½x17½. 294 p. Green wraps. Found with and without "Revue technique de l'exposition universelle de Chicago en 1893" at head of t.p. title.

---- Hc: 27x18. 2 *l*, 1-294 p, 2 pink *l* of ads. Brown cloth hc, black print and design. C.t.: "Revue technique de l'exposition universelle : de Chicago : 1893." On spine: "4ME partie."

Atlas: Grille, [Antoine], and H. Falconnet. *La mécanique générale a l'exposition de Chicago : moteurs a vapeur, a gaz, a air hydraulique, pompes grandes installations mecaniques.* Paris: Bernard & Cie, imprimeurs-éditeurs, 1894. 37x29½. 2 *l*, 120 plates, diagrams. Brown cloth hc, black print and design. C.t.: "Revue technique de l'exposition universelle de Chicago : 1893 : Atlas : 4ÈME Partie." Companion to hc text.

410.1 France. Grille, [Antoine], and H. Falconnet. *Les nouvelles chaudières a vapeur : chaudières fixes et chaudières marines.* Paris: E. Bernard et Cie, Imprimeurs-Editeurs, 1894.

Text: Part 2 of 10 part set. No part 8; two parts 9. See #411.

Trans: The new steam boilers : regular and naval boilers.

---- Wraps: 26½x17½. 176 p. Green wraps. Collaborateur: M. Lelarge. Found with and without "Revue technique de l'exposition universelle de Chicago en 1893" at head of title. May be found without "Les nouvelles chaudières a vapeur" on t.p.; that is, the title would then be *Chaudières fixes et chaudières marines.*

---- Hc: 27x18. 1 *l* bound-in light green front wrap, 2 *l*, 1-174, (2) p, (2) pink p ads, back wrap. Brown cloth hc with black print and design. C.t.: "Revue technique de l'exposition universelle : de Chicago : 1893." On spine: "2ME partie."

Atlas: Grille, [Antoine], and H. Falconnet. *Revue technique de l'exposition universelle de Chicago en 1893 : Deuxième Partie. -- Chaudières fixes et chaudières marines.* Paris: E. Bernard & Cie, imprimeurs-éditeurs, 1894. 37x29½. 2 *l*, 48 plates printed one side. Brown cloth hc, black print and design. C.t.: "Revue technique de l'exposition universelle de Chicago : 1893 : Atlas : 2ÈME Partie." Companion to hc text. ☺ . (CCA,CU,MIT)

411. France. Grille, [Antoine], and H. Falconnet. *Review technique de l'exposition universelle de Chicago en 1893 : Première Partie.--Architecture.* Paris: E. Bernard et Cie, Imprimeurs-Editeurs, 1894.

▶Replace entry with the following:

Part 1: *Architecture.*

---- Wraps. 26½x17½. Green wraps with black print and design. C.t. = t.p. At head of title: "Review technique de l'exposition universelle de Chicago en 1893."

---- Hc. 27x18. 2 *l*, 1-176 p. Brown hc with black print and design. C.t.: "Revue technique de l'exposition universelle : de Chicago : 1893." On spine: "1RE partie."

Atlas: 37x29½. 2 *l*, 106 plates of photo reproductions and diagrams printed one side. Brown cloth hc, black print and design. C.t.: "Review technique de l'exposition universelle de Chicago : 1893 : Atlas : 1.ÈRE Partie^." Companion to hc text.

Part 2: *Chaudiére fixes.* Moved to #410.1.

☺ . (BRA,CCA,Col,CU,MIT)

411.1 France. Grille, [Antoine], and H. Falconnet. *...Les travaux publics aux États-Unis.* Paris: E. Bernard et Cie, Imprimeurs-Editeurs, 1896.

Text: Part 10 of a 10 part set. No part 8; two parts 9. See #411.

Trans: Public works in the U.S.

---- Wraps: 26½x17½. 240 p + 2 tables. Green wraps. Variants found. C.t. may or may not = t.p. At head of title: "Revue technique de l'exposition universelle de Chicago en 1893 : Dixième Partie:..." may or may not be printed. The work was in collaboration with M. Laborde whose name may replace Falconnet in some versions, i.e., Falconnet's name may be omitted on t.p.

---- Hc: Grille, [Antoine], and Laborde. *Les Travaux publics aux États-Unis : par M. Grille M. Laborde.* 2 *l*, 1-240 p. includes tables. Brown cloth hc with black print and design C.t.: "Revue technique de l'exposition universelle : de Chicago : 1893." On spine: "10ME partie."

Atlas: *Les travaux publics aux États-Unis : par M. Grille M. Laborde.* Paris: Bernard & Cie, imprimeurs-éditeurs, 1896. 37x29½. 2 *l*, 105 plates of diagrams and photo reproduction printed on one side. Brown cloth hc, black print and design. C.t.: "Revue technique de l'exposition universelle de Chicago : 1893 :

Atlas : 10ÈME Partie." Companion to hc text.
☺ . (BRA,CCA,Col,CU,MIT)

End of *Review technique de l'exposition universelle de Chicago en 1893*

---

412. France. Gruel. *Catalogue des Reliures de Style*: (BRA,Col,CWM,FLP,ICRL,LBA,MIT,UCB,UTA,WM,Yale)
▸Add annotation: For Gruel's personal scrapbook, see #2447.UMD.

412.1 France. Henry, J.-A. *Quelques notes : sur : l'exposition : colombienne : de : Chicago : (1893).* Lyon: Imprimerie Mougin-Rusand, 1894.

25x16½. 66 p, 2 *l* of plates (1 folded). Illus. Buff wraps, black and red print. Trans: Some notes on the Columbian Exposition at Chicago (1893). ☺ . (CCA)

412.2 France. Lamy, Étienne. *Oeuvre libre d'assistance : office central des institutions charitables : Première Assemblée générale et inauguration de la maison de travail (foundation Laubespin) discours de. M. Étienne Lamy.* Paris: Au siège de l'œuvre [Imprimerie Nouvelle A. Bellier et Cie, Bordeaux], 1892.

19x12. 45, (1) p printer info + text on inside both wraps. Gold wraps, black print and border. C.t. = t.p. Lamy founded the free charity organization. No WCE content; from intact WCE collection. (WM)

412.3 [France]. Laurent-Mouchon. *...Grand culture de blés pour semences : graines de betteraves a sucre.* N.p.: [Imp. Le Bigot frères], n.d.

27x21½. (4) p. Folded thin buff sheet, blue and red print, illus of heads of grain and Paris 1889 medals. C.t. At head of title: "Chicago—exposition universelle de 1893 : Exposant : Collectivité de la Société des Agriculteurs du Nord." In French. Growth of seed for wheat and sugar beets. See #405.1 for another French grain pub. WM)

414. France. Lavasseur. "Coup d'aeil sur l'ensemble: (Col,CU)

414.1 [France]. Librairie Firmin-Didot et Cie. *Publications : de la : Librairie Firmin-Didot et Cie : imprimeurs de l'institut de France.* Paris: n.p., 1892.

26½x16½. 93, (2) p. Buff self-wraps, black print with illus of "Institut de France" in a circle. C.t. Issued with laid-in (4) page supplement for 1893 addressed to prospective judges of printers. Catalog of books with prices; printers for the Institute. No mention of WCE; from an intact WCE collection. ☺ (WM)

419. France. Ministère du Commerce. *Rapports publiés sous* [7 vol]: (CU,ICRL)

419.1 France. Ministère du Commerce, de l'Industrie, des Postes et des Télégraphes. *...Rapports : publiés : sous la direction : de : M. Camille Krantz... : Comité 8 : L'Horticulture française à Chicago.-- L'Horticulture aux États-Unis.* Paris: Imprimerie nationale, 1894.

29x20. 3 *l*, (3)-231 p. Wraps. French language. At head of title: "Ministère du commerce, de l'industrie : des postes et des télégraphes : exposition internationale de Chicago en 1893." Trans: French horticulture at Chicago.—Horticulture in the United States.
---- Also listed: With author Maurice Leveque de Vilmorin.
☺ . (CU,HU,NDU,SML)

420.1 France. Ministère du Commerce, de l'Industrie, des Postes et des Télégraphes. *...Rapports : publiés : sous la direction : de : M. Camille Krantz... : Comité 15 (primier volume) : La Mécanique générale américaine à l'Exposition de Chicago.* Paris: Imprimerie nationale, 1894.

28½x19. vii, 630 p. Gray wraps, black print. C.t. At head of title: "Ministère du commerce, de l'industrie : des postes et des télégraphes : exposition internationale de Chicago en 1893." Trans: American machinery at the WCE. ☺ . (BRA,HML)

420.2 France. Ministère du Commerce, de l'Industrie, des Postes et des Télégraphes. *...Rapports : publiés : sous la direction : de : M. Camille Krantz... : Comité 15 (deuxième volume) : Les Machines à bois américaines.* Paris: Imprimerie nationale, 1894.

28½x19. 147 p. Gray wraps, black print. C.t. At head of title: "Ministère du commerce, de l'industrie : des postes et des télégraphes : exposition internationale de Chicago en 1893." Trans: American woodworking machines (at the WCE). ☺ . (BRA)

420.3 France. Ministère du Commerce, de l'Industrie, des Postes et des Télégraphes. *...Rapports : publiés : sous la direction : de : M. Camille Krantz... : Comité 16 : Materiel des chemins de fer.* Paris: Imprimerie nationale, 1895.

28½x19½. 3 *l*, (3)-316 p+ 26 numbered folded plates of railroad engines and apparatus. C.t. = t.p. Description of railroads. (Stfd)

424.   France. Ministère du Commerce. *Rapports...Comité 22*: (VAM)
426.   France. Ministère du Commerce. *Rapports...Comité 24*: (UMD)
434.   France. Ministère du Commerce. *Rapports...Comité 31*: (Col)
435.   France. Ministère du Commerce. *Rapports...Comité 34*: (Col,HU,UCLA,UIC,uiuc,UMD)

437.1 France. Ministère du Commerce, de l'Industrie, des Postes et des Télégraphes. *...Rapports : publiés : sous la direction : de : M. Camille Krantz... : Commissariat spécial de l'agriculture.* Paris: Imprimerie nationale, 1894.

29x19. 135 p. Gray wraps, black print. C.t. At head of title: "Ministère du commerce, de l'industrie : des postes et des télégraphes : exposition internationale de Chicago en 1893." Trans: Special commission on agriculture. ☺ . (BRA)

439.   France. Ministère du Commerce. *Rapports...Congrés tenu*: (Col)
▶Delete from title: commissaire général du gouvernement français.

440.   France. Ministère du Commerce. *Rapports...Rapports administratif*: (Col)
441.   France. Ministère du Commerce. Délégation ouvrière. *Rapports...Rapports de la délégation*: (Col,ICRL,UIC)

441.1 France. Ministère du Commerce, de l'Industrie et des Colonies. *...Avis important. I. Instruction relative au transport des colis destinés à l'exposition de Chicago.* Paris?: [Imprimerie Nationale, 1893.]

27x21½. 2 p. At head of title: "Exposition Internationale de Chicago. (1893.)." Trans: Important advice. Instruction for the transport of parcels destined for the Chicago exposition. (UMD)

442.   France. Ministère du...et des Colonies. *Catalogue de l'exposition*: (GLD,HU,NSW,SML,UBO,Yale) $40 - 80
▶Correct paging: 3 *l*, (3)-108 p includes some b/w illus + 11 single plates and 3 double plates; all plates have letter press tissue guards.
---- Also found: Red pebble-textured leatherette on flexible cardboard, gilt print.

☞ Memorabilia from the American War of Independence were shown in the French Bldg.

444.   France. Ministère du...et des Colonies. *Section...Catalogue officiel*: (NSW,SML,UBO)
445.   France. Ministère du...et des Colonies. *Section...Palais des femmes*: (Col,SML,UBO)

448.1 France. Ministère du Commerce et de l'Industrie. *...Règlement général de la section française.* [Paris: Imprimerie des Journaux officiels, 1892].

30½x24. (2) p. The names Jules Roche and Camille Krantz are on p (2). List of 19 articles: general rules, admission, and installation. At head of title: "République française : Ministère du commerce & de l'industrie : exposition internationale de Chicago (1893)." (UMD)
---- Also found: Paris?: [Imprimerie Nationale, 1892]. 27x21. (2) p. Font differs. Date same. (UMD)

448.2 France. Montceau-les-Mines. *...Inauguration de la statue de M. Jules Chagot Ancien Gérant de la Compagnie des Mines de Blanzy le 2 Aout 1891.* Montceau-les-Mines: Rajaud Frères, imprimeurs, 1891.

21½x13½. (2) p, 1 *l* frontis illus of statue on stiff stock, 1 *l*, (5)-96 p. Blue-flecked wraps with black print. C.t. = t.p. At head of title: "Ville de Montceau-les-Mines." This is a two-part book: A tribute to Chagot ends on p 68 and there follows a second frontis and a Blanzy tribute to labor unions. In French. See #394. No WCE content; from intact WCE collection. (WM)

448.3 [France]. *Note sur l'Exploitation Agricole : du : domaine de Monthorin : Arrondissement de Fougères (Ille-&-Vilaine)*. Fougères: Imp. de la chronique de Fougères, 1892.

> 24x15½. 1 *l* (t.p.), (3)-27 p, (1) p printer info. Pale gray-green wraps, black print. C.t. = t.p. Production of various farms in the Monthorin district surrounding Fougères. Milk, cheese quantities and aggregate value in francs. List of medals won to 1892. No WCE content; from intact collection. ☺ (WM)

449. France. *Notice sur la société générale d'éducation*:
▶Add: 23 p. [The Société also handed out its magazine at the Fair: *Bulletin de la société générale d'éducation et d'enseignement*. Vol 1 (1892). 67 p, 11 p ads. The issue had no WCE content.] ☺ (WM)

450. France. *Paris Chicago exhibition*: (GLD,S) $30 - 60
▶Correct paging: vi, 122 p. Pulp paper text.

450.1 [France]. Paris. *...Paris Xth municipal district : Municipal benefit society*. N.p.: n.p., n.d.

> 27x21½. 1 *l*. Black print, illus of town hall, decorative border. At head of title: "Republic of France... Chicago Universal Exhibition of 1893." Gives number of members and pensions paid. Notation of their gold and silver medals from Paris expo, 1889. ☺ (WM)

451.1 [France]. Piet & Cie. *Blanchisseries : désinfection : lavoirs publics : installations : Procédés et Appareils spéciaux*. Paris: [Imp. Baré, à Guise (Aisne)], 1892.

> 24x15½. 1 *l* frontis, 1 *l* (t.p.), 2 p preface, 1 *l*, 200 p. Drab olive wraps, black and red print. Frontis of laundry methods old and new. Their illus 1893 catalog of laundry equipment and installations. One was a laundry installed on a river barge for a good water supply. C.t. = t.p. Exhibited and awarded in 1889 Paris expo. No WCE content; from intact collection. ☺ (WM)

452. France. *Section Française beaux-arts Catalogue officiel*: (Stfd)

454.1 [France]. *...Société anonyme Franco-Belge : pour la : construction de machines & de matérials : de chemins de fer*. [Paris : Auto. A. Gentil], n.d.

> 27x20. 8 p with 4 *l* interspersed folding plates of their locomotives. Blue-flecked tan pulp wraps, black print. C.t. At head of title: "Exposition Universelle Internationale de Chicago 1893." Offices for their railroad hardware in France and Belgium. ☺ (S)

454.2 [France]. Société Centrale des Architectes Française. *Caisse de défense mutuelle des architectes... architects' mutual defense fund...* Paris: Imprimerie Chaix, 1893.

> 27½x21. (3) p. Folded sheet, black print. English/French languages. As described, a handout at their WCE exhibit, Class 37, Social Economy. The society's group for legal defense of members. ☺ (WM)

455.1 [France]. Société d'Initiative pour la Propagation de l'enseignement scientifique par l'aspect. Jardin, H., et G. Serrurier. *Société d'enseignement par les projections lumineuses...statuts*. Havre: Siège de la société, [Janvier 1893?].

> 22x14. 8 p. Blue-flecked wraps, black print and border with illus of their Paris expo award. Society for teaching optical projection; their bylaws in French. Last dated on p 8: "Le Havre, 24 Janvier 1893." No WCE content; from intact collection. (WM)

455.2 [France]. Société d'Initiative pour la Propagation de l'enseignement scientifique par l'aspect. Serrurier, G. *...Monographie*. Havre: Imprimerie du Journal le Havre, 1889.

> 21x13½. 48 p + foldout illus of projector between pp 28-29. Robin's-egg blue wraps, black print and border design with single medal. At head of title: society name and info; rubber over-stamp "Médalle d'ob. a l'exposition universelle de paris." About the society of optical projection; list of talks made on the subject. In French. No WCE content; from intact collection. (WM)

455.3 [France]. Société de Secours Mutuels. *...Compte rendu de l'assemblée générale du 6 mars 1892*. Paris: Siège social [Imprimerie Charles Blot], 1892.

21½x13½. 102 p. Self-wraps not in paging; black print and border. C.t. At top of cover: "Exposition universelle : Paris 1889 : medaille d'or." Also society info at head of title. Trans: recognition of the mutual aid society in the Seine area in 1892. No WCE content; from intact collection. (WM)

455.4 [France]. Société de Secours Mutuels. ...*Statuts : de la : société de secours mutuels.* Paris: Imprimerie Chaix, 1893.

24x16. 16 p. Lime wraps, black print. At head of title: "Blanchisserie et teinturerie de thaon (Vosges)." Trans: Laws of the mutual aid society. C.t. = t.p. Union society founded in 1872 which gave medical and financial aid to sick workers. No WCE content; from intact collection. (WM)

455.5 [France]. Société Toulousaine d'Électricité. ...*Notice : sur : L'usine d'électricité : du Bazacle : a Toulouse (Haute-Garonne) : France.* Toulouse: Imprimerie douladoure-privat, 1893.

23½x15½. 16 p. Wraps, black print. C.t. = t.p. Report on the properties of their DC power plant and amperage output. At head of title: "Exposition internationale de Chicago 1893." (WM)

456.   France. *Some words about the société de l'industrie minérale*:
▶Completed citation: 18½x13. Blue-flecked gray wraps, black print. C.t. = t.p.

457.   [France]. Varigny. *En Amérique souvenirs de voyage*: (Col,CU,IHi,UdM,UIC)

457.1 [France]. Vossion, Louis. *Exposition de Chicago : l'inauguration : souvenirs personnels.* Paris: E. Dentu, Éditeur, [1892].

22½x15. 32 p. Frontis of the Court of Honor: "Exposition colombienne. La cour d'honneur, la nuit." The author's personal account of the WCE dedication ceremonies. Dated Nov 1892. ☺. (UPa)

-G-

457.2 [Germany]. Acker, Carl [Co.]. ...*Original- und Cabinets- Abfüllungen aus der Königl. Preuss. Domanial-Kellerei.* Wiesbaden: L. Schellenberg'sche Hof-Buchdruckerei, n.d.

22½x14½. (8) p includes self-wraps. Chocolate brown and red print and crest illus, pale blue border. C.t. A listing of available wines with New York and Chicago prices. Becklin, Chicago agent, printed at bottom. In German. No WCE content; from intact collection. ☺(WM)

457.3 [Germany]. ...*Agricultural-Chemical Experiment Station...Collection of selected Laboratory Apparatus.* [Bonn: Printed by Charles Georgi], n.d.

28x18½. (2) p. Single glossy sheet, black print. At head of title: "World's Columbian Exposition, U.S.A." In English. List and description of 13 apparatus. (WM)

457.4 [Germany]. Albert, H. & E. [Co.]. *The Best Methods of Restoring Nutritive Materials to the Soil.* London: H. & E. Albert (Printed by A. Southey & Co.), 1893.   P↑

21½x14. 28 p. Light blue wraps decoratively printed in shades of blue. C.t.: "Souvenir of the Centennial Columbian Exhibition at Chicago 1893 : presented by H. & E. Albert...Agricultural-Chemical Manure Works." Located: Biebrich-on-Rhine. Illus of plant cultivation. ☺.(WM)

457.5 [Germany]. Allgemeine Elektricitäts-Gesellschaft. *Exhibition of the Allgemeine Elektricitäts-Gesellschaft : at the : World's Columbian exposition : Chicago 1893.* [Berlin: Printed by H.S. Hermann], 1893?.   P→

15x22½. (32) p. Illus. Buff wraps with blue print and design of woman hoisting light bulb and sitting on winged

wheel atop globe. C.t.: "Allgemeine Elektricitäts-Gesellschaft : Berlin." Back wrap illus of both sides of commemorative medal. ©. (HML)

458. Germany. *Amtlicher Bericht*: (ICRL,IHi,LHL,MIT,SML,UTA)

459. Germany. *Amtlicher Katalog*: (Col,CU,HU,Merc,MSI,NLI,NSW,SML,Stfd,UBO,UBW,Yale)
▶The first 9 *l* can be correctly paged as (16) p, 1 *l*

459.1 [Germany]. *The Apollinaris Spring : Valley of the Ahr : Rhenish Prussia, Germany.* London: Spottiswoode & co., 1893.

24½x17½. 15 p., (1) p printer info, 12 *l* plates—2 folding. Pink smooth wraps with black print and illus of "The Apollinaris Church." C.t. = t.p. English co exhibited in the German section of the Ag Bldg, Group 10, Class 64. No mention of WCE; from intact collection. © (GLD) $20 - 40

460. Germany. *Ausstellung*: (ICRL,MIT,SML,UBO,UTA)
▶Correct paging: 3 *l*, (7)-51 p.

460.1 Germany. Bavaria. Lang, Georg. *Biological Collection : of the most destructible* [sic] *insects to forests : and their enemies : exhibited by the Zellstofffabrik Waldhof : (Waldhof Sulphite Co.) : at the : Columbian World's Fair : Chicago 1893.* [Bayreuth?]: Waldhof Sulphite Co., n.d.

22x15. 31 p. Olive wraps, black print. C.t. = t.p. List of Waldhof's WCE exhibit content. At the bottom of odd pp: "This paper is made out of pure Waldhof Sulphite Wood Pulp." [The pulp paper of a pristine copy found at the FM in 1996 is browned with age, but otherwise in excellent condition.] (FM)

461. Germany. Bayerischer. Gmelin. *Das Deutsche Kunst*: (Col,UMD,VAM,Yale)
462. Germany. Bayerischer. *Verzeichniss der auf den*: (MSI,WM)   P➜

462.1 Germany. *Der : Bergbau und Hüttenbetrieb : der : Lahn-, Dill- und benachbarten Reviere : (Nassau).* Siegen: Druck von C. Buchholz, 1893.

22½x14. iv, 79 p. Written expressly for the WCE as stated on p iii; table of contents on p iv. Wraps. German language. Trans: The Mining and Metallurgy of Lahn range, Dill range, and neighboring ranges. Subject: chemical content and mining activity in these mountain ranges. See #462.2 for a related publication. ©. (SML)

462.2 Germany. *Der Bergbau und Hüttenbetrieb des Siegerlandes.* Siegen: Druck von C. Buchholz, 1893.

22½x14. 28 p. Tan red-flecked wraps, black print and decorative border. C.t. = t.p. German language description of mining in the Rhine-Westfal mountains. Mineral content described. Charts and table; table of content on p 28. No mention of WCE; from an intact WCE collection. See #462.1 for a related item. (WM)

462.3 [Germany]. *Berlin-anhaltische maschinenbau-actien-gesellschaft... Transmissions-Gruppe der Ausstellung in Chicago.* Berlin: n.p., n.d.

23x14½. (2) p. Sheet, black print, illus of their WCE exhibit. List of contents on back. In Portuguese, German, and English. Berlin company's catalog of couplings, pulleys and clutches for power transmission. (WM)

463. Germany. Berlin. *Beschreibung*: (GLD,HU,ICRL,LBA,UTA)   P➜ $40 - 75

464.1 [Germany]. Braun, Gottfried H. *Sociale fragen des Columbischen katholiken-congresses (Sept. 1893), bei gelegenheit der Chicagoer weltausstellung. ...* Freiburg i. Br.: 1893.

8°. 88 p. Trans: Social questions of the Columbian Catholic congress on the occasion of the Chicago World's fair. (Col)

465.   Germany. *Catalog of the Collections in the Museum*: (WM)   P➜

466.   Germany. *Catálogo oficial*: (NLI,NSW,SML,UBO,UTA)
▸Add: Spanish version of #459.
▸Correct paging: (16) p, 1 *l*, 347, 90 p ads.

468.   Germany. Central-verein. Weigel. *Führer durch*:
(Col,FM,HU,KBS,MIT,NAL,PSU,S,SML,UBO,UCLA,WM,Yale)
---- Also found: 1 *l* (t.p.), 1 *l* "Buchgewerbliche," (v)-xii, 1 *l*, 149 p.

469.   Germany. *Chicago und die Columbische*: (LHL)
472.   Germany. Deutsche gesellshraft. *Special catalogue*: (ICRL,MIT,WM)
473.   [Germany]. *Das Deutsche haus*: (LBA)

475.   Germany. *Der Deutsche Tag*: (HU,S)

475.1 [Germany]. Deutsche Warte. *...Neujahrs-Gruss : nebst : Wegweiser : zur : Columbia Weltausstellung : in Chicago : 1893. Den Lesern der : Deutsche Warte : dargeboten vom Herausgeber.* Chicago: Deutsche Warte, n.d.

18x11. (38) p. Illus, map. The last (16) pages are on 4 sheets 18x21 folded to 18x11. Cream wraps, black print and border. C.t. At head of title: "Supplement to D[eutsche] Warte No. 4, Chicago, Ills." Trans: New Years greetings plus guide to the WCE in Chicago. Printed by German-American organization for its readers. B/w WCE views and WCE text in old German script. 1893 calendar on back. One fold out is an A. Zeese bird's-eye view entitled "Weltausstellungsplatz" ᶜ1892. ☺ . (IHi)   P➜
---- Also found: Germania [author]. Milwaukee: [Germania Publishing Co.], n.d. Cover subtitle "Germania." At head of title: "Supplement to Germania No. 64, Milwaukee, Wis." (GLD) $44

476.1 Germany. *...Deutsches Reich. Abtheilung für ingenieurwesen. Ausstellung der stadt Köln. Auszug. Schwemmkanalisation.* N.p.: n.p., n.d.

19½x15½. (3)-19 p. Self-wraps, black print. At head of title: "Columbische welt-ausstellung in Chicago 1893." Catalog describing designs no 21 to 26 exhibited at the WCE concerning layout and implementation of city services such as gas, water, sewer, and electricity. Trans: German empire. Division of engineering technology exhibit of Cologne. Summary of city infrastructure. ☺ (GLD) $25 - 50

477.   [Germany]. Dümmler. *Die Ziegel-*: (LHL,VAM)
---- Also found: 3 *l*, 180 p, illus, 13 plates, diagrams. Half leather over purple textured cloth hc, gilt spine print. Blue, brown, white marbled end papers.

478.   Germany. Dyck. *Special-Katalog der mathematischen*: (HU,MIT)

478.1 Germany. Ebermayer, Gustav, Georg Ehrne von Melchthal, and Valentin Zehnder. *Bericht über eine im auftrage der k. bayer. staatsregierung ausgeführte reise nach Nordamerika und zur columbischen weltausstellung in Chicago vom 30. Mai bis 5. August 1893.* München: n.p., 1896.

Octovo. Text plus atlas of 128 plates. The subject is US railways. Trans: Report about a trip sponsored by Bavaria to North America and the WCE. (HU)

479.   Germany. Ehrenbaum. *Bericht über eine Reise*: (HU)

480.1 [Germany]. Fitzner, W., [Co.]. *...W. Fitzner Boiler and Bridge Building Works. Speciality: Welded Sheet Work. ...World's Columbian Exposition Chicago 1893. Section for German Machinery : № 3751. Class 49.* Leipzig: Eckert & Pflug, Kunstanstalt, n.d.

26x20½. 3 *l*, 6 p. White stiff wraps with black and gilt print, decorative floral design in shades of peach and green. C.t At head of title: "Awarded the First Gold Medal in Prussia." Laurahütte, Prussia co. In English. Beautiful ad. ☺ .(WM)　　　　**P→**

480.2 [Germany]. Förstel, C. ...*Specialität: obstverwerthung. Preparations of fruits.* Jena: [Lithogr. Anstalt von Karl Wesser], n.d.

14x11. (4) p. Folded buff card. Chromoliths of flowers on yellow-tan background, blue and red borders. At head of title: co name boldly printed diagonally across cover in brown. German p (2); English p (3). Flowers around lithographic info on back. No WCE; from an intact collection. (WM)

481. Germany. *Führer durch die Ausstellung der Chemischen*: (HU,SML,WM) ▶Correct paging: W. Berlin: Julius Sittenfeld, n.d. v, 1 *l* index, (4) exhibit plan, 115, (1) p colophon.
---- Also found: Berlin: Carl Heymanns Verlag, 1893. 22½x15. Olive-green textured stiff wraps, black print. C.t. = t.p. German language.

482. Germany. *Führer durch die ausstellung für das höhere mädchenschulwesen*: (HU,Yale)

482.1 Germany. ...*Führer durch die ausstellung für das höhere schulwesen.* Chicago: Press of Max Stern & co., [1893].

22x15. 1 *l*, (3)-20. Light blue wraps, black print and border. C.t. = t.p. At head of title: "Deutsche Unterrichtsausstellung in Chicago 1893." Trans: Guide through the exhibit for high schools. ☺ .(HU)

483. Germany. Gängl. *Das berg- und hüttenwesen*: (MIT)
484. [Germany]. *German Village : Das Deutsche Dorf*: (ref,wslb)　　　　$84

484.1 [Germany]. *German Village. Sunday, June 4, 1893. Two Grand Military Concerts by the German infantry band...* N.p.: Gindele printing co., n.d.

22½x15. (4) p. Folded pulp sheet, black print and cover illus of village. Inside pp (2)-(3)are programs for two concerts; bill of fare at the concert garden on back. ☺ (WM)

485.1 [Germany]. Güttler, H[ermann], [Co.]. ...*Arsenik- Berg-u. Hüttenwerk : "Reicher Trost" : der gruppe deutschen Collectiv-Ausstellung,...* Reichenstein: Lith. Carl Flemming, Glogau, n.d.

19x13. 16 p. Dark burnt-orange wraps with black print and design, including several medals. After the cover is sheet with identical front cover design but title in English: "Arsenic- Mine and Works : 'Reicher Trost' : Group of the German Collective Exhibition..." German and English text each page. .(WM)　　　　**P→**

486. Germany. Graesel. *Special-katalog der bibliotheks*: (HU,LBA,MIT,MSL,WM,Yale)

486.1 Germany. Grossheim, C. *Das Sanitätswesen auf der Weltausstellung zu Chicago.* Berlin: Verlag von August Hirschwald, 1893.

21½x14½. Contains 92 plates. Part 7 of *Veröffentlichungen aus dem Gebiete des Militär-Sanitätswesens Herausgegeben von der Medizinal-Abtheilung des Königlich Preussischen Kriegsministeriums* (a work of the Medical division of the Royal Prussian Ministry of War). Title trans: Sanitary Science at the World's Fair in Chicago. ☺ .(UBW)

487. Germany. *Guide through the exhibition of the German chemical*: (HU,S) ▶Clarification: The 3 *l* could have been paged as 1 *l*, (4) p.
---- Also found: Berlin: Carl Heymanns Verlag [Printed by Julius Sittenfeld, Berlin], 1893. On bottom of

t.p.: The International News Company of New-York and London. English language version of the "also found" in #481. (SML)

---- Also found: Gray-green textured wraps, black print and border.

487.1 [Germany]. Haarmann, A. *Eine Fahrt zur Kolumbus-Ausstellung : Mitgleid der Iurn fur die Ingenieur-Abtheilung auf der Weltausstellung zu Chicago 1893.* Osnabruck: J.G. Kisling, 1894.

23x__. 116 p. In German. Trans: A trip to the WCE and description of the Engineering Congress. (ref)

488. [Germany]. Hofmann. *Chicago-Reise*: (HML)
489. Germany. Imperial Insurance. Zacher. *The Workmen's*: (HU,LBA)

490. [Germany]. Badische Anilin- & Soda- Fabrik. *...Guide to the exhibits of the : Badische Anilin- & Soda- Fabrik.* [Ludwigshafen on Rhine: Weiss & Hameler, 1893?]. P➔

22x14½. 3 *l*, 3 *l* plates separated by tissue guards, 1-24 p+ tipped-in folded chart at back cover. Very decorative cream (or caramel color) stiff cardboard wraps, brown print and design with gilt rays, red dyed edges. Red decorative border around text pages. At head of title: "The World's Columbian Exposition : Chicago : 1893. .(UMD,WM)

▶Delete Interessengemeinshaft as author. Citation rewritten and complete.

492. *John Rotzer's Gasthof*: (WM)
▶Add author and info: Rotzer, John, [Co.]. N.p.: [A. Goldsmith manufacturing stationer], n.d. (8) p. Cover design includes Columbus landing scene. Ad for Adams-Smith Co., Chicago, inside back cover. Exhibit on the Midway.

493. Germany. *Kaiserlich deutsche reichsdruckerei*: (CU)
494. Germany. *Katalog der ausstellung...mädchenschulwesen*: (HU,ICRL,S,Yale)
495. Germany. *Katalog der ausstellung...schulwesen*: (HU,ICRL,UCLA)
496. Germany. *Katalog der Deutschen Ingenieur-Ausstellung*: (ICRL,LU)

497. Germany. *Katalog der Universitätes-Ausstellung*: (HU,NAL,NSW)
---- Also found: Blue-flecked wraps, black print.

498.1 [Germany]. Kloss & Foerster [Co.]. *Sparkling Wines : Kloss & Foerster...Deutscher Sect.* Freyburg: n.p., n.d.

12x9. (4) p. Folded buff stiff card. Green and black cover, gilt medal at top front and back. Litho of winery, back. C.t. Prices. In English. ☺(WM)

498.2 Germany. Komités für die Amerika-feier. *Hamburgische festschrift zur erinnerung an die entdeckung Amerika's.* 2 vol. Hamburg: L. Friederichsen & C̲o̲, 1892. P➔

26½x17½. Vol 1 includes 2 plates and 25 illus in text; vol 2 includes 1 map. Decorative hc with old German script; circular cover design labeled: "Rosa nautica der Weltkarte des Juan de la Cosa 1500." Title trans: Early writings from Hamburg recalling the discovery of the Americas. ☺.(Col)

498.3 Germany. *Königl. Preussische bergwerks-direction zu Saarbrücken. Direction of the royal Prussian coal mines at Saarbrücken. Weltausstellung zu Chicago 1893. The Columbian World exposition Chicago 1893.* N.p.: n.p., n.d.

19x11½. 35 p+ 1 folded *l* labeled "table of pit-wire-ropes." Very dark wine-red wraps with gilt print and border. C.t.= t.p. Even pages are in German; odd, in English. No illus. ☺.(MIT,SML,UBO)

499. Germany. Königlichen Bibliothek. *Verzeichniss der in Deutschland*: (Col,MIT,NSW,UMN,wslb,Yale)

499.1 Germany. Königlichen Preussischen Ministeriums. Arndt, Otto. *Verzeichnis der pädagogischen Zeitschriften, Jahrbücher und Lehrerkalender : Deutschlands.* Berlin: Druck von A.W. Hayn's Erben, 1893.

> 26x17½. 71 p. Gray paper covered boards, black print, gray cloth spine and corners. C.t. = t.p. List of papers and magazines published in Germany for schools and teachers. No mention of WCE; from an intact collection. Same format as #499.2 and #499.3. (WM)

499.2 Germany. Königlichen Preussischen Ministeriums. Lange, Helene. *Entwickelung und Stand des höheren Madchenschulwesens in Deutschland.* Berlin: R. Gaertners Verlags buchhandlung, 1893.

> 24½x16½. 1 *l* (t.p.), 69 p. Robin's-egg blue paper covered boards, black print, gray cloth spine and corners. C.t. = t.p. Trans: Development and current situation with German women's high schools. No mention of WCE; from intact WCE collection. Same format as #499.1 and #499.3. (WM)

499.3 Germany. Königlichen Preussischen Ministeriums. Rethwisch, Conrad. *Deutschlands höheres Schulwesen in neunzehnten Jahrhundert. Geschichtlicher Überblick...* Berlin: R. Gaertners Verlagsbuchhandlung, 1893.

> 24x17. viii, 206, 53, (1) p. Gray paper covered boards, black print, gray cloth spine and corners. In the foreword it says that this book was written for WCE. C.t. = t.p. Trans: Germany's high schools in the 19th century. Historical overview. Same format as the two above. (WM)

500. Germany. *Königreich Preussen. Höhere Lehranstalten*: (HU)

501. Germany. *Königreich Preussen. Statistisches über Volks- und Mittelschulen*: (HU)
▶Completed citation: 1 *l*, 3-25, (1) p. Gray wraps, black print and border.

502. Germany. *Königreich Württemberg*: . (HU,ICRL)
▶Correct pub info: There is no date printed on the t.p.

503. Germany. Lexis. *Die Deutschen universitäten*: (Col,CU,DC,NDU,UMN,Yale)
▶See #723.2 for a prospectus.

504. Germany. Bavaria. *List of exhibitors : from : Nuremberg and Fuerth : (Bavaria) : at the : Columbian World's Exhibition : Chicago 1893.* Nuremberg: G.P.J. Bieling-Dietz Printer to the Royal Bavarian Court, n.d.

> 17½x12. 92 p+ unpaged stiff ad before p 81. White glossy stiff wraps, black print, diamond design on rectangular blue background. C.t.: "The exhibitors of Nuremberg-Fuerth Bavaria at the Columbian World's Exhibition. Chicago 1893." In English. Lists exhibitors and some "Bavarian manufactures not exhibited" starting on p 81. ☺. (SML,WM) **P→**

504.1 [Germany]. *Ludowici Roofing tile Company.* [Chicago: Kirchner, Meckel & Co. Printers, 1893].

> 15x20. 1 *l* folded illus of the factory, 5-32 p. Bone-white glossy wraps, black and red print, illus of red tile on black circle. C.t. On cover: "Manufactures and exhibitors at this exposition of the Roof of the German Government Building on the Lake Front and the Pavilion in Northwest Corner of Mining Building." Dated on p 5: "Chicago, July 25th, 1893." In English. ☺ (WM)

504.2 [Germany]. Ludowici-Falz-Ziegel [Co.]. *Carl Ludowici : Ludwigshafen & Jockgrim...1891.* [Würzburg: Kgl. Universitätsdruckerei von H. Stürtz], n.d.

> 18x12. 1 *l* folded illus of the factory, 45, (3) p "Notizen" + many scattered unpaged *l* of photo illus. Gold pebbled wraps, bold black print with red roofing tile on a black circle. Blue-black text and lithos. In German. Manufactured interlocking roofing tile and roof ornaments. [Manufacturer of tiles for the German Bldg.] No WCE content; from intact collection. ☺ (WM)

505. [Germany]. *Old Vienna. Alt Wien*: (ICRL,MSL,UBW,wslb,Yale)

506. Germany. *Official Catalogue*: $45 - 95
(GLD,CLP,CU,FM,HML,HU,ICRL,LBA,Merc,MIT,NLI,NSW,SML,UBO,UCLA,uiuc,UMD,WM)

▶Published by the Imperial Commission; printed by the Reichsdruckerei in Berlin. Introd by Otto N[icolaus] Witt; see #513 for another Witt item.
▶Correct paging: (16) p, 1 *l*, 312, 90 p ads.
▶Improved cover description: Olive green flexible cloth hc.   **P➔**

506.1 Germany. Pappenheim, E., Emanuel Vogelgesang, and Otto Janke. ...*Bericht : des Sonderkomitees IX der : "Deutschen Frauen-Abteilung bei der Weltausstellung in Chicago 1893" : uber Krippen, Kinderschutzvereine, Oberlinschulen, Bewahranstalten, Fröbelsche Kindergärten, Kinderhorte und Anstalten zur Ausbildung von Kleinkinder-...* Berlin: L. Oehmigke's Verlag, 1893.

20½x13. 252 p. At the head of the title: "Unter dem Protektorat ihrer Königl. Hohiet der __? Friedrich Karl von Pruessen." Henriette Schrader, Director. Trans: Report of special committee IX for the German women's work at the WCE. ☺. (BRA,UBW)

506.2 [Germany]. Paulsen, Friedrich. *The German Universities : Their character and historical development.* Trans. E.D. Perry. New York [and] London: Macmillan and Co., 1895 [ᶜ1894 By Macmillan and co.].

19½x13½. xxxi, 254, (8) p ads. Rebound. In his preface, the translator states that this is an English translation of the introductory part of W. Lexis's 2-vol work from the WCE, #503. ☺(DC)

506.3 Germany. ...*Preis-Verzeichnisse der Deutschen Aussteller der Gartenbau-Abtheilung. Price-Lists of the German Exhibitors of the Horticultural Department. World's Columbian Exposition : Chicago 1893.* N.p.: n.p., 1893?; Cambridge, MA: HULMS, [1983]. Film Mas C 978.

24x16½. 48 p. Deep red glossy wraps. At head of title: "Columbus-Welt-Ausstellung : Chicago 1893." ☺. (HU)   **P➔**

506.4 [Germany]. *Programm der : Königlichen Bergakademie : zu : Clausthal. Lehrjahr 1893-94.* Leipzig: Druck von Breitkopf & Härtel, n.d.

22½x15. 64 p+ large folded map of hiking routes about Clausthal in the Harz Mountains. Buff smooth wraps, black print and border. C.t. = t.p. A technical school curriculum in the mountains. No mention of WCE; from an intact WCE collection. ☺(WM)

508.   Germany. Reichs-Versicherungsamt. Zacher. *Leitfaden zur:* (CU,HU)
---- Also listed with paging: 26, (4) p.

509.1 Germany. Reusche, Friedrich. ...*Chicago und Berlin. Alte und neue Bahnen im Ausstellungswesen.* Berlin: Verlag von Carl Ulrich & Co., 1892.

ca 21x14. Pt 1 of *Deutsche Weltausstellung-Bibliothek : Erscheint in zwanglosen, einzeln käuflichen Heften* (German World Exposition Library : Easy single purchasable parts) by Reusche. At head of title: "Deutsche Weltausstellung-Bibliothek. Heft 1." Trans: Chicago and Berlin. Old and new exposition methods. ☺. (UBW)

509.2 [Germany]. Riedler, A. *Ein Rückblick auf die Weltausstellung in Chicago. Vortrag gehalten im Verein zur Beförderung des Gewerbfleisses.* Berlin: Verlag von Leonhard Simion, 1894.

22x15. 35 p. 15th annual ed of *Volkswirthschaftliche Zeitfragen. Vorträge und Abhandlunger : herausgegeben von der Volkswirthschaftlichen Gesellschaft in Berlin*, pt 117. Trans: A retrospective view of the international exposition in Chicago. Lecture held to promote the industrial union. (Col,KBS,ONB,Yale)

510.   Germany. *Die sächsische Textil-Industrie:* (WM)
▶Add: Two-tone dark green wraps, black print. Title on a diagonal banner. Exhibit floor plan on back.

510.1 [Germany]. Schröder, Max. *Die wasserfreie : flüssige : schwefligesaüre : und ihre verwendung in der industrie von Dr. Max Schröder...* Oberhausen: Buch- und kunstdrukerei Richard Kühne, n.d.

15x10½. 27 p. Gun-metal gray wraps, black print. C.t.= t.p. In German. Trans: Uses of waterless liquid sulfuric acids in Schröder's business. No WCE content; from an intact collection. (WM)

510.2 [Germany]. Schuchardt, Theodor, Chemical Works. ...*Catalogue of the Exhibit of Dr Theodor Schuchardt : Chemical Works, Goerlitz, Germany : Manufacturer of Chemicals of every description for scientific, medico-pharmaceutical,...* N.p.: [Printed by Goerlitzer Nachrichten and Anzeiger], n.d.

20x13½. 29 p, 1 *l* printer info. Bone-white wraps, red and blue print, black/red/blue border design. Text in English, blue ink. C.t. At head of title: "Chicago 1893 : World's Columbian Exposition." Back cover ad for "plastilina (an excellent stuff for moulding)." ☺ (WM)

510.3 [Germany]. Schüking, Dr. *Gruppen-Ausstellung der Deutschen Bäder und Brunnen. Weltausstellung : Chicago 1893.* Pyrmont: n.p., [1893].

21½x14½. 31 p. Dark lavender wraps, black print and ornate border. Text in old German script. Date and author on p 5. Trans: The group exhibit of German spas and baths. See #510.4. ☺ (S)

510.4 [Germany]. Schüking, Dr. *Joint Exhibition of the German bathes and springs. World's Exhibition: Chicago 1893.* Pyrmont: n.p., [1893].

21½x14. 30 p. Robin's-egg blue wraps, black print and ornate border. Schüking was manager of Pyrmont, one of the baths. English version of #510.3. ☺ (S)

511. Germany. *The Textile Industry of Saxony*: (Col,FM)
512. Germany. *Verzeichnis der seit 1850*: (CU)

512.1 Germany. Wenzel, Otto. <u>*Prospect*</u>. *Adressbuch und Waarenverzeichniss der Chemischen Industrie des Deutschen Reiches. 1892.* Berlin: Verlag von Rudolf Mückenberger (Druck von Fischer & Wittig im Leipzig), n.d.

14½x10. 64 p. Buff wraps, black print and German phoenix shield, orange decorative border. C.t.: "The Chemical Industries of the German Empire 1892." Product directory for Germany with company addresses. German language. C.t.= t.p. No mention of WCE; from an intact WCE collection. ☺ (WM)

513. [Germany]. Witt. *Die chemische industrie auf der Columbischen*: (MIT,NAL,URI,Yale)

513.1 [Germany]. Witte, Friedrich, Chemical Works. ...*List of the Chemical, pharmaceutical and scientific preparations exhibited by Friedr. Witte chemical works...* [Rostock: Adlers Erben], n.d.

31½x23½. (12) p includes self-wraps. Blue-black print throughout. C.t. At head of title: "International Columbian exhibition : Chicago 1893 : German department." In English. ☺ (WM)

514. Germany. Wittmack. *Gartenbau*: (NAL)
515. Germany. Wittmack. *Landwirthschaftliche Erzeugnisse*: (NAL)

517.1 Great Britain. Cotton, W.J.R. *A tributary ode. Victoria, of Great Britain and Ireland—Queen. 1837–1887.* London: Printed by W.H. & L. Collingridge, n.d.

20½x16½. 1 *l* (t.p.), 3 *l*, 6-16 numbered pp only printed on rectos. Blood-red glossy wraps with gilt print. C.t.= t.p. Poem. Subject: 50th anniversary of Queen Victoria's reign. No WCE content; found with a uniform WCE collection; "Chicago Exposition 1893" handwritten years ago at top of t.p. ☺ . (SML)

518. Great Britain. [McCormick]. *The future trade relations between Great Britain*: (HU)
519. Great Britain. Royal Commission. *Baroness Burdett-Coutts*: (CU,Smth,uiuc)

520. Great Britain. Royal Commission for the Chicago Exhibition, 1893. Burdett-Coutts, ed. ...*Woman's Mission : a series of congress papers on the philanthropic work of women : by eminent writers.* London: S. Low, Marston & company, limited, 1893.

25x17½. xxiv, 485 p. Red pebble-textured cloth spine over red cloth boards, gilt British seal. Gilt spine print. At head of title: "Royal British commission, Chicago exhibition, 1893." Papers given by English

women for the congress in the WCE Woman's Bldg. Includes Coutts' introd: a letter to Princess
Christian of Schleswig-Holstein, chair of the women's committee. © (DC) ▶Completed citation.

521. Great Britain. Royal. *Handbook of Regulations*: (FM,RSA,SML,VAM,WM)
▶Also found: Same paging and cover except "Final edition" is not printed
on cover.

522. Great Britain. Royal. *Official catalogue*: (Amh,BNCR,BRA,CCA,CLP,Col,CU,EPL,FLP,
FM,HU,ICRL,LBA,Merc,MSL,NAL,NLA,NSW,RSA,S,SML,Stfd,UBO,UBW,UMC,UMD,UPa,UTA,VAM,WM,Yale)
---- Also found: 1st ed. 19x14½. xlii, 1 *l* printed with "xx and, xxi" (all
ads), 544, xxii-cix (ads, some interspersed in text), (1) p ad. Royal blue
hc, gilt design and print, gilt spine print. "Presentation copy" on front
cover. Canary yellow end papers. Stationery with embossed blue seal of
the "Royal commission Chicago exhibition 1893" tipped-in below seal on
front fly leaf: "With Sir Henry Trueman Wood's Compliments." Wood's
name crossed out in ink and Mrs. P.E. Cope's written in. Wood was the
indefatigable Secretary for the Royal Commission; Cope was an exhibitor.
☺. (GLD)   P➔ $60 - 95

523. Great Britain. Royal. Pascoe. *An Illustrated*: (HU,ICRL,S,slpl,UTA,WM,Yale) P↘

525. Greece. *Catalogue of casts exhibited*: ☺. (HU,ICRL,UTA)
▶Completed annotation: 25x17½. 20 p. Steel gray wraps, black print.
C.t. = t.p. Catalog lists 112 sculpture items exhibited at WCE.

526. [Greece]. Graf. *Catalogue of the Theodor Graf*: (HU,LBA,S,UCB,UPa,WM)
▶Cover info: Pale green wraps, black print, no cover illus. Back cover:
"The Hellenistic portraits,…"

527. Greece. *Greece. Official catalogue World's Columbian*: (ICRL,UTA)

527.1 [Greece]. Greek Metallurgical Company of Laurium. Cordella, A[ndré].
*The mining and metallurgical industries : of Laurium : for : the exhibition
of Chicago U.S. America.* Athenes: Printing offices Alexandre
Papageorgiou, 1893.

22x14½. 16 p. Pale green wraps, black print. Cordella was general manager of the company. ☺. (CCA)

527.2 Greece. *Greek Section : World's Columbian Exposition : Chicago, 1893. Take this home : important to all
housekeepers…Currants…* N.p.: n.p., n.d.

16x9. (4) p. Card folded at top edge, blue print, vignette of Greek seal. C.t.
Includes various currant recipes. ☺. (GLD,KS)   P➔ $18 - 36

527.3 [Greece]. Negris, Ph. *La société des travaux publics et communaux : a
l'exposition de Chicago.* Athenes: n.p., 1893.

22½x15. 1 *l* (t.p.), (3)-12 p includes tables. Blue-green wraps, black print.
C.t. = t.p. Describes the Society's activities in the magnesium carbonate mines
at Milo, Greece. In French. Trans: The society of public and social works at
the Chicago exposition. ☺. (MIT,S)

528. Guadeloupe. Guesde. *Guadeloupe (West Indies)*: (S)
▶Completed citation: 15½x10. Peach wraps, black print. C.t. = t.p. A brief
history of Guadeloupe, its products, politics, etc.

529.1 Guatemala. Department of Public Works. *A Descriptive Account of the republic
of Guatemala : Central America.* Chicago: Press of the Courrier de Chicago
[for the] Department of Public Works, 1893.

19x13½. 39 p. Red (or yellowish-green) wraps, black print. C.t. History and present condition of the country. No WCE; from intact collections. ☺ . (FM,LBA)   **P→**

-H-

531.1 [Haiti]. Easton, William Edgar. *Dessalines, a dramatic tale : a single chapter from Haiti's history.* [Galveston, TX]: J.W. Burson-Co., 1893.

20x__. viii, 138 p, illus. Includes Frederick Douglass's WCE oration, see #531. (UMA)

532.1 [Holland]. *Koninklijke fabrick van metaalwaren : Lakwerken : W. Reijenga. Tᵉ Amsterdam.* Amsterdam: Roeloffzen & Hüber, n.d.

16½x11½. (4) p. Folded sheet, black print and illus of their ceramic and coated metal trays, office, and kitchen wares. C.t. No WCE content; from intact collection. (WM)

532.2 Holland. *Netherlands Day.* ___: ___, 1893?

20½x14. (6) p. Tri-fold buff card with inserted loose song sheet printed in Dutch. Pale blue print; coat of arms in pale blue, red, black, and gilt; vignette port of Queen Wilhelmina. C.t. At head of title: "31st of August, 1893." At the bottom of the cover: "World's Columbian Exposition." (D) $25 - 40

-I-

534.   India. Office of I-G of Forests. *Hand-book to accompany:* (GLD,FM,NAL,S)
---- Also found: No t.p. and no (1) p at end. (SML)
---- Also found: Hand annotated copy signed by C.F. Millspaugh of West Virginia, who was "Installation Preparator." Used to number and install the woods sent by India to the Forestry Bldg.

534.1 [India]. Telléry, S.J., & Co. *The Industrial Art Manufactures of the Indian Empire.* Dehli: S.J. Telléry & Co., n.d.

23x15½. 36 p. Gray wraps, blue print and elaborate tower trade-mark design. Caption title: "The Art Work of the Indian Empire." WCE handout; found in intact collections. ☺ . (CCA,LBA)

534.2 Ireland. Irish Industries Association. *Guide to the Irish Industrial Village.* [Chicago]: Rand, McNally & co., printers, n.d.

23x15½. (4) p. Folded sheet. Caption title. Cover titled: "Bird's-eye view of the Irish industrial village in midway plaisance." Illus caption: "Come and Kiss the Blarney Stone." (ref,WM) $18 - 38

535.   Ireland. IIA. *Guide to the Irish Industrial Village:* (NLI)
536.   Ireland. IIA. *The Irish Village:* (NLI)

536.1 Ireland. Irish Industries Association. *Why should we encourage Irish industries? The exhibit...at the World's Columbian Exposition, Chicago. President, The Countess of Aberdeen.* [Chicago]: Irish village book store, 1893.

22x__. 32 p of ports, plates. (NLI)

537.   Ireland. Johnson. *Description and history of Irish:* ☺ . (FM)
▶Completed citation: 17x12½. 108 p. Tan cardboard cover with brown print and design of "The Terra Brooch." On front cover: "British Section : Depart' H. Group 98." [The Columbian Field Museum purchased these metal art work items at the close of the WCE.]

537.1 [Ireland]. Richardson, J.N., Sons & Owden, Ld. *Some of the Great Textile Industries of Ireland.* Belfast: n.p., n.d.   **P→**

18½x25. (8) p. Sky-blue wraps with rust-red print, floral design with lion symbol and swallow. Illus description of Irish linen manufacture; brief description of their planned WCE exhibit, p (2). On cover: "Reprinted from the Irish Textile Journal Belfast." Cover over-stamp shows exhibit was purchased by Mandel Bros. in Chicago. Ad. ☺. (WM)

537.2 [Ireland]. Robertson, Ledlie, Ferguson & Co. Ltd. *Historical sketch of flax and linen : In Ancient and Modern Times. With special reference to the Irish Linen Manufacture in and around Belfast.* Belfast: Robertson, Ledlie, Ferguson & Co. Ltd. (by Marcus Ward & Co., Ld.), [1893?]. **P→**

17x10½. 32 p. Light blue wraps, black print, illus of weaver. Frontis port: "Her Majesty Queen Victoria at work with Irish spinning wheel." Preface dated 1 May, 1893. C.t.: "...Flax & Linen in Ancient & Modern Times." At head of c.t.: "Souvenir of the World's fair, Chicago, 1893." (UMD,WM)

538. Italy. Brazza. *A guide to Old and New*: (EPL,FLP,ISU,KSU,UAT,UCB,URI,UWM,VAM,VT,Yale)
---- Also listed: Edition de luxe. 28x__. 148 p, 1 *l*.

538.1 Italy. Buckingham, H. *Guida italiana allo spettacolo americano dall'Italia a Chicago in 150 minuti.* Traduzione di I.F. Firenze: tip. Cooperativa, 1893.

8°. 77 p. (BNCF-missing)

539. Italy. Candiani. *L'industria chimica*: (BMF,BNCF,BNCR)
▶Add annotation: Various countries' chemical exhibits are listed by WCE group and class. Largest reports are on the exhibits of Italy and Germany; 17 countries are included.
---- Also found: Same size and paging. Pale green wraps, red and black print. C.t. = t.p. T.p. in red and black.

540. Italy. Capacci. *L'esposizione ed i congressi di Chicago*: (BNCF,LHL)
541. Italy. *Catalogo Ufficiale delle sezioni Italiane*: (Col,MSI,NLI,SML,UBO)

542.1 Italy. *Comitato per L'Exposizione di Merletti Italiani a Chicago.*

Book plate. These numbered bookplates are found on a series of books at FM and are from a library display at the WCE on tatting. The vols at FM have plates numbered #1-#11, #12 (2 titles), #13-#16, #20, #21, #30, #34. Trans: "Exposition committee of Italian Lace at Chicago."

543. Italy. Barbèra, Piero. *...Educational publications in Italy, notes by Piero Barbèra.* Florence: Printed by G. Barbèra, 1893.

23½x15. 14 p. C.t. = t.p. At head of title: "World's educational congress in Chicago–July 1893." Barbèra is listed as honorary vice pres of the dept congress of educational pubs. See #2130-33 and #2181-86 for other educational congress items. ☺. (UPa,Yale) ▶Completed citation.

543.1 Italy. *...Chicago. Guida illustrata del viaggio e della città di Chicago, con riguardo speciale all' esposizione universale in memoria di Cristoforo Colombo, al porto di Genova quale luogo d'imbarcazione ed al porto di New-York qualo luogo di sbarco. Con 38 illustrazioni.* Milano: Max Kantorowicz editore, 1893. **P↑**

19½x12½. (8) p ads, 1 *l* frontis, 1 *l* (t.p.), (2) p index, 1 *l* litho, 1-60 p, (1)-16 p ads for the editor's other books. Interspersed unpaginated illus (printed one side). Frontis litho: "Veduta di Chicago dal Nord." The 1 *l* litho: "Il monumento di Cristoforo Columbo a Genova." Light green stiff wraps, navy print with highlights in red. Sepia vignette of Native American statue. Contents: guide to Genova, ship trip to NY, guide to NYC, train guide to Chicago by various routes, Chicago guide, and WCE guide beginning at p (54). C.t.: "Chicago : Guida M. Kantorowica Editore Milano 1893 : Esposizione Mondiale Colombiana." At head of title: "Guide illustrate di città e paesi : di tutto il mondo," which trans: Illustrated guides to city and country and all the world. [Series]. ☺. (BNCF)

543.2 Italy. Ferraris, Galileo. *Opere.* Vol. II. Milano: Ulrico Hoepli : editore-libraio della real casa [Tip. Bernardoni di C. Rebeschini e C.], 1903.

> 22x16. T.p. in red and black. Article by Galileo Ferraris: "Sul congresso internazionale de elettricità in Chicago. Relazione." On t.p.: "Pubblicate per cura della : associazione elettrotecnica italiana" [published by the Italian electronic association]. The article relates to the International Congress on Electricity at the WCE. (BNCF–missing).

543.3 Italy. *Italian Day : Thursday, Oct. 12, 1893. Grand Concert...to celebrate the discovery of America...* N.p.: n.p., [1893].

> 20x13. (3) p. Folded glossy sheet, black print. C.t. A "Programme" of music in Festival Hall at the WCE. ☺. (S)   P➔

543.4 Italy. Tappari, Pietro, and Camillo Cerruti. *L'italiano : alla fiera mondiale di Chicago : guida pratica.* [Firenze: Tipografia di G. Barbèra, 1893].

> 16½x11. 1 *l*, 1 *l* (t.p.), (5)-121 p. T.p. has litho of "The Metropole Hotel : Chicago." A four-panel foldout, "F. Henry Humbert" travel schedule from Firenze to NYC—Mar 1 to Oct. 31, 1893, is tipped-in behind p 115 and is included in paging. Index pp (119)-21. ☺ (BNCF)

543.5 Italy. Ungaro, Errico. *L'italia alla esposizione di Chicago : relazione del R.° commissario generale duputato E. Ungaro.* Napoli: R. tipografia Francesco Giannini & Figli, 1894.

> 28x19. 1 *l* (t.p.), (3)-28 p. Beige flecked wraps. C.t. = t.p. Short description of the following Italian exhibits topics: 1) Belle Arti, 2) Manifatture, 3) Arti liberali, 4) Agricottura ed Orticoltura, 5) Lavori femminili, 6) Macchine, elettricità, trasporti, 7) Miniere, 8) Premîe ricompense. Dated on p (3): "Chicago, 10 Novembre 1893." Three letters to Ungaro; two from John Boyd Thacher and one from James Allison, are reproduced as appendices on pp 26-28. Trans: Italy at the Chicago Exposition : report of the deputy commissioner general, E. Ungaro. ☺ (BNCF,BNCR,uiuc)

543.6 Italy. Zeggio, Vittorio. *L'Italia : all' esposizione di Chicago : ricordi, note, commenti, lista ufficiale dei premiati.* Firenze: Bernardo Seeber, editore, 1894.

> 23½x16. (7), 6-114 p. Wraps. C.t. = t.p. Zeggio was "Commissario ufficiale all' Esposizione mondiale Colombiana di Chicago." Title trans: Italy at the WCE, records, notes, comments and list of official awards. ☺. (BNCF,UCLA)
> ---- Also listed: 164 p.

-J-

544.   Jamaica. Ward. *World's Fair Jamaica at Chicago* [95 p]:
          (Col,CU,cul,CWM,DC,FM,HML,HU,Merc,MIT,NDU,NLA,NLI,PSU,S,SML,Stfd,UAB,UBO,UCB,UCLA,uiuc,UMC,UMD,UPa,WM,Yale)
545.   Jamaica. Ward. *World's Fair Jamaica at Chicago* [63 p]: (CU,S,WM)
548.   Japan. Batchelor. *An itinerary of Hokkaido*: (HU,WM)

549.1 Japan. *A brief description of the figures of the Japanese horses and cattle exhibited in the World's Columbian exposition published by the agricultural bureau of the department of agriculture and commerce, Japan. 1893.* N.p.: Agricultural Bureau of the Dept. of Agriculture and Commerce, 1893?.

> 20½x15. (1) p tipped inside a slightly stiffer folded leaf; title on front cover. Black text on white paper. C.t. Animals were not displayed; this is a description of the illustrations of the Japanese horses and cattle exhibited at the WCE. ☺. (SML,UBO)

551.   Japan. *A brief description of taxidermic specimens of Ohiki*: (HU,ICRL,SML,UBO)
553.   Japan. *Catalogue of objects exhibited at the World's Columbian exposition*: (Col,CU,HU,ICRL,LBA,UCB,UPa,WM,Yale)

554.   Japan. CMO. *Explanatory notes on the exhibits*: ☺. (ICRL,SML,UBO,UTA,WM)
          ▶Completed citation: No comma after "U.S.A." in title. Tokio: Central meteorological observatory of

Japan, n.d. 22½x15. 1 *l* (t.p.), 14, (1) p. Light blue (or gray) wraps, black print. C.t. = t.p. List of their meteorological publications on back cover. Text explains meteorological exhibit items, Japanese temperature data, etc.

555.   Japan. CMO. *Organization of the meteorological system*: (NLI,NSW)

555.1 [Japan]. Central Tea Association of Japan. *The Japanese Tea House.* Tokyo: Kokubunsha Type, n.d.

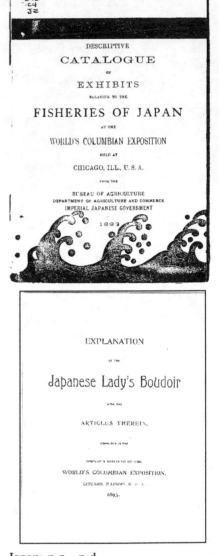

37½x27. 1 *l*. Fine rice paper sheet, black print and illus. Large illus of the Tea House which fronted the driveway leading from the Illinois Bldg to the Fisheries Bldg. Consisted of three "Tea Saloons": "Common," "Special," and "Ceremonial." ☺ (WM)

557.   Japan. *A description of bees, honey*: (NAL,UBO)

558.   Japan. *Descriptive catalogue of exhibits relating to the : fisheries of Japan : at the World's Columbian exposition : held at Chicago, Ill., U.S.A. : from the bureau of agriculture : department of agriculture and commerce : imperial Japanese government : 1893.* N.p.: n.p., 1893?   P➔

22x14½. xii, 38 p. Decorative wraps with gilt wave design, purple print. C.t. = t.p. ☺ . (FM,HU,WM)   ▶Improved citation.

559.   Japan. *A descriptive catalogue of Japanese forage*: (CU,NAL,SML,UBO,WM)

560.   Japan. *A descriptive catalogue of Japanese wild birds*: (HU,SML)
    ▶Actual size: 22½x15.

561.   Japan. *A descriptive catalogue of the agricultural products*:
    (GLD,CLP,CU,DU,FM,ICRL,LBA,KSU,LBA,NAL,NLA,NSW,SML,UBO,UMD,UMN,WM)
562.   Japan. *Details of the industrial*: (DU,HU,ICRL,MIT,NLA,NSW,SML,UBO,UIC,WM)
563.   Japan. *Details of the weights*: (HU,MSL,NSW,PSU,SML,Stfd,UBO,WM)

564.   Japan. *Explanation of the Japanese Lady's Boudoir*: (GLD,WM)   P➔
    ▶Add: String-tied. Description of boudoir from the Tokugawa period. "Explanation of the various articles of the Japanese Lady's Boudoir" starts on p 9; "Explanation of the ornamental articles..." from p 13.

564.1 [Japan]. Fukai, K. *Memorandum of exhibit. Chōshi superior shōyu.* Chōshi, Japan: n.p., n.d.

21x?14 (incomplete). Dark pink pulp sheet, black print. Exhibit of water packed beans. Price list and list of previous awards. (WM)

565.   Japan. *General view of commerce*: (Amh,FM,LBA,SML,UPa,UVM)
    ▶Add cover description: Maroon cloth hc with gilt title on front cover and spine.

566.   [Japan]. Hasegawa, T[akejiro]. *Exhibition of Figures representing life in Old and New Japan.* Tokio: T. Hasegawa, Designers and Printers], n.d.

18½x12½. (26) p includes inside of covers. All pages folded Japanese-style. String-tied wraps with block print of 2 women in full traditional dress. C.t.: "Japan Old & New." Explains the large collection of life-like figures especially designed for the WF and exhibited in the section for the sale of Japanese products. Manners and customs of various periods. Many b/w illus; color inside front wrap. ☺ . (NYPL,WM)   P➔
    ▶Improved citation.

567.   [Japan]. Hayashi. *Twelve bronze falcons*: (HU,ref,S,UMD,WM) $255
    ▶Add: Plates and text are loose in a gray paper covered folio that has three flaps folded in, black print.

569.   Japan. *History of the Empire of Japan*: (GLD,CUA,DC,FM,GMU,GU,HU,NLA,ref,S,SHB,SPL,Stfd,UCLA,UI,UPa,USFr) $100-250

570.   Japan. *Imperial geological survey*: (FM)
   ---- Also found: 49, (1) p + 3 *l* maps + 1 *l* in Japanese.

570.1 Japan. Imperial Japanese Commissioners. [Dinner invitation]. Chicago: A.C. McClure & Co., 1893. P✔

   23½x18. (1) p. Steel engraved invitation with vignette of Hō-ō-den at top of sheet. Commissioners: N. Yamataka, L. Tegima, and C. Matzudaira. Dinner given July 29, [1893?], at the Auditorium. ☺. (S,UMD)

571.   Japan. *Japanese Woman's Commission*: (WM)   P↑

572.   Japan. Japanese Woman's Comm. *Japanese Women*: (CLP,Col,CU,FM,HU,SHB,slpl,Smth,Stfd,UMN,UPa,UVM,Yale) P↑
   ---- Also found: 22½x14. 2 *l*, (1)-159 p. Tan stiff wraps, flower design outside and inside front cover and on back. First *l* is t.p. C.t. = t.p.

572.1 Japan. Kawashima, Jimbei [Co.]. *Art fabrics exhibited at World's Columbian exposition by Jimbei Kawashima, Nishijin, Kyōto, Japan*. N.p: n.p., n.d.

   30½x21½. iv, double-page insert, (2) p award medals, (1)-22 p+ unpaged plates between p 10 and 11. Pale yellow wraps with large white trademark in background. C.t.: "J. Kawashima's art fabrics." Double-page insert illustrates a tapestry shown at WCE representing Nikkō Temple. Beautiful ad. (WM)

573.   [Japan]. Kubota. *Kakuryu sekai*: (ref) $1000
   ---- Also found: 2 vol set. 32 woodblock printed plates. Japanese text. Accordion folded. [Kubota, an illustrator, won a gold medal for art, Paris Expo, 1889.]

574.   Japan. Kyoto Exhibitors' Association. *Kyoto*: (NLA,WM)

574.1 Japan. [Murayama, M.]. *...Brief history & preparation : of the : Japanese tea : exhibited in the World's Columbian exposition*. Tokyo: Printed by Kokubun-sha, 1893.

   19x12½. 1 *l* (t.p.), 16 p. Buff stiff wraps, black print; tissue guard before t.p. C.t. = t.p. At head of title: "Japan. Agricultural bureau, department of agriculture and commerce." Dated on t.p.: "April, 1893." Murayama's name appears below caption title on p (1). ☺. (SML)

574.2 [Japan]. Nishimura, Sozayemon [Co.]. *Nishimura Sozayemon, Kyoto, Nippon*. N.p.: [Printed by Osaka Kokubunsha & co.], n.d.

   18x12½. 1 *l*, (21) p, 8 *l* illus on stiff paper interleaved with text pages. Beautiful string-tied block-printed wraps, black print. C.t. Most text on Japanese-style folded tissue pages. Their 1889 Paris Expo award is reproduced. Made art fabrics in Kyoto. No mention of WCE; from an intact collection. (WM)

575.   Japan. Okakura. *The Ho-o-den (Phoenix Hall)*: (GLD,Col,FM,HU,ICRL,S,UCLA,UTA) **P➔**
▸New publisher: Cambridge, MA: HULMS, 1983. Film Mas C 978.

☞ A Japanese Pagoda from the WCE was moved to Walter Reed Annex in Washington, DC. *Washington Post*. 18 July 1966, sec. B: 1.

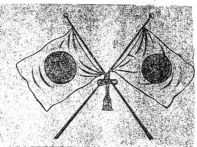

$30 - 65

575.1 Japan. *Outlines of the history of telegraphs in Japan.* N.p.: n.p., n.d.

18½x12. 56 p. Green wraps, black print and design of crossed rising sun flags. C.t. In English. No WCE content; from intact collection. ☺ . (LBA)

576.1 Japan. *A short account of the educational society of Japan.* Tokyo: Published by the society [Printed at the Tokyo Tsukiji type foundry], 1892.

21½x14. (2), (1)-26 p+ 2 folding graphs of Society data tipped-in at back cover. Front cover has a pretty multicolor design border plus two vignettes of warriors. C.t. = t.p. No direct reference to the WCE. GLD copy shows it was a handout at the Fair since the t.p. is inscribed: "T.J. Kanematsu, ana (?) Japan, Liberal Arts Bldg-." ☺ (GLD)
---- Also found: Inscribed "T.J. Kanematsu : Liberal Arts Bldg. : Japan Section." (S)

576.2 [Japan]. Suzuki, S[hirozaymon]. *Compliments of S. Suzuki, manufacturer of and dealer in : Cloisonné Enamel (Shippo) Ware. Japanese section, Manufactures and Liberal Arts Building and Fine Arts Building. World's Columbian Exposition.* N.p.: n.p., n.d.

13½x19. 12 p. Light gray pulp wraps, crossed white/red Japanese flags joined with a printed red tasseled tie. Illus ad. ☺ . (ICRL,WM)   **P➔**

577.   Japan. Takahashi. *Descriptive notes on silks*: (NAL,SML,WM,Yale)
---- Also found: Brown cloth spine over tan paper covered boards, gilt print. C.t. = t.p.

577.1 Japan. Wada, Tsunashiro. *The mining industry of Japan : during the last twenty five years. 1867–1892.* Tokyo: Tsukiji type foundry, 1893.

29x23½. 1 *l* (t.p.), 1 *l* weights and measures, (2) contents, 304 p, 1 *l* plus 1 loose errata sheet, plus unpaged folding maps and plates. Light brown cloth hc, gilt print and design of rising sun and crossed miner's mallets. Top edge dyed black. Report of Japanese mines and their production. The author signed the FM copy in the upper right corner with "Metallurgist, W.C. Exposition Chicago, Ill." No specific mention of WCE in text but part of intact WCE accession collection, #3661, at FM. ☺ . (FM)

578.   Java. *The Javanese Theater, Java Village*: (HU,KS,LBA,S,UIC)

☞ G.J.L. de Bruyn was manager of the Java Village on the Midway Plaisance.

579.   Java. *The Java Village : Midway Plaisance : World's Columbian Exposition.* [Chicago: Java Chicago Exhibition Syndicate], n.d.

20½x14. (3) p. Folded leaf of pulp paper, black print. Caption title. Handout describes items housed in the Village, such as the coffee shop and the Orang-outang named "Klass." ☺ . (GLD,csuf,R,S,WM) $16 - 35
▸Corrected title and paging.

-K-

579.1 Korea. Royal Korean Commissioners. [Dinner invitation]. N.p.: n.p., n.d.

20x15. (1) p. Stiff stock. Commissioners: Chung Kyung Won and Ye Sung Loo. Engraved invitation to "Dinner at the Auditorium, Tuesday evening, the fifth of September, [1893], at seven o'clock." The three Syun Cho Dae characters at top of invitation translate "Great Korea." ☺ . (S,UMD)

579.2 Korea. Royal Korean Commissioners. [Dinner souvenir]. N.p.: n.p., 1893.

19x13½. 3 *l*. Stiff stock; string-tied, steel engraved. Striking red/white/ blue cover with Korean and US flags. The three Syun Cho Dae characters in the center of a silver wreath translate "Great Korea." For "Chicago, September 5th 1893. Auditorium Hotel." Companion to #579.1. ☺. (S,UMD)

-L-

580.   Liberia. *Liberia 1847–1893*: (GLD,CLP,Col,FM,ICRL,WM)   **P➜**

-M-

583.1 Mexico. Campos, Ricardo de Mária, comp. *...Datos : mercantiles*. México: Oficina tip. de la secretaría de fomento, 1892.

> 23½x17. 1 *l* (t.p.), iii preface, 776 p, xiv p index. Sand wraps, black print. C.t. = t.p. At head of title: "Estados unidos mexicanos. Secretaría de fomento, colonización é industria. Sección 2ª." 2nd edition to the commerce report issued for the 1889 Paris expo; this edition for the WCE (preface). ☺ (WM)

583.2 Mexico. *...Catálogo oficial : de la : exposición : de los : estados unidos mexicanos : en el certamen universal colombino : de Chicago*. México: Oficina tip. de la secretaría de fomento, 1893.

> 24x17½. 333 p. Lacks covers. At head of title: "Exposición universal colombina de Chicago : 1893." Complete listing of Mexico's exhibits by group and class. No illus. See also #588.2. ☺. (FM)

584.   Mexico. Comisión. Díaz. *Comisión geográphico-exploradora*: (HU,NAL,UTA)
         ---- Also listed: 24 p, 28 plates.

586.   Mexico. Junta. *Explicación de las cuatro*: (S)

587.   Mexico. Martinez Baca. *Estudios de Antropologia*: (ref,Stfd)   Presentation copy: $400
         ---- Also found: Inscribed presentation copy in ornate blind-stamped cover, full leather, gilt print.

588.1 Mexico. *The National Commission of the Republic of Mexico to the World's Columbian Exposition requests the pleasure of your presence at a concert to be given in honor of Mexico Day, Wednesday, October the fourth, from four until six o'clock, Music Hall, Jackson Park*. N.p.: n.p., n.d.

> 20x15. (4) p. Folded white stiff leaf. Steel engraved, black print. ☺. (E)

588.2 Mexico. *Official catalogue : of : exhibits : of the : Republic of Mexico : World's Columbian Exposition : Chicago, Ill, U.S.A. : 1893*. Chicago: W.B. Conkey co., Printers and Binders, n.d.

> 21½x15½. 1 *l* (t.p.), (3)-91 p. Rust wraps, black print. C.t. = t.p. In addition to a listing of Mexico's exhibits, this pamphlet names the Mexico commissioners, p (3). See also #583.2. ☺. (FM)

590.1 [Mexico]. Sánchez, Ramón. *Lijera descripcion de Un viaje de Jiquilpan de Juárez, á la ciudad de Chicago, por...* Segunda edicion. Zamora: Imprenta Moderna, 1894.

> 21x15½. 21 p. Self-wraps. Small illus of paddle wheel steamer on cover. C.t. A brief description of a trip to the city of Chicago. ☺. (UCB)

590.2 Mexico. Sessé, Martino, and Jospeho Marianno Mociño. *Plantæ novæ Hispaniæ : nutú, ope, et auspicio benignissimi regis Caroli IV, hucusque colectæ, et Linneano systemate ordinatæ, quarum tercentæ aut plures a nemine...* Ed. Ricardo Ramirez. Editio secunda. México: Oficina tip. de la secretaría de fomento, 1893.

> __x__. viii, 175 p, xiii. Maroon cloth hc. Content: Plants of New Spain [Mexico]. Published for presentation at the WCE. ☺. (UPa)

591.1 Mexico. Tabasco. Rovirosa, C. José N. *Catalogo de los Objetos enviados por el Gobierno del Estado de Tabasco : a la exposicion universal colombina : Que se verificará en la Ciudad de Chicago, del 1° de Mayo al 31 de Octubre de 1893, formado por el comisionado oficial...* San Juan Bautista de Tabasco: Tip. del Gobierno dirigida por Felipe Abalos. Callede aldama, 1893.

>21x15 (cut down copy). 1 *l* cover (may be the t.p. of booklet with missing cover), (3)-33 p. The 1 *l* is same paper as text, black print. Found bound with unrelated pamphlets at UCB. ☺. (UCB)

592.   Mexico. Vigil. *Poetisas Mexicanas*:   (HU,nmsu,UCI,UCLA,uiuc,UTA)

592.1 Mexico. Yucatan. Espinosa, Félix Martín. *Exposicion universal de Chicago. Informe : que presenta el comisionado especial...a la H. Junta recolectora de objetos para esta exposicion.* Mérida de Yucatan: Imprenta "Gamboa Guzman," 1893.

23x15½. 1 *l* (t.p.), (3)-23 p. Rose wraps of same light weight stock as text, black print. C.t. = t.p. Page (3) caption title: "H. Junta recolectora de objetos para la exposicion de Chicago." ☺. (UCB)

593.   Monaco. Mackie. *Monaco at the World's*:   (SML,UBO,Yale)

-N-

594.   New South Wales. New South Wales Commissioners. Department of Woman's Work. ...*Catalogue...of woman's work*:   **P➔**
▸Added authors and improved cite: 24½x16. (1) p (half-title), pp 716-42. At head of p 716: "Committee XII on Woman's Work." Lady Windeyer, Pres. Exhibits and exhibitors in all depts. ☺. (GLD,CLP,ICRL) $40 - 80

594.1 New South Wales. ...*Exhibition of Woman's Work in the centennial hall, from which the exhibits for the woman's department in the Chicago exhibition will be selected. Sydney, 1892. Official catalogue.* Sydney: Wm. Andrews & Co., Printers, 1892.

21x14. 48 p. Buff wraps, black print and border design. At head of title: "World's Columbian Exposition, 1893." At bottom of t.p. and cover: "Price 3d." Exhibition, preliminary to the WCE, at Centennial Hall in Sydney.
☺. (NLA,NSW)   **P⬂**

595.   New South Wales. NSWC. Brewer. *The drama and music*:   (GLD,HU,NLA,UMN) $40 - 60
▸Completed cite: Brewer, F[rancis] C[ampbell]. 24½x15½. Pale aqua wraps, black print. C.t. = t.p.

596.   New South Wales. NSWC. *Catalogue of...Dept A*:   (GLD,CLP,FM,MSI,UMD) $40 -80
---- Also found: Peach wraps, black print. Printed with half t.p. C.t.:
"...Catalogue of New South Wales Exhibits. Department A. : Agriculture, food and its accessories, machinery and appliances."

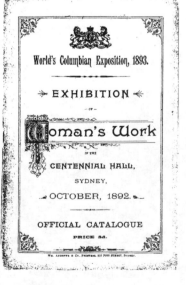

596.1 New South Wales. New South Wales Commissioners. ...*Catalogue of New South Wales Exhibits. Department D. Fish, fisheries, fish products, and apparatus of fishing.* Sydney: Charles Potter, Government Printer, 1893.

24½x15½. (1) p (half title), pp 198-213. Bright red-brown wraps, black print. C.t. At head of title: "World's Columbian Exposition, Chicago, 1893." At head of p 198: "Committee VI, on Fish and Fisheries." William McMillan, President. List of exhibit contents and exhibitors. ☺. (GLD,HU) $40 - 80

597.   New South Wales. NSWC. *Catalogue of...Dept E*:   (GLD,FM,HML,MIT,UPa)

597.1 New South Wales. New South Wales Commissioners. ...*Catalogue of New South Wales Exhibits. Department F. Machinery.* Sydney: Charles Potter, Government Printer, 1893.

24½x15½. (1) p (half title), pp 372-83. Bright green wraps, black print. C.t. At head of title: "World's Columbian Exposition, Chicago, 1893." ☺. (GLD,MSL,UMD) $40 - 80

598.   New South Wales. NSWC. *Catalogue of...Dept G*: ☺ (GLD) $40 - 80
▸Completed citation: 24½x15½. (1) p (half title), pp 386-403. Yellow wraps, black print. C.t.

598.1 New South Wales. New South Wales Commissioners. ...*Catalogue : of : New South Wales Exhibits. Department H. Manufactures.* Sydney: Charles Potter, Government Printer, 1893.

24½x15½. (1) p (half title), pp 406-28. Deep orange wraps, black print. C.t. At head of title: "World's Columbian Exposition, Chicago, 1893." Lists their exhibits in the Manufactures and Liberal Arts Bldg. ☺ (MSI)

598.2 New South Wales. New South Wales Commissioners. ...*Catalogue : of : New South Wales Exhibits. Department K. Fine arts, painting, sculpture, architecture, decoration.* Sydney: Charles Potter, Government Printer, 1893.

24½x15½. (1) p (half title), pp 430-42. Yellow wraps, black print. C.t. At head of title: "World's Columbian Exposition, Chicago, 1893." Lists committee members and art work displayed and the artist. William McMillan, President. ☺ . (GLD,FM) $40 - 80

599. New South Wales. NSWC. *Catalogue of...Dept L:* (GLD,KBS,UPa) $40 - 80
▸Completed citation: 24½x15½. (1) p (half title), pp 444-642. Pink wraps, black print. A complete listing of all their exhibit contents in this section as well as exhibitors.

599.1 New South Wales. New South Wales Commissioners. ...*Catalogue : of : New South Wales Exhibits. Department M. Ethnology, archæology, progress of : Labour, and invention.* Sydney: Charles Potter, Government Printer, 1893.

24½x15½, (1) p (half title), pp 644-76. Ochre wraps, black print. C.t. At head of title: "World's Columbian Exposition, Chicago, 1893." Extensive aboriginal exhibit material described: clothing, weapons, implements, etc. Chairman: James Charles Cox. ☺ . (GLD,FM) $40 - 80

600. New South Wales. NSWC. *Catalogue of...Dept N:* (GLD,FM,HU,MSI,UMD)
▸Corrected paging: (1) p (half title), pp 678-714.

601. New South Wales. NSWC. *Catalogue of...courts:* (FM,MSL,NLA,SML,UBO,Yale)
---- Also found: Dark tan pebbled cloth hc. No cover print; gilt spine print.

602. New South Wales. NSWC. Coghlan. *Sheep and:* (GLD,NLA,SML,WM) P➔ $40 - 80
▸Corrected paging: 1 *l* (red/white bar-graph frontis), 23 p.

603. New South Wales. NSWC. Cohen. *The marine fish:* (GLD,FM,HU,NLA,SML)
▸Completed citation: 24½x15. 30 p, one folding color map. Salmon wraps, black print. $40 - 80

604. New South Wales. NSWC. Dept of Mines. *Extracts from the:* ☺(GLD,WM)
▸Completed citation: T.M. Slattery (author). 24½x15½. 1 *l* (t.p.), 1 *l* mineral area list, 85 p. Salmon (or rose) wraps with black print. C.t. = t.p. Also at the head of the title: "Department of mines, New South Wales. $40 - 80

604.1 New South Wales. New South Wales Commissioners. Dowling, Edward. ...*Australia and America in 1892: a contrast.* Sydney: Charles Potter, Government Printer, 1893.

24½x15½. 2 *l*, viii, 172 p. Salmon wraps, black print. At head of title: "Published by Authority of the New South Wales Commissioners for the World's Columbian Exposition, Chicago, 1893." A description of Australia and its products; exhibits at previous WFs, and comparisons with their US production counterparts. ☺ . (FM,NLA,SML)
---- Also listed: Cloth hc, gilt print. (ref) $55

604.2 New South Wales. New South Wales Commissioners. ...*Exhibits from New South Wales to the Chicago exposition. (Return respecting.)* [Sydney: Govt. printer, 1893.]

F°. 12 p. At head of title: "1892-1893. Legislative assembly. New South Wales." (MSL-missing)

605. New South Wales. NSWC. Fraser. *The Aborigines of New South Wales:* (FM,HU,NLA,ref,SML,UMN,UPa) $80
▸Correct size and paging: 24½x15½. 1 *l* (color fold map), 102 p+ 3 unpaged heleotypes + one unpaged folded illus between pp 10 and 11.

606.   New South Wales. NSWC. Gill. *South Pacific and New Guinea*: (FM,NLA,SML,UCLA,UPa)
     ---- Also found: 1 *l* (t.p.), 38 p.

607.   New South Wales. NSWC. Greville. *NSW statistics*: (GLD,FM,HU,MIT,MSL,NLA,SML,UCLA,WM) $40 - 80
     ▶Add authors: Kendall, Henry, and W[illiam] C[harles] Wentworth.

608.   New South Wales. NSWC. Hanson. *Geographical encyclopædia*: (Col,CWM,DU,HU,NDU,NLA,NSW,Stfd,UCLA,UPa,Yale)

608.1 New South Wales. New South Wales Commissioners. Hill, Richard, and George Thornton. *...Notes on the aborigines of New South Wales : with personal reminiscences of the tribes formerly living in the neighbourhood of Sydney and the surrounding districts.* Sydney: C. Potter, Government Printer, 1892.

     24½x15½. 8 p. Pale blue wraps with black print. C.t. At the head of title: "Published by authority of the New South Wales Commissioners for the World's Columbian Exposition, Chicago, 1893." ☺ . (GLD,CU,NLA,SML,UPa,WM) $40 - 80

609.   New South Wales. NSWC. Hyman. *An Account of the Coins*: (UMC)
610.   New South Wales. NSWC. Hyman. *Catalogue of Coins*: (NLA,NSW,WM)

611.   New South Wales. NSWC. Miller. *The Prison system*: (NLA,WM)
     ▶Add: Blue-green wraps, black print.

612.   New South Wales. NSWC. *NSW wool exhibits*: (GLD,FM,HU,ICRL,SML,UBO,WM) $40 - 80
     ▶Completed citation: 24½x15½. Olive wraps, black print. C.t.

613.   New South Wales. NSWC. Olgilby. *Edible Fishes*: (SML,UMN)
     ▶Actual size and paging: 24½x15½. 1 *l* (t.p.), ii, 212 p, 51 *l* (plates of fish).

614.   New South Wales. NSWC. O'Sullivan. *Social, industrial, political*: (HU,NLA,NSW,WM)

615.   New South Wales. NSWC. *Pamphlets issued by the New South Wales Commissioners*: (NLA)
     ▶These 2 vols contain those pamphlets separately issued as #602-603, #613, #616, #617-619, and #620.1.

616.   New South Wales. NSWC. Pulsford. *The rise, progress*: (GLD,CU,FM,HU,NLA,UCLA,WM) $40 - 80
     ▶Completed citation: 24½x15½. Blue wraps, black print.

616.1 New South Wales. New South Wales Commissioners. *...Report of the president : of the : New South Wales commission : &c., &c., &c.* Sydney: Charles Potter, government printer, 1894.

     24½x15½. 104 p. Red cloth hc, gilt print. At head of title: "1894. New South Wales. World's Columbian Exposition, Chicago, 1893." ☺ . (NLA)

616.2 New South Wales. New South Wales Commissioners. *...Report of the President : of the : New South Wales commission : &c. &c. &c. : Presented to Parliament by Command.* Sydney: Charles Potter, government printer, 1894.

     33½x21½. 1 *l* (t.p.), 69 p. At head of title: "1894. (Second session.) New South Wales. World's Columbian Exposition, Chicago, 1893." ☺ . (SML)

617.   New South Wales. NSWC. Russell. *Physical geography*: (DC,FM,HU,MSI,ref,SML,WM) $40 - 80
     ▶Completed citation: 24½x15½. 1 *l* (t.p.), 35 p+ 2 folding diagrams + 1 folding map. Rust-orange wraps, black print; C.t. = t.p.

618.   New South Wales. NSWC. Thompson. *History of the fisheries*: (FM,HU,MSL,ref,SML,UMN) $200
     ▶Actual size and paging: 24x15. 1 folding color map, 2 *l* (t.p. and contents), 126 p, 8 *l* (plates and explanation), 6 folding color maps.

619.   New South Wales. NSWC. Tregarthen. *A sketch of the progress*: (GLD,FM,HU,NLA,SML,UMN) $45 - 90
     ▶Completed citation: 24½x15½. 4 *l*, 47 p+ 10 unpaged interspersed charts; tan wraps, black print.

620. New South Wales. NSWC. Warren. *Australian timbers*: (LHL,NLA,SML,Stfd,UCB,UPa,URI)
▶Correct paging: Fold map tipped-in at front, 3 *l*, 67 p+ 44 (i.e. 45) plates of which 36 are folding.

620.1 New South Wales. New South Wales Commissioners. Wilkins, William.
...Agriculture in New South Wales. Sydney: Charles Potter, Government
Printer, 1893.

24½x15½. 1 *l* (t.p.), 50 p. At head of title: "Published by Authority of the
New South Wales Commissioners for the World's Columbian Exposition, Chicago,
1893." ☺. (NAL,NSW,SML)

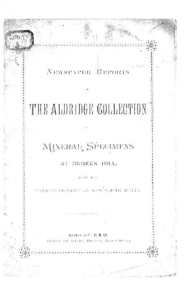

620.2 [New South Wales]. *Newspaper Reports : on : the Aldridge collection : of :*
Mineral Specimens : at Broken Hill, from the : barrier district of New South
Wales. Broken Hill, N.S.W.: Fiveash and Attkins, Printers, [1892]. **P➡**

21x14. (3)-24 p. Buff wraps, black print. C.t. = t.p. Recounts articles
from various papers urging Edward Aldridge to display his extensive
mineral collection at the WCE. Citizens offered to pack the stones per his
specifications and pay his way to Chicago. No evidence has been found
showing that Aldridge ever exhibited at the Fair. ☺. (FM)

621. New South Wales. *Report of the Executive*: (HU,ICRL,LHL,MSL,NLA,SML,UCLA,UTA)

622. Norway. Andersen. *Vikingefærden*: (DC,UBO,UIC)
---- Also found: Presentation copy at UIC.

☞ Andersen also wrote about his visit to Chicago's 1933 Century of
Progress: *Skoleskibet Sørlandets utstillingstokt til verdensudstillingen.* (UBO)

623.1 Norway. *Beretning : om : Norges deltagelse : i : Verdensudstillingen i Chicago*
1893. Kristiania: Trykt hos W.C. Fabritius & sønner, 1895.

__x__. 4 *l*, 134, (1) p+ 4 *l* of unpaged interspersed plates (one is the Norway
Bldg at the WCE). Leather spine over mottled purple paper covered boards,
gilt spine print. Trans: "Report of Norway's Participation in the World's Fair
in Chicago 1893." ☺ (UBO,WiHx)

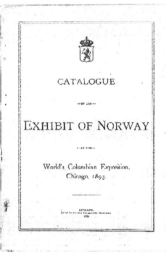

624. Norway. *Catalogue of the exhibit*: (CLP,Col,HU,ICRL,NAL,NLI,S,SML,WM) **P↗**
▶Correct paging: 1 *l* (frontis), (3), (5)-84 p.
---- Also listed: 79 p. (Col)

624.1 Norway. *Norway : midnight sun.* Kristiania (Oslo): Lithogr. Akliebulag, n.d.

15x10. (12) p. Multicolored wraps with bold "Norway" and illus of men
fishing with the midnight sun in the background. Caption title: "Norway."
From intact WCE collection. English language travel guide. ☺. (LBA) **P➡**

-P-

625. Paraguay. Comision. Aceval. *República del Paraguay*: (HU,Yale)

626.1 [Portugal]. *Notice : sur les : travaux d'amélioration : du : port de Lisbonne.*
Lisbonne: Imprimerie nationale, 1893.

26x17½. 33 p. Buff wraps, black print. C.t.= t.p. French language. Their
easier-access port is described; documentation of its ship traffic, including
shipping improvements; rules for using the port. ☺. (Stfd–bound WCE Trans Dept Collection)

627. Portugal. Society. *Portugal contribution of the society*: (LHL,LU,MIT)
▶Catalog of 25 chapters, each for a photo album displayed at the WCE; the albums depicted bridges,
railways, monuments, churches, harbors, and other Portuguese infrastructure.

-R-

629. Russia. *Account of the ore deposits*: (Col)

630. Russia. *Catalogue of exhibits of the Imperial Russian state paper*: (Col,HML,MSI,UBO)
---- Also found: A loose sheet laid in this catalogue, printed both sides, showing 22 vegetable-fiber photomicrographs that are described in the catalog, p (4). Also a loose sheet printed one side describing three types of paper they manufactured.

631. Russia. *СИБИРЬ* [Siberia]: (Col,Stfd,Yale)
▸Add: Cyrillic head of title: "Министерство Финансовъ : Департаментъ Торговли и Мануфактуръ. [Ministry of Finance : Department of Trade and Manufacturers.]" Published in St. Petersburg in 1896.
---- Also found: 1893 edition. Different t.p. and publisher. С.-Петербургъ [St. Petersburg]: Тинографія В. Киршваума, Дворцовая площадь [Tipographia V Kirshbauma], 1893. At head of title: "Всемірная Колумбова Выставка 1893 г. : Вь Чикаго. [World's Columbian Exposition 1893 in Chicago.]" 309 p.   **P➔**

633. Russia. Dept Trade. *The industries*: (Col,CU,DC,FM,HML,HU,LU,Merc,MIT,MSI, NAL,NLA,NSW,PSU,SHB,slpl,SML,Stfd,UBO,UCB,UCI,UCLA,UMA,UMD,UMN,UPa,URI,Yale)
---- Also found: 5 vols in blue-gray wraps, black print.
---- Also found: brown cloth hc stamped in gilt, black, and blind.
▸Additional info for Vol IV: *Mining and metallurgy : with a set of mining maps : by A*[lexsei] *Keppen.* ix, (1), 97, (1) p errata, 5 *l* of plates (one folded).

634. Russia. Депавтамента Торговли ию [Industry and commerce of Russia]: (HU,UCB,Yale)
635. Russia. *Detailed list of articles exposed by the St. Petersburg*: (CCA)

635.1 Russia. Dokoutschaïeff, W.W., and N.M. Sibirtzeff. *...Short scientific review : of Proffessor Dokoutschaïeff's and his pupils : collection of soils, exposed in Chicago, in the year 1893.* St. Petersburg: Типографія Е. Евдокимова, 1893.

22x16. 40 p. No illus. Trans of authors names: V.V. Dokuchaev (see #635.2) and Sibirtsev. ☺.(NAL)

635.2 Russia. Dokuchaev, V.V. *The Russian steppes : study of the soil in Russia, its past and present...for the World's Columbian exposition at Chicago.* Ed. John Martin Crawford. St Petersburg: Department of agriculture ministry of crown domains, 1893.

23x15. 52 p. No illus. Crawford, US Consul General to Russia, was editor of this English translation. See #635.1 for another Dokuchaev item. ☺. (NAL)

637. Russia. Glukhovskoj. *ОТЧЕТЬ* [Report]: (HU,ICRL,MIT,Stfd,UCB,UCLA,UMN,UTA,Yale)
▸Cover annotation: Pale green glossy wraps, black print and illus including façade of the Russian exhibit, Admin Bldg, and Columbus's bust.

638. Russia. IRC. *Catalogue of the Russian section*: (Amh,CCA,CLP,Col,CU,DC,FM,HU,ICRL,KBS,KSU,LBA,Merc,MIT,MSL,NAL,NSW, slpl,SML,Stfd,UAB,UBO,UBW,UCB,UCLA,UMC,UMD,UMN,UTA,UVM,Yale)
639. Russia. Ismailoff. *Russian Horses*: (GLD) $30 - 60

640. Russia. Кирпитева, В. Л. [Kirpichev, V.L.]. *...Отчеть : о командировкь Вь Сьверную Америку* [Otchet o komandirovkie v Sievernuiu Ameriku \ Report on a Business Trip to North America]. С.-Петербургъ [S.-Petersburg]: Типографія Кн. В. П. Мешерскаго [Izd. Departamenta torgovli i manufaktur Ministerstva finansov \ Published by Department of Trade and Manufactures of the Ministry of Finances], 1895.

25x16½. 69 p, 8 *l* of plates. Illus. C.t. At head of title: "Всемірная Колумбова Выетавка Вь Чикаго. [Vsemirnaia Kolumbova vystavka v Chikago \ World's Columbian Exposition at Chicago.]"
▸Improved citation. Cyrillic added.

---- Also listed: 23½x__. 65 p.
☺ . (Col,LC,NLA,UDe)

640.1 Russia. Коновадова, Д. [Konovalova, D.]. ...*Промышленность : Соединенныхь Штатовь Съверной Америки : и Современные Пріемы ; Химической Технологіи.* [Promyshlennost' Soedinennykh Shtatov Sievernoi Ameriki i sovremennye priemy khimicheskoi tekhnologii \ Industries of the United States of North America and present-day methods of chemical technology.] С.-Петербургь [St. Petersburg]: Тинографія В. Демакова [Published by V. Demakova], 1894.

25½x17½. iv, 158, ii p. Edition of the Department of Trade and Manufactures. At head of title: "Всемірная Колумбова Выставка Вь Чикаго. [World's Columbian Exposition in Chicago.]" ☺ . (Col)

641. Russia. Kovalevsky. Сельское и: (Col,HU,UBO)
▶Add: Romanized title listed as: "Sel'skoe i lesnoe khoziaistvo Rossii." S.-Petersburg, V.S. Balasheva, 1893. 25½x17. (2), ii, xxvi, 647 p, 1 *l* (large fold map) + 2 loose fold tables + interspersed diagrams (color and some double) that are not included in paging. Gray-flecked wraps, black print. Russian language. Romanized head of title: "Vsemirnaia Kolumbova vystavka 1893 g.v. Chikago \ World's Columbian Exposition 1893 in Chicago." A collection of articles on agriculture.

643. Russia. MIV. Bocharoff. *Russia city of Ivanovo-Voznesensk*: (FM)
647. Russia. MNP. *Russian Ministry of public education*: (Stfd,UCLA,UPa,Yale)

648.1 [Russia]. Nadiein, M. *New apparatus for House and City Sanitation and Economical Canalization. (Patented in Europe and America.) System of M. Nadiein, Captain of the Russian Army. Chicago, World's Columbian Exposition, 1893.* N.p.: n.p., n.d.

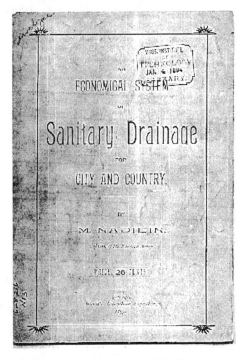

24x16. 1 *l*, (3)-15 p+ fold out. Yellow-tan wraps, black print and design. The large fold out is a parts illus and functional description of the Nadiein apparatus—a water-saving system which separated solid from liquid waste. C.t.: "An economical system of Sanitary Drainage for city and country." ☺ . (MIT) **P➔**

651.1 Russia. *The Russian imperial state paper manufactory.* St.-Petersburg: Printed at the Imperial State Paper Manufactory, 1893.

23x16½. 36 p. Tan stiff wraps, black print, small rust border. Text on stiff stock with rust decorative border. C.t. Paper making and printing. No WCE content; from intact collection. See #630. ☺ (WM)

652. Russia. *Russie bureau des dames institué*: (UPa)

653.1 [Russia]. [St. Petersburgh]. *"Russian Coprolites..."* С.-Петербургь [St. Petersburgh]: Типографія Р. Гопике [Published by R. Gopiky], 1893.

18½x12½. 23 p. Burnt-orange wraps, black print includes diagonal banner title. C.t. = t.p. In English. Coprolites have chemical composition $Ca^3(PO_4)^2$ and differ by their polymerism or allotropic modification. Descriptions and production costs. Phosphorites sent to the WCE, p 22. (WM)

654.1 [Russia]. *Vladikavkaz railway company : Russia : Novorossisk : Black Sea : its : shipping and facilities.*

71½x57½. Folding folio. Part of the Russian transportation exhibit at the WCE; FM accession number 10195. Folio held closed by ribbon. Silver print. The folio cover is gray-green pebble textured cloth hc. It contains 4 large maps, 6 mounted real photographs of train engines, ship, and the harbor, 2 booklets explaining exports and rolling stock. The items have titles and keys in Cyrillic and above them is the English translation beautifully written in red ink. The English titles of two display books are: "Vladikavkaz Railway Rolling Stock" and "Plans of the buildings for the storage and export of goods at Navorossisk." A unique display collection. ☺ (FM)

655.   Russia. War Dept. *Sketch of the articles exposed by the War*: (WM)
    ▶Add: Gray-flecked white thin wraps, black print.

-S-

656.   Siam. Mayer. *The Siamese Exhibits*: (Col,FM,LBA,MSI,NAL,SML)
    ---- Also found: Peach-tan wraps, black print.

658.   South Africa. *Orange Free State (Republic)*: (GLD,S)   **P➔** $40 - 80
    ▶Completed citation: 22x15. 15 p. Off-white wraps, black print, color
    crossed flags and shield. Color map on back: "Oranje Vrijstaat." Dated on
    p 15: "May 1, 1893." No WCE content; handout.

662.   Spain. CGDE. *Catálogo de la Sección Española*: (CLP,FM,NSW,SML.UBO)
664.   Spain. CDGE. Faura. *La meteorología*: (CU,UPa,Yale)
668.   Spain. Puig. *Viaje á América*: (LU,HU,UAT,UCB,UTA)

668.1 Spain. *Recopilación : de : Estudios é Investifaciones : efectuados per la : Comisión obrera Catalana en la Exposición de Chicago. Subvencionada al electo por la Exema. Diputación Provincial de Barcelona y el Misisterio de Pomento.* Barcelona: Establectmiento tipográfico de Redondo y Xumetra, 1893.

    24x16. 215 p. Pale blue cloth hc stamped in black and gilt. Illus with engravings. Trans: Account of the studies and investigations put into effect by the Spanish commission at the WCE. ☺ .(CCA)

668.2 Sweden. [Bendz, Olaf P.] *Catalogue of articles from the Farriery school at Alnarp (Sweden) exhibited at the World's Columbian exposition in Chicago.* Malmo: Stenström & Bartelson, 1893.

    19½x13. 8 p. Wraps. C.t. ☺ .(KBS)

669.   Sweden. Bohlin. *Genom den stora västern*: (UCB,UMN)

669.1 Sweden. *The Commissioners from Sweden and Ladies : will be happy to receive yourself and ladies : at the : Swedish Pavilion, on Monday afternoon, June twenty sixth, at three o'clock : 1893.* N.p.: n.p., n.d.

    26½x20. 1 *l.* Folded sheet printed on front only. C.t. Illus of Swedish Bldg and black print. Invitation. ☺ .(S)   **P➔**

669.2 [Sweden]. Dannemora Iron and Steel Works. *Price-List : from : Aktiebolaget Österby Bruk : Iron and Steel works...* Dannemora: [printed by Central-tryckeriet, Stockholm, 1893].

    27x19. 20 p+ 2 *l* color repro of sample steel labels between pp 12-13. Stiff cardboard wraps, chromolith border and award medals to 1889. Properties of their steel with testimonials. No WCE content; from intact collection. ☺ (WM)

669.3 Sweden. *...Eisen-& stahl-manufakturen. Eisen-& stahlwerk domnarfvet.* Falun: Falu nya boktr.-aktieb, 1891.   **P➔**

    21x14. 23 p. White glossy alligator-textured stiff wraps with rounded corners, black print. At head of title: "Stora Kopparbergs Bergslags Aktiebolag, Falun, Schweden." The Stora company was granted the king's rights in AD 1347; a German company operating in Sweden. Their iron and steel production from Swedish ranges. Illus of their trade marks. German version of #672. No WCE content; from intact collection. .(WM)

669.4 Sweden. Fries, S.A. *Betydelsen : af : religionkongressen : i Chicago.* Stockholm: K.J. Bohlins förlag [Norrköping : M.W. Wallberg & Co. Boktryckeri, 1895].

20x13½. 66 p. Light green flecked wraps with black print and border. C.t. = t.p. Ad on back for a Swedish translation of John H. Barrows' book on the Parliament of Religions. Trans: The Importance of the Congress of Religions in Chicago. ☺. (UMN)   P➔

671.   Sweden. Gullberg. *Boken om Chicago*: (UMN)
▶Complete pub info: Stockholm: Fr. Hellbergs förlag [Iduns tryckeri aktiebolag], 1893.
---- Also found: Orange-peach wraps, black print.

671.1 Sweden. Hemborg, Carl A[ugust]. *"Gån in" : ett Jesu rop till den stora folkvandringen*. Moline, IL: [C.A. Hemborg], 1893.

15½x11. 64 p. Gray paper-covered boards, all print and design is navy blue except "Gån in" in red. Hemborg was pastor of an Evangelical Lutheran church in Moline, Illinois. In Swedish. Trans: "Go In" A Jesus call to the big migration. (UMN)

672.1 Sweden. L[ee], C[harles]. *Verldsutställningen i Amerika : eller : arbetarerörelsen enligt guds dubbla plan*. Stockholm: A. Ohlssons förlag [F. Mällborns konkursm:s tryckeri, 1892].

20x14. 40 p. Yellow thin wraps, black print and ornate border, string-tied. Biblical archeology. Trans: World Fair America : or : the labor movement according to God's double plan. [F. Mällborns bankruptcy creditors printing office, 1892]. C.t.: "Amerika : verldsutställningen : samt : arbetarerörelsen : enligt : guds dubbla plan." ☺. (UMN)   P➔

673.1 Sweden. Lundbohm, Hjalmar. *Om Juryarbetet vid chicagoutstallningen*. Stockholm: Tryckt hos A.L. Normans boktryckeri-aktiebolag, 1895.

22½x14½. 16 p. Wraps. C.t. Technical journal rpt. Trans: About the work of the jury at the Chicago Fair. ☺. (KBS)

673.2 Sweden. Odelstjerna, E. G:son. *Meddelanden från ett besök vid världs-expositionen i Chicago 1893 och en i sammanhang därmed företagen resa till amerikanska järnverk*. [Stockholm: K.L. Beckmans Boktryckeri, 1896].

20½x13. 236 p + 9 fold plates. Blue-flecked wraps. Caption title given. Trans: Reports from a visit to the World Fair in Chicago 1893 and in connection herewith a travel made to American steelworks. According to this personal account in Swedish, Odelstjerna was an awards judge in mineralogy and metallurgy who stayed at the WF for 75 days, July 23–Oct 5, 1893. FM's copy is inscribed by the author to F.J. von Skiff, WCE Mines and Mining Dept. (FM,UMN)

674.   Sweden. *Öfversigt af den:* (FM,HU,SHB,Smth,Stfd,uiuc,UMN,UoC,UVM,WM,Yale)   P➔

675.   Sweden. *Reports from*: (Col,HU,ICRL,KBS,SHB,SML,Smth,Stfd,UBO,uiuc,UMN,UVM,Yale)
▶Add: Blue stiff wraps, black print and border. C.t. = t.p.

677.   Sweden. Royal Swedish Comm. *Swedish catalogue*:   2 vol. $50 - 85
(GLD,Col,FM.HU,KBS,LBA,MSI,NLI,SML,UBO,UBW,UMN,Yale)

677.1 [Sweden]. *Skånska Cement Aktie-Bolaget : Malmö : Sweden*. Malmö: Skånska Lith. Aktiebolaget, [1892].

21½x14. 1 *l* (t.p.) with color Swedish flag, 19 p, (5) p tables. Tan wraps, black and red print and seal of the company, illus of previous WF awards. C.t. = t.p. Red and black text. Ad for their Portland cement. Uses, mixtures, and testing results of their concrete. Also found bound as part of #1017.1, WCE exhibit catalog. ☺. (WM)   P⬇

681.   Switzerland. Escher. *Mitteilungen aus dem Gebiete*: (MIT)

683.1 Switzerland. Grobet, H. and Th. Otto Schweitzer. *...Rapport : sur la :
    situation des ouvriers en Amerique.* N.p.: Imprimé par les soins du syndicat
    des maitres imprimeurs de la suisse romande, 1894.

    22½x15. 92 p. Pulp paper. At head of title: "1893 : Exposition Universelle
    de Chicago." In French. Title trans: Report on the condition of American
    workers. Questions posed to the delegates by the federal inspector of factories
    regarding conditions in American factories. What were the popular foods,
    illnesses of invalids, availability of supplemental schools for children (e.g., pre-
    school), public hygiene facilities, factory salaries. ☺. (SML)

684.   Switzerland. Houriet, Charles. *...Rapport concernant la petite mécanique
    et ses applications a la fabrication de l'horlogerie aux États-Unis...* Chaux-
    de-fonds: Imprimerie R. Haefeli & Cie, 1894.

    23x15. 72 p. Wraps. At head of title: "Exposition universelle de Chicago
    1893." In French. Trans: Report on micro-machining and its applications
    in the fabrication of time pieces in the US. ☺. (NYPL,SML)   ▶Corrected citation.

686.   Switzerland. Hunziker. *Das Schweizerische*: (HU)

690.   Switzerland. Meyer-Bæschlin, Jos. and J. Lepori. *...Architektur, Baukonstruktionen und Baueinrichtung :
    in : nordamerikanischen Städten.* Bern: Fritz Haller & Co. (Haller'sche Buchdruckerei), 1894.

    22½x15. 44 p. Pulp paper. At head of title: "Weltausstellung in Chicago, 1893 : Berichte der
    schweizerischen Delegierten." German language. Subject: Architecture and the construction industry in
    North American cities. ☺. (NYPL,SML)   ▶Improved citation.

692.   Switzerland. Moos, Hans. *...Die Landwirtschaft : der : Vereinigten Staaten von Amerika in ihrem Lande
    und an der Weltausstellung in Chicago.* Bern: Fritz Haller & Co. (Haller'sche Buchdruckerei), 1894.

    22½x15. 180 p. At head of title: "Weltausstellung in Chicago, 1893 : Berichte der schweizerischen
    Delegierten." Subject: Agriculture in the US, its territories, and at the WCE.
    ---- Also listed: 1 *l*, 180 p, 1 *l*.
    ☺. (BPL,NYPL,SML)   ▶Improved citation, including correct spelling of author and title.

692.1 Switzerland. Palaz, A., and René Thury. *L'Industrie électrique : a : l'exposition de Chicago : et : aux
    États-Unis : rapport : présenté au : département fédéral des affairs étrangères.* Berne: Imprimerie
    Gebhardt, Rösch & Schatzmann, 1894.

    23½x15. 118 p. Wraps. Trans: The electrical industry at the WCE and of the United States; report
    presented to the federal department of foreign affairs. French language. ☺. (CCA,SML)

692.2 Switzerland. *...Rapport : du : commissaire spécial : au : département des affaires étrangères : division du
    commerce.* Berne: Imprimerie Gebhardt, Rösch & Schatzmann, 1894.

    23½x15. 80 p. No illus. Pulp paper text. At head of title: "Exposition universelle de Chicago, 1893." Trans:
    Report of the special commissioner to the [Swiss] department of foreign affairs, commerce division. French
    language. ☺. (SML)

693.   Switzerland. Ritter. *Der brückenbau*: (HU,MIT,SML,Yale)
    ▶Completed size and paging: 22½x15. 66 p with 60 b/w text illus, "XII" double plates (i.e., 24 *l*).
    ▶Add publisher: New Haven, CT: Yale U Photographic Services, 1979. Neg. film N575.7.

695.   Switzerland. Schweitzer, Th. Otto. *...Die Baumwolle : nebst : Notizen über deren Kultur und
    Verarbeitung in Amerika.* Bern: Fritz Haller & Co. (Haller'sche Buchdruckerei), 1894.

    22½x15. 79 p. Pulp paper. At head of title: "Weltausstellung in Chicago, 1893 : Berichte der schweizerischen
    Delegierten." Subject: Cotton cultivation and processing in America. ☺. (NYPL,SML)   ▶Improved citation.

697.   Switzerland. *Switzerland*: (ICRL,S,SML,UBO)   **P➜**
▶Better cover description: Buff wraps, black print and design of woman
overlooking the Alps; pale green background.

-T-

698.   Trinidad. TCWF. Clark. *"Iëre" the land of*: (GLD,CLP,Col,FM,LBA,NSW,UCB,uiuc)

699.   Turkey. *Souvenir Programme Turkish Theater*: (ICRL,S,sfpl)
▶Better description of [American Engraving Co.]: (16) p+ text inside
covers. Colorized photo of "Rosa" on back. Contents: eight programs
and captioned photos.
---- Also found: Same c.t. [Chicago: Economy Engraving Co.], n.d.
(13) p. B/w front cover without either "Price 10 Cents" or "Pierre
Antonius & Co. : Managers." Back blank. Contents: one program (on
t.p.) for the Kalamounic Drama.   (S)

699.1 Turkey. Turkish Village Bazaars. Covas, Mary. *Souvenir of the World's
Columbian Exposition. Photogravure Views of the Holy Land and
Costumes worn in Turkey.* N.p.: n.p., n.d.   **P⬇**

13½x23. 12 *l* plates with captions are 6 *l* plates of ethnic people in costume plus 6 *l* plates of Holy Land
views; no text. Pea green wraps, black print and arabesque borders top and bottom. C.t. © (GLD) $40 – 80

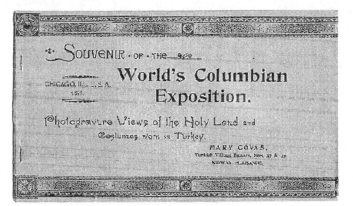

-U-

700.   Uruguay. Castro. *Estudio sobre los ferrocarriles*: (Col,DU,HU,MIT,sfpl,SML,Stfd,UCB,UCLA,UTA)
701.   Uruguay. Castro. *Treatise on*: (Amh,Col,CU,DU,HU,LHL,LU,MH,NDU,NLA,NUL,OU,sfpl,SML,Smth,Stfd,UCLA,UMA,UMC,UMN,UTA,UVM,Yale)
703.   Uruguay. Dirección. *La Instrucción Pública*: (UTA)
705.   Uruguay. Peña. *The Oriental Republic of Uruguay*: (BRA,CLP,FM,HU,MSI,NAL,NLI,NSW,SML,Yale)

-V-

706.   Venezuela. *Los Estados Unidos de Venezuela*: (ICRL,SML,UCB)

707.   Venezuela. *The United States of Venezuela*: (Amh,BNCR,CLP,Col,CU,DC,DU,FM,FU,HU,ICRL,LBA,LHL,LU,MIT,NLI,SML,Stfd,UBO,
UBW,UCB,UCLA,UMC,UPa,UTA,Yale)
---- Also found: 21½x14. Bound without the two folded color crest plates between pp 108 and 109.

708.   Venezuela. Rojas. *Objetos historicos de Venezuela*: (Col,FM,HU,UCB)

Chapter 5

GENERAL

709.   Abbot. *Carter Henry Harrison*: (UTA)
  ▶See #2362.2 and #2362.3 for publications by Harrison's son.

   ☞ Mayor Harrison's assassin, Patrick Prendergast, a lawyer, was defended by the renowned Clarence Darrow using an insanity plea. In spite of this defense, Prendergast was speedily tried and hung.

710.   *Acme : The Perfection of all Plastering Material*: (WM)

710.1 Adamek, Anton [Co.]. *...Toilet soaps, fruit soaps and perfumes.* Vienna, Aus.: n.p., n.d.

   7x13½. Card printed in blue. At head of title: "World's Columbian exposition, Chicago, '93. Agricultural building, and 34 Old Vienna, Midway Plaisance." On back "Old Vienna No. 34." © (WM)

712.1 Ahrenfeldt, Charles, & Son. *...M. Redon's French China, at the Columbian World's Fair at Chicago, (manufactures building).* New York: Charles Ahrenfeldt & Son, 1 May 1893.

   28x21½. Single letter sheet with black script font. At head of title: "Dear Sir: we take pleasure to inform you that we take charge of the large and exquisite Exhibit of..." Highest award at 1889 Paris Expo. Notice that they would only sell china to dealers (no private parties) at the WF. Ad. (S)

713.1 Albert, Alexander, [Co.]. *K.K. Hof- Kunsttischler.* Vienna, Aus.: n.p., n.d.

   11x16. (4) p. Folded tan sheet, gilt and black decorative cover. Ad for joiner and upholsterer. Red and black text print. Notice of their past awards. From an intact WCE scrapbook. © (S)

713.2 *Album.* N.p.: n.p., n.d.

   26x20½. 12 *l.* Red velvet cloth covered thick boards with silver design and title embossed on a large copper band. Gilt edges. C.t. = t.p. A period photo album with slots for card portraits. Eight leaves have two b/w lithos of WCE bldgs each. For a similar albums see #806.1, #1017.3. © (GLD) $60 - 100

713.3 Alexander & Co. *...Columbian coin book.* Boston, Mass: Alexander & Co., ᶜ1893.

   21½x14½. 16 p. Pink wraps with graph paper-like background lines and image of Columbian half-dollar (verso and recto) and bird's-eye of WCE grounds. C.t. At head of title: "6ᵗʰ edition." (ref) $160

714.   *All the World at the Fair*: (UCB)
  ▶Add: White wraps with fancy lady standing on globe. Blue and black illus, red title print. Very colorful little booklet.

714.1 Allen, S.L., & Co. *The "Planet Jr." 1893.* Philadelphia: S.L. Allen & Co., n.d.

   22x14½. 32 p. Yellow-tan stiff wraps with gilt, white, and black print and gilt Saturn and floral design. Their planet plow line of farm implements. No mention of WCE; from intact WCE collection. (WM)

714.2 Alliance Carriage Co. *Styles for 1893. Capacity 10,000 vehicles per year. Alliance Carriage Company.* Cincinnati, OH: n.p., n.d.

   6½x9½. 44, (4) p (price list). Tan wraps, green print, design showing factory. C.t. Blue print text and illus of their carriages. "No. 170" carriage illus on back. No mention of WCE; from an intact WCE collection. © (WM)

714.3 Allis, E.P., Co. *Northwestern Lumberman.* Rpt. Milwaukee, WI: n.p., 1893.

   39½x28. Pp 4-5. Folded sheet. Rpt of *Northwestern Lumberman* article, 12 Aug. 1893, which featured the Allis saw mill and equipment at WCE. Used as ad. Two illus of mill in WF Mill Bldg. (WM)

714.4 Allsopp & Sons. *Chicago exhibition. Messrs. Samuel Allsopp and sons, limited.* N.p.: n.p., 1893?

28½x21½. Buff *l*, black print. Large illus of exhibited ales. Rpt from *British Trade Journal*, April 1, 1893. Brewers from Burton-on-Trent, England. (WM)

714.5 Alvin Mfg. Co. Norris-Alister, B.F., & Co. *The official souvenir spoon : World's Columbian exposition 1492 1892–3.* Chicago: J. Manz & co., n.d.

15x9. (4) p. Folded sheet, dark brown print and illus. Page (2) illus of a tea and coffee spoons with Columbus in wreath at handle tops and Santa Maria in bowls. Illus of "I Will" Chicago symbol standing before Machinery Hall on back. C.t. ☺. (WM)　　[Front & back] P➔

714.6 American Bell Telephone Co. *American Telephone and Telegraph Company.* Boston: Rand Avery supply co., engr's, 1 June 1893.

20½x9½. (12) panels. Sheet unfolds to 41x28. Back (6) panels show US map with installed AT&T copper phone lines in red as far west as Chicago and Milwaukee; left side of map lists "public stations. World's Columbian exposition." Pale blue front panel, b/w print; illus of elaborate pay phone booth. Advertises connections at "1000 miles and return in 5 minutes." Chicago phone book, #715.10. ☺ (WM)

715.　American Bell. *Exhibit of The American Bell Telephone Co:* (HML,ICRL)

715.1 American Bell Telephone Co. *Speaking Tube Telephones of The American Bell Telephone Co. : Columbian Exposition, 1893.* Boston: Alfred Mudge & son, printers, n.d.

19½x10. (6) panels. Glossy sheet tri-fold unfolds to 19½x29. Black print, green illus. Description of their office intercom system. ☺. (S)　　P➔

715.2 American Bell Telephone Co. *Telephone switchboard in operation in the exhibit of The American Bell Telephone Co. in the Electricity Building, World's fair, Chicago.* N.p.: n.p., n.d.

23x10. (6) panels. Glossy sheet tri-fold unfolds to 23x30. Black print, sepia illus. Caption title. ☺ (S)

715.3 American Bible Society. *Abstract of the Seventy-Sixth Annual Report, May 12, 1892.* New York: The American Bible Society, 1892?

14x8. 12 p. Folded sheet unfolds to 14x47. On p 8 is their plan to distribute Bibles at WCE because many foreign visitors would take them home. ☺ (S)

715.4 American Biscuit & Mfg. Co. Rorer, Sarah T[yson]. *Some Dainty Ways For Serving Crackers.* N.p.: American Biscuit & Mfg. co. (Woodward & Tiernan printing co., St. Louis), ᶜ1893 by American Biscuit & Mfg. co.

15½x8½. (8) p. Coated white wraps, black print and illus. Copyright info is overprinted on front wrap in purple. Recipes and ads. Rorer is described as "Demonstrator in Model Kitchen at Columbian World's Fair, Chicago, 1893." See #1565 for another American Biscuit item and #999.1 and #1000 for other Rorer items. ☺ (GLD)　　P➔　　　　$20 - 40

715.5 *American Box Machine Co. : home office and manufactory, Amsterdam, New York, have a complete exhibition of : paper box manufacturing machines : at the World's Columbian exposition, Chicago, 1893.* N.p.: n.p., n.d.

14x20½. (4) p. Folded buff stiff card, black print, embossed illus of child in yellow and gilt dress holding gilt bouquet. Scalloped card edges. C.t. Illus of Machinery Hall on back. Illus of box making machines, pp (2)-(3). ☺. (WM)

715.6 American Carpet & Floor Duster Co. *The Carpet Duster : a woman's Invention for housekeepers.* Chicago: n.p., [1893].

23x15½. (4) p. Folded sheet, brown print and cover illus of a woman dusting floor. Rpt excerpt from Aug 13, 1893, *Inter Ocean* on p (4) locates exhibit at "invention rooms, Woman's Building." C.t. (WM)

715.7 American Cement Co. *History of the Portland Cement Industry in the United States.* Philadelphia: American Cement Co., n.d.

24x17½. 75, (1) p of co logos in color. Wraps illus by Geo. E. Harris and Sons are in shades of green and gray; logos for "Egypt Cement" and "Giant Cement" on back. No mention of WCE; intact collection. ☺ (WM)

715.8 The American Cereal Co. *...America's : Cereal Foods : and : how to cook them : The American Cereal Co., we feed the world.* [Akron, OH: The American Cereal Co., ᶜ1893 by The American Cereal Co.]

17x11½. 68 p. Chromolith front and back wraps: Front shows a US flag-draped woman holding wheat and standing behind two globes; back wrap has colorful box of "Quaker rolled white oats." C.t. Pp 1-2 is a tear-out coupon for WCE souvenirs. Pp 34-35 have chromoliths of 8 different cereal products. B/w lithos inside both wraps. At head of title: "Souvenir coupon in this book." Their exhibit is described on pp 7-8. Beautiful ad with many recipes. ☺ (GLD) P➔ $30 - 60

715.9 The American Cereal Co. *World's Fair souvenir; the great pictures by H. Bolton Jones and Francis C. Jones in the panorama "The procession of the seasons," shown at the exhibit of the American Cereal Co. (The Quaker booth) Gallery of Agricultural Building...* [Chicago: American Cereal Co., 1893].

13x19. 12 chromoliths. (HML)

715.10 American District Telegraph. *Chicago : telephone : directory.* Chicago: Reuben H. Donnelley, publisher, 1893.

21x14½. 458 p+ 2 p of maps showing toll lines. Tan stiff wraps, red and black print. Issued "October 1, 1893." WF telephone numbers pp 385-87. For example, the Columbian Guards office in the Service Bldg was "World'sFair-3." ☺ (GLD) P➔ $140 - $260

717.1 American Hosiery Co. *We cordially invite you to inspect our exhibit at the : World's Columbian Exposition : in : Manufactures and Liberal Arts Building : Section P.* [New York: H. E. Rowland, Lith.], n.d.

9x16½. (4) p. Folded white card with hinge at top, black print. C.t. Litho of factory on back. They made "fine knit underwear and hosiery" from "silk-wool-merino-balbriggan." ☺ (GLD) $20 - $36

717.2 American Institute of Architects. Bloor, A[lfred] J[anson]. *Report of A.J. Bloor, delegate of the New York chapter A.I.A. to the twenty-sixth annual convention of the institute, held in Chicago, October 20th, 21st and 22nd, 1892.* [New York: Press of Isaac A. Blanchard], n.d.; New Haven, CT: RPI, 1971.

15x__. 39 p. American architectural books; based on the Henry Russell Hitchcock bibliography. Microfilm reel 13, no 193a. WCE buildings. [The A.I.A. convention took place in Chicago at the same time the WCE buildings were dedicated.] ☺. (CCA, Col)

718. American Jersey Cattle Club. *The Jersey herd at the World's Columbian:* (NAL.S.UAH.UMA)
▸Add pub: Chicago: Library Resources Inc., 1970. Microfiche. LAC-40032.

718.1 American Jersey Cattle Club. *The Jersey : the most economic dairy cow. Demonstrated in official tests at two World's expositions: Chicago, 1893 : St. Louis, 1904.* New York: The American Jersey Cattle Club, 1910.

21x__. 98 p. See #277.c and #1337.1. (NAL)

718.2 American Library Association. *...A.L.A. Meeting. Chicago, 13–22 July, 1893. Railroad Routes and Hotel Accommodations.* N.p.: n.p., May 1893.

25x20. (4) p. Folded sheet. At head of title: date/circular info. Sent by Frank P. Hill, Secretary, Newark, NJ. [Like many other organizations, the A.L.A held its 1893 annual meeting in Chicago; members participated in Congresses and attended the WF.] [See A.L.A. in index for related items.] ☺ (WM)

718.3 American Library Association. *Papers and proceedings : of the fifteenth general meeting : of the : American library association : held at Chicago, Ill. : July 13–22 : 1893.* N.p.: American Library Association, 1893.

24x19. 1 *l*, 106 p. Meetings consisted of 8 sessions, 1 per day, which were held both at the Art Institute and WCE locations. Melvil Dewey presiding. [See A.L.A. in index for related items.] ☺ . (UMA)

718.4 American Library Association. *Program of the 15th general meeting : Chicago : 13–22 July 1893.* N.p.: n.p., n.d.

12½x7½. 11 p+ back cover lists of officers for 1892–93. Self-wraps, black print, no design. At head of title: "American Library Association : Organized 1876." Sessions were adjourned at 1 p.m. for afternoon study of the various library exhibits at the WF. [See A.L.A. in index for related items.] (WM)

720.   American Philatelic Association. *Catalogue of the : American Philatelic Association's : loan exhibit of : Postage Stamps : to the United States post office department at the : World's Columbian exposition : Chicago, 1893.*

▶Corrected title capitalization. ☺ . (GLD,HU,KS,S,UCLA,UMD,Yale)
---- Also found: Light green wraps, black and brown print with brown border.
---- Rpt.: Baltimore: Braemar Press, 1991. (csuf)

720.1 American Philatelic Association. *Official circular : of the : General Committee : in charge of the : Postage stamp exhibit : to be held at the : World's Columbian Exposition, Chicago, 1893...* [Birmingham, CT: Press of D.H. Bacon & co.], n.d.

23½x15. (8) p. Pistachio colored smooth wraps, black print, string-tied. C.t. List of committee members, the exhibit plans and rules. Albert R. Rogers, Chairman. Back cover illus of Govt Bldg where the stamp exhibit was located. ☺ . (S)   P➔

720.2 American Philatelic Association. Rogers, Albert R. *Executive committee of the American Philatelic Association's Exhibit of Postage Stamps at the World's Columbian Exposition, Chicago, 1893.* New York: n.p., 1893.

22x14. (3) p. Folded sheet, black print. Caption title. Request for donations for exhibit and sale of their WF catalogue, #720. Dated: "April 3, 1893." ☺ (S)

720.3 American Projectile Co. *Government reports on projectiles.* [Lynn, MA]: n.p., n.d.

21½x14. 16 p. Self wraps, blue print on buff paper, string-tied. C.t. Front wrap projectile illus captioned: "Projectiles being now delivered to the Army and Navy of the United States." (WM)

721.   *The American Republic*: (CU,UMD)
---- Also found: [°1892 by John W. Iliff]. 28x__. 3 *l*, 9-206 p. Burgundy cloth pebbled hc, gilt print. T.p. in red and black. Frontis of 13 colonial flags in color.

721.1 American Screw Co. *World's Columbian exposition. Exhibit of Cold-Forging Machinery, in Machinery Hall Annex, Section 29-K 50. Exhibit of product, Etc., in Manufactures and Liberal Arts Building, Section P, Block 3, No. 2.* Providence, RI: American Screw co., n.d.

14x20½. (16) p. Pale green wraps with co's "Trade mark": eagle clutching screws in talons and perched on a sphere marked 1838. Trademark also shown on t.p. Illus of factories, products, and previous awards and medals. Ad handout. ☺ (GLD) $25 - 40

721.2 American Writing Machine Co. *The Caligraph : Manufactured by...* Hartford, CT: n.p., [1893].

12½x9. (8) panels. Folded buff sheet opens to 12½x34½. Black print and illus of their typewriter on front cover. Lists advantages and previous awards. No WCE content; from intact collection. ☺ (WM)

721.3 Amieux Frères. *...Extract of the general price current.* Chantenay-lès Nantes, France: n.p., n.d.

32x24. (4) p. Folded pulp sheet, black print and illus of one of their 9 factories. C.t. At head of title: distributor info. Price list of their packed products: sardines, tuna, mackerels, etc. No WCE content; from intact collection. (WM)

721.4 Andrews, A.H., & Co. *The Andrews Bank and Office Furniture and Fittings.* Chicago: A.H. Andrews & Co., n.d.

9x11. (8) p. Die-cut pamphlet in the shape and color of an oak roll top desk. Front wrap shows desk open; back wrap shows desk closed. Centerfold color litho of their counter and furniture used in the World's Fair Bank. ☺ (GLD) **P➔** $25 - 50

721.5 Andrews-Demarest Seating Co. *Columbia chair.* [New York: Andrews-Demarest Seating co., n.d.

13x10. (4) p. Folded white coated card. Red and gilt chair on cover has under-seat hat holder. C.t. Back cover shows their folding bench chairs. Caption title: "Souvenir : Columbian exposition ; 1893." Manufacturer of chairs, pews, and settees. ☺ (GLD) $22 - 45

721.6 Andrews, E. Benjamin. *The history of the last quarter-century in the United States : 1870–1895.* 2 vols. New York: Charles Scribner's sons, 1896 [ᶜ1895, 1896 by Charles Scribner's sons].

24½x17½. Vol 1: xxii, 1 *l*, 390 p. Vol 2: xxi, 1 *l*, 409 p. Maroon cloth hc, beveled boards; gilt design, spine print, and top edge. Rough-cut fore and bottom edges. A detailed history in a high quality binding. Vol 1, chap 8: "The Centennial exposition." Vol 2, chap 8: "The World's Columbian Exposition illustrated from initial plan to its burning." Vol 2, chap 9: "Impact of the World's Columbian Exposition after the fair." (ref,SPL)

721.7 Androvette , Geo[rge] E., & Co. *...Ecclesiastical Glass : Designers & Makers of Memorial Windows.* Chicago: n.p., n.d.

22x14. (4) p. Folded sheet, black print, illus of window. C.t. No WCE content; intact collection. (WM)

721.8 *...Apperly, Curtis & Co. Woollen Manufacturers; Dudbridge Mills, Stroud. West of England.* N.p: n.p., n.d. **P➔**

13x7. (4) p. Folded card. Beautiful dark green metallic print, pale pink and pale yellow design and accents inside. C.t. At head of title: "Chicago 1893." Illus of the factory and medals won. Their exhibit was in the Great Britain section in the west gallery of the Manuf Bldg. ☺ (E)

721.9 Appleton, D., and Co. *The American cyclopædia. Supplement edition.* New York: D. Appleton and co., n.d.

26x17½. Variously paged, 4 mm thick. White wraps, black and red print, litho of the encyclopedia set in a case, dark tan paper spine. Compilation of sample pp from various vols. Endorsements on back. Text in red and black. No WCE content; from intact collection. ☺ (WM)

721.10 Appleton, D., and Co. *Appleton's annual cyclopædia and register of important events of the year 1893.* New York: Appleton and co., 1894 [ᶜ1894 By D. Appleton and co.].

__x__. viii, 875 p. Maroon textured cloth with gilt spine print. Frontis port of Phillip Brooks. Details of WCE listed on several pages. ☺ (S)

721.11 Arctic Whaling Expedition Co. Coffin, G.A. *There She Blows : or the story of the : progress.* Chicago: Arctic whaling expedition co. [Palm, Knott & Co., Printers and Binders], [°1893 By Arctic Whaling Expedition Co.]. **P➔**

18x18. 46 p, 1 *l.* Fine-lined blue wraps, red print and litho of sailor in blue looking for whales. C.t. = t.p. "Progress" was the name of the whaler, the first to visit Chicago; the occasion was the WCE. The Progress was an exhibit at South Pond within the WCE fairgrounds and was also moored in the Chicago River for a time. On cover: "price, 25 Cents." ☺ . (FM)

721.12 Ardeshir & Byramji Co. *...East Indian Art-Ware.* Jubilee, Bombay and Jawanji, London: n.p., n.d.

24x16. 1 *l.* Broadside ad for Indian arts. Buff sheet, blue-black print and illus of Indian Palace. At head of title: "World's Fair. Chicago, 1893 : Ardeshir & Byramji East Indian palace, Midway Plaisance, and E. Indian Section Manufactures and Liberal Arts Bldg." ☺ (S)

721.13 *Armour institute : Corner of Thirty-third Street and Armour Avenue. ...Department of mining engineering and metallurgy.* N.p.: n.p., n.d.

21x14. (4) p. Folded tracing paper, blue print. Prof. Haupt of the school's mining dept and his students visited WCE mining exhibits as part of class work for the coming semester. ☺ (WM)

722.1 *Art building. Columbian exposition 1893 Chicago Ills.* N.p.: The John Dodds Mfg. Co., n.d.

6x12½. 30 *l.* Blue-lined graph note paper. Black paper covered boards, gilt illus of the Art and Woman's bldgs and print, red dyed edges. Opens at top edge; intended as a memo booklet. Cover style similar to #978 (illustrated). Advertiser listed in gilt on back cover: "The John Dodds Mfg. Co. : Dayton, Ohio, U.S.A. Agricultural Implements." ☺ (GLD) $20 - 40

723. *Artisan expedition to the World's fair:* (Col,HML)

723.1 Aschaffenburger Herdfabrik und Eisengiesserei. Koloseus, H. *World's Fair Columbian Exposition, Chicago. German Section, Group 115, No. 3940.* Aschaffenburg, Germany: Aschaffenburger Herdfabrik u. Eisengiesserei, n.d.

20½x11. (6) p. Single sheet tri-fold unfolds to 20½x33. Tan paper with black print and engraved illus of five ranges. C.t. Ad handout. Herdfabrik is German for stove factory. ☺ (GLD) $20 - 40

723.2 Asher, A., & Co. *List of works published by A. Asher & Co. Berlin : Unter den Linden 13...exhibited at the World's Columbian Exposition, Chicago 1893.* [Berlin: Printed by H.S. Hermann], n.d.

29x23. 6 p includes back wrap. Buff heavy rag stock, black print, tied with red/white/black string. List of Asher's WCE publications plus "Miscellaneous works." Issued with a laid-in (4) p prospectus for #503. Prices in marks with US equivalent given as $1 = 4 marks 20 phennig. ☺ (WM)

724. Associated Manufacturers. *Tin and terne plate exhibit:* (GLD,HML,WM)
▶Cover description: Tan wraps, black print and double line border; back wrap blank. Purple overprint gives exhibit location. The US industry, only 2 years old, was spawned by legislated higher US protective tariffs against English plate.   **P➔**

724.1 *Athens Cottage Hotel, 7321-7327 South Chicago Avenue,... Chicago, Ill.* N.p: n.p., n.d.

8x14. (2) p. Single card printed in black both sides. Front has illus of the hotel facade in green ink. "Only ten Minutes Walk to Main Entrance of World's Fair Grounds." Rooms were 50¢ per day per person. ☺ . (E)

724.2 *The audiphone : For The deaf : at the : World's fair.* Chicago: Rhodes & McClure Pub. Co., n.d.

21x14. Single thin sheet, black print. Caption title. The company claimed improved hearing through the medium of the teeth. Ad announcing demonstration, hearing test, and sale in "Section E, Manufactures and Liberal Arts Building, in the Gallery, at the north end, about the center of the north end of the Building." [The only company fitting this description is Boughton & Smith, which dealt in dental specialties.] ☺ (GLD,WM) $20 - 40

725. *The Audubon*: (WM)

725.1 Austin, F.C., Mfg. Co. *Well Sinking Machinery.* N.p.: n.p., n.d.

27½x20. 81 p includes inside back cover. Stiff wraps with chromoliths by Phoenix Lith Co of Chicago show cherubs at water pump and trough; back cover illus of Austin's well drill. Illus catalog of their gas and water drills and parts. No mention of WCE; from intact collection. ☺ . (WM)

725.2 "Autobiography : of : A Glacial Tramp." Rpt from the *Oberlin Review*, 25 Apr. 1894.

14½x10½. 13 p. Self wraps, black print. Engaging and unusual story from the jasper rock's point of view of its travels via glacial ice from Canada to Kentucky and thence to the WCE Anthropology Bldg for an Oberlin College exhibit. At the end of the text: "Mary I. Pinneo." ☺ (FM)

726.1 Avery, B.F., and Sons. *Bunny, the postman.* Philadelphia: ©Sunshine publishing co., n.d.

8½x11. (8) p. Beige wraps with black print and chromolith of 2 rabbits under an umbrella. Stapled at fold. Title is caption title for the first of 3 children's poems. Four chromolith bunny illus in B. Potter style. Ads inside wraps and on back cover for their plows, planters, and other farm implements. No mention of WCE; from an intact WCE collection. Sunshine copyrighted the poems. (WM)

726.2 Axford, H.W., [Co.]. *H.W. Axford's Columbian exhibit : 1893. ...Electric incubator.* Chicago: n.p., n.d.

14x9. (6) panel tri-fold. Newspaper sheet tinted in greens and reds unfolds to 14x25½; text in both portrait and landscape orientation. On back: "World's Fair Exhibit : South End Gallery of Electric Building." Caption title: "The Axford Incubator and Brooder Combined." ☺ (WM)

727. Bailey. *Annals of Horticulture...1889*: (CU,HU,UCB,UMN)
728. Bailey. *Annals of Horticulture...1893*: (FM,HU,NSW,UMA,UMC)

729.1 Baker, Joseph, & Sons. *World's Columbian Exposition : Chicago, 1893 : Exhibits of Joseph Baker & Sons : Engineers and Patentees.* London, Eng.: Joseph Baker & Sons (Rand, McNally & Co., Printers, Chicago), n.d.

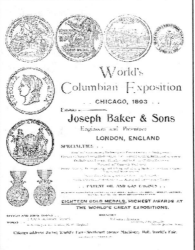

30½x23. (4) p. Folded buff sheet, black print and illus. C.t. is surrounded by previous awards to 1892. At bottom of cover: "Northeast corner Machinery Hall, World's Fair." Two large lithos of exhibited machines on p (4); inside, their 5 exhibits of baking and cooking machinery are detailed. Ad. ☺ (GLD,WM)   P➔ $22 - 45

729.2 Baker, L.A., & Co. *The McCornack Shingle nailer.* Elgin, IL: [L.A. Baker & Co.], n.d.

9x15. (9) p including inside back wrap. Buff self-wraps, navy print and illus of nailer. C.t. Red-line border on covers and text pages. On p (5): "World's Fair Work : Michigan Building." (S,WM)

729.3 Baker Mfg. Co. *Monitor pumping wind mills.* Evansville, WI: n.p., [1893].

22½x15. (4) p. Folded green thin sheet, black print with illus of mill with vanes which open like a fan when rotation starts. Testimonials. No WCE content; from intact collection. ☺ (WM)

729.4 *Baker Wire Co. Chicago. Exclusive manufacturers of the celebrated Baker perfect barb wire. World's Columbian edition. 1892 1893.* N.p.: Baker Wire Co., n.d.

16x9. 1 *l*, 64 p, 1 *l* + unpaged plates. Gray glossy wraps, black print, litho of eagle on globe. C.t. Leaves and plates are illus of WCE bldgs. WCE description. Ad catalog. ☺ (IHi)

729.5 Balcom, P.A., Soap Co. *Story about Geyserite...A Perfect Toilet Soap.* Denver, CO: n.p., n.d.

23½x15. (2) p. Pulp sheet, black print both sides. Prize winner in the French Salon of 1892. A product of geyser action. No WCE content; from intact collection. ☺ (WM)

730. Baldwin. *Exhibit of locomotives*: (CU,FLP,HML,S,SHB,Stfd,UPa)
▶Add company name: Burnham, Williams & Company.

730.1 [Ballard, Harlan H.]. *The Agassiz Association.* [Pittsfield, MA: The Agassiz Association, 1893].

15x8½. 12 p. Self-wraps, black print, string-tied. Caption title. Assn purpose: "to encourage the personal observation of nature." Overprinted in red at top of p (1): "Do not Fail to Visit the A.A. exhibit and reception rooms in gallery of Anthropological Building! Next to Pennsylvania exhibit!" ☺ (S)

731.1 Baltimore & Ohio Railroad. *Baltimore and Ohio R.R. station, foot of Liberty St. : Royal blue line.* N.p.: [C.G. Burgoyne, New York], 1893?

21½x10. (8) panels. Folded sheet. Center map across 3 panels shows B&O route and "World's fair" label at Chicago. Dated at bottom of front cover: "May 15, 1893." (WM)

732. Baltimore & Ohio RR. Phelps. *World's fair via B&O RR*: (GLD,DU,E,HML,UMD,WM,Yale) $30 - 60
▶Cover variant: Buff wraps. Red and blue fancy print: "World's fair via Baltimore & Ohio Railroad."

732.1 Baltimore and Ohio Railroad. *Routes and Rates to the World's Columbian Exposition at Chicago, Ill. via Central Railroad of New Jersey. Reading Railroad System. Baltimore & Ohio Railroad.* N.p.: n.p., n.d.

28x21½. (4) p. Folded white sheet, black print. Only a small B&O logo on back. Caption title p (2): "Picturesque B&O. The Most Attractive Route to the World's Fair." Eight routes described. (WM)

732.2 Bancroft, Hubert Howe. *Achievements of Civilization : The Book of Wealth : Wealth in Relation to Material : and : Intellectual Progress and Achievement...* 10 vol. New York: The Bancroft Company, Publisher, 1896–1900 [ᶜ1896 by Hubert H. Bancroft. Press of The Blakely Printing Co., Chicago].

56x43½. 1000 p. Paged continuously. Ochre silk hc with hand painted recessed cover illus., each named; all edges gilt, decorative end papers. Each vol provided with a folding silk covered case, string-tied. Edition Cygne Noir limited to 150 copies and signed by the author. Preface explains that this is a "consort" to #733. Vol 9 includes WCE and Field's donations to start the FM. FM has set No 24 printed for Marshall Field. Impressive publication by the prolific and respected Bancroft. ☺ (FM,ref)   [Vol I] P➔ $3000

733. Bancroft. *The Book*: (B,CCA,CLP,Col,CU,cul,DC,DU,EPL,EvP,FLP,GBP,HML,HPL,HU,IHi, ISU,KCPL,Knox,LBA,LL,Merc,MIT,MOHx,MSL,NAL,NDU,NLA,NPG,PSU,RPL,SPL,UAT,UBO,UCB,UCD, UCLA,UGa,UH,UMC,UMD,UMN,URI,UTA,UVM,UWM,Yale)

734. Bancroft. *The Book.* (Author's ed): (ref)
---- Also listed: 1893. 10 vol + 2 folding portfolios containing 16 matted plates. Vol 1 is inscribed and signed by Bancroft.

735. Bancroft. *The Book.* (Columbian ed): (Amh,S,UPa)
▶Add annotation: Limited to 1500 copies.
---- Also found: Brown and tan hc, brown print.

737.   Bancroft. *The Book*. (Fin de siècle ed): (HU,IHi,MSI,ref,ULC)   Incomplete plates, no box: $2300
▶Citation clarification: This set was issued with 10 text vol and 10 matching ribbon-tied folios, each folio with 10 matted plates with letterpress tissue guards. The 10 vol text and 10 vol of folios were shipped in a special box. The price in the original bibliography was for the 10 vol of text only.
---- Also found: Gilt stamped presentation copy in wooden case with 10 sliding shelves for the 20 vols: 10 vol text bound as above and 10 vol plates bound in morocco. (ULC)

738.   Bancroft. *The Book*. (Imperial ed): (FPL)
739.   Bancroft. *The Book* (Rpt): (FLP,HU,LACL,LHL,MIT,NAG,NPG,sapl,SHB,UCI,UH,UMD,UPa,wsu)

740.   [Banks]. *The artistic Guide*:
(CCA,Col,CU,cul,HU,IHi,IStU,MH,S,Smth,UAB,UAT,UCLA,UMA,UMC,UMD,UPa,UTA,VT,WM)
---- Also found: Gray wraps with same design as hc but design is sepia, white and black print with red sun burst (rather than gilt). 23x15. (4) p, 1 *l* folding bird's-eye of Chicago, 233, (4) p ads + many unpaged plates on smooth stock; text on pulp paper. ☺ (S)

741.   Banks. *The artistic Guide*: (bgsu,HML,IHi,MOHx,OU,PSU,UCD,VT)

741.1 *The Barber Asphalt Paving Co. : Columbian year, 1893. Columbus discovered Trinidad on his third voyage in 1498. Genuine Trinidad Asphalt Pavements. 1893.* Buffalo, NY: The Matthews-Northrup co., complete art-printing works, n.d.   **P➜**

19x12½. (2)-48 p. Peach wraps with black, white and red print. They used Trinidad pitch as did Warren, #1050.7. Lists streets paved in US and square yards used. Fair handout. ☺ . (FM,WM)

741.2 Bardeen, C[harles] W[illiam]. *...Book on Teaching*. Syracuse, NY: C W Bardeen, Pub., n.d.

17x12. (56) p. Dark slate-blue flecked wraps, black print. At head of title: co address and illus of 1889 Paris expo award. Partial catalog of available books; full catalog index on front cover. Ads inside both covers and on back. See Bardeen paper at #2181. No WCE content; from intact collection. (WM)

741.3 Barker, Moore & Mein Medicine Co. *Barker's Komic Picture Souvenir*. Philadelphia: n.p., n.d.

17x27. Unpaged 8 mm thick book of cartoons advertising Barker's patent medicines. Color cartoon cover depicts rail transportation converging on the Fair; cloth spine. Five cartoons relate to WCE. ☺ . (S)

741.4 Barlow & Jones, Ltd. *...An Old World Industry at Chicago*. Manchester & Bolton, England: Barlow & Jones, Ltd., n.d.   **P➜**

11x14. 30 p. Illus. Pale blue illus wraps, blue print, blue string-tied. C.t. At head of title: "1893 : Barlow & Jones." Text in landscape and cover in portrait orientation. Front wrap illus: draped U.S. and English flags, heads of state, and partial bird's-eye of WCE. Illus of "the Columbian Celebration Quilt," p 28. Frontis litho of Barlow & Jones office bldg. Ad for cotton textile manufacturing. ☺ . (GLD,ICRL) $25 - 50

741.5 Barre Granite Mfg. Co. *World's Columbian Exposition : Exhibit of Barre Granite : Barre. Vt. : 1893.* N.p.: [Barre Granite Manufacturing Co.], n.d.

14½x23½. 15, (2) p. Yellowish-tan (or pale pink or bright green) wraps, dark blue-green print and illus of their exhibit. C.t. Frontis illus of VT state capitol in Montpelier which was built of Barre granite. Photos on versos; text on rectos, except last (2) p, which are both illus. Ad. ☺ . (GLD,S,UVM) $24 - 50

741.6 *The Barrett House. Souvenir and Visitors' Guide to the World's Columbian Exposition and Chicago.* Chicago: Vandercook engraving and publishing co., n.d.

11x7. (4) p. Folded blue card, navy blue print. Accordion fold-out tipped onto p (2). C.t. Barrett Hotel illus on back cover. Located at Cottage Grove and Bowen Ave. B/w accordion foldout has 12 panels of WCE bldgs on one side and 11 panels of Chicago info on the other. Ad variant of #1160. ☺ (S)

741.7 Bartholomay Brewing Co. *A miniature brewery on exhibition at the World's fair, Chicago 1893.* [Rochester, NY: Bartholomay Brew. Co.], n.d.

15x9. (4) p. Folded coated card. Front cover litho of their WCE exhibit, a working model of a miniature brewery producing one barrel per day. Chromolith of their brewery inside. Trademark litho on back is a woman on winged wheel. Ad. ☺ (GLD) $30 - 60

742.   Barton. *Columbus the Catholic*: (NDU)

742.1 Barton Mfg. Co. *Testimonials*. New York: n.p., n.d.

17½x11. (2) p. Single buff sheet, blue print. Testimonials for their vulcanized rubber kits used for making rubber stamps. Appropriately rubber stamped in red at top "Column S-45, Machinery Hall, World's fair." Caption title. ☺ (WM)

744.1 Battle Creek Sanitarium. *Chicago branch of the battle creek sanitarium : 26, 28 college place : Chicago.* N.p.: n.p., n.d.

20½x14. (4) p. Buff folded thin sheet, black print. Illus of the sanitarium entrance on front, view from a distance on back. C.t. Caption title p (2): "Rates and Information." Room charges included meals, weekly bath with attendant, and medical attendance and examination for elderly. Last paragraph: "The location seems to be an exceedingly convenient one for visiting the Fair." (WM)

744.2 *The Bay State hotel, (Between 63rd and 64th Streets,) : Stony Island Avenue, Chicago, Ill.* N.p.: n.p., n.d.   **P➔**

THE BAY STATE HOTEL.

16½x15. (8) p including self-wraps. Folded glossy sheets, blue-black print and illus. C.t. Cover illus of the hotel. "J.A. Nutter, Hotel Manager" at bottom of front cover. The center, pp (4)-(5), has bird's-eye of WCE grounds and Bay State location. Back cover illus of child with caption "I'm Going To the World's Fair. Are You?" ☺ . (S,WM)
---- Also found: 16x15. Without Nutter's name on cover. Reference to him has been crossed out on p (7) and prices lowered, both in red ink. (S)

744.3 Beaman & Smith Co. *Patent Safety Drill and Tap Holders.* Providence, RI: n.p., 1892.

15½x8½. (8) panels which unfold to 15½x34½. Buff stiff stock, black print. Issued with tipped-in purple and black price guide. Text and illus on taps, chucks, and spanner wrenches for lathes. Issued with ten ads in similar format, each (4) p, for their lathes. No WCE content; from intact collection. [Their exhibit location in Machinery Hall was 28-K-47, Group 71, Class 433.] ☺ (WM)

744.4 Belding Bros. & Co. *Slate Drawings : useful & instructive.* Chicago: n.p., n.d.

11x15½. (16) p. Tan stiff smooth wraps, green print and border design of child's slate with wooden frame. C.t. Green print and illus of silk products inside both covers. White line drawings on black background each page. "Manufactures Building World's fair Chicago" on p (13). ☺ . (WM)

745.   Belfast and NCRC. *Irish scenery at the World's Columbian exposition*: (WM)
▶Complete citation: 34x21. (4) p. Folded buff smooth sheet, black print. Exhibit scenery described in paragraphs by location. Pp (3)-(4) same format but exhibit by "Great Northern (Ireland) Railway Company." Capitalize "Transportation" in title. ☺ (WM)

745.1 Belknap Motor Co. *B.C. Standard Dynamos and electric motors. Price List. ...* N.p.: n.p., [1893].

16x9. (4) p. Folded white sheet, navy and red print. Illus of dynamo on front, factory on back. C.t. Parts and price list. "Revised Jan. 2, 1893." No WCE content; from an intact WCE scrapbook. ☺ (S)

745.2 Belknap Motor Co. *B.C. Standard Dynamos and Electric Motors : for : power, arc and incandescent lighting.* N.p.: n.p., [1893].

20x15½. (4) p. Folded cream coated sheet, black print. Front cover illus of "B.C. standard 10 H.P. motor." C.t. WCE exhibit mentioned on pp (3)-(4). Testimonials to May 4, 1893. (WM)

745.3 Belknap Motor Co. *The Belknap Little Giant Water Motor : improved.* N.p.: n.p., n.d.

30x23½. (4) p. Folded yellow sheet, black print. Illus of turbine pump with cut-away views. "Our Next Exhibit will be at Chicago, 1893, World's Columbian exposition." Testimonials to 1892. Ranged from 1-8 HP depending on nozzle pressure. ☺ (WM)

745.4 Belknap Motor Co. Brown, Geo[rge] W. *Belknap Motor Company, Portland, Maine, U.S.A. World's Columbian Exposition, May 1ˢᵗ to November 1ˢᵗ [sic], Electrical Building, Section E, Space 2, Ground Floor...We Would Welcome You.* N.p.: n.p., n.d. P➔

15x13. (4) p. Folded white coated sheet, black print, red illus of Electrical Bldg. C.t. Jackson Park illus on back shows exhibit location in red. Motor exhibit described on pp (2)-(3). ☺ . (S,WM)

745.5 Belknap Motor Co. *The New Cyclone Coffee Mill, No. 5.* N.p.: n.p., n.d.

14x13. (4) p. Folded white sheet, black print and mechanical drawing of the mill. C.t. On back: "Space 2, Section E, Electricity Building, World's Columbian Exposition, Chicago, Ill." ☺ (WM)

745.6 Belknap Motor Co. *Price list. B.C. Standard Dynamos and Electric Motors.* N.p.: n.p., n.d.

17x14. (4) p. Folded sheet, black print and illus of 10 HP motor as in #745.2. C.t. User list on back. Variant of #745.1. No WCE content; from intact collection. ☺ (WM)

745.7 Beloit College. *Proceedings : At the Presentation of : The Fisher Collection : of : Antique Greek Sculpture, On the Occasion of the Fiftieth Anniversary of the : Inception of Beloit College. June 20th, 1894.* [Chicago: Peter F. Pettibone & co., 1894].

26x18½. 1 *l* (Lucius Fisher, Jr. port), 73 p, 1 *l* publication info, 8 *l* plates of casts. Navy blue cloth spine over cream cloth hc, blue and gilt print, Greek state seal. Fisher, son of a founder of the college, outbid other Chicago businessmen including Marshall Field for the Greek government's collection of accurate statue casts which it had exhibited at the WCE. The Wright Museum of Art at Beloit College houses the collection. See #2321.2 (BC)

745.8 Bensdorp & Co. Bartlett, Steven L. *A few choice cooking receipts for the use of Bensdorp's Royal Dutch Cocoa.* [Boston: Steven L. Bartlett, Importer (Boston Bank Note & litho co.)], n.d.

10x7½. 16 p+ text inside front and back wraps. White coated paper wraps, sepia and yellow illus and print. Lists four companies at the WCE using Bensdorp cocoa and their locations on the grounds. Handout which included a sample packet of cocoa. ☺ (GLD)   P➔ $20 - 45

745.9 Bent, Geo[rge] P., [Co.]. *The "Crown" : Pianos & Organs.* Chicago: n.p., n.d.

14x9. 16 p. Cream stiff wraps, black and purple print with vignette of crown in purple and gold. C.t. Text and piano illus in brown ink. WF state and foreign bldgs for which Crown Pianos were chosen are listed on back cover. (WM)

746.1 Bernheim Brothers. *A chat about good whiskey.* Louisville, KY: n.p., n.d.

15½x8½. (4) p. Folded green sheet, black print and cover illus of a rustic building. Ad for "I.W. Harper" whiskey. No WCE content; from intact collection. ☺ (WM)

746.2 Berry Brothers, Limited. *Description of the Mammoth Redwood Plank.* Detroit, MI: n.p., n.p.　　　　　　　　**P➜**

12½x10½. (3) p. Folded tan sheet, black print. C.t. At cover bottom: "World's Columbian exposition, 1893." B/w illus of the redwood plank on p (2). Plank was cut June 1890, in Humbolt County, for exhibit at the WCE. Ad for their varnish and hard oil finish. ☺(GLD,E,WM)　　$20 – 40

☞ The 16 foot wide redwood plank is currently on display at the Muir Woods National Park north of San Francisco. It is attached to an outside wall of the concession building, just inside the park entrance.

☞ In addition to paper souvenirs, several wood and finish manufacturers issued souvenir trade cards printed on wood veneers.

☞ Berry Brothers also exhibited at the 1901 Pan-Am Fair in Buffalo, NY.

746.3 Berry Brothers, Limited. *A talk on varnish for users of varnished things. World's Columbian exposition, 1893.* Detroit, MI: n.p., n.d.

15½x11½. (4) p. Folded pink sheet, black print and illus of factory. Includes description of their exhibit. Branch office list on back. ☺(WM)

746.4 Best, John, & Co. *John Best & co., Paterson, N.J. : Manufacturers of : Illuminated Pure Silk Book Markers...exhibit at World's Columbian Exposition, machinery hall, Section 29, Column 51, Right Main Aisle.* N.p.: n.p., n.d.

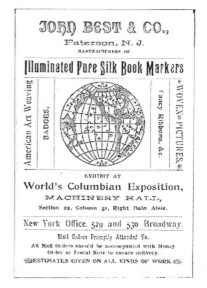

11½x7½. (3) p. Folded sheet, black print with illus of globe. C.t. They wove WCE souvenirs at their exhibit. The styles are described in the text, which is a *Chicago Dispatch* article. ☺.(WM)　　　　**P➜**

746.5 Betz, John F., & Son, Limited. *World's Columbian Exposition Souvenir. John F. Betz & Son, Limited, brewers, bottlers and maltsters. ...* Philadelphia: John F. Betz & Son, Limited, n.d.

30½x24. (8) p. White coated paper wraps and text. Black print and red borders throughout. B/w litho of their Philadelphia plant on front wrap. Handout describes the Betz WCE exhibit and reprints previous awards from the Cotton Centennial in New Orleans, 1884. ☺(GLD)　　　　$35 - 70

746.6 Bilgram, Hugo, [Co.]. *Perfection in bevel gearing : bevel gearing cut theoretically correct...* Philadelphia: n.p., n.d.

20½x14. (4) p. Folded sheet, black print and illus of two bevel gears. Framed at bottom cover: "Exhibit at Columbian Exposition Machinery Hall, Sec. 15. H.J. 28. Group No. 69. Class 416." Describes their methods using beveled blanks. They were glad to give "Estimates." ☺(WM)

746.7 Bilin Springs. *Bilin and Saidschitz Springs. The Acidulous Waters of Bilin in Bohemia. Wells Near the Saurerbrunn (Bilin-Water)...* Teplitz-Bux. (Bohemia): C. Weigend, n.d.

17x11. 16 p. Fold-out graph between pp 2-3. Pale green wraps, black print. C.t. Illus of Bilin spa on back cover. No mention of WCE; from an intact WCE collection. ☺(WM)

746.8 Bilin Springs. *Natural Spring in Bilin : Renowned medicinal spring. Bilin digestive tablets.* Bilin-Sauerbrunn [and] New York: n.p., n.d.

15½x9. (10) panels. Sheet unfolds to 15½x44½. Chromoliths of various spa views one side; other side has a description of "The Acidulous Water of Bilin in Bohemia" in brown print, two seals in blue. The water was said to reduce stomach disorders. No WCE content; from intact collection. ☺(WM)

746.9 *Billet. Sardines, Mushrooms and Peas : From net and field to table.* [Buffalo, NY: The Matthews-Northrup co.], n.d.

14x18. (8) p+ self-wraps. String-tied. Bold "Billet" at cover center, other print brown. C.t. French packing co ad; lists awards to time of Paris 1889. No WCE content; from intact collection. ☺ (WM)

747.　*The biographical dictionary* (Chicago and WCE): (HU,S,ULC)
　　☞ Later editions have no reference to the WCE, e.g., *Biographical dictionary and portrait gallery of the representative men of the United States*. Chicago: The Lewis publishing co., 1896. Same size and format to the 1893 editions. The Illinois volume was edited by John Moses, see #939 and #940.

748.　*The biographical dictionary* (Chicago, Iowa and WCE): (IHi)

748.1 *The biographical dictionary and portrait gallery of representative men of Chicago, Milwaukee and the World's Columbian exposition.* Chicago and New York: American Biographical publishing co. (Press of Knight, Leonard & co.), 1892.

　　29x23½. 1 *l* (frontis), 913, (3) p index. Frontis port: "The Gunther Columbus." Black leather hc; gilt border design, spine print, and all edges. Gilt and black decorative end pages. Tissue guards. ☺ (S)

749.　*The biographical dictionary* (Chicago, Minnesota and WCE): (UWM)
750.　*The biographical dictionary* (Chicago, St. Louis and WCE): (ref,slpl)　　　　　　　$150
751.　*The biographical dictionary* (Chicago, Wisconsin and WCE): (RCHx)

751.1 Birkenhead Iron Works. *List of models & pictures of sundry vessels built at the Birkenhead Iron Works from 1830 to 1892. World's Columbian exposition, U.S.A., Chicago, 1893.* [Birkenhead, Gt. Brit.: E. Griffith and son, printers], n.d.

　　18½x12. 8 p. Self-wraps, black print. C.t. Ad handout in the Trans Bldg. ☺ (Stfd,WM)

752.　Blaine. *Columbus and Columbia:* (B,bgsu,BrU,CWM,E,GPL,HML,HU,IHi,nmsu,OU,Stfd,UCLA,UMD,UTA,UVM,Yale)
　　---- Also listed: Omaha [and] Denver: W.A. Hixenbaugh & Co., [ᶜ1892]. 1 *l*, (17)-832 p.

753.　Ridpath, John Clark, and James W. Buel. *Pictorial history of the United States,...to which is added the : Story of Columbus and the New World,...Two Books in One Volume.* Philadelphia: Historical Publishing Co., 1894 [ᶜ1892 by H.S. Smith].

　　27x20½. 1 *l*, (17)-832 p. Light gray-green cloth hc, black print and border, gilt print spine. Colored frontis of Columbus landing. Illus include ports. James G. Blaine is not the primary author, but he and Benj. Butterworth wrote sections of this book; they are not listed on the t.p. Also pub in 1892 under the title *Columbus and Columbia*, #752. (GLD)　　　▶Corrected citation.　　　　$18 - 40

753.1 Blair Camera Co. Cannon, Annie J[ump]. *In the footsteps of Columbus.* Boston: L. Barta & co., printers, 1893 [ᶜ1893 Annie J. Cannon].　　　　　　　　　　P➔

　　13x17½. 33 p. Pale yellow glossy wraps, black print, illus of Columbus statue in Spain. C.t. = t.p. Description of Cannon's trip to Spain and photo-illus from pictures she took with her "Kamaret," made by Blair in Boston. Back cover: "This Souvenir of the World's Fair Presented by..." Ad. ☺ (S,WM)

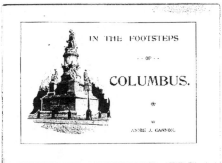

753.2 Blair Camera Co. *Two new Blair cameras. The "Columbus" and "The 400" : Designed especially for visitors to the world's fair.* Boston: n.p., n.d.

　　22x15. (4) p. Folded smooth sheet, black and red print. Illus of "Columbus" box camera, p (2), and "The 400" folding, p (3). WF info on back. Cameras appear to be modeled after Kodak's line, or vice versa, e.g., "The 400" = Kodak "4," etc. Issued with laid-in sheets printed one-side. ☺ (WM)

753.3 Blair, Edward T. *A history of the Chicago Club.* Chicago: [Printed by R.R. Donnelley and sons co. under the direction of Herbert S. Stone & co.], 1898.

17½x11½. 3 *l*, 5-116, (1) p. Green cloth hc with gilt print and blind-stamp cover design. Boxed. Describes the interaction of the Chicago Club with the Art Institute and the WCE in 1893. Membership list at the back includes WCE dignitaries. (ref) $65

755.1 Blanchard, Rufus. *Discovery and Conquest of the : Northwest : with the : history of Chicago.* 2 vol. Chicago: R. Blanchard and Co., 1900.

25x17½. Vol 2: 681, (4), (3) p index. Illus and tables. "Northwest" in title in red. WCE described from pp 386-462. ☺ (IHi)

755.2 Bleyl, J., Co. *Catalogue of the Publications of Gilbers' Royal Court Publishing House : J. Bleyl : in : Dresden. Speciality: Architecture and Art-Industry.* [Dresden: Printed by C.C. Meinhold & Sons], n.d.

15½x12. 31, (1) p includes buff self-wraps, black print. Illus. C.t. In English. No WCE content; from intact collection. ☺ (WM)

755.3 Blooker, J. & C., [Co.]. *World's Columbian Exposition 1893. J. & C. Blooker, Cocoa manufacturers, Amsterdam (Holland.).* N.p.: J. & C. Blooker, n.d.

14x9. Single stiff card printed both sides. Front side chromolith of their WCE exhibit bldg, an 1806 windmill near South Pond; title from print on back. Red over-stamp on back lists their representative and office on Wabash Ave in Chicago. ☺ (GLD)　　P➜　　$16 - 32

☞ The Blooker exhibit was dismantled after the close of the WCE and moved to 20 Netherlands Road, Brookline, Massachusetts. P➜

755.4 Blum, Emil. *...Städte und Landschaften in Wort und Bild : Amerikanische Städtebilder. Serie I. Chicago : und die Columbische Weltausstellung 1893... ___ : J. Laurecie?, ___ .*

21x14. ca. 48 p. Attractive light gray wraps with dark green lithos and red and dark gray print. C.t. Part of extended series: "Illustrirte Welt- und Reisebibliothek- Lfg: 1." Series info and price at head of title. WCE and Chicago text and pictures. Cover lists Blum as US Correspondent. . (wslb)

755.5 Boericke, R., & Co. *R. Boericke & co., manufacturers of : The Depew Convertible Operating Chair, Physicians' Cabinets,...* Chicago: Geo. Gregory, Printer, n.d.

The Blooker Chocolate Bldg 1992
(Courtesy J. Emple)

25½x17½. 32 p. Sepia wraps, black print. Catalog of their professional office chairs. Back cover illus of "Columbia rolling chair," which was used at the WCE. ☺ . (Stfd–bound WCE Trans Dept Collection)

756.1 Borden, Selleck & Co. *The Harrison Conveyor Irrigating Pump.* Chicago: n.p., n.d.

28x18. 1 *l*. Robin's-egg blue sheet printed in black. Illus of two horses working the pump. No WCE content; from intact collection. (WM)

756.2 Boston and Albany Railroad. *The Boston and Albany To The World's Columbian Exposition at Chicago, 1893.* Buffalo, NY: The Matthews-Northrup co., complete art printing works, n.d.

21x10½. Sheet unfolds to 41x103; cover printed in red and black. Large map on one side in red and black and labeled: "The Only Double Track Route Between New England and the West." Other side has smaller map of Chicago and WCE plus info on WF and hotels. (WM)

756.3 Boston & Maine Railroad. Bay State Hotel. *Twenty-five Trips to the World's Columbian Exposition, via Boston & Maine Railroad's World's Fair Special, Leaving Boston between May 6 and October 28, 1893.* N.p.: n.p., n.d.

16x14½. (10) p including inside covers. White wraps, black print. Centerfold bird's-eye of WCE area including Bay State at 64th and Stony Island Ave. Info about the excursion hotel and rail specials. © (S)

756.4 Boston & Maine Railroad. Varnam, A.C. *The World's Columbian Exposition. Elegant special Pullman trains with dining cars, For the Exclusive Accommodation of the people of Lawrence and vicinity...* [Boston: American Printing and Engraving Co.], n.d.

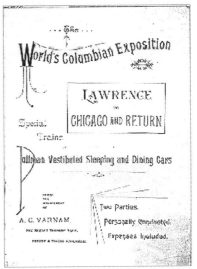

19½x13½. 16 p. White wraps, black print Bird's-eye view of WCE grounds on back. Caption title: "Two Lawrence excursions." Describes excursion accommodations to the WCE in detail. . (ref,WM) **P➜**

756.5 Boston Camera Mfg. Co. *Stray Bits at the World's Fair by a Bull's-Eye Camera.* [Boston: L. Barta & Co., Printers, 1894].

13x10. 32 p. Tan textured wraps. C.t. 12 halftone reproductions from a lot of 143 pictures taken at the WCE with an $8 "Bull's-Eye" camera using "Light-proof Film Cartridges." Two cuts of cameras, film case; price list. Ad. (E,HML,ref) $30

757.1 Boswell, Russel Thomas. *A trip to the fair.* Philadelphia: Russel Thomas Boswell, [1893].

23½x15½. 8 p. Caption title; unbound text. At bottom of p 8: "Monday Literary Club : November 20, 1893." Description of full trip from Philadelphia, Sept 5–18, 1893. © (8)

757.2 Boughton & Linville [Co.]. *Interior Decorations : & : artistic wood floors.* Boston: John W. Boughton, Manufacturer, ©1893.

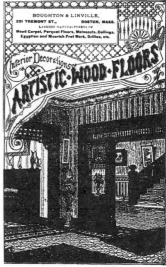

23½x14½. 66 p. Yellow, brown, and orange decorated wraps showing their fancy interior woodwork. C.t. Verso cover photo illus of their ornate WCE exhibit with parquetry, fret work, and grilles. Pretty ad. © . (HML) **P➜**

757.3 The Bovinine Co. *1492. Columbian exposition. 1892. Bovinine : Compliments of THE BOVININE COMPANY, Chicago, New York, Boston, London.* [New York: The Bovinine co.], n.d.

Envelope 16½x25½. Bold black and red print and illus of bull. Back of envelope printed in purple: "North east gallery, section F.F. 4 (up stairs.) Agricultural building, 'Worlds [sic] fair.'" Bovinine was a "highly condensed raw food extract" touted as a medicinal food. Handed out at the WCE, the enveloped contained the two pamphlets below. © (GLD) **P➘** All: $30 - 60

a. *Bovinine The Original Raw Food.* New York: The Bovinine Co. (Art press, Dempsey & Carroll), n.d. 20x15. 8, (8) p+ 1893 and 1894 calendars are printed in blue inside front and back wraps. C.t. Cover chromoliths ©1893 by Trautmann, Bailey & Blampey of New York. No mention of WCE but this pamphlet was handed out at the WCE in the above envelope.

b. *BOVININE.* [New York: The Bovinine Co., n.d.] 19½x14. 8 p include printed self-wraps. Buff paper with black print. C.t. Gives medicinal uses for this beef extract.

757.4 Bowers, R.C., Granite Co. *R.C. Bowers Granite co.,...Spaulding's Granite and Marble power polisher.* Montpelier, VT: [Union card co., power job printers], n.d.

21½x14, (4) p. Folded green-flecked green sheet, black print with illus of polisher. C.t. On cover: "Call at R.C. Bowers granite co's exhibit, in north west corner of Manufacturers [sic] Building, Section H, Block 2." Machine cost $75; price list for wheels and grinding powders, pp (3)-(4). © (WM)

758.1 Bowsher, N.D., Co. *...Mill cogs a specialty. Made to order.* South Bend, IN: n.p., n.d.

28x21½. (4) p. Folded sheet, black print and illus of cog teeth blanks. Red print headers. At head of title in red: "Read this!...Keep it!" Method for making wooden cog wheels with interchangeable teeth of maple wood and linseed oil to minimize maintenance time. Testimonials p (4). No WCE content; from intact collection. ☺ (WM)

759.   Boyd. *Columbia: From Discovery in 1492 to the World's Columbian Exposition*: (ref) $45
---- Also found: Red cloth hc, black print and design. (ref)
---- Also listed: Philadelphia and St. Louis: P.W. Ziegler & co., [ᶜ1893]. 768 p. (ref)

759.1 Bradley, David, Mfg. Co. *Map of a part of Chicago showing Streets, Street Railways, Railroads, Railway Depots, Etc.* Chicago: n.p., n.d.

17x12½. (4) p. Folded white card, black print. Cover port of co president, Bradley, captioned: "The Oldest Plowmaker in America." Centerfold map shows co's location and nearby Art Institute; illus of factory on back. No WCE content; from intact collection. (WM)

759.2 Bradley, Milton, Co. *...Bradley's Kindergarten Material and School Aids.* Springfield, MA: n.p., n.d.

23x15. 74 p. Buff self-wraps, black print with port of Columbus and Admin Bldg. C.t. One product was "Columbus sewing cards," p 56. At head of title: "Columbian Edition." ☺ (S)

761.   *Brandreth Columbian ABC for The Little Ones*: (E,S,WM)   P➔
▶Added annotation: In the middle are 2 p of chromoliths of WCE bldgs. Illus parody with children, rather than Columbus, discovering America.
---- Also found: With "A.J. Barker, Druggist & Apothecary, Taunton, Mass." on back cover.

761.1 *Braunscheweigische Maschinenbau – Anstalt : Braunscheweig. Deutschland.* Braunscheweig: n.p., n.d.

13½x22. (2) p. Buff stiff card, blue-black print and border both sides. Bold diagonal orange over print "World's Columbian Exposition Chicago 1893." Back has exhibit list printed in five languages. They made pumps, filters, and presses for the sugar and alcohol industry. ☺ (WM)

761.2 Brennan and Co. *...The Improved Kentucky Shoe Drill.* [Louisville, KY]: Brennan & Co. South-Western Agricultural Works, n.d.

15x23. 15 p. Rust smooth wraps, black print. C.t. At head of title: "1893." Illus of shoe drill on back. No mention of WCE; from an intact collection. ☺ (WM)

762.   Brewer. *The World's Best Orations* (10 vol): (FPL)

762.1 *The Bridgeport Chain Co., manufacturers of the "Triumph" Chain. ...Display in department of transportation exhibits building, World's Columbian exposition, Chicago.* Bridgeport, CT: Bridgeport Chain Co., n.d.   P➔

22x14. (4) p. Folded buff sheet with black print. C.t. Caption title: "The 'Triumph' Chain." Compares English welded chain with "Triumph." ☺ . (Stfd-bound WCE Trans Dept Collection)

762.2 Bridgeport Gun Implement Co. *World's fair price-list. Chicago, May 1, 1893. The Forstner auger bit.* New York : n.p., n.d.

9x15. (4) p. Folded sheet, blue print and illus of auger. Mentions that their WCE exhibit was made with Forstner bits. Landscape orientation; folds at top. Sizes and price list. The Forstner, still used today, is a circular cap bit on a shank; the cutting edges are sharp openings in the cap sides. ☺ (WM)

762.3 Brigg, T.H., Co. *...Great Economy of Horse Power.* London: n.p., n.d.

23x15½. 12 p. Buff wraps, black print and ornate design with port of T.H. Brigg. C.t. At head of title: "World's Columbian Exposition : Chicago, Ill. : 1893." Contains lithos of their English hauling buggies. Exhibited in the Trans Bldg Annex, Group 83, Class 511. (ref) $27

762.4 Brigg, T.H., Co. *On Friday Oct. 27ᵗʰ at 11-30 a.m. Pavilion A. In The Hall Of the National Commission...A Descriptive Lecture : on "Haulage by Horses."* N.p.: n.p., n.d.

20½x13½. (2) p. Buff stiff card printed both sides, brown print and illus of Admin Bldg on front; black print on back. Admin Bldg was the "Hall of the National Commission." Invitation. ☺ . (S)

763. Brooklyn Eagle. Chicago Bureau. *World Columbian*: (GLD,S) **P→**
▶Add annotation for 4th ed: *A hand-book to the World's Fair.* Chicago: Brooklyn Daily Eagle, Chicago Bureau, 1893. 14x9. 56 p. White glossy wraps, gray-blue (or green) print. Color "Miniature map of Chicago and the World's Fair" tipped-in at front cover. This is the t.p. title. Includes "How to See the Fair." (S)
---- Also found 5th ed: 60 p. Yellow wraps, blue print; blue ink text. T.p. title same as 4th ed. (GLD) $30 - 50

☞ During the WCE, the *Brooklyn Eagle* had a presence in Chicago. With its office in the Auditorium Bldg on Wabash, it was the headquarters for residents of Brooklyn and Long Island, who could secure rooms for the Exposition through the office. See #1998.1.

764. Brooks. *Exhibit of Locomotives made by Brooks*: (S,Stfd,UPa)
---- Also found: Black leather flexible hc cover, gilt print. (S)

764.1 Brotherhood Wine Co. *Souvenir : Columbian : Exposition : 1893.* [New York: Brotherhood Wine Co.] (Heffron & Phelps, lith.), n.d.

14x8½. 24 p including 6 numbered "Memoranda" pages. Chromolith stiff wraps, black print. C.t. This ad describes the monastery wine as both food and tonic. ☺ . (OU,WM) **P→**

764.2 Brown & Sharpe Mfg. Co. *The Brown & Sharpe Chucking Machine.* N.p.: [Printed by Kilbourne Tompkins, NY], n.d.

25x18½. 1 *l*, (4) p testimonials, 1 *l* litho of chucking machine, (4) p. Deep teal-flecked wraps with red print, red string-tied. C.t. Testimonials dated 1889. No mention of WCE; from an intact WCE collection. (WM)

764.3 Brown & Sharpe Mfg. Co. *Catalogue and price lists of Brown & Sharpe Mfg. Co.* [Providence, RI]: n.p., [ᶜ1893 by Brown & Sharpe Mfg Co.].

14½x9. xiv, 306 p. Dark blue wraps, black print. Illus catalog of their machinery, tools, castings; also catalog for Darling, Brown & Sharpe rules, try squares, etc. No mention WCE; intact collection. (WM)

764.4 Brown & Sharpe Mfg. Co. *Illustrated Supplement to the catalogue of Brown & Sharpe Manufacturing Co....* Providence, RI: Brown & Sharpe manufacturing co. (Printed by Kilbourne Tompkins, NY), 1889 [ᶜ1889 by Brown & Sharpe Manufacturing Co.].

26½x18. 67 p. Blue wraps, navy print. Illus of their works on back cover. C.t. = t.p. Illus catalog printed on maize backgrounds. No mention of WCE; from an intact WCE collection. (WM)

764.5 Brown & Sharpe Mfg. Co. *Messrs. Brown & Sharpe Mfg. Co. cordially invite you to the World's Columbian exposition, to be held in Chicago, in 1893, and to visit their works in Rhode Island.* [Providence, RI: Printed by Livermore & Knight co., ᶜ1893 by Brown & Sharpe mfg. co.].

17½x13½. 1 *l* frontis, 2-66 p, map. Frontis illus of factory "prior to 1872." Light blue (or gray) paper wraps glued over stiff card stock, navy blue print with decorative upper border. The tri-fold Rand, McNally 1892 bird's-eye of WCE after p 66 has red overlay numbers at their WF sites. (S,WM)

765.1 *Brownies at the Columbian Exposition.* N.p.: n.p., n.d.

23x15. Unpaged ruled writing tablet hinged at top with tan cloth. C.t. Card wraps with different illus. Examples: "Arrival" (Brownies entering WCE entrance at Terminal Station) and "Indulge in Boat Racing" (Brownies racing sculls in front of Manufactures Bldg). ☺ (S)

765.2 Brun, A., & Co. ...*Noveau Medoc Vineyards.* Oakville, CA: n.p., n.d.

12½x7½. (4) p. Folded white glossy sheet, black print and thin border. C.t. Chicago representatives: Delafield, McGovern & Co (see #825.4). No WCE content; from intact collection. ☺ (WM)

765.3 Brunner, Mond & Co., Limited. ...*Pure alkali.* Northwich, Eng.: n.p., n.d.

27x15½. 1 *l.* Light blue stock, black print. At head of title: co name and address. Soda used in "manufacture of glass, soap, paper, wood pulp, starch or colors." No WCE content; from intact collection. (WM)

765.4 Bryant, Robert, Limited. *Robert Bryant,...manufacturers of all kinds of : Wood & Leather Gun & Pistol Cases, cartridge bags and belts,...World's Columbian exposition, Chicago, 1893.* London: n.p., n.d.

10½x17. 16 p. Pale blue wraps, black print and border. C.t. = t.p. On back cover, "Catalogue No., 4449. Position of exhibit, no. 173, facing Indian and New South Wales sections." Illus catalog of their sturdy English hunting cases. ☺ (WM)

765.5 Bryn Mawr Hotel. *Bryn Mawr, where you may live as if at home while visiting the World's fair.* Chicago: Charles A. Barker, n.d.

30½x24. (3) p. Folded buff sheet, black print. Back blank. C.t. Pp (2)-(3) map in black and red with "Bird's Eye View shows a portion of Bryn Mawr and the World's Fair grounds." Attractive ad. ☺ (S)

766.   [Buck]. *Amy Leslie at the fair:* (RU,UCLA,UMD)
---- Also found: 27½x20½. Brown cloth beveled-board hc, gilt print, gilt top edge. The signed presentation copy at UMD is #62 of 200.

766.1 Buckeye Incubator Co. *Farmer Slows Visit to The World's Columbian Exposition.* Springfield, OH: Buckeye Incubator Co. (The Orcutt Co. Lith.), n.d.

7½x13. (6) p includes inside front and back wraps. Chromolith illus front wrap shows fowl pecking for food; on back, chicks are seen emerging from the "Invincible Hatcher." Text in verse with illus in dark blue and red. Story's characters are Nancy and Silas Slows. Attractive ad. ☺ (GLD,E,HML) $25 - 50

766.2 *Buckeye Iron & Brass Works, Dayton, Ohio, manufacturers of Hot Water and Natural Gas Fittings.* Dayton, OH: n.p., n.d.

23½x16. (4) p. Folded cream smooth sheet, dark chocolate print. Illus of valves pp (2)-(4). Gives size and price list for "Brass, Phosphor Bronze and Aluminum castings." ☺ (WM)

766.3 Bucyrus Steam Shovel & Dredge Co. ...*Improved process : of : Placer Mining : by the "Bucyrus": patent amalgamator, in combination with Dredging and Excavating Machinery.* Milwaukee, WI: Bucyrus Steam Shovel & Dredge Co., [1893]

17½x25½. (18) p. Tan stiff wraps, brown print. At head of title: "2d edition. World's fair." Mentions their exhibits in the Mining Bldg, Main Floor, and Trans Bldg Annex, X5, Posts 4 to 8. ☺ . (Stfd)

766.4 Buff & Berger Co. *A complete list of the instruments of precision exhibited by Buff & Berger of Boston, Mass., at the World's Columbian exposition in Chicago. 1893. This exhibit will be found in the building of manufactures and liberal arts; gallery floor, north end. Group 151: Classes 867, 868, 869.* Boston: Printed by C.H. Heintzemann, n.d.

20½x13½. 8 p. Self-wraps, black print on light beige stock. Ad. (WM)

767.   *Buffalo Bill's Wild West and Congress of Rough Riders:* (BBM,ref,S) $345
[See index under Buffalo Bill for related Cody items.]

767.1 ...*Buffalo Bill's wild west : congress of rough riders of the world.* Chicago: Blakely printing co., 1893? **P➔**

Single sheet folds to 18x9. Unfolds to (8) panels text one side; on the reverse, a large red and black WCE plan-map showing the rough rider exhibit location just outside the fairgrounds. "Nate Salsbury, Manager." At head of title: "Chicago, Summer 1893 : the [key] to all : The open sesame to the World's Fair Subject is..." [See index under Buffalo Bill for related Cody items.] ☺ . (UIC)

☞ Literature from the Buffalo Bill Congress for 1895 and 1902 continues to refer to the shows held at the WCE.

767.2 Bullock, M.C., Mfg. Co. ...*Williams Patent Central-Valve Engine : M.C. Bullock Manfg. Co. : Sole American Manufacturers. Chicago.* Chicago: n.p., n.d.

28x20½. (4) p. Folded buff smooth sheet. C.t. Title printed on the diagonal. At head of title: "Columbian Circular. No. 26." P (2) shows engine at WCE; list of engines in use in Machinery Hall and Electricity Bldg. ☺ (WM)

767.3 *The Burgess Gun Co. Buffalo : New York : USA : 1893.* Buffalo, NY: Burgess Gun Co. [The Matthews-Northrup co.], n.d.

12x20. 2 *l*, (15) p + tipped-in errata sheet printed in red ink. Turquoise wraps, dark blue print and illus of the factory. Blue text print and illus of gun products. C.t. Purple overprint on first leaf: "Our Agent W.H. Skinner has charge of our exhibit in Manufacturer's Bldg., Section 'Q' Block 3. Please call." Errata: apology for imperfect printing in rush to print for the WCE. Ad. ☺ (GLD) $35 - 75

767.4 *Burley & Company, Sole Chicago Agents : for : The Libbey Glass Co., Superior Cut Glass. Manufactures & Liberal Arts Building, World's Columbian Exposition.* Chicago: n.p., n.d.

7x11½. (4) p. Stiff folded card, black script font print outside, black and red print inside. Description of "The Plaisance Factory" on back. ☺ (WM)

767.5 Burlington Blanket Co. *Catalogue of : Burlington Blanket Co. : Manufacturers of the Burlington "Stay on" Stable Blanket.* Burlington, WI: Burlington Blanket Co. (Henry Gugler Co., Milwaukee), n.d.   **P➔**

17½x11. 32 p. Color litho wraps in pink, yellow, and orange; illus of blanketed horse surrounded by flowers. C.t. Descriptive catalog of their horse blankets. ☺ . (Stfd–bound WCE Trans Dept Collection)

767.6 Burnett, Joseph, & Co. *How to use : Burnett's : Standard Color Pastes.... Columbian Exposition, 1893.* Boston and Chicago: Joseph Burnett & Co., n.d.

13½x9. (6) p + text on inside both wraps. Cream wraps, red and black print, string-tied. C.t. Back wrap has list of "World's Fair Columbian Catering Companies" using their coloring and flavoring extracts. Recipe for "Columbian Ice Cream" on p (6). Nice ad. ☺ (GLD) $20 - 45

767.7 Burnham & Morrill Co. *Columbian Exhibition 1893. Compliments of Burnham & Morrill Co. Packers of the World Renowned Paris Corn, Succotash, Machias Bay Lobster, Baked Beans, Canned Meats Etc.* N.p.: [Forbes litho co.], n.d.

15½x10½. (4) p. Folded card. Beautiful chromoliths on all pages. Front cover shows a large globe featuring the Americas; back cover, a red lobster and medals won at previous fairs; inside illus of their products made in Portland, Maine. [The company is famous today for its beans under the B&M label.] ☺ . (E.ref)   **P➔** $48

768.   Burnham. *The book of the builders*: (Amh,CCA,CLP,Smth,UAH,UCB,UIC,UTA,UoC,WM)

768.1 Burns, Paul O., & Co. *Strawberry Brandy : Yerba Buena Vineyard : Paul O. Burns Wine Co.* San Jose, CA: n.p. (H.S. Crocker & Co., Lith. S.F.), n.d.

34½x10. 1 *l.* Color illus of large bottle of Strawberry Brandy on greenish-gold background. Stamped at top: "Exhibit No. 141, So. End : Horticultural hall, Please call B.C. Quigley, manager." (WM)

768.2 Burns, Paul O., & Co. *Yerba Buena : Vineyard : Paul O. Burns & Co. Burgundy.* San Jose, CA: n.p., n.d.

34½x10½. White sheet filled with large color illus of burgundy bottle. Stamped at top: "Exhibit No. 141, So. End : Horticultural hall, Please call B.C. Quigley, manager." (WM)

769.1 The Busiest House in America. *...Seventeenth annual illustrated Catalogue : containing Illustrations and Prices...* N.p.: Busiest House in America, 1893.

26½x18½. 868 p. Blue-black cloth hc, gilt print. Stepped fore-edge index. At head of title: "1893 A.D. World's Columbian exposition edition 1893 A.D." Fine period illus catalog containing illus and lists of their WCE souvenirs. ☺ (S)

770.1 Butler Brothers. *..."Our Drummer."* New York and Chicago: Butler Brothers, Nov. 1893.

33½x24½. 116 p. Blue wraps, black print. C.t. At head of title: "Santa Claus edition." Toy catalog includes several toys related to the WCE, such as banks and purses. (S)

770.2 Butterworth, Hezekiah. *The Story of America. ...Revised and Enlarged...* New York [and] Akron Ohio [and] Chicago: The Werner co., [ᶜ1893 by The Werner Co.].

21x16. 7 *l*, 12-692 p. Dark tan cloth hc, gilt print; black, blue, and red design of Native Americans viewing "modern" Washington, DC. T.p. in red and blue. WCE: pp 578-81. US history school book. Butterworth was at the WCE; see #6 and #2209. ☺ (GLD) $10 - 20

770.3 California Fig Syrup Co. *World's Columbian Exposition. Compliments of California Fig Syrup Co.* San Francisco, CA: California Fig Syrup Co., [ᶜ1893 by Calvert Lith. & Eng. Co., Detroit, MI].

13½x10. (8) p. Single sheet unfolds to 13½x40. Chromolith wraps show seated woman holding fig leaf with Admin Bldg in background (front); illus of Manufactures Bldg (back). Text in blue ink. C.t. Ad for their "syrup of figs" + description of the WCE on (6) pages. ☺ (GLD,E,WM)   P➔ $30 - 55

770.4 Cambiaghi, Giuseppe, [Co.]. *Large mechanical hats manufacture.* Monza, It.: Lit. Clivio, Milano, n.d.

18x13½. (2) p. White sheet printed both sides in blue; one side English, one side French. At bottom: "Agents for Chicago's exposition: [list of names]." ☺ (WM)

770.5 Cambridge Hotel. *The Cambridge Club Family Hotel : Cor. 39ᵗʰ and Ellis Ave.,...* N.p.: n.p., n.d.

8½x16. (2) p. Stiff card printed both sides in black. Photo-illus of hotel with caption: "Six minutes from the exposition." On back: Chicago map showing hotel and WCE locations and hotel floor plan. "Special to Members of the World's Congresses." (WM)

771.   Cameron. *History of the World's Columbian Exposition*: (CCA,Col,Fess,HU,MSI,NSW,RU,sfpl,slpl,UCLA,UIC,UMD,UoC,Yale)
▶Cover variant: Stuffed black leatherette hc with gilt print and design, red dyed edges. (Fess)

772.   Cameron. *The World's Fair being a pictorial history*: (CCA,CU,HML,IHi,NDU,RU,slpl,UAT,UCLA,UVM,VT)
▶Add publishers:
---- Boston: Desmond Publishing Co., [ᶜ1893 by J.R. Jones]. Blue cloth hc and leather; marbled edges.
---- Boston: MacConnell Brothers & Co., ᶜ1893. Listed at 816 p.

---- Boston: John K. Hastings, [ᶜ1893 by J.R. Jones]. 816 p.
---- Cincinnati, OH: W.H. Ferguson, ᶜ1893. Listed at __ p.
---- Grand Rapids, MI: P.D. Farrell & co., [ᶜ1893 by J.R. Jones]. Listed at 814 p.
---- [Philadelphia: Co-operative Pub. Co.], ᶜ1893. Listed at __ p.
---- Philadelphia: Gately & Fitzgerald, [ᶜ1893]. Listed at 816 p.

772.1 Camp Lincoln. *World's Fair : Camp Lincoln : Six month's encampment.* Chicago: E.C. Cook & Bro., Proprietors, n.d.

22½x15½. (4) p. Folded buff sheet printed in navy and red. C.t. Cover illus of soldier in front of tent; back cover map of their location. "A delightful, beautiful and safe home : For Grand Army Posts, Camps of Sons of Veterans, Old Soldiers and their families, Sons of Veterans..." ☺ (S)

772.2 ...*Campbell & Zell Co., : manufactures of : the Zell improved : Water Tube Safety Boiler,...* Baltimore, MD: [Campbell & Zell] Guggenheimer, Weil & Co., prs., n.d.

24½x20. 56 p. Blue-green cloth hc, blind stamped, silver print and anchor design. Frontis litho in green and apricot with vignettes of their factory and steam boiler. C.t.: "World's Columbian exposition : edition : How To Generate Steam Economically : 1892 1893." At head of title: "Enterprise Iron Works, Canton. Enterprise Marine Works, Locust Point." Ad. ☺ (HML)

772.3 Campbell Cutlery Co. *Campbell's : practical : sliding display trays. Patented Dec. 1ˢᵗ, 1891. Can be made...* Syracuse, NY: n.p., n.d.

25½x16½. (4) p. Folded blue sheet, black print. C.t. Issued with peach sheet listing firms using their cases and a folded sheet showing case and how to size and custom order trays. The trays were inserted in guides placed in any typical showcase. No WCE content; from an intact WCE collection. ☺ (WM)

773. Campbell, James B. *Campbell's Illustrated History*: (GLD,CLP,FLP,LL,MOHx,MSI,NDU,NLA,RU,UCB,UIC,UMN,UWM)
▶Add new publisher: Toledo, OH: Carothers pub. co., 1894 [ᶜ1894 James B. Campbell].
---- Also found: Red (or green) cloth hc.

774. Campbell, J[ames] B. *Official List of state boards*: (GLD)   P➔ $22 - 45

774.1 Canadian Copper Co. *Descriptive list of samples exhibited by The Canadian Copper Co. Cleveland, Ohio. Ontario court, Mining Building, World's Columbian Exposition, Chicago, 1893.* Sudbury, Ont.: n.p., n.d.

23x15½. (4) p. Folded buff sheet, black print. C.t. Lists their Ontario ores and mines and describes their Cleveland refinery. Exhibit described. ☺ (WM)

775. *Canadian Pacific RR at the World's fair*: (E,WM)
▶Add: Peach background, navy blue print.

775.1 Canadian Pacific Railway. *Banff and the Lakes in the Clouds : by the Canadian Pacific Railway.* N.p.: [Canadian Pacific Railway], n.d.

13x17½. 19 p. White wraps, blue and black print, illus of mountain lake. On t.p.: "The Canadian National Park. Outings in the Mountains. The C.P.R. Hotels." No WCE; from intact collection. ☺ (LBA)

775.2 Canadian Pacific Railway. Scidmore, Eliza Ruhamah. *Westward to the far east : a guide to the principal cities of China and Japan with a note on Korea.* 4th ed. [Montreal]: The Canadian Pacific Railway Co., 1893.

23x15½. 76, (2) p+1 fold color map of Japan, served by the co's steamship line. Multicolored litho wraps depict Oriental junk with Mount Fuji in background. Illus and text in brown and blue. Date "January, 1893." Lithos by American Bank Note Company of NY. No mention of WCE; from an intact collections. ☺ (LBA,WM)

776. *The Canadian Pacific : the new highway to the Orient*: (LBA)

776.1 Carborundum Co. *Price List of the Celebrated Carborundum Wheels.* Monongahela, PA: [Mackenzie, Davis & co. pr.], n.d. P→

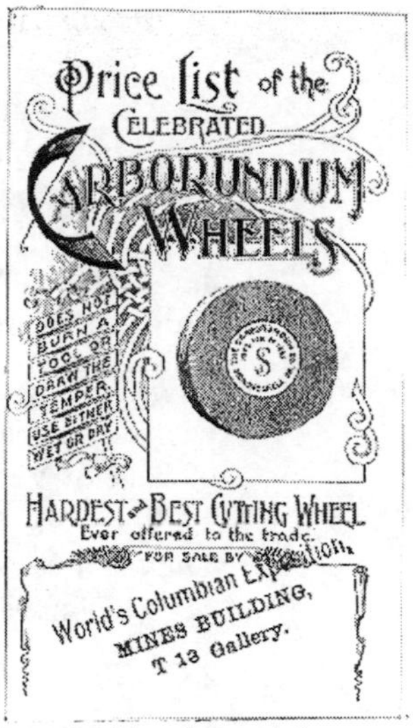

16x9. (4) p. Folded bright yellow card, black print and illus of wheel. C.t. Sizes and price list p (4). Bottom of cover stamped "World's Columbian Exposition Mines building, T 13 Gallery." ☺. (WM)

776.2 Carbutt, John, Co. *The Oldest Dry Plate Factory in America : 1878–1893 : Keystone : Dry Plate and Film Works,...* Philadelphia: n.p., n.d.

18x15½. (4) p. Folded white glossy sheet, black and red print. "Carbutt's Exhibit, Section E, Liberal Arts Building," p (4). Sold photo plates and kerosene safe lights. Issued with laid-in b/w price list for Jan 1893. Products included "Carbutt's Columbian Plates." ☺ (WM)

776.3 Cardwell Machine Co. *Little giant : Hydraulic Cotton Press : self packer.* Richmond: n.p., n.d.

24x15½. 1 *l.* White glossy sheet, black print, illus of press. Caption title. Printed vertically along right margin: "Takes the premium wherever exhibited." No WCE content; from intact collection. (WM)

776.4 ...*The Carriage Monthly Daily : Chicago, 1893.* Philadelphia: Ware Brothers publishers, [1893]. P→

25x20½, 94 p. White stiff wraps, gilt print; design in green, blue and red. C.t. At head of title: "Columbian Edition." Illus of Trans Bldg entrance. WCE text and illus especially of the Trans Bldg where carriages were displayed. A special WCE ad with no vol number? See #1260.2. ☺. (S)

777.1 Casino Cafe. *Wines : Casino Cafe, World's Fair : August 16, 1893.* [Chicago: A.L. Swift & co.], 1893.

8x12. (4) p. Folded blue stiff card, maroon and dark blue print with illus of casino at WCE. "California wines" listed pp (2)-(3), e.g., "Zinfandel $.85/quart $.50/pint." ☺ (WM) P↘

777.2 Casino Restaurant. *Dinner Bill of Fare : Saturday, September 16, 1893.* [Chicago]: A.L. Swift & co., 1893?

26½x17. (2) p. Single buff sheet printed both sides in black ink. At upper left, "Columbia Casino Restaurant" with b/w vignette litho of casino at the south end of the peristyle; Wm. Werner, Mgr. Entrees averaged 50¢, but soup, salad, vegetable, and dessert were extra. Draught Budweiser was 10¢. "Wine list" on reverse. ☺ (GLD) $25 - 45

777.3 The Castree-Mallery Co. *The Star No. 109 Land roller.* [Flint, MI]: n.p., n.d.

14½x8½. (8) panel from accordion folded sheet. C.t. Illus ad for several rollers on tan backgrounds. Red overprint: "Now Manufactured Exclusively by The Lansing Wheelbarrow co., Lansing, Michigan." No mention of the WCE; from an intact WCE scrapbook. ☺ (S)

778.1 *Catalogue of more than one thousand of oriental rugs and carpets from the looms of Turkey, Persia and India.* Providence, RI: B.H. Gladding Co., [1894?]

24x__. 24 p, 4 *l* plates. Illus and ports. "The official exhibits for the Ottoman Empire and Persia at the World's Columbian Exposition..." Auction catalog "by order of H.H. Topakyan, Commissioner for Persia." (HML)

779. *Catalogue of Singer Sewing Machines for family use*: (csuf,E,HML,ICRL,VAM,WM)

▸Correction: Illus shown in original bibliography is for Singer pamphlet #1005.12.

780.1 Cately & Ettling [Co.]. *Cately's Carriage Attachments*. Cortland, NY: n.p., n.d.

    23x14. (4) p. Folded white sheet, black print and five illus of carriage parts. C.t. At bottom: "Exhibited at World's Fair, Transportation Building, Chicago, Ill." (WM)

780.2 Cately & Ettling [Co.]. *Cately's Carriage Attachments. Cately's buggy prop spring*. [Cortland, NY: Cately & Ettling], n.d.

    23½x14½. (4) p. Folded sheet, black print and three figures of buggy springs. C.t. At bottom: "Medal Awarded on Our Exhibit at the World's Fair, Chicago." ☺ . (Stfd -bound WCE Trans Dept Collection)

781.   Catholic Educational Exhibit. *Catalogue* (1894): (Col,CUA,NDU)
    ---- Also found: Full leather hc with beveled edges, gilt print, gilt text edges.

782.   Catholic Educational Exhibit. *Catalogue* (1893): (CUA,NDU,UTA)
    ---- Also found: Presentation copy stamped on cover: "Right Rev. J.L. Spalding, D.D. : Bishop of Peoria." Prussian blue leather hc with gilt print and design, gilt edges.

782.1 Catholic Educational Exhibit. *...Catalogue of Albums sent by Pupils of the Sisters of Notre Dame, in Academies and Parochial Schools*. N.p.: Archdiocese of Boston, n.d.

    17½x13½. 88 p. Full leather beveled hc with gilt print, gilt edges. No frontis. At head of title: "A.M.D.G. : Catholic Educational Exhibit. World's Fair, Chicago, 1893." Upper right corner of cover: "Ad majorem dei gloriam." ☺ . (CUA)

782.2 Catholic Educational Exhibit. *Catalogue of the Catholic educational exhibit of the archdiocese of Chicago at the World's Columbian exposition 1893*. Chicago: C.M. Staiger, printer, n.d.

    22x15. 90 p. Illus, plates. Black leather hc with gilt print. ☺ . (CUA,ICRL)

782.3 Catholic Educational Exhibit. *Catholic educational exhibit at the World's Columbian Exposition,...* Chicago: The Catholic Home, Print, 1890.

    __x__. 12 p. Report submitted by the committee appointed Oct 8, 1890, by the committee of the American archbishops. Members: E.A. Higgins, S.J., M.F. Egan, W.J. Onahan. (CUA-Misc. Scho. 34:7)

783.   Catholic Educational Exhibit. *The Catholic educational exhibit at the World's*: (CUA,ISU,MCHx,NDU,PSU,S)
784.   Catholic Educational Exhibit. *Circular of information and directions*: (NDU)

784.1 Catholic Educational Exhibit. Eaton, John. *The Catholic Educational Exhibit at the Columbian Exposition*. Rpt. from *The American Catholic Quarterly Review*. Jan. 1895. Philadelphia: Charles A. Hardy, n.d.

    23½x15. 16 p. Gray wraps. C.t. = caption title. Eaton was ex-commissioner of the US Bureau of Education, see #265. ☺ . (CUA)

785.   Catholic Educational Exhibit. *Final report. Catholic Educational Exhibit : World's Columbian Exposition, Chicago, 1893. By Brother Maurelian F.S.C., Secretary and Manager. To Right Reverend J.L. Spalding, D.D., Bishop of Peoria and President Catholic Educational Exhibit, World's Fair, 1893*. N.p.: n.p., n.d.
    ▸Added: Full title. (GLD) $40 - 80
    ---- Also found: Full leather hc with gilt print. C.t.: "Final report. Catholic educational exhibit : Chicago, 1893." ☺ . (CUA)

787.   Catlin. *Switzerland The St. Gothard Railway*: (ref)
    ▸Add: 38 p, 2 l. Illus of offices at Lucerne. White wraps with colorful litho, brown and red print. Color maps tipped-in at front and back covers.

787.1 *...Caw's Ink & Pen Co*. New York: n.p., n.d.

    14x7½. (12) panels. Buff thin strip unfolds to 14x47, black print. C.t. Ads for Caw's "Dashaway" and stylographic pens, etc. Price list. Chicago agent info at bottom of cover. No WCE content; from an intact collection. ☺ (WM)

787.2 Celadon Terra Cotta Co., Limited. *...Artistic Roofing Tiles.* Alfred Center, NY: n.p., n.d.

21½x16½. (4) p. Folded buff coated sheet, print and illus in brown ink. C.t. Bottom p (1): "Columbian Exposition, Liberal Arts Building, Section I., Col. H." Illus of their exhibit on back. At head of title are co name and address. ☺ (WM)

787.3 Central Vermont Railroad. *Summer Homes among the Green Hills of Vermont, and along the shores of Lake Champlain.* St. Albans, VT: The St. Albans Messenger Co. Job Print [for The passenger department : Central Vermont Railroad], 1893.

22x14½. 151 p, maps. Pale yellow wraps; red, brown, and white print; illus of pastoral scene. C.t. = t.p. No mention of WCE; from intact collection. ☺ . (LBA)

787.4 Century Co. *The century illustrated monthly magazine.* New York: The Century co. [The deVinne press], ᶜ1893 by The Century Co. **P➜**

12x8½. (12) p+ text inside front and back wraps. Tan wraps, brown print, string-tied. C.t. Illus of Lundborg's perfume exhibit bldg on back wrap. Mentions upcoming article on Olmsted and his WF landscapes; Notes Mark Twain serials to appear in *Century*. Ad. ☺ (GLD) $15 - 30

787.5 Century Co. *The St. Nicholas Autograph Book : what some well-known people say of the bound volumes of St. Nicholas for 1892 : written in November and December, 1892.* New York?: The Century Co.?, n.d.

8½x15. 16 p includes self wraps, black print, cover illus of St. Nicholas book. One testimonial per page, e.g., Oliver Wendell Holmes. No WCE content; from an intact collection. (WM)

787.6 Century Co. *...St. Nicholas : For Young Folks : conducted by Mary Mapes Dodge.* New York: The Century Co., ᶜ1893 by The Century Co.

12x8½. 12 p+ text inside front and back wraps. Tan wraps, brown print, string-tied. C.t. The only WCE content is illus of Lundborg's perfume exhibit bldg on back wrap. Companion ad to #787.4 (identical back covers). No mention of WCE; from intact collection. ☺ (GLD) $15 - 30

787.7 Champion Wagon Co. *...The Champion Wagon is the Horse's Friend.* Owego, NY: n.p., n.d.

14½x8½. (8) p. Folded white sheet, blue print. C.t. At head of title: "'A Merciful Man is Merciful to his Beast.'" Illus of wagons and parts, prices on back. No WCE; from intact 1893 scrapbook. ☺ (S)

787.8 Chase, A.B., Brothers Pianos. *The Alla Unisono or Octavo Pedal.* [Chicago: J.C. Winship & Co. Printers], n.d.

12½x10. (4) p. Folded cream glossy sheet, purple and red print. C.t. WCE location on back. ☺ (WM)

787.9 Chase, A.B., Brothers Pianos. *Chase Bros. Pianos. Columbian Souvenir Catalogue.* Muskegon, MI: Chase Bros. pianos (Novelty Card & Adv'g Co., Chicago), [1893].

13½x9. Shocking pink wraps, black print and design. Tipped-in accordion folded strip, 13x103½, folded to make 13 panels per side. One side of strip has illus and testimonials for pianos; the other side has 13 WCE views ᶜ1892 by A. Zeese. C.t. Illus inside front wrap captioned: "Chase Bros. Exhibit at World's Fair." Illus of their Muskegon factory on back. Testimonials to July 1893. ☺ (GLD,IHi) $23 - 45

787.10 Chase, A.B., [Brothers Pianos]. *...Practical Points for Piano Purchasers. Improves by Age and Use.* N.p.: n.p., n.d.

8x14½. (16) p. Gray-blue wraps, black print. C.t. At head of title: "No. 2." Piano ad. No mention of WCE; intact collection. (WM)

787.11 Chase & Sanborn. *Photographs of all the government and state buildings at the World's fair, Chicago, consisting of fifty different views, will be sent to any applicant on receipt of twelve cents in stamps.* Boston: Chase & Sanborn, n.d.

10 cm diameter. 50 individual paper discs each with a b/w WF view.
Title from back of discs. Front title: "Chase & Sanborn's : Served
Exclusively at the World's Fair." ☺(GLD,E,L)   P➜   Each: $8 - 18

787.12 Chase & Sanborn. *Chase & Sanborn's "Seal brand" coffee : served
exclusively at the World's fair.* N.p.: Chase & Sanborn (Forbes Co.), n.d.

7½x11½. (4) p. Folded card die-cut in shape of coffee cup.
Chromoliths of ornate coffee cups throughout, women with coffee and
tea cups. Ad. ☺(GLD,E)   P↘ $22 - 42

787.13 *The Chatauqua : Corner of Forty-eighth Street and St. Lawrence Ave. :
Chicago.* [Chicago: The W.J. Hayne co., printers and engravers], n.d.

25½x18. (4) p. Folded white matte sheet, teal cover illus of hotel.
Red and teal print throughout. C.t. Back cover map shows location.
Rates and room diagrams. (S)

787.14 *Chattanooga Plow Co.'s : Plow Catalogue : manufacturers of Chilled
Plows, Plow Repairs...* [Chattanooga, TN: Lake-Kuster publishing co.,
print], n.d.

22½x15. 16 p. Gray wraps, blue print and design showing their plow
trade mark. Illus of factory on back. Illus catalog of farm products.
No mention of WCE; from intact WCE collection. ☺(WM)

787.15 Cheesman, James. *The Columbian dairy cattle tests : at the : World's Fair, Chicago, 1893.* Southborough,
MA: n.p., 1894.

23x15. 1 *l* (t.p.), (2), (5)-32 p. Wraps. Rpt from *Journal of the British Dairy Farmers' Association.*
Introd is copy of letter from the British Assn, to James Cheesman of Southborough, MA, dated Sept 28,
1893, requesting review of the American dairy tests and an explanation of the divergence in results found
in American and England. [See #277.c. and e. for related items.] ☺.(CU,NAL,UMA)

787.16 Chesapeake & Ohio Railroad. *Virginia in black and white.* Washington, DC: Chesapeake & Ohio R'y
(The Matthews-Northrup co. Complete Art Printing Works, Buffalo, NY), [°1893 by H.W. Fuller].

16½x14. 64 p+ color route map tipped-in at back cover. White stiff wraps, red and black print and
design. Frontis illus of Alleghenies. Gilt illus on back. "World's fair special" on pp 62-63. ☺(S)

787.17 Chicago & Alton Railroad. *World's fair folder : Chicago & Alton R.R. Perfect passenger service to the
World's fair and all points east and north via Chicago.* Chicago: Rand, McNally & Co., 1893.

21x11. Folded sheet unfolds to 42x90. Illus, maps. Printed in red and black on both sides. C.t.
Informational brochure and schedule. (csuf)

787.18 Chicago Athletic Association. *The World's fair championships : under the auspices of the : amateur athletic
union : of the : United States : given by the Chicago Athletic Association : Saturday, September 16, 1893 :
south side ball grounds : Chicago.* ___: ___, 189_.

22x28. 1 *l* ad, 24 p, 1 *l* ad. C.t. (ref,S) $50

787.19 Chicago, Burlington, and Quincy Railroad. *Ocean to
Ocean : San Francisco, Chicago, New York.* San
Francisco, CA: The Burlington Route, n.d.

11x17. 24 p. Illus, map. Gray wraps, red and dark
gray print, Poole Bros illus of oncoming train. C.t.
On cover: "Compliments of T.D. McKay. Pacific
Coast : Passenger Agent : Burlington Route." Illus
include sketches of the WCE bldgs. ☺.(IHi)   P➜

787.20 Chicago Clothes Dryer Works. *The Chicago Combined Clothes Dryer and Laundry Stove for residence flats etc.* Chicago: E.G. Christoph Lith Co, n.d.

> 15x10. (4) p. Folded yellow-tan card. Decorative cover, text and illus in black. C.t. References on back include Potter Palmer and Geo. Pullman. No WCE content; from intact collection. (WM)

788. *The Chicago Record*: (GLD,HU,S,UIC,WM,Yale) P➔ $25 - 55
---- Also found: Bright blue hc, bold gilt print, gilt spine print, red dyed edges.

789. The Chicago Daily News. *The Daily News Almanac*: (MSL)

789.1 Chicago, Milwaukee & St. Paul Railway. *For the Foreign Journalists.... A brief description of the Chicago, Milwaukee &...1893.* [Chicago: Keogh & Schroeder co. printers, 1893.]

> 19½x10½. 17 p. Paged on rectos including inside back wrap; paged A-P on versos; i.e., 33 pp total. Pink wraps, black print and red co logo. C.t. Printed "in English, German, Scandinavian, French." "One effect of the World's Columbian exposition" by Luis Jackson on p 16. Describes locals served by the RR. Last dated June 30, 1893. ☺ (GLD) $25 - 55

790. Chicago, Milwaukee. *How to See the World's*: (UMD)
791. *Chicago of To-day*: (IHi,ref,S,VT) P➔ $250

791.1 Chicago Police Department. *Department police. City of Chicago : 1893.* N.p.: n.p., n.d.

> 13½x8. 16 p. Beige wraps, black print and Chicago city seal. C.t. Caption title: "List of hotels in the World's Columbian Exposition district." Alphabetical hotel list with addresses. [The police helped travelers find lodging.] ☺. (IHi) P➘

791.2 *The Chicago Rawhide Manufacturing Co. manufacturers of rawhide belting lace leather.* Chicago: [Chicago Rawhide Mfg. Co. (Skeen Baker & Co., Printers and Publishers)], n.d.

> 16x9. 32 p. Deep peach wraps, black print. Litho of the plant (front) and 1883 award medal (back). Calendars for 1893 and 1894 printed inside covers. Ad. Testimonials and price list. No mention of WCE; from an intact WCE collection. (WM)

791.3 Chicago, Rock Island & Pacific Railway. *The World's fair line : The great Rock Island : Route : June 1893.* Chicago: Rand, McNally & co., printers, n.d.

> 23x10. Sheet unfolds to 60x45½. Map route in blue and red ink. Chicago map inside shows location of the WF and electric lines from Englewood to the gates overlaid in red. ☺ (WM)

791.4 Chocolat-Menier. *Souvenir : Chocolat-Menier.* Chicago: The Winters art litho co., n.d.

> 14½x20. (16) p. Light green (or bright yellow) wraps, blue print. Brown text print. C.t. Chromolith of their WCE pavilion on p (1); pavilion contractors listed on next page. Also chromoliths at centerfold and on p (16) of factory in Moisiel, France. ☺. (E,WM)

792.1 *Church's Tours to the World's Fair.* [Boston: W.H. Church (Livermore & Knight Co., Providence, RI), 1893].

> 14x12. 32 p. Sepia wraps, black print, string-tied. Centerfold of Allen Compartment Hotel Car for train excursions. Boston to Chicago round trip advertised at $85. ☺(GLD,E,WM) $20 - 42

792.2 Civet, Crouet, Gautier & Cie. *Notice sur les Pierres dont les Echantillons sont déposés.* N.p.: n.p., n.d.

> 26x18. 6 p. Ultramarine wraps, black print, string-tied. Published version of a handwritten text. Trans: Account of the sample stones on exhibit. Their quarried rock and granites with prices per cubic meter. No mention of WCE; from an intact WCE collection. ☺(WM)

792.3 Clark, Francis E. *World Wide Endeavor : the story of the Young People's Society of Christian Endeavor : from the beginning and in all lands...* Philadelphia: Gillespie, Metzgar & Kelley, 1895 [ᶜ1895].

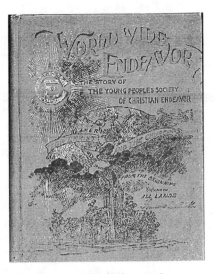

26½x20½. 1 *l* frontis, 644 p. Turquoise cloth hc with gilt, black, and silver design and print. In Portland, Maine, Clark founded Christian Endeavor in 1873. Description and illus of their WCE exhibit on pp 472-76. See #1127 for hotel description. ☺(GLD)   P➔ $16 - 35

794.   Clemens. *The Depew story book*:
    ▸Add: Green cloth hc with black print. Pulp paper.

794.1 Cleveland Baking Powder Co. *Cleveland's Superior Receipts.* New York: Cleveland Baking Powder Co., n.d.

17x11½. 76 p+ printing inside covers. White glossy wraps with blue, black, and red print and a chromolith of a can of their powder. On p 3: "Cleveland's was the baking powder selected for use in the Model Kitchen of the Woman's Building at the World's Fair." Not listed as a WCE exhibitor in the *Official Directory*, #1207. Recipes by Sarah T. Rorer, M. Harland, and Ms. Parloa. Ad. ☺(GLD) $16 - 35

794.2 Clipper Chilled Plow Co. *Strait's Lever Spring Tooth Harrow.* Elmira, NY: n.p., n.d.

14½x9½. (6) panel tri-fold buff sheet unfolds to 14½x26½, chocolate and black print. Two illus of harrows on outside panels. Caption title. No WCE content; from intact collection. ☺(WM)

794.3 Clipper Chilled Plow Co. *Strait's Patent Reversible Sulky Plow.* Elmira, NY: n.p., n.d.

29x23½. (1) p. Sheet with black print. Plow illus. Testimonials dated 1888–91. Caption title. No WCE content; from an intact collection. (WM)

794.4 Clipper Chilled Plow Co. *Strait's Self-Dump Horse Hay Rake.* Elmira, NY: n.p., n.d.

14x9. Tri-fold buff sheet, chocolate and black print, unfolds to 14x26 making (6) panels. Two illus of hay rakes on outside panels. Caption title. No WCE content; from intact collection. ☺(WM)

794.5 Colbert, Sarah M. and E. *Washington, : Shakespeare : and St. George.* Chicago: Western British American, 1893.

20x14. 1 *l* (t.p.), (3)-53 p. Blue-black cloth hc, gilt print. Written for the WCE as stated on p (3). Explains George Washington's British ancestry. On t.p.: "Respectfully dedicated to the St. George Society of this [Chicago] City." ☺ . (SML)

795.   *Columbian bazaar given under the auspices of the Friday*: (S)

795.1 Columbian Bazaar. *Mrs. Potter Palmer and The Friday Club invite you to attend The Columbian Bazaar, given for the benefit of The Children's Home of the World's Fair, on the afternoons and evenings of December seventh and eighth. 100 Lake Shore Drive.* N.p.: n.p., n.d.

16½x13. (4) p. Fold card, black print. Invitation. See #795. ☺(IHi)

795.2 *Columbian Compositions : Three Americas.* N.p.: n.p., n.d.   P➔

21x17. Unpaged blue-lined composition book. Dark tan embossed stiff wraps, cloth spine. Shield design with leaf border; illus of Machinery Hall inside shield printed in black and khaki. ☺ . (S)

796.   *Columbian Day, October 21, 1892*: ☺(GLD,WM) $22 - 45
    ▸Add alternate authors and info. National Educational Association. Executive Committee. (8) p. Newspaper format, black print with illus of Columbus Landing. Illus of Columbus scenes, ads, national

and Boston programs for that day. Five committee members listed. Note change in date from original plans, see #942.5. Participants received a silk ribbon; see the illus. **P→**
---- Also found: Issued by city of Providence, RI. (GLD)

796.1 Columbian Endeavor Association. *...The Hotel Endeavor.* Chicago: n.p., n.d.

> 20x12½. (2) p. Single pale yellow sheet, black print both sides. C.t. Illus of hotel. Hotel open to all "Christian Endeavorers and their friends." Reservation payments due by Dec 1, 1892. For more about Christian Endeavor, see #792.3, #1127, and #1308.1. ☺ (S)

797. *Columbian exhibit New York Condensed Milk:* (Col)

798. *The Columbian Exposition and World's fair illustrated:* (GLD,CUA,EPL,FLP,LU,S,Smth,UH)
▶Add copyright: [ᶜ1893 by M. McIntyre]. Add printer: [Avil Printing Co., Phila.]
---- Also found: Brown cloth hc, gilt print and edges.

799. *Columbian exposition Dedication Ceremonies memorial:* (ICRL,MSI,UIC,UTA)

799.1 Columbian Exposition Excursion Co. *...Hotel Elmore.* Chicago: n.p., n.d.

> 30x20½. Buff sheet printed in black one side, Columbus port upper left. At head of title: co name and info. Hotel Elmore was the only "cottage hotel," each a 2-story house accommodating 24 guests. ☺ (WM)

800. Columbian Exposition International. *Columbian Exposition International Exhibit and:* (KNM)

801.1 *...The Columbian Fair excursion company. Of Chicago, Ill. : Room 4 Mallers Building...* Chicago: n.p., n.d.

> 16½x9. (8) panels unfold to 16½x36. Tan pulp paper, black print and two panel illus of a hotel they used. C.t. At head of title: "Boston rate, $48.00." Ad. ☺ (GLD) $18 - 38

801.2 *The Columbian Fair Excursion Company, of Chicago, Ill. Room 806, Royal Insurance Building.* Chicago: n.p., n.d.

> 13½x8. 9, (1) p (i.e., 10 panels). Strip unfolds to 13½x40. Pink pulp paper, black print. Illus of a Chicago hotel that was used by the company covers three panels. ☺ (S)

803. *Columbian Intramural Railway the First and only:* (E,KS,S,WM)
▶Add annotation: Found printed with different advertisers. Found with and without red overprint across inside panels: "good only up-stairs between 2 and 6 p.m." [See also Intramural RR in index.]

803.1 *Columbian Intramural Railway Co. : The first and only Electric Elevated...* Chicago: Regan Printing House, n.d.

> 26x14. (2) p. Single sheet, black print. Back ad: "Good for 10 Cts" at French Bakery. [See also Intramural RR in index.] ☺ . (WM)

804. *The Columbian jubilee : Or Four Centuries of Catholicity in America : being a Historical and Biographical Retrospect from the Landing of Christopher Columbus to the Chicago Catholic Congress of 1893. ...Illustrated : With Colored Frontispieces and Many Rare and Beautiful Engravings from Paintings by Gregori and others,...* 2 vol. Chicago: J.S. Hyland & co. [(La Monte, O'Donnell & co., printers and binders), ᶜ1892 by J.S. Hyland & co.].

> 25x18½. Vol I: 1 *l* Columbus landing frontis, 4 *l*, (vii)-xix, (1) p, 1 *l* Columbus port, (9)-500. Vol II: xi, (1), 5ll p. Half leather over rust cloth boards; gilt print, Columbus landing design, and edges. ☺ . (GLD,CUA)
> ---- Also found: Dark blue cloth hc, gilt print and round vignettes of Columbus landing linked to port of Catholic priest. (S)   **P→**

804.1 *Columbian Liberty Bell Committee. Circular Letter, No. 13.* N.p.: n.p., 1893?

> __x__. __ p. Dated Nov 22, 1893. See #828 for another Columbian Liberty Bell. (WM)

804.2 Columbian Liberty Bell Committee. Desha, Mary. "To the Daughters of the American Revolution:" N.d. Letter. Washington, DC.

23½x14½. (4) p. Folded buff sheet, black print. Desha, founder of the DAR, describes the plan to have the bell cast on Apr 30, [1893] and gives the intended travels of the Columbian (New) Liberty Bell during the WCE up through the Paris Expo of 1900; she requests money donations and metals for the casting, including pennies. ☺. (DAR,HU)

☞ The new Columbian bell is lost. One theory is that it was loaned to Russia during WW II and was melted down to make bullets. See #1365.3.

804.3 Columbian Liberty Bell Committee. Desha, Mary. "To the Sons of the American Revolution:" 16 May 1893. Letter. Washington, DC.

23½x14½. (4) p. Folded buff sheet, black print. Same info as #804.2, updated. The bell cost $6,500. ☺. (DAR)

804.4 Columbian Liberty Bell Committee. McGee, Howard Hawthorne. *The new liberty bell.* N.p.: n.p., 1893?

__x__. __ p. (HU)

804.5 Columbian Liberty Bell Committee. *Members of the Columbian Liberty Bell Committee.* N.p.: n.p., n.d.

24x15. (4) p. Folded sheet, black print. Members list with no other text. Members included Desha and Mickley of DAR; H. Butterworth, J. Winfield Scott, Frances E. Willard, and John H. Barrows. ☺ (WM)

804.6 Columbian Liberty Bell Committee. Stocking, Patty Miller. "To the Daughters of the American Revolution:" N.d. Letter.

23½x14½. (2) p. Buff sheet, black print. Lists express companies that would deliver parcels of metal to be smelted into the Columbian Bell free of charge to the DAR. (HU)

804.7 Columbian Liberty Bell Committee. Wagner, Madge Morris. *Liberty's bell.* N.p.: n.p., n.d.

__x__. __ p. See #804.4. (HU)

806.1 *Columbian Souvenir : 1492 1892.* N.p.: n.p., n.d.

27x22x8½ thick. Album. 1 *l* (t.p.), 16 *l.* T.p. in gray-green and gold shows Columbus standing atop two globes with background bird's-eye view of the WCE. Engraved aluminum front cover with bass-relief celluloid insert of Columbus landing; insert border made from gold-plated scrolled metal rope. Spine and back cover in olive plush velvet. All edges silver and blind-stamped in a floral pattern. Clasp. A period picture album for family portraits. Every other leaf (8 total) is decorated with 2 lithos each of scenes and bldgs from the WCE. See #713.2 for another photo album. ☺ (GLD) $100 - 200

807.   *Columbian souvenir institute Note Book*:
---- Also found: 21½x13½. (8), 64 (ledger sheets with printed headers), (8) p. Tan wraps, blue print and photo illus. Twelve of the unnumbered pages have illus of the WCE. (GLD)   P➔ $25 - 55

807.1 *Columbian visitors' association.* Chicago: n.p., n.d.

9x15½. (16) p+ laid-in "addenda." Light gray wraps, black print. Illus of their "South Shore" hotel on back. Gives rates, etc, for accommodations. "[O]rganized for Christian people and their friends under Christian management." ☺ (E)

807.2 ...*Columbian Visitors' Association "The South Shore" : Corner Bond Avenue and Seventy-Third Street. Will open April 15, 1893.* Chicago: n.p., n.d.

24½x16. (4) p. Folded sheet, blue-green print and illus. Caption title with bird's-eye illus of hotel 7 blocks south of Jackson Park, "away from the confusion of the crowded Exposition." Co info at head of title. Lists rules and conditions and payments. Reservation form on back. (WM)

807.3 *Columbian Visitors' Association : owners of : Hotel "South Shore."* Chicago: n.p., n.d.

26½x35½. Sheet printed one side in burgundy; three green illus include one photo-illus of the WCE taken from the "South Shore." ☺ (WM)

808. *The Columbian World's Fair Atlas*: (B,E,FM,IStU,KCPL,PSU,UMD,UMN)
---- Also listed: Northampton, MA: C.P. Pettis, 1893?
---- Also listed: Mackinaw, IL: Smith Bro., 1893?
---- Also found: Sioux Falls, SD: Markham & Densmore for <u>The Fair</u>, n.d. The Fair was a dept store.
---- Also found: Published for McColm dry goods co., Muscatine, IA. 2 *l*, 1 *l* (i.e., p 9), 11-194. Pp 15-79 paged rectos only (blank versos included in paging); pp 81-194 maps and text both sides of pages.

810.1 *The Columbus Buggy Co. of today : supplying the World with the Finest Vehicles.* [Columbus, OH: Columbus Buggy Co.] (The Henderson-Achert-Krebs Lith. Co., Cin.), n.d.

15½x8½. (4) p. Folded card stock. Chromolith front and back wraps. Front: factory. Back: "Columbus first sighting the New World 1492." Inside there are world and US maps. The US map shows routes to "the World's Fair at Chicago." C.t. Beautiful ad. ☺ (GLD) $22 - 50

810.2 *The Columbus Caravels : and : The Norse Viking In America, A.D. 1893 : illustrated.* New York: E.H. Hart, n.d.

15½x24. 24 p. Pale blue wraps, blue-black print and illus of Santa Maria and WCE Viking ship. Blue-black text print and photo-illus by Hart. Describes the Viking ship, Capt. Magnus Andersen, and the trip from Norway to NY harbor and on to the WCE. ☺ (GLD) $25 - 55

810.3 *The Columbus Letters. Souvenir of the monastery of La Rabida, World's Fair Grounds, Chicago.* New York: Edward Brandus & co., ᶜ1893.   **P➜**

25½x16½. (10) p includes inside of both wraps. Tan high rag content paper, rough-cut edges, self-wraps, brown text and cover print, yellow string-tied. C.t. Rpt of 3 Columbus letters, their translations, and explanatory text. Issued with manila mailer envelope which has the return address: "Souvenir La Rabida. World's Columbian Exposition Chicago, 1893." ☺ (GLD) $26 - 55

811. *Columbus Memorial 1492 400 years*: (HU,UCB,UCI,UMC)

811.1 *The Columbus shield. Sold for the benefit of the teachers' home fund. Chicago, 1893.* N.p.: n.p., n.d.

17x14½. White sheet, blue print and border. Text starts: "This shield is the exact reproduction of the coat-arms bestowed on Columbus..." To accompany exhibit? ☺ (WM)

812. Colville. *World's fair text book of Mental Therapeutics*: (E,HML,S)
---- First ed: 1 *l* frontis, 139 p, xi appendix + ads at end. Frontis port of Colville. (S)
---- Second ed, 1893: 3 *l*, 3-139, 1 p, iv-xi (ads), (1) p. Frontis port of Colville. Red textured stiff wraps, gilt print. "Introduction" on p 3 discusses intent of book for the WCE.
---- Fifth ed. (HML)

812.1 Commercial Cable Co. *Concise history of the atlantic cable and the commercial cable company.* 2d ed. N.p.: [The Commercial Cable Company], 1893?   **P➜**

14x21. 32 p. White wraps, black print and illus of their WCE exhibit and an underwater scene. C.t.: "World's Columbian Exposition : The Commercial Cable System : in operation at Chicago." Also on cover: "compliments of the cable company." ☺ . (CCA,IHi,LBA,S,WM)

☞ The Commercial Cable Company exhibit was in the Electrical Building. Visitors could send and receive a

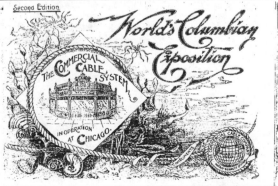

"souvenir cablegram at the World's Columbian Exposition." IHi has a cable received on "Chicago Day, Oct 9th 93."

812.2 Commissioners of Lincoln Park. Bryan, I.J., comp. *Report of the commissioners and a history of Lincoln park*. Chicago: Published by the commissioners [printed by R.R. Donnelley and sons co. at the Lakeside Press], 1899 [^c1899 By The Commissioners of Lincoln Park].

23½x31. 6 *l*, (13)-188, (1) p. Frontis collage of Lincoln monument in the Park. Dark green cloth hc, bold gilt print: "LINCOLN PARK : 1899." States the Commissioners bought WCE launches for the ponds in the park. Several illus show the re-erected Ferris wheel at its North Chicago location. [The Chicago Historical Society is located at the southern end of Lincoln Park.] (ref) $80 - 170

812.3 *Compañia general de tabacos de filipinas...Price current of the "Flor de la isabela" factory, at Manila*. Barcelona, Sp.: Louis Weiss & Co., Printers, New York, n.d.

61½x22½. Buff tracing paper. Price list for cigars, tobacco, cigarettes. Bold at bottom: Fabien & Mendy, General Agents. No WCE content; from intact collection. (WM)

812.4 Concord & Montreal Railroad. *...Lakes, Ponds and Streams : On the C. & M.* Concord, NH [and] Boston: Passenger Department Concord & Montreal Railroad, 1892.

20½x14. 64 p, maps. Pale yellow wraps, red and black print, lake scene illus. C.t. = t.p. At head of title: "Concord & Montreal railroad. Merrimack Valley Route." From intact WCE collection. ☺ . (LBA)

812.5 Continental Fire Insurance Co. Moore, F.C. *Economical fire-resisting construction. A Treatise on Building*. Rev. ed. New York: n.p., 1890, 1892.

21x14. 37, (29) p. Dark tan wraps, black print underlined boldly in red. C.t. = t.p. The (29) p are ads on versos with color plates of construction methods on rectos. At top of cover: "Price, 25 cents." Moore was Continental's president. Gives building tips that could have altered the outcome of the 1871 Chicago fire. No WCE content; from an intact collection. (WM)

812.6 Cook, C. Ward, Manager. Cook's World Fair Trips. *...Cook's Special Teachers' Tour, With Friends, to the World's Fair*. Boston: n.p., n.d.

28x21½. 1 *l*. Buff sheet, chocolate print. At head of title: "$60! $60!" Trip from Boston to WF described. Illus of young girl with cat in upper left. Different company from Thos. Cook & Son. ☺ (WM)

812.7 [Cook, C. Ward, Manager]. Cook's World Fair Trips. *What you want to know at a glance. Come with me to the World's fair at Chicago,...* Boston: n.p., n.d.

16x9. (4) p. Folded buff sheet, black print. Cover illus of young girl with cat on shoulder. Pp (2)-(3) description of $75 for 10-day and $50 for 10-day trips. On back: "Our routes." (WM)

812.8 Cook, E.C., & Brothers. *Camp Lincoln*. Chicago: n.p., n.d.

14x7½. Buff card, black print. Ad for WF tent encampment on the lake shore 600 ft south of WCE at "South Shore station" on the Illinois Central South Chicago suburban train. Six or eight beds per tent, 50¢ per day and 25¢ per meal. (WM)

812.9 Cook Railway Development Co. *...Cook Elevated Electric Railway*. Chicago: W.G. Russell & Co., n.d.

24x16. (4) p. Folded buff sheet, blue-black print and illus. At head of title: "Time and Distance Annihilated : World's Fair Souvenir." Ad for passenger car system with speeds to 200 mph. "Working model one-twelfth the scale, near the Canadian Pacific exhibit in the Transportation Building." ☺ (WM)

812.10 Cook, Tho[ma]s, & Son. *Cook's Tours : to the World's Columbian exposition : Chicago, 1893 : For Personally Conducted & Independent Travelers*. Boston: n.p., n.d.

22x9½. (6) p. Tri-fold white sheet opens to 28x22, navy print and illus throughout. Inside caption title: "The World's Columbian Exposition." Trips started Apr 26, 1893, from Boston. (WM)

813.   Cook, Thomas. *The World's Fair at Chicago*: (bgsu,CCA,FLP,Stfd,WM)

814.   Cook, Thomas. *Programme of Cook's Tours to the World's Columbian Exposition*: (GLD,UMD) $22 - 55
▸Additional info: "Son," not "Sons." Self-wraps and print inside each cover, dark blue print. Sepia cover illus of the Admin Bldg. C.t.: "Cook's tours to the World's Columbian Exposition : Chicago : 1893." Round-trip cost from Boston for a week at the Fair was $120 with hotel, meals, and admissions.

814.1 Cook, William. *Cook's perfect folding carriage.* New York: William Cook, patentee, n.d.

28x17½. 1 *l.* Single sheet, black print. Caption title. Illus of baby carriage erected for use and folded for carrying and storage. ☺. (Stfd-bound WCE Trans Dept Collection)

814.2 Cooksey & Co. *Retail stores : Cooksey & Co. Hat manufacturers.* London: John Levy, litho, n.d.

12x12. (6) p. Teal and peach tri-fold card, black print and illus of their London shop; the two folding panels are half width so when folded, they meet in the middle of the card. Factory illus on back. Associated with E.M. Knox hats exhibit; see #1080. ☺. (E)   P➜

814.3 Cork-Faced Collar Co. *Illustrated Catalogue : Cork-Faced Collar Co. : Manufacturers of the Only Cork-Faced Horse Collar.* Lincoln, IL: Cork-Faced Collar Co. (Pantagraph ptg. & stat'y co., Bloomington, IL), n.d.

12x17. 96 p. Burgundy pebbled stiff wraps, gilt bold print. Bird's-eye of WCE, p 2; "Souvenir Book of the World's Fair," p 3. Text and illus in sepia/aqua/blue. . (Stfd-bound WCE Trans Dept Collection)   P➜

814.4 Cork-Faced Collar Co. *Lincoln Souvenir book : Cork-Faced Horse Collars,...* Lincoln, IL: Cork-Faced Collar Co. (Courier print), n.d.

14½x9. Peach card forming folded wraps; tipped-in (12) panel accordion foldout, six panels each side. C.t. Cover b/w port of A. Lincoln. Across two panels: "The highest medal of award ...World's fair, Chicago, 1893." . (Stfd-bound WCE Trans Dept Collection)

814.5 Corticelli Silk Co. *...Florence : home needle-work : Subjects: {scarfs belts garters} Crocheted. 1892.* [St. John, NB] Can.: Corticelli Silk Co., n.d.

20½x12. 8 p. Folded pulp sheet opens to 20½x48½, black and red print, black illus. C.t. At head of title: "Abridged edition"; text and illus are rpt from the 1892 magazine, *Florence Home Needle-work*, which shows Corticelli and Florence silk balls. Bottom of front cover and printed in red: "Silk Work can be seen in the Canadian section of the Manufacturers [sic] Building...on Columbia Avenue." Ad. ☺ (GLD,WM) $22 - 45

814.6 Cortland Howe Ventilating Stove Co. *The Only Successful Ventilating Stove. The famous Cortland Howe Ventilator.* Cortland, NY: n.p., n.d.

17x13. Sheet unfolds to 34x26. B/w print, turquoise background. Two Brownie cartoons (Palmer Cox) show room heat in color with and without the Ventilator. Black text print, cut-away illus of the stove, user list. Stove took in outside air through a pipe in its bottom. From intact WCE collection. ☺ (WM)

814.7 *The Cotgreave Library Indicator.* N.p.: n.p., n.d.

21x13. (4) p. Folded buff sheet. Indicator invented by a librarian, A. Cotgreave of West Ham, England, and manufactured by W. Morgan, Birmingham, England. For recording and showing books out on loan. No WCE content; from an intact collection. ☺ (WM)

814.8 Coudsi, G.A., and A. Andaloft [Co.]. *Oriental bazaar of G.A. Coudsi and A. Andaloft Manufacturers of oriental goods at Damascus and Constantinople...* N.p.: n.p., n.d.

11x13. (4) p. Folded bright pink stiff card. Photo-illus on cover is Mosque of Omar Il Khattab in Jerusalem. Caption title. On p (2): "Midway plaisance—Turkish bazaar No. 6 and 8." Back cover: "Exhibitors at the Manufactures Building, Turkish section." © (WM)

814.9 Courtauld, Samuel, & Co., Ltd. *Of Special Interest to : Buyers of Mourning Apparel.* London: n.p., n.d.

10½x8. (8) p. Black wraps with silver print and 2 small designs. Caption title. C.t.: "Columbian : Fair : 1893." Blue string-tied. No illus. Describes their black silk funeral products made in Britain. [They exhibited in the Manufactures Bldg, Group 100, Class 630.] © (ref) $50

814.10 Cox Duplex Printing Press Co. *The new cox duplex printing press.* [Battle Creek, MI]: n.p., 1893.

30½x23. (4) p. Folded white sheet. Large illus of press on front. Caption title. Testimonials from early 1893. Stamped in purple at top: "World's fair station Ills. : Machinery Hall P. No. 32." (WM)

814.11 Cox Duplex Printing Press Co. *New cox stop cylinder : Front Delivery Country Press.* Battle Creek, MI: n.p., n.d.

32x20. 1 *l.* White sheet, black print with large illus of press. Caption title. For printing newspapers of moderate circulation. Long testimonial from Lincoln County News, Waldoboro, ME. Stamped in purple at top: "World's fair station Ills. : Machinery Hall P. No. 32." (WM)

814.12 Crane Co. *...Crane company : Manufacturers. Exhibiting at the World's Columbian Exposition : In the Machinery and Transportation Buildings.* [Chicago]: n.p., n.d.

13x17½. 24 p. Beige wraps, black print with decorative border. At head of title: "Established 1855. Incorporated 1865." C.t.: "Crane Company." Text in red and black. Producers of iron pipes and fittings, valves, and railroad supplies. (WM)

814.13 Crane Co. *7000 articles are manufactured and carried in stock : by : Crane Company : Chicago : exhibiting at the World's Columbian exposition : machinery hall.* [Chicago]: n.p., n.d.

12½x17½. 32 p. Pale teal wraps, black print. Photo illus of Crane exhibit on back cover. C.t. Ad catalogue for their steam, water, and gas supplies. Exhibit at Section 26, Column O, Number 28. (WM)

814.14 Crane Elevator Co. *Crane Elevator Company : builders of : Passenger and Freight Elevators : operated by : hydraulic, steam and electric power.* Chicago: Crane Elevator Co., n.d.

13x17½. 22, (2) p. Buff stiff wraps, black print and illus of elevator. T.p. in red and black. C.t.: "Crane Elevator Co. : Chicago." Illus of WCE Admin Bldg with Crane elevator. "Our Exhibit" gives location: "Machinery Hall Annex, West End, Section 29, Column L, Numbers 51, 52, and 53." © . (S,Stfd)

814.15 Crane Elevator Co. *...Improved Duplex Power Pumps : for elevator service.* Chicago: Crane Elevator Co., 1890. **P→**

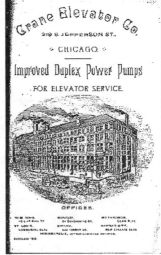

24x15. (4) p. Folded buff glossy sheet, black print and factory illus. C.t. At head of title: "Crane Elevator Co. : 219 S. Jefferson St., Chicago." © . (Stfd-bound WCE Trans Dept Collection)

815. Crane. *Columbia's Courtship: a picture history of the United:* (S) ▶Cover descriptions: Brown cloth hc, gilt and black print. Also found with white cloth hc, gilt and blue print.

815.1 Crane, W[illia]m M., & Co. *The Hall keramic kilns, with New and Improved Gas Burners, for firing decorated china, Glass, and Bisque,...* New York: [Press of Styles & Cash], n.d.

24x14½. 6 p. Green tri-fold sheet unfolds to 24x43, black print, kiln illus. Price list and testimonials, pp 2-6. No WCE content; intact collection. (WM) ---- Also found: 24x14½. Green *l* printed with p 1 above. Bottom: a suggestion to request full ad. (WM)

815.2 [Cranston and Curts, Agents.] *...New pronouncing parallel family bible.* N.p.: n.p., n.d.

17½x13½. (18) p includes self-wraps, black print. Caption title. Illus of bibles throughout. At head of title: "Just issued: our." Handout to prospective canvassers. No WCE content; intact collection. (WM)

815.3 [Cranston and Curts, Agents.] Western Methodist Book Concern. *General catalogue of Publications of the western Methodist book concern.* Chicago?: n.p., n.d.

23x16½. 64 p. White wraps, brown print over bldg in background, border in pale greens and golds. C.t. Front cover: "1893." Back cover: "Visitors to the exposition will find the headquarters of the Western...a very convenient and pleasant place at which to spend time when in the city [Chicago]." (WM)

815.4 *Crédit Lyonnais : French : banking company limited.* N.p.: n.p., n.d.

24x15½. (4) p. Folded sheet, black print. Cover photo-illus showing their bank bldg in Paris plus a listing of available branches. C.t. Ad handout at the WCE; their "Chicago Representative : (During the World's Exhibition), J.H[Y] Stutz, First Nat'l Bank Bldg., 164 Dearborn St." ☺ (GLD,WM) $17 - 34

815.5 *Crescent City Hotel : Mrs. E.M. Gillen, Mrs. L. Curlett, Proprietors.* Chicago: n.p., n.d.

20½x12½. (3) p. Folded buff sheet, black print and illus of hotel on State Street. C.t. Rooms for 300 people at $2 per day. Back blank. ☺ (S)

815.6 *Criterion European Hotel, Stony Island Ave. and 64[th] St. : Chicago. Opposite World's Fair Gate.* ___: ___, ___.

12x15½. (8) p includes self-wraps, black print. Front cover illus of hotel; back cover map shows location. On pp (4)-(5) are floor plan and rates: $1.50/day single to $12/day for four people. (S)

815.7 Crittenden, J.P., and Cha[rle]s B. Helffrich. *New York Securities : A Descriptive and Statistical Manual of the Corporations of New York City and Brooklyn, and the Railroads of the United States.* New York: New York Securities, 1893.

24x19. 1094, 782, (52) index, (30) index, (2) p ads. Maroon cloth hc, bold gilt print. Financial information on p 449 for the "World's Fair Tourist Co." Gen. Joshua L. Chamberlain is listed as a director of the co. See #1075.2 for one of their WCE ads. This book lists all the rail lines into Chicago and their financial assets; a great railroad reference work. ☺ (DC)

815.8 Croly, J[ennie] C[unningham]. *The history : of the : Woman's Club Movement : in America.* New York: Henry G. Allen & co., [ᶜ1898 by Jennie Cunningham Croly].

25½x21. (2), 2 l, (ix)-xi, (2), 1 l, 1184 p. Illus. No frontis. Half leather over maroon cloth hc, gilt emblem on cover, gilt spine print. See #2442.1, a related history of women's clubs; also #2264.1. (LPL)

☞ The Chicago Woman's Club (CWC) was one of the finest. They were literary clubs until 1894 when they broadened their scope. The CWC was a strong advocate for Sunday opening at the WF. The federated clubs met in Woman's Bldg as part of the congresses of women, May 1893; many women dignitaries attended. Ellen M. (Mrs. Charles) Henrotin was President.

815.9 Crone & Hoefer. *Kiebitz...The celebrated German Egg-nog.* Dresden: Druck von Albert Hille, 1893?

29x20½. Buff sheet, navy print and illus of cherub holding Kiebitz sign. A liqueur composed of egg, sugar, and cognac. Lists reasons why it is good and good for you. List of awards to "London 1893." No WCE content; from an intact collection. (WM)

815.10 *The Crosby Invalid Furniture Co.* Nashua, NH: n.p., n.d.]

19x11½. (24) p. Aquamarine wraps, black print and illus of the bed with clamp-on food tray. Factory illus back cover. C.t. Caption title: "The Crosby invalid bed." Illus catalog with testimonials. Bed was adjustable and had slats as a base (illus). A chamber pot slid below the buttocks and removal of the correct slat allowed elimination into the pot. No WCE content; from an intact collection. ☺ (WM)

815.11 Crossman Brothers. *...Garden and Farm Annual. 1893.* [Rochester, NY: Crossman Brothers (Stecher lith. co.), n.d.

23½x15½. 1 *l* color flowers, 68 p+ table printed inside back cover. Brown and tan floral wraps, brown print. C.t. At head of title: Crossman Brothers. No 23" and their address. 1 *l* of flowers is titled: "Our Columbian collection." Back cover: "Columbian Year." (s)

816.   *Crystal Water Palace*: (ICRL)

817.   Cunard. *The Cunard line and The World's Fair*: (cul,FM,HML,MSL,UMD)
▸Cover description: Red cloth hc, black border, gilt print.

817.1 Cunard Steamship Line. *The Cunard Line : Royal Mail Steamers*. London: The Electrotype co., 1893.   P➔

13x10½. 23 p text, (5) p ads. Chromolith of crossed US and British flags and flowers on white wraps, brown print on green background. Pulp paper text describes their steamers. "The Cunard Exhibits in the World's Columbian Exposition," pp (16)-23. ☺ (GLD) $25 - 50

818.   Cunard. *The Cunard Royal mail twin-screw*: ☺. (Col,LHL,Yale)
---- Also found: 36x27½. 1 *l*, 134 p, 1 *l*. Illus (includes diagrams), 13 plates (includes 2 plans; part double). C.t. = t.p. Stamped below imprint: "D. Van Nostrand co., New York." See #1292.

819.   Curtis (Part 2). *Christopher Columbus*: (GLD,FM,ICRL,S,uluc,UMN,UPa,UTA)
▸Add cover annotation: Buff wraps, red and black print, vignettes of Columbus and La Rabida. Upper right cover: "Price 25 Cents." B/w litho of Santa Maria on outside back cover.

820.   Curtis (Part 1). *The Relics of*: (GLD,B,Col,CU,DC,E,FM,FPL,HU,ICRL,KCPL,NDU,OU,SHB,slu,UCB,UCLA,UIC,UMN,UPa,USFr,WM,Yale)
▸Add: [ᶜ1893 by William E. Curtis]. Printer info: [W.B. Conkey Co., Printers and Publishers].
---- Also found: Blue-flecked gray wraps, black print; same design as red-brown wrap. 216 p. (GLD)

821.   Curtis. *First edition of World's fair Blue Book*: (s)

822.   Cutler. *The World's fair its meaning and scope*: (RU,UIC)
---- Also found: San Francisco: King, 1892. In full morocco leather.

822.1 *The cyclopedic review of Current History : Columbian annual 1892 : Illustrated*. Buffalo, NY: Garretson, Cox & Co., 1893.

18½x12½. ca (800) p. Black cloth hc. Contains 14 A. Zeese & Co. plates of WCE bldgs. (ref) $35

822.2 Daemicke, Paul J., & John Tobin [Co.]. *The Chicago Fish Scaling Machine*. Chicago: n.p., n.d.

16x9. (4) p. Folded tan stiff card. C.t. On front: "Group 40, class 279, Section A, department fisheries." Illus of machine on back. (WM)

822.3 Daimler Motor Co. *Daimler Motor Company : marine catalogue : 1893*. New York: E.P.P. McClure, stationer and printer, n.d.   P➔

15x24. 40 p. Light blue stiff wraps, fancy navy blue print, illus of a trim power boat. C.t. ☺. (Stfd-bound WCE Trans Dept Collection)

822.4 Daisy Mfg. Co. *Daisy dishwasher. A family blessing*. [Chicago: Daisy Mfg. Co.], n.d.

15x8½. (6) panel tri-fold. Pink sheet, black print. C.t. "Saves 30 to 60 minutes each day." From intact WCE collections. ☺ (S,WM)

822.5 *Dandicolle & Gaudin Lᴅ. Factories...Bordeaux...London*. N.p.: [F. Javanaud & Cº Angouléme], n.d.

14x10½. (6) panel tri-fold. Buff stiff card stock. C.t. Cover in greens, red, blue with many medals in gilt; green print. Listed on the 3 inside panels are items they pack (vegetables, olives, fruits, fish) and their specialties. Back panel has chromolith of early plan for WCE grounds, unrealized. ☺(WM)

822.6 Davis & Rankin Co. *Compliments of Davis & Rankin bldg. and mfg. co.* [Chicago: Davis & Rankin co.], n.d. **P➔**

13½x7½. (10) p+ text on inside both wraps. Brown print and design on white smooth stiff wraps. Caption title: "The World's Fair." Five pages text on Chicago + five pages ads for their creamery machinery and dairy supplies. ☺(GLD) $20 - 45

822.7 Davis Coal & Coke Co. *Description of coal and coke exhibited by Davis...from their mines at Thomas, W. VA.* [Cumberland, MD: Frank B. Jenvey], n.d.

14x10½. (4) p. Folded buff smooth sheet, black and red print. C.t. Their products listed with chemical analyses. "Stephen B. Elkins, President." No WCE content; from intact collection. ☺(WM)

822.8 Davis Sewing Machine Co. *The : Davis : vertical feed : sewing machine : Best on Earth.* [Watertown, NY]: The Davis Sewing Machine Co. (W.W. White Co., Print), n.d.

16x9½. 24 p+ ads inside both wraps. Wraps are without title but have beautiful chromoliths showing 4 women of different ethnic extraction in front of a US flag and WCE lagoon. Cover images are ᶜ1892 by Schumacher & Ettlinger. Title from verso of front wrap. Illus with descriptions and prices of their machines. Attractive ad. ☺(GLD)   **P➔** $26 - 55

822.9 Day, M.J., Co. *Peerless Waist and Sleeve Ironing Board. Exhibited in Invention Room : Women's* [sic] *Building, World's fair...* New York: n.p., 1893.

23x15. Single ad sheet, black print one side. Illus of narrow pointed ironing board with list of users. In text: "For Sale at Sales Dept. Woman's B'ld'g." ☺(WM)

822.10 Dayton Autographic Register Co. *The Invincible Autographic Register. How is this, Sir?* Dayton, OH: n.p., n.d.

8½x16½. (6) panels. Sheet unfolds to 8½x49. Black print and tan-shade litho of register for stores, front and back. Three sales slips printed with one copy automatically staying in the register when the other two were removed for clerk and customer; intended for chronological store reference. ☺(WM)

822.11 *The De La Vergne Refrigerating Machine Company : Manufacturers of : Refrigerating and Ice Machines. : Machinery hall, Main Section 26, Column O-29, and Ice railway, Midway Plaisance, Jackson Park, Chicago, Ill.* New York: n.p., n.d.

28x20½. (4) p. Folded sheet, black print and border. Illus of 500-ton refrigerator on p (4). List of sizes and users. [Their WCE exhibit category was Group 69, Class 417.] ☺(WM)

823.   Dean. *The World's fair city and her enterprising sons*: (HML,IHi,ref,S) $50

824.   Dean. *White city chips*: (GLD,bgsu,CLP,HML,ICRL,IHi,RU,S,Yale)
▸Add cover description: Light gray-green cloth hc with gilt print. $30 - 60

824.1 Dederick, P.K., & Co. *Testimonials.* [Albany, NY: P.K. Dederick & Co], n.d.

8½x16. 22 p. Red wraps, bold black title. Text in portrait orientation. Agriculture and Machine works. User comments on Dederick lever and belt presses. From an intact WCE collection. (WM)

825.1 Deere, John & Co. *No. 25 : illustrated Catalogue : season of 1893-94 : Deere and company...* Moline, IL: Lowman publishing co., n.d.

24x16½. 336 p. Light blue cardboard wraps, maroon cloth glued spine, rounded corners. Deere port on t.p. C.t.: "1893–94 Illustrated...Catalogue No. 25." Green decorative border on each page. Illus catalog of their extensive farm implements, parts, and prices. Logo on back cover. No WCE; intact collection. ☺ . (WM)

825.2 Deering, William, & Co. *The Deering victorious in every field.* [Chicago: William Deering & co., n.d.].   P➔

9 cm diameter. (14) p. Silver embossed stiff covers. Metal eyelet allows fanning of pages for viewing. C.t. Circular die-cut ad. On p (1) is a welcome to the WCE and Deering exhibit. WCE souvenir catalog from "manufacturers of grain and grass-cutting machinery."
---- Also found: Text in German.
☺ (GLD,E,IHi) $25 - 45

825.3 Deering, William, & Co. *One of the Triumphs of the 19th Century.* [Chicago: William Deering & co., 1893?].

12½x10½. 32 p+ text inside both wraps. Pale green wraps, brown print and b/w design. C.t. Illus of WCE Administration Bldg on p 1; also references to WCE on pp 14-15. C.t. = caption title. The year "1893" is found on catalog items pp 16-17. ☺ (GLD,WM)   P➔ $27 - 55

825.4 Delafield, McGovern & Co. *California Wines. Vineyard la Feld...Noveau Medoc Vineyards.* Chicago: n.p., n.d.

22½x14½. 1 *l.* Water-marked rag sheet, red and black print. In text: "We offer...wines...entered for award competition and exhibited at the World's Fair." Caption title. ☺ (WM)

825.5 Denver & Rio Grande Railroad. Hooper, Shadrick, comp. *Rhymes of the Rockies : or, what the poets have found to say of the : Beautiful Scenery : on the...* Chicago: Poole Bros., Printers and Engravers, 1893, ᶜ1887.

11th prt. 21½x17. 64 p. Pale blue-green smooth wraps, gilt print. Handout "Compliments of" but no mention of WCE. Poems, text and illus of scenery on the route. From an intact WCE collection. (WM)

825.6 Denver & Rio Grande Railroad. *The Natural Resources of Colorado : with map of the : Denver & Rio Grande System.* Denver?: Denver & Rio Grande Railroad, [1893].

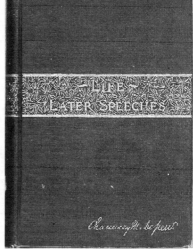

19½x10. Tan stiff card forming folded wraps, brown print and design. Brown print inside both covers. Tipped-in leaf unfolds to 38½x45; colored route map on one side and 10 p black print text panels on other side. Shows standard gauge (in red) and narrow gauge (in green) routes; narrow gauge was confined to CO and NM. No WCE content; from intact collection. ☺ . (GLD) $30 - 60

826.   Depew. *The Columbian oration:* (GLD,S,UMN,UPa,Yale)

826.1 Depew, Chauncey M[itchell]. *The Columbian Oration, delivered at the dedication ceremonies of the World's Fair at Chicago, October 21st, 1892,...* N.p.: n.p., n.d.

47x14½. 8 p. Printed one side of page. Caption title. Printer's galley proof of #826. Stapled at top edge; no cover. ☺ (GLD) $25 - 50

826.2 Depew, Chauncey M[itchell]. *Life and later speeches of Chauncey M. Depew.* Introd. Joseph Gilder. New York: The Cassell publishing co. (The Mershon co. press), [ᶜ1894 by the Cassell publishing co.].   P↑

20½x15. xxiii, 510 p. Blue-black cloth hc, gilt print and design. Speech I is the Columbian Oration (see #826, #826.1); speech II is Depew's dinner speech for the WF commissioners at Delmonico's (see #192). Gilder's bio of Depew includes Depew's assoc with the WCE. ☺ (GLD) $25 - 50

827.1 Deroy Fils Aîné. *1893 New brandy still 1893*. [Paris: Imp. Michels et fils, n.d.].

32½x24½. (4) p. Folded pulp sheet, black print and illus of elaborate stills. Text in English. Sizes of their stills are given in liters, prices in francs. No WCE content; from intact collection. © (WM)

828.1 ...*The Detrick & Harvey Machine Co. : Baltimore, Md. : manufacturers of : the open side iron planers,...* Baltimore, MD: n.p., [1893].

24½x16. (4) p. Folded sheet, black print. Illus pp (2)-(3) of their large industrial bed planers. C.t. At head of title: "World's Columbian Exposition Chicago, Ill. 1893." List of references; 4 testimonial letters reproduced on back. (WM)

828.2 Detroit Boat Works. *Detroit Boat Works, builders of : Steam and Sail Yachts...* Detroit, MI: [Gulley, Bornman & co. Printers], n.d.

20x17. 80 p. Light blue wraps, white and blue print with illus of sails, boat steering wheel and boats. On cover: "Catalogue 1892." Their extensive exhibit in the Trans Bldg was located at D-1-22. See #828.3. © . (Stfd–bound WCE Trans Dept Collection)

828.3 Detroit Boat Works. *Electric launches : Detroit boat Works.* [Detroit, MI: John Bornman & son, printers], n.d.

19½x15. 4 p (miss-paged) includes inside front and back covers. Sepia print on cream glossy stock. Back cover illus of Director of Works, Daniel H. Burnham, in their electric launch before the Manufactures Bldg. © . (Stfd–bound WCE Trans Dept Collection)

828.4 Deuscher, H.P., Co. *The McColm : Soil Pulverizer and Field Roller.* Hamilton, OH: n.p., n.d.

15x8½. 16 p includes both covers. Buff self-wraps, black print and illus of "compress field roller." Description of the rollers with testimonials. No mention of WCE; from an intact collection. (WM)

828.5 *Deutsche Gold-& Silber-Scheide-Anstalt : vormals Roessler : and its Branch Establishments. At the World's Columbian Exposition : Chicago.* Frankfurt o/M, Germany: Deutsche Gold-& Silberscheide-Anstalt [J. Maubach & Co. Frankfurt a/M], n.d.

20x11½. (8) p. Sheet opens to 20x46. Cream heavy coated paper with heather green and brown ornate print and design. C.t. Two-page illus of their WCE exhibit. They made chemicals from precious metals. Beautiful ad for their world-wide branch offices. © (GLD,WM)   P➔ $25 - 50

828.6 Devens, R.M. *American Progress: or the great events of : The Greatest Century,...* N.p.: C.A. Nichols co., 1893 [ᶜ1893 by C.A. Nichols co.].

28½x20. 769 p. Calf leather hc, two black spine labels with gilt print. Frontis illus of signing of the Declaration of Independence. A US history; chap 86 describes WCE, illustrated, pp 740-56. © (ref) $20

829.1 *Dexter Brothers' English shingle stain.* Boston: n.p., n.d.

22x18. (4) p. Folded sheet, black and red print. User list. A linseed and vaseline oil based stain available in many colors. No WCE content; from an intact collection. (WM)

829.2 *Dibble publishing company's : World's Columbian Exposition : pocket record book. Illustrated with cuts and...* Chicago: Dibble publishing co., 1893, ᶜ1893.

17½x10½. 57 p, 1 *l* + laid in fold grounds map ᶜ1893 by A. Zeese & co. Tan wraps, black print. © (S)

829.3 Dietz, R.E., Co. *Beware of imitations. 1840. 1893. Dietz standard tubular goods.* New York [and] Chicago: n.p., n.d.

15½x14½. Sheet unfolds to a 61x58 poster printed one side and meant for wall display. Black print title arranged in large center circle; many illus of their wide line of kerosene lanterns, lamps, and wicks outside circle. At top stamped in purple: "R.E. Dietz Company 25 Lake St., Chicago Ills." Wonderful bold ad.

No WCE content; from intact collection. [Their exhibit was located in the Manufactures Bldg, Section N, Block 3, South; Group 114, Class 720.] (WM)

829.4 Dixon, Joseph, Crucible Co. *Hints : Of what we manufacture in Graphite.* Jersey City, NJ: [G.H. Buek & co. lith. NY], ᶜ1893 by J. Dixon Crucible co.

8½x15½. 16 p. Chromolith wraps with port of Dixon, a crucible, and their pencil. Product descriptions in black ink. Factory chromolith on back. C.t. = caption title. From an intact WCE collection. [Dixon pencils are still available.] © (WM)

829.5 Dolge, Alfred, Felt Shoes. *Facts Felt by Folks' Feet together with Felt Facts for Folks' Feet.* New York: n.p., n.d.

7½x10½. Buff stiff card forming folded wraps; tipped-in (12)-panel accordion folded sheet which unfolds to 43½x10. C.t.: "A Foot Note." Touts the advantages of felt shoes and soles: absorb perspiration, ventilate, and generate electricity to aid body force and vitality. Hinge at top, accordion-folded text sheet unfolds down. No WCE content; from intact collection. © (WM)

830.1 Douglas High School. *Commencement themes : of the : class of 'ninety-four : Douglas High School : Cairo, Illinois : June the fifteenth : 1894.* N.p.: Press of the Citizen company, 1894.

20x16½. 1 *l* frontis, 115 p. Forest green cloth hc, silver print. Frontis of Douglas High School is protected with a tissue guard. Thirty-four essays by the Class of 'Ninety-Four.' "The World's Fair as an Educator" by Florence Bennie Ellis, pp 24-27, is her eye-witness heartfelt account of a trip to the WCE in '93. Several references to the fair in other essays. © (GLD) $20 - 40

830.2 Doulton & Co. *Doulton & Co. : General and Art Potters.* Works in England *at Lambeth, London. Burslem, Staffordshire. ...* N.p.: n.p., n.d.

24½x16½. 2 *l*, (3)-64 p. Frontis illus titled: "Doulton's show rooms and works, Lambeth, London." Half title precedes frontis: "Doulton & co. at Chicago exhibition, 1893." Ornate t.p. has five litho vignettes of potters working. © , (FLP)

830.3 Doulton & Co. *Doulton & Co. : General and Art Potters.* Works in England *at Lambeth, London. Burslem, Staffordshire. ...* N.p.: n.p., n.d.

19x12. (6) panels. Green smooth sheet unfolds to 19x36½. Dark green and gilt print. Illus of Doulton WCE pavilion and interior. C.t. given is on center panel and has five litho vignettes of potters working same as in #830.2. Ornate ad describing their exhibit. (WM)

830.4 Doulton & Co. *...The Doulton Exhibits will be found in the following Sections.* Lambeth and Burslem, Eng.: n.p., n.d.

23x15. (2) p. Pink sheet, black print and no illus. At head of title: "World's Columbian Exposition, Chicago." Lists six WCE exhibit locations. (WM)

830.5 Doulton & Co. *Notes on the Doulton Potteries. Burslem, Staffordshire, England. I.–The acquisition of the works and its progress. II.–Description of a few of their works exhibited at Chicago.* London: Waterlow & Sons, Limited, Printers, n.d.

19x12. 16 p. Red wraps with gilt print. C.t.: "Doultons Art Potters." History of the company and description of their WCE exhibits. (WM)

830.6 Doulton & Co. *A sketch of the Doulton potteries.* N.p.: Waterlow & Sons, printers, London, [1893].

19x__. 40 p, 5 *l* of plates. Illus. Description of the works and their WCE exhibit. (HML)

830.7 Dowagiac Mfg. Co. *Compliments of Dowagiac Manufacturing Co. : Dowagiac Shoe Grain Drill,...* Kalamazoo, MI: Ihling bros. & Everard, n.d.

15½x8½. (8) p+ testimonials inside both covers. Pale peach stiff wraps, shaded brown and red print, wheat shock illus (front), shoe drill illus (back). C.t. Explains pronunciation of the company's Indian name on pp (1), (3), (5): "Doe"-"Waugh"-"Jack." Tipped-in glass mirror on p (5). From Dowagiac, MI. No mention of WCE; from an intact WCE collection. (WM)

830.8 Downie Pump Co. *The Downie double-acting Geared pump! For Artesian Wells.* Valencia, PA: n.p, n.d.

23½x15½. (4) p. Folded sheet, black print and illus. C.t Rubber stamped at top of cover: "Well drilling exhibit south of machinery hall." Used belt driven wheel and crank system. ☺ (WM)

831. Dredge. *Chicago and Her Exposition of 1893. A Stereopticon Lecture:* (UCB)
832. Dredge. *A record of the transportation exhibits:* (Col,DC,HML,HU,LU,MIT,MSL,NSW,RSA,S,slpl,Stfd,Yale)

832.1 Dreydoppel, William, [Co.]. *Light and Shade : use Dreydoppel soap : no finer made.* [Philadelphia: William Dreydoppel, ᶜ1892–93 by Wm. Dreydoppel].

9½x13½. (16) p. Chromolith wraps. Text and wrap illus of cartoon "Negroes." Story of a black boy who, unable to wash the black off with other chemicals, goes from black to white by using this soap. Ad which describes their awards at previous WFs and expectancy of "the same from Chicago." [They exhibited in Agricultural Hall, Section F-M-6.] ☺ (GLD) $50 - 85

832.2 Dudley, C.E. *The Great New Combination. Woman's friend. The Elward combined Swing Churn Washer and Dishwasher.* [Grand Crossing, IL: C.E. Dudley (Langton & Flach, ptrs., Chicago), 1893].

20½x14. (4) p. Buff paper, black print, illus of machine. Exhibited in the Ag Bldg, "South Gallery, Division H, Col. G. H. ɪ." Price list and operating instructions. Testimonial dated Aug 1893. ☺ . (E)

832.3 *Due southwest. Through fields of virgin soil. For the farmer and planter, stockman, lumberman and business man generally. A description of the country : Traversed by the "Cotton Belt Route," from Cairo, Illinois, through Southeastern Missouri...* St. Louis: Woodward & Tiernan Printing Co., 1891.

23½x17½. 176 p, map. Turquoise wraps, black print, design of surveyor in compass. C.t.: "Due Southwest over the Cotton Belt Route." WCE handout. [This route was run by the St. Louis Southwestern Railway. See #1022.6.] ☺ . (LBA)

832.4 Duluth Imperial Mill Co. *"The old mill." Agricultural Building, World's Fair, Chicago, 1893.* [Duluth, MN: Duluth Imperial Mill Co. (Corbitt-Skidmore Co., Chicago)], n.d.

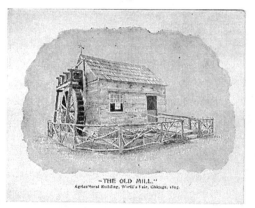

"THE OLD MILL."
Agricultural Building, World's Fair, Chicago, 1893.

11½x14. (4) p. Folded pale pink coated card, black print and illus. C.t. Front shows their WCE exhibit, a reproduction of a 150 year old company flour mill which was still operating in Reading, PA. Barrel of Imperial flour shown on back cover. Ad. ☺ (GLD)   P➜ $16 - 35

832.5 *Duplex Color Disc Co's Exhibit : At the World's Columbian Exposition, Chicago, 1893.* Chicago: n.p., n.d.

28x21½. Sheet with green and red print one side. Palmer Cox "Brownie" cartoon characters. Ad printed with the 2-color disc plate on a "12x18 Chandler & Price press," printing 2 inks per pass. ☺ (WM)

832.6 *...Dwight Lyman Moody : The Great Evangelist : of the : nineteenth century : Last Scenes; Generous Tributes...* Chicago: Classic publishing co., [ᶜ1900 by Donohue, Henneberry & co.].

19x13. xiii, 15-318 p. Red cloth hc, silver print and silver/black design, pulp paper. At head of title: "Memorial Edition." Chap 10 (pp 213-23), "The World's Fair Campaign," describes Moody's religious activities at the WCE. See #865 and #932.3 for other Moody entries. [Moody died in 1899.] (ref)

833.1 Eckert, H.F., [Co.]. *Illustrierter special-katalog : über : pflüge : und Landwirthschaftliche Geräthe : der actien-gesellschaft...* [Berlin: Lewent'sche Buchdruckerei], 1893.

22x15½. (4), 3-74 p. Dark peach wraps, black print and illus. Dated Jan 1893. Their illus horse-drawn plow and farm implement catalog. In German. No WCE content; from intact collection. ☺ (WM)

833.2 Eclipse Wind Engine Co. *The Eclipse Windmill : for Pumping, Shelling, Elevating, Irrigation,...* Beloit, WI: n.p., 1893? **P➔**

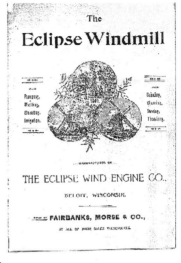

> 25½x17. 24 p. Blue wraps, dark blue print and 3 red circle illus of old and modern (1893) windmills. Full-page blue illus of their windmill on back. C.t. Text and illus in dark blue. On front: "Sold by Fairbanks, Morse & co." No mention of WCE; from intact collection. ☺ (WM)

833.3 Edison, Thomas A. *Mimeography.* N.p.: [R.R. Donnelley & Sons co. printers], n.d.

> 16x8½. __ p. Gray wraps with red print. C.t. On last page: "Samples of work free : A.B. Dick company Chicago." Gives benefits of the mimeograph in business. No mention of WCE; probable handout. ☺ (S)

834.   Eggleston. *Four days at Chicago*: (DU,UGa)

834.1 *The Eick bottle-Cleansing machine is an assured success. ...* Philadelphia: n.p., n.d.

> 27x20½. (4) p. Folded smooth sheet; black print and illus of their belt driven bottle loader, which used a metal rack to hold 8 bottles for washing. Price $450 with 20 metal crates. Mentions their WCE exhibit. Illus of example shop operation on back. (WM)

834.2 *The Electric Cake Beater and Dropper.* N.p.: n.p., n.d.

> 20x16. Light green pulp sheet, black print and illus of the beater. Last paragraph: "The Exposition C East 5, Agricultural Building for a demonstration by the inventor herself." ☺ (WM)

834.3 Electric Light Hygiene Co. *Safe Application of the Electric Light as a Therapeutic Agent. ...as an Exhibit at the World's Fair.* Newark, NJ: n.p., n.d.

> 15½x12. (4) p. Folded sheet, black print and illus. Illus pp (2)-(4) of their light studios and lamps. C.t. Explains antiseptic properties of their equipment. [Early use of UV lamps.] ☺ (WM)

834.4 Electric Light Hygiene Co. *Therapeutics of the electric light.* [Newark, NJ]: n.p., n.d.

> 20½x13. 8 p. Pulp sheet unfolds to 20½x51, black print. Rpts from journal article describing their lights as curative, generating ozone, etc. No WCE content; from intact collection. ☺ (WM)

834.5 Electrical Machine Co. *The Caldwell Electric Cloth-Cutting Machines.* Chicago: n.p., [1893].

> 21½x28. (4) p. Folded sheet, blue-black print and illus. On front: "During the world's fair this machine will cut clothing in northwest gallery of electricity building." Electric cord from ceiling powered a hand-held motor with oscillating blade at 2500 strokes/minute in an elliptical pattern to simulate a typical knife cut. Illus of factory using machine on p (2). Testimonials. ☺ (WM)

835.   Elliott. *Art and handicraft*: (Amh,BrU,CCA,CLP,D,DC,DU,GBP,GU,HML,HU,ICRL,IHi,LBA,MIT,MSI,NAG,NDU,NHL,NLA,NPG,NSW,PPL,PSU, RU,sfpl,SHB,slpl,Smth,SPL,Stfd,UAB,UBO,UCI,UCLA,UGa,UIC,uiuc,UMD,UMN,UPa,UTA,UVM,UWM,VAM,VT,Yale)
> ▶Add publisher: Ann Arbor, MI: UMI, 1977.
> ---- Also found: Rand, 1894 (Cover design 2): "Rand" is not printed on spine.

836.   Ellis. *Chicago and the World's Columbian Exposition with a portrait gallery*: (GLD,sfpl) $120 - 250
> ▶Cover description: Full leather, beveled boards, all edges gilt. Gilt c.t.: "The Quadri centennial memorial: Chicago and The World's Columbian Exposition."

836.1 Emerson Drug Co. *Pocket Memorandum and Some Valuable suggestions to Friends when in distress- illustrated.* Baltimore, MD: Emerson Drug Co. (S.C. Malone), n.d.

> 11½x7. 16 p+ text inside both wraps. Brown stiff wraps, tan print. Humorous illus and poems on even pages; ruled note paper on odd pages. Listing of the Bromo-Seltzer collection of 54 popular songs on p 15. See #1509.1 for sample song handout from the WCE. No WCE; from intact collection. ☺ (GLD) $20 - 40

836.2 Empire Drill Co. *Thirty-Seventh Annual Catalogue. Read carefully. 1892.* Shortsville, NY: J. Ottmann Lith Co., Puck Bldg, n.d.

    19x14. 30 p. Buff wraps with pretty blue-black print and gilt spiral design with wheat ears. Caption title. Farm drills for seeding. No mention of WCE; from an intact WCE collection. ☺ (WM)

836.3 The Empire State Cigar Machine Co. *On exhibition at the World's Columbian Exposition, Chicago, Ill. : Cigar : Manufacturing Machinery. ...* Philadelphia: The Empire State Cigar Machine Co., n.d.

    27x16½. (4) p. Folded coated sheet, black and red print and b/w illus of three cigar bunching machines. C.t. At bottom of cover: "World's Columbian Exposition, agricultural hall, annex No. 206 E, Chicago, Ill., U.S.A." Ad. ☺ (GLD,WM) $22 - 55

836.4 Engle Sanitary and Cremation Co. *The exhibit : of the : Engle sanitary & cremation company : at the : World's Columbian Exposition, Chicago, Ill., U.S.A. : A.D. 1893.* Des Moines, IA: Engle Sanitary and Cremation co., [ᶜ1893].

    20½x14½. 12 p. Buff wraps, black type. Illus on p 2 of the working Engle Crematorium in the SE part of the WCE grounds. Ad describing their sewage/refuse disposal capabilities. ☺ . (CCA,S)

836.5 Enterprise Chamois Works. *Price list : Enterprise chamois works.* Philadelphia: Walther print, n.d.

    13x8. (8) p. Blue sheet with black print unfolds to 25½x16. C.t. On cover: "On Exhibition at : The World's fair : Leather and Shoe Building." Prices for six different types of chamois. ☺ (WM)

836.6 Epworth World's Fair Association. *Application for membership in the Epworth World's Fair Association.* N.p.: n.p., n.d.

    20x13½. 1 *l.* Tan sheet, brown print one side. Special rates for members at their hotel for up to 2 weeks during the WCE. Methodist association. Confirmation by printed post card. ☺ (S)
    ---- Also found: 7½x13. Post card for confirming remittance. (S)
    ---- Also found with above post card: "Facts for Epworth Leaguers." 15½x9. 8 p. Equipment list for Leaguers: Bible, Methodist Hymnal, and 1892 *Methodist Discipline.* (S)

836.7 Epworth World's Fair Association. *The Epworth World's Fair Association is incorporated...* [Chicago: Epworth World's Fair Association], n.d.

    14x20½. (4) p. Folded sheet unfolds to 14x42. White glossy paper, red print and hotel illus. Jackson Park map on back. Caption title. Gives objectives of the Methodist organization and hotel info. ☺ (S)

836.8 Erard, S. & P., [Co.]. *Erard Harps : at the : Chicago exhibition, 1893.* [London: Feilden, McAllan & Co., Ltd., 1893].

    21x26. 8 p. White wraps, teal print; brown illus of founder, Sebastian Erard, and "The Prince of Wales' Harp" that was given by Erard on the occasion of the Prince's marriage. C.t. Brown text print. Harp info and testimonials. . (WM)   **P➜**

837.1 Evans, F[rederick] W[illiam]. *Russian famine : A shaker protest against closing the World's Fair on Sunday.* Mt. Lebanon, NY: n.p., 1891; Glen Rock, NJ: Microfilming Corporation of America, 1976.

    __x__. 6 p. Western Reserve Historical Society Shaker Collection, no. 95. One microfiche. (MH,ref)

837.2 Evans, F[rederick] W[illiam]. *Shakers' Sabbath : composed of seven days.* Mt. Lebanon, NY: n.p., [1892]; Glen Rock, NJ: Microfilming Corporation of America, 1976.

    15x__. 7 p. C.t. Caption title: "World's Fair." Western Reserve Historical Society Shaker Collection, no 94. One microfiche. (MH,ref)

838.   Evans. *The World's Fair!:* (MH,ref)

▶Add publisher: Glen Rock, NJ: Microfilming Corporation of America, 1976. Western Reserve Historical Society Shaker Collection. No 93. One microfiche.

838.1 Evans, George G., ed. *Illustrated history of the United States mint : with short historical sketches and illustrations of the branch mints and assay offices, and a complete description of American coinage...with photo-illustrations and fine engravings and twenty-four plates of rare coins.* Rev. ed. Philadelphia: George G. Evans (Dunlap printing co.), 1893 [°1885 and 1892 by George G. Evans].

23½x15½. vii, (1), 179, (5) p. No frontis. Interspersed plates on glossy stock are not included in paging. Navy blue smooth (or burgundy pebbled) cloth hc, blind-stamped, Christopher Columbus medallion in gilt on front cover. Gilt spine print title: "History of the U.S. mint and coinage : Columbian edition : 1893." Text does not mention Columbian coinage. ☺(GLD,B,S) $50 - 100

839.   *Excelsior Diary*: (GLD,S) $25 - 45
---- Also found: Black cloth hc with extended fold-over back flap, gusset pocket at back cover with loop made from a strip to hold a pencil, marbled edges.

839.1 *Excelsior Electric Co. Plating Machines.* N.p.: n.p., n.d.

21x14½. 8 p. Very pale green wraps with litho of dynamo on front cover. C.t. Offices in NY and Chicago; works in Brooklyn, NY. Ad. No mention of WCE; from an intact collection. (WM

839.2 *Exhibit of games in the Columbian exposition.* N.p.: n.p., n.d.

8°. Pp 205-27. No t.p. Bound in a collection of pamphlets on games at UPa. [The bound collection is also listed in this supplement, #2446.UPa] (ref,UPa) $60

840.   *Facts on Cut Glass*: (HML,LBA)
▶See #911.7, #912, and #2352.5 for other Libbey Glass items.

840.1 *Fair View Hotel: Corner 72ⁿᵈ Place and Jefferson Ave. Chicago. Only Six Short Blocks South from the World's Fair Grounds.* Chicago: M.A. Fountain & Co., Hotel Supply Printers, n.d.

17x16. (4) p. Folded buff sheet with red and black print. "Our Rates are as follows: 50 and 75 cents for each person per day, two in a room." Location map on back cover showing Fairgrounds. . (E,S)

840.2 Fairbank, N.K., & Co. *Cottolene.* [Chicago: N.K. Fairbank & co.], n.d.

14x9. (8) p+ text inside both wraps. Chromolith on white wraps depicts "Entrance to Cottolene exhibit Chicago, 1893." Illus of company's trade mark on back wrap. Cottolene was a cooking oil preparation made from cotton seed oil and beef fat. Ad. ☺(GLD,E,WM)

840.3 Fairbanks, E. & T., & Co. ...*Fairbanks' : scales : The World's Standard.* Chicago: Rand McNally Co. Printers for E. & T. Fairbanks & co., n.d.

17½x13½. 20 p. Tan wraps with orange Admin Bldg litho (or lime or tan wraps with rose Admin Bldg), black print. At head of t.p. title: "1492, discovery of America : 1830, invention of Fairbanks' scales : 1893, World's Columbian exposition." The c.t. reads: "1492 : 1830 1893. Fairbanks' Souvenir : of the World's Columbian Exposition : Chicago." See #2088.1 for Vermont's exhibit using these scales.
☺(GLD,CCA,IHi,S,VtHx,WM)   P➔ $22 - 45

840.4 Fairly, Jno. S. *Answer to bishop H.C. Potter on Sunday opening of the Columbian exposition.* Charleston, SC: The Daggett Printing Co. Printers and Binders, 1893.

22½x14. 1 *l* (t.p.), (3)-15 p. Tan flecked wraps with black print and border. C.t. = t.p. Potter was for Sunday opening at WCE. ☺. (HU)

840.5 Falk, Zsigmond. *Budapesttöl San-Franciscoig : Amerikai uti jegyzetck.* Budapest: Magyar Kereskedelmi közlöny kiadása, 1902.

24x17. 196, (1) p. Gray-blue cloth hc with gilt and black print. Illus. The author's visit to WCE described pp (50)-78. (csuf)

840.6 Famous Mfg. Co. *"Champion giant" self timing large bale continuous travel Portable Baling Press.* Chicago: n.p., n.d.

20½x26. (4) p. Folded buff newspaper stock sheet, black print and illus of the press "at Work in the Field." C.t. No WCE content; from intact collection. (WM)

840.7 Famous Mfg. Co. *Champion self-tieing* [sic] *baling press.* Chicago: n.p., n.d.

17½x22. 1 *l*. Shiny sheet printed one side in blue. Caption title. Illus of the press is labeled "self-tying." No WCE content; from intact collection. ☺ (WM)

840.8 Fargas y Vilaseca, Miguel. *Fabricacion de cuero repujado para silleria y decoracion de habitaciones.* Barcelona, [Sp.]: Imp B. Arnaud, Lyon-Paris, n.d.

17½x11. (8) panels. Buff sheet unfolds to 17½x43½; dark green print and illus of factory and medals won at Paris expo, 1889. C.t. Manufacturers of leather goods for chairs and rooms. No WCE content; from intact collection. (WM)

840.9 Faries, Robert, [Co.]. *Catalogue : of : Revolving and : Stationary Window : display fixtures.* Decatur, IL: Robert Faries, 1893.

16½x9. 65, (10) p testimonials and purchasers. Gray pulp wraps with black print; chocolate overlay print: "World's Columbian exposition : 1893." No "window" in c.t. Staple and hinge at top. (WM)

840.10 Farina, Johann Maria, Co. *Eau de Cologne : (Kölnisches Wasser) : by the most ancient distiller : Johann Maria Farina.* 18th ed. N.p.: n.p., n.d.

22x14½. 1 *l*, 10 p, 2 *l*. Blue-green wraps, black print. C.t. Description of their cologne, its properties and uses, and awards at previous WFs. No WCE content; from intact collection. (WM)

841. Farmer. *The National Exposition souvenir:* (GLD,HML) $40 - 80
▶Add: Advertised as "A complete epitome of Woman's Work in all departments of life." See #1744.2.

841.1 Farnley Iron Co., Ltd. *"King & Humbles's" patent safety detaching hook...The Chicago exhibition : department E.–Mines and Mining. British section. Stand 115.* Leeds, Eng.: n.p., n.d.

22½x14½. (4) p. Folded buff sheet, black and red print. C.t. Illus of hook on front cover; description of industrial hook and its features. "Testimonials" on back. ☺ (WM)

841.2 *...The Farnley Iron Company, Limited whole Mines, Collieries...* Leeds, England: [The Leadenhall Press, Ltd.: London, May, 1893].

27x21. (2) p. Single high-rag sheet with black print both sides. Bird's-eye illus of factory at Leeds on front. At head of caption title: "Columbian Exposition, Chicago, 1893. Mines and Mining Building. Stand No. 115." Gives properties and prices of their iron. C.t. ☺ (WM)

841.3 Farquhar, A[rthur] B., Co., Limited. *"The Pony."* York, PA: n.p., n.p.

23x16½. (2) p. Blue-fleck sheet printed both sides in black. Illus of "'Pony' Spring-Tooth Cultivator" (front), "The Pennsylvania All Steel Frame Spring-Tooth Harrow" (back). Caption title. No WCE content; from intact collection. [Farquhar was active in PA's state exhibits; see #2042 to 2044.1]. ☺ (WM)

841.4 Felt & Tarrant Mfg. Co. *The Arithmetic Machine. The Comptometer...* Chicago [and] New York: Geo. E. Cole & co., printers, n.d.

16x12½. 27, (1) p. Tan wraps, black print and design. C.t. Ad with photo-illus showing proper and improper use of machine. Testimonials. No mention of WCE; from an intact WCE collection. (WM)

842.1 Fenno, Isaac, & Co. *The Fenno Cloth-cutting Machines.* Boston: J.A. Lowell co., n.d.

21x15. (2) p. Buff sheet, black print both sides. Illus of "The climax" and "The improved" models. Top of back side: "World's Columbian Exposition, Machinery Building, Section 29, Column O-52." Operator used a belt-driven rotating blade mounted on articulated swivel arms to make cuts. ☺ (WM)

842.2 Fenton, J.H., Co. *The J.H. Fenton Co. Manufacturers Jobbers and Dealers in Fine Harness, Ladies and Gents Riding Saddles and Bridles.* Chicago: J.H. Fenton Co., n.d.

19½x13½. 47, (1) p+ index on inside back cover. Silver-gray wraps, black print, illus of horse team and a woman on horseback. C.t. No t.p. Catalog of harness items. ☺ . (Stfd-bound WCE Trans Dept Collection)

842.3 Fenton, J.H., Co. *The J.H. Fenton Co. Manufacturers Jobbers and Dealers in Fine Turf Goods of Every Description.* Chicago: J.H. Fenton Co. (P.F. Pettibone & Co., printers), n.d.

19½x13½. 104, (4) p index and ad. Aqua wraps, white and black print, illus of sulky cart and driver. C.t. No t.p. Catalog of their trotting gear and horse maintenance products. ☺ . (Stfd-bound WCE Trans Dept Collection)

842.4 Fenton Metallic Mfg. Co. *"The Fenton" 1893: High Grade Bicycle.* Jamestown, NY: Fenton Metallic Mfg. Co., n.d. **P➔**

16½x8½. (4) p. Folded pink stiff card, black print and illus. C.t. Their bicycle illus on back cover. On p (3): "Medal awarded World's Columbian exposition." ☺ . (Stfd-bound WCE Trans Dept Collection)

842.5 *Férét's hygenic* [sic] *elevating table.* Paris: Férét, n.d.

25x33½. 12 p includes covers. Pulp self-wraps, black print. Caption title. Illus catalog and price list of ergonomic adjustable school desk system. List of awards at previous fairs. No mention of WCE; from an intact collection. ☺ (WM)

843.1 [Ferris Wheel Company?] *...The honor of your presence is requested by the Board of Directors, at the formal opening of the Ferris Wheel. Wednesday, the twenty first of June, at three o'clock P.M. To___.* N.p.: n.p., n.d.

17x11. 1 *l.* Folded sheet printed on front. Blue illus of wheel at top, black print with blank line at end for the recipient's name. At head of title: "Midway Plaisance : World's Columbian Exposition." It is not clear which Board issued this invitation. ☺ . (S) **P➔**

843.2 Fibre Conduit Co. *Office of the fibre conduit company.* New York: n.p., n.d.

28x21½. 1 *l.* Sheet printed one side. Black print, no illus. Virtues of their insulating underground electrical conduit. No WCE content; from intact collection. (WM)

843.3 Fidelity Mutual Life Association. *Proceedings of the Columbian Convention of Agents of The Fidelity Mutual Life association of Philadelphia, Pa., held August 10 to 17, 1893, at the Cornell Avenue Hotel, Chicago, Ill.* N.p.: [Press of Billstein & Son], n.d.

20x13½. 124, (1) p+ 3 *l* fold outs of b/w illus including photos of agents and PA State Bldg. Navy cloth with silver print and scroll design. Minutes and speeches from their convention. Attendees were encouraged to visit the WCE (p 7) and had a reception at the PA Bldg (p 33). ☺ (S)

844. Field Columbian Museum. *Annual report...1894–95:* (GLD,FM)

845. Field Columbian Museum. Curtis. *The Authentic Letters of Columbus:* (GLD,FM)
▶Correction: "Publication 2. Vol. 1. No. 2." is printed on the cover and t.p., not "Publication 1."

846. Field Columbian Museum. *An historical and descriptive account of the Field:* (GLD,FM,VAM)

846.1 [Field] Columbian Museum. *The Property, now on Exhibition in the (blank) Building at The World's Columbian Exhibition, Chicago, Illinois, described as follows; (blank) is hereby presented to The Columbian Museum of Chicago,...* Chicago: n.p., 1893.

28x21½. Single sheet. Black ink. Used by the fledgling museum to obtain unwanted exhibits and exhibit materials from the WCE at the close of the fair. ☺ . (FM-Archives)

848.1 Flanagan & Biedenweg [Co.]. *Leaded art glass : Flanagan & Biedenweg,...* [Chicago: Globe Litho & Print Co.], n.d.

15x9½. (4) p. Folded buff stock, black print and illus of a stained glass window. Map of grounds on 2 inside pages in red and black shows location of exhibit in Manufactures Bldg; this is a manufacturer's ad variant of #1166. Illus of "Ecclesiastical glass" on back cover. ☺(GLD) $18 - 40

848.2 Flanagan & Biedenweg [Co.]. *Souvenir : World's Columbian Exposition : Chicago, 1893 : Flanagan & Biedenweg, Stained Glass : Manufacturers. Manufactures and Liberal Arts Building. Exhibit Nos. 96 and 98. Section F.* N.p.: n.p., 1893.

17x13. (16) p. Light blue wraps, red print, illus of winged woman. Factory illus on back. Caption title. C.t.: "1492 : Exposition souvenir : 1892." Text in red. Explains works; many testimonials. (WM)   P➔

849.1 Flint & Walling Mfg. Co. *The Hoosier Regulator!* N.p.: n.p., n.d.

30½x20. 1 *l*. Pink sheet, black print, illus of the Lowe automatic wind mill regulator. Caption title. Stock watering tank regulator prevented overflow. No WCE content; from intact collection. ☺(WM)

849.2 Foos Mfg. Co. *The Scientific Special Machinery For Crushing, Grinding and Pulverizing.* Springfield, OH: n.p., n.d.

15½x23. 48 p. White wraps, burgundy print, bordered and decorated in light green. Illus of factory in Springfield on back cover. C.t. Illus and description of their mills, rock crushers, etc. No mention of WCE; from an intact WCE collection. (WM)

849.3 Forbes, J.P., & Co. *...Castalian.* Chicago: n.p., [1893].

30x23. (4) p. Folded pulp sheet, black print. C.t. At head of title: "Samples Free! At World's Fair, Agricultural Building, up stairs, I.E. 6 : try it!" Water-based natural liniment claimed to cure many ailments. Testimonials to March 1893; analysis of the solution listed. ☺(WM)

849.4 Fort Wayne Organ Co. *The Packard Organ.* [Fort Wayne, IN?]: n.p., n.d.

15½x12½. (12) p. Folded stiff card wraps with color illus of man in rowboat on lake near country cottage, dogwood border design. C.t. Inside both covers are ads for Packard. All pages have illus children's poems titled "Peep show" by Uncle Harry; London: Pictorial Literature Society, n.d. No mention of WCE; from an intact WCE collection. (WM)

849.5 Fortis Powder & Explosives Co. Ltd. *Extracts from Official and other Reports : on the : "Fortis" explosive.* Brussels [and] London: Fortis Powder & Explosives C^Y L^D, n.d.   P➔

21x13½. 12 p. Green fleck wraps, black print and illus. Both wraps illus by Evermorcken, Bruxelles. C.t.: "The Fortis explosive : trade mark." It is stated on obverse of t.p. that the company took space at the WCE "where they will be pleased to receive inquiries." A series of 1888 testimonials for the company's explosives. WCE handout ad. ☺(GLD) $20 - 45

849.6 Fourteenth Regiment of Infantry, O.N.G. *Camp "Buckeye"...Seventy-first Street and Cottage Grove Avenue, Chicago, Ill., September 4 to 15, 1893.* N.p.: n.p., 1893.

12x9. (4) p. Folded card, gray-blue print. The Ohio National Guard (O.N.G.) is featured in "prominent ceremonies" list, p (4), including WCE dedication, 1892, and Duke de Veragua, 1893. © (S)

849.7 Fox, A.O., [Co.]. *Columbian Souvenir Catalogue of Woodside Farm, the property of A.O. Fox, Oregon, Dane County, Wis.* Madison, WI: M.J. Cantwell, book and job printer, 1893.

17x12. 42, (6) p. Red wraps with black print and vignette of sheep. Horse illus on back cover. Sections on sheep, horses and cattle; two folding illus of horses. C.t.: "Columbian Catalogue 1893 : Woodside Farm." The farm was 134 mi. from Chicago. Ad for sale of their animals. © (S)

849.8 Francis & Co., Limited. *Portland Cement.* London: n.p., n.d.

26½x20½. (2) p. Sheet printed both sides in red and black. Illus of past WF medals up to the Paris expo, 1889. No WCE content; from intact collection. © (WM)

849.9 Frazer, Persifer. *The Columbian exposition. A hasty glance taken in August, 1893, at the ores of the noble and of the useful metals in the Mines and Mining Building.* Rpt. N.p.: n.p., 1893–94.

22x15. Pp 376-94. Also pp 49-62 editorial comment. Beige cardboard hc. Caption title. Rpt from the *American Geologist* 12 (1893) and 13 (1894). See #1224.2 (*American Geologist*). © . (UPa)

849.10 Freeport Bicycle Mfg. Co. *Elliptic World's Records.* [Freeport, IL: Freeport Bicycle Mfg. Co., 1893?]

28x19½. (4) p. Folded sheet, black print. Caption title top of p (1). Bicycle with a "patent Elliptical sprocket." Testimonials dated through Jan 1893. Statistics. Prices. © . (Stfd-bound WCE Trans Dept Collection)

849.11 Frick, A.O., Co. *General Catalogue, 1893. Frick company engineers, "eclipse," traction and portable engines, saw mills, small stationery engines, and steam boilers.* Waynesboro, PA: [Deutsch lith. & prtg. co. Balto. MD], n.d.

24½x21. 55, (1) p index. Gold wraps with colorful lithos of globe, machinery and ferns in peach and blue. C.t. in bold white print: "Frick Company : eclipse : Machinery." Litho of factory on back. Stamped on back cover: "A.O. Frick, Machinery Hall, World's Fair, column–30-31." . (WM)

849.12 Frick, A.O., Co. *...Ice Making and Refrigerating Machinery. ...* [Waynesboro, PA: (The Friedenwald Co., Baltimore, MD), 1892?].

25x20½. 1 *l*, pp 67-75. Brilliant light green wraps, navy print. Plan of Frick Co. shops on back. At head of title: "Division number four." C.t. = t.p. except after c.t.: "1892." No mention of WCE; from an intact collection. (WM)

849.13 Frick, A.O., Co. *...Improved traction engines : also : Manufacturers of Frick company's "Eclipse."* Waynesboro, PA: Deutsch lith & print. co., Baltimore, MD, [1893?].

15½x8. (8) panels. Sheet unfolds to 15½x32, black print both sides. They made tractors and especially friction clutches for them. Stamped: "A.O. Frick, Machinery Hall, world's fair : column 30-31." Company also known as Frick & Co. Engineers. (WM)

849.14 Frick, H.C., Coke Co. *Connellsville Coke.* Pittsburgh, PA: [Duquesne printing & publishing], n.d.

15x22. (44) p. Dark gray-green stiff wraps, bold copper print, red string-tied. Back cover photo illus of "Works No. 1." C.t. Half title page in red and black: "A brief outline of the development of the great Connellsville Coke Region..." Many b/w and color illus. From intact WCE collections. (LBA,WM)

849.15 Fritzsche Brothers. *Catalogue of Essential Oils and Chemical Preparations... exhibited at the World's Columbian Exposition : Chicago : 1893.* New York and Garfield, NJ: Fritzsche Brothers (The Cherouny Print, NY), 1893?

14x22. 20 p. Buff wraps, black print. C.t. = t.p. Lists their oil products and oils chemical structures. Interesting ad since many of the oils are used today. © (GLD,WM) $25 - 50

849.16 Fritzsche Brothers. *Fritzsche Brothers : New York. Manufacturers of essential oils & chemical preparations. Exposition 1893 : Chicago, Ill.* [New York: Fritzsche Brothers (J. Ottmann, lith. co.)], n.d.

16½x10. (4) p. Folded stiff coated card stock. On back cover: exhibit architect listed as DEL E.V. FINTEL, ARCH'T. with litho of their exhibit and map of its location on the "ground floor : manufactures & liberal arts bldg." Front cover litho of the bldg. Ad. © (GLD) P↙ $24 - 55

849.17 Fromm, J., [Co.]. *...J. Fromm : Frankfurt a/M. Preisgekrönt aufallen beschickten-Ausstellungen.* Frankfurt, Germany: Friedr. Schoembs, Offenbach a/M, n.d.

13x8½. (6) p. Tri-fold sheet. Light blue outside with dark blue text and illus of products and medals; white inside with black text. At bottom of cover in red: "Agents: World's Exposition Exhibitor's [sic] Representing Company : Chicago." In German, English, and Spanish. At head of title: "World's Columbian Exposition : Chicago 1893. Königl. u. Grossherzogl. : Hoflieferant." Medicinals ad. (WM)

850.1 *...Fuller & Johnson : Manufacturing co. : Manufacturers of Corn Planters, Plows, Cultivators, Hay Rakes, Harrows, Mowers.* Madison, WI: [M.J. Cantwell, printer], n.d.

23x15½. 47 p. Dark tan stiff wraps, black print, illus of factory. Illus of corn planter on back. "Catalogue for 1892." C.t. At head of title: "Established 1846..." Issued with 3 loose ad sheets on colored paper. No mention of WCE; from intact collection. © . (WM) P↓

850.2 *Garden Café : Woman's Building : Chicago Day : Monday, October 9th, 1893 : World's Columbian exposition.* Chicago?: A.L. Swift & co., n.d. P↘

17½x11½. (4) p. White glossy wraps, green and red print and design, blue string-tied. Front cover red vignette of Woman's Bldg. C.t. At the top of the cover: "Mrs. E.W. Riley   H.F. Sawford." The extensive menu is printed in blue ink. Food prices ranged from 5¢ for tea to 50¢ for lobster salad. © (GLD) $35 - 60

850.3 *Garis-Cochran : dish-washing machine : for : hotels : restaurants : club houses : steam-ships and : private houses.* [Shelbyville, IL.: Barnum & Pennington, printers], n.d.

19½x13½. 12 p. Dull yellow wraps, black print. C.t. Illus of their elaborate machines; testimonials all dated Nov/Dec 1892. Catalogue with port of inventor "Mrs. Josephine G. Cochran." No WCE content; from intact collection. © . (WM)

850.4 Gas Engine and Power Co. *The only Naphtha Launch.* [Morris Heights, NY: Gas Engine & Power Co. (The Knapp co., lith.)], n.d. P→

12 cm diameter clam shell shaped die-cut. (16) p+ text and illus on insides of both wraps. Front wrap chromolith depicting the launch. C.t.

Last (10) p for testimonials about the Naphtha launches. Bottom inside front wrap: "World's Columbian Exposition 1893. Exhibit on main aisle of transportation building." ☺ (GLD,WM) $30 - 60

850.5 Gas Engine and Power Co. *The only naphtha launch.* [Morris Heights], NY: [Gas Engine and Power Co.] (Press of Bartlett & Co.), [ᶜ1893].

13½x17½. (2)-16 p. Frontis litho of Naphtha launches on p (2). Ornately embossed cream glossy stiff wraps depict launch. Gold string-tied. Text in brown ink; dark green illus. C.t. = caption title on p 5. T.p. title: "Gas Engine and Power Company." At the bottom of t.p.: "Exhibit on the main aisle of the transportation building : Worlds [sic] Columbian exposition." Beautiful ad. ☺ (GLD) $25 - 50

851.1 Gaze, Henry, & Sons. *Henry Gaze & Sons, Programme of Arrangements : for : traveling and hotel accommodation : at the : World's Columbian Exposition : Chicago, 1893.* N.p.: n.p., n.d.   **P→**

23½x13. 45, (2) p. Blue wraps, navy print, small illus of Admin Bldg. Bird's-eye of the WF ᶜ1892 by A. Zeese on back. Top of p (1): "First edition.—March." On p (2) dated Jan. 20, 1892: President W.T. Baker appointed the company "Inter-national Tourist Agents" for the WCE. (WM)

851.2 Gaze, Henry, & Sons. *...Henry Gaze & sons' : special program : with details of ocean steamers, American railway routes, hotel accommodations, principal sights, conducted tours, and the World's fair.* London: Henry Gaze & sons, n.d.

25x16. 48 p. Cream wraps, navy blue print, title printed over faint litho of Admin Bldg. C.t. At head of title: "World's Columbian Exposition, Chicago, 1893." Top p 1: "Gaze's Chicago program.—Second edition." Ads on wraps. European travel brochure for WF trips. The WCE is described, pp 1-5. ☺ . (UMD)   **P→**

851.3 Gaze, Henry, & Sons. *...Henry Gaze & Sons' weekly excursions to the World's Columbian Exposition, at Chicago. Leaving Boston every Tuesday at 4.20 p.m., By a Special Vestibuled train of Wagner Palace Cars.* N.p.: n.p, n.d.

13x16½. 16 p. Pale green wraps, navy print. Navy WF bird's-eye view on back. C.t.: "Weekly Excursions to the World's Fair." All expenses paid, $90 for one week. (WM)

851.4 General Electric Co. *General Electric Company.* Schenectady, NY: General Electric co. (Press of Bartlett & co.), n.d.   **P→**

19x9. (28) panels from sheet opening to 38x56. White paper, brown print and design, black illus. Front illus of an angel holding a light bulb above globe and WCE grounds. Ad describing their many plants and products; and uses of their products at the WCE, e.g., intramural railway [see also Intramural RR in index], cold storage bldg, and the electric fountains. ☺ (GLD,E,L,S,WM) $25 - 50

851.5 General Electric Co. *General Electric co.'s electric locomotive for B&O tunnel.* Chicago: Rand, McNally & co., n.d.

9½x19½. 36 printed panels; 29 are paged. Glossy sheet unfolds to 85x39. C.t. Brown print; illus in dark green. C.t. Illus and text of their exhibited electrical railroad apparatus. Six unpaged panels show map of WCE grounds and route of Intramural RR in red. The RR was run by GE motors. Last unpaged panel is the cover. [See also Intramural RR in index.] ☺ (S)

851.6 General Electric Co. *...Triumphant Industries. General Electric Company.* New York: [Electrotyped and printed by Publishers' printing company], 1893.

23½x16½. 1 *l*, 14 p. Tan wraps, black print. C.t. At head of title: "Reprinted From The Forum for February, 1893." Text and illus of their WF fountains and Intramural Railroad at the WCE. (WM)

851.7 Genesee Fruit Co. *Price List of 1893 : Genesee Fruit Company : Proprietors of S.R. & J.C. Mott Brands of fine ciders & vinegars : and Manufacturers of Apple Products.* New York: Genesee Fruit Co., n.d.

9x14½. (4) p. Folded buff sheet; gilt, black, and red print. Colored lithos of three different fancy cider bottles on back. C.t. Early Mott juice ad. Exhibited in the Hort Bldg, Section N-70. No WCE; from an intact collection. © (GLD) $18 - 42

851.8 Genoa Hotel. *The Hotel Genoa.* [Chicago: Palm, Stevens & Co. : printers], n.d.

The Hotel Genoa.

12½x17½. (32) p+ 1 *l* "engagement blank" to sign up for a stay. Tan wraps, black print, illus of the hotel and first floor cafe. C.t. = caption title. WCE Bldgs every other page ᶜ1892 by A. Zeese. Map of Jackson Park with Genoa location 3 blocks NW of the fairgrounds. Located at "5311-13-15 Lake Avenue, Chicago, Ill." (Hyde Park area). [This is the prospectus that may be requested below.] ©. (WM)   P➔

851.9 Genoa Hotel. *Hotel Genoa : Illustrated Prospectus of World's Fair Buildings Sent on Application.* Chicago: n.p., n.d.

7½x14. Buff stiff card, print both sides. Same hotel illus as #851.8. Caption title. The prospectus mentioned in this title is #851.8. Back: "Shall you visit the World's Columbian exposition?" © (WM)

852.1 Gérard, E., and J. Dufraisseix & Cie. *E. Gérard, Dufraisseix & co., manufacturers of the "Ch. Field Haviland" China, Limoges, France.* New York: H.A. Rost, printer, n.d.

13½x11½. 24 p. Yellow wraps, dark brown print, green floral design borders with vignette of a potter, string-tied. C.t.: "Nearly a century old" (very small print). Their exhibit explained pp 11-14. . (WM)

852.2 ...*Germain Fruit Company. Wine department : ...Buy your Wines from California direct.* Los Angeles: Germain Fruit Co. (Lazarus & Melzer), [1893].

16x9. (4) p. Folded green sheet, black print and design, illus of wine bottles. Illus of co's fruit farm on back. At head of title: "Incorporated January 1ˢᵗ 1884." Ad came with a typewritten form letter in blue ink on pink stationery and an order envelope addressed to the company. No mention of WCE, from an intact collection. [Their exhibit was in the Hort Bldg, Sec F-4.] © (GLD) $25 - 50

853. German Kali-Works. *Potash*: (E,KS)
▶Variant: Different words at top and bottom margins of cover, otherwise the same c.t. and illus of their exhibit entrance.

853.1 Gill, Wilson L[indsley]. *A Children's Palace : For the World's Fair.* N.p.: n.p., 1892?

20x14. 15 p. Buff wraps, black print and design. Illus. C.t. On cover: "Reprint from THE CHRISTIAN AT WORK, April 28, 1892" (See #1273.1). Cover litho of young girl with dove. Frontis and back cover drawings of the proposed children's dept palace. ©. (ICRL)   P➔

854.1 Goldman, Henry. *Goldman's Advanced System for Locating Errors : Without Re-checking or Copying Entries.* N.p.: n.p., n.d.

15x8½. (4) p. Folded white sheet. Text in English, French, German, and Spanish—1 page each. Exhibited in: "Lib. Arts Build'g. N.E. Gal., Sect. E, U–105." Goldman, author and inventor, was editor of *Office Men's Record*, a "Magazine of practical Knowledge." (WM)

854.2 Goldschmidt, Theodore, [Co.]. *Th. Goldschmidt : Chemical Works : Essen-Ruhr : (Germany).* New York: A. Kern & Co. agent, n.d.

27x20. (3) p. Folded glossy sheet, black/gilt/red print on pale green background with light brown border. C.t. List of items exhibited as part of United Chemical Works in the Germany pavilion. (WM)

854.3 Goldsmiths' & Silversmiths' Co. *The exposition clock, Columbian shield, : and : Shakespearian gold casket, specially designed and manufactured for the world's fair by,,,* London: n.p., n.d.

32x24½. (2) p. Single sheet printed both sides, black print and illus. Illus of 3 items listed in title (front); description of the 3 items (back). (WM)

854.4 Goldsmiths' & Silversmiths' Co. *The Manufacturing Goldsmiths' & Silversmiths* [sic] *Company. .. The exposition clock. Specially Designed & Manufactured for the World's Fair, 1893.* London: Goldsmiths' and Silversmiths' Co., n.d. **P➜**

14x9½. (8) p. Folded buff card opens to 14x37. Pale yellow background, blue print and illus. Shows and describes the company's other WCE showpieces: "The Columbian Shield," "The Shakespearean Casket," and "Exhibit of Diamond & Gem Work." C.t. Beautiful ad. For more on the Exposition Clock, see #1256.3. ☺ (GLD,E,WM) $35 – 65

☞ The clock is now located in the lobby of the Waldorf Astoria Hotel on Park Ave, New York City. **P↘**

854.5 Goodyear Shoe Machinery Co. *Worlds* [sic] *Fair Souvenir : A Pair of Goodyear Welt Shoes.* Chicago: [Goodyear Shoe Machinery co.] Shober & Carqueville lith. co., n.d.

15½x9. 11, (1) p+ text inside front wrap. White stiff wraps. Chromolith front cover includes "The Goodyear pagoda." C.t. At bottom of front wrap: "In Gallery Shoe and Leather Building : World's Columbian Exposition : Chicago, 1893." Photo-reproduction of their working exhibit on back wrap. Ad describing their machinery and shoe assembly process. ☺ (GLD,E) $20 - 45

855.1 Gore, J.W., Tours. *Grand tours to the World's Columbian Exposition, Chicago : May 1st to November 1st, 1893.* [Boston : Press of Geo. E. Crosby & co.], n.d.

9½x15½. 12, (3) p. Lavender wraps, navy print, white string-tied. C.t. Double page panorama of Michigan Columbian Club Hotel on last pp. Centerfold unpaged photo-illus of two private hotel cars. Worcester Excursion Car illus on back. (WM)

855.2 Gorham Mfg. Co. *Columbus Statue. Sterling Silver.* New York and Providence: Gorham M'f'g Co., Silversmiths, n.d.

20½x14. (4) p. Folded white coated sheet, black print, cover litho of the "Columbus Statue." C.t. This statue, displayed in their exhibit [Manufactures Bldg, Section N, Block 1, South], was modeled by Bartholdi, who also designed the Statue of Liberty. Ad. ☺ (GLD,WM) $20 - 45

856. *The Gospel according to Saint John*: (GLD) $20 - 42
---- Also found: Blind stamped bright red paper covered boards.

856.1 Gouben, Albert, [Co.]. *...Breton Apéritive : S-Servais's Wine : tonic, digestive balsamique without any bitter.* Saint-Servan, France: Merlaix, imp. A. Chevalier, n.d.

42x20. 1 *l.* Orange sheet, black print in 3 large columns: English, French and Portuguese. At head of title: "Chicago exposition : Palace Horticulture B." (WM)

856.2 Graham, Passmore & Co. *...Philadelphia lawn mower.* Philadelphia: Graham, Passmore & Co. [J. Ottmann Lith, NY], n.d.

16x9½. (4) p. Folded sheet (fold at top), black print, lithos of a different push mowers on each page. At head of title: "World's Columbian Exposition : Chicago 1893." [Exhibited in Hort Bldg, Group 26, Class 192. North end of the bldg.] ☺ (GLD) $18 - 40

856.3 Grand Detour Plow Co. *Pocket catalogue of the Grand Detour Plow Co.,...goods of its manufacture : as shown at the : Columbian Exposition, Chicago, Ill, A.D. 1893.* Buffalo, NY: Gies & co., printers, n.d.

15½x8½. 44 p includes unpaged color plates of their plow and cultivator line. White stiff wraps with chromolith of child's head, brown print. At top of cover "Worlds [sic] Fair Greeting." Text pages have a green background rectangle under black print. Pretty ad. ☺ (WM)

857. Grand Trunk RR. *How to visit the World's Fair at Chicago*: (NLA)
▸Add paging: 20 p.
▸Add publisher: CIHM microfiche series no. 60895, 1986. One microfiche (17 frames).

858. Grand Trunk RR. *Pen and Sunlight*:
▸Paging correction: (11), 11-99, (6) p.
▸Add cover description: Blue cloth beveled hc with gilt print. Contains WCE section with illus.

858.1 *Granger's : roller stamp mill.* Denver, CO: n.p., n.d.

16½x9½. (4) p. Folded yellow sheet, black print, illus of mill. C.t. Rubber stamped on back: "World's Columbian Exposition N.E. Section T. 13, Mines & Mining Building. Chicago." A lobed cam apparatus crushed ore, then stamping occurred at 120 five-inch drops per minute. Section view of mill on back. ☺ (WM)

858.2 Granite Manufacturers' Association. *Souvenir of the World's Columbian Exposition. 1893.* Quincy, MA: Granite Manufacturers' Association. (McIndoe Bros. Printers, Boston), 1893?.

9x16. (4) p+ text inside front and back wraps. Coated white stiff wraps, black print and design. Text pages are glued to wraps' hinge (unusual). Monument illus on back wrap captioned: "Exhibit in Section H, Manufacturers' Building, World's Fair." Ad. ☺ (GLD) $25 - 45

859. *The graphic history*: (CCA,cul,GBP,MIT,MSI,PSU,sfpl,SPL,SStu,UIC,UTA,UWM) **P➜**
---- Also found: Dark blue pebble-textured cloth hc, silver print and design.

Graphic Cover Design, #859.

859.1 Gray National Telautograph Co. *Gray National Telautograph Company.* New York: Gray National Telautograph Co., 1893?

8x13½. Single buff stiff card, brown print. On bottom front: "Heth Lorton, manager of exhibition, electricity building, World's fair." On verso: "The Telautograph transmits *instantaneously, in fac simile, writing to any distance*" and lists 12 advantages. Ad. ☺ (GLD) $30 - 65

☞ Elisha Gray (1835-1901) was the near-inventor of the telephone and the inventor of the telautograph, the very first fax machine. In a legal contest with Alexander Graham Bell over the invention of the telephone, he lost. He was professor of dynamic electricity at Oberlin College, Ohio.

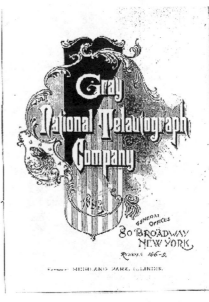

859.2 Gray National Telautograph Company. *Gray national telautograph company.* New York: American Bank Note Company, 1893.

23x15½. (12) p. Robin's-egg blue stiff wraps, navy print and shield decoration by American Bank Note Co. C.t. = t.p. Shows samples of the machine's facsimiles. Company info and bio of Gray. Illus of machine in operation. Factory in Highland Park, IL; offices in NYC. No mention of WCE; from an intact collection. . (ref,WM)   **P➜** $107

859.3 Gray National Telautograph Company. *"Telautogram : The writing attached hereto is a sample of work done on Prof. Elisha Gray's Telautograph,..."* New York: Gray National Telautograph Co., n.d.

11x26½. (2) p. Single sheet printed both sides in blue ink. Illus: 1) transmitter record, 2) receiver copy. At bottom of front: "Heth Lorton, manager of exhibition, electricity building World's fair." On verso the derivation of the name is explained along with a list of 12 advantages. Ad. ☺ (GLD,WM) $30 - 65

☞ WM has the mentioned actual sample of a handwritten WCE message and its excellent facsimile.

859.4 Gray's, A.W., Sons. *Gray's : Latest Improved Patent : horse powers. Threshing Machines and Wood Sawing Machines.* Middletown Springs, VT: A.W. Gray's Sons (Plimpton manufacturing co. press, Hartford, CT), n.d.

23x15½. 50 p. Beautifully illus wraps with horses head and wheat shafts in gilt and dark blue; illus of machinery in gilt and dark blue on back cover. C.t. Stamped on front cover: "F.M. Clemons, R-11, Agricultural Annex. World's Fair, Chicago." Banner on p (1): "1893. Gray's 1893." (WM)

859.5 ...*Great Eastern Fertilizer Company : manufacturers of : high grade : Fertilizers.* N.p.: (Gies & co., Buffalo, NY), n.d.   P➔

16½x9. 48 p. Ad booklet stapled on tri-fold buff card stock, rounded corners on inside flap; red and black print. C.t. At head of title: "World's fair edition : 1893." Sales office was in Rutland, VT. ☺ . (E)

860. *The Great School Exhibits*: (MSL)
▶Add: Ivory glossy wraps, black print. C.t. (no t.p.). First *l* is publisher's introduction followed by plates from various school exhibits shown by the Liberal Arts Dept in the Manufactures and Liberal Arts Bldg.

860.1 *The Great Western Railway of England : illustrated guide.* [London Wall, London: Waterlow & Sons Limited, Printers], May 1893.

21½x14. (4), 24 p. Pale green wraps, brown print, b/w illus of scenes on the railway route. Blue text and illus. From intact WCE collection. ☺ (WM)

861. Green. *Food Products*: (GLD,CU,KCPL,NAL,SPL,UMC,UMN) $30 - 60
▶First ed. description: 20x14½. xi, 249 p., vii. Red and white interwoven fiber cloth hc, black print. Dedicated to cook and author Juliet Corson. Articles on WCE food exhibits. Green was a food judge. P➔
▶Add another edition: 6th edition.

861.1 Greene Register Co. *The Greene Cash Register.* Chicago: n.p., n.d.

21½x14. (4) p. Folded white sheet, blue-black print, register illus. At bottom of cover: "World's fair exhibit, Gallery, Sec E, 101 R." Patented Apr 30, 1893. AKA Jno. T. Greene & Co. ☺ (WM)

861.2 Gregory, James M. *Frederick Douglass the Orator. Containing an Account of His Life; His Eminent Public Services; His Brilliant Career as Orator; Selections from His Speeches and Writings.* Springfield, [MA]: Willey & Co, 1893.

21x14. 215 p. Cloth hc, illus and ports. Introduction by W.S. Scarborough. Contains Douglass's WCE speech for Haiti Day, pp 192-98. (ref) $75

861.3 Griswold Mfg. Co. ..."*Erie*" *hollow ware. American Waffle Iron. American Damper.* Erie, PA: n.p., n.d.

15½x9. (4) p. Folded light tan card, green and red print and spider decoration. At head of title: co and exhibit info. On cover: "World's Columbian exposition : Manufacturers' [sic] Building, Section G, Block 4." Inside illus of 2 waffle irons. ☺ (WM)

☞ Griswold was noted for quality cast iron goods. Their products and ads are still collected today.

861.4 Grover, R.B., & Co. ...*Emerson shoe : Exclusively for gentlemens* [sic] *wear.* Brockton, MA: n.p., n.d.

14x6½. (8) panels. Sheet unfolds to 14x26. C.t. in rust and black. Illus catalog with two shoes per panel. At head of title: "Spring Catalogue of a few leading styles of the celebrated." No mention of WCE; from an intact collection. (WM)

861.5 Grusonwerk. ...*Excelsior Mill (Gruson's System)...Kibbling and Grinding Mill for Agricultural purposes, Flour Mills,...* [Magdeburg, Germany]: n.p., 1891.

29x22½. 20 p includes front and back of self-wraps; red and black print. Front cover list of exhibition award won with the mill. Illus catalog; no WCE content. C.t. At head of title: "Grusonwerk, Magdeburg-Buckau. (Germany.)" Item found with those below; all assumed to be WCE handouts: (WM)
a. Gruson, H. [Co.]. *The cosine governor.* [Magdeburg, Ger.: Walter Ochs & Co.], 1886. 38 p. (WM)
b. Grusonwerk. *Case-hardened Steam-hammer blocks.* [Same as Gruson above], 1887. 57 p. (WM)

861.6 Grusonwerk. ...*Sombart's geräuschloser patent-gasmotor.* Magdeburg-Buckau: [Walter Ochs & comp., 1893].

29x22½. (4) p. Folded yellow-tan sheet, black and red print. Black illus of engines. Laid-in sheet listing engine sizes and horsepower. Purple rubber stamp: "World's Columbian Exposition, Chicago, 1893 Machinery Hall." © (WM)

861.7 Guckenheimer, A., & Bros. *Guckenheimer Pure Rye Whiskey. The Standard of Perfection, Absolutely Pure, Always Reliable.* Pittsburgh, PA: A. Guckenheimer & Bros., n.d.

18½x10½. (4) p. Folded white coated paper. Gilt print and blue illus of distillery in Freeport, PA; back cover has gilt and dark blue ad banner. C.t. No mention of WCE; from intact collection. Their exhibit was in Ag Bldg, Section I-L-5. © (GLD,E) $25 - 65

861.8 Gurley, W. & L.E., [Co.]. *Souvenir catalogue. World's Columbian exposition.* [Troy, NY]: n.p., 1893.

Oblong octavo. (64) p. Catalog of their civil engineers' and surveyors' instruments. (HU)

862.   *Hagenbeck's Arena and World's Museum:* (S,UIC)
---- Also found: White glossy wraps, blue background, black print.

862.1 Hagenbeck's Zoological Arena. *Hagenbeck's Zoological Arena : midway plaisance World's fair.* N.p.: n.p., n.d.

9½x13. (8) panels. Folded ad sheet unfolds vertically to 38x13. Front has black print and illus of the arena and a Midway location map; the back has chromolith illus of wild animals. © . (E,S) $25 - 55

862.2 Hagenbeck's Zoological Arena. *Price List : of : Ethnographical Collections : Exhibited at : Carl Hagenbeck's Zoological Arena and World's Museum. Midway Plaisance. World's Columbian Exposition.* N.p.: Hagenbeck's Zoological Arena, n.d.

ELEVATOR TOWER
To Roof of Manufactures and Liberal Arts Building.

23x15½. (4) p. Buff paper, black print. List of 27 grouped items from Africa. On back: "Capt. Adr. Jacobsen" was in charge of the sale. © . (FM-Anthropology Acc-81)

☞ The Field Columbian Museum purchased all 27 Hagenbeck lots for $6000. For correspondence associated with the sale see #2446.FM-C.

862.3 Hale Elevator Co. *Elevator tower : To Roof of Manufactures and Liberal Arts Building.* [Chicago?: Hale Elevator co., 1893?].   P➔

17x9½. (4) p. Folded card. Pale green (or yellow) card stock, sepia print and illus of the elevator tower on front and bird's-eye view of WCE grounds on back. C.t. Gives statistics of 300,000 visitors to the roof by Sept 1, 1893. Late ad. © (GLD,E,S,WM) $20 - 52

862.4 Hallet & Davis Piano Co. Howes, C.F., comp. and ed. *Music in Literature : Quotations from Literati of All Nations.* Philadelphia: Ketterlinus Printing House, 1894 [ᶜ1894 By Hallet & Davis Piano co.].

23x15. 112 p. Pale drab green wraps with royal blue and gilt print and small floral decoration. Back cover ad for Kimball pianos. Clever cartoon ad on p 17 showing H & D pianos in place of cars on the Ferris wheel. Sent to all who signed their guest book at the WCE exhibit. ☺ (S)

862.5 Hamburg-American Packet Co. *Across The Atlantic.* [New York: Moss Eng. Co.], n.d.

10x14½. 40 p. White glossy wraps, brown print, illus of steamer in blue. Illus of three Columbus caravels on inside front cover. Illus comparison of Columbus' voyage with a "modern" trip on Hamburg ships. No WCE content; from an intact collection. ☺ (WM)

862.6 *Hamburg-American Packet Co.* [New York: Press of John C. Rankin, Jr.], n.d.

14x21½. 20 p. Chromolith stiff wraps in portrait orientation, black print and illus of ships and harbors. C.t. No WCE content; from intact collection. ☺ (WM)

862.7 Hampden Hotel. *The Hampden : a residential hotel. 39ᵗʰ street & Langley avenue. Chicago.* Chicago: Vandercook Engraving and Pub Co., n.d.

13x17½. (12) p+ 1 *l* fold map of location relative to Chicago and WF at back cover. Tan glossy wraps, chocolate brown print, illus of the hotel, blue ribbon tied. C.t. The hotel was midway between downtown and Jackson Park; directions to hotel and WCE given. On back: illus of coach drawn by four horses with banner "Between The Hampden and World's Fair." ☺ . (WM)

862.8 Hancock Inspirator Co. *...The Hancock inspirator. The Standard.* Boston: The Hancock inspirator co., n.d.   **P➔**

23x15½. (8) p+ text on self-wraps. C.t. At head of title: "1893." Ad for inspirators, lifters, and ejectors for steam systems such as railroads and stationary boilers. From an intact WCE collection; assumed to have been handed out with the following two items which were found with it. ☺ . (WM)
a. "The Hancock Inspirator Co. Manufacturers of Inspirators, Ejectors and general jet apparatus." 8½x15½. Light green card printed 1 side. (WM)
b. "1893. 1893. The Hancock Inspirator for Feeding Stationery Boilers." 15½x8½. (4) p. Folded buff sheet. Product price list. ☺ (WM)

863. *Handbook of General Information for university men*:
▶Add: Light green wraps, black print and top and bottom border design.

863.1 Hardy, F.A., & Co. *F.A. Hardy & Co. : Wholesale Opticians.* Chicago: n.p., n.d.

9x14. (2) p. Buff card, black print. C.t. On back is WCE location, "Machinery Hall Annex." ☺ (WM)
---- Also found: 7½x13. (2) p. Cream card, black print. On back is a plan of Machinery Hall showing their exhibit location. ☺ (WM)

863.2 *Harper & brothers' : exhibit at : The Columbian World's Fair.* N.p.: n.p., n.d.

16½x13½. (4) p. Folded coated sheet, black print and illus of cabinet. Description of the publisher's exhibit. Title given is the caption title from p (2). (WM)

863.3 Harper, Thomas, [Ltd]. *With Compliments of Thomas Harper : Phoenix Needle Works, Redditch, England : Souvenir of the World's Columbian Exposition Chicago, U.S.A.* Redditch, Eng.: Thomas Harper, n.d.

11½x8. (6) p. Sheet printed both sides unfolds to 11½x18½. Chromolith of two ladies talking over tea; hostess is sewing with Harper's needle. C.t. A needle sample case is tipped-in on the inside of this pretty folded ad. ☺ (GLD,S)
$30 - 60

863.4 Harris, Hatch & Abbott. *The Louis J. Harris' : Grand "World's Fair" tours.* Boston: Louis J. Harris (Press of the Evening Journal Company, New Bedford, MA), [ᶜ1893 by Louis J. Harris].

15x21. 40 p. Blue-green wraps, black print, railroad car illus. C.t. Harris had Midway Plaisance WF headquarters. All-expenses-paid tours to WCE: $75 and $100. Harris used a private car, "Jeannette." (WM)

863.5 Hartford Courant Co. *An Almanac for the year 1893 : With Some pictures and information Concerning Columbus and the Worlds* [sic] *fair.* Hartford, CT: The Hartford Courant Co., n.d.

20½x13. (6) ads, (66) text, (24) p ads. Sienna colored wraps, black print and litho of the Courant Bldg. C.t.: "The Courant almanac, 1893. Price, 10 Cents." Frontis: "The Landing of Columbus." Extensive text and illus of the WCE and its bldgs along with info on previous fairs and typical almanac data.
© (GLD,HML,S)   P➜ $20 – 45
---- Also Found: Phoenix Mutual Life Insurance Co. Hartford: Phoenix Mutual Life Insurance Co., n.d. 20x13. (48) p. Tan wraps, blue and red print. 1893 calendar on p 1. (Fess,ref,S)

863.6 *Hartmann & Braun's : Electrical-Instruments at the World's Columbian Exposition : Chicago. 1893.* Frankfort o.M. [Ger.]: Bockenheim (Printed by Julius Bahlke, Berlin S.), 1893.

23½x16. 2 *l*, (1)-36 p. No frontis. Leaves are t.p. and illus of co's bldg. Page 36 for "Notes." Tan wraps with gray/silver/tan/black illus and print on front cover. "HB" and "Hübel & Denck Buchbinderei Leipzig." Decorative end pages, red dyed edges. Scientific instrument and electrical apparatus. Exhibit No 1349, group 123. 119. Catalog of 112 items in their exhibit. © . (E)

863.7 Hartmann Bros. & Reinhard. *Souvenir of the World's Columbian exposition : Chicago, 1893. High grade musical instruments.* New York: n.p., 1893?

15½x8½. (12) p. Lemon-yellow stiff wraps, gilt print both covers. C.t. Last testimonial dated Feb 15, 1893. Illus catalog of their instruments: "Zithers, Guitars, Mandolins, and strings a specialty." (WM)

864.   Hartzell. *Life of Columbus*: (GLD,E,UMD) $20 - 40
▸Add: At top of cover: "PLEASE PRESERVE this BEAUTIFUL SOUVENIR of Your First Visit to the WORLD'S COLUMBIAN EXPOSITION. You Will Not be Sorry." Found with and without this cover statement.

865.   Hartzler, H[enry] B[urns]. *Moody in Chicago or the World's fair gospel campaign*: (Amh,DU,FLP,IHi,UIC)
▸Add pub: Chicago: The Bible Institute colportage Association, [ᶜ1894 By Fleming H. Revell Co.].

865.1 Harvard University. "American college exhibits at Chicago 1893".

25x18. Tan cloth hc. Title from spine. Unique collection from the WF education exhibits. Harvard's bound volume of school pamphlets each a hand out at the WCE. None of the pamphlets except Lehigh U, #911, specifically mention the WCE. Other schools include Columbia College, Illinois State Normal U, Johns Hopkins U, U of Michigan, Mount Holyoke College, Princeton, St. Lawrence U. (HU-Widener Econ)

865.2 Harvey World's Fair Hotel and Entertainment Co. *One Dollar : The World's Fair : headquarters : at Harvey, Ill.* ... Chicago: The Harvey World's Fair Hotel and Entertainment Co., [1892?].

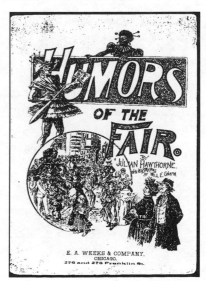

23x10. Sheet unfolds to 45x29, printed both sides. Illus of Harvey Co's two World's Fair hotels and map location. One dollar per person per day for two persons in a room. Managed by Mrs. E.A. Russell of Minneapolis, MN. The hotel at Harvey had 740 rooms, 1714 feet of street frontage, 1.2 miles of verandah, and 10 acres of floor space. © (GLD,S)

866.   Hawthorne. *The fairest of the fair*: (FLP,GU,Merc,NPG,ref,S,SHB)

867.   Hawthorne. *Humors of the Fair*: (Col,UCB,UPa,UR,Yale)   P➜
---- Also found: Light green glossy wraps, black print and illus. 205 p.

867.1 *Heine & C° : Leipzig : manufacturers of essential oils essences and chemicals for perfumery...* [Leipzig: Printed by Oscar Fürstenau], n.d.

> 18x12. (4) p. Folded stiff card, black and red print, black border. At top of pp (2)-(3): "Products exposed at Chicago 1893..." C.t. ☺ (WM)

867.2 Heinemann, T.W., Co. *New light on old facts. O-P-C...Suspensory.* Chicago: n.p., [°1893 T.W. Heinemann Co.].

> 14½x8½. (12) p. Cream smooth wraps, brown and yellow print and scroll work design. At bottom of cover in red overprint: "Exhibit : Manufactures and Liberal Arts Building : North Gallery, Sec. E. Post I." Advantages of their men's scrotum sack; illus on back wrap. [Early version of the jock strap for athletic activity.] ☺ (WM)

867.3 Heinze, Hermann. *Souvenir Map of the World's Columbian Exposition at Jackson Park and Midway Plaisance : Chicago Ill. U.S.A. : 1893.* Chicago: Hermann Heinze (A. Zeese & co. engravers), °1892 by Hermann Heinze.

> 21½x10½. Red stiff folder containing laid-in color map that unfolds to 63x63. Folder is printed in black. Map has ornate black border and is printed one side in 3 colors. Title from map. At top of folder: "Attention!" followed by ad for "The New Section Liner : Invented by Hermann Heinze, Chief Draughtsman, Surveys and Grades Department, World's Columbian Exposition." Found priced 15 (or 25) cents. ☺ (GLD,WM) $70 - 150

867.4 Helvetia Milk Condensing Co. *Highland Brand Evaporated Cream by Helvetia milk condensing co.* [Highland, IL: Helvetia Milk Condensing co.], n.d.

> 12x7½ die-cut in shape of a can. The accordion folded panels unfold to 12x45½. 6 panels printed both sides make (12) p. One side of the "strip" has 6 chromoliths which includes an illus of their exhibit in the Ag Bldg. The other side is all text and testimonials printed in black ink. Beautiful color WCE handout ad. ☺ (GLD) P➔ $30 - 60

867.5 *Hemmets drottning kokbok : tva tusen vardefulla recepter for matlagning och hushallning, matsedlar, bordskick, toalett, m.m. : bidrag fran ofver 200 af Verldsutställningens ledande damer, guvernorernas fruar och andra framstaende damer.* Chicago: Fort Dearborn, [°1899 by The Fort Dearborn Publishing Co.].

> 24x15½. 1 *l* (frontis port of Juliet Corson), 604 p. Pebbled white oil cloth hc with black print. Swedish version of *The "Home Queen" World's Fair souvenir Cook Book*, #885. Same cover design showing the Admin Bldg. This later edition of #867.6 mentions the WCE and has recipes from the WCE. Illus of WCE bldgs throughout. (UMN)

867.6 *Hemmets drottning : Verldsutställningens souvenir kokbok.* Chicago: Swedish book co., [°1893].

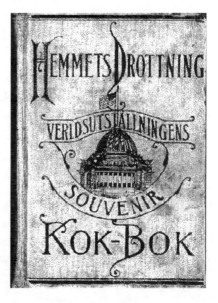

> 24x15½. 1 *l* frontis port of Juliet Corson, 604 p. Pebbled white oil cloth hc with black print. Swedish version of *The "Home Queen,"* #885; same cover design showing the Admin Bldg. ☺ (S)
> ---- Also found: Chicago: The Fort Dearborn Publishing Co., [°1893 by Geo. F. Cram : °1894 by Jno. F. Waite]. Same book by another publisher: ☺ (GLD) P➔ $60 - 120

867.7 Hendey Machine Co. *The Norton improved screw-cutting engine lathe.* Torrington, CT: Hendey machine co., 1893.

> 9x22. (4) p. Tri-fold sheet, printed one side, unfolds vertically to 22x38½. Black print and litho of the lathe. Rubber stamped on back: "Sec 28, col. K-L-38, machinery hall annnex [sic], World's fair." ☺ . (E)

867.8 Hendrick, D.B., Co. *Hendrick's portable bailing press, for Bailing Hay, Straw, Cotton, Husks, Rags, Paper, Manure, &C.* N.p.: n.p., n.d.

14x20½. (8) p. Lime green wraps, black print, illus of horse-drawn bailing press. Text inside both covers. Testimonials and company info with illus. No mention of WCE; from intact collection. (WM)

869. Heron, Addie E. *Dainty work : for : pleasure and profit.* Chicago: Thompson & Thomas, 1893; Grand Rapids, MI: P.D. Farrell & co., Publishers, n.d.

Thompson: 24x18. 444 p. Red-brown cloth hc, gilt print. 2 *l* preface dedications to the WCE and Mrs. Potter Palmer. "How to" book on darning, crocheting, embroidering, and other craft work. (S)

Farrell: 24x19. 1 l (t.p.), 2 *l* (dedications), xv, 444, (1) p. Four interspersed color plates not included in pagination. C.t. = t.p. Red-brown cloth hc, gilt print, red dyed edges. Same preface dedications to Mrs. Potter Palmer and the WCE as found in #869.1 and #869.2. "How to" book with many b/w illus of various types of embroidery, crochet, knitting, etc. ☺ (GLD) $30 - 65

▶Delete: 3rd ed. Chicago: Thompson and Thompson, 1904. ▶Delete: ---- 1904: 24x19. 458 p. Dark brown cloth hc. See #869.1 for correct placement of this 3rd ed citation.

869.1 [Heron, Addie E.]. *Dainty work : of the Dainty Series. Compiled and written by editor of "home art," Journal devoted to interior decoration and author...* 3rd ed. Chicago: Thompson & Thomas, 1904.

24x19. 458 p. Dark brown cloth hc. See #869 and #869.2 for related Heron publications. ☺ (S)

869.2 Heron, Addie E. *Fancy work : for : Pleasure and Profit.* Chicago: Thompson & Thomas, 1905 [ᶜ1894 by Deanks & co. : ᶜ1905 by Thompson & Thomas].

24x18. (10), 6-496, (12) p+ four unpaged interspersed color plates. Red-brown cloth hc with gilt lettering. Same preface dedications to Mrs. Potter Palmer and the WCE as found in *Dainty Work, #869* and #869.1. (ref) $65

869.3 Hersey Mfg. Co. *Hersey Mfg. Co.,...Exhibits at World's Columbian Exposition, machinery hall annex, Section 31, column T53. Water meters.* N.p.: n.p., n.d.

33x20. Buff sheet, black and red print. Caption title. Illus of water meter in upper left corner. Includes map showing location of exhibit in red. (WM)

869.4 Hersey Mfg. Co. *Map of the grounds of the World's Columbian Exposition at Jackson Park showing the General Arrangement of Buildings and Grounds 1893.* N.p.: n.p., n.d.

33x20. Buff sheet, black print. "Our exhibit is located in Machinery Hall, annex, section 31, as shown in red upon the plan." Map caption title. Hersey made sugar and soap machinery, water meters. (WM)

869.5 *...Herts brothers : artistic furniture : interior decorations.* New York: n.p., [May 1893].

17½x11. (4) p. Folded pale blue sheet, dark blue-gray print and illus. C.t. At head of title: "1893." Illus of store p (3) and factory p (4). They made bank and office furniture and fittings. No WCE content; from intact collection. ☺ (WM)

871. [Hill, M]. *Fame's tribute*: (GLD,CC,CU,E,FLP,IHi,KCPL,slpl,Stfd,UAB,UR)   Either 1st or 2nd edition: $50 - 100
▶Correct paging: Hayes 2nd ed: Part I: 6 *l*, 15-84 p, Part II: 4 *l*, 7-101 p. (Delete: 6 *l*, 15-101 p, 1 *l*.)
---- Hayes 2nd ed: White cloth spine over decorative cloth covered boards.
---- Hayes 2nd ed: Half-leather over black cloth covered boards.

872. Hill. *Hill's album of Biography and Art*: (D)

872.1 Hilles & Jones Co. *Catalogue of New & Improved machine tools : Built by Hilles & Jones Company.* Wilmington, DE: [Press of Edwd. Stern & co., Phila., 1893].

28½x20. 32 p. Buff wraps, red print, illus of whimsical woman and a gear. C.t. All pages with a litho or photo illus of their wares and caption for text. On p (1): "Illustrations of the Special Line of machine tools..." No mention of WCE; from an intact collection. (WM)

872.2 Hilles & Jones Co. *Exhibit of New & Improved machine tools Built by...* Wilmington, DE: n.p., n.d. **P➔**

15½x9. (4) p. Folded white stiff card, green and red print. C.t. On cover in red "World's Columbian Exposition : Space 53 J : Machinery Hall Annex." Exhibit content listed; announced sale of exhibit hardware after the WF closed. ☺. (WM)

872.3 Hillger, Hermann. *Amerika und die Columbische Welt-Ausstellung : Chicago 1893 : Geschichte und Beschreibung.* Chicago: Verlag der Columbian History Co. The Temple, [°1893].

ca. 48x35. 504 p. Beautiful red half leather over boards covered in green, bold gilt print. C.t.: "Amerika und : die Columbische Weltausstellung : Chicago : 1893." T.p. trans: America and the Columbian World's Fair : Chicago 1893 : History and Description. See #771 for another Columbian History Co. publication. ☺. (HML,ONB)

872.4 *History and commerce of Central New York. With illustrated supplement of the Columbian World's fair at Chicago. ...1893.* New York: A.F. Parsons publishing co., 1893?

27x21. xi, (33)-234 p, 1 *l* ad, (15) p. Tan wraps, color litho of field and farm blending into city scene, also a diamond shaped vignette of blacksmiths. At the top of the front wrap: "Compliments of Oswego Starch Factory." Sepia illus of mill scene entitled "Bygone Days" on back wrap. The last (15) p have b/w lithos of the WCE buildings by A. Zeese & Co each with caption text. ☺ (GLD,CU) **P➔** $25 - 55

873. *History of Chicago and Souvenir of the Liquor Interest*: (IHi)
---- Also listed: 1891. 25x__. 254 p.

876. Hitchcock. *The art of the world* (Artist's Facsimile Japan ed): (ref.UMC)
---- Also listed: 4 vol.

877. Hitchcock. *The art of the world* (Edition de Luxe): (CLP,CU,HU,MSI,slpl,UMD,UPa)
---- Also found: Cover variant (10 vol ed). Maroon cloth spine over pebble-textured paper covered boards, gilt print. (S)
---- Also found: Custom bound in green half leather over green cloth covered thick wood boards in 3 vols; a massive and impressive set. (MSI)

878. Hitchcock. *The art of the world* (Grand Columbian Edition de Luxe): (S,UMC)
---- Also found: Bound in 3 massive folios. (S)

880. Hitchcock. *The art of the world*: (Amh,Berk,CCA,CLP,Col,DC,DU,ESU,FLP,HU,ICRL,IStU,ISU,MH,MSI,NAG,NPG,NUL,sfpl,SHB, Smth,SU,UCB,UCLA,UIC,uiuc,UMD,UMN,UTA,UVM,UWM,VAM,VT,WM)

881. Hitchcock. *The story of the exposition*: (Amh,MSU,UCLA)

881.1 Hoffmann, Julius, Publisher. *Verlags Verzeichniss von Julius Hoffmann in Stuttgart.* [Stuttgart: Hoffmannische buchdruckerei], n.d.

29x22. (12) p includes tan self-wraps, black print. C.t. Catalog of decorative frontis engravings and fancy script lettering for book publication. Examples of some of their published work. No WCE content; from intact collection. ☺ (WM)

881.2 Hofmann & Schoetensack. *The Chemische Fabrik vormals Hofmann & Schoetensack : Ludwigshafen °/Rhine : (Germany)...* [Ludwigshafen: Buchdruckerei Weiss & Hameler], n.d.

18x12. 31 p. Pale green stiff wraps with narrow red and black border, black print and illus of award medals. Illus of factories on inside covers and back cover. Printed sequentially in 4 languages. Catalog. T.p. states chemical products exhibited at the WCE are marked with an asterisk. . (HU,WM)

882.1 Hohmann & Maurer Mfg. Co. ...*The H. & M. Special Thermometers and Gauges.* N.p.: [A.B. King, NY], n.d.

12x16½. Self-wraps with black print enclose 2 folded sheets each 12x33 making (8) printed panels; text inside both covers. C.t. At head of title: "World's Columbian : Exposition : Chicago : 1893" and the co's name and address. Nice lithos of their products. (WM)

882.2 Holmes & Edwards Silver Co. *Holmes & Edwards Silver Co., Bridgeport, Conn. U.S.A. World's fair exhibit: Manufactures and Liberal Arts Building, Section N.* Bridgeport, CT: n.p., n.d.

16½x9½. (10) panels. Sheet unfolds to 16½x45½, printed both sides in blue. C.t. Illus of table service patterns, types, and prices. ☺ (WM)

882.3 Holmes & Edwards Silver Co. *Sterling Silver inlaid Spoons & Forks.* Bridgeport, CT: n.p., n.d.

17x29. Single sheet, black print with illus of spoons (front), and green print replica of their "Guarantee Certificate" shipped with each box (back). C.t. No WCE content; from intact collection. ☺ (WM)

882.4 Holmes, E.B., [Co.]. *High class wood working machinery.* Buffalo, NY: n.p., 1893.

23x31½. 24 p. Sand wraps, black print and illus of factory. C.t. At bottom of cover: "Specimen Pages from Catalogue D." Text and illus in dark green. Bold overprint: "Stop at our exhibit : Section 12 Column F 50, Machinery hall annex." ☺ (S)

884.   *Home Almanac:* (B,E)
---- Also found: Other advertisers and cover variants.   **P➜**

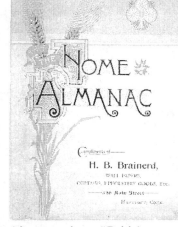

885.   The *"Home Queen" World's Fair souvenir Cook Book*:
▶See #867.5 and #867.6 for the Swedish versions.

886.   *Homes for visitors to the World's fair:* (UMD)

886.1 Homacoustic Apparatus Co. *The telephone entirely superseded for indoor purposes : by : the homacoustic.* N.p.: n.p., [1893].

28½x20½. (4) p. Folded thin smooth sheet, black print and illus of machine and its operation. "British section, electrical building, World's Columbian exposition." An acoustic voice speaking tube exhibit; it was used by the British navy because there was no static. Testimonials pp (3)-(4). ☺ (WM)

886.2 Hooper, Charles, & Co. ...*Woollen Manufacturers, Eastington Mills, near Stonehouse, Gloucestershire.* London: Herbert Fitch & Cᵒ lith, n.d.

13½x9½. (6) panels. Accordion folded buff stiff card unfolding to 13½x27½. Black and gilt print. C.t. Co's name at head of title. WCE fabric exhibit illus on p (6); exhibit contents on 4 panels. Location: "Stand Nᵒ 322, British Section, Manufactures Building." ☺ (WM)

886.3 Hoover and Prout Co. *The Hoover : Columbian catalogue.* N.p.: n.p., n.d.

8½x15½. 27, (2) p. Green wraps, black print, illus of an elevator digger. Illus of potato sorter on back cover. C.t. Caption title: "A word with you, Potato Growers!" (WM)

886.4 [Hornsby, Richard, and Sons, Ltd.]. *All the Marble Blocks used in This Monument Were Quarried Solely with The "Rio Tinto" Drill. World's Columbian Exposition : Chicago 1893.* [Eng.]: n.p., n.d.   **P➜**

29x22½. (4) p. Folded coated sheet, red ink print and illus. C.t. Cover illus captioned: "The 'Centenario' Columbus Monument at the Rabida, Hispania." Illus of drill on back. Inside pages in red and black ink. Location: "Stand No. F 28, British Section Machinery Hall." Striking, large format ad. ☺ (GLD,WM)

$30 - 60

886.5 Horticultural Society of Chicago and National Chrysanthemum Society of America. *World's fair :
Chrysanthemum Show : under the auspices of : The Horticultural Society of Chicago and The National
Chrysanthemum Society of America.* N.p.: n.p, 1893?

21½x15½. 11 p. Self-wraps with illus of Hort Bldg on outside back. Illus. C.t. Also on cover: "To be
held in the horticultural building, World's fair grounds, Chicago, Ill. : to open on Saturday, November 4,
1893, at 12 o'clock noon, and be continued until November 14, inclusive." This call for exhibits contains
a loose entry blank to be mailed to W.C. Egan, Secretary, Hort Bldg. [The event occurred on the
fairgrounds after the WCE closed.] ☺ . (ICRL)

886.6 Houghton, Mifflin and Co. *An account of the work of Houghton, Mifflin and Company of Boston and New
York : Chicago and London.* [Boston: Houghton, Mifflin and Co.], 1893.

17x10½. 15, (1) p+ print on inside back wrap. Also 2 unpaged plates with letterpress tissue guard
between pp 8-9 and 12-13. String-tied white stiff wraps with green print and The Riverside Press logo. At
bottom of front wrap: "Presented with the compliments of the publishers to the visitors at the Chicago
exposition of MDCCCXCIII." Ad. ☺ (GLD) $25 - 50

886.7 Houghton, Mifflin and Co. *...Autumn Announcement of Messrs. Houghton, Mifflin and company : Boston
and New York : The Riverside Press : Cambridge.* [Boston: Houghton, Mifflin & co.], 1893.

25½x17. (24) p including covers. Buff paper with black print. C.t. At head of title: "September,
1893." On p (3): illus with description and location of their WCE exhibit, "An American Library."
Their catalog of authors and new books. ☺ (GLD) $25 - 50

886.8 Houghton, Mifflin and Co. *Christopher Columbus and how he received and imparted the spirit of discovery
by Justin Winsor.* Boston and New York: Houghton, Mifflin and co. : Cambridge: The Riverside Press, 1891.

21½x14½. 8 p. Self-wraps. C.t. Illus and listing of chapter contents in Winsor's book. No WCE
content; from intact collection. ☺ (WM)

887.   Houghton. *Descriptive list of the five hundred and forty eight books*: (Col,UMD)
888.   Houghton. *Four old portraits of Columbus*: (S)

888.1 Houghton, Mifflin and Co. *...The Holiday Bulletin of Houghton Mifflin & Co : Boston and New York: The
Riverside Press : Cambridge MDCCCXCIII.* Boston, New York, and Chicago: Houghton, Mifflin & Co., 1893?

25½x17. 42 p. Tan wraps beautifully illustrated by Walter Crane in blues and reds with "flowers,
figures, and fancies." Catalog of books and contents for Jan 1894 *Atlantic Monthly*. At head of title: "For
the Christmas holidays MDCCCXCIII." No WCE content; from intact collection. (WM)

888.2 Houghton, Mifflin and Co. *The Riverside Press : Where it is, What it is, Why it
interests You. ...* [Boston [and] Cambridge, MA: Houghton, Mifflin & Co.;
The Riverside Press], 1893.

21x10½. 22, (2) p includes self-wraps. White paper, black print, b/w illus.
C.t. Description of the company and list of then current authors. Back wrap
has partial map of WCE with their exhibit location at "'An American Library'
in the northwest corner of the manufactures building...Section E, in the
Gallery. Columbian exposition : Chicago." Ad. ☺ (GLD)   P➜ $25 - 50

888.3 *Howard Iron Works : Buffalo, N.Y. : manufacturers of book trimmers,
Embossing presses, smashing machines. Hand & power paper cutters...*
[Buffalo, NY: The Courier Lith. co.], n.d.

27x18½. 23, (1) p. Highly decorated wraps in shades of brown on beige
background. C.t. Brown litho of factory on back. Illus catalogue with
prices. No mention of WCE; from an intact WCE collection. (WM)

888.4 Howell Condensed Milk & Cream Co. *Howell's purified and sterilized
evaporated milk.* Goshen, NY: n.p., n.d.

29x19. Buff thin sheet, black print and cow trade mark at top of page. Gives chemical analysis of milk and directions for infant use. No WCE content; from intact collection. ☺ (WM)

---- Also found: Same title/text. 27½x17½. At page bottom: "Mead & Roys, Printers, Goshen, NY."

888.5 Huber Mfg. Co. *Fair catalogue : The Huber Mfg. Co. : Engines : Threshers.* Marion, OH: The Huber Mfg. Co. (Gies & co., Buffalo, NY), n.d.

10½x15½. (8) p+ illus inside front and text inside back wrap. White wraps with tan background, black print and port of Huber (front) and factory (back). C.t. Illus of threshers. Their exhibit was in the Ag Bldg, E-A-7. WCE handout. ☺ (GLD,E) $25 - 50

888.6 Hunt, C.W., Co. *The C.W. Hunt Company : Cordially invite you to visit their Exhibit in the Transportation Building of the World's Columbian Exposition.* [New York?: C.W. Hunt Co. (Press of A.H. Kellogg, New York), ᶜ1893.]

25x16½. 7 p. Self-wraps. Illus, maps, and a plan which shows their location in the Trans Bldg. C.t. Ad describes their hoisting and conveying machinery for railroad applications. ☺ . (CCA)

888.7 *Hyde Archer and Co., Coach Lace and Trimming Manufacturers, Coach & Harness Curriers,...* [London: J. & C. Cooper printers], n.d.

16½x18½. 10 p. Blue-black wraps, gilt print. Title from first half title page. Extract from *Coach Builders' Art Journal*, Jan 15, 1893. Illus ad catalog. ☺ . (Stfd–bound WCE Trans Dept Collection)

888.8 *Iliff's Imperial Atlas of the World.* Chicago: John W. Iliff & co., 1892.

37x29½. >190 p. Color maps; includes 16 p on the WCE. Red cloth hc, black and gilt print. Similar to #808. See #721 and #811 for other Iliff items. (ref) $60

888.9 Illinois Alloy Co. *...Anti-Friction Metals for Railroad Cable and Electric Roads, Electric Lighting and Power Plants...* [Chicago: Illinois Alloy Co.], n.d.

21½x14. (8) p+ ads inside covers and outside back cover. Robin's-egg blue wraps, gilt print and design, small navy logo mid-page, text in navy. C.t. At head of title: "Special." No mention of WCE; from an intact WCE collection. (WM)

888.10 *Illustrated programme and descriptive souvenir of the International Naval Review : New York bay, April 27th 1893.* New York: Press of Nevius & Kane, n.d.

26x17½. (64) p. White glossy wraps, blue print and illus of tall ship. See #890.1 for another naval review item and annotation. ☺ (S)

889. *Illustrations of the different languages and dialects in which the Holy Bible*: (CCA,E,UMD)
---- Also found: 61 p. Self-wraps. (ref) $35

889.1 India Alkali Works. *Facts and some figures : about the buildings at : The World's Columbian exposition.* Boston: India Alkali Works, [1893].

28x21½. (4) p. Buff paper, black print. Caption title on p (2). Map of WCE grounds on back. Ad for Savogran cleaning powder, which was used in the Admin Bldg and other WCE bldgs. Intended as a folded mailer. ☺ . (E,WM)

889.2 Ingram Hotel. *Visitor's Guide to the World's Columbian Exposition and Chicago.* Chicago: Vandercook engraving and pub. co., n.d.

13½x8½. Folded white card forming wraps, teal print and design. (3) p of hotel info tipped to inside front cover. (23) panel accordion sheet which unfolds to 13x90 is glued to inside back cover. One side of the accordion is (12) panels of teal ink text; the other side is 11 illus panels of WCE bldgs. C.t. Fold out is titled: "For Guide and Points about Chicago : Hotel Ingram." ☺ (S)

890. International Linguistics. *The World's Columbian Exposition Phrasebook*: ▸See supplement #1132.

890.1 ...*International Naval Parade. Commemorating the discovery of America. New York Harbor : Wednesday and Thursday, April 26 and 27 1893. Admiral Gherardi's official programme. Illustrated.* N.p.: n.p., n.d.

20½x14. (8) p includes self-wraps, black print, and b/w line drawings of 3 ships. Back cover is full page ad for Knapp's root beer. C.t. At head of title: "1492 COLUMBUS. 1893." Contents: b/w line drawings of US and foreign ships in order of parade appearance. ☺. (E)

☞ This parade commemorated the arrival of the Spanish built replicas of Columbus' ships in New York harbor. Later they sailed to Chicago for the WCE. Do not confuse this parade with the Columbian Naval Parade held in New York in October 1892 to commemorate 400 years since Columbus' landing.

890.2 International Navigation Co. *American Line : New York : Southampton : London : International Navigation Company : Red Star Line : New York & Antwerp : Philadelphia & Antwerp.* [Philadelphia: International Navigation Company], 1893? **P➜**

14x11½. 31 p. White wraps, blue and red print, gilt diagonal band. Crossed flags of the lines are illus on back wrap. Blue and red text and illus. C.t. General agent was located in Chicago. Gives 1893 sailing schedules. No WCE; intact collection. [They exhibited in the Trans Bldg, Sec D-9-23.] ☺ (GLD) $25 - 50

890.3 ...*International Room Renting Agency.* Chicago: n.p., n.d.

8x13½. (16) p includes self-wraps. Buff paper, black print and illus of WCE bldgs. C.t. Describes the need for rooms for 45,000 WCE employees plus visitors. Agency owned and managed hotels and also made contracts for 100,000 rooms held by private parties. Rates from $1–$2 per day or less. ☺ (S)

890.4 *The Intramural Railway. World's Columbian Exposition.* Chicago: Rand, McNally & Co., Printers, n.d.

18x14. (2) p. Single sheet printed both sides. Rand, McNally map of grounds has railroad loop overprinted in red. [See also Intramural RR in index.] ☺ (S)

890.5 *"Ironclad."* New York: G.H. Buek & co. lith., [ᶜ1893 by Iron Clad Mfg. Co.].

8x10½. (8) p+ text inside both covers. The "U.S. Cruiser 'New York'" chromolith on the front cover wraps around to the back cover. On back: "World's Fair Souvenir : Iron Clad Mfg. Co. New York." The illus text describes their cookware. ☺. (E,WM)

890.6 *Ivorine Collar and Cuff Co. Section G Block 3 Gallery Floor. World's Columbian Exposition,* Chicago Ivorine Collar and Cuff Co., n.d.

15x8 (8) p. Strip unfolds to 15x32. Pale green paper, black print. C.t. Gives facts, price list, and illus of their various designs styles exhibited in the Manufactures Bldg. ☺. (E,WM)

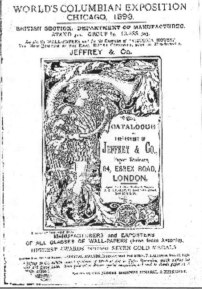

892.1 *The Jefferson Hotel : Headquarters for Clubs, Lodges, Parties and all Masonic Orders*: Chicago: Rand, McNally & Co. Printers, n.d.

12½x17½. (32) p. Gray glossy wraps, large illus of the hotel. Hotel info on versos, illus of WCE bldgs on rectos, all in blue-black ink. From an intact WCE scrapbook. ☺ (S)

892.2 Jeffrey & Co. ...*Catalogue of the exhibit of Jeffrey & Co., Paper Stainers, 64, Essex road, London.* N.p.: n.p., n.d. **P➜**

25½x17. (6) panel. Tri-fold buff sheet, red/brown print and design of horn blower amongst foliage. C.t. At head of title: "World's Columbian exposition Chicago, 1893. British section.—department of manufactures. Stand 321. Group 89. Class 563." Lists their 99 exhibited items. ☺. (S)

892.3 Jeffrey Mfg. Co. *World's fair greeting. 1893. The Jeffrey Mfg. Co. Columbus, Chicago, New York. Engineers, Founders, Machinists.* [Columbus, OH: The Jeffrey Manufacturing Co. (Gies & co. print, Buffalo, NY)], n.d.　　　　　　P➔

9x14½.　8 p+ text inside both wraps.　Tan coated stiff wraps, brown print and design, red string-tied.　C.t.: "The Jeffrey Manufacturing Co. ...Chain Belting."　Text in brown and red ink.　Their two exhibits are noted inside of front and back wraps; located in Machinery Hall and Mines and Mining.　Illus on outside back wrap of their electric coal mining machine. ☺ (GLD,WM)

$25 - 50

894.1 Johns, H.W., Mfg. Co. *Artistic House Painting.*　New York: n.p., [ᶜ1893 by H.W. Johns m'f'g co.].

6x9.　(16) p.　Tan stiff wraps, gilt print, vignette of lake landscape in green and brown.　C.t.　(12) p of pretty color plates of houses they had painted.　Their trade mark was "asbestos," see #894.2.　Their six WCE exhibit locations are listed inside back cover. (WM)

894.2 Johns, H.W., Mfg. Co. *...Asbestos.*　New York [and] London: H.W. Johns M'f'g Co., ᶜ1893.

18x12.　23, (1) p.　Pale green wraps, navy print.　Back cover illus: "Specimen of Asbestos in its natural state."　C.t.　At head of title is copyright info and "February 15ᵗʰ, 1893.　Descriptive price list.　H.W. John's M'f'g Co."　Navy text.　Ad catalog.　No mention of WCE; from an intact collection. (WM)

894.3 Johns, H.W., Mfg. Co. *...Insulation.*　New York [and] London: H.W. Johns M'f'g Co., ᶜ1893.

18x12.　__ p.　Light tan wraps, black print.　C.t.　At head of title is copyright info and "May, 1893."　Navy text.　Ad catalog of their electrical insulators.　"Western Branch...Chicago" is stamped on cover.　No mention of WCE; from an intact WCE collection. (WM)

895.　Johnson. *A history of the World's Columbian Exposition held in Chicago*:
(Amh,CCA,CLP,CU,EvP,Fess,FLP,FM,GBP,HU,IHi,Knox,MCHx,Merc,MH,MIT,MSI,NSW,OU,ref,RPL,sfpl,slpl,SPL,SZB,UH,UIC,UMN,UPa,WM)
▶Note:　The original citation (morocco/marbled papers/gilt) is for a limited edition of 500 copies.　　　$1100
---- Also found:　Red coarse cloth hc, black border, gilt design and spine print.

895.1 Johnson, Geo[rge] T. *...Johnson's eradicator (extract of soap tree bark).*　Chicago: n.p., n.d.

21½x14.　White sheet, black print.　At head of caption title: "Unparalleled on earth!　A grand success!"　Clothes and glove cleaner made from Quillaia bark.　No WCE content; from intact collection. ☺ (WM)

895.2 Johnson Peerless Works. *New : <u>Have You Seen it?</u> Combination of Cylinder and disk distribution at will. "Peerless."*　New York [and] Chicago: n.p., n.d.

18½x14.　(4) p.　Folded sheet, black print and illus of their printing press.　C.t.　Cuts show how rollers distribute ink on transfer plate prior to each print cycle.　Rubber stamp in purple on cover "Presented by R.M. Unger, Col. T-35; machinery hall, world's fair."　Found with mailing envelope with same WCE stamp and other Johnson ad cards that do not mention the WCE. ☺ (WM)

896.　Johnson. *"My Country 'Tis of Thee!"*: (GLD)
▶Add:　1893 Blue cloth hc version: A 2-page frontis bird's-eye of grounds by A. Zeese & Co. that is different from the 2-page frontis view in the 1892 edition.

896.1 Jones National Fence Co. *...Dead-lock : The Jones locked-wire fence. Stock proof lock.*　Columbus, OH: n.p., n.d.

24x15½.　(4) p.　Folded sheet, black print and farm fence illus.　At head of title: "Circular No 1."　Issued with 15½x15 "Price list" and illus envelope to hold ad items.　No WCE content; from intact collection. ☺ (WM)

896.2 Jones National Fence Co. *The Jones Locked Wire Fence.*　Columbus, OH: n.p., [1893?].

28½x18. (4) p. Folded sheet. Dated on p (3): "April 1, 1893." List of tensile strengths and comparisons of both light and heavy weight wires. Extensive list of agents. Fits in envelope above. No WCE content; from intact collection. ☺ (WM)

896.3 Judson & Co. Excursions. *Teachers' World's Fair Party : July 5, 1893.* Boston: n.p., n.d.

28x22. 1 *l.* Sheet, black print one side. Eleven day trip with 7 days at Bay State Hotel, Chicago, (see #744.2) and six WCE admission passes for $85. ☺ (WM)

896.4 Julian Hotel Co. *Office of The Julian Hotel Co. Cor. 63d Street and Stewart Boulevard, Chicago, Ill.* N.p.: n.p., n.d.

28x20½. (4) p. Folded white sheet, navy print and illus of hotel. C.t. Back cover WCE bird's-eye ᶜ1892 by Knight, Leonard & Co shows hotel location. Letter format: "To the Public:–" ☺ (S)

896.5 Kalk Limited. *Chemische Fabrik : Kalk : G.m.b.H.* Köln: [Druck von J.P. Bachem in Köln], n.d.

18x12. 1 *l* (factory view), 14 p. Gray textured stiff wraps, gilt print, blue illus of boy and Köln city. Inside in English, p (1): "Chemical Works : Kalk : (limited) formerly Vorster & Grüneberg : Cologne (Germany). Various potash, ammonia and acid products described. No WCE; intact collection. ☺ (WM)

896.6 Kane, Thomas, & Co. *Catalogue of Kane's Regan : vapor marine engines and vapor launches.* Chicago: [P.F. Pettibone & co., printers], 1892.

17x25. 11 p. Navy blue wraps, gilt print. Blue text print and illus. "June 1892" at bottom of t.p. Kane had 3 exhibits in the Trans Bldg, Group 85, Classes 528, 529, and 532; this and the next 2 catalogs are one from each exhibit. ☺ . (Stfd–bound WCE Trans Dept Collection)

896.7 Kane, Thomas, & Co. *Catalogue of Racine Automatic Engines and Boilers : Marine and Stationary. Steam Launches : yacht fittings.* Chicago: Thomas Kane & Co., 1892.

19½x27½. 32 p. Light brown wraps, chocolate print. "October, 1892" at bottom of t.p. Pretty illus catalog of their hardware. ☺ . (Stfd–bound WCE Trans Dept Collection)

896.8 Kane, Thomas, & Co. *Illustrated catalogue : Boats and Canoes : rowing, sailing and paddling : and boating hardware.* [Chicago: press of W.T.P.A.], 1893. P➔

17x25½. 36, (2) p. Glossy stock self-wraps, black print with 2 vignettes of boats on lakes. Date at top of t.p.: "July, 1893." ☺ . (Stfd–bound WCE Trans Dept Collection)

896.9 Kansi Trading & Co. *Note : Kaiki : manufactured at Tsurugori : Kainokuni Yamanashi Ken : Japan.* Tokio, Printed at Seishibunsha, n.d.

21x14. (4) p. Folded sheet, black and gilt print. Chromolith of 2 ladies weaving Kaiki silk with Mt. Fuji and red rising sun in background. Black text print. Tsuru district, Yamanashi Prefecture, had 86 silk merchants. Pretty ad. In English. No WCE content; from intact collection. [Exhibited in the Manufactures Bldg, Group 100, Class 629 along with 577 other silk companies from Japan!]. ☺ (WM)

896.10 Karlsbader Mineralwasser-Versendung. *Chicago 1893. Notice : les eaux thermales de Carlsbad.* Karlsbad, [Austria]: Karlsbader Mineralwasser-Versendung (Schlesische Buchdruckerei), n.d.

30½x23. (4) p. Folded sheet, black and red print, b/w cover litho of ancient hunters finding the Carlsbad thermal water fountain. C.t. French language description of the water properties. Exporter: Löbel Schottländer. Other than the bold "Chicago 1893," there is no mention of WCE; but this item was purchased with an intact set of WCE handouts. Ad. ☺ (GLD) $20 - 45

897.   [Keeler]. *America focalized at the Columbian World's Fair.* (UCB,UCLA)

899.1 Kentucky Wagon Mfg. Co. *Brief Descriptive Circular of the Kentucky Wagon M'f'g. Co....and of the "Old Hickory" and "Tennessee" farm wagons.* Louisville, KY: Kentucky Wagon M'f'g. Co. (Kentucky Litho Co.), n.d.

> 16½x9. (8) panels. Folded sheet unfolds to 16½x36. White stock with black print and decoration. C.t. At bottom of cover: "Presented as a souvenir of the World's Columbian Exposition." Illus ad. (S)

899.2 *Kette : Deutsche Elbschiffahrts-Gesellschaft : Schiffswerft Uebigau. : recommends Hydraulic Steering gears.* Dresden: Lithograph Anstalt von Theodor Beyer, n.d.

> 30½x21½. __ p. Light blue wraps, blue print and litho of their system. Hinged at top edge. Blue text in 2 columns: German and English language. C.t. = t.p. Describes the advantages of hydraulic steering based on "Schleicher's Patent." ☺ . (Stfd–bound WCE Trans Dept Collection)

899.3 Keystone Mfg. Co. *Catalogue of Agricultural Implements : Manufactured by...Issued July 1, 1893.* [Chicago: The Foster press, art printers], n.d.

> 24½x16½. 32 p. Brown stiff wraps, brown/white/green print and green design. Illus catalog of farm disks, planters, hayers. Co's logo on back. No WCE content; from an intact WCE collection. ☺ . (WM)

899.4 Keystone Watch Case Co. *Souvenir World's Columbian Exposition, Chicago, 1893. Compliments of Keystone Watch Case Company, Philadelphia, Pa.* [Philadelphia: Keystone Watch Case Co., ᶜ1893.]

> 14½x20. (40) p+ text inside both wraps. Blue ink print on cream wraps, string-tied. C.t. Keystone factory illus on outside back wrap. Illus by A. Zeese & Co. (CCA,UMD)

899.5 King, William C., ed. *The World's Progress : as wrought by men and women in art, literature, education, philanthropy, reform...* Springfield, MA: King-Richardson Publishing Co., 1896 [ᶜ1896].

> 21½x16½. 1 *l* frontis, A to Z p, 49-701 p+ 7 *l* plates interspersed. Frontis illus of Statue of Liberty. Gray cloth hc, black print and design of globe. Many references to the WCE and Congresses and the people who made them successful. ☺ (GLD,CU) $20 - 40

899.6 Kingsford & Son. *Columbian Souvenir.* Oswego, NY: T. Kingsford & Son (Forbes co., Boston), ᶜ1893 by T. Kingsford & Son.

> 15½x10½. 12 p+ (4) p of chromolithographs of starch products as a centerfold. Front cover chromolith of Indian maiden sitting on a rock in the mountains with an eagle in the background; illus of Kingsford starch exhibit at the WCE on back cover. C.t. ☺ . (E)

899.7 *Kinnard Press Co. : manufacturers of : flour city hay presses : and powers.* Minneapolis, MN: n.p., n.d.

> 15½x23. 12 p. Gray wraps, black print. Back cover: "Columbian Number." Kinnard exhibited hay balers for the field in Ag Bldg. B/w litho of a hay press and caption description on each page. (ref) $45

900. Kinney. *Why the Columbian Exposition Should be Opened on Sunday:* (ICRL)

901. Kirkland. *The Story:* (GLD,bgsu,CCA,Col,CU,DC,EvP,HU,IHi,KCPL,NDU,RPL,UCLA,UIC,UMC,UMN,UPa,UTA,VT,WML,Yale) $30 - 65
▶Correct paging and add to first listing (1st ed). Vol 1: 3 *l*, vii-xxiii,... Brown cloth hc, gilt print and design in black, decorative end papers. Frontis is a photo of the "Robert Cavelier, Sieur de La Salle" bronze monument; tissue guard.

902. Klein. *Unsere Weltausstellung Eine Beschreibung der Columbischen:* (CUA,Fess,ICRL)

902.1 Kleinschmidt, G. *Zwei lemnische Inschriften.* Insterburg: Druck von C.R. Wilhelmi, 1893.

> 21½x14½. 1 *l* (t.p.), 19 p. Tan wraps, black print. C.t. = t.p. In German script plus Greek text. "Separatabdruck aus Heft III der Zeitschrift des Insterburger Alterthumsvereins." Translation of 2 ancient Greek texts by the Insterburg antiquarians. No WCE content; from intact collection. ☺ (WM)

902.2 Knutsford Hotel. *Souvenir of the World's Columbian Exposition : Chicago.* Chicago: Vandercook engraving and pub. co., n.d.

13½x8. (4) p. Folded beige card, brown print and illus of Admin Bldg. C.t. Blue ink accordion fold out tipped-in on p (2). Fold out has 9 panels of WCE bldgs one side, and other side has 8 panels of info about Utah and Salt Lake City, the hotel's location. Ad variant of #1160. ☺ (S)

903.1 Krupp Pavilion. *Ausstellungs-Katalog der Gussstahlfabrik Fried. Krupp : Essen a. d. Ruhr (Rheinpreussen). World's Columbian Exposition : 1893 : Chicago.* Essen a. d. Ruhr: Buchdruckerei der Gussstahlfabrik von Fried. Krupp, 1893.

17½x11½. 208 p. Probably original Krupp catalog pub; German version of #906 (cover same). ☺ . (Yale)

904. Krupp. *Cast-steel works of Fried Krupp*: (S,UMD,WM)

904.1 Krupp Pavilion. *Catálogo de la exposición de las acerias de Fried. Krupp, Essen sobre el Ruhr (Prusia rhenana). Chicago, Exposición colombina universal, 1893.* Essen a. d. Ruhr: Krupp'sche gusstahlfabrik, n.d.

17½x12. 210 p, 2 *l*, (4) p, 1 *l*, (2) p, 1 *l*. Illus, tables and diagrams. Spanish version of the Krupp catalog #906. (Col)

904.2 Krupp Pavilion. *Catalogue du matériel exposé par les aciéries Fried. Krupp : Essen sur Ruhr (Prusse Rhénane). World's Columbian exposition : 1893 : Chicago.* N.p.: n.p., n.d.

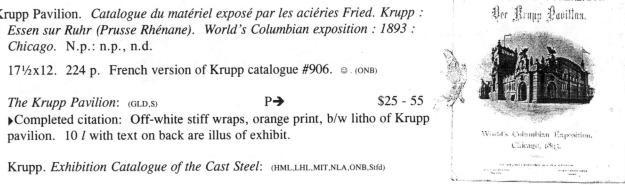

17½x12. 224 p. French version of Krupp catalogue #906. ☺ . (ONB)

905. *The Krupp Pavilion*: (GLD,S)   P➔ $25 - 55
▶Completed citation: Off-white stiff wraps, orange print, b/w litho of Krupp pavilion. 10 *l* with text on back are illus of exhibit.

906. Krupp. *Exhibition Catalogue of the Cast Steel*: (HML,LHL,MIT,NLA,ONB,Stfd)

907. Kurtz. *Official illustrations (three hundred and*: (Amh,bgsu,CCA,CLP,Col,CU,CUA,D,DC,GU,HML,HU,IHi,KCPL,Knox,LBA,LU,MH, MSI,MSL,NDU,NLA,NLI,NPG,OU,PSU,SAL,SHB,slpl,Smth,Stfd,UCB,UCD,UCLA,UIC,uiuc,UMD,UMN,UoA,UPa,UTA,UVM,UWM,VAM,VT,Yale)
▶Add pub: Microfiche. [New York]: M. Knoedler, ᶜ1973. Four microfiches.

907.1 Labatt, John, Brewer. *Labatt's London Ale and Stout.* London: n.p., n.d.

28½x21½. Glossy white sheet, black print decorated with colored Labatt labels, yellow and gold medals. Reports of 4 analytical chemists are excerpted. Lists Naylor Rogers & Co., Chicago, as representatives. No WCE content; from intact collection. (WM)

907.2 Lake Shore & Michigan Southern Railway. *...The Lake Shore route : to the : World's Fair.* N.p.: Cleveland plain dealer, printers, July 1893.

22x10½. Sheet unfolds to 44x112. Covers in red and black print with bird's-eye of WCE. C.t. Includes time tables for the "World's Fair Special," illus of WCE buildings, and map of Chicago with instructions to WCE. At head of title: "America's best railway." Dated at bottom of cover. (GLD,WM) $28 - 60
---- Also found: Dated at bottom "Form M – Aug. 1893." (GLD)

907.3 Lake Shore & Michigan Southern Railway. *...Official local time tables.* Battle Creek, MI: Wm. C. Gage & sons, railroad printers, 1893?

24x20. 23 p. Covers printed in black and red, pulp paper. Many ads. Calendar for July 1893 on front. At head of title: co's name and address. Includes times for WF special trains. ☺ (WM)

907.4 Lamson Consolidated. *...Automatic Coin Cashiers and Coin Storage and Counting Trays.* [Boston]: n.p., n.d.

14½x8½. (4) p. Folded white sheet, purple print and product illus. At head of title: co info. No WCE content; from intact collection [Exhibited in Liberal Arts Bldg, Group 154, Class 898, Gallery E]. (WM)

907.5 Lamson Consolidated. *Cash Carriers Extraordinary.* Boston: n.p., n.d.

9½x16½. (6) panel. Tri-fold from white glossy sheet, purple print and illus of cash carriers. C.t. No WCE; from intact collection. [Liberal Arts Bldg, Group 154, Class 898, Gallery E]. ☺ (WM)

907.6 Lancaster Mills. *Lancaster ginghams.* Clinton, MA: Lancaster Mills, n.d.

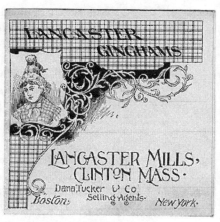

9½x9½. (4) p. Folded card stock, b/w print and illus. Factory illus on back. C.t. A swatch of plaid gingham is tipped onto p (3) with words underneath: "See Dana & Tucker Co.'s Exhibit in Manufacturers' [sic] Building, Section O, Post 79, Oak Case." Colorful and interesting ad.
☺ (GLD,WM)   P➜ $20 - 55

908.1 Lanston Monotype-Machine Co. *Prospectus of The Lanston Monotype-Machine Company.* N.p.: n.p, n.d.

23½x14½. 7 p. Tan-flecked wraps, black print and design. C.t. = t.p. Also on t.p.: "World's Fair Exhibit: Machinery Hall Annex, column, S-34." Their main office was in Washington, DC. They made a complex printable surface from a single plate. (WM)

909.1 Larkin Soap Mfg. Co. *Illustrated History of the World's Columbian Exposition Free With a Combination Box of "Sweet Home" Soap.* Buffalo, NY: Larkin Soap M'f'g Co., n.d.

32x23½. 1 *l.* Blue and red print. Ad for a free copy of #771 which is described in detail. ☺ (GLD) $20 - 40

909.2 Lazarus, Rosenfeld & Lehmann. *...Victoria China Works : Altrohlau, Carlsbad, Austria.* N.p.: n.p., n.d.   P➜

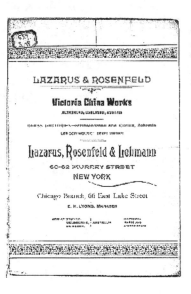

23x15½. (12) p. White wraps, black print and bands of dots. C.t. At head of title " Lazarus & Rosenfeld." They were US distributors with Chicago branch, E.H. Lyons, Mgr. Caption title: "Vases. 'Liberty' and 'Progress' by the Victoria China Works : Carlsbad Austria." Describes their exhibit and fancy named vases in the Manuf Bldg, Austrian Section. Factory illus on back. ☺ . (FM)

911. Lehigh. *Catalog of Articles in the exhibit of the Lehigh:* (Col,HML,HU,LU)

911.1 Leiblee, C., Residence. *Give the inside pages your attention if you propose going to the World's fair.* Chicago: C. Leiblee, n.d.

21½x14. (4) p. Folded sheet, brown print and illus of their furnished home for rent during the WCE. C.t. Back cover map of WCE grounds showing location at 6617 Ellis Ave. Caption title on p (2): "Visitors to the World's Columbian Exposition." ☺ (S)

911.2 Lemming, Tho[ma]s, & Co. *Let Me Taste it! : BABIES.* [New York: Thos. Lemming & co. (Jersey City printing co.)], ᶜ1892 by Thos. Lemming & co.

14½x8½. (4) p. Folded white card, red print, green design. B/w photos of babies in cribs on both covers. Title across p (2)-(3): "Who Said Nestle's Food? Let Me Taste it! Give The Babies what is far more important..." Ad for Nestlés Milk Food manufactured in Vevey, Switz. No WCE; from intact collection. [Probably exhibited in Ag Bldg with the Milk Society of Vevey.] ☺ (GLD) $20 - 40

911.3 Lemp Brewing Co. *Souvenir : Wm. J. Lemp : Brewing Co. : Saint Louis, Mo. U.S.A.* [St. Louis, MO: Wm. J. Lemp Brewing Co.], 1893?   P➜

8x13. 45 plates, 7 p. 24x14 map folded to 12x8 and tipped-in at end. Orange wraps with green, yellow, and pink design of hops and grain. C.t. On folded map: "Standard guide map of the World's Columbian Exposition at Chicago, 1893." Ad. ☺ . (HML,ref) $55

911.4 Lemp Brewing Co. *Visitors to the World's Columbian Exposition are respectfully...Agricultural Hall Building. ...will be found at the Banquet hall east of the Fisheries building...* [St. Louis, MO: Wm. J. Lemp Brewing Co.], n.d.

15½x10. (4) p. Folded yellow card, black print. Includes illus of Banquet Hall, their St. Louis plant, and their ornate label. (ref) $35

911.5 Lewis, Williams, & Sons. *Wm. Lewis & sons, Hosiers, Glovers, Shirt-Tailors and Men's Furnishers. ... Exhibit at World's fair, Chicago, 1893.* [London: Wm. Lewis & Sons (W.P. Griffith & Sons, Ltd., Printers, &c.)], 1893?

19½x12. 19, (1) p. String-tied cream wraps with black and red print. Black and red text on fine rag paper. Lists WCE exhibit and product prices. At bottom of front wrap: "World's Fair, Chicago, 1893." Ad. ☺ (GLD) $25 - 50

911.6 Lexington Hotel. *Souvenir of the Lexington Hotel. Chicago : E.A. Bacheldor, Proprietor.* [New York Boston: Published and copyrighted by J.L. Bridgford & Co], n.d.

27½x20. (40) p. Brown wraps. T.p. drawing of lobby scene. Beautifully photo-illus booklet of the grand hotel and its amenities. [A family hotel located at 22nd and Michigan Ave.] ☺ (S)

911.7 Libbey Glass Co. *Libbey Glass company's factory : In full operation at the World's Fair : Located on the Midway Plaisance, adjoining Illinois Central R.R.* [Toledo, OH: Libbey Glass Co.], n.d.

9x13. (4) p. Folded white coated sheet, blue print and brown illus of their exhibit bldg. C.t. Illus of WCE glass activities include spinning and weaving. Ad. ☺ (GLD,E,WM) $25 - 50
---- Also found: Issued with company mailing envelope and folded loose Jackson Park map which was printed for Libbey and shows their location on the Midway. (ref)   [Damaged]: $90

912.   *Libbey Glass Company World's Fair 1893*: (E)
▶See #840, #911.7, and #2352.5 for other Libbey Glass items.

914.1 *Life of Christopher Columbus : World's Fair Souvenir Edition : After the most Authentic Documents. Faithfully abridged. ...* N.p.: n.p., 1891?.

15x23. 12 p+ 12 plates. Tan wraps with gilt, brown, and red print and illus of Columbus and globe. At top of front cover "1492—1892." At bottom of each plate: "ᶜ1891, University of Notre Dame." The twelve plates are reproductions of paintings by Gregori of Florence, Italy. Ad for Larkin Soap Mfg. Co. on back. ☺ (GLD) $20 - 40

914.2 Lightening Check Punch Co. *Paper Insurance.* Bridgeport, CT: n.p., [1893].

15x8. (4) p. Folded light tan sheet, black print and illus of two different punches. C.t. Testimonial on p (4) dated Apr 25, 1893. No WCE content; from intact collection. [Lightening Check exhibited in the Liberal Arts Bldg, Group 154, Class 898, Gallery E.] (WM)

915.   Lipscomb. *James D. Lynch Poet-Laureate of the World's Columbian*: (UTA)

915.1 *The Lodge & Davis improved Standard Machine Tools.* Cincinnati, OH: n.p., n.d.

24x16½. Sheet unfolds to 94½x64. Striking and magnificent poster printed one side only, black and red print and b/w lithos of many large lathes and other shop machines. Intended for mounting for reference. No WCE content; from an intact collection. ☺ (WM)

915.2 London and North Western Railway. *Queensland Harbour. Europe. Stratford-on-Avon : Lime Street Station Hotel, Liverpool. London.* [London: London and North Western Railway of England], n.d.

22x15½. (4) p. Folded sheet, chocolate print and illus of woman, ship, hotel, and London scene. Caption title: "In the Old Country." On p (4) a RR route map and "Transportation Building (Annexe), British Section, Group 80, Catalogue No. 205, World's Columbian Exposition." (S,WM)

915.3 London and North Western Railway. *Ye olde Countrie : ye London and North Western Railway Co of England sends Greeting to ye Visitors to ye World's Faire...* N.p.: [Winchell press, NY], ᶜ1893.

10x17. 2-19, (1) p (printer's mark). Vellum wraps, brown print and red seal. C.t. Illus catalog of their WCE Trans Annex exhibit including model of Rocket engine and company statistics. ☺ (WM)

☞ The Field Columbian Museum bought the engine after the fair. See #2446.FM for an illus of the original accession record for the Rocket engine.

915.4 London Times. *The Chicago World's fair. From The Times.* London: The Times (printed by George Edward Wright), 1892.

14x10½. 38 p includes front cover. Self-wraps, black print. C.t. Rpt compilation of 3 WCE articles that appeared in *The Times*, October 12, 17, and 20, 1892. See #187 for *Times* article by Cook. ☺ (SML)

918. Lord's Day Alliance. *Brief In Favor of Keeping the World's Fair Closed on Sunday*: (HU,S)

919.1 Lothrop, D., Co. *The best histories and fiction.* [Boston: D. Lothrop co.], n.d.

14x8½. (4) p. Folded cream sheet, blue-black print and port of Elbridge S. Brooks. Listing of Brook's books, including #3. Bottom of front cover gives their exhibit location: "North Gallery, Section E, Manufactures and Liberal Arts Building." ☺ (GLD,WM) $20 - 45

919.2 Lothrop, D., Co. *...Books by Willis Boyd Allen.* [Boston: D. Lothrop co.], n.d.

14x8½. (4) p. Folded cream sheet, blue-black print and port of Allen. Listing of Allen's books including the "Pine Cone Stories." At head of title: "'Hearty, Wholesome, Entertaining.'" Bottom of front cover gives their exhibit location, same as #919.1. ☺ (GLD,WM) $20 - 45

919.3 Lothrop, D., Co. *Margaret Sidney's Books.* N.p.: [D. Lothrop co.], n.d.

14x8½. (4) p. Folded cream sheet, blue-black print and port of Sidney on front. Listing of her books including the "Five Little Peppers and How They Grew" series. Bottom of front cover gives their exhibit location, same as #919.1. ☺ (GLD) $20 - 45

THE PANSY BOOKS

"PANSY" (MRS. G. R. ALDEN)

Orders for these books may be left at D. Lothrop Company's exhibit, " An American Book Corner," in the North Gallery, Section E, Manufactures and Liberal Arts Building, where samples are shown.

919.4 Lothrop, D., Co. *The pansy books.* N.p.: [D. Lothrop co.], n.d.

14x8½. (4) p. Folded cream sheet, blue-black print and port of "Pansy" (Mrs. G.R. Alden) on front. Listing of over 100 Pansy children's books priced from 50¢ to $1.50. Bottom of front cover gives their exhibit location, same as #919.1. ☺ (GLD,WM) P➔ $20 - 45

919.5 Low's Art Tile Soda Fountain Co. *Souvenir : World's Fair : new tile top...* Buffalo, NY: n.p., n.d.

19x10½. (4) p. Folded white coated sheet, royal blue print and illus. C.t. "[L]argest and Most Magnificent Soda Fountain in the World at Manufacturers' [sic] building, Section H 107, Col. 3." ☺ (WM)

919.6 Ludwig, P., [Co.]. *P. Ludwig : Proprietor of clay-pits : Coblenz-Lützel : °/Rhine, Germany. Represented at the Universal Exhibition of Chicago : Group 46, number of order 3735.* Coblenz-Lützel: Gebr. Breuer, n.d.

17x11½. (3) p. Folded buff sheet, black print and ornate border. C.t. Analysis of the "dark-blue Mülheim clay" used in the steel industry. Analysis by Dr. Bischof of Wies-bade. ☺ (WM)

919.7 Luther, G., Machine Works. *...Carl Haggenmacher's Patent Plansifter : Arrangement with overhead driving pulley.* Brunswick, Ger.?: n.p., 1893?

29x22½. (4) p. Folded sheet, navy print on tan paper, brown illus of the machine. C.t. At head of title: company info and "April 1893." No WCE content; from intact collection. [They exhibited in the German section, Machinery Hall, Group 69, Class 415]. ☺ (WM)

919.8 Luther, G., Machine Works. *...Combined Grain-Ending-, Scouring- and Brushing –Machine.* Brunswick, Ger.?: n.p., 1893?

29x22½. (2) p. Sheet printed both sides in navy ink, brown illus of the machine. At head of title: co info and "March 1893." No WCE content; from intact collection. Same p (1) format as above. © (WM)

919.9 Luther, G., Machine Works. ...*Roller Mills (Luther's System 1892). Chilled Cast Rolls.* Brunswick, Ger.?: n.p., 1893?

29x22½. (8) p includes both sides of both self-wraps. Navy print on tan paper, brown illus of mill on cover. C.t. At head of title: company info and "March 1893. I.B.2." Catalog of mills. No WCE content; from intact collection. Same p (1) format as above. © (WM)

919.10 Lyman Brothers. *Hotel Beatrice, Chicago.* Chicago: Lyman Bros., n.d.

20½x12½. (4) p. Folded buff sheet, black print and large illus of hotel. C.t. Map on back shows location "only three blocks from World's fair grounds." Rental terms and routes to WCE. © (S)

920.1 Mabie, Hamilton W., and Marshall H. Bright. *The memorial : story of America : comprising the important events, episodes, and incidents which make up : the record of four hundred years : from : 1492 to 1892. ...With over 350 illustrations, mostly by noted artists.* Philadelphia and Chicago: John C. Winston & co.; Toronto, Ont.: Winston, Phillips & co., 1893 [ᶜ1892 by John C. Winston].

26½x21. 1 *l*, v-xxvii, 1 *l*, 21-851 p. Chocolate cloth hc, gilt title and design. C.t.: "Story of America : 1492 1892 : Illustrated." Lower right: "Authors [sic] Edition." Chap XLI (pp 710-24): "World's Fairs," includes WCE. Small b/w illus of WCE bldgs interspersed in text. Early ed of #920. (ref) $50

921. Magee. *The Alphabet and Language...Three essays*: (GLD,UCB,UoC,USFr,Yale) $30 - 75
▸Add copyright info: [ᶜ1894 by William Doxey]
---- Also found: Maroon cloth hc; blind-stamped design, gilt print. GLD copy is signed by Magee.

921.1 Maine Central Railroad. Waldron, Holman D. *Crown of New England : Mt. Washington and the White Mountain Range via the Crawford Notch.* Boston: The Passenger Department of the Maine Central Railroad, 1893.

14½x19½. (40) p. Red, blue, and white wraps with illus of New England mountain scene. String-tied. Illus by Harry D. Young. See another Waldron, #1908. No WCE; from intact collections. © . (LBA,SML)

921.2 Maine Central Railroad. ...*Personally conducted World's fair tours for $75 : Including Tickets, Pullman Cars, Meals in Transit, Hotel Accommodations, Seven Admissions to Fair, &c.* N.p.: n.p., 1893?

14½x8½. Sheet unfolds to 29x40: (10) panels on front; illus of WCE and bldgs on back (10) panels. C.t. At head of title: "10 DAYS." Trips starting June 5, [1893], from Portland, ME, continued weekly until the Fair ended. Accommodations at "The Hotel" near Ellis and Midway Plaisance. © . (E)

921.3 Majors, M.A. *Noted negro women : their triumphs and activities.* Chicago: Donohue & Henneberry, Printers, Binders and Engravers, [ᶜ1893 by M.A. Majors, M.D.].

23½x16½. xvi, 17-365 p. Frontis port of Majors with tissue guard. Royal blue cloth hc, black design, gilt print and design in center of cover. Biographies of Negro women include Ida B. Wells, pp 187-94. See #1053, and #2441.1. © (WML)

921.4 Manhattan Silver Plate Co. *Souvenir Reference Book : 1492 1893.* [Lyons, NY]: Manhattan Silver Plate Co. [Chas. E. Krone & co., art printers, Chicago], [1893?].

13½x8. (32) p. Pale pink stiff wraps with rounded corners, blue and red print. WCE bird's-eye, p (1); grounds map showing co's exhibit location, p (2); their exhibit illus, p (6). B/w lithos ᶜ1892 by A. Zeese & Co. on even pages; facing odd pages are ruled for notes. © (GLD,E) $25 - 50

921.5 Manitou Mineralwater Co. ...*Original : "Manitou" : Absolutely Natural : the only water on the : American continent : bottled recharged...* Manitou, CO: The Manitou Mineralwater Co., [1893].

27½x20. (4) p. Folded sheet. Chromolith cover with gilt border front and back: Spring water bottles (front) and bottle labels (back). Blue-green text print inside. Caption title on p (2): "1793 Original

'Manitou' spring water. 1893." No WCE content; from intact collections. [Found with a variety of Manitou ad cards with no mention of WCE.] ☺ (GLD,WM)　　　　　$25 - 50

921.6 Mann Brothers. *Mann Bros.' Cable-Ware.* [Chicago and Milwaukee]: Mann Brothers, 1893?

15x8½. (4) p. Folded buff sheet, blue print and illus of Mann's exhibit in the Forestry Bldg. C.t. Back cover illus of their exhibit in the Fisheries Bldg. Manufactured welded-wire pail hoops with indents to prevent slippage. ☺ (GLD,E,WM)　　　$18 - 38

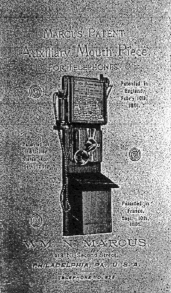

921.7 Manning, Warren H[enry]. "Classification. [Notes concerning the horticultural exhibits...]"

Unpaged vol of typescript. (HU Loeb Design: Microfilm NAB 5625 Chi; Loeb Design VF NAB 5625 Chi)

921.8 Manning, Warren H[enry]. ["...Report on landscape gardeners' plan.]

Unpaged vol of typescript. At head of title: "World's Columbian Exposition." (HU Loeb Design: Microfilm NAB 5625 Chi; Loeb Design: VF NAB 5625 Chi)

921.9 Marcus, W[illia]m N., [Co.]. *Marcus' Patent : Auxiliary Mouth Piece : For Telephones.* Philadelphia: n.p., n.d.　　　　**P➜**

15x8½. 10 p. Gray-green wraps, black print, illus of phone with the special mouthpiece. C.t. Inside front cover: "on exhibition in : Department of Electricity : Exhibit Y-12, World's Fair, Chicago, Ills." Price $3 for a rotating elbow mouthpiece that adjusted to user's height. User list. ☺ . (WM)

921.10 *...Marezzo Marble Company, manufacturers of artificial marble.* Chicago: n.p., June 1893.

24x15. Robin's-egg blue sheet, navy print one side. Caption title. At head of title: co's officers. Dated after title. At bottom: "We will also have a display of these goods in the Manufactures Building at the World's Columbian Exposition, main floor, northwest, Section H,..." (WM)

921.11 Marks, A.A., Co. *A.A. Marks : established 1853. Inventor, patentee & manufacturer of : Artificial limbs : with rubber hands and feet.* New York: n.p., n.d.

13x11. (4) p. Folded stiff card, black print, steel engraved illus of previous award medals. C.t. On pp (2)-(3) in landscape orientation: "World's Columbian exposition, Chicago, 1893. ... Manufacturer's [sic] Building, Department of Liberal Arts, Section D, Column D 103." (WM)

☞ The Marks Company also exhibited at the 1901 Pan American World's Fair in Buffalo, NY.

921.12 Marks, A.A., Co. *Caution : To those who intend purchasing Artificial Limbs.* New York: n.p., n.d.

21½x10. 3-14 p. Buff self-wraps, black print, illus with a border of past award medals. Cover is table of contents. Caption title. Inside back cover: "World's Columbian exposition, Chicago, 1893. Our display of Artificial Legs, Feet, Arms and Hands can be seen in the Manufacturer's [sic] Building, Department of Liberal Arts, Section D, Column D 103." Catalog of products with prices. ☺ . (WM)

921.13 Marks, A.A., Co. *Highest Award for Artificial Limbs At The Columbian Exposition Chicago 1893.* N.p.: n.p., n.d.

21½x10. (8) p. Off-white smooth wraps, black print, and image of tied blue ribbon. C.t. Includes litho of their exhibit and its location, pp (4)-(5). (ref)　　　　[damaged] $33

921.14 Marquart & Schulz Co. *Chemical Works : Bettenhausen : Marquart & Schulz : Bettenhausen-Cassel (Hesse) Germany.* N.p.: n.p., n.d.

23x16. 19 p. Gray wraps, red/blue/black print, green leaf border. C.t. Title in German on p 1. Text alternates German/English. Text pages have red borders. Railhead at Bettenhausen; wharf at Cassel. Chemical products listed and described. No mention of WCE; from an intact collection. (WM)

921.15 *...The Marquette...* N.p.: The Foster press, n.d.

> 12x20. (16) p. Sepia illus of the hotel on cover. C.t. At head of title: "European." Sepia text. Text plus floor plans of hotel. Inside covers have illus of WF bldgs. (ref.S) $20 - 50

921.16 Mason & Hamlin Organ & Piano Co. *The opinions of five American musicians regarding the Mason & Hamlin Piano-Forte.* N.p.: n.p., n.d.

> 17½x15½. (6) p. Self-wraps, black print and filigree design. C.t. Opinions by Chadwick (see #1481), Huss, Lang, Mason, and Sherwood, one page each. No mention of WCE; from an intact collection. (WM)

921.17 Massey-Harris Co. Harris, S.M., ed. *Food For Plants.* N.p.: n.p., n.d.

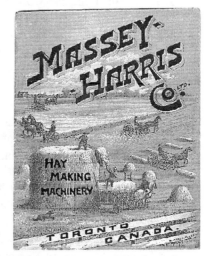

> 19½x13. 32 p+ "Contents" on verso front wrap and Harris's address on inside back wrap. Pale green wraps, black print. C.t. Bottom of cover in small print: the 3 WCE exhibit locations for their fertilizers. Pulp text. Original article by John Harris. © (GLD,WM) $22 - 45

921.18 Massey-Harris Co. *Massey-Harris Co. LTD. Hay Making Machinery : Toronto : Canada.* [Toronto, Can.: Massey-Harris Co. Ltd.] (Toronto eng. co.), n.d.

> 20½x15½. (28) p+ print and illus inside both wraps. Blue print with harvest scene litho in brown ink. C.t. Back cover illus of maple leaves on banners. Text in blue, dark brown illus of product line. WCE exhibit noted inside back cover: "Implement Annex, off the Agricultural Building." Ad. © (GLD) **P→** $30 - 60

921.19 Massey-Harris Co. *Massey-Harris Co. Limited : Largest Makers : of Farm Implements : Under the British Flag.* Toronto: Massey-Harris Co. (Toronto Lith Co.), n.d.

> 7½x12. (30) p includes inside both wraps. White wrap, white/yellow/black print with chromolith of the Canadian flag of the time. C.t. is repeated on back wrap. Color flags and product line throughout. Ad handout. No mention of WCE; from intact collection. © (GLD) $25 - 60

921.20 Massey-Harris Co. *Massey-Harris Co LTD ... Seeding and Cultivating Machinery.* Toronto, Can.: Massey Harris Co. ltd., n.d.

> 20½x16. (22) p includes inside both wraps. White wraps, blue-black fine-line block print with red fine-line illus. Back wrap illus in same colors. C.t. Text and illus in dark blue-black and red. Handout ad. No mention of WCE; from intact collection. © (GLD) $30 - 60

921.21 Mast, Foos & Co. *The Columbia Steel Wind Mill.* Springfield, OH: (The Henderson-Acher & Krebs litho co. Cin.), n.d.

> 15x8½. (4) p. Folded sheet. Front and back cover chromoliths of the wind mill on a farm; also back cover illus of two children operating Mast's force pump from a well. Text in black. Mast made punched metal rail fence and lawn mowers too. No WCE content; intact collection. See Foos, #849.2. © (WM)

921.22 Mast, P.P., & Co. *The latest : Buckeye Grain Drills.* Springfield, OH: P.P. Mast & Co., n.d.

> 24½x17. (8) p+ text inside front cover. Red wraps, black print, design includes grain drill. C.t. Back cover factory illus: "Buckeye Agricultural Works." No mention of WCE; from intact collection. (WM)

921.23 Masten [Co]. *Political joker.* Chicago: Masten, n.d.

> 10½x6. (6) p. Tri-fold white card opens to 10½x18. Chromoliths of the three 1892 Presidential candidates. Two of the panels are cleverly split down their centers so the holder can seat the candidate of his choice (Cleveland, Harrison, or Bidwell) in the president's chair. In this ad, Masten, a clothier, offered a "special discount to World's fair employees." Most likely issued in 1891 or 1892, since Cleveland sits in the presidential chair and the Fair was under construction. © (GLD) $35 - 60

922.1 *The McAdams marine brake, : a sure preventative of : All kinds of Marine Collisions with Ships, Icebergs, Rocks, Bottom, etc.;...The Brake will be shown in a few minutes.* [Brooklyn, NY]: n.p., n.d.

24x15. (2) p. Sheet, black print both sides. Caption title. Describes exhibit demonstration. Testimonials. McAdams used fold out vanes to decelerate ships. Ad. ☺ . (Stfd-bound WCE Trans Dept Collection)

922.2 McClain, George M. *Yachting Trip to the World's Fair : For the Limited Number of Sixty...* N.p.: n.p., n.d.

20½x14. (3) p. Folded white sheet, black print. Back blank. C.t. Ad for 2-month boat trip, Boston to Chicago for $125. On front: "Starting from May 20th to June 1st, 1893." Capt. McClain's name at end. ☺ (WM)

923. McClure. *The World's Columbian exposition complete with:* (Berk)

923.1 McClure, J[ames] B[aird]. *The World's Columbian exposition : with illustrations and descriptions of the public and state buildings...* Chicago: Rhodes & McClure, pub. co., 1893.

18x12. (7), 33, (37), 229-296, 403-409, (7) p. Yellow wraps, black print. Front cover and frontis both have Moro port of Columbus. At top of cover: "Standard No 58. Library." Illus and maps. Back cover ad for "The audiphone for the deaf at the World's fair" (see #724.2). Also see #923 for another McClure item. ☺ (GLD,S)   P➔ $22 - 50

923.2 McCormick Harvesting Machine Co. *Bindlochine.* [Chicago: Rand, McNally & Co., Printers & Engravers], n.d.

24½x18. 39, (1) p. Front cover chromolith by Orcutt Co of children playing on reaper. A scene from 1876 Centennial harvesting demo on back. Text and illus in blue. C.t. "January 1, 1892" on p (3). Illus of their harvesters and of Chicago bldgs including WCE Admin Bldg. Pretty ad. ☺ . (WM)

923.3 McCormick Harvesting Machine Co. *The historical egg. Discovery of America by Columbus 1492. Invention of the reaper by McCormick 1831.* [Chicago: Donohue & Henneberry, printers and binders], n.d.

24x18. 47, (1) p. Chromolith wraps showing Columbus landing and McCormick port in an historical egg. On back is illus of 3 caravels on high seas with globe in background. Dark blue text and illus. On p (3), "Chicago, January 1893." Vignettes from 1871 Chicago fire. Each page heading is a train with a foreign country's name in the engine smoke. No WCE content; from an intact collection ☺ . (WM)

☞ Upon his return to Spain, Columbus demonstrated standing an egg on end and told friends the secret of the simple trick. He analogized to his discovery of the Indies—easy once you know how.

923.4 McCormick Harvesting Machine Co. *Souvenir Calendar and Memorandum Book : Compliments of McCormick Harvesting Machine Co.* Chicago: McCormick Harvesting Machine Co. (Orcutt Co. Lith), n.d.   P➔

12½x6½. (20) p+ product lithos inside both wraps. Glossy coated wraps, chromolith illus. C.t. Monthly calendar from June to Dec 1893. Memorandum sheets are headed with description of awards from previous WFs; these awards were displayed at their WCE exhibit, which is described on p (7). Centerfold map of Chicago business district. ☺ (GLD,WM) $25 - 60

923.5 McCully & Miles. *...Interior Decorations : Stained Glass : Glass and Marble Mosaics.* [Chicago]: n.p., n.d.

29x22. (4) p. Black print and illus on glossy paper. Last (3) pages are photo illus of their ornamental work. At head of title: "Fine Wall Papers : Draperies : special Furniture Designs : Fresco Painting." No mention of WCE; from an intact collection. (WM)

923.6 McCully & Miles. *Interior decorations : stained glass : glass and marble mosaics.* [Chicago]: n.p., n.d.

24x16. (4) p. Folded pink card, sepia print and design. Illus on back is captioned "Plastic relief work." No mention of WCE; from an intact collection. ☺(WM)

923.7 McDaniel, R.E. *...My church.* 4th ed. N.p.: n.p., 1893.

18½x11. (4) p. Folded sheet. C.t. At head of title: "Souvenir World's Fair." Contents: a description of the Evangelical Lutheran Church. ☺. (KS,ref) $26

923.8 McDowall, J., & Co. *Chicago exhibition, 1893. Department A Group 14. J. M°Dowall & C°. The royal horse & cattle condiment Manufactory.* Glasgow: n.p., n.d.

15½x10½. (8) panels. Folded light mauve sheet opens to 15½x42, black print. C.t. A liquid tonic and supplement for farm animals. (WM)

924. McDowell. *Liberty primer:* (csuf,DAR,UoC)
▸Alternate author: Columbian Liberty Bell Committee. History of the bell, telling when it was rung. Contains a 2-page poetic Liberty Bell tribute by Madge Morris Wagner (#804.7). Describes smaller souvenir bells for schools; this primer was meant to accompany each replica.
---- Also found. 23½x15. 32 p. Self wraps. ☺. (DAR)

925. McKee. *US "Snap Shots" An Independent, National:* (HU,UCLA)

925.1 McKim, J.M. *...Souvenir of the Worlds* [sic] *Fair : Celebrating the four hundredth anniversary of the discovery of uncle sam.* N.p., n.p., n.d.

20½x14½. 32 p. Yellow wraps, black print, Columbus port. C.t. At head of title: "1492 1892." Dr. McKims' ad for "Wonderful Eight" patent medicine includes lithos, testimonials. (ref) $30

925.2 McNeal, D.W., and Co. *If you use Dr. McNeal's hair tonic...* Chicago: n.p., n.d.

14½x9. (4) p. Folded sheet, brown print, illus of the back of a bald man's head. C.t. At bottom: "Exhibiting at the Manufactures Building, Gallery, World's Fair." Rubber stamped below this: "Directly East of Roof Elevator." ☺(WM)

925.3 McPherson, Edward, ed. *...Tribune Almanac : and political register for 1891.* New York: The Tribune Association, 1891.

19x13. 364 p. Blue-green wraps, black print. C.t. At head of title: "Library of Tribune extras. Vol. III. January, 1891. No. 1." Illus of the Tribune Bldg on front cover. WCE described on p 41 (House votes and Act) and pp 146-50 (listing of state managers and nat'l committees). ☺(GLD) $15 - 32

925.4 *McVicker's theater : Bill of Play.* Chicago: W.J. Jefferson printing and publishing co., 1893?

21½x15. (32) p+ print inside covers. Buff wraps, green print and design. Pulp paper. Play bill for theater's week commencing Sept 17, 1893. No relationship to WCE but many great WCE exhibits ads, and the back cover is a full-page ad for Alley "L" transportation to the fair—5 cents. ☺(GLD) $12 - 30

925.5 *Medical agents of the Chemical Works : (vormals E. Shering), Berlin. 1893.* Walbrook, E.C.: M.S. Rickerby, Printer, 1893?

21x14. viii, 112 p. Black hide-grained stiff wraps, gilt print and logo. Shering founded Chemische Fabrik auf Actien, Germany, to develop pure chemicals for photography and medical uses. In English. Dated "February, 1893." No mention of WCE; from an intact collection. ☺(WM)

926.1 *...Memorial to Mrs. Emma Willard.* Chicago: n.p., 1893.

14x__. 12 p. Issued unbound. Port. At head of title: "World's Columbian Exposition." Chiefly Mary Ellen West's "Mrs. Emma Willard." Willard, an early educator of women, lived 1787–1870. (Amh)

926.2 Merchant & Co. *What visitors will be shown at the World's Fair by Merchant & Co's. Brownies.* [Philadelphia?: Merchant & Co., 1892?].

13½x20½. (41) p. Buff wraps, blue design of Palmer Cox brownies (see #7.3 for book with his brownies). Illus. Buff t.p. has blue design and gilt print. Calendar for 1892 with Uncle Sam, eagle, and brownies on back cover. Ad. ☺. (HML,S) **P➜**

926.3 Mercier, A., and Co. ...*Sugar-manufactories. Bresles (Oise).* Beavais, Fr.: Imprimerie de Moniteur de l'Oise, 1893.

24x16. 8 p. Bright blue wraps, black print, string-tied. C.t. = t.p. Mrs. A. Mercier's first exposition. Co info and processing methods. No mention of WCE; from intact collection. ☺ (WM)

927. Merck. *Catalogue of the exhibitions of \Katalog der aussstellungen:* (UMD)
▶Clarification: Title given is c.t.; published without t.p.

927.1 Mergenthaler Linotype Co. *The Linotype and its advantages.* [New York]: n.p., n.d.

26½x20½. (2) p. Buff sheet, chocolate print. Front lists advantages, back is same as cover of #927.2. No WCE content; from intact collection. [Exhibited at Machinery Hall, Group 74, Class 455.] ☺ (WM)

927.2 Mergenthaler Linotype Co. *The Linotype : construction : advantages : records : endorsements.* New York: Mergenthaler Linotype Co. [Bartlett & Company, Designers, Engravers and Printers], 1893?

24x17. 1 *l* frontis, (4), 7-72 p. Maize wraps, brown print and design with center b/w litho of the machine. Frontis litho of their Brooklyn factory. Testimonials as late as Apr 1, 1893. Illus of newspaper banners printed on the Linotype. No mention of WCE; from an intact WCE collection. (WM)

☞ The Linotype won the race for automated typesetting over the Paige typesetter (not exhibited at WCE) which was heavily backed by Mark Twain. Twain was thrown into bankruptcy by the failure; he traveled around the world lecturing and wrote a book about the trip to pay all the creditors at no loss.

928.1 Merritt's World's Fair Accommodation Bureau. *Save money by securing your rooms through Merritt's.* N.p: n.p., n.d.

7x11½. Stiff card with navy print one side. ☺ (WM)

928.2 Metallic Rod-Packing Co. *Columbian : Metallic Rod-Packing Co. self-adjusting. no springs.* Philadelphia: [Metallic Rod-Packing Co. (Edwd. Stern & Co. Prs.)], n.d.

10x19½. (12) p. Gray wraps, black print. C.t. Rubber stamped in purple ink on cover: "Exhibit Machinery Hall, 31-32 section F." ☺. (GLD,E) $22 - 45

928.3 Michigan Central Railroad. *The North Shore Limited.* [Chicago: Rand, McNally & co., engravers, embossers, printers and binders, Jan. 1893].

17½x13. 1 *l*, (34) p. Pale blue textured wraps, green and red print, string-tied. Illus. C.t. = Caption title. Describes Chicago and WCE terminus. Timetable and sights along route to NY/Boston. ☺ (WM)

928.4 Michigan Central Railroad. *To the World's Columbian Exposition : Chicago from New York Boston and the east : Michigan Central : "The Niagara Falls Route."* Chicago: Rand,, McNally & Co., Printers and Engravers, n.d.

21x10½. Sheet unfolds to 43x82½. Folded "cover" in red and black shows WCE scenes of Admin Bldg and MacMonnies Fountain. Route map. Inside panels have illus of seven WCE bldgs. ☺ (WM)

929. Midland RR. *The Midland Railway of England:* (GLD,WM) **P➜** $24 - 55

929.1 Miller, Henry F., & Sons Piano Co. *Henry F. Miller : piano-fortes. World's Fair, Chicago, Ill.* Boston: n.p., n.d.

> 12x18½. (4) p. Folded cream glossy sheet, blue-black print. Illus of fancy pianos on pp (1) and (4). C.t. On p (2), WCE exhibit at: "Liberal Arts Building, Sec. I, Col. V6." Styles listed. ☺(WM)

930. Millet. *Some artists at the fair*: (CCA,Col,CU,CWM,DU,EPL,EvP,HU,LBA,Merc,NDU,NPG,NSW,sfsu,UMD,UPa,RU,sfpl,UVM,VAM,Yale)

931.1 Milwaukee Gas Stove Co. *"Perfection" Gas Stoves.* Milwaukee, WI: Milwaukee Gas Stove Co., [1893].

> 11x7½. 26 p. White glossy wraps, blue print and design in landscape orientation (text in portrait). C.t. On back cover: "Columbian edition" printed around eagle on stars and stripes shield. Ad catalog dated "Milwaukee, Jan. 1ˢᵗ, 1893." (WM)

931.2 Milwaukee Harvester Co. *Fifteenth annual illustrated catalogue of the World's best and lightest draft : Grain and Grass Cutting Machinery. 1893.* [Milwaukee, WI: King, Fowle & co., printers], n.d.

> 16½x25½. 20 p. Buff wraps, gray and black print, illus of barefoot girl in hay. Illus of oxen plowing on back. Illus catalog of farm implements. No mention WCE; from an intact collection. ☺(WM)

931.3 Minerva Chiffonier Trunk Co. *A Woman's invention : verily there are...* Chicago: n.p., n.d.

> 16x18. Yellow stiff card with black print. Caption title. "On exhibition at The World's Fair in the Patent Department, in the Woman's Building, and in the South Dakota Building..." Illus of "Fall River, Hot Springs, So. Dak." on back. Modified chiffonier with curtains for women's travels. ☺(WM)

931.4 Missouri Pacific Railway. *Statistics and information : concerning the : state of Nebraska, taken from state and national reports, showing the advantages, and giving information...* 2d ed. N.p.: General passenger department of the Missouri Pacific Railway, n.d.

> 19½x14. 64 p. Pink wraps, black print. Map. C.t.: "Nebraska." WCE handout encouraging immigration to Nebraska. ☺. (LBA)

931.5 Missouri Pacific Railway. *Statistics and information : concerning the : State of Texas : with its Millions of Acres of Unoccupied Lands, for the farmer and stock raiser, unlimited...* 8th ed. N.p.: General Passenger Department of The Missouri Pacific R'y Co., [1893].

> 19½x14. 93 p, map. Orange wraps, black print and illus of Lone Star. C.t.: "Texas." WCE handout encouraging immigration to Texas. ☺. (LBA)

931.6 Moffat, David, & Co. *...Tanners of Harness Leather. ...The World's Columbian Exposition, Chicago, Ill. 1893.* [New York: Burr printing house], n.d.

> 14½x12. (4) p. Buff rag paper self-wraps, red and black print, red string-tied. Text in red and black. C.t. Co info at head of title. Explains harness leather exhibit. ☺. (WM)   P➜

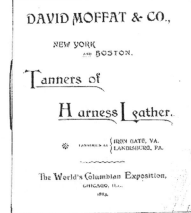

DAVID MOFFAT & CO.,
NEW YORK and BOSTON.
Tanners of
Harness Leather.
TANNERIES AT { IRON GATE, VA. / LANDISBURG, PA.
The World's Columbian Exposition,
CHICAGO, ILL.
1893.

931.7 Monarch Shirts. *A little history of a big : Monarch.* N.p.: N.p., n.d.

> 8x11½. (6) p includes text inside both covers. Pale blue-gray wraps, blue print, trade mark "Monarch" in red. Blue text print. C.t. Title and text refer to their shirts as monarchs among shirts and real monarchs (kings). No mention of WCE; from an intact collection. ☺(WM)

932. Monroe. *John Wellborn Root : a study of his life and work*: (MIT,Smth)
---- Also listed: Rpt ed: Park Forest, IL: Prairie School Press, [1966]. 23x__. xxii, 291 p.

932.1 Montaudon, A., [Co.]. *Classic Anatomy of Dr. Auzoux, officer of the legion of honor. Manufactured by...* [Rochester, NY: R.W. Lace, printer], n.d.

> 26½x18. 18 p. Light blue smooth wraps, blue print and illus of a skinned human model on a stand. Illus of horse model on back cover. C.t.: "Auzoux anatomical models..." Price catalog for their elaborate full-

sized humans and animal models. Montaudon was Dr. Auzoux's nephew. "Agents: Ward's Natural Science Establishment" in Rochester, NY. For laboratory and teaching. No WCE content; from an intact collection. ☺. (WM)

932.2 Montserrat Co. *The Montserrat : World's Fair : Souvenir.* Chicago: Columbian Eng. Co., n.d. **P➜**

14x10. (4) p. Folded buff card, gold/teal/green showing litho of Admin Bldg. C.t. The company made lime and arrow root juice preparations. In 1493 Columbus discovered this island in the Antilles and named it Montserrat. ☺. (E)

932.3 Moody, William R. *The Life of Dwight L. Moody.* New York, Chicago [and] Toronto: Fleming H. Revell Co., 1900 [ᶜ1900 by Fleming H. Revell co.].

25x18. 2 *l*, 590 p. Morocco half leather over black cloth boards, gilt print. Marbled edges and end papers. Frontis port of D.L. Moody. T.p. in red and black. C.t.: "The Life of Dwight L. Moody by His Son." Chap 36, "World's Fair Campaign," describes Moody's WCE activities. Illus are included in pagination. See #865 for another Moody item. ☺ (GLD) $15 - 35

932.4 Moore, L. Murray, [Co.]. *L. Murray Moore, manufacturer of : Trucks and Shoe Racks.* [Rochester, NY: Parkerson Printing and Engraving Co.], n.d.

15½x9. 23 p. Red glossy wraps, black and gilt print, black border design top and bottom. C.t. WCE location in the Trans Bldg, "Vehicle Department, Section A., Block I2" given on p (3). Catalog for 1893 for industrial wheeled metal baskets and hand trucks. ☺ (GLD) $20 - 50

932.5 Morgan, D.S., & Co. *...D.S. Morgan & Co. Agricultural Machinery. Spading Harrows, Reapers, Mowers, Binders, Rakes : Novelties in Implements.* Brockport, NY [and] Chicago: D.S. Morgan & Co., [1893].

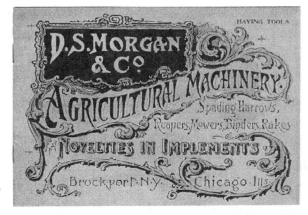

14x20. 12 p+ text inside both wraps. Pale blue-gray wraps, dark blue bold print and design. C.t. At head of title: "Haying tools." Contains 9 lithos of their mowers and rakes. Columbus landing and Magellan ship lithos in blue ink on back. Testimonials to Oct 1892. Exhibited in the Ag Bldg, Sec E-N-3. No mention of WCE; from an intact collection. Ad. ☺ (GLD)   **P➜** $20 - 40

933. Morgan. *Annual Statement of the trade and commerce of St. Louis:* (WM)

934. Morgan, H. *The Historical WCE and Chicago guide:* (Berk,CCA,CUE,ESU,FLP,IHi,MOHx,slpl,UIC)
---- Also found: Mason 1892 cover variant: Full morocco binding blind stamped with gilt print.
---- Also listed: New publisher: Springfield, MA: Wiley, [ᶜ1892].
---- Also listed: New publisher: St. Louis: P.M. Vanderwalker & co., 1893.
---- Also found: This book's t.p. found in book #936. See second "also found" at #936 below.

935. Morgan. *The Historical World's Columbian Exposition and guide to Chicago:* (IHi)
▸Correct spelling: [ᶜ1892 by J. L. Hebert].

936. Morgan. *The Historical World's Columbian Exposition and guide to Chicago:*
(GLD,A,HU,IHi,Merc,NPG,UTA,UoC)   Hardcover or Paperback: $25 – 45
---- Also found: St. Louis and San Francisco: The Pacific publishing co., 1892, [ᶜ1892 J.L. Hebert].
24x16½. 1 *l* (fold color bird's-eye), 1 *l* (Columbus Statue illus), (2) p (t.p./copyright p), 1 *l* (dedication), 3-480, 20 p. Light blue hc; red, black, and gilt print ; small port of Columbus upper left; design of Columbus landing and WCE Court of Honor. Outside back cover is blank. C.t.: "1492 : The World's Columbian Exposition : and guide to Chicago and St. Louis : the carnival city of the world : 1893 :

Illustrated." The last 20 pages are "Publishers' appendix" devoted to St. Louis industries.

---- Also found: St. Louis and San Francisco: The Pacific publishing co., 1892 [°1892 by J.L. Hebert]. This vol is exactly the same as the book described directly above (c.t., pub info, size, paging, color) except it has the title page of #934 and an illus outside back cover—a pretty embossed black and gilt ad for Pauly Jail Building and Manufacturing Co., one of the industries advertising in the final 20 p.

---- Also listed: New pub: St. Louis: Vanderwalker & Co., [°1892].

---- Also found: Paperback ed: St. Louis and San Francisco: The Pacific publishing co., 1892 [°1892 by J.L. Hebert]. 23½x15½. 1 *l* (fold color bird's-eye), (2) p (t.p./copyright), 1 *l* (dedication), 3-480 p. Light tan wraps, sepia and gold print; small port of Columbus upper left; blue-black illus of Columbus landing and WCE Court of Honor. Except for coloring, the c.t. and design are duplicates of Pacific hc editions above.

936.1 Morris, B.N., [Co.]. *Description of the Boats and canoes : on exhibition at the : World's fair, Chicago, 1893.* Veazie, ME?: B.N. Morris, n.d.

15x11½. (4) p. Green-gray folded sheet, black print. Caption title. Litho of one of their models in top and side view. "Canvas covered." ☺ . (E)

936.2 Morris, Nelson, & Co. *Nelson Morris & Co., extract of beef : beef and pork packers : lard refiners : Fairbank Canning Co., packers and preservers of meats : union stock yards : Chicago.* [Chicago & East St. Louis, IL: Nelson Morris & Co., 1893].

16x9. (4) p. Folded white card, red and black print. Back cover illus of 3 old women drinking extract of beef tea. C.t. No WCE content; from intact collections. [The company exhibited in the Ag Bldg, Sec D, 1st Floor, Col C.0.] ☺ (GLD,WM) $20 - 45

936.3 Morris, Nelson, & Co. *Nelson Morris & Co. : Matchless.* N.p.: n.p., n.p.

12½x6½. (4) p. Folded die-cut card in the shape of a ham, brown design and chocolate print. C.t. Inside illus of pork processing in brown and tans and "See our Exhibit at the worlds [sic] fair." Back cover title: "Nelson Morris & Co. : Supreme." ☺ (GLD)   P➔ $20 - 50

937. Morse, W[illiam] F[rancis]. *The disposal of the garbage and waste of the World's Columbian Exposition. A paper read at the International Congress of Health, Chicago, October 11, 1893.* (CCA,HML,NYPL)

▶Completed title.   ▶Add second author: International Congress of Health.

938.1 Moses, John. *Supplement to Illinois : Historical and Statistical.* N.p.: n.p., 1896.

24½x15½. Pp 1317-79. Blue wraps are signed and dated in ink by John Moses with compliments, Jan 1, 1896. C.t. The title given is also written on the cover but in a different hand. Caption title: "Supplementary. Chapter LIV." Not contained in #939 or #940. (IHi)

939. Moses. *History of Chicago*: (DC)

▶WCE content: Chap 10 is devoted to the WCE; there are many other scattered references to the WCE.

940. Moses and Selby. *The white city*: (GLD,Col,CU,CWM,GPL,IHi,MOHx,MSI,NLA,OU,RU,UIC,wsu,Yale) $24 - 48

▶Add copyright info: [°1893 Chicago World Book Co.].

▶Clarified paging: 5 *l*, (1) p, xii-xix, 6 *l*, (9)-170 p, 2 *l*, 132 p, 2 *l*, 166 p+ many interspersed unpaged *l*.

☞ Some confusion exists about the content and intent of this book and especially Moses's #1055. Parts of these two books came from his 1887 treatise, *Illinois, Historical and Statistical.*

940.1 *Mount Pleasant wine co. : Wine Growers : Wholesale Dealers in the best Grades of : native wines.* Augusta, MO: (The Orcutt Co. Lith, Chicago), n.d.

18½x13. (2) p. White coated stiff card, black print both sides. C.t. Illus of their WCE exhibit on back with a scene of their Missouri vineyards in background. (WM)

940.2 Muhr's, H., Sons. *...H. Muhr's sons : Columbian Exhibition : Manufactures & Liberal Arts Building : Section O : Block 1.* New York, Philadelphia [and] Chicago: H. Muhr's sons [R.W. Stern & co. prs, Phila.], n.d.

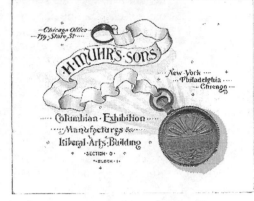

12x15. (8) p+ text inside back wrap. Blue print and banner illus, also embossed gilt watch case and diamond ring. String-tied. C.t. At head of title: "Chicago Office." Text and photo illus of their production lines in jewelry and watch cases. Ad.
© (GLD,E,WM) P➔ $25 - 55

941.1 Musallem Brothers. *City of Damascus!* N.p.: n.p., n.d.

22½x15. 1 *l.* Broadside on tan pulp with black print. "No. 30 Turkish Village, Midway Plaisance" at bottom. Eastern arts and crafts for sale. © (S)

942. Muybridge. *Descriptive zoopraxography:* (NLA,UCB,UCLA)
▶Add: 20x14. 1 *l* (frontis), (2) p (t.p. and copyright), xi, 44, 34, 14, (2) p. Brown cloth hc, black print. Although the t.p. bears the imprint "University of Pennsylvania," the book was actually printed by the Lakeside Press in Chicago.
---- Also found: Presentation copy, inscribed "Charles M. Kurtz with the warm esteem of The Author 23 Septr 1893" on the front flyleaf. (ref) Presentation Copy: $1,650
---- Also found: Wraps edition: 19x13. 1 *l* (frontis), (2) p (t.p. and copyright), ii, 4, 34 [imperfect paging], 14 [imperfect paging] p. Yellow pebble-textured stiff wraps with "University of Pennsylvania : 1893" at bottom. Inscribed by the author. (UCLA)

942.1 Myers American Ballot Machine Co. *Continued, complete success of the Myers Ballot Machine.* [Rochester, NY]: n.p., n.d.

23x15. 12 p. Self-wraps, black print, illus of box in use. Caption title. Testimonials. Overprint in red on p 12: "At Columbian Exposition Section O, Electrical Building, near north west entrance." (WM)

942.2 National Cash Register Co. *...All Nationalities At the World's Fair Use Our Registers. World's fair exhibits of The National Cash Register Company.* Dayton, OH:, n.p., n.d.

32x24. White sheet printed both sides in red and blue. At head of title: listing of nationalities using the register plus "All in the Costumes of their Respective Countries." Illus of 8 people surround the words: "All Nationalities." On back is a partial list of those at the WF using NCR. © (WM)

942.3 National Cash Register Co. *The Hustler : A change in circumstances.* [Dayton, OH: National Cash Register Co., °1893 by the National Cash Register Co.].

32x23. (7) p includes inside front cover. Small newspaper format. Color wraps illus a couple dining in poverty and then in elegance. Color litho of NCR registers and Dayton factory on back cover. C.t. Title refers to improved life using NCR. Lists main exhibit in Manuf Bldg and branch exhibits. © (WM)

942.4 National Christian Association on Freemasonry. *Worlds* [sic] *fair list of standard illustrated rituals. ...On freemasonry. ...On odd-fellowship. ...Other secret society rituals.* [Chicago]: National Christian Association, n.d.

16x8. (4) p. Folded card, blue print. Caption title. Lists available books with prices. At bottom of p (1): "These and many other Secret Society Books may be seen and ordered at Exhibit of National Christian Association, in North West corner of gallery of Manufactures Building..." © (GLD) $18 - 35

942.5 National Educational Association. Executive Committee. *Columbus Day, October 12, 1892. Message to the public school teachers of America.* N.p.: n.p., 1892.

28x21½. (4) p. Folded buff sheet, black print. Flyer addressed: "To the Teachers of the American Public Schools." Developed the idea for a uniform school celebration to coincide with the WCE dedication ceremonies; it was intended to "interest youth of the county in the Exposition." Uniform press release rpt on p (4). Originally proposed by *Youth's Companion.* The celebration was held throughout the US, but was moved to Oct 21 to match the new WCE dedication date. © (WM)

942.6 National Key Opening Can Co. *Masonic Temple : Chicago : This Building is the highest commercial...* Chicago: The National Key Opening Can co., n.d.

17½x10½. (4) p. Folded sheet of buff stiff paper, black print, b/w illus of Masonic Temple. Inside are b/w illus of a variety of key opening cans. Advantages of these cans listed on back. The Company's offices were in the Temple Bldg. No WCE content; from an intact collection. © (GLD) $20 - 45

942.7 National Live Stock Association. *Final report of the National Live Stock Association by its committee of eighteen : appointed to represent the live stock industry of the United States before the World's Columbian commission.* Springfield, IL: Illinois State Register Book Publishing House, 1894.

22x15. 21 *l*, (5), 4-211, (1) p. Wraps. C.t. = t.p. The 21 preliminary leaves each have a half-tone image of one of the Committee members. Verso of p 211 is the Treasurer's Final Report. © . (UCLA)

942.8 *The National Wall Paper Co's : exhibit : Columbian exposition.* N.p.: National Wall Paper company, n.d.   P➜

35x25. 10 *l*. Tan wraps, full-cover chromolith of their WCE pavilion, red string-tied. Leaves are coated and of very stiff stock. Five text leaves alternate with 5 full leaf chromoliths of their exhibit interior that was decorated with various wall papers. Gray text print. C.t. = t.p. Back cover chromolith of the "'Efficient' Shade Roller Pavilion : Section F - No. 276 – N.E. Gallery : Manufactures and Liberal Arts Building" provided by Nevius & Haviland, NY. Lists branches responsible for the exhibits. Gorgeous ad. . (WM)

944.   Naylor. *Across the Atlantic*: (IHi)

944.1 Neal, John R., & Co. *Sea Food. A brief HIstory of The New England Fisheries with a Few Statistics and Interesting Facts. Where the Fish Are found, the Methods Used in Catching and Preparing Them for the Market. Also the History of Finnan Haddies, and How They Are Cured. Souvenir, World's Columbian Exposition, Chicago.* Boston: A.T. Bliss & Co., 1893.

25x17. 32 p. Wraps. Illus, fold map. Ad describing Atlantic fishing. (HML,ref) $25

945.1 New England Grocers. *New England Grocer's World's fair excursions.* N.p.: [New England Grocers], n.d.

13½x8. 2 p+ (8) p blank for trip diary. Tri-fold soft leather cover with window pocket for "membership certificate in New England Grocer's Plan of World's fair excursions during 1893." Caption title. Gusset pocket in back for business cards. On front flap in gilt: "World's fair : 1893." Given to each tour customer. See #945.2 to #945.4 and #1070. (S)

945.2 New England Grocers. *Latest circular! Superceding All Others. Personally Conducted Tours : every five days to the Columbian exposition.* Boston: [New England Grocers, 1893].

21x14½. (7) p including back wrap. Self-wraps, black print and co logo. Dated "Chicago, April 15, 1893." C.t. Litho of "Our Chicago homes" on p (2) and floor plans pp (5)-(7). Benj. Johnson's name on cover. Contents exactly the same as #945.4. (S)

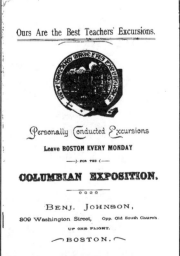

945.3 New England Grocers. *Ours Are the Best Teachers' Excursions. Personally Conducted Excursions : Leave Boston every Monday for the Columbian exposition.* Boston: Benj. Johnson [New England Grocers], n.d.   P➜

23x14½. 10 p. C.t. Back cover illus of "Our Chicago Homes." See adjacent citations and #1070 for other Grocer's excursion items. © . (E)

945.4 New England Grocers. *"We are Advertised by Our Patrons." Personally Conducted Excursions : leave Boston every Monday : for the : Columbian exposition.* Boston: [New England Grocers, 1893].

21x14½. (7) p including back wrap. Self-wraps, black print and co logo. Dated "Chicago, April 15, 1893." C.t. Litho of "Our Chicago homes" on p (2) and floor plans pp (5)-(7). "Benj. Johnson" on cover. Contents the same as #945.2. (S)

945.5 New England Ticket Agents Association. *New England Cottage, 301 53ʳᵈ Street, Hyde Park, Chicago, Ill.* Boston: n.p., n.d.

16x8½. Buff stiff card, blue ink. Center card on front: "Only 6 blocks from 57ᵗʰ Street Gate of World's fair, eight minutes walk." Eight rooms, $1 to $3 per day for 1 or 2 people. (WM)

946.1 New Home Sewing Machine Co. *VALUABLE INFORMATION : Where to go while in Chicago. What to see at THE FAIR. : FACTS WORTH KNOWING.* [Chicago: The New Home Sewing Machine Co.], n.d.

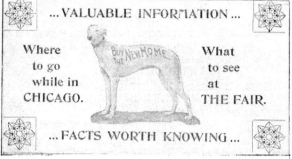

8½x15. (6) panels. Sheet unfolds to 24½x15 printed both sides. Coated paper, red-purple print and illus. Exhibited "in the manufacturers [sic] and liberal arts building." Back three panels give WCE "Pointers!" ☺ (GLD,WM)　　　　　　P➜　　　　$18 - 35

946.2 New Orleans Brewing Ass'n. *Worlds* [sic] *Fair 1893. Exhibit of the New Orleans Brewing Ass'n at Chicago.* [New Orleans, LA: New Orleans Brewing Ass'n (The Milwaukee litho & engr co)], n.d.

15½x8½. (6) panels. Tri-fold unfolds to 15½x25. Three illus panels each side. Tan paper, gilt borders, illus of their exhibit. C.t. Contains a 14½x24 tipped-in "Standard guide map of the World's Columbian exposition at Chicago, 1893" showing their exhibit location on "2ⁿᵈ Floor – Agricultural Hall, –West." Beautiful chromoliths of 3 product beers, 1 per inside panel. Ad. ☺ (GLD)　　　　　P➜　　　　$35 - 65

946.3 *The New Popular Atlas of the World.* Philadelphia: Mast, Crowell & Kirkpatrick, ᶜ1892.

36x29. 220 p+ fold color map of Maine tipped-in at first flyleaf. Black cloth hc, gilt print. Color maps, some folding including Illinois. WCE text and illus pp 126-30; "Christopher Columbus" bio pp 131-32. Similar in style and format to #808. (ref)　　　　　　　　$150

948. *New Year's greeting and welcome to Chicago*: (ICRL)

948.1 New York and New England Railroad. *...Boston and New England to Chicago and the west.* Boston: Cashman, Keating & co., printers, n.d.

9½x21. (8) panels. Sheet unfolds to 21x38½. Route map across inside four panels showing Boston to Chicago. Across tops of panels in red: "The 'Isabella Express' for the World's Columbian Exposition." At head of title: "World's Columbian Exposition" and co's name. (WM)

948.2 New York and New England Railroad. *...Chicago Tours : Summer of 1893.* N.p., n.p., n.d.

21½x14. (2) p. Folded blue sheet, printed on the 2 rectos in navy and red ink. At head of title: co's name. Tour No. 1, "Isabella Express to Chicago," traveled 3 times a week from June 20. (WM)

948.3 New York Central & Hudson River Railroad. *"America's greatest railroad." New York Central & Hudson River Railroad. Direct line New York to Chicago via Niagara Falls.* New York: New York Central & Hudson River Railroad (The Matthews-Northrup co., complete art-printing works, Buffalo, NY), n.d.

15½x8½. (4) p. Folded buff sheet, dark green print, illus of moving train. Illus Niagara Falls on back. Solicited travelers from New York to the Chicago WF; trains leaving every hour. Ad. ☺ (GLD)　　$24 - 50

948.4 New York Central & Hudson River Railroad. …*The Lake Region of Central New York : Reached Via The New York Central & Hudson River RR.* [New York: New York Central & Hudson River R.R. Co. (The Giles co., NY), 1892.]

20½x10½. 32 p+ text inside both wraps. Folding color map before p (1). Multicolor wraps. C.t. At head of title: "Four-track series." No mention of WCE; from intact collection which contained the companion piece, #948.3. © (GLD) $25 - 55

948.5 New York Central & Hudson River Railroad. *Local time table of New York Central & Hudson River Railroad.* New York: [New York Central & Hudson River R.R. (The Matthews-Northrup co, complete engraving and printing works, Buffalo, NY)], 1893.

20½x10½. Buff sheet unfolds to 41x101½, black print. Map in green, buff, black. Title from caption of timetable inside. On map, next to Chicago: "World's Columbian Exposition." Lower right: "between the East and Chicago, the World's Fair City." At bottom of cover: "July, 1893." (WM)

948.6 New York Central & Hudson River Railroad. *This is all about "999" of the New York Central & Hudson River RR.* [New York: New York Central & Hudson River R.R. (The Matthews-Northrup co. complete art printing works, Buffalo, NY), 1893].

16x9. 12 panels. Single strip unfolds to 16x54, printed both sides. C.t. Describes this high speed engine of the Empire Express as exhibited at the Trans Bldg at the WCE. The "999" is illus on panel (12). On panel 11: a poem, "Plenty Quick, Ho Gan," and printer's date, "Oct. 11, '93." © . (E)

☞ Engine "999" is on permanent display at the Museum of Science and Industry (the original Fine Arts Bldg at the WCE) in Chicago. Its light overall weight and oversized drive wheels precluded its use as a passenger locomotive; in fact, it had to be pushed to start and never saw daily service. Photo-illus at #2446.MSI.

948.7 New York Central and Lake Shore Railroads. …*The "Exposition Flyer" (Limited).* New York: [New York Central and Lake Shore Railroads (American Bank Note co.), 1893].

15½x9. (12) p. Folded buff card stock opens to 15½x54. Front cover illus of their WCE bldg. Printed in red and blue-black ink. C.t. At head of title: "'America's greatest railroad' : Fastest : finest : best." Contains the Exposition Flyer time table, illus of elegant car interiors, illus of "999", and a route map to Chicago on back. Grand WCE handout ad. © (GLD) $30 - 55

948.8 New York Life Insurance Co. *How a New-York Life man may attend the Columbian Convention and The World's Fair.* N.p.: n.p., n.d.

13½x22½. 6 *l* of Winters Art Litho chromoliths of WCE bldgs, followed by p 13: "Our Calendar." Smooth card wraps, blue print, string-tied. C.t. Calendar of contest to write "Accumulation Policy" from Apr 3 to June 10, 1892; winners to attend Columbian Convention July 10–15, 1893. Winners listed in #948.11 © (WM)

948.9 New York Life Insurance Co. Kingsley, D.P., comp. *Proceedings : Columbian Convention "70" : New York Life Insurance Co. : Chicago : July 10-15, '93.* [Chicago: Press of J.F. Leaming & Co.], n.d.

23x14½. 120 p. Pale blue-green wraps with black print and litho design of flags, banners, and building. "Kingsley" on bottom of front wrap. Illus. Ad. . (HML.WM)   P➔

948.10 New York Life Insurance Co. *New York Life : Insurance Co. : John A. McCall, pres't.* [New York: New York Life Insurance Co.], n.d.

8x5½. (28) p+ text inside both wraps. Interspersed chromolith views of WCE bldgs. Chromoliths on white paper wraps: eagle (front), co's bldg with port of Columbus and "1492 1892" (back). Wraps in portrait orientation; landscape text. C.t. Calendar pages Apr 1893 through Mar 1894. © (GLD) $22 - 50

948.11 New York Life Insurance Co. *This : Roll of Honor : Contains the Names of the Representatives of the New York Life Insurance Company Who wrote and placed ten or more : Accumulation Policies...* [New York: New York Life Insurance Co.], n.d.

13½x20. (20) p. White glossy stiff wraps, embossed design of leaves and eagle in circle, pale blue and gilt print, yellow string-tied. T.p. in red and black. Lists winners in Sept 1892 contest to write policies (see #948.8); winners went to annual meeting and WCE in Chicago. Striking ad. (WM)

948.12 New York Life Insurance Co. *Woman's Building.* [New York: New York Life Insurance Co.], n.d. **P➔**

5x8. (24) p+ text on inside both wraps. Chromolith wraps illustrating the Woman's Bldg (front) and Govt Bldg (back). C.t. Monthly calendars (Apr 1893 through Mar 1894) with 12 chromoliths of WCE bldgs. Co's ad and WF handout. ☺(GLD,WM) $20 - 30

948.13 *Niagara Hotel : European Plan.* [Chicago: Vandercook engraving & pub. co.], n.d.

11x7. (4) p. Folded pink card, black print and hotel illus. C.t. Accordion strip glued to p (3) folds out to 13 panels one side showing 11 WCE views in green hues; 12 panels on the back side have info for the visitor. Ad variant of #1160. ☺(S)

948.14 Noble, Brown & Co. *New era in pumps! Motive power from operator's whole weight. The "Nobro" portable pump.* Leeds, Eng.: n.p., n.d.

33½x21½. (8) p. Buff paper, black print, richly illus with company's products including self-pump fire extinguisher, showers, plant watering, and window washing devices. Title from p (1). Issued with blue-flecked envelope, 12½x22½, with illus captioned "Nobro portable bath" in upper left. ☺(WM)

948.15 Noble, Brown & Co. *"Nobro" portable fire engine.* N.p.: n.p., n.d.

12½x7½. 1 *l*. Black print, illus of the engine. At bottom: "164, British Section, Machinery Hall, Chicago Exhibition." ☺(WM)

949.1 Norfolk & Western Railroad. *The Industrial Future of the South : Prize Essays.* Norfolk, VA?: Norfolk & Western R.R., n.d.

22½x15½. 16 p. Faded orange wraps. C.t. On cover: "Published for gratuitous distribution." Contains three prize winning essays from a contest held by *Public Opinion* [weekly], Mar 1891. From intact WCE collection. ☺. (LBA)

949.2 Norfolk & Western Railroad. *Virginia; its Climate, Soil, productions, Manufacturing Industries, and mineral wealth.* [Baltimore, MD]: Norfolk & Western railroad co. (press of Record printing house), n.d.

22½x15. (4), 36 p. Buff wraps, black print and border. C.t. On cover: "For gratuitous distribution in the interest of emigration to the State of Virginia." First (4) p are bound in and on tan pulp paper; the section is captioned: "A word from : The Virginia Agricultural Development Com'y." Caption title on p 1: "A Great Railroad System"; this section is on buff paper. No mention of WCE; from intact WCE collections. . (LBA,WM)

950.1 North American Phonograph Co. *Recuerdo : de la exposición universal columbina de Chicago.* Chicago New York: n.p., n.d. **P➔**

15½x16½. 2 *l*. Folded cream glossy sheet printed on rectos. Red and black print. C.t. Illus of Edison and audience listening to his phonograph. WCE location noted: "Space 2, Seccion S, En el Edificio de la Electricidad, Jackson Park." Edison co's ad in Spanish. ☺. (WM)

950.2 *North German Lloyd : Bremen. World's Columbian Exposition : 1893.*
Bremen: [The Matthews-Northrup co.; complete art-printing works,
Buffalo, NY], 1893?

22x16. 39 p. Pale green decorative wraps, navy print, illus of one of
their steam-sail passenger ships. Their WCE pavilion illus on back.
History of the North German Lloyd steamships; description of trans-
Atlantic voyages in the 1890s. Ad. (ICRL,Stfd) P→

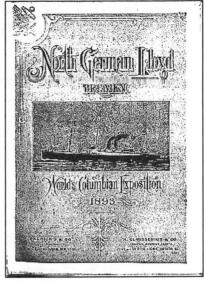

950.3 North German Lloyd. *Norddeutscher Lloyd ، Bremen : 1893 World's
Columbian Exposition 1893.* [Berlin: Julius Sittenfeld, 1893?].

20x16. 24 p, 9 *l* colored graphs. Pink-tan wraps, black print, illus of
steamer and decorative border top and bottom. C.t. Illus of their WCE
pavilion on back. History of the Lloyd. ☺ (WM)

950.4 North Press Co. ...*North Web-Feeding Press : both colors at each
impression.* Chicago: J. Mantz & co., n.d.

20½x14½. 1 *l*. Red and black print, illus of the press. At head of title "Printed in Machinery Hall (In
Section 32, Column Q-42), World's Columbian Exposition, from a roll, on an Eighth-Medium..." ☺ (WM)

950.5 Northern Pacific Railroad. ...*World's fair exhibit of products : of the : Seven Great Northwestern States :
traversed by the line, viz.: Wisconsin, Minnesota,...* St. Paul, MN: n.p., n.d.

30½x23. 1 *l*. White sheet, black print, no illus. "Exhibit in the Transportation Exhibits Building."
Name of "Gen'l Emigration Agt" at end of text: "P B Groat." ☺ (WM)

951. Northrop. *Four Centuries of Progress or Panorama of:* (bgsu,CWM)

951.1 Northrop, Henry Davenport. *Königin der Republiken : oder : Eine ausführliche Geschichte der Vereinigten
Staaten.* N.p.: n.p., [ᶜ189_ by J.R. Jones].

25x__. Presentation page, 1 *l*, 948? p. Hc. US history with WCE in the last chap. German language.
Similar to #951. (sapl)

952.1 Northrop, Henry Davenport. *Popular history of America including the period of discovery and settlement;
...Revised and enlarged.* Springfield, MA: Hampden Publishing Co., 1900 [ᶜ1898 by J.R. Jones].

25x18½. xvi, 17-497 p+ unpaged plates. Dark green cloth hc, gilt print. Frontis of Columbus landing;
WCE p 392-97. ☺ (GLD) $18 - 38

953. Northrop. *Story of the new world:* (ref)
---- Also found: Buffalo, NY: Callahan & Conneally, [ᶜ1892 by J.R. Jones]. 916 p+ unpaged illus.

954. Northrop. *The World's fair as seen in One Hundred Days:* (FLP,HML)
---- National, 720 p: ▶Add: Philadelphia: National publishing co., [ᶜ1893 by Henry Davenport Northrop].
23½x16½. Presentation page, 1 *l*, iii-xxii (with interspersed unpaged plates not counted in pagination), 1
l, 17-720 p (with interspersed unpaged plates not counted in pagination). Turquoise cloth hc, title
embossed in chocolate and silver, marbled edges. The difference between this and the 736 p editions is
additional description of international fairs in the longer book. (GLD)

955.1 *The North-Western Line : "Summer Outings."* [Chicago]: The North-Western Line?, n.d.

21½x10. Color illus of couple relaxing outdoors (front) and boat scene (back) by Rand McNally. C.t.
Sheet unfolds to 77x42½. When unfolded, one side is a large colored map (litho by Orcutt) of routes
including Chicago and the "World's Fair." Map title: "The Lake Resort Regions of Illinois, Wisconsin,
Northern Michigan & Minnesota. Reached by the North-Western line." The other side has text and illus
of scenic resorts along the routes. Ad. ☺ (GLD) $25 - 50

955.2 Northwestern Brewing Co. *Our Worlds* [sic] *Fair Exhibit 1893. Worlds* [sic] *Columbian Exposition.* [Chicago: Northwestern Brewing company, n.d.].

> 16½x11½. (4) p. Folded card die-cut in shape of a pretty blue beer stein. Caption title from p (2). Illus of their exhibit on p (2). Located at 781 to 831 Clybourne Ave, Chicago. Nice ad. (Fess)

956. Norton. *World's fairs from London 1851 to Chicago*: (CCA,FM,HML,IHi,LBA,slpl)

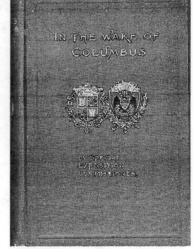

956.1 Norton Emery Wheel Co. *The Worcester drill grinder.* Worcester, MA: n.p., n.d.

> 14x20½. (4) p. Folded sheet, illus of bench grinder with angled drill-bit holder used for sharpening twist drills. C.t. Illus of floor grinder and bit holder on back. Includes price list. Rubber stamped on front: "Column E-52-53. Machinery hall annex; world's fair." ☺ (WM)

957. Ober. *In the wake of Columbus*: ☺ (GLD,DC,HU,SHB,slpl,UAH,UCLA,UMD,UTA) **P➔**
> ▶Add cover descriptions: Maroon (or green) cloth hc, gilt print and illus of two shields. Gilt top edge; other edges rough cut. Handsome. $40 - 75
> ---- Also found: Signed limited ed of 250 copies. 25x18. 1 *l* (signature), 1 *l* (frontis), 8 *l*, 515, (8) p. T.p. in red and black. Half morocco over golden satin cloth covered boards, gilt and colored seals of the West Indies, gilt spine print. Gilt top edge, uncut fore and bottom edges; marbled end papers. Frontis of Columbus with Catholic Kings. Unpaged folding map between pp 54-55. (GLD)   Limited Edition: $80 - 170

958.1 Office Specialty Mfg. Co. *Labor-saving devices : for : Mercantile and Public Offices, Banks, Trust Companies, Insurance and Railroad...* Rochester, NY: Press of A.J. Wegman, n.d.   **P➔**

> 24x16. (12) p+ text inside both self-wraps. Black print with litho of a fully equipped office. C.t. Illus of their filing cases, cabinets, drawers. Catalog, no prices. No mention of WCE; from intact collection. ☺ . (WM)

959. *Official hand book of the Retail Furniture Dealers'*: (S)
> ▶Add author and info: Retail Furniture Dealers' Association. 24x31. (60) p. Red cloth pebbled hc with black print. Text and illus on heavy stock. Eight full page b/w WCE illus by "J. Manz & Co. Eng. Chicago" on rectos, pp (45)-(59). Bylaws and ads.

960. *Official Souvenir Programme: Dedicatory Ceremonies*: (E,IHi,S,UIC,UTA)

960.1 Old Bangor Slate Co. *The Old Bangor Slate Co. : to the roofing slate trade.* Bethlehem, PA: The Old Bangor Slate Co., 1893.   [Back] **P➔**

> 10x13. (4) p. Folded card stock, b/w lithos of slate roofs on front and back; back is their WCE exhibit roof. Caption title. Specially cut slate tiles conformed to curves of towers and domes. Ad. [This was a Pennsylvania mining exhibit. A more complete picture of their exhibit is found in #2044 facing p 60, with description p 88.] ☺ (GLD,WM) $18 - 30

960.2 Olsen, Tinius, & Co. *Olsen's Little Giant Testing Machine.* Philadelphia: Garber, Printer, n.d.

> 30x23. (4) p. Folded sheet, black print and illus of floor model tester. C.t. Stamped on cover: "Tinius Olsen & Co, Machinery hall, column O-24, world's fair, Chicago." Illus and properties of their different tensile strength testing machines. ☺ (WM)

960.3 Olsen, Tinius, & Co. *Olsen's New Automatic and Autographic Testing Machines.* Philadelphia: Garber, Printer, [1893].

30x23. (4) p. Folded sheet, black print, illus of pull tester. Machine recorded tests; tension provided by a series of levered weights. Same rubber stamped WCE location as above. ☺ (WM)

961. [O'Neil, J.S.]. *The Columbian Celebration. The part taken by the congregation of St. Louis Bertrand, with full text of the lecture on catholicity in the discovery of America.* Louisville: n.p., 1892.

20x13½. 1 *l*, 95, (1) p. Blue cloth hc, gilt print and blind-stamped. ☺ (ref) ▶Completed cite. $20 - 40

961.1 Onstott, J.P., Grower. ...*Thompson's Seedless Grapes. This Grape Makes the Finest Seedless Raisins Known.* Yuba City, CA: n.p., n.d.

14½x7½. 4 p. Folded sheet, black print and design. Data through the 1892 season. At head of title is Onstott's name. No WCE content; from an intact collection. (WM)

961.2 Ortmayer, A., & Son. *California Brand : horse boots.* Chicago: A. Ortmayer & Son? (Dies & co., Buffalo, NY), n.d.

19x14½. 24 p of color lithos of their horse products. Gold wraps, black and gilt print, bold star design. C.t. ☺ . (Stfd–bound WCE Trans Dept Collection) P➡

961.3 Osborne, D.M., & Co. *Worlds* [sic] *Fair Souvenir : Presented with Compliments of : D.M. Osborne & Co. ...* Auburn, NY: D.M. Osborne & Co. (Forbes Co., Boston), n.d.

15½x9. (4) p. Folded white coated card. Front cover chromolith of girl with banner plus a small illus of "Agricultural building." C.t. Back cover chromolith of the "Masonic Temple, Chicago, Ill. U.S.A." Inside b/w lithos and black print: "Manufacturers of Harvesting Machinery, Farm Implements, Binder Twine and Oil." Ad. ☺ (GLD,E) $18 -40

961.4 Ottmann Lithographing Co. *Compliments of the Ottmann Lithographing Co.* New York: J. Ottmann Lithographing Co., [ᶜ1893].

8½x14. (4) p. Folded card. Beautiful chromolith of 3 children on front cover. C.t. Ottmann offices were located in the Puck Building in NY and in the Puck Bldg at the WCE, illus on p (3). This card is particularly prized by collectors of Victorian color prints. ☺ . (GLD,E) $40 - 90

961.5 Otto, C., & Co. ...*Dr. C. Otto & Comp. Dahlhausen a. d. Ruhr : Westfalen. Otto-Hoffman Koksofen mit Gewinnung der Nebenproducte. Otto-Hoffman Coke-Oven with utilization of by-products.* Dahlhausen a. d. Ruhr, Germany: Dr. C. Otto & Co., [ᶜ1893].

17½x12. (13) p. Pale salmon wraps, black print and ornate border design. C.t. At head of title: "Weltausstellung in Chicago : 1893." Ad with descriptions in German and English. ☺ . (CCA)

961.6 Overleigh, Herbert. *The evolution of the typewriter.* [New York: The Remington Standard Typewriter co.], n.d.

20½x14. 8 p. Self-wraps. Caption title. "Reprinted from Belford's Magazine for April, 1892, by courtesy of the publishers." No mention of the WCE; from an intact collection. Ad handout. (WM)

961.7 *Overman Wheel Co.* [Chicopee Falls, MA?: Overman Wheel Co.], n.d.

15x9½. (4) p. Folded stiff card with fancy cover illus of their Victor bicycle. C.t. Back cover illus of their factory in Chicopee Falls. Caption title: "Victor Facilities." ☺ . (Stfd–bound WCE Trans Dept Collection)

961.8 Pabst Brewing Co. *An Invitation.* Milwaukee, [WI]: Pabst (The Gugler lith. co.), n.d.

12½x7½. (12) p+ text inside both wraps. Chromolith front and back wraps + 6 chromoliths inside. Red Pabst logo on covers and each illustrated page. C.t. Caption title: "An Invitation to Milwaukee." "Pabst Exhibit: Agriculture, West end." Rail routes from Milwaukee to Chicago on p 12. Colorful WCE ad. ☺ (GLD) $45 - 90

☞ After the WCE, the ornate Pabst exhibit building was moved to Milwaukee, Wisconsin, and erected as a wing of the Pabst Mansion. Today it serves as a museum gift shop. **P**◥

961.9 *Pacific mills : Lawrence, Mass.* Lawrence, MA: John Andrews & Son Co, n.d.

15x9½. Folded pale-green stiff card, black print. Cover illus in landscape of the mills that wove cotton and wool fabric; back cover illus in landscape of the "worsted department" bldg. No WCE content; from intact collection. [The mill buildings are still there by the Lawrence River but are not operating factories today.] © (WM)

961.10 Page Belting Co. *Twenty-Fifth Anniversary Souvenir of the Page belting company : founded at Manchester, N.H., May, 1868 : special exhibits at the Columbian exposition, May, 1893.* [Manchester: Page Belting Co. (Republican press association, Concord), °1893 by Page Belting co.].

16½x24. 32 p. Tan stiff wraps, tan cloth spine, black and gilt print over illus of a stretched tanned hide. T.p. title given. History of the company with descriptions of their pavilions in Mach Hall and the Elect Bldg. Issued with 14x9½ ad sheet illus with a hide marked for cutting into "Crown belts." . (S,WM)

Joy Bliss at the Pabst Pavilion

961.11 Palmer, Elizabeth R. *A Long-Felt Want : A trunk that can be elevated to a desired height for convenience in packing or unpacking.* N.p.: n.p., n.d.

23x14½. 1 *l.* Black print one side, illus of trunk. Invented by Palmer, its hinged legs were enclosed in the trunk's bottom; when extended, they elevated the trunk; legs could be curtained to hide shoes, etc. "It is now on exhibition in the Patent Department of the Woman's Building, World's Fair,..." (WM)

962. *Panorama of the Swiss Alps*: (LBA)

☞ Although Switzerland did not exhibit art in the Fine Arts Bldg, it was awarded an arts medal for its Panorama painting that was exhibited on the Midway Plaisance. Exhibits on the Midway Plaisance were not meant to be in competition for awards.

963.1 Panton, J[ane] E[llen]. *Elton ware : designed by : Sir Edmund Elton baronet : at The Sunflower Pottery : Clevedon Court, Somerset, England.* N.p.: n.p., n.d.

24½x15½. (4) p. Folded buff sheet. C.t. Rpt from *The Illustrated London News*, Dec 8, 1888. "World's Fair, Chicago, Manufactures Building, British Section, facing Canadian Exhibit." Caption title: "Clevedon Court and its pottery." "J.E. Panton" at end. Ad. . (ICRL)

963.2 Parkhill Mfg. Co. *Columbian Exposition : 1893 : "Toile du Nord" : Trade mark.* Fitchburg, MA: Parkhill M'f'g Co., n.d.

15½x12. (4) p. Folded buff card with black and embossed gilt print and design on a green background. C.t. Toile du Nord was a fabric sold by Denny, Poor & Co. Inside black print and bold green "1492" and "1893." WCE ad. © (GLD)

964. Parloa. *Choice Receipts*: (csuf,E,HML,WM) **P**→

964.1 Parry Mfg. Co. *World's Columbian Exposition : Chicago. 1893.* [Indianapolis, IN: Parry Mfg. Co., 1893?].

11½x16. (12) p. Wraps with cover illus same as #1687. Color illus of WCE bldgs with captions are on the rectos of 6 pages; b/w illus of Parry horse drawn carriages on versos. (ref)

$15 - 30

964.2 Patek, Philippe & Co. *List and description : of : Watches & Movements : exhibited by : Patek, Philippe & Cº : Geneva : at : Chicago 1893.* [Geneva: Printed by Haussmann & Lips], n.d.

> 15½x11. 42 p. Light tan stiff wraps, red and blue-black print and Geneva seal. T.p. title. At top of cover: "World's Columbian Exposition : Chicago 1893." Illus of co's bldg on back cover. (WM)

964.3 *The Patent. World's Fair Edition. A journal devoted to the interests of every patentee.* ___: ___, ___.

> 30x22½. (16) p. Gray wraps, bold black print. C.t. "Sample Copy" rubber stamped at top. Text explains this WCE handout to be sample pages from their five year old magazine. Contains ads for patents, patent sales, investors, etc. (WM)

964.4 Patterson, G[eorge] W.S. *The World's Fair and my trip round the world. ...A description of cities visited and scenes and scenery witnessed in some of the chief cities and countries of the old and new world.* Auckland, NZ: H. Brett, General Printer, 1894.

> 19x12½. 126 p. Illus. Frontis port of Patterson. Hc. C.t.: "The World's Fair and A Trip Round the World." Description of his trip to the WCE. ☺. (Yale)

964.5 *The Peach Bottom Roofing Slate.* Delta, PA: Delta Times print, 1893.

> 14½x8½. (6) panels. Tri-fold sheet, blue-black print both sides, no illus. C.t. Six manufacturers listed for this slate, which came from PA and MD quarries. No WCE content; from intact collection. ☺ (WM)

964.6 Peake, Thomas, [Co.]. *...Roofing Tiles. Trade Mark: "Perfecta." Color: Dark Red and Mottled.* Staffordshire, Eng.: E.H. Eardley Printer Tunstull, [1893].

> 20½x13. (4) p. Folded buff sheet, brown print and design. At head of title: co's name and address. Testimonials pp (2)-(4) dated Jan and Feb 1893. No WCE content; from intact collection. (WM)
> ---- Also found: Page (1) above as single sheet printed one side in brown. Printer: "Atkinson Brothers, Lithographers, oriel works, Hanley, England." No WCE content; from intact collection. (WM)

964.7 Pearson, William, & Co. *Creolin-Pearson : Acknowledged by the scientific world as the most effective : Disinfectant...* N.p.: n.p., n.d.

> 13½x10½. 9 p includes inside front cover. Light blue wraps, black print. C.t. Back cover rpt of Higinbotham's letter authorizing the use of Creolin-Pearson in WCE medical dept. At bottom front cover: "Adopted by World's Fair Authorities as a general disinfectant for the grounds and buildings of the World's Columbian Exposition." (WM)

965.1 Peattie, Elia W. *The story of America : containing ; the romantic incidents of history, from the discovery of America to the present time.* Chicago: Mid-continent publishing co., 1892 [°1889 by R.S. King publishing co.].

> 24½x19. 1 *l*, (3), (7)-844 p. Blue pebble-textured cloth hc; gilt spine print. Frontis (1 *l*) is illus of "DeSoto on the March." Chap CXII, pp (838)-44, describes the WCE; includes an unpaged A. Zeese & Co., 1892, bird's-eye view of the early but unrealized grounds. (ref) $38

965.2 Penn Salt Mfg. Co. *Lewis' 98% Lye : The Ready Family Soap Maker.* Philadelphia: Penna Salt Mfg. Co., n.d.

> 15x9. (4) p. Folded card, cover lithos of product. C.t. Inside pages have black ink product info and yellow and green decoration. From an intact WCE scrapbook collection. ☺ (S)

965.3 Pennsylvania Railroad Co. *A Estrada de Ferro Pennsylvania : e a : exposição quatrocentennial de Chicago, com notas descriptivas das cidades de New York, Philadelphia, Washington, Chicago, e uma descripção completa dos : Terrenos e Edificios da Exposição, Com Mappes e Illustrações.* Philadelphia: Companhia da Estrada de Ferro Pennsylvania, 1892 [°1892].

> 19½x16. 128 p, 14 *l* of plates. Maps and illus. Dark red quarter morocco over decorated paper hc, gilt print. Portuguese version of #971. ☺. (CCA)

966. Pennsylvania RR. *Catalogue of the exhibit of the Pennsylvania Railroad Company:*
(GLD,Amh,CLP,Col,CU,DC,FLP,FM,FU,GU,HML,HU,ICRL,KSU,LU,MIT,MSI,NLA,SHB,SML,Stfd,UMC,UMN,UPa,UVM,WM,Yale)

▶Add to Large Format: Black cloth spine over gray linen boards. C.t. is printed in open block lettering: "The Pennsylvania railroad company at the World's Columbian exposition : Chicago : 1893." Text contains 50 unpaged plates on glossy stock of diagrams and illus which are printed one side. They are interleaved between pp 7-158. C.t. = t.p.

---- Also found: Large Format Presentation copy. Same cover, etc, as above but with tipped-in 16x12½ slip with a blank for the recipient's name followed by "Compliments of the Pennsylvania Railroad Company..." (MIT)

---- Also found: Large Format wraps.

---- Also found: Small Format hc: Blue cloth spine over blue-gray cloth boards.

967.   Pennsylvania RR. *Chemin de fer Pennsylvanie* (French): (GLD,FM,Stfd,Upa) $30 - 65

967.1 Pennsylvania Railroad Co. *Columbian exposition.* Presentation Copy. [Philadelphia: Pennsylvania Railroad Co., 1892].

20x16½. 1 *l* port of J. R. Wood, 2 blank *l*, #967 except wraps, #970 except wraps, #971 except wraps. Brown half leather over blue marbled paper covered boards. Spine title. Handwritten inscription paragraph on first blank page after his port is signed by J. R. Wood, General Manager of the RR. Original owner: "Wm. Elmer Jr. Princeton, N.J. May '93." One-of-a-kind. (GLD) $150 - 300

☞ William Elmer Jr. was a mechanical engineer for the Pennsylvania Railroad having been trained at Princeton University. He also served in the New Jersey State Building at the WCE.

968.   Pennsylvania RR. *El Ferrocarril de Pennsylvania* (Spanish): (UPa)

968.1 Pennsylvania Railroad Co. *Exhibit of department of chemical and physical tests at the World's Columbian exposition, 1893, under the direction of Theo. N. Ely...J. Elfreth Watkins...* Chicago: Rand, McNally & Co., Printers, 1893.

18½x13. 15 p. Buff paper, self-wraps. Describes the dept the Railroad set up for national testing of railroad rolling stock. ☺ (GLD) $20 - 50

969.   Pennsylvania RR. *Ferrovia Pensilvania* (Italian): (BMF,E,UMD)

969.1 Pennsylvania Railroad Co. *Med Pennsylvania jernvägen till Columbia Utställningen, samt vyer och skisser af städerna : New York, Philadelphia, Washington, Chicago, jemte fullständig beskrifing af Utställningsplatsen och Byggnaderna, Med Kartor och Illustrationer.* Philadelphia: Pennsylvania Railroad Co., 1893.

19x16. Color fold train route map, 1 *l* frontis, 112 p. Color fold map of NY Harbor before p (3). Light blue-green wraps. Frontis: Statue of Liberty with caption title in Swedish. C.t.: "Pennsylvania Railroad to the Columbian Exposition." Swedish version of #971; same cover design. ☺. (UBO,UMN)

970.   Pennsylvania RR. *Mit der Pennsylvania eisenbahn* (German): (HML)
---- Also found: 131 p.

971.   Pennsylvania RR. *Pennsylvania Railroad to the Columbian* (English): (CLP,FLP,HML,MSI,PSU,UVM,WM)

972.1 Pennsylvania Railroad Co. *Special information concerning passenger transportation over the Pennsylvania short lines to and from Chicago and "The World's Fair."* Chicago: Poole Bros., 1893.

19½x__. Folder. Maps. (Information folder no 2). "Corrected to September 20th, 1893." (HML)

972.2 Pennsylvania Railroad Co. *Supper : Pullman Dining Cars in service on : The Pennsylvania Lines : West of Pittsburgh.* [Pittsburgh, PA: Pullman Dining Cars, 1893].

18½x11½. (4) p. Folded card. Inside, pp (2)-(3), is the menu for June 27, 1893, for dining car "Carleton." Supper cost $1. ☺ (WM)

973.1 Phelps, J.H., [Co.]. *...Wonderful improvement in pianos. "A supreme success." Phelps Harmony Attachment. ...* [Sharon, WI]: n.p., n.d.

15½x21½. (16) p+ text inside both covers. Blue wraps, black print. C.t. At head of title: "World's Fair Edition." Inside front cover: "Malcolm Love Piano Exhibit, and Strauch Bros. Piano Action Exhibit in "Section I of Manufactures and Liberal Arts Building." (WM)

974. *Philadelphia Record Almanac 1893*: (S)

974.1 *Phoenix Glass Company. Catalogue No. 5.* [Pittsburgh, PA: H.L. Lockwood press, New York, 1893.].

30½x38. 2 *l* index, 32 numbered plates, 32 *l* description of facing plate interleaved. Brown cloth hc, black print and design. Numbered plates are on stiff stock and have pale yellow backgrounds and blue illus. Back cover blind-stamped design matching front cover. C.t. = t.p. T.p. has large sepia illus of their WCE exhibit, which had their light fixture globes illuminating their elaborate glassware. (WM)

974.2 Photo-Materials Co. ...*Price list : of : enlarging and finishing...* Rochester, NY: n.p., n.d.

16½x9. (4) p. Folded sheet, purple-brown print. Bromide papers to 40x70 inches. Properties, sizes and prices. Boldly printed on p (4): "Try Kloro." No WCE content; from an intact collection. (WM)

975. *Picturesque Chicago and Guide to the World's Fair*: (Amh,CCA,DU,HPL,HU,MH,UCI,UCLA,UMD,UMN,WM,Yale)
---- Also listed: N.p.: Lenox Pub. Co., 1893. xiii, 318 p.
---- Also found: *Picturesque Chicago and Guide to the World's Fair.* Hartford, CT: The Christian secretary, n.d. xiii, (2), 318 p. Brown cloth hc, black and gilt print, design as illustrated for the 304 p version. T.p. lacks the words "profusely illustrated." See #994 for a later version. ☺ . (SStu)

976. Pierce. *Photographic history of the World's fair and sketch*: (CCA,CLP,cul,FLP,HML,PSU,RU,UIC,UMD,WM)

976.1 Pilcher's, Henry, Sons. ...*Pneumatic pipe organs.* Louisville, KY: n.p., n.d.

22x14½. (6) p includes insides of both wraps. White wraps, black print and illus of cherubs at the organ. C.t. Co's name at head of title. No mention of WCE; from an intact collection. (WM)

977. Pinchot. *Biltmore forest*: (DC,DU,HU,MSL,NAL,Stfd,UCB,UCLA,UMA,UMN,Yale)
▶Rpt ed: New York: Arno Press, [1970]. 49 p. (NAL)

977.1 Pittsburgh Locomotive Works. ...*Locomotives Exhibited : by the : Pittsburgh Locomotive Works, Pittsburgh, Pa., U.S.A.* Allegheny, PA: [Pittsburgh Locomotive Works], 1893?

22½x15. 1 *l* (frontis), 41 p, 4 *l* plates of locomotives illus at end. NB: There are 6 *l* plates interspersed in text that are counted in paging. Frontis illus of the company's WCE exhibit. Brown cloth hc, gilt print and black border design. Decorative end papers. At head of title: "World's Columbian exposition, : Chicago, 1893." Very attractive ad. ☺ . (SML)

977.2 *Plano : souvenir : World's Columbian Exposition : 1892-3.* [Chicago: Plano], n.d.

12½x18. (28) p. Gray wraps, gray and white print, red port seal of Columbus. Text in brown ink. Chromoliths are by Shober & Parqueville, Lith. Co., Chicago. Half the pages have color lithos of WCE bldgs; the remainder of the booklet is ad text in German for plows and other farm machinery. Pretty ad. ☺ (GLD,UIC)   P➔ $30 - 60

977.3 Platform Binder Co. *What the Users Say of the Platform Binder.* Rockport, OH: n.p., [1893].

22½x15. (4) p. Folded sheet, black print. Full illus of binder for farm use on p (2). Testimonials dated to Apr 17, 1893. No WCE content; from an intact collection. ☺ (WM)

977.4 Platt Brother & Co. Limited. *Catalogue of Machinery for opening, carding, drawing, and combing cotton.* Oldham, Eng.: n.p., n.d.

22x14½. 3 *l*, (5)-24, (4) p. Fire engine red cloth on stiff cardboard, gilt print. C.t. = t.p. Illus of their cotton machinery. At bottom of cover: "World's Columbian Exposition, Chicago,...1893" ☺ (WM)

978.1 Pokagon, Simon. *The red man's rebuke. By chief Pokagon.* [Hartford, MI: C.H. Engle, Publishers, ᶜ1893 by Simon Pokagon].   P➜

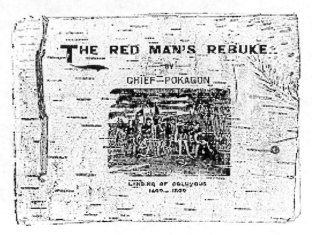

9x12. (3), 2-26 p. Natural birch bark covers, black ink. Cover vignette of "Landing of Columbus : 1492–1892" (front) and Indian chief vignette and poem (back). Tied with birch bark ribbon. Speaking for the "Red Man," he says in part, "We have no spirit to celebrate with you the great Columbian Fair now being held in this Chicago city." Pokagon later gave a more conciliatory speech at the WCE on Chicago Day, Oct 9, 1893; see the text in #2348.3. A special WCE item. ☺. (DC)

978.2 Pomeroy Brothers, Mfg. *Pomeroy Duplex Duplicator or Pomeroy Automatic Duplicator and The Pomeroy Compressed Inks...* N.p.: n.p., n.d.

21½x14. (2) p. Sheet printed both sides in blue ink. Caption title. A stencil process. No WCE content; from an intact collection. ☺ (WM)

978.3 Pomeroy Brothers, Mfg.. *We believe in The Metric System.* Newark, NJ: n.p., n.d.

33x38. (2) p. White sheet, black print both sides. Illus of products: mucilage in metric containers. Bottles ᶜ1892. Metric system strongly supported. No WCE content; intact collection. ☺ (WM)

980.   [Pope]. *A Memorial to Congress on...comprehensive exhibit of roads*: (GLD,HML,HU,MSL,S,UMN,UTA,WM) $18 - 36
981.   [Pope]. *A Memorial to Congress on...Road Department*: (HU,UMC,WM,Yale)

982.1 Pope, Albert A[ugustus]. *An Open Letter to the People of the United States.* [Boston: Albert A. Pope, 25 May 1892].

28x21½. (3) p. Folded buff sheet, black print. Caption title. Pope's proposal for a unified exhibit and road department. At end of text: Albert A. Pope and dated "Boston, Mass. : May 25, 1892." ☺. (HU,UMD)
---- Also found: Above "Open Letter" accompanied by mimeographed typed letter dated June 13, 1892, which is personally signed by Pope, requesting write-in support for his proposal for a Road Department at the WCE. [Pope's plan for a department was not realized]. (UMD)
---- Also found: Same "Open Letter" dated: "Boston, Mass., April 12, 1892." (WM)

983.1 Porter, J.E., [Co.]. *Illustrated catalogue : of the : Porter hay tools.* Ottawa, IL: J.E. Porter (Ottawa Free Trader Print), n.d.

13½x19. 24 p. Pinkish beige wraps, black print. C.t. = t.p. Awards and testimonials are mentioned on inside back cover. Boldly printed on back: "1892." No mention of WCE; intact collection. (WM)

984.1 Potter, C., Jr. & Co. *C. Potter, Jr. & Co. Printing Presses.* New York: [E.D. Slater, Printing, Engraving, Lithography, Blank book], n.d.

26½x17½. 15, (1) p. Powder blue wraps, dark blue print, red string-tied. C.t. Each page has a thin red border and dark olive-green print. Their seven presses are illus on versos. No mention of WCE; from intact collection. (WM)

984.2 Power, Sir John, & Son. *Descriptive particulars : of the : exhibits : of : Sir John Power & Son : at : the World's fair : Chicago : 1893.* Dublin: John's Lane Distillery, 1893.   P➜

19½x12. 16 p. Multi-color wraps, brown and gilt print. Frontis port of Powers from a picture in ivory and needlework. Distillery illus on front wrap; exhibit illus on back. Handsome ad. ☺ . (FM)

984.3 Prang, L., & Co. *L. Prang & co., Fine Art Publishers and Lithographers, …Exhibit at the World's Columbian exhibition, (North Gallery, Building of manufactures and Liberal Arts.) Chicago, 1893.* Boston: L. Prang & co., 1893?

18x12. 7, (1) p includes string-tied self-wraps. Buff paper, black print. Illus. Lists paintings in their exhibit and their 6 Columbian publications, which include #35, #810, and #815. Ad. ☺ (GLD,HML) $24 - 55

984.4 Prang, L., & Co. *…Souvenir of the World's Columbian Exposition : presented by L. Prang & Co. : Fine Art Publishers and Lithographers : Boston, U.S.A. : Exhibit: North Gallery, Liberal Arts : Chicago, 1893.* Boston: L. Prang & Co., 1893?

14½x9. (4) p. Folded white stiff card, brown print. C.t. Inside card is single chromolith entitled "The vision of Columbus : 1492 1892–3." Shows Columbus viewing stylized WCE lagoon and MacMonnies Fountain. Ad. ☺ (GLD,E) $24 - 55

985.   Pratt. *Exhibit of the Women Graduates:* (GLD,MSL,UMD)   P➜ $25 - 60
▸Add: Tan wraps (or self-wraps), black print and illus, string-tied. The 16 p include front and back covers. Brief descriptions of items on display made by students and graduates of the Institute.

985.1 Price Baking Powder Co. *Dr. Price's Cream Baking Powder; World's Fair Highest Award.* ___: ___, ___.

18½x12½. 58, (3) p testimonials. Self-wraps, black print, red string-tied, punch hole in upper left corner in the manner of almanacs. C.t. Facsimile of their St. Gaudens WCE award medal printed below title. Their exhibit was located in the Ag Bldg, Section F-H-9. (KSU)

985.2 Price Baking Powder Co. *Opinions of leading Chicago Physicians on the use of ammonia and alum in Baking Powders…* N.p.: [Price Baking Powder co.], n.d.

45x20½. (2) p. Buff sheet, black print both sides. Caption title. Extols the virtues and purity of Price Powder and lists "Instances of fraudulent advertising" by a competitor, Royal Baking Powder. No mention of WCE; from intact collection. [WCE location: Ag Bldg, Section F-H-9]. ☺ (GLD) $20 - 45

985.3 Price Baking Powder Co. *Table and kitchen : a compilation of : Approved Cooking Receipts : Carefully Selected for the Use of Families and Arranged for Ready Reference.* Chicago: Price Baking Powder co., n.d.

18½x12½. (3), 61 p+ text inside both wraps. Pistachio colored wraps; red, silver, and black lettering and borders. Punch hole upper left corner for string loop. C.t.: "Table and Kitchen." No mention of WCE; from an intact collection. [WCE location: Ag Bldg, Section F-H-9]. ☺ (GLD) $20 - 45

986.   *Proceedings of the Convention of Southern Governors:* (FM,LBA,MIT,SML)
▸Corrected and completed citation: 82 p+ 16 unpaged interspersed plates. The plates are b/w illus on coated paper. Lime green wraps, black print.

986.1 Providence and Stonington Steamship Co. Whittemore, Henry. *The past and the present of Steam Navigation on Long Island Sound.* N.p.: Providence and Stonington Steamship Co., [1893].

22½15. 71 p. Turquoise wraps. C.t.= t.p. No mention of WCE; from intact collection. ☺ . (LBA)

986.2 Prudential Insurance Company of America. *All the world at the fair : 1893.* [New York: The Giles co., lith], n.d. P➜

11x14. (8) p+ co data inside both covers. Blue speckled white wraps with chromolith of four children in a national costume each with a numeral of "1893" on her frock. Brown text print describes their exhibit; color illus of Manuf Bldg. C.t. Beautiful ad. ☺. (WM)

986.3 *Public Ledger : 1893 : Almanac.* Philadelphia: Geo. W. Childs, 1893.

19x13. 1 *l*, 77 p+ 5 *l* interspersed photo illus. Light blue and yellow printed stiff wraps, red lettering with black lithos and border design front and back. C.t. Usual period almanac issued by the Ledger. WCE described on p 62. ☺ (GLD,S) $20 - 40

987.1 Putnam, G.P., Sons. *The Story of The Nations.* New York and London: G.P. Putnam's Sons, n.d.

19½x13½. 56 p. Illus. Dark green glossy wraps with gilt print and design. C.t. Gives title, content, and what critics say about each vol in the series. No WCE content; from intact collection. ☺ (WM)

987.2 Queen & Co. *Some features : of the : World's Columbian Exposition.* Philadelphia: Queen & Co., n.d.

23½x14½. 16 p. Buff wraps, brown print; also brown print t.p. C.t. = t.p. [Queen & Co. dealt in optical and scientific apparatus for educational work. Their liberal arts exhibit was in the Manuf Bldg, Gallery E.] Ad. ☺. (HML)

987.3 Queen Isabella Association. Starr, Eliza Allen. *Isabella of Castile, 1492-1892.* Chicago: C.V. Waite (Daniels & Pitkin, printers), 1889 [1889 by the Queen Isabella Association].

21½x15. x, 11-134 p. Buff stiff wraps, gilt center design with white print and port of Isabella, gilt top edge. Frontis port of Isabella. Formative document of the association and history of the Queen. ☺ (S)

988.1 Quibell Brothers. *"Home, sweet home." Quibell's infallible disinfectants : Liquid, Powder, & Soaps, for Toilet, Household & Hospital purposes. Hurrah for Quibell's soap.* Newark, Eng.: n.p., n.d.

25x15½. (4) p. Folded blue sheet, black print. Illus of baby in bath on cover, woman p (2), dog p (3). Testimonials on p (4). Vertical red overprint on right edge of front cover: "Exhibit No. 299, British Section, World's Columbian Exposition." (WM)

988.2 Quibell Brothers. *Quibell's infallible Disinfectants : Liquid, Powder, Soaps.* Newark, Eng.: [T. Forman & sons, Nottingham], n.d.

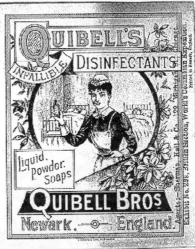

15½x12½. 19, (1) p. Light gray wraps, brown print with illus of nurse in ward. C.t. Text on blue paper. Vertical red overprint on right edge of front cover: "Exhibit No. 299, British Section, World's Columbian Exposition." ☺. (WM)   **P→**

988.3 Quibell Brothers. *Quibell's Liquid Sheep Dip...* Newark, Eng.: n.p., n.d.

28½x22. 1 *l*. Buff sheet, black and red print one side. Red overprint at bottom "Exhibit No. 299, British Section, World's Columbian Exposition." Illus of three sheep. Ad for disinfectant. ☺ (WM)

988.4 Quibell Brothers. *Quibell's "prize" sheep dips.* Newark, Eng.: n.p., n.d.

22x28½. 1 *l*. Single yellow pulp sheet in landscape orientation, black and red print and illus of four sheep. Disinfectant. WCE overprint in red at bottom as in #988.3. ☺ (WM)

988.5 Quint, A.D., Co. *Quint's patent Six Spindle Turret Drill.* Hartford, CT: A.D. Quint, [1893?].

23x14½. (8) p includes self-wraps. Black print and drill illus. Caption title. Stamped on top of p (1): "Machinery Hall, Column K-44, World's Fair, Chicago." Testimonials from early 1893. (WM)

988.6 Rachmann Brothers Co. *Exhibitors at the World's Fair Chicago 1893 Austrian Section. Manufactory of Atomizers (Spray Diffusers) and Toilet Articles.* N.p.: n.p., n.d.

10½x15½. (4) p. Folded buff stiff card; fold at top with text landscape. Black and red print. Illus of their containers and trade-mark. C.t. (WM)

988.7 The Railroad Gazette. Gilbert, Bradford Lee. *Sketch Portfolio : of : Railroad Stations and Kindred Structures, with nearly two hundred illustrations,...* New York: The Railroad Gazette, °1895 by the architect [Gilbert].

26x34. 70 *l.* Dark and light green cloth hc, silver print and decorations. Contains designs and drawings by Gilbert that were displayed at the WCE. Handout at the Cotton States Expo, Atlanta, 1895. ☺ . (CCA)

988.8 Raleigh Cycle Co. Ltd. *...Compliments : British exhibit, Transportation Building, gallery stand 20.* New York: T.C. Crichton?, Print, n.d.

15½x15. (6) p. Pink wraps, red print; illus of bicycles and text in brown ink. Catalog with race finish placements. Back cover illus: "A.A. Zimmerman on his Raleigh racer." ☺ . (Stfd–bound WCE Trans Dept Collection)

988.9 Raleigh Cycle Co. Ltd. *The "Raleigh" : The First Racing Safety ridden to victory by Arthur Augustus Zimmerman, N.Y.A.C.* [Nottingham, Eng.: Raleigh Cycle co.], n.d.

21½x28. (3)-10 p. Company ad info inside both covers. Blue stiff wraps, red print and photo illus of Zimmerman and his racer; listing of all his 1892 prizes. C.t. Caption title: "1893 (June) catalogue of the Raleigh cycle co., Ltd." Back cover illus of their factory in England. ☺ . (Stfd–bound WCE Trans Dept Collection)

989.   Ralph. *Harper's Chicago and the World's:*
(bgsu,CCA,CLP,CU,E,FM,HML,HPL,HU,ICRL,IHi,IStU,Knox,LBA,LL,MSL,NSW,RU,S,SHB,SPL,UAB,UCB,UIC,UMD,UPa,UTA,WM,Yale)

989.1 Rand, McNally & Co. *...Educational catalogue : maps and globes.* Chicago and New York: Rand, McNally & co., n.d.

22½x15. 23 p+ unpaged centerfold Chicago map, WF location in red. White wraps, red title, globe on green background. Red and black text. C.t. Illus of roller wall maps and globes. At head of title: "World's fair edition, with program of N.E.A., plan of educational exhibit and map of Chicago." ☺ (WM)

989.2 Rathbone Sard & Co. *Compliments of the Manufacturers of Acorn Stoves and Ranges.* [Albany, Chicago [and] Detroit: Rathbone Sard & Co.], n.d.

8x15. (8) p+ text inside both covers. Chromolith covers: two mariners (front) and Santa Maria (back), red print. C.t. Text and illus of stoves and WCE exhibit in blue. ☺ . (E)   P➜

989.3 Raymond and Whitcomb. *Essex Institute Party : Salem May 27 1893 : Raymond & Whitcomb excursion : to : World's Columbian exposition, Chicago.* N.p.: n.p., n.d.

21x17½. (3) p. Folded white glossy sheet, dark blue print. List of members in two cars leaving May 27 and returning June 7 in Salem, MA. C.t. Private trip for the Institute; see MA in States Chapter for more on the Institute at the WCE. H.M. Brooks, Institute Secretary. ☺ (WM)

989.4 Raymond and Whitcomb. *...Excursion of the Massachusetts Mutual Fire Insurance Union : with ladies and friends : to the World's Columbian Exposition, in Chicago. Leaving Boston Monday, May 15, and Returning Thursday, May 25.* Boston?: Raymond & Whitcomb (American printing & engraving co.), 1893?

11½x14. 48 p+ fold map of WCE grounds tipped-in at back cover. Wraps. At head of title: "1893. A solid insurance train." In Chicago, the travelers stayed in the Raymond & Whitcomb Grand Hotel. Tour price of $125 covered all expenses including 12 admissions to the WCE. ☺ (GLD) $20 - 42

☞ The four-story Grand Hotel was located at Washington and Madison Avenues, fronting the Midway.

989.5 Raymond and Whitcomb. *Raymond's Vacation Excursions : A Winter in California : Nine Grand Trips. Leaving Boston October 13,...1892;...March 7 and 9, 1893.* Boston: Raymond & Whitcomb, n.d.

11x14. 192 p. Same cover type and format as #991 below. C.t. T.p.: "Season of 1892–93. A winter in California. Nine Magnificent Trips Across the Continent. ...A week's visit to Chicago during the World's

Columbian exposition." Note that the last trip date precedes the official opening of the WCE—i.e., May 1st. See #989.6 for a New York departure. ☺ . (S,ref,UCI) $15

989.6 Raymond and Whitcomb. *Raymond's Vacation Excursions : A Winter in California : Nine Grand Trips. Leaving New York October 13,...1892...* Boston: Raymond & Whitcomb, n.d.

11x14. 192 p. See #989.5 for Boston departure. (S)

989.7 Raymond and Whitcomb. *Raymond's Vacation Excursions : Trips to the World's Columbian Exposition, Leaving Philadelphia between May 22 and October 12, 1893 and tours beyond Chicago.* Boston: Raymond & Whitcomb (American printing & engraving), [1893].

11x14. 111, (1) p. Illus plus map. C.t. ☺ (S)

989.8 Raymond and Whitcomb. *Souvenir List of Members of Columbian Exposition Party : Raymond's Vacation Excursions : Leaving Boston Saturday, May 13, 1893.* [Boston: Raymond & Whitcomb], n.d.

9x15½. (8) p. White wraps, brown illus of four vacation scenes, black print. C.t. Cover in landscape; text in portrait. Passenger list. [Listed in original #991 as an also found.] ☺ (GLD) $20 - 42
---- Also found: Leaving Boston May 27, 1893. (GLD,S,WM)
---- Also found: Leaving Boston May 30, 1893. (S)

989.9 Raymond and Whitcomb. *The World's Columbian Exposition. Arrangements for a special party from Nashua.* N.p.: n.p., n.d.

11x13½. (3) p. Folded lavender sheet, back blank. Ad for special train leaving Boston 3 June. Rooms assigned at Grand Hotel, Chicago. Name at end "Mrs. Anna March Danforth, Nashua, NH." ☺ (WM)

991.   *Raymond's Vacation Excursions : trips to the World's...April 28 and October 21:* (GLD,csuf,HML,HU,S,WM)
▸Add cover description: 11x14. White glossy wraps, black print and vignettes of travel locations on gray background. "Bird's-eye view of exposition grounds" on outside back ᶜ1892 by A. Zeese & Co.

992.1 Reed & Carnrick [Co.]. *Kumysgen The Ideal Food.* New York: The Winthrop Press, n.d.

25½x16½. (4) p. Folded white sheet, black print. Ad for a powdered milk preparation. Lists 7 products, e.g., "Carnrick's Lacto-preparata." No WCE content; from an intact collection. ☺ (WM)

993.1 Reliable Incubator and Brooder Co. *Illustrated Catalogue and Price List : of the : Reliable Incubator and Brooder Co. Incorporated. Agricultural building. The Worlds* [sic] *Fair Hatcher.* Quincy, IL: Richmond lith co. Buffalo, NY, [1895].

19½x13½. 1 *l*, 112 p. Chromolith wraps, black print and illus of Ag Bldg, border of yellow baby chicks. First leaf is a folded color illus of brooder. Their "Tenth annual catalogue and guide." WCE award and exhibit content throughout, especially pp 45-47. ☺ (S)

994.   Religious Herald. *Picturesque Chicago and guide:* (GLD,CU,DC,HU,UCB,WM,wsu) $22 - 55
---- Also found: 7 *l*, v-xiii, 1 *l*, 334 p. Brown (or gray) cloth hc, same print and design as the red cloth. NB: This is exactly the same paging as the original first entry, and the first 7 *l* are 6 *l* ads and 1 *l* t.p.

994.1 Remington Typewriter Co. *Compliments National Association of Women Stenographers. Missipi (Edna Eagle Feather.) Honorary Member National Association Women Stenographers.* N.p.: n.p., n.d.

17x11. Card printed both sides. Front side photo-illus of Missipi at the typewriter; Remington ad on back. Remington engaged Missipi to exhibit her typing skills at its booth during July 1893. Exhibit location: "Landing, Southeast Stairs, Woman's Bldg., World's Columbian Exposition." ☺ (WM)

994.2 Renfost Hotel. *The Renfost, Chicago, Ill., U.S.A. : 52d Street and Cottage Grove Avenue.* [Chicago: Vandercook engraving and pub. co.], n.d.

10½x16. (10) p. Pink stiff wraps, dark maroon print and hotel illus. C.t. Hotel floor plan, map of Chicago with WCE grounds and hotel location to the northwest near the end of the Midway, bird's-eye of WCE, illus of Manuf and Liberal Arts Bldg and other WCE Bldgs. ☺ . (WM)

994.3 Renfost Hotel. *The Renfost : Fifty-Second Street and Cottage Grove Ave.* [Chicago: Renfost Hotel], n.d. **P➜**

17½x13. (12) p. Pink stiff wraps, black print and decoration, string-tied. C.t. Illus of hotel on p (1). Illus of scenes in Washington Park. WF references throughout including inside front/back covers. ☺. (WM)

994.4 *Rice & Hutchins, Twelve Leading staple shoes.* Boston: n.p., n.d.

20x26. Sheet printed with 2-tone yellow background and blue illus of shoes and factories. At bottom in black: The Continent Shoe Co., Chicago agents. No WCE content; from intact collection. (WM)

994.5 Rice & Whitacre Mfg. Co. *World's Columbian exposition : Rice & Whitacre Mfg Co. : Steam Engines and Boilers : Complete Steam Power plants.* Chicago: Rice & Whitacre Mfg Co., ᶜ1892 by Rice and Whitacre M'f'g Co.

16½x8½. 8 p+ text inside both wraps. White coated stiff wraps, black print and illus of boiler. Punch hole in upper left corner. C.t. WCE ad. ☺ (GLD) $20 - 30

994.6 Richardson & Boynton Co. *Catalogue. Richardson & Boynton Co. ...Manufacturers of the Celebrated : "perfect" : Warm-Air Heating Furnaces, Cooking Ranges, Fire-Place Heaters, &c.* N.p.: n.p., n.d.

24x14½. 10 p. Folded strip unfolds to 24x72½ with five panels each side. Prussian blue print. Illus of their coal-fired furnaces and stoves. C.t. From intact WCE collection. ☺. (WM)

995.1 Ridpath, John Clark. *...Family history : of the : United States.* Chicago, Philadelphia [and] Oakland: Monarch book co., [ᶜ1897 by C.R. Graham.].

26½x20. 3 *l*, (2), 19, 570 p, illus, color plates. Light brown cloth hc, brown border and design, gilt print. At head of title: "Standard 1897 Edition." Description of the WCE in chap 31 and 32. A standard US history which includes this WCE summary. (ref) $30

995.2 Ridpath, John Clark and James W. Buel. *Our Country and the World's Fair : A Pictorial Description of the Great Columbian Exposition...A Complete History of America,...Two books in one volume.* Boston: Union publishing co., [ᶜ1892 by H.S. Smith]. **P➜**

27x21. xiv, 1 *l*, 821, (1) p illus of State Street in Chicago. Gray cloth hc, black floral design and gilt print. The first 62 p are on WCE; pp 781-821 are Butterworth's WCE description as contained in #752; page headers "Columbus and Columbia," #752. ☺ (GLD) $20 - 45

995.3 Riedel, J.D., [Co.]. *Chicago : J.D. Riedel, Berlin.* Berlin: E. Wundsch, n.d.

17½x10. 19 p, 3 *l*, 25-38 p, 1 *l*. Chromolith cardboard cover, gilt print, cloth spine, illus of cherub and dove with rising sun. C.t. First half in German on yellow paper, blue print; second half in English on pale blue paper, blue print. Complete drugstore installations and wholesale druggist preparations. No mention of WCE; from an intact collection. (WM)

995.4 *Riehlé Bros. Testing Machine Co.* Philadelphia: n.p., n.d.

8x13½. Buff stiff card, black print (front) and red print (back). C.t. WCE location noted on front: "Section 25, Group 77, Class 490. Engineers, Iron founders, General Machinists." Partial plan of WF grounds on back shows their location in north center Mach Hall. Issued with many 29x23 sheets without WCE content but describing and illus their machines and testing equipment. ☺ (WM)

995.5 Rio Grande Western Railway. *The Promised Land : information for the visitor to the World's fair : Chicago. 1893.* [Chicago: Rio Grande Western Railway], n.d.

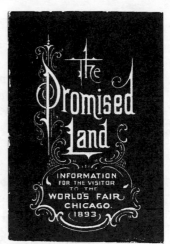

11½x7½. 32 p. Wraps. C.t. Illus. Caption title on p 2: "Utah and the great west. 'The Promised Land.'" Map of US rail routes on inside back cover are printed by Matthews-Northrup company, Buffalo, NY. Poem on p 1. WCE handout enticing visitors to Utah by rail. ☺. (NHL,WM) **P➔**

995.6 Ritter, Julius Léon von Wernburg, [Co.]. *...Portrait of Francis Joseph I, emperor of Austria-Hungary, woven on the power-loom.* N.p.: n.p., n.d.

31x24. Folded buff smooth sheet making (2) panels printed in black. Illus of F. Joseph woven port on front cover. At head of title: "World's Columbian Exposition Chicago U.S.A. 1893." They wove detailed ports from cotton/silk fiber. Ad for loom using punched cards to make images. ☺(WM)

995.7 *Rochester Lamp Co. Largest lamp manufacturers in the World.* New York: Rochester Lamp Co., n.d.

8x11. (4) p. Tan folded card, black print, Arabesque period border with lamp at top. Illus of lamp and stand on back cover and reference to the close of the Columbian Exposition. Two photo reproductions of their lamps used in the Waldorf Hotel, NYC, on pp (2)-(3). ☺. (E)

996.1 Rogers, Tho[ma]s L. *Mexico? Si, Señor.* Boston: n.p., 1893.

18½x12½. 294 p, map, index. White wraps with green and red lettering and illus of Mexican cowboy on horse. C.t.= t.p. A 2-line poem by Wilhelm Meister is on the t.p. From an intact collection. ☺. (LBA) **P➔**

996.2 Rogers, William, Mfg. Co. *Genuine Rogers goods.* Hartford, CT: n.p., n.d.

15½x9. (4) p. Aquamarine wraps, black print, string-tied. C.t. Illus and trademark definitions for their tableware (illus inside both covers). No WCE; intact collection. ☺(WM)

996.3 Rogers, William, Mfg. Co. *Silver Plated Spoons & Forks : Rogers & Bro. A.1.* Waterbury, CT: Rogers and Brother Works, n.d.

16x11. (4) p. Folded glossy card, black print, illus of dancing nymphs. C.t. Their WCE display illus on back with caption: "Worlds [sic] Fair, Chicago, Ill, U.S.A. : 1893. Pavilion of Rogers & Brother, Waterbury, Conn." Ad for "Electro Silver Plated" flatware. ☺(GLD,B,WM) $24 - 50

996.4 Rogers, William, Mfg. Co. *Silver Table Ware : How it is made.* Hartford, CT: n.p., n.d.

12x18½. 20 p. Pale gray-green string-tied wraps, black print. C.t. Back cover illus of "Our Exhibit World's Fair." Their WF souvenir spoon shown inside the back cover. ☺(WM)

997.1 Rome, Watertown & Ogdensburg Railroad. *Great highway and favorite route for fashionable travel... World's fair route : via Niagara Falls.* Oswego, NY: Oliphant's print, 1893.

21½x10½. Yellow sheet unfolds to 82½x21½, black print both sides. Route map and time table. RR superintendent located in New York City. (WM)

999. *Ropp's Commercial Calculator:* (S)
▸Completed citation: [1887 by C. Ropp]. Maroon stiff wraps, gilt print and border design. Red dyed edges. WCE from pp 129-44.

999.1 Rorer, S[arah] T[yson]. *How to cook vegetables.* 5th ed. Philadelphia: W. Atlee Burpee & co., 1895 [°1890 By W. Atlee Burpee & co.].

18½x13. 1 *l*, (v)-viii, 9-182, (10) p ads. Pale blue-green wraps with dark blue print. Booklet does not mention WCE but one ad in back is for Burpee WCE item #2276. ☺(GLD) $15 - 32

1000.   Rorer. *Recipes used in Illinois Corn Exhibit Model Kitchen*: (E,S,UIC)

1000.1 *Royal Worcester : England : ...Manufacturers of Porcelain by special: Royal Warrants : to : Her Most Gracious Majesty.* [Worcester: Baylis, Lewis & co.], n.d.

7½x13. White coated stiff card; two half-width panels fold to meet in center and form the c.t. given, using both panels. Beautiful chromolith borders, brown print. Back of card "Royal Worcester at the Chicago Exposition and Worlds' Fair, 1893" followed by a list of "The Specimens Exhibited." ☺. (WM)

1000.2 Rudolph Indexer Co. *The Rudolph Continuous Indexer.* [Chicago]: n.p., [June 1893].

28x21½. (4) p. Folded white sheet, blue print and 2-view illus of indexer. Info about the machine followed by testimonials on pp (2)-(4). On back: "Indexer is now on exhibition with the Bureau of Education's exhibit in the Government Building." Dated at end. ☺ (WM)

1000.3 Rudolph Indexer Co. *The Rudolph Indexer Case.* [Chicago]: n.p., [July 1893].

28x21½. (4) p. Folded white sheet, blue print and illus of case. Ads inside. On back: "[T]he Indexers are now on exhibition with the Bureau of Education's exhibit in The Government Building." ☺ (WM)

1000.4 Rudolph Indexer Co. *Some Good Words from California. San Francisco free public library.* [Chicago]: n.p., [July 1893].

21½x14. (4) p. Folded white sheet, blue print and 2-view illus of indexer. S.F. library replaced their card catalog with on indexer on Mar 26, 1893. Testimonials from the library staff; dated at end. No WCE content; from an intact collection. (WM)

1000.5 Runyan, Georgie D. *400 years of America: her : Discovery, History, Achievements and Politics.* Springfield, OH: The New Era Co., 1892 [ᶜ1892 by The New Era Co.].

20½x14. 1 *l* (frontis port of Runyan), 592 p+ 16 *l* of interspersed plates with tissue guards (14 are C. Graham chromoliths of WCE bldgs, 2 are non-WCE). Maroon cloth hc, gilt spine print. Chap II is about Columbus. "The World's Fair Buildings," pp 587-90. US history of the time. ☺ (GLD) $25 - 60
---- Also found: 3rd ed. Springfield, OH: The New Era co., 1893 [ᶜ1892 by The New Era Co.]. (IHi)

1000.6 Russell, Adolph, Publisher. *Gesammt-Verlags-Katalog : für den deutschen Buchhandel.* [Leipzig: Oscar Brandstelter], 1893?

26x17. 12 p. Paged with roman numerals. Paging includes self-wraps. Black print. C.t. Ad in German for their bibliography of German literature to 1893, with listings by publisher, author, and subject; cost for cloth ed is given as 65 marks. No WCE content; from intact collection. ☺ (WM)

1000.7 Russell Process Co. *...The Russell process, the Improved Method of Lixiviation,...* Park City, UT: Russell Process Co., 1893?

23x14½. (4) p. Folded gray-green sheet, black print. At head of title: "January, 1893." Chemical process to extract unprocessed gold and silver from mine tailings. On p (4) rubber stamped in blue: "The Russell Process Co., Sec. 25-26 B-, S.W. Gallery, Mining Building,– World's Fair." (WM)

1002.1 Sack, Rud., [Co.]. *Catalogue : of : Agriculture Implements : and : Machinery : manufactured by : Rud. Sack : Plagwitz-Leipzig.* Plagwitz-Leipzig: [Printed by E. Stephan], n.d.

18x11½. 138 p. Blue-flecked wraps, black and red print and design. Illus of 26 ploughs on back cover; index inside back cover. List of previous WF awards. No WCE content; from intact collection. ☺ (WM)

1003.   Sala. *Sunlight*: (S)

1003.1 Sanderson Brothers Steel Co. *To Workers of Sanderson Brothers Steel Co.'s Tool Steel.* N.p.: n.p., n.d.

14x10. (4) p. Folded sheet, black print. Lists their numbering system for grading different steels for various applications. On back: "World's fair, 1893. Mines and Mining Building." ☺ (WM)

1003.2 Sandwich Enterprise Co. *The new champion : double acting : spray pump.* Sandwich, IL: n.p., n.d.

20x13½. (4) p. Folded sheet, black print and illus of man spraying orchard. C.t. Their hand pump was listed at $14. They also made a tilting "Red Cross Cart" for gardening. No WCE content but found issued with pulp envelope, black print: "World's Fair Exhibit," listing 3 WCE exhibit locations. ☺ (WM)

1003.3 Santa Fe Railroad. Higgins, C.A. *Grand cañon : of the : Colorado river, Arizona.* Chicago?: Passenger department Santa Fe route, 1893.

22x18½. 1 *l* frontis, (3)-31, (1) p map. White coated wraps, black print and vignette illus. Frontis of stage coach; map of Santa Fe route from Arizona to Chicago. C.t. = t.p. No mention of WCE; from an intact collection. ☺ . (FM)

1003.4 Santoni, Jules [Co.]. *General supply for the army : Fournitures Générales des Armées : France, Colonies, Étranger. Foreign countries.* Marseilles, Fr.: House Jules Santoni, n.d.

28x21½. (4) p. Folded buff sheet, black print and lithos. Text in French and English. Inside is a beautiful double-page chromolith of Santoni uniforms and accouterments for the French Colonies. At top of p (3): "Chicago International Exhibition 1893 : French colonies : Algerian & Tunisian troop' uniforms." Same text in French at top of p (2), the two language headings are separated by a brown ink litho of the Santoni exhibit. Interesting ad. ☺ (GLD) P➔ $30 - 65

1003.5 Sargent Mfg. Co. *...Illustrated Catalogue of Sargent's patent ball bearing : Rotary Book Cases.* New York: n.p., n.d.

24½x16. (8) p. Sheet unfolds to 49x32. Buff stock, black print. C.t. At head of title: "Catalogue D." Contains 4 catalogues with A, B, C, D at tops section pages. At bottom of p (4): "Exhibit at Columbian Exposition, Dept. D, Main Floor, Anthropological Building." ☺ . (WM)

1003.6 *Scandinavian World's fair Lodging Bureau.* Chicago: n.p., n.d.

28x21½. 1 *l*. Single white sheet with black print one side. Caption title. Text in old Norwegian. ☺ (S)

1003.7 *Schall & Co.'s Exhibit : World's Columbian exposition : Department of Agriculture, Section G, Second Floor.* [New York: Schall & Co.], n.d.

14x9. (4) p. Folded pale pink card, blue print and illus of their display of Columbus landing. Covers in landscape and inside text in portrait orientation. C.t. Schall's was a confectioner supplier, cake baker, etc. Ad for the co's imported goods. ☺ (GLD) $18 - 42

1003.8 Schieffelin, W.H., & Co. *A Complete Compendium and : reference handbook : Of the Products of the Farbenfabriken vormals Friedr. Bayer & Co. ...* New York: n.p., [1893].

18x11½. (3)-48 p. Yellow stiff wraps, navy print. C.t. = t.p. Blue text print. Properties and list of Bayer aspirin products. Bottom p (5), "May 1893." No mention of WCE; from intact collection. (WM)

1003.9 Schieren, Cha[rle]s A., & Co. *Catalogue of "Novelties" Curiosities in Belting...Leather Link Pavillion* [sic], *Electrical Hall : Columbian World's Fair Grounds : Chicago 1893.* N.p.: n.p., n.d.

21½x15. 7 p. includes front cover. Buff self-wraps, green print. C.t. Green ink text. Illus of their New York City factory on back cover. Ad. (WM)

1003.10 Schieren, Cha[rle]s A., & Co. *Chas. A. Schieren & Co., are the leaders in the manufacture of Leather Belting for Electric Light and Railway Plants.* N.p.: n.p., n.d.

9x10½. (8) p includes both covers. White wraps with red and green print. C.t. From an intact WCE scrapbook. ☺ (S)

1003.11 Schieren, Cha[rle]s A., & Co. *Chas. A. Schieren & Co.: manufacturers and tanners of : Electric Leather Belting for Street Railroads.* [New York: Watkins], n.d.

27x20½. (4) p. Folded cream glossy sheet, black print and illus of man at the company's shipping door with two huge rolls of belting. C.t. No WCE content; from intact collection. ☺(WM)

1003.12 Schieren, Cha[rle]s A., & Co. *Chas. A. Schieren & Co., Sole manufacturers and patentees of the : Electric and Pat. Perforated Belt.* N.p.: n.p., n.d.

11x10. (4) p. Folded cream glossy sheet, dark-green print. On p (2) they note their "Black Belts" in use in WCE Mach and Elect Bldgs. Trademark, "Electric," was printed every 10 ft on belt. ☺(WM)

1003.13 Schmidt, C. Ch. [Co.]. *...Description of the Oils exhibited by the Chemical-technical Laboratory : C. Ch. Schmidt : Riga.* [Riga: Printed at Mueller's printing works, 1893].

25½x17. 18 p, 1 *l* color graph titled "Table IV." Buff wraps with gray and black litho, red elliptical logo, and two coins. Fancy cover pinpoints Chicago and Riga, Latvia, on globes. C.t. At head of title: "The World's Fair-Chicago Exhibition : 1893." Color illus ad. [Oils included terpene now used for cleaning.] ☺(CCA,ICRL,WM)   **P➜**

1003.14 Schutte, L., & Co. *L. Schutte & Co. : Engineers and Machinists : Philadelphia : Columbian Exhibition : 1893.* Philadelphia: L. Schutte & Co., [1892?].

16x10. 42 p. Paging includes the numbered text inside the front and back covers. Plain gray wraps, black print. First of several product caption titles is on p 2: "The universal double tube injector." Illus of valves and boilers. Handout at their exhibit: Mach Bldg 26-M-27. Date on p 40. ☺(GLD) $20 - 50

1003.15 Seamon, H., & Son. *Cheapest Smoke in the world : mild or strong.* [Wheeling, WV]: n.p., n.d.

20x13½. 1 *l*. Glossy sheet, black print one side and illus of their WCE tobacco exhibit. C.t. ☺(WM)

1003.16 Seeger, Eugene. *...Chicago, Die Geschichte einer Wunderstadt.* 2d ed. Chicago: [Geo. Gregory Printing Co.], 1893 [ᶜ1893 By Eugene Seeger].

22½x14½. x, 1 *l*, (2) p, 1 *l*, 542, (2) p. Hc. At head of title: "1837 1871 1893." Printed in German. Many b/w illus. Three chap on the WCE, pp 457-537; complete descriptions of Germany and Austria on the Midway Plaisance and the German Day speeches. Trans: Chicago, the history of an amazing city. See #1003.17 for the English language ed. ☺.(UIC)

1003.17 Seeger, Eugene. *...Chicago, the Wonder City.* Chicago: [The Geo. Gregory Printing Co.], 1893 [ᶜ1893 By Eugene Seeger].

24x16½. xii, 451 p. Hc. At head of title: "1837. 1871. 1893." Marbled edges. "The World's Fair. Chicago 1893," pp 383-451 with illus. See #1003.16 for the German language edition. ☺(DC,Fess,IHi)

1003.18 Sell, Henry. *Catalogue of British newspapers from the earliest period, 1632, to the middle of the nineteenth century : exhibited by Henry Sell at the World's fair : Chicago, 1893.* London: n.p., [1893].

Octovo. 32 p. (HU)

1003.19 Seventh-Day Baptists. *Catalogue of the Seventh-day Baptist Exhibit : World's Columbian Exposition : 1893.* [Alfred Centre, NY: Press of the American Sabbath Tract Society], n.d.

15x10½. 15 p. Self-wraps. C.t. List of 84 items in their exhibit. Associated with Alfred U. ☺.(NHL)

1003.20 Seventh-Day Baptists. *Sabbath Souvenir.* N.p.: n.p., [1893].

18x12. 3-11 p includes inside back wrap. Blue text and illus. C.t. Cover illus of "Steinheim, Alfred University" (one of their schools). On back: "From The Seventh-Day Baptist Exhibit : at the : World's

Columbian Exposition in Chicago, 1893. Manufactures and Liberal Arts Building, Gallery–, post 102, D." Description of church and references to their World's Congress. (S)   P➜

1003.21 Seydoux & Cie. *Maison : Seydoux & Ce : Ancienne Maison Paturle-Lupin.* Le Cateau, Fr.: Typographie et lithographie Samaden et Roland, 1893.

23x15. 29 p, 1 *l* printer's name. Green pulp wraps, black print. Trans: Seydoux company formerly Paturle-Lupin. At top of cover "Exposition Internationale de 1893 : Chicago." Describes their woolen mills with sales office in Paris. List of employee benefits and WF medals won. In French. ☺ (WM)

1004. *Shakespeare Boiled Down*: (B)
▶Alternate author: New Home Sewing Machine Company.

1004.1 Shaw, George, & Co. *Shaw's limited, (George Shaw & Co.), Fibre and Bristle Dressers.* Manchester, Eng.: n.p., [1893].

26½x20½. (4) p. Folded buff sheet, black print. C.t. Illus on p (2) of their brushes and brooms. Testimonials p (3). Mentions their exhibit and "Catalogue No. 177, World's Fair, Chicago." Ad. (WM)

1004.2 Shayne, C.C., and John T. Shayne. ...*High Class furs.* New York [and] Chicago: n.p., n.d.

12½x9. 16 p. Chromolith textured wraps with illus of a polar bear. C.t. At head of title "Columbian Exposition." Color illus of the offices in NY and Chicago on back. On p 1: "In presenting this Souvenir of our Exhibit in the World's Columbian Exposition." ☺ . (ref,WM)   P➜ $43

1005.1 Sheppard, Isaac A., & Co. *Condon's mixing machinery for Bakers...* Baltimore, MD: n.p., n.d.

23x15½. (4) p. Folded buff sheet, black print. One large illus of a machine per page. Inventor's name stamped on cover: "J.W. Condon, Chicago." No WCE content; from intact collection. ☺ (WM)

1005.2 *Sheridan hotel : John McGrath, Proprietor. 6142 Oglesby Ave., Chicago.* N.p.: n.p., n.d.

6x10½. 1 *l*. Ivory card printed on one side in black ink. Gives location as a 5 minute walk from the Fair. The board and room rate was $1.50/day. ☺ . (E)

1005.3 Sheridan, T.W. & C.B., [Co.]. ...*T.W. & C.B. Sheridan, manufactures of Paper Cutters of every description. Bookbinders and paper-box makers machinery.* Champlain, NY: n.p., n.d.

30x21. 16 p including covers. Self-wraps, black print. C.t. At head of title: "Established 1835." Illus catalogue with prices. Chicago office address stamp. No mention of WCE; from intact collection. . (WM)

1005.4 Shoninger, B., Co. *Shoninger Pianos.* [New Haven, CT: B. Shoninger Co.] (Valley ETF? eng. & print. co., Grand Rapids, MI), n.d.   P➜

22x17½. 24 p. White pebbled wraps, black and gilt print, illus of muses playing musical instruments. C.t. Back cover illus of New Haven, CT, office and factory. Catalog with testimonials. See #1530 for a Shoninger music piece. No mention WCE; from an intact collection. . (WM)

1005.5 The Short Electric Railway Co. ...*Silence and Speed. The Gearless Motor :
The Short Electric Railway Co. Cleveland, O.* Cleveland, OH: W.J.
Morgan & co. lith, [1893].

8½x14. (4) p. Folded ivory card; blue, red, and brown print. C.t. At
head of title: "World's Columbian Exposition." Page (2) caption title:
"Exhibit of The Short Electric Railway co." Diagram and description of
their exhibit in Section L in the Electricity Bldg. ☺ . (E)   P➔

1005.6 *Siegel, Cooper & Co. : Columbian Exposition Catalogue. 1893.* Chicago:
Siegel, Cooper & Co. (W.B. Conkey co., printers and binders), n.d.

29½x22½. 368 p. Off-white wraps, black and brown print, litho of women
overlooking WCE grounds. C.t. This cover title is repeated at the top of
each page. Siegel also published view books, #1668 and #1668.1. ☺ (S)

1005.7 *Simonds Rolling Machine Company : steel balls and rolled forged specialties
: Fitchburg Mass U S A.* [Fitchburg, MA: Press of Livermore & Knight co.
Providence, RI, 1893?].

11½x15. 63, (1) p index. Maize wraps, orange decoration, black print and co. logo. C.t.: "Simonds
Rolling Machine Company Fitchburg Mass USA : steel balls and..." Yellow pages with green and orange
print. Frontis photo-illus of factory, Testimonials to May 18, 1893. ☺ . (Stfd–bound WCE Trans Dept Collection)

1005.8 Simpson McIntire & Co. *Simpson's Top-O-Can Brand of Diamond Creamery Butter.* N.p.: n.p., [1893].

16x11½. (4) p. Folded white sheet, gilt and red print. Dated May 1, 1893. List of previous fair awards
to 1892. No WCE content; from an intact collection. (WM)

1005.9 Singer, A.L., & Co. *The Polygon Cutting Tables.* Chicago: n.p., n.d.

9x15½. (4) p. Folded buff stiff card, black print. On p (4): A cutting table illus and "On Exhibition at
Machinery Palace, Sec. 28, Col. A.–47." A table with 3 faces like a prism, which could be rotated on its
axis for triple the fabric layout areas and cutting ease. ☺ (WM)

1005.10 Singer Mfg. Co. ...*Costumes of All Nations.* N.p.: n.p., n.d.

14x8½. Boxed set of 36 chromolith cards. White box, sepia and green print and decoration. Title from
box. At head of title: "Singer Mfg Co." At bottom: "Souvenir : World's Columbian Exposition : 1893."
"National costume studies"—each card illus a different foreign costume. (GLD,DC,GPL,S,WM) $70 - 160

1005.11 Singer Mfg. Co. *The Golden Harvest : 54 first awards : gathered at the World's Columbian exposition.*
N.p.: n.p., n.d.

15½x9½. (8) p. Folded buff strip unfolds to 15½x38, blue print and illus. Three sewing machines are
shown. Describes two large tapestries exhibited and their WCE awards. Handout ad. ☺ (GLD) $18 - 38

1005.12 Singer Mfg. Co. *The Singer Manu'f'g Co's exhibit of Family Sewing Machines and Art Embroidery.*
N.p.: n.p., n.d.

13½x10½. (8) p. Pretty chromolith stiff wraps. (4) p text and (4) p b/w lithos. C.t. [Cover illus shown
with #779 in original book is in error and belongs to this item, #1005.12.] ☺ (GLD,E,VAM) $24 - 55

1005.13 *Skandia Plow Co. : Rockford, Ill. : manufacturers of Plows, Cultivators, Corn Planters, Check Rowers,
Harrows...* [Rockford, IL: Skandia Plow Co. (Rockfords-Posten electric print)], n.d.

16x8½. 48 p+ text inside wraps. Tri-fold beige stiff wraps with green and black print and design.
Orcutt illus of plow (front); factory illus (back). On folding flap: "Pocket Annual." Calendar for 1893 on
p 2. No mention of WCE; from an intact collection. ☺ (WM)

1005.14 Smalley Mfg. Co. *Smalley goods. Directions for setting up and operating : Smalley Ensilage...*
Manitowac, WI: n.p., n.d.

21x14. 18 p. Tan stiff wraps, black print. C.t. No illus. Their farm implements, parts, and prices. No WCE; from an intact collection. (WM)

1005.15 Smith, Elbert C., Owner. *World's fair visitors* [sic] : *rooms : south side, Chicago.* Chicago: n.p., n.d.

21½x14. Folded sheet printed only on the inside, i.e., pp (2)-(3). Caption title. Offer to rent Smith's home at 5063 Lake Avenue, 5 blks north of the WF. The home was also listed with the Bureau of Public Comfort. ☺ (WM)

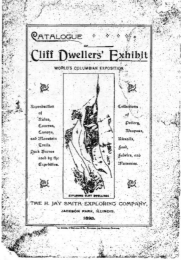

1006. Smith Exploring. *Catalogue of...weapons:* (GLD,FM,S)   P➔ $22 - 50

1006.1 Smith Exploring Co., H. Jay. *Cliff-Dweller Exhibit : World's Columbian Exposition.* N.p.: H.J. Smith Exploring Co., n.d.

15x9. Single buff card printed both sides in black and red ink. Grounds map has red star designating Cliff-Dweller exhibit. ☺ (GLD,S,WM)

1007. Smith Exploring. *Cliff Dwellers The H. Jay Smith:* (HU,S,UCB,UPa,UTA)

1008. Smith, Frank. *Art History Midway Plaisance:* (MSI,S,Stfd,UCLA)
▶Cover description "(second edition)": Brown cloth hc, no illus on back.
---- Also found for first citation: Brown satin-like cloth over pliable boards, gilt print, gilt Ferris wheel illus on back.

1008.1 Smith, John E., & Sons. *Illustrated Catalogue and price list of the celebrated Smith's buffalo choppers with self-mixers and spice attachments.* N.p.: (F.W. Burow & son, Printers, Buffalo, NY), 1892.

23½x15½. 40 p. Green wraps, black print and litho of the chopper. Back wrap award info in German. C.t. Office and factory in Buffalo. Machinery for butchers. Ad. Handout included laid-in 23x15 ad sheet for their "Buffalo spice mill." No mention of WCE; from an intact collection. (WM)

1008.2 ...*The Smith Premier Typewriter Co. : Syracuse, N.Y....* Chicago: Western Bank Note Company, n.d.

14x14. (4) p. Folded pale pink stiff card, black print. On cover at bottom: "World's Columbian Exposition Dept. Manufactures & Liberal Arts Bldg. Section F. Block 2. Chicago, Ill." Back cover Illus of Admin Bldg. C.t. At head of title: "Improvement the order of the age. Souvenir." Text in 4 languages. Inside back cover is an (8) p tipped-in elegant silver and black ad for the Smith Premier, which is die-cut in the shape of the typewriter. ☺ (WM)

1009. Snider. *WF Studies* (entire book):(CLP,ICRL,ISU,MOHx,MSI,OU,RU,S,UCLA,UIC,UMC,UTA,WM)
▶Add cover description: Blue cloth hc, gilt spine print.

1010. Snider. *WF Studies : number one:* (S)
1011. Snider. *WF Studies : number two:* (S)
1012. Snider. *WF Studies : number three:* (S)
1013. Snider. *WF Studies : number four:* (S)
1014. Snider. *WF Studies : number five:* (S)
1015. Snider. *WF Studies : the Plaisance--First:* (S)
1016. Snider. *WF Studies : the Plaisance--Second:* (S)

1016.1 Sohmer Piano Co. *Souvenir of Sohmer Cartoons, From Puck, Judge, and Frank Leslies.* N.p.: n.p. [Sackett & Wilhelms litho. co., NY], n.d.

15½x12. (12) p. Buff stiff wraps, red & light green print and design. Trademark on back. C.t. Ad with series of cartoons showing pianos; Sohmer's name is on each cartoon. One Columbus cartoon from "Christmas Puck," 1892. No WCE; from an intact collection. (WM)

1017. *Something of Interest to All : The South-Land:* (S,WM)
▶Completed citation: N.p.: [St. Louis, Iron Mountain and Southern Railway Co. (Woodward & Tiernan printing co.)], n.d. 30 p+ text inside both covers. Self-wraps, black print. Arkansas is main content.

1017.1 *The Sound Exhibition : Sweden : Chalk : Portland Cement : Fire-bricks :*
Front bricks : Draining pipes. [Malmö, Swed.: tr. Skånska lith. a.-b.,
1893].　　　　　　　　　**P➜**

21½x14½.　48 p includes 6 plates.　A very confusing pagination (e.g., p
5 somewhere in the middle after p 10 and some unpaged pages); mostly
no pagination at all.　Multicolor wraps with the Swedish flag a pale green
background; lettering in blue, yellow, white, and red.　C.t.　Compilation
of manufacturer's catalogs.　List of Swedish companies that constructed
the Swedish Bldg, WCE.　The "Sound" is the strait between Sweden and
Denmark.　☺. (KBS,WM)

1017.2 Southern Pacific Co.　*Comparative Climatic Map of California.*　San
Francisco: Southern Pacific co. (F.S. Crocker co., SF), 1892.

25x9½.　Sheet with colorized map unfolds to 25x77.　Cover in orange
and black print.　C.t.　CA statistics in panels on back of sheet.　No WCE
content; from intact collection.　☺(WM)

1017.3 *Souvenir : Album : Columbian Exposition Chicago 1893.*　N.p.: n.p., n.d.

27x22x8½ thick.　1 *l* (t.p.), 18 thick *l* cut for inserting photographs.　Heavy front cover in ivory and
brown has celluloid in deep relief; yellow plush cloth back cover; all edges gilt; brass clasp on fore edge.
Admin Bldg chromolith and port of Columbus on t.p.　An ornate photo album with WF buildings
chromoliths.　See #713.2, #806.1　☺(GLD)　　　　　　　　　　　　　$150 – 320
---- Also found:　Brown cover with Columbus medallion, red plush back.

1017.4 *Souvenir Calendar of the World's Fair at Chicago.*　Lynn, MA: Souvenir
Publishing Co., ᶜ1892.　　　　　　　**P➜**

28x18.　12 *l*.　White coated stiff card stock wraps, black print, string-tied
at top.　C.t.　Each leaf has a banner, illus of WCE bldg, and calendar
month at bottom— one for each month.　☺. WM)

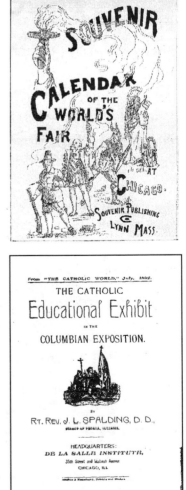

1018.　*Souvenir of a ride on The Ferris Wheel*:　(Col,GPL,HML,IHi,NLA)
▶Also listed:　Collins Shackelford as author.

1022.　Spalding, J[ohn] L[ancaster].　*The Catholic Educational*:　(CUA,UCB)　**P↘**

1022.1 *The Sperry Electric Railway company.*　Cleveland, OH: [Press of The F.W.
Roberts Co.], 1893.

19½x13.　31 p.　Navy coated cloth flexible wraps, bold silver print.
C.t. = t.p.　Sperry made motors for electric street cars.　No mention of
WCE; from an intact collection.　(WM)

1022.2 Sprenger, Ed., [Co.].　*Nivellir-Instrumente.　Aus zug aus dem Preis-*
Verzeichniss.　Berlin SW: [Wilhelm Baensch], n.d.

24x16.　(11) p.　Self wraps.　C.t.　Illus price catalog of 126 items.　No
WCE; intact collection.　☺(WM)

1022.3 Sprenger, Ed., [Co.].　*...Theodolite, kleinere Winkelmesser und Auftrage-*
Instrumente.　Auszug aus dem Preis-Verzeichniss.　[Berlin SW: Druck von
Wilhelm Baensch], n.d.

24x16.　(24) p.　Green wraps.　Issued with envelope with English title:
"Illustrated Catalogue of the Engineer's and Surveyor's Instruments, made
by Ed. Sprenger."　Catalogue of 105 items with prices.　At head of title:
co info and illus.　No WCE content; from intact collection.　(WM)

1022.4 Springer Torsion Balance Co. *A few new styles. Just out.* New York: n.p., n.d.

    30½x23. (2) p. Sheet with black print with illus. Chicago agent stamped on front. Large trademark has 2 children "See-Sawing on a Torsion Balance." No WCE content; from intact collection. ☺(WM)

1022.5 Springfield Scale Co. *McClelland Automatic Improvement in druggists' prescription scales.* Springfield, MO: n.p., 1893?

    16x10½. (4) p. Folded peach sheet, black print, color illus of a scale. On p (3) is a price list for three scales. Testimonials dated to March 1893. No WCE content; from intact collection. (WM)

1022.6 St. Louis Southwestern Railway. Stevens, Walter B. *Through Texas. A series of Interesting Letters by Walter B. Stevens, special correspondent of the St. Louis globe-democrat.* [St. Louis: St. Louis Southwestern Railway], 1892.

    22x15. 108 p. Pale turquoise wraps, black print. C.t.: "Through Texas." WCE handout. ☺.(LBA)

1022.7 Standard Sewing Machine Co. *The Nation's Pride : The Standard of Conquest.* Cleveland, OH: The Standard Sewing Machine Co. [Geo. S. Harris & sons, lith., Philadelphia], n.d.

    8½x14½. (12) p+ text inside both wraps. White coated wraps with chromolith depicting Columbus, Isabella, and Ferdinand. The text is a poem about them. Blue ink text and text illus. C.t. No mention of WCE; from intact collection. [They exhibited in the Manuf Bldg, Gallery, Sec G.] ☺(GLD,E) $20 - 35

1022.8 Star & Crescent Mills Co. *Turkish Toweling at the World's Fair.* [Philadelphia: Star & Crescent Mills Co.], n.d.

    12.7 cm diameter card folded at top. (4) p. Pale peach card, dark blue star and crescent designs. Caption title. Dark blue text print and two illus of people using towels. On p (3) they note that their weaving exhibit was at Sec 29, Col N 50, Machinery Hall. Frank Leake, President. ☺(GLD)   P➔ $24 - 55

1022.9 Starr Piano Co. *...Standard Styles of Starr Pianos.* Richmond, IN: Register publishing co., printers, n.d.

    18x13½. (8) panels. Cream glossy sheet unfolds to 18x54. Black print descriptions and illus of pianos. C.t. No WCE content; from intact collection. ☺(WM)

1023. Stead. *If Christ came to Chicago*: (GLD,FPL)   P➔ $25 - 50
    ▶Corrected citation: (3)-472 p, 1 *l.* Illus of Admin Bldg on last leaf and front cover (Christ pointing to it). This books puts the dirt on nearly every organization and leader in Chicago! The WCE mentioned throughout.

1023.1 *Steam Gauge & Lantern Co. manufacturers of tubular safety lanterns, tubular street lamps,... World's fair edition.* Syracuse, NY [and] Chicago: Steam Gauge & Lantern Co., n.d.

    15½x10½. 64 p. Green wraps, black print. C.t. Back cover: "Our exhibit is in the Manufactures Department : Ground Floor, Section N, Block 3." Illus catalog of their lamps. (WM)

1023.2 Steel Protecting Glove Mfg. Co. *...The only Steel Protected Glove in the World.* Chicago: n.p., n.d.

    24x15½. Single sheet ad, black print, illus of chain-mail glove at top. At head of title: "World's Columbian Exposition." ☺(S,WM)

1024.1 Stern, Charles, & Sons. *...California Wines and Brandies.* N.p.: n.p., n.d.

    12½x8. (6) p. Stiff card unfolds to 12½x23½, blue-black print. C.t. Litho of WCE Hort Bldg on p (5). Product list. Based in Fresno and Los Angeles; offices in Chicago, NY, and Boston. ☺(WM)

1026.   Stevens. *Six months at the World's fair*:   (HML,UIC,UMC,UMD)

1026.1 Stevenson-Hoggson Electric Co. *"The Hoggson" Automatic Perpetual Calendar and Time Stamp*. St. Louis, MO: n.p., 1893?

27½x21½. (2) p. Buff sheet, black print, center illus of the machine. Back stamped twice in purple by the machine: 1) "This Machine is on Exhibition in N.E. Corner, Ground Floor, Electricity Building. (E.S. Greeley's Co. Exhibit.)" and dated, e.g., "Sep 12, 1893" (as on WM's copy); 2) "Visited World's fair : (date): The Hoggson Time Stamp, St. Louis, MO." ☺ (WM)

1026.2 *The Stever Railway Rail Joint company*. Chicago: n.p., n.d.

15½x8½. (4) p. Folded white sheet, red and black print, litho of their joints. C.t. At bottom of cover: "Transportation Building, World's Columbian Exposition." ☺ (S)

1026.3 Stoddard Mfg. Co. *The Beck Side Delivery hay rake*. Dayton, OH: n.p., n.d.

16x9½. (4) p. Folded gold sheet, black print. Full 2-page illus of the rake inside. No WCE content; from intact collection. ☺ (WM)

1026.4 Stoddard Mfg. Co. *Tiger Tedder*. Dayton, OH: n.p., n.d.

15½x8½. (6) panels. Tri-fold maize sheet, black print. C.t. Caption title: "Special points on the tiger tedder." For tedding hay. No WCE content; from intact collection. Found with ad card for "The Tiger : King of Rakes" by J.W. Stoddard & Co., Dayton, which shows that the co's name had changed. ☺ (WM)

1026.5 Stoll, H., & Co. *H. Stoll & Co's. : Knitting and Hosiery Machinery : Works: Reutlingen (Wurtemberg) Germany*. N.p.: n.p., n.d.

28½x23. 6 p. Yellow-tan self-wraps which are included in paging, black and red print. C.t. On p 3: "World's Columbian Exposition." Illus and description of their knitters. ☺ (WM)

1028.   *The Story of Columbus*:   (CSL,IHi,S,UMD)
▸Add annotation: Issued with souvenir manila mailing envelope.

1029.   *The Story of Columbus and the World's Columbian Exposition*:   (CCA,UMC,UNO,uofs)
▸Add: Introd. Tyron Edwards, Detroit, MI. Found cataloged with Edwards as author.

1030.   *The story of Pullman*.   (HML)
▸Add author and additional info: Pullman Co. [Chicago: Blakely & Rogers], 1893? 15x10. 40 p. Gray green wraps. C.t.= t.p. Outside back wrap: "Pullman exhibit : World's Columbian exposition : 1893."

1031.   Straus. *Modern art creations A collection of artotypes*:   (BrU,WM,Yale)

1032.1 Superior Drill Co. *...Beet Drill, Superior to any other...* Springfield, OH: n.p., n.d.

28x21½. (4) p. Folded buff sheet, black print, illus. C.t. At head of title: co info and "Manufacturers of the new superior solid steel..." For sugar beets. No WCE content; from intact collection. ☺ (WM)

1032.2 Superior Drill Co. *The superior 5 hoe drill*. Springfield, OH: n.p., n.d.

24x16. (2) p. Sheet printed both sides in red and black, large illus of the hoe drill on front. Caption title. Used for wheat or corn. No WCE content; from intact collection. ☺ (WM)

1032.3 Superior Drill Co. *Superior solid steel frame grain drills...* Springfield, OH: n.p., n.d.

15x8½. (12) panels. Sheet unfolds to 15x50. Printed both sides in red and black. C.t. Seven illus of equipment including "The No. 2 Superior Solid Steel Frame Drill for 1893." No WCE content; intact collection. ☺ (WM)

1032.4 *...Susquehanna fertilizer company of Baltimore City*. Baltimore, MD: n.p. (Guggenheimer-Weil, prs.), n.d.

16x10. 33, (1) p. Tri-fold tan stiff wraps, brown print and illus of their factory, string-tied. C.t. At head of title: "World's fair edition." Illus and description of WCE bldgs constitute most of text. Bird's-eye of WCE grounds on back is ᶜ1892 by A. Zeese & Co. Ad. ©(GLD)   P➔ $25 - 55

1032.5 Swift and Co. *Cotosuet : Made only by Swift and Company : Chicago, U.S.A.* Chicago: Swift and Co., ᶜ1893.

15x9. (4) p. Folded card, chromolith illus of bull in cotton patch with pail of cotosuet (beef suet and prime cotton seed oil). C.t. No mention of WCE; from an intact collection that includes the next 4 Swift items. Ad. [Exhibited in Ag Bldg, Sec D, Main Fl, Col E.0.] ©(GLD,F,WM) $16 - 45

1032.6 Swift and Co. *Swift and Company, Butterine department. Man'f'r's of fine Butterine and Neutral Lard. Union stock yards. Chicago, U.S.A.* Chicago: Swift and Co., n.d.

15x9. (4) p. Folded card with chromolith illus on front and back. C.t. Front illus is of their Butterine exhibit in Ag Bldg, Sec H, 2nd Fl, Col J.9. Caption title: "Exhibits of Swift and company, Union Stock Yards, Chicago, U.S.A. : At the World's Columbian exposition." Ad. ©(GLD,E,F,WM) $16 - 45

1032.7 Swift and Co. *Swift and Company, Glue and Fertilizing Materials. Union stock yards. Chicago, U.S.A.* Chicago: Swift and Co., n.d.

15x9. (4) p. Folded card with chromolith illus on front and back. C.t. Front illus of their WCE glue exhibit in Ag Bldg, Sec H, 2nd Fl, Col I.9. Caption title: "Exhibits of Swift and company, Union Stock Yards, Chicago, U.S.A. : At the World's Columbian exposition." Ad. ©(GLD,E,F) $16 - 45

1032.8 Swift and Co. *Swift and Company, Packers. Union stock yard. Chicago, U.S.A.* Chicago: Swift and Co., n.d.

15x9. (4) p. Folded card with chromolithograph illus on front and back. C.t. Front illus of their WCE "Swift Refrigerator line. 9999. : Fresh meat express" exhibited in Ag Bldg, Sec D, Main Fl, Col E.0. Caption title: "Exhibits of Swift and company, Union Stock Yards, Chicago, U.S.A. : At the World's Columbian exposition." Ad. ©(GLD,F,WM)   P➔ $16 - 45

1032.9 Swift and Co. *Try Our New Package : Swift and Company : Chicago. U.S.A. : Pure Leaf Lard...and You Will Always Use It.* Chicago: Swift and Co., 1893.

15x9. (2) p. Card with chromolith showing product (front) and description in black ink (back). [Lard was exhibited in Ag Bldg, Sec D, Main Fl, Col E.0.] No mention of WCE; from an intact collection with Swift items above. Ad. ©(GLD,F) $16 - 45

1033. Sylvestre. *The marvels in art of the fin de siecle*: (FLP,NDU,UMN,UWM)
---- Also found: Grand Edition Deluxe: 52x37. 10 vol. One of 55 copies. Burgundy half-leather with mocha color textured boards, gilt print and design, satin ties. No color plates. (ref) $2600

1033.1 *Syracuse Chilled Plow Co., manufacturers of the Syracuse Patented Steel, Iron and Wood Beam, Chilled and Steel Plows, for Level Land and Hillside.* Syracuse, NY: The Moser & Lyon co., press, n.d.

23x15½. 32, 4 p. Buff wraps with beautiful royal blue and gilt print and design; back cover illus of factory. Issued with 9x14 trade card. No mention of WCE; from intact WCE collection. © . (WM)

1033.2 Taft, Lorado. *Lectures upon the Fine Art Department : At 11 o'Clock Daily, Agricultural Assembly Hall : Lorado Taft.* N.p.: n.p., n.d.

21½x14. Bright pink card stock, black print. Also announces Taft's 9 a.m. meetings with the art class for a tour through the galleries. At bottom "Price per Course, $3.00 : per Lecture, .50." ☺ (WM)

---- Also found: 21x13½. On thin pink paper, otherwise the same.

1033.3 Taylor, B.C., Rakeworks. *Taylor Hay & Grain Rake : 38,000 in use.* Dayton, OH: Dayton Journal Print, n.d.

14½x8½. White strip unfolds accordion style making (10) panels, purple print. Cover illus of Taylor Rake in use by a farmer. No WCE content; from intact collection. ☺ (WM)

1033.4 *Tea Room.* N.p.: n.p., n.d.

23x13. 1 *l* menu. Buff glossy sheet, black print. At top: large Charles Graham b/w illus of "Woman's Building : World's Columbian exposition" at night. At bottom: "No Lunch Baskets Allowed." All menu items "10 Cents." ☺ . (NHL,WM)

1033.5 Teachers' Columbian Hall. *1893 : souvenir : World's Fair.* N.p.: n.p., n.d.

20x13½. (16) p. Off-white smooth wraps, black print. C.t. Describes their boarding establishment on Woodlawn Ave one block south of Midway and 5 blocks west of WCE. Seven illus of WCE bldgs ᶜ1892 by A. Zeese; WCE map inside back cover shows their location. (GLD) $22 - 50

1034. Telang. *A World's Fair Souvenir Impressions of the World's Fair:* (IHi,UCLA)

1034.1 Textile Club. *Souvenir. Columbian Exposition, 1893 : Textile club excursion : Tuesday, October 10th to Saturday, 21st.* N.p.: n.p., n.d.

14½x12. (4) p. Folded stiff card, purple print. Lists officers for 1893 and members of 4 chapters. President W.E. Parker. On front: "'Yarn' spinners we!" Rare souvenir. [Found in travel packet of WCE tour originating in Boston.] ☺ (GLD) $20 - 55

1034.2 Thames Ironworks and Shipbuilding Co. Ltd. ...*Catalogue of models of ships and general engineering works. Specially prepared for World's Columbian Exposition, Chicago, U.S.A., 1893.* [London: Waterlow & Sons Limited, Printers], n.d. **P➜**

24x18½. 65 p. Buff stiff wraps, black print and illus of their docks at Orchard yard, Blackwall, London. Co name at head of title. "World's Columbian exposition" at top of front cover. ☺ . (Stfd-bound WCE Trans Dept Collection)

1034.3 Thatcher, H.D., & Co. *How to Test baking powder, illustrated and explained for the practical use not only of the scientist but the common people and the ordinary cook, with description of : Thatcher's sugar of milk : baking powder : and selected : cooking recipes.* Potsdam, NY: H.D. Thatcher & co., n.d.

20x12. 23, (1) p+ text inside both wraps. Yellow-tan wraps, black print and illus. Their WCE Ag Hall exhibit location is noted on p 10 and is illus on back cover. They participated at the "Great Columbian Food Exposition held in Madison Square Garden in [Oct] 1892." Ad. ☺ (GLD) $25 - 50

1034.4 Thiele & Steinert [Co]. ...*Manufactorers of Military, Theatrical and Society Goods.* Berlin: Reuter & Siecke Berlin C., n.d.

15½x10½. (6) panels. Tri-fold buff card, dark green print and illus. Inside 3 panels repeat the text in German, English, Spanish, starting "Gold- and Silver-wire. Factory at Freiburg illus on back. No WCE content; from an intact collection. (WM)

1035.1 Thompson, Edward, Co. *Are you going to the World's Fair? If so : be sure and visit our Office at 115 Monroe Street, Chicago, Ill. Which we have placed at the disposal of all visiting lawyers as their Headquarters & Corresponding Room During their Stay in the City.* Northport, NY: Edward Thompson Co. (Ketterlinus, Philadᐞ & NY), n.d. **P⬇**

16½x15½. 1 *l.* Single steel-engraved sheet, blue-black ink, two circular illus of lawyers looking for information. At bottom: "Publishers of American and English Encyclopædia of Law." © . (WM)

1035.2 *Thompson's pocket speller.* 20th ed. Danbury, CT: F.M. Thompson, ᶜ1890–92 by F.M. Thompson.

14x6½. 133, (3) p memoranda. Burgundy leather hc with print and illus of Govt Bldg stamped in silver. Rounded corners, gilt edges, front edge is notched for alphabetical finger tabs. C.t.: "World's Columbian exposition 1893 : government building." © (GLD) $20 - 55

1036. Tiffany. *Catalogue of Tiffany & Co's exhibit*: (FM,WM)
---- Also found: Dark blue embossed stiff wraps, gilt design and illus of royal shield. A complete list of art items and precious stones exhibited.

1037. Tiffany. *Diamond cutting as shown in the Mines and mining*: (HML)
---- Also listed: 6, (1) p.

1038. Tiffany. *A Glimpse at the Tiffany Exhibit*: (FM,LBA,WM) **P➔**
▶Add author and pub info: Heydt, Geo[rge] Frederic. N.p.: n.p., n.d. On 1 *l* (t.p.): "Tiffany Exhibit : Chicago, 1893."
---- Also found: N.p.: n.p., n. d. 13 p. Deep royal blue wraps with silver print and design of their exhibit exterior.

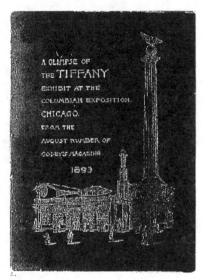

1038.1 Tiffany & Co. Kunz, George Frederick. *Natal Stones : sentiments and superstitions : connected with precious stones.* New York: Tiffany & Co., [ᶜ1892 by Tiffany & Co.].

16½x12. 17 p. String-tied navy wraps with gilt print. Text on untrimmed heavy rag paper. No WCE; from intact collection. (WM)

☞ H.N. Higinbotham purchased the George Frederick Kunz gem collection and donated it to the (Field) Columbian Museum. See #1360.2 for more about Kunz and his WCE collection.

1039. Tiffany. *A synopsis of the exhibit of the Tiffany Glass and Decorating co*: (WM)

1039.1 *Tompkins Avenue Congregational Church, Brooklyn, N.Y. : programme of three special excursions to the World's Columbian Exposition at Chicago, organized under the auspices of the above named church, Rev. Robt. R. Meredith, D.D., Pastor, Leaving New York, Tuesday, June 20th, Tuesday, July 11th, & Tuesday, Aug. 22d, In a Special Train of Pullman sleeping, parlor & dining cars...* New York [etc.]: Henry Gaze & sons, 1893?

14x18. 30 p. Hc. Colored frontis litho copyright by The Winters Art Litho Co, Chicago. . (Yale)

1039.2 Tooth, Arthur, & Sons. *Catalogue of Etchings, Engravings and Photo-Engravings.* [Chicago: P.F. Pettibone & co, stationers & printers], 1893.

19x13. 19 p. Blue-flecked wraps, black print. Assumed to be a numbered catalog of their exhibits at the WCE; however, Tooth also had a Chicago showroom on Michigan Ave. No mention of WCE; from an intact WCE collection. (WM)

1040. Towne. *Rays of Light from all Lands*: (CU)

1041.1 Tracy Sewing Machine Co. *The Tracy Gravity Safety Elevator, with automatic platforms.* N.p.: n.p., n.d.

17x10. (2) p. Buff sheet, black print. "World's Fair, Chicago, N.E. corner gallery, section F, col. 103, Liberal arts building." Elevator used 2 off-center pull ropes for redundancy; if 1 broke, the resulting cant of the car caused ratchets to lock between elevator and shaft. © (WM)

1041.2 Tracy Sewing Machine Co. *The Tracy Lock-Stitch and Chain-Stitch sewing machine.* N.p.: n.p., n.d.

22½x15½. (4) p. Folded sheet, black print and illus of machine and bobbins. Testimonials on p (4). Gives same WCE location as #1041.1. 1000-yd capacity bobbin with 3 pt rotary shuttle. © (WM)

1041.3 The Travelers of Hartford. *Note Book for Visitors to the World's Fair.* Hartford, CT: The Travelers, n.d.

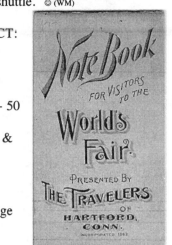

10½x6. (24) p. Dark tan stiff wraps, black print and design. C.t. Hinged at top edge. Pages are lined for notes, each with an illus of a WCE bldg. Ads on inside front and back wraps. © (GLD,WM) P➜ $20 - 50

1041.4 Trimmel, Joh[ann]. N., [Co.]. *Joh. N. Trimmel : Wien.* [Wien, Aus.: Otto Maass & Sohn], n.d.

14½x9. (4) p. Folded pale blue stiff card, black print and ornate floral design. Description of their Austrian accordion models with price list in French p (2), English p (3), and German p (4). At top of each price list in the respective language "Columbian World's Exposition Chicago 1893." © (WM)

1041.5 Troy Laundry Machinery Co. *Price List of Laundry Supplies and Specialties.* Chicago: Hughes litho. co., 1 Feb. 1893.

15½x9. (4) p. Folded pale green and silver paper, decorative print in black and silver. Price list on pp (2)-(3) in red and black. Co logo on back. No WCE content; from intact collection. (WM)

1042. Truman. *History*: (B,BD,bgsu,CCA,CLM,Col,CU,cul,D,ESU,EvP,FM,HML,HU,ICRL,ISU,Knox,KS,Merc,MH,MIT,MOHx,MSI,NDU,NLA,SHB,slcl,slpl, SML,SPL,UCB,UCLA,UIC,UMD,UMN,UTA,UVM,WM)
▶Correct spelling of pub's name: Kelley.
---- Also found: Cover variant for Mammoth (Chicago and Philadelphia), 610 p: Deep blind stamped morocco leather showing two muses and the Manuf Bldg, gilt print, all edges gilt.
---- Also found: Four more publishers. Chicago: J.S. Goodman & Co., 1893; New York: E.B. Treat, [c1893]; Providence, RI: W.W. Thompson & co., [c1893 by Ben C. Truman]; Vancouver, BC: MacGregor Publishing Co., 1893.

---- Rpt ed: (CC,CCA,LU,KSU,NDU,sapl,sfpl,UCD,UCI,UI,UH,uiuc,UMD,UMN,UoA,VCU)
▶Correct spelling of pub's name: Kelley.

1042.1 Turner Machine Co. *The Turner Painting Machine : for spraying : calcimine : whitewash : disinfectants and : oil paints : By which the interiors of most of the buildings in the : World's Columbian Exposition : Were painted.* Brooklyn: n.p., n.d.

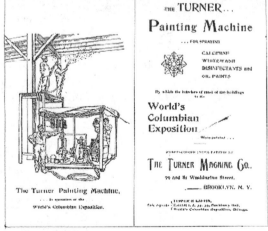

15½x8½. (4) p. Folded sheet, black print. Illus on back. C.t. Cover bottom: "Exhibit I, J, 34, 35, Machinery Hall,..." 25 gallon size cost $500 complete with 5 HP compressor. [One of the important inventions spawned by the WCE.]
* © (WM) [back and front] P➜

1042.2 Turner Machine Co. *The Turner Rotary Engine : combining the qualities of an air compressor, vacuum pump,...* Brooklyn, NY: n.p., n.d.

15½x8½. (8) panels. Folded buff strip unfolds to 15½x34. C.t. Details engine they made before inventing the paint sprayer. Mentions their painting of interiors of WCE bldgs. Gives sizes, weights, and costs. On bottom of front cover: "I, J, 34, 35, Machinery Hall, World's Fair." © . (WM)

1042.3 Underberg-Albrecht's, H., [Co]. *Export to all parts of the World. Chicago 1893 : The only genuine H. Underberg-Albrecht's Boonekamp of Maag - Bitter.* [New York: Luyties brothers, Sole Agents, 1892?].

15½x8½. (8) p. Folded sheet unfolds to 15½x34. Black and red print. The medicinal beverage was manufactured at Rheinberg on the Niederrhein, Germany. © . (E,WM) P⬇

1044.   Union Pacific. *Sights and scenes in Idaho*: (csuf)
▶Completed citation: 92, (2) p+ color Union Pacific map tipped-in at back cover. White wraps, colored mountain scene, navy and red print.

1044.1 United Indurated Fibre Co. *...The star pail*. [New Jersey: United Indurated Fibre co., "copyright 1889 : World's fair : 1893."]

10x9 die-cut in the shape of pail. (4) p+ text inside both wraps. Front wrap is a brown litho of pail with "Trade mark" at head of title; back wrap shows men around spittoons at the Union League Club in Chicago. C.t. Brown text and lithos. Cute ad for durable seamless pails. ☺ (GLD,E,WM)   P➜ $22 - 50

1044.2 United States Mailing Case Co. *United States Liquid Mailing Cases,...* Boston: n.p., [1893?].

16x14½. (4) p. Folded sheet, black print and illus of their hard-walled padded tubes with brass lids for shipping liquids through the mail. C.t. Sizes and price list for 1893. No WCE content; from intact collection. ☺ (WM)

1044.3 United States Wind Engine and Pump Co. *Gem Steel Wind Engine*. Batavia, IL: The Milwaukee Litho & Engr. Co., n.d.

8½x15. (8) panels. Sheet unfolds to 33½x15 (landscape). Chromoliths of 4 windmills with farm backgrounds on one side, black print description of each mill on back side. No WCE content; from intact collection. [Exhibit located in Ag Bldg, West extension, Group 16, Class 88.] ☺ (WM)

1044.4 *The University of Chicago : announcement of accommodations for World's fair visitors*. Chicago: [University of Chicago], 25 Apr. 1893.

15½x9. (4) p. Folded buff paper, black print. University offering single-bed rooms for $7.50/week and suites for $18/week. Dorms were open to "friends and the educational and religious public," May 15 to Sept 25, 1893. Illus caption on back: "Graduate and divinity dormitories." ☺ (S)

1045.   U of Chicago. U Extension. Taft. *Syllabus of a course of six lecture-studies*: (ref)
▶Add at head of title: "The art of the World's Columbian exposition."

1045.1 *Van Dusen's World fair tourist trips. Personally conducted*. N.p.: n.p., 1893?.

15½x10½. (6) panels. Tri-fold unfolds to 15½x30½, black print. Ad for a 7-day $20 trip with lodging and two meals per day on the Pennsylvania RR starting Aug 7, 1893. Last dated July 12, 1893. ☺ (S)

1045.2 Van Houten, C.J., & Zoon [Co.]. *Exhibit of : Van Houten's Cocoa : at the Worlds* [sic] *Columbian Exposition*. [Weesp, Holland: C.J. Van Houten & Zoon, 1893?].   P↗

8½x15. (10) p includes inside both wraps. C.t. Ad. Chromolith wraps and color illus of their pavilion's exterior and interior. Their bldg is shown on the fairgrounds near the NE corner of the Manuf Bldg, dating this item to 1893. Attractive. ☺ (GLD) $22 - 55

1045.3 Vendome Club. *World's Columbian Exposition 1893. Membership Certificate for the use of* (blank) *Member of Vendome Club Chicago*. Chicago: n.p., n.d.   P➜

11½x7. Round-corner cream card printed in black both sides. Blanks for entering holder's name and address. Back side listing of rates: $2 to $5 per day, good only during the WCE. Club was located at Oglesby Ave and 62nd St, not far from the Midway. Card no. 1232 reproduced here was issued to Silas Chapman Jr. of Hartford. See #1683 for another Vendome item. ☺ (GLD) $25-55

---- Found with *Application for Membership* stub, 9½x19½, printed in black one side with numbers matching card above. Stub gives dues as $25 and lists Chapman's occupation as fire insurance. WCE not mentioned on application stub.

1045.4 *The Venice & Murano Exhibiting Co. of Venice, Italy. At the World's Columbian exposition, Chicago, Ill., 1893...glass and mosaic.* Venice, London [and] Murano: The Venice & Murano Exhibiting Co. [W.B. Conkey co. printers and publishers, Chicago], n.d. **P➜**

12½x17. 24 p+ illus inside both self-wraps. Navy ink print and illus throughout. Frontis (the inside of front wrap) illus of their office in Venice. C.t. On front cover: "[A]dmittance fee refunded on purchase." Caption title: "The Venice & Murano Exhibiting Co. of Venice. At the Chicago World's fair, 1893. Glass and mosaic." They exhibited on the Midway next to Hagenbeck's Arena. ☺ . (E,FM,HML,ref) $85

1045.5 *Vereinigte Fabriken : Zimmer & Co. : Frankfort º/M. : Germany.* N.p.: n.p., n.d.

16x11. Folded stiff card forming wraps, tipped-in (4) p folded sheet. Chromolith cover with 2 factory illus and floral design. C.t. = caption title. On p (3): "Articles exhibited at World's Columbian exposition Chicago 1893." Dr. Julius von Jobst, company president, was a WCE German commissioner. Lists awards. Ad for pharmaceuticals. ☺ . (WM) **P➜**

1045.6 Vermont Hotel. *The Vermont : American and European. 51st Street Boulevard and Drexel Boulevard, Chicago.* N.p.: n.p., n.d.

14x9. (4) p. Folded buff sheet, black print, illus of path leading to hotel in the distance. C.t. "In walking distance of the Exposition." ☺ (S)

1045.7 Vessot, S., and Co. *Vessot's grain grinder and car-axle lubricator.* Joliette, PQ, Can.: n.p., n.d.

22x13½. (4) p. Folded maize sheet, black print, illus of both products. Vertically at front left margin: "Souvenir of the 'Vessot' exhibit in the year 1893, at the World's Columbian Exposition,... (WM)

1045.8 *Victoria Hotel, Chicago. Illustrated Map of Chicago and The Worlds* [sic] *Fair.* Chicago: Victoria Hotel, n.d.

11½x16½. 12 *l.* Buff stiff wraps, blue and gilt print and logo, maroon string-tied. Text and plates of hotel exterior and interior. C.t. Located at Van Buren and Michigan Ave downtown. Also describes trips from the WF to "The Fountain Spring House Hotel Waukesha, Wis.," their sister hotel. ☺ . (WM) **P➜**

1045.9 *The Vieille Montagne zinc co. : at : the World's fair, Chicago, 1893. Zinc and its Applications.* [London: Waterlow & Sons Limited, printers], n.d.

28x22. 15 p. Inside back cover is paged. Light blue wraps, blue and brown print and decorative border. Buff text stock with orange and black print, orange border each page. C.t. Description of their products and exhibit at WCE. ☺ . (WM)

1045.10 *Villeroy & Boch : Dresden.* N.p.: n.p., n.d.

17x11½. (4) p. Folded stiff sheet, blue-black print and floral and trellis design. Describes their detailed kiln-fired art tiles used for interior decoration. No WCE content but found with company ad cards marked WCE. ☺ (WM)

1045.11 Vilmorin, Andrieux & Co. *A few points of general interest : referring to : Vilmorin, Andrieux & Co. : wholesale : seed growers, Paris. On the occasion of Chicago's World fair.* Paris: Vilmorin-Andrieux & co., ᶜ1892.

22½x13½. 12 p. Pale gray-green wraps, dark green print, illus of carnations. C.t. Description of the company and their WCE exhibit. Large chrysanthemum illus on back cover. ☺. (WM)

1045.12 Voris, Emma Frances. *The new Columbian White House Cookery : containing toilet, medical, and cooking receipts,...* Introd. Grace Townsend. Chicago, Philadelphia, and Stockton, CA: Monarch Book Co. (Formerly L.P. Miller & Co.) Publishers, [ᶜ1893 by Charles S. Sutphen].

25½x19. 1 *l* (frontis), (4) p, 2 *l*, (2) contents, 17-527 p+ 15 interspersed unpaged glossy paper plates ᶜ1892 by A. Zeese. Deep slate blue oil-cloth hc, black lettering and design, marbled edges. Frontis port of "Mrs. Potter Palmer." Pulp paper text. Same as #1041 but with different author; Grace Townsend wrote #1041. Complete book; see its salesmen's sample, #1770. (GLD) $90 - 180
---- Also found: Philadelphia: World Bible house, [ᶜ1893 Charles S. Sutphen]. Same as above. ☺ (S)

1045.13 Vuitton, Louis, [Co.]. *Louis Vuitton (Chicago fair–Group 111–leather palace) : 1893.* N.p.: n.p., n.d.

23x16. (4) p. Folded sheet, black print. WCE exhibit content and advantages of Vuitton luggage such as 1-key custom fitting all your pieces. No illus. [They are still in business.] ☺ (WM)

1045.14 Vuitton, Louis, [Co.]. *Louis Vuitton : 1. Rue Scribe : Paris : London : 454 Strand Charing.* [Paris: Louis Vuitton (Imp. Hauducoeur), 1892].

22x14. (1) ad, 38, (1) p ad. Tan wraps with litho of state seals, award medals, and trunks; black print; string-tied. C.t. Illus ad catalog with prices. Vuitton designed and manufactured high quality trunks, hand bags, etc. No WCE content; from an intact collection. [Their trunk exhibit was in the Leather Trades Bldg.] ☺ (GLD)   P➔ $25 - 60

1045.15 Wabash Railroad. *The Wabash Line. A Few facts for visitors to the Columbian Exposition : Chicago. 1893.* N.p.: [Knight, Leonard & Co., Printers, Chicago], n.d.

42½x99. Unfolded map with route and Wabash logo in red, state borders outlined in gold. The two wing panels on either side of map have 6 chromoliths of WCE bldgs each. Other side printed with gold background, chocolate ink railroad illus, and chromolith panels of Dearborn and Detroit stations. Title given is c.t. of folded map; it is printed in black on a light blue banner. On back of folded map: "The banner route to the Columbian Exposition." (WM)

1046.   Wabash RR. *The Wabash line the banner route to Chicago:* (HML,UMD)

1046.1 Wachtel, D., [Co.]. *Kartoffel-Pelanzloch-Maschine.* Breslau, Germany: Schlef. Buchdr., Kunst und Verl. Anstalt v. S. Schottlaenderi, n.d.

28x22½. (4) p. Folded buff sheet, red and dark blue print. C.t. In German front and back and English pp (2)-(3). English title on p (3): "Potato Planting Machine." At top of p (2) in bold red block print: "Worlds [sic] Fair, Chicago 1893." Rough-cut page edges. Attractive ad. (WM)

1046.2 Walburn-Swenson Co. *Beet Sugar. The coming industry.* N.p.: n.p., n.d.

15½x9. (4) p. Folded buff high-rag sheet, black print. "Our exhibit at the World's Fair Agricultural Building Annex represents a modern Beet Sugar factory (1/20 actual size)." C.t. ☺ (WM)

1046.3 Waltham Watch Co. *Catalogue : of : Historical and Antique : Watches : From the famous Collection of : Mr. Evan Roberts, Manchester, Eng., kindly loaned to the American Waltham Watch Company for exhibition at the World's Columbian Exposition, Chicago, U.S.A., 1893.* [Waltham, MA: Waltham Watch co., 1893.]

21½x16½. 23 p. Gray wraps, black print, no design. Text on buff rag stock. List and description of each watch in the exhibit, no illus. ☺ (HU,WM)

1047.　Walton. *Art and Architecture:*　　　　　　　　　　　　　　　　　　$400 - 800
(CCA,CLP,Col,CU,CUA,DC,FLP,HML,HU,KCPL,KSU,Merc,MH,NLA,NPG,PSU,RU,sfpl,slpl,Stfd,StLa,UCB,UIC,uiuc,UMC,UMD,UMN,UPa,UTA,VAM)

1047.1 Walton, William. *...Art and Architecture.* Columbus Edition. Philadelphia: G. Barrie, 1893.

57x40½. 11 vol limited ed. Blue cloth hc, gilt print and design. Has edge ribbons with which to tie cover. SLP has copy no 846. (S,SLP)

1049.1 Walton, William. *...Art and Architecture.* Edition of the White City. Philadelphia: G. Barrie, 1893.

49x37. 11 parts bound in 11 vol. Blue cloth hc with gilt print and design. Text on glossy stock with matted plates. Wide margin version of #1047. KCPL copy no 679 to "Graham C. Lacy." (KCPL)

1049.2 Walton, William. *...Art and Architecture.* Indo-Japan edition. Philadelphia: G. Barrie, [°1893-95].

51x__. 11 parts bound in 2 vol. Limited to 500 copies. (Copy #86-Yale)

1050.　Ward. *Columbus Outdone an exact narrative of the voyage of:* ☺ . (S)
---- Also found: Maize pebble textured wraps; otherwise identical to the hc version. (GLD)　　　　　　　　P➔　　　　　$22 - 50

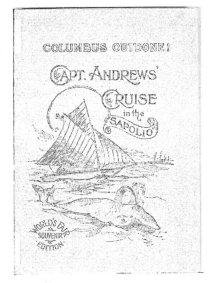

☞ As the book explains, the little "Sapolio" sailed to Spain in late 1892 so Captain Andrews could attend the Columbian Madrid Exposition (see #2448-57). After the Madrid Exposition, which was held in the Monastery of La Rabida, the Sapolio was shipped back to New York, then by rail to Chicago where it was made a part of the Sapolio soap exhibit in the Manufactures Bldg.

1050.1 Ward, Montgomery, & Co. *...List of new views taken during June and July, 1893, for Magic Lantern Slides, The City of Chicago and The World's Fair, the Columbian naval review at Hampton Roads, Va., and New York.* Chicago?: Montgomery Ward & co.?, 1893?

22½x14½. (7) p including back cover. Self-wraps, black print. At head of title: "Extra." C.t. Catalog of available slides by category. (WM)

1050.2 *Ward, Montgomery, & Co's : Special Catalogue of : Organs, Pianos and Sewing Machines : With Fac-simile Lithographic Plates of each style.* Chicago: Montgomery Ward & Co. [The Milwaukee litho & engr. co.], n.d.

20x13. 24 p+ text inside both covers. Rich tan wraps elaborately decorated with yellow and black print, illus of 2 factories. C.t. Beautiful wood-tone chromoliths of their pianos. No mention of WCE; from an intact collection. ☺ . (WM)

1050.3 Warder, Bushnell & Glessner Co. *Champion grain & grass cutters.* [Springfield, OH]: n.p., n.d.

15x22½. 24 p. White glossy wraps, b/w print, bold red dot design with black banner. C.t. Their farm and field machinery. There is a map of the WCE grounds on inside back cover. (WM)

1050.4 Warder, Bushnell & Glessner Co. *Chicago : Compliments of Warder, Bushnell & Glessner Co.* [Springfield, OH and Chicago]: Warder, Bushnell & Glessner, Co.? (G.H. Dunston, Buffalo, NY), n.d.

15½x9. Folded card with chromoliths forming covers: globe and reclining Columbus (front) and factory (back). C.t. A tipped-in folded sheet printed both sides opens to 29½x50½. One side has b/w lithos and text about co's farm machinery, other side has a 3-color map of downtown Chicago with Warder's office location and route to WCE of World's Fair Steamship Co. Ad. ☺ (GLD,E) $25 - 50

1050.5 Ward's Natural Science Establishment. *Ward Exhibit on Mineralogy, World's Columbian exposition, Chicago, Ill.* Rochester, NY: n.p., June 1893.

24½x16. (4) p. Folded sheet, black print. Very long "A–Z" list of exhibited minerals/gems. ☺ (WM)

1050.6 *Warner & Swasey : manufacturers of : Astronomical Instruments.* Cleveland, OH: (Western B.N. co. Chicago), n.d.

8½x14½. White stiff card, black print and fine steel engraved illus of Yerkes telescope. Description of their Yerkes 40-inch diameter objective telescope exhibit in the Manuf and Liberal Arts Bldg. ☺ (WM)

☞ Charles Yerkes gave the telescope to the University of Chicago at the close of the WCE; at the time, it was the largest refractor in the world. It is now located and operating near Lake Geneva, Wisconsin.

1050.7 Warren Chemical and Mfg. Co. *...Asphalt from the Pitch Lake on The Island of Trinidad.* New York: Warren Chemical & M'f'g Co., n.d.

19x13. 32 p. Wraps. Illus. C.t. At head of title: "Columbian Exposition : 1492–1892." Describes their Trinidad pitch and how it was used on roofs and pavements. Ad. ☺ (HML,WM)   **P➔**

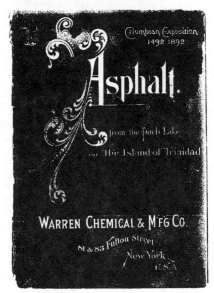

1050.8 Warren, Fuller & Co. *Silver medal Paris : 1889 Warren Fuller Co.* [New York: Warren, Fuller & Co., n.d.

16x11. (4) p. Folded sheet of coated paper. Silver design with black illus of obverse of an Exposition Universelle medal, 1889; awarded to Warren Lange & Cie as shown on medal's reverse, back cover. "Branch of the National Wall Paper Co." No WCE content; from intact collection. ☺ (GLD) $18 - 42

1050.9 *Washburn, Crosby Co. : Flour Mills : Minneapolis, Minn. : World's Columbian exposition 1893.* Minneapolis, MN: Washburn, Crosby Co. (Armstrong & co. lith Boston), n.d.

12½x17½. (32) p+ text inside both covers. Tan stiff wraps, brown print with illus of mill and its two founders. C.t. Brown text print and illus. Mill story, flour, baking with recipes. ☺ (GLD,WM)   **P➔** $16 - 44

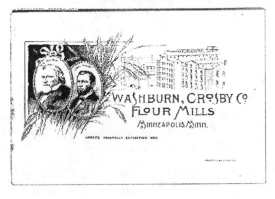

1050.10 Water Circulating Grate Co. *This is the : Only Automatic Water Circulating and : Shaking Grate in the World.* Philadelphia: n.p., [1893].

21x15½. Buff sheet unfolds to 42x30½. Illus of furnace and grate; print in blue ink. Testimonials. Stamped at top: "Don't fail to see the exhibit of our grate boiler house extension, section D, machinery hall, Columbian exposition, Chicago." (WM)

1050.11 *Waterbury Rubber Company, Manufacturers and Owners of : The Sphincter Grip...armored hose patents.* New York: n.p., n.d.

14½x8½. Tan card unfolds to 14½x25. Blue-black print. Price list and testimonials for their woven core hose. No WCE content; issued in a bright orange envelope with: "World's Columbian exposition, Chicago. 1893. Exhibit machinery building annex. Section No. 8, Column A.-43." (WM)

1050.12 Waterbury Watch Co. *The Waterbury Watch Company's century clock.* Waterbury, CT: The Waterbury Watch co., n.d.

8½x7. (8) p. Pale blue-gray wraps, blue print, blue litho of the Century Clock exhibited at the WCE. C.t. Caption title: "The Century Clock." Text explains the exhibited clock: 20 feet high and 6 foot square. Ad. See #854.4 and #1256.3 for other WCE clock information. ☺ (GLD)   P↓ $25 - 55

1050.13 Waterloo Organ Co. *Illustrated Catalogue : of the : Waterloo Organs.* Waterloo, NY: [The Courier printing company, printers and binders, Seneca Falls, NY, 1893].

23x14½. 24 p. White wraps with decorative brown print. Back cover illus of organ. C.t. Dated p 4: "July 1, 1893." Illus catalog of their pump organs. No mention of WCE; from intact collection. . (WM)

1050.14 Watt Mining Car Wheel Co. *...Watt's Patent Self-Oiling Mine Car Wheel.* Barnesville, OH: [Buchanan], n.d.

16x13. (4) p. Folded white sheet, black print. Illus of factory (front) and car (back). On cover: "You will find our exhibit at World's Columbian Exposition, Mines and Mining Building, N.E. Section—Ground Floor." At head of title: co's name and address plus "sole manufacturers of..." (WM)

1050.15 Waukesha Hotel. *The Waukesha Family Club : Jackson Park : Chicago : A select Club for Members visiting the : World's Columbian Exposition : 1893.* [Chicago: S.D. Childs & co., stationers and printers], n.d.   P→

13½x20. 19, (1) p illus of "The Columbia steel cottage." Pale pink stiff card wraps, string-tied, gilt print. Text in blue ink. C.t. Their hotel was 1 block from WCE at 64th and Grace plus sites at "Annex No. 1" and "Annex No. 2," which were a collection of the Columbia steel cottages for visitors. ☺ . (S)

1050.16 Waukesha-Hygeia Mineral Springs Co. *A silver line : An Aqueduct of Health Giving Water.* Waukesha, WI: Waukesha Hygeia, n.d.

16x9. Folded card with a tipped-in folded sheet together making (8) p of text. Black print with blue co logo on front. C.t. Map showing blue pipe line from Waukesha, WI, to Chicago and WCE. 200 drinking booths were available at the WF. Description of request by the WCE for installation of the line; an analysis of the water is given. Their bottled water was also available for city hotels. "Telephone, World's Fair No. 48." Important ad on WF water supply. * . (WM)   P→

1050.17 *Webster Manufacturing Co. Catalogue no. 14. Columbian edition. Engineers, Founders and Machinists. Workers in Metal.* Chicago: Webster M'f'g Co (Thayer & Jackson stationery co.), 1893.

__x__. (2), 209, (3) p index. Brown stiff wraps, silver print and decoration. Back cover silver co logo and "Columbian." C.t.: "1893 : Webster M'f'g Co : Chicago." (S)

1050.18 Wegman & Co. *The Wegman pianos Are First Among the Acknowledged Leaders of America.* N.p.: (Shubel print Chicago), n.d.

15x23. 16 p. Shocking green wraps with gilt print. C.t.: "The Wegman Piano with its wonderful Turning Pin." Twelve pages testimonials. Illus ad. No mention of WCE; from intact collection. (WM)

1051.   Wellesley. *World's Columbian Exposition 1893 Wellesley College:*

☞ The women students of Wellesley and Vassar College were waitresses at the Old Tyme Farmers' Diner on the Midway Plaisance.

1051.1 *Wellington Catering Company : Electric Restaurant (D) : World's Fair Grounds, Jackson Park.* N.p.: n.p., 1893?

> 24x14. Buff card with menu for June 3, 1893, in blue ink (front) and list of their restaurants at WCE in brown ink (back). Patrons paid the waiter; smoking, including cigars, allowed in all restaurants. © (WM)

1052. Wells, Fargo. *Catalogue : Wells, Fargo and Company:* (GLD,csuf,HML,sfpl,UCLA,WM,Yale)
---- Also found: Dark tan (or olive-green) wraps.

1053. Wells, Ida B, et. al. *The Reason Why : The Colored American is not in the World's Columbian Exposition. The Afro-American's Contribution to Columbian Literature.* Chicago: Ida B. Wells, [1893]. P➔

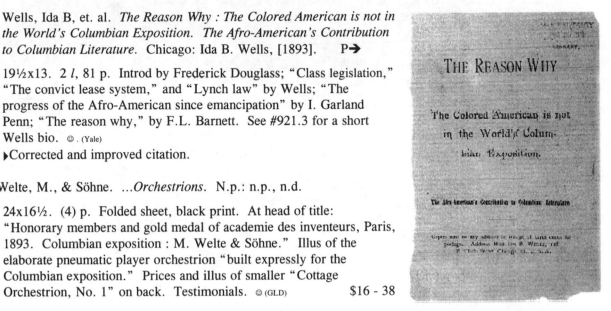

> 19½x13. 2 *l*, 81 p. Introd by Frederick Douglass; "Class legislation," "The convict lease system," and "Lynch law" by Wells; "The progress of the Afro-American since emancipation" by I. Garland Penn; "The reason why," by F.L. Barnett. See #921.3 for a short Wells bio. © . (Yale)
> ▸Corrected and improved citation.

1053.1 Welte, M., & Söhne. *...Orchestrions.* N.p.: n.p., n.d.

> 24x16½. (4) p. Folded sheet, black print. At head of title: "Honorary members and gold medal of academie des inventeurs, Paris, 1893. Columbian exposition : M. Welte & Söhne." Illus of the elaborate pneumatic player orchestrion "built expressly for the Columbian exposition." Prices and illus of smaller "Cottage Orchestrion, No. 1" on back. Testimonials. © (GLD) $16 - 38

1053.2 Werner & Pfleiderer [Co.]. *Specialities of our works : "Universal" Kneading and mixing machines : "Universal" steam ovens.* Cannstatt: n.p., n.d.

> 14x9. (4) p. Folded pale yellow satin-textured stiff card. Co's name boldly printed diagonally on a black background. Caption title taken from pp (2)-(3). Co's three WCE locations shown on back. (WM)

1053.3 Werner, Emerik A. *Die Columbia-Welt-Ausstellung in Chicago 1893.* N.p.: n.p., [1893].

> __x__. 9 p, 13 plates. WCE description rpt from "Allgemeine Bauzeitung," part 1-4, 1893. (UoC)

1053.4 Wessell, Nickel & Gross [Co.]. *Illustrated Catalogue of Piano-Forte Actions.* New York: Wessell, Nickel & Gross (Lindner, Eddy & Clauss, Lith. NY), ᶜ1893 by Wessell, Nickel & Gross.

> 12x16½. 64 p. Drab olive cloth wraps. C.t. Co history and description; factory and piano parts illus. C.t.: "Wessell, Nickel & Gross Piano-Forte Actions." No WCE; from an intact collection. (WM)

1053.5 West Virginia & Pittsburgh Railroad. *Timber and coal. West Virginia : A Manufacturing State.* Baltimore: Juggenheimer, Weib & co., prs., n.d.

> 22x9½. (36) panels. Folded giant sheet opens to 108½x131, black print and illus of the area one side; magnificent multicolor map and "plan of Camden-on-Gauley West Virginia" on the back (18) panels. Promo for development of the area and the RR. No WCE content; form intact collection. © (WM)

1053.6 Western Druggist. Engelhard, G.P., & Co. *Druggists' Columbian Souvenir. With the Compliments of G.P. Engelhard...* Chicago: G.P. Engelhard & Co., Publishers, n.d.

> 16x8½. (8) p. 32x17 sheet folds in quarters like greeting card. Outer sheet face is gold with black print; inner is white with b/w maps labeled "Western Druggist map of the World's Columbian Exposition" and "21 Druggists' Directory to City of Chicago." Floor plan showing exhibits of Pharmacy, vignettes of Manuf Bldg. List of exhibits. Ad for the *Western Druggists' Journal.* © (WM)

1053.7 *Western Electric Company, : Manufacturers of : Electrical Apparatus.* Chicago: n.p., n.d.

7x11½. Buff stiff card, black print both sides. On front: "World's Fair Exhibit, Electrical Building, Section A, Spaces 4, 4 & 5. W.F. Telephone, 156." Exhibit map on back. ☺ (WM)

1053.8 Western Gas Association. *Proceedings of the Western Gas Association.* [St. Louis]: Published by the Association [Flammger & Grahl Co., Publishers], 1900.

23x16½. 545 p+ 4 *l* perforated tear sheets for membership application. One fold out is not included in paging, other plates are included. Dark hunter green cloth hc, blind-stamped, gilt spine print. Contains proceedings of four annual meetings, 1892–95. A WF exhibit was discussed at length during the May 1892, meeting in Detroit (pp 26-45). The 16th annual meeting was held in Chicago, May 16, 1893; no mention of the WCE. There never was a WCE Western Gas Association exhibit. ☺ (GLD) $15 - 35

1053.9 Western Wheeled Scraper Co. *The celebrated Western Wheeled Scraper : or : self-loading and self-dumping cart.* [Aurora, IL: Western Wheeled Scraper Co.] (Slason Thompson & co., printers, Chicago) n.d.

12x21. 40 p. White smooth wraps, ornate b/w print of a scraper and work site. Manufactured at Aurora. Caption title. ☺ . (Stfd–bound WCE Trans Dept Collection)   P➔

1053.10 Western Wheeled Scraper Co. *Western Wheeled Scraper Company : Manufacturers of Earth Moving Machinery.* Aurora, IL: Western Wheeled Scraper co., n.d.

8½x14½. 24 p. Pale yellow wraps with green and black print and illus. C.t. Back cover illus of horse-drawn scraper leveling a country road. Illus catalog of the scrapers. ☺ . (Stfd–bound WCE Trans Dept Collection)

1053.11 Western White Bronze Co. *...Open this Book and see what I have to say to you. ...* N.p.: [(Iowa Printing company, Des Moines), 1893].

22x14½. 32 p. White wraps with black print and illus of newspaper boy. C.t. Testimonials inside front cover and listing of purchasers inside back cover. At head of title: "White Bronze Co." No mention of WCE; from intact collection. (WM)

1053.12 Westinghouse Electric and Mfg. Co. *Alternating current arc system. Some opinions.* [Pittsburgh, PA.: Westinghouse Electric and Manufacturing Company (Davis & Hoburg, prs.)], n.d.

17½x15. (13) p. Green wraps, black print, border design top and bottom. C.t.: "Some opinions of the Alternating Current Arc System." Litho of generator on back. No WCE; from intact collection. ☺ (WM)

1053.13 *Westinghouse Electric and Manufacturing Co. ...The automatic circuit breaker.* Pittsburg: n.p., ᶜ1893.

16½x12. (4) p. Folded sheet, black print, illus of the breaker open and closed on front cover. C.t. For AC lines based on the N. Tesla inventions. No WCE content; from an intact collection. (WM)

1053.14 *Westinghouse Electric and Manufacturing Co. ...The ground detector.* Pittsburg: n.p., n.d.

16½x12. (4) p. Folded sheet, black print. Illus of the detector with 2 indicator lamps (front) and electrical circuit diagram of the detector (back). C.t. For AC lines based on the N. Tesla inventions. Same format as above. No WCE content; from intact collection. (WM

1053.15 Westinghouse Electric and Mfg. Co. Stillwell, L.B. *Transmission of Power. Description of systems and apparatus furnished by Westinghouse...* Pittsburg, PA: Fort Pitt Engraving Co., 1893 [ᶜ1893 Westinghouse Electric & Manufacturing co.].

25½x19½. 97 p. White cord-tied stiff wraps with gray and black bold print and surrounding design. Illus of their equipment with descriptions and details of power transmission including distances and electromotive force. No mention of WCE; from an intact collection. ☺ (WM)

1053.16 Westinghouse Electric and Mfg. Co. *Type E compensator.* N.p.: n.p., ᶜ1893.

15½x11½. 8 p includes covers. Self wraps. Caption title = C.t. Cover illus of the compensator. No mention of WCE; from an intact WCE collection. (WM)

1053.17 *Westinghouse Electric and Manufacturing Co's Apparatus : at the : Columbian Exposition.* N.p.: n.p., n.d.

24x16½. (12) p includes front cover. Self-wraps. C.t. Description of the AC and DC power plants in Mach Hall which generated all of the electricity for the WCE, including the Midway Plaisance. Gives WCE bldg locations of their other power plants. Nikola Tesla's magnetic coil apparatus is described on back cover. ☺(GLD,ICRL) [cover print] P➜ $28 - 65

Westinghouse Electric and Manufacturing Co's Apparatus ...AT THE... Columbian Exposition.

1053.18 Westinghouse Electric and Mfg. Co. Wetzler, Jos[eph]. *A Visit to the Westinghouse Electric Works at Pittsburgh.* Pittsburgh, PA: The Westinghouse Electric and Manufacturing Co., 1892.

30x23. Pp 369-383. Illus. Buff wraps, navy print and design. Rpt from *The Electrical Engineer*, Oct 19, 1892. No WCE; from an intact collection. (WM)

1053.19 *The Weyburn Special Machine Company's : cloth cutting machines...* Chicago: n.p., n.d.

29½x22. (4) p. Folded burnt sienna sheet, black print. Illus of cutter. Used belt-driven flexible drive shaft for maneuverability of a rotating blade unit. No WCE content; from intact collection. ☺(WM)

1053.20 Wheeler, Candace, ed. *Household art.* New York: Harper & Brothers Publishers, 1893.

16x__. xi, 204 p. The last paper, "Decorative and Applied Art," was written by Wheeler for the "Columbian Exposition Art Congress." (HML)

1055. *The white city the Historical, Biographical, and* (Virginia): (GLD,Yale)
▶NB: The spine and the last page refer to this eclectic work as a "prospectus" leading to an intended larger work covering all states and the World's Fair in detail. This may account for the unusual arrangement of content.

1056. *White Star Line of Steamships A Résumé of Twenty Years*: (bgsu,Stfd,WM,)

1056.1 *White Star Line : United States : and : royal mail steamers, exhibit : at the : Worlds* [sic] *fair : Chicago, 1893.* N.p.: White Star Line, n.d.

17½x8½. (8) panels. Sheet unfolds to 17½x34. Brown and red cover print. Illus of their WCE bldg designed by McKim, Mead & White. Caption title: "White star line pavilion, Chicago Exposition. Ad handout. ☺. (S,Stfd,WM)

1057. White. *The World's Columbian Exposition*:
(BD,bgsu,CC,CCA,CU,cul,DC,DU,FLP,FM,GBP,GPL,HML,HU,IHi,NDU,NPG,PSU,RU,SStu,UIC,UMD,UPa,URI,VtHx)
---- Also found: Boston: J.K. Hastings, [ᶜ1893].

1057.1 White, W[illia]m R. *An invention of a farmer who was involved in debt.* Jerseyville, IL: [Jerseyville Republican Print], n.d.

30½x22. Sheet printed in black with illus of White's swinging gate. White was the patentee. In the text: "[T]he government will exhibit it as the best gate in the patent office at the Columbian Exposition at Chicago, the commissioner having sent to me for a model." ☺(WM)

1059. Wilberforce, Archibald, ed. *The capitals of the globe : The political, commercial, artistic and sacred capitals of Europe, Asia, Africa, North America, South America and the West Indies : with graphic and accurate descriptions of...* New York: Peter Fenelon Collier, 1893 [ᶜ1893 by Peter Fenelon Collier]; New York: Peter Fenelon Collier, 1894 [ᶜ1893 by Peter Fenelon Collier]. ▶Completed title.

1893 version: Described in original bibliography. (S)

1894 version: 34½x27½. 4 *l*, 586 p. Tan (or brown) cloth hc, gilt and black print and ornate design of 4 capitals and 4 people of various ethnic extraction, marbled edges. The section entitled "Chicago," pp 495-513, with illus, describes the WCE. © (GLD,ref) $25 - 45

1060.1 Williamson, Mary A. *Miss Mary A. Williamson, designer of embroideries.* Indianapolis, IN: n.p., n.d.

7½x12½. (3) p. Folded stiff card, black print, back blank. C.t. On p (2): "Manager of Decorative Art Needle Work for Indiana for World's Fair." © (WM)

1060.2 Wilovid Hotel. *Hotel Wilovid, 5811 & 5813 Madison Avenue...* Chicago: n.p., n.d.

27½x21. 1 *l*, black print. Illus of hotel in upper left. Located within one block of WF entrance; telephone: "110—World's fair." Could also be booked through the Bureau of Public Comfort. © (WM)

1060.3 Wilson, Francis. *The Eugene Field I Knew.* New York: Charles Scribner's Sons, 1898 [ᶜ1898 by Charles Scribner's Sons].

21x13½. 8 *l*, 128 p, 6 *l*. Illus (some folding) found within the text are not included in paging. Half white vellum over pale blue paper covered boards, gilt print. Rag paper, rough cut edges. T.p. in red and black. Facsimile of Field's work in pocket inside back cover. Limited to 204 copies. GLD has autographed copy no 140. Field was a poet who lived in Chicago. Brief mention of Field giving tour of the WCE to friends. © (GLD) $25 - 75

1060.4 Winchester Hotel Co. *When you visit The World's Fair : Stop at the Winchester Cor. Sheridan Ave. and 64ᵗʰ Street. "Only Four Blocks Away."* [Chicago]: n.p., n.d.   **P→**

13½x20½. (16) p. Pale green wraps, black print, illus of hotel. C.t. Admin Bldg illus inside front wrap. Map giving hotel's location on back. Hotel info. Registration coupon on p (15). Illus of WCE bldgs by A. Zeese; captions include dimensions and costs. © (GLD,S) $22 - 55

1060.5 Windermere Hotel. *Hotel Windermere : Jackson Park, Cornell Avenue and Fifty-Sixth Street.* Chicago: [Windermere Hotel], n.d.

17½x13. 16 p. Buff stiff wraps, hotel's logo in gilt. Caption title. Litho of hotel on caption page. Brown print and lithos. Gives plan and room costs, as well as location relative to WCE. Commendation issued by WCE dignitaries, rpt on p 2. WCE train trip to Windermere by "J.J. Grafton, NY." © . (WM)

1061.   *Windsor Castle at Chicago To which is added The Home of Sunlight Soap:* (CCA,csuf,HML,ICRL,LBA,UIC,WM)

1061.1 Winslow Bros. Co. *...Exhibit of The Winslow Bros. Co. : in the : manufactures and liberal arts building, Section H, Block 3.* [Chicago: Winslow Bros. Co.], n.d.

23x10. (8) p. Sheet unfolds to 23x40. At the head of title: "Columbian Exposition, 1893." Illus of the exhibit, the factory, and a gate. Makers of ornamental iron, bronze, and brass for architectural construction. Office in Chicago. (WM)

1061.2 Winterhoff & Wessel Co. *Curled grass : exhibited by : Winterhoff & Wessel, at the : Agricultural Building. F.G. 4, Gallery. World's Columbian exposition.* Chicago: Heun & Lichtner, printers, n.d.

28x20. (2) p. Sheet printed on green (or blue) pulp. English on one side; German on other side. © (WM)

1061.3 Wire Mat Co. *Every Home, Office, Business House, School House, Church, Hotel, Soda Fountain and Street Car in the World needs them : The Best Wire Mat and Matting in the World...* [Decatur, IL: Wire Mat Co.], n.d.

8½x15. 8 p+ text inside wraps. Light maize wraps, litho of matting encircling the globe. Stamped on back: "See World's Fair Exhibit, Manufactures B'ld'g., Department Q-104. N.E. Entrance." C.t. (WM)

1062. Wisthaler. *By Water to the Columbian Exposition*: (HU)
▶Add cover description: Brown cloth hc, gilt print.

1062.1 Woman's Christian Temperance Union. Wright, Elvirton. ...*Tested*. Chicago: n.p., [1893].

15½x10. 6 p. String-tied buff wraps, green print and illus of woman on pedestal. At head of title: "National leaflet. L.T.L. no. 202." C.t.: "Exposition Souvenir 1893." Exhibit ad. ⓒ (S)

1062.2 *Woman's Directory, Purchasing and Chaperoning Society*. Chicago: n.p., n.d.

18x15½. (4) p. Folded pink sheet, blue-gray print. Caption title. Describes their WF services: finding room and board, guides at $1/hour, run errands, and chaperone men or ladies—$1 to $2/evening. ⓒ (WM)

1063. *Wonderful Chicago and the World's fair*: (IHi)
▶Add author: George W. Melville.

1063.1 Wooten Co. ...*Miniature catalogue of : Remodeled Wooten Desks : strictly high grade*. Richmond, IN: n.p., 1893?

15x9. (8) p includes self-wraps. Black print. C.t. At head of title: "1893 : Remodeled Desks! Greatly Reduced Prices!" Illus and descriptions of their roll top desks with swing-out file drawers. No WCE content; from intact collection. ⓒ (WM)

1063.2 Worcester Corset Co. *Royal Worcester : W C C*. [Worcester, MA: Worcester Corset co.] (G.H. Buek & co. lith., New York), n.d. P➔

15x9. (8) p+ text inside both chromolith wraps. Caption title on inside front wrap: "A souvenir from our exhibit of Royal Worcester WCC Corsets. World's Columbian exposition, Chicago, 1893." Five chromoliths of fancy corsets from this exhibit. Beautiful ad. ⓒ (GLD) $30 - 65

1065.1 *World's Columbian edition : "The Blue Book" : textile directory of the United States and Canada, comprising Cotton, Woolen, Silk, Jute, Flax and Linen... including a history of textiles, colored illustrations of the World's fair buildings, state buildings, etc., with cost and size of same*. New York: Davison publishing co., ᶜ1893 by the Davison Publishing Co.

24x16. 469, (1) p. Royal blue cloth beveled hc, gilt print and a small black illus; black leather spine with gilt print. T.p. in blue ink. On t.p.: "Sixth annual edition. 1893–4." Gilt ads on back. [St. Louis WF, 1904, edition also exists.] (S,Stfd)

1067.1 *The World's Columbian Polyorama : Three exhibitions in one*. N.p.: n.p., n.d.

61x23½. (2) p. Sheet printed both sides in black ink. Overprinted: "Nov. 1, Port Mills, Vt." Large illus of lecturer pointing to a projected image on a screen. Admission 20 cents. One of the 3 exhibitions ("Sec. III") featured the WCE. ⓒ (UVM)

1067.2 *World's fair*. N.p.: n.p., n.p.

25½x17½. Unpaged lined writing tablet, purple cloth hinge at top edge. Cardboard wraps with color litho of Uncle Sam sitting on a money-filled barrel atop a globe with ethnic peoples gathered below. ⓒ . (S)

1068. *World's Fair and the Journey Thereto, by We Four*: (PSU)

1069.1 *World's Fair Columbian Souvenir : for the pacific coast. Composed of All the Principal World's Fair Buildings, with full and complete description of same*. San Francisco: H. & P. Fredrick, 1893, ᶜ1893.

47x31. 2 *l*, 49 p. Light blue cloth beveled hc, decorative end papers. Each litho is opposite a descriptive text page. ⓒ . (sfpl)

1069.2 *The : World's fair : combination : Needle and Toilet : pin case. Containing a complete assortment of the best : Elliptic Large Eyed Needles : bonnet, shawl, toilet pins, etc.* [Germany]: n.p., n.d.   **P➜**

18½x11½. (6) panels. Elaborate triptych pin case opens to 18½x33½. C.t. The c.t. panel is lime green, peach, and maize with black and open block white print. The outsides of the two folding panels have b/w lithos: "Marriage of Pocahontas the Indian princess to John Rolfe in Virginia 1613" and "Columbus at the court of Spain–Queen Isabella sacrificing her jewels." Pinned to the 3 inside panels is a large assortment of "Cantbendem trademark" needles, pins, and hat pins. Ad likely from the German exhibit in the Manuf Bldg where several needle companies exhibited. ☺ (GLD) $40 - 85

1069.3 *The World's Fair Co-operative Bureau : Organized for the Purpose of Assisting People who wish to Visit the : Great World's Fair : Columbian Exposition : in Chicago, in 1893.* Chicago: R.R. Donnelley & Sons Co., Printers, n.d.

18½x14½. 3, (5) p including covers. Buff wraps with black print. C.t. Back cover illus of "The Great Western." Endorsements dated 1891–92. Map at center shows location of the Bureau and The Great Western Hotel of 400 rooms. ☺ (S)

1069.4 World's Fair Encampment Co. ...*World's fair encampment and Hotel Fraternity.* ___ : ___, ___.

8½x15. 14, (2) p+ text inside front cover and location map inside back cover. Tan wraps, black print. C.t. At head of title: "Incorporated under..." Illus of hotel and tents on back cover. Located at 71st and the Lake Shore. Rental ad for tents of various styles and sizes "with good floor and a fly, making it absolutely waterproof." Conducted on the European plan. See #1127.1 for more Hotel Fraternity. (S)
---- Also found: Same covers in maize, black print. Different text on p (1). (S)

1070.   *World's Fair Excursions. Special features of the "New England grocer's" plan. A Simple, Business-Like Arrangement, which all can Understand. Payments can be made in cash or installments.* Boston: Benjamin Johnson, Manager, Grocers' Exchange, [1893].

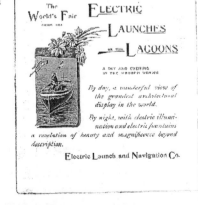

24½x15½. 26 p includes front wrap. Tan wraps, black print, illus of Admin Bldg by A. Zeese. Frontis port of Johnson. WCE bird's-eye view on back. C.t. Caption title: "World's fair excursions. The 'New England grocer's' plan." Their rooms were at Ellis and 65th St. See #945.1-4 for other New England Grocers' items. ☺ (GLD,BPL,CCA,CHx,S,WM) $18 – 44
▶Completed and improved citation
---- Also found: Self-wraps with illus of Admin Bldg. 23 p. Frontis port Johnson. Illus of "Our Chicago Homes," Woodlawn, on back. (S)

1071.   *The World's Fair from the Electric Launches*: ☺ (S)   **P➜**
▶Alternate author and added info: Electric Launch and Navigation Co. Folded off-white glossy sheet, dark blue and olive-green print. C.t. Jackson Park map pp (2)-(3) with the Launch route and stops in red. Images of launch, front and back.

1071.1 *The World's Fair : 1492 1892 : Souvenir.* [Germany]: n.p., n.d.

7x12½. (4) p. Folded tan card. Yellow background with red and blue print and color illus of [Palmer Cox?] brownies. C.t. On back: "Household Treasure : Family Friend." Inside is pastel green with 5 tipped-in "Sharps : superior" needle packets plus samples of larger needles and pins in a cloth swatch. [Ad most likely from the German exhibit in Manufactures Bldg where several needle companies exhibited.] ☺ (GLD,E)   **P➜** $30 - 55

1071.2 World's Fair Hotel [and Boarding] Bureau. *Go With Us. Eastern Agency of World's Fair Hotel Bureau of Chicago.* N.p.: n.p., n.d.

11½x7½. (4) p. Folded buff card. C.t. Advertisement for round-trips from Boston for $60 first class to $35 for "room in good location." Special excursion described on back. © (S)

1071.3 World's Fair Hotel and Boarding Bureau. *Will you stop in Chicago? This is the authorized agent of the World's Fair hotel and boarding bureau.* Chicago: n.p., n.d.

22x10. (2) p. White (or yellow) sheet printed both sides in black ink. Description of Bureau. Chicago map on back. A handout given to passengers during railroad trips. © (GLD,S,WM) $15 - 30

1072.   World's Fair Hotel and Boarding Bureau. *World's Columbian Souvenir hand-book*: (S)
---- Also found with author: World's Columbian Tourist Co. Pink wraps, black print. C.t. At head of title: "Compliments of Columbian Tourist Co., Boston." (S)
▶NB: For another Chicago Hand-book Company guide, see #1210.

1074.   *The World's Fair In Commemoration of the World's*: (MSI,WM)

1074.1 *World's fair : military tournament : at stock pavilion.* N.p.: n.p., n.d.

13½x6½. Tan paper, orange print and design. Cover illus of Hussar in full uniform; vertical print beside illus: "A glittering spectacle : 200 men and 100 horses." Memoranda at centerfold. Back cover: "12,000 good seats at 50¢." © (WM)

1074.2 World's Fair Protective Entertainment Association. *The Problem Solved. A Visit to the Columbian exposition brought within the reach of all by the World's Fair Protective...* [St. Louis], n.p., [1892?].

30½x23. (4) p. Fold buff sheet, black print, illus of West Pullman depot. Caption title. Illus of West Pullman grounds p (2); bird's-eye of WCE p (3); map of Chicago, WCE, and West Pullman south of Jackson Park on back. $3/week in tent city with wooden floors. Rules, conditions, entertainment. © (WM)

1074.3 World's Fair Protective Entertainment Association. *Special advantages of the World's Fair Protective Entertainment Association.* [St. Louis]: World's Fair Protective Entertainment Association, n.d.

22x15½. (4) p. Folded sheet, blue print. Ad for the "Encampment," a tent city south of the fair on the Lake Michigan shore. $2.50 per week plus cot and linen fees; entertainment secured for $5/week. © (IHi)

1074.4 World's Fair Protective Entertainment Association. *The World's Fair Protective Entertainment Association. An economic entertainment encampment at Chicago during the World's Fair.* St. Louis, MO: World's Fair Protective Entertainment Association, n.d.

15½x8½. 14 p. Self wraps, buff pulp paper, black print. C.t. © (IHi)

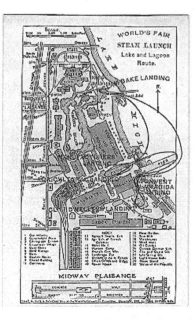

1074.5 *The World's Fair Steam Launch : Lake and Lagoon Route.* Chicago?: [World's Fair Steam Launch], [ᶜ1892 by Rand McNally & Co.].   P➔

14x9. (2) p. Buff stiff card with yellow background WCE grounds map one side, text on the other in red and black. Map is overprinted in red with the 5-mile launch route. A "Rand, McNally & Co.'s Card Map of the World's Columbian Exposition." Fare 25¢—50¢ for viewing the WCE fireworks. © (GLD) $18 - 40

1075.1 World's Fair Sunday School Building. Jacobs, B.F. *Circular No. 3. World's Fair Sunday School Building.* [Chicago]: n.p., n.d.

28x21½. (3) p. Folded white sheet, black print. At end: "B.F. Jacobs, Chairman of the International S.S. Committee." Describes bldg in the planning stages before the WF opened. Chicago S.S. workers raised $10,000, and a bldg was erected on Stony Island Ave between the 57th and 61st St entrances. © (S)

1075.2 *World's fair : Temperance Encampment Association,...* Chicago: World's Fair Temperance Encampment Association, [1893].

> 23x15½. (4) p. Folded sheet, black print. Map of WCE grounds and south Chicago on back. Encampment occupied a square block at Indiana Ave and 57th St, west of Washington Park. They rented tents and furnishings at $10 per week, sold meals for 50¢, provided day care for 25¢ per day, and offered 5¢ fares to the WCE. Ad. Each tent was 10x14 feet and had a slop pail and water bucket supplied without extra charge. © (GLD) $20 - 45

1075.3 *World's Fair Tourist Company.* New York: World's Fair Tourist Co., 1892?

> 15x8. (6) p. Tri-fold cream sheet opens to 15x24, black print. C.t. = caption title. Solicits contract payments of $1/week for 37 weeks (plus lodging costs) for a 1-week WCE visit originating in New York. Included $3000 accidental death insurance. "Gen. Joshua L. Chamberlain, President." © (GLD) $30 - 50

> ☞ Joshua Lawrence Chamberlain, a hero at the Civil War battle of Gettysburg and leader of the Grand Army of the Republic, was later president of Bowdoin College, Brunswick, Maine, and Governor of Maine. His Brunswick home has been restored and is open to the public.

1076. *World's Fairs from London 1851 to Chicago 1893*: (GLD,FM,UBW,UCB)
> ---- Also found: 25x17½. 1 *l* frontis, (6) p tri-fold bird's-eye, (1)-82, (1) p, 1 *l*. Frontis is Columbus port. Maize wraps with black print, lighter maize design and border. Horse illus on outside back cover. Ads inside both covers. Found with and without a tipped-in letter, reproduced in blue ink, from the WCC Director-General attesting to the value and accuracy of this authorized publication. $40 - 70

1076.1 *The World's Inn : Midway Plaisance : facing the fair grounds : Chicago. Chas. E. Leland. Manager.* Chicago: Rand, McNally & Co., Printers and Engravers, n.d. **P➜**

> 15½x9. (8) p+ map that unfolds to 19x24. Colored wraps and text. C.t. Text begins on verso of cover. Lodging ad. ☺ . (csuf,Stfd)

1076.2 Yates, May. *World's fair children's building. "The joyous message of vegetarianism."...Address at the woman's building, "What shall we eat?"* N.p.: n.p., [1893].

> 23x15½. (2) p. Sheet with black print and red overprint: "Children's building!...Aug. 3d and 5th." Port of Yates on front. Yates represented the "Vegetarian Federal Union" in England; as noted in this lecture ad, the Union's WCE exhibit was in the Vegetarian Annex, Manufactures and Liberal Arts Bldg, British Section. ☺ . s)

1076.3 Young, W.D., [Co.]. *American Made : and the only : practical : Stained Glass Substitute : designs unlimited.* Philadelphia: W.D. Young, n.d.

> 16x10. (5) p including inside back cover. Mottled light blue and pink self-wraps, blue print. Illus of Christ and children done in "Stained Glass Substitute" on back. Inside front cover: Sefton Brothers, Chicago agent. No WCE content; from an intact collection. (WM)

1077. Young. *How to celebrate the Four Hundredth Anniversary*:
> ▸Add annotation: Very early plea for NYC as site of an 1892 Columbian Fair. William Euclid Young worked for the NY Stock Exchange and was "Secretary of the Committee of the Christopher Columbus Exposition of 1892." He doesn't appear as author on later NY Committee for the International Exposition of 1892 documents.

1078. Zimmerman. *Vierhundert Jar Amerikanischer*: (S)

Chapter 6

GUIDES

1079. *The ABC guide*:
  ▸Correction to original Nickle Pub citation: T.p. title given (not c.t.)
  ---- Also found: Chicago: Nickle publishing co., ᶜ1893 (on cover).
  17x13. C.t.: "The A-B-C Guide of Chicago and the Worlds [sic]
  Columbian Exposition." At top: "New and revised : Edition for 1893."
  At bottom: "May, 1893." (S)   **P→**
  ---- Also found: *The ABC guide of Chicago and the World's Columbian
  exposition. Replies to questions asked every day by the guests and citizens
  of the World's fair city.* [Chicago: Walter J. Van Derslice, ᶜ1893].
  17x13. 128 p+ print inside covers. Beige wraps, red print and borders.
  T.p. title given. C.t.: "Guide to Chicago and the World's Fair." At top
  of cover: "New and revised : edition for 1893."

1080. *American-Hispano Pocket Guide of the*: (CCA,FLP,HML,ICRL,Merc,PSU,UPa,UTA)

1080.1 *Appleton's general guide to the United States and Canada illustrated...* New York: D. Appleton and Co.,
  1893,

  17½x12. 20, 616, 16 p+ plus folding maps and plates. Flexible paper-covered cardboard covers stamped
  in gilt. WCE discussed on pp (585)-99. (csuf,HU,OU)

1080.2 *...Authentic daily programme of the midway plaisance : This Programme is given FREE that you may see
  the leading attractions in systematic order.* N.p.: n.p., n.d.

  22½x15. (4) p. Folded sheet in newspaper format, black print. At head of title: "Ice Railway—greatest
  attraction in Midway—South of Ferris Wheel." Ice Railway ads at top and bottom of all pages. (S)

1081. *Authentic guide to Chicago and the World's Columbian exposition*:
  ▸Add: [ᶜ1893 by A.J. Burton]. Folding map follows front cover.
  ---- Also found: Maroon pebbled wraps, gilt print. (GLD) $30 - 50

1085. *The buildings of the World's Fair with map* [Montgomery]: (ICRL)
  ---- Also found: *The buildings of the World's fair with map of the grounds. A useful souvenir.* Chicago:
  The Standard guide co., n.d. Light gray coated wraps, black print. Map by Flinn. (ICRL)

1088. *Chicago and the World's Columbian Exposition*: (GLD,S,UCB,uiuc,WM)
  ---- Also found: Chicago: Midway Publishing Co., ᶜ1892. Peach (or rose-tan) wraps with black (or
  brown) print and globe logo of Dept of Publicity and Promotion. After title at bottom of cover:
  "Department of publicity and promotion, Rand, McNally building, Chicago, Ill." © (GLD,S)
  ---- Also found: Chicago: Midway Publishing Co., ᶜ1893. Rose-tan wraps, brown print. (UCB)

1089. *Chicago and World's Fair guide*: (UIC)
1091. Chicago Cottage Organ. *Map and Pocket Guide of Chicago*: (WM)

1091.1 *Chicago Exposition : guide & description.* Bruxelles: E. Lyon-
  Claesen, éditeur, n.d.

  23x15½. 79 p. Carmine-red cover. Frontis bird's-eye view with
  caption and key in French. (BRA)

1093. Chicago Jewelers. *Columbian souvenir Visitors Directory*:
  (GLD,MOHx,NLA)   **P↗** $25 - 50
  ▸Alternate author and added info: Committee of the World's Fair Bureau of Information of the Chicago
  Jewelers Association. (44) p includes 18 plates of WCE and state bldgs ᶜ1892 by Zeese. Tan wraps,

brown print and design of woman with shield; Columbus Memorial Bldg at the SE corner of Washington and State St illus on back cover. Illus list of 54 jewelry businesses in Chicago area, many with WCE exhibits. WCE bird's-eye view inside front cover, map of Jackson Park inside back cover.

1094.1 *The Columbian guide : to : Chicago : and the : World's Fair.* N.p.: G[rosvenor] K. Glenn, Publisher [Hamblin Printing Co., Chicago], ᶜ1893.

19½x13½. (6), (11)-114, (12) p. Maps, illus, ads. Blue-gray wraps, navy blue print, bird's-eye view. After c.t.: "Magnificently illustrated." WCE throughout, especially chap X-XIII. ☺(GLD)   P➜ $18 - 45

1094.2 Conkey, W.B., Co. "To the Exhibitor:" Letter. 21 Apr. 1893. Chicago.

28x21½. (1) p. Printed letter on letterhead stationery: "Office of the official publications of the World's Columbian Exposition..." Requests exhibitor data for the *Official Catalogue*, #1176. The charge for each exhibit's listing was $5/line up to seven lines maximum. ☺. (UMD)

1095.   *Conkey's complete guide to the World's Columbian:* (GLD,CCA,IStU,LBA,WM)
---- Also found: 221 p. Flexible brown cloth hc, gilt print. Marbled edges.
---- Also found: 221 p. Decorative wraps: color litho of Peristyle, lettering in black and red. Frontis of Admin Bldg and horse statue.

1095.1 *"Counting the Cost." World's Fair : Chicago, 1893. Midway Plaisance : Unique Attractions : Never before seen in this Country : directory including Official Charges : And also Special Features in Jackson park.* [Chicago?]: Miller & Marsland, n.d.

16½x7. (4) p. Tri-fold rose sheet opens to 16½x21; print on 4 of the 6 panels. One line descriptions of each Midway exhibit including admission cost. Bottom of cover: "Price, 5 Cents." ☺. (csuf)

1095.2 Davis, Augustine. *...Chicago in a nut shell : A Convenient and Reliable Reference Book.* Chicago: [Columbian exposition savings co.], ᶜ1892 by Augustine Davis.

12x8. 32 p. Lavender stiff wraps, black print. Text only, no illus. A brief city history, demographics, and quick guide to Chicago. Includes "secret societies" and "colored societies." WCE on last 7 p. ☺(GLD)   P➜ $18 - 38

1095.3 *Deere & Company's indexed standard guide map of the World's Columbian Exposition at Chicago, 1893.* [Chicago]: Rand, McNally & Co., 1892.

Map on 33x59 sheet. Part colored. On verso: "Deere & Company's handy map of Chicago World's Fair, 1893," with inset: "Rand McNally & Co.'s card map of Chicago." Text in margins. Similar to other Rand McNally maps: #1130.1, #1156.2, and #1170.1. (IHi)

1097.   Dredge. *The Columbian exposition of 1893: what to see and:* (Col)

1098.   *The economizer how and where to find the Gems:* (HML,IHi)
▶Cover title: "Rand, McNally & Co's : economizer : How and Where to Find the : Gems of the Fair."

1099.   *The English-German Guide to the City of Chicago:* (ICRL,UTA)

1100.   *Facts about the World's fair:* (GLD,WM)   P➜ $25 - 65
▶Add author: Evans, C.H., & Sons.

1102. Flinn. *The best things to be seen*: (CCA,CU,HML,HU,ICRL,MOHx,NDU,NLA,S,UGa,UIC,WM)

1103. Flinn. *Chicago the Marvelous* [1891]: (FLP,FU,HU,IHi,ISU,UAT,UIC)

1104. Flinn. *Chicago the Marvelous* [1892]: (GLD,CU,FLP,FU,ISU,Stfd,UIC,USFr) $35 - 70
    ▶Standard n.d.; Bright royal blue cloth hc, gilt and black print. Has the
"Chicago has arisen" frontis facing the t.p. and bird's-eye plate inserted
before text begins on p 17.   **P➜**

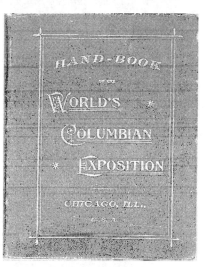

1104.1 Flinn, John J[oseph]. *Chicago : The Marvelous City of the West : a
history, an encyclopedia : and a guide : second edition : illustrated :
1893.* Chicago: National book and picture co., n.d.

    17x13½. viii (ads), 1 *l* frontis "Chicago has arisen," (10), xvii, (1) p, 1
l bird's-eye view, 17-632 p with interspersed unpaged plates, iii-xxxii
(ads). Red cloth hc, gilt and black print, marbled edges. Spine title:
"Standard guide to Chicago : 1893 : Flinn : illustrated." The 1893 issue
of #1103 and #1104. ☺ (UIC)

1107. Flinn. *Guide to...grounds and buildings* [40 p]: (BCHx,ICRL,S)

1108. Flinn. *Guide to...grounds, buildings* [67 p]: (UIC)

1109. Flinn. *Hand-book of the World's*: (GLD,ICRL,IHi,UTA) $30 - 60
    ▶Add cover description [1st ed]: Black leather hc, gilt print and gilt
spine print.   **P➜**

1110. Flinn. *Official Guide to Midway Plaisance*: (E,Yale)

1111. Flinn. *Official guide to the WCE*: (Amh,B,Berk,bgsu,BrU,CCA,CLP,Col,CU,cul,DC,DU,FLP,
HML,HU,ICRL,IHi,IStU,KSU,LBA,LU,MCHx,Merc,MIT,MOHx,MSI,MSL,NDU,NLA,NPG,OU,RSA,sfpl,SHB,
SML,Smth,SPL,SStu,UAB,UCD,UCLA,UGa,UIC,UMD,UMN,UTA,UVM,Yale)

1112. Flinn. *Offizieller Führer durch den Columbischen*: (ICRL)

1112.1 Flinn, John J[oseph]. *The Standard Guide to Chicago : illustrated :
World's Fair Edition : 1893...* Chicago: The Standard Guide Co.
[Donohue & Henneberry, printers and binders], n.d. [© by The Standard
Guide co.].

    17x12. L, 584 p. Red cloth hc with black print; black diagonal cover
banner with "CHICAGO" in gilt. Same frontis as #1104 and #1104.1:
"Chicago has arisen." ☺ . (HU,ISU,Knox,S)

1114. *Godey's Illustrated Souvenir Guide to Chicago*: (GLD) $25 - 55

1117. *Guide book to the Joss House*: (GLD,WM)   **P➜** $18 - 48
    ▶Add: At head of c.t.: "Wah Mee Exposition Company, World's fair,..."
Self-wraps.

1118. *Guide to Chicago valuable and reliable information*: (GLD) $18 - 40
    ---- Also found: (20) p. Turquoise wraps, black print. (GLD)

1119. *A guide to the Columbian World's Fair*: (GPL,ICRL,UTA)
    ---- Also found: 65, (2) p. (ICRL)

1120. *Guide to the Exhibits of American Wool Manufactures*: (UMD)

1121. *Guide to the Field (Columbian) Museum*: (GLD,FM,MSI)
    ▶Completed listing of the first seven editions of the guides. All are 19x12½ and have gray wraps with
black print (except presentation copy below). C.t. = t.p. Each has information about the early Field
Columbian Museum collections that came from the WCE by gift or purchase.
    ---- [1st ed]: 1894. 248 p. No index; many blank leaves interspersed.

---- Also found [1st ed]: Maroon leather-bound-gilt-edged presentation copy, No 17, to Frederick J.V. Skiff, Director of the Museum and Chief of the WCE Dept of Mines. Laid-in blank pages with tipped-in tickets, opening announcements, clippings. (FM)

---- 2nd ed: 1894. 263 p. includes index.

---- 3rd ed: 1895. 251 p. includes index.

---- 4th ed: 1896. 267 p. includes index.

---- 5th ed: 1897–98. 277 p. includes index.

---- 6th ed: 1900. 176 p. includes index.

---- 7th ed: 1903. 168 p. includes index. Tipped-on notice sheet on front cover: "The collections of the Division of Transportation have been withdrawn from exhibition." [No documentation at FM explains where they went or what happened to them.]

☞ Even though there are additional editions of the guides, after the Transportation exhibits were removed, the overall exhibit content became less and less related to the initial WCE acquisitions. See #844-846.1 and 2446.FM for other Field Museum publications and info on their collections.

1122.   *Guide to World's fair buildings. And toilet rooms*: (S)

1123.   Hamilton. *The Time-Saver*: (csuf,D,HML,NUL,S,UIC)

1123.1 Handy Guide Co. *...Handy Guide to the Columbian exposition containing Alphabetically Arranged Information of Buildings and Grounds*. Chicago: Handy Guide Co., 1892.

15x9. 32 p+ folded map of Jackson Park at back cover. At head of title: "price 10 cents." © (S)

1124.1 *The Heart of Chicago at a Glance. Free guide to the Theatres, Art Galleries, Museums, Parks, Panoramas, Palaces, Clubs, Libraries, societies*. 20th ed. [Chicago]: n.p., 1891.

20x10. 24 p. Tan stiff wraps, black print and heart design. The front wrap opens into a map of "The Heart of Chicago" and the rear wrap into a panorama of the World's Fair. (ref) $45

1126.   Hill. *Hill's souvenir guide to Chicago and the World's fair*: (GLD,E,FLP,IHi,SHB,uiuc) $22 - 46
---- Also found 1893 ᶜ1892: 248 p.

1127.1 Hotel Fraternity. *The hotel and guide map to the World's fair and vicinity. A.N. Marquis & Co.'s official Guide Map of the World's Columbian Exposition and vicinity*. Chicago: A.N. Marquis & Co., Publishers, ᶜ1893 by A.N. Marquis & Co.

51x38. Unfolded map with black print and red and gold overlay. City sections numbered in red: 1-56. Hotel Fraternity info and rates at bottom of map, see #1069.4. Indices on 4 backside panels. © (S)

1128.   Hull. *Illustrated world's fair guide containing map*: (CU,S)

1129.   Igleheart. *A "fair" companion*: (CCA,WM)
---- Also found: 26x20. Pale green wraps, black print. C.t.: "A 'Fair' Companion." Lower left front cover: "Price 50 Cents." Double page map is of Jackson Park.

1130.   *Illustrated guide to the World's fair and Chicago being a complete directory*: (HML,S,UMD)
---- Also found Wanamaker: Light blue wraps with black print and no design.

1130.1 *Indexed : Guide Map : and Key to : World's Fair Buildings, Grounds and Exhibits*. Chicago: Rand, McNally & co., printers, n.d.

14x7. 50½x39 sheet tipped-in tan stiff wraps, black print. On front wrap: "Old Times Distillery Co. Louisville, Ky." Distillery's WCE exhibit bldg illus on map.
---- Also found: "With Compliments of C.J. Van Houten & Zoon" on front cover and illus of their bldg exhibiting chocolates on map. See #1045.2 for another Van Houten item.
© . (E,ICRL,WM)

1132.   International Linguistics Institute. *Linguistics guide in Thirty Foreign Languages*: (MH,NDU)
▶Add annotation: Found at Library of Congress under alternate title, see #890. 3 *l*, (ix)-xx, 202 p.

1134.   Kenny. *Illustrated guide to Cincinnati and The World's Columbian Exposition*:   (GLD,Yale) $30 - 60

1134.1 *Knight, Leonard & co's : MAP : and : birds-eye view of Chicago.* Chicago:
Knight, Leonard & Co., ___ .

> 17x9. Wraps with folded colored map which opens to 94x66. Violet wraps
> with black print. Back wrap blank. Bird's-eye view map of WCE is drawn in
> perspective.   . (IHi)   P➜

1135.   Marquis. *A.N. Marquis & Co.'s Ready Reference Guide to Chicago*:   (S,WM)
---- Also found: Tan wraps with red and black print.

1137.   Melville. *Gems of wonderful Chicago and the World's*:   (FLP,HU,PSU,UCB,UIC,WM)

1138.   *Methodist headquarters at Chicago*:   (S)
▶Alternate author and added info: Epworth World's Fair Association. The
Johnson-White ptg. co. Also found in tan wraps. Centerfold illus of hotel;
Govt Bldg illus on back. Hotel and association info.

1139.   *The Moorish palace and its startling wonders*:   (HML,MSI,S,UMC)

1139.1 *The Moorish Palace : Midway Plaisance : The great blue dome just east of Ferris Wheel. The best show on
the Midway.* N.p.: n.p., n.d.

> Buff broadside in red print. At bottom: "Admission 25 cent." ☺ (S)

1139.2 Moorish Palace. *The original Guillotine that executed Marie Antoinette : Every part just as it stood on that
eventful day.* N.p.: n.p., n.d.

> 12x7½. (4) p. Folded tan sheet, black and red print. The show was in the Moorish Palace. List of
> Palace contents on last page. On back: "25 cents admits you to two floors." ☺ (S)

1141.   Murphy. *Authentic visitors' guide to the World's Columbian*:   (CCA,FLP,HU,ICRL,LBA,UMD,UMN,WM,Yale)
▶Completed pub info: New York: The Union News Co. [Stromberg, Allen & Co., printers, Chicago,
1893, ᶜ1892 by Richard J. Murphy]. Two folding maps: Grounds map after p 34 and map tipped-in at
back cover, ᶜ1890 and printed with date 1893, entitled "The Union News Company's new and correct map
of Chicago."
---- Also found soft cover: (3) ads, 67 text, 9 p ads + the 2 tipped-in folding maps.

1142.1 *The Niagara Falls and World's fair guide,...* [Niagara
Falls, NY]: The Niagara Falls publishing co. (The
Matthews-Northrup co., complete art printing co.,
Buffalo, NY), 1892.

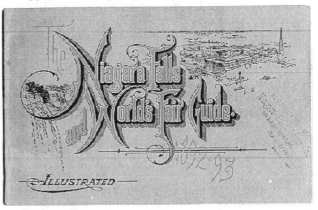

> 16x24½. (48) p. Light gray-green wraps, red and
> black lettering and b/w bird's-eye of the fairgrounds
> and Niagara Falls. C.t.: "The Niagara Falls and
> World's Fair Guide. 1892–93. Illustrated." Text on
> buff paper includes local ads and illus. Brown and
> green print and illus. Last (17) p are an illus guide to
> the WCE. ☺ (GLD)   P➜ $25 - 55

1143.   Otis Bros. *Diagrams of World's Fair Buildings showing location of exhibits*:   (HML,ICRL,LBA,S,Stfd)
---- Also found: Burnt-orange wraps. Yellow, black, red diagrams.   (stfd)
---- Also found: Tan wraps. Black and red diagrams (no yellow).   (ICRL)

1145.1 Photo-mezzo Art Co. *...Directory and Map of Special Exhibits in Midway plaisance and Jackson Park...*
Chicago: n.p., ᶜ1893.

> 16x9. (12) panels. Folded yellow pulp sheet unfolds to 32x25½. Black print. Back is a 6-panel map of
> entire WCE with key, ᶜ1893 by N.C. Miller. Front panel c.t. ☺ (WM)

1146.   *Pictorial Guide to Chicago and the World's Columbian exposition*:   (WM)
1147.   *Plan of World's Columbian Exposition and Handy Map of Chicago*:   (CCA,DC,HML)

1148.1 Plymouth Rock Pants Co. *The best guide-book to the World's Fair.* Boston: Plymouth rock pants co., __.

> 14½x10½. 66 p. Blue wraps, black print and thin border. Branch offices listed on front cover. Illus, maps, ads. Fair guide with several ads besides the Pants Co.   (ref) $35

1150.   *Rand, McNally & Co.'s a week at the fair*:
(CCA,CLP,Col,CU,cul,DC,FPL,HML,HPL,HU,ICRL,IHi,LBA,MSL,NJHx,NLA,NLI,slpl,SML,SPL,SStu,UAT,UCLA,UIC,UMN,UNC,UPa,VAM,VT,WM,Yale)
▶Add pub: Cambridge, MA: HULMS, 1989. Film Mas 19076.

1151.   *Rand, McNally & Co.'s advance guide to the World' Columbian Exposition*:   (ICRL,S)
---- Also found: Blue wraps, black print and litho of Columbus standing in New World.

1152.   *Rand, McNally & Co.'s bird's-eye views and guide to Chicago*:   (E)
1153.   *Rand, McNally & Co.'s Diagrams of the World's Fair Buildings*:   (HU,WM)
1154.   *Rand, McNally & Co.'s guide to Chicago and the World's Columbian Exposition*:   (S)
1155.   *Rand, McNally & Co.'s handbook of*:   (Berk,CCA,CWM,D,FM,HU,ICRL,IHi,LU,Merc,NDU,sfpl,slpl,SPL,UGa,UIC,UMC,UTA,WM,Yale)

1156.   *Rand, McNally & Co.'s handy Guide to Chicago and the World's Columbian*:   (DC,GBP,HML,IHi,MSL,UMD,UPa,Yale)
---- Also found: Flexible red cloth hc, gilt print. (12), 216, (27) p index, ads, and folded map. First (12) p are ads on pink paper.

1156.1 *Rand, McNally & Co.'s handy map of Chicago and the World's Fair, 1893.* Chicago: Rand, McNally & Co., ᶜ1893.

> 14½x10½. Colored map unfolds to 49x32. Issued by advertisers, e.g., Henry R. Worthington.   (HML,UIC)

1156.2 *Rand, McNally & Co.'s new indexed standard guide map of the World's Columbian Exposition, Chicago, 1893.* Chicago: Rand, McNally & Co., ᶜ1893.

> 46x33. Color map folds to 14x7 and is tipped into a red stiff cover with black print. C.t.: "Rand, McNally & Co.'s indexed Guide Map and key to World's Fair Buildings, Grounds, and Exhibits, with handy map of Chicago." Also issued for advertisers. © (CU,UIC)

1156.3 *Remington typewriter : map of : World's Columbian Exposition, Chicago, U.S.A., 1893.* New York: Wycoff, Seamans & Benedict [Press of A.H. Kellogg, M. Fay Hoawley, engraver, ᶜ1893].

> 56x43. Single sheet folds to 14x7½. Blue print ad with illus of typewriter on front panel; when unfolded, the inside is a blue ink map with red flags showing use locations of Remington typewriters on the WCE grounds. C.t. "Compliments of Wycoff, Seamans & Benedict." [Remington exhibit was located in the Manuf Bldg, Sec F, Block 2.] © (GLD,WM)   P➔ $30 - 60

1156.4 Roy, Peter. *Bird's eye view of Chicago, 1893.* Chicago: n.p., ᶜ1892.

> 37x76. Color view map. Inset: "View of Chicago in 1832." On verso, map of the buildings and grounds of the WCE at Jackson Park and Midway Plaisance. (CU)

1158.   *A Scamper Through The States*:   (WM)
▶Completed citation: 23x16. 120, (4) p ads. Navy blue cloth hc, gilt print, beveled boards. Frontis litho of Battleship Illinois exhibit at WCE. Promotional book for trips to "Chicago and Back In One Month for 25 Guineas inclusive." Dredge contribution starts on p 45. Text and illus on coated stock. See #831 and #832 for other Dredge items.
▶Alternate authors: Polytechnic Magazine. Dredge, James.

1159.1 Shonfeld, Peter, comp. *Columbian Exposition : and : World's fair. Chicago : 1893. Origin, History and Progress of Chicago; Guide Book to the Exposition; Illustrations of the Principal Buildings : Advantages to Canada.* N.p.: n.p., n.d.

22x15. 74, (6) p ads including back cover. Pulp wraps and text. C.t. ☺ (HU)

1160. *Souvenir and Visitor's Guide to the World's Columbian Exposition and Chicago*: (csuf,HU,WM)
▶Add pub: Cambridge, MA: HULMS, 1983. Film Mas C 978.

1161. *Souvenir of the World's Columbian Exposition* [Mandel Bros]: (GLD) $18 - 38

1161.1 *Souvenir of : The World's Columbian Exposition, Chicago, with street guide.* Chicago: Vandercook engraving and pub. co., n.d.

12x7. Folded glossy smooth card wraps, blue print with illus of Admin Bldg. (24) panel (total both sides) accordion strip tipped-in, blue print and illus of WCE bldgs one side and city guide other side. Ad for "Lake Michigan and Lake Superior Trans. Co." Variant of #1160. ☺ (WM)

1161.2 *Souvenir of The World's Columbian Exposition. 1893. And Condensed Guide to Chicago.* Chicago: The Michigan Stove Co., 1893.

10x17. 48 p. Black leather hc with pretty gilt print and logo design: "Garland stoves and ranges : The World's Best." Gilt edges. Attached black cloth strap to keep item closed. First 16 p are Chicago guide. 15 color plates by C. Graham. ☺ (GLD,KS,PSU) $18 - 40

1162. Stone. *Chicago and The World's Fair a popular guide*: (UIC)

1163.1 *The Strangers Guide To Chicago & World's Fair. Giving Location and Information Concerning All Points Of Interest Including Parks,...* [Chicago: Metropolitan Business College], n.d.

17½x8½. 16 p+ folded map of Chicago tipped-in at inside back cover. Tan wraps, brown print. C.t. At top of front wrap: "Price. 10 cents." Back wrap illus of Metropolitan Business College. ☺ . (E.S)   **P→**

1164.1 *Sykes & Street : Guide to Chicago and World's Columbian Exposition. Illustrated. What to See and How to See It.* Chicago and New York: Rand, McNally & Company, Publishers, 1893 [ᶜ1893 by Rand, McNally & Co.].

17x11. (3) p memoranda, frontis of The Temple, 216, (10) p index, map, and memoranda pages. Tan wraps, black print. Variant of #1154. ☺ (BPL,CHx,S)

1166. *A True Guide Through The World's Fair Grounds*: (IHi,WM)
---- Also found: "Compliments of George M. Clark & Company, Chicago." Brown print front and back. Stove illus on back. They exhibited gas and gasoline stoves in the Manufactures Bldg–No. 113–NE Quarter–Sec O–Block 3–No 76. (WM)
---- Also found: "Compliments of American Biscuit & Mfg. Co." Navy print front and back. (WM)
---- Also found: "Compliments of Globe Lithographing and printing co." Blue print. Globe ad on back. Exhibited in Manuf Bldg, "No. 113 (in this guide) N.E. Quarter, Sec. E., Gallery Floor." (WM)

1166.1 *The Union News Company's indexed map of the World's Columbian Exposition at Chicago, 1893.* [Chicago]: n.p., [1893].

34x46. Unfold sheet. Color map of grounds. [Union News had concession stands at the WCE.] (HML)

1166.2 *Di velt-oysshtelung in Tshikago in 1893.* [A. o.: o. fg.], n.d.; HULMS microfilm, N.S. 14564 -Item 70.

ca 23x15. 34 p includes plates. Wraps. Caption title given is anglicized from Hebrew. Illustrated WCE guide book in Hebrew. Captions for illus of fair bldgs are also in Hebrew. ☺ . (Stfd)

1168. *Vest pocket directory of the Leading Business Houses of Chicago*:
▶Add annotation: 95, (1) p. The (1) p (i.e., verso of p 95) is an unpaged map of the Midway Plaisance. This map and the folding map were engraved by A. Zeese & Co. (GLD,HML,IHi,S,UIC) $18 - 42
---- Also found: Red cloth flexible hc, gilt print.

1168.1 *Vest pocket guide of Chicago. And the World's Columbian Exposition. The Whole Thing in a Nutshell. Handy and Reliable.* Chicago: Vest Pocket Guide Publishing Co., [°1892 by the Vest pocket guide publishing co.].

8x6½. 144 p. Tan stiff wraps, brown print, rounded corners. "[C]ompliments of Ames Sword Co. Chicago." Truly full of WCE facts and illus. ☺ (S)

1168.2 *Visitors' Memoranda Book, giving the Attractions and Prices in Jackson Park and midway plaisance. Also The Buildings. Price 10 Cents.* N.p.: n.p., °1893 by W.L. Hutchings.

18x9. (7) p tabulation and listing of WCE places+ many blank sheets for notes. Tan stiff wraps, black print, black cloth spine at hinged top edge. Opens like steno note book. ☺ (S)

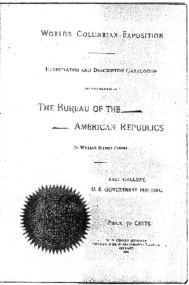

1169. [Vynne]. *Chicago by Day and Night*: (Knox,Stfd)
---- Also found: N.p.: "Published for the Trade," ca 1891 or 1892. 8x13. 168, (5) p ads. White wraps with b/w illus of Chicago street, gray print. Describes Chicago theatre, vaudeville, parties, cab and tallyho rates, massage parlors, parlors etc. WCE in preparation mentioned on pp 53, 11, 118, and 162. (Knox)
---- Also found: Philadelphia: Royal Publishing Co., [1892?]. (Stfd)

1170. Wade. *"The nut shell" The ideal pocket guide to*: (GLD,csuf,HU,S,uiuc,UMD,UoC) $24 - 48

1170.1 Ward, Montgomery, & Co. *Montgomery Ward & Co.'s : New and Concise map of Chicago : showing the new city limits and location of The World's Columbian Exposition, Streets, Parks, Boulevards, Railroads, Street car lines, etc.* Chicago: Montgomery Ward & Co. (Rand, McNally & Co., printers), 1893, °1890.

14x7. Multicolored map unfolds to 69x40. Tipped into brown (or gray-green) stiff wraps, black print. C.t. ☺. (GLD,UIC,WM) $25 - 50

1172. *What to see and how to find it...10,000 facts*: (CU, UMC)

1173. WCE. Bureau of Amer Republics. Curtis. *Illustrated and Descriptive Catalogue*: (WM)   P↗
▶Add cover description: Peach wraps, red seal lower left corner. "Price, 50 Cents."

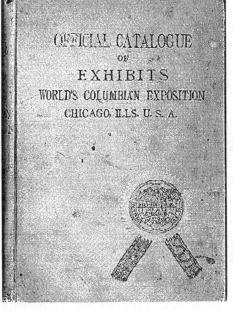

1174. WCE. Dept Publicity. *Condensed catalogue of Interesting*: (NJHx,UMD)
1175. WCE. Dept Publicity. *Condensed official catalogue of*: (E,GU,UMC)

1176. WCE. Dept Publicity. *Official Catalogue.* (multiple parts):
(GLD,bgsu,CCA,CLP,D,FM,HML,HU,IHi,LU,Merc,NAL,NDU,NLA,NPG,NSW,SAL,sfpl,SML,Stfd, UIC,uiuc,UMD,UMN,WM)
---- Also listed: "Revised ed." Parts 1-3, 5, 8, 11-15.
---- Also listed: "Revised ed." Parts 1, 2, 5-8, 11, 14.
---- Also found: "Preliminary issue." Parts 1, 2, 4-9, 11-14.
---- Also found: Orange cloth hc with 12 parts in one vol. Illus is a black and gilt seal on lower right front cover. Edges not dyed or cut for tabs.   P→

☞ These volumes were bound with many variations since the individual guide books were continually being updated as the Columbian Exposition and the exhibitor entries were submitted to the Publicity and Promotion Department. Charges for inclusion in the *Catalogue* are found at #1094.2.

Start of *Official Catalog* section in individual parts:

Pt. 1. Department A: Agriculture building and dairy building

1177.   WCE. Dept Publicity. *Official Catalogue : Part I*: (CLP,FM,HU)
▶Add: Globe-seal is red (color was omitted in original).

Pt. 2. Department B: Horticulture building, Wooded Island, lawns and Midway Plaisance nursery

1177.1 World's Columbian Exposition. Department of Publicity and Promotion. ...*Official catalogue : part II. Horticulture building : wooded island : and midway plaisance nursery : Department B. Horticulture : viticulture, pomology, floriculture, etc. : J.M. Samuels, Chief : Edited by The Department of Publicity and Promotion : M.P. Handy, Chief.* Chicago: W.B. Conkey co., Publishers to the World's Columbian Exposition, 1893.

21½x15. 54 p. Orange-red wraps, black print. Lacks WCE globe-seal; no cover illus. At head of title: "World's Columbian Exposition : 1893." C.t.: "Official Catalogue of exhibits. World's Columbian Exposition : Department B. Horticulture Building : part II. Price 10 cents." ☺. (HU,S)

1178.   WCE. Dept Publicity. *Official Catalogue : part II* [119 p]: (FM,WM)

Pt. 3. Department C: Live stock exhibits

1179.   WCE. Dept Publicity. *Official Catalogue : part III*: (E,S)   **P➜**
▶Correct paging: 98, (1), (5) p "MEMORANDA." Gray smooth wraps, black print and red globe-seal.

Pt. 4. Department D: Fisheries building and aquaria

1180.   WCE. Dept Publicity. *Official Catalogue : part IV* [36 p]: (GLD) $25 - 55

1180.1 World's Columbian Exposition. Department of Publicity and Promotion. ... *Official catalogue : part IV. Fisheries Building and Aquaria : Department D. Fish, fisheries, Fish Products and Apparatus of Fishing : J.W. Collins, Chief : Edited by The Department of Publicity and Promotion : M.P. Handy, Chief.* Chicago: W.B. Conkey co., Publishers to the World's Columbian Exposition, 1893.

21½x15½. 27 p. Deep peach wraps, black print with illus of men in dory pulling in fishnet. Red globe-seal in lower left corner of cover. C.t.: "Official catalogue of Exhibits. World's Columbian Exposition : Department D. Fish & Fisheries : Price. 10 cents." Not a revised edition. ☺. (WM)   **P➜**

Pt. 5. Department E: Mines and mining building

1182.   WCE. Dept Publicity. *Official Catalogue : part V*: (FM)
▶Correct paging: 96 p. Brown-red wraps, black print.

1183.   WCE. Dept Publicity. *Official Catalogue : part V* [revised, 198 p]: (FM)

1183.1 World's Columbian Exposition. Department of Publicity and Promotion. ...*Official catalogue : part V. Mines and Mining Building : Department E. Mines : mining and metallurgy : F.J.V. Skiff, Chief : Edited by The Department of Publicity and Promotion : M.P. Handy, Chief.* Chicago: W.B. Conkey co., Publishers to the World's Columbian Exposition, 1893 [°1893 by The World's Columbian Exposition].

21½x15. Folding map, 1 *l* frontis, 186 p. Gray wraps with black print. At head of title: "World's Columbian Exposition : 1893." C.t.: "Revised edition. Official Catalogue of Exhibits. World's Columbian Exposition : Department E. Mines and mining building : Price, 25 cents." WCE red globe-seal lower left; cover illus of miner with tool (pick). ☺ (GLD,FM,WM)
$25 - 55

Pt. 6. Department F: Machinery hall and machinery annexes

1183.2 World's Columbian Exposition. Department of Publicity and Promotion. ...*Official catalogue : part VI. Machinery Hall and Machinery Annexes : Department F. Machinery : L.W. Robinson, U.S.N., Chief : Edited by The Department of Publicity and Promotion : M.P. Handy, Chief.* Chicago: W.B. Conkey co., Publishers to the World's Columbian Exposition, 1893 [ᶜ1893 by The World's Columbian Exposition].

21½x15. Folding map, 1 *l* frontis, 48 p. Tan wraps with black print. At head of title: "World's Columbian Exposition : 1893." C.t.: "Official Catalogue of Exhibits. World's Columbian Exposition : Department F. Machinery Hall : Price, 10 Cents." WCE red globe-seal lower left; cover illus of ancient and modern machines and gear same as in #1184. ©(GLD,WM) $25 - 55

1184.   WCE. Dept Publicity. *Official Catalogue : part VI* [revised, 51 p]: (MIT,WM)
▸Completed citation: Issued with folding ground plan at front cover, 51 p. Rosy-tan wraps with black print and design as shown.
▸Correction: The 48 p version originally listed as an "also found" is actually #1183.2 above.

Part 7. Department G: Transportation exhibits building, annex special buildings and the lagoon

1184.1 World's Columbian Exposition. Department of Publicity and Promotion. ...*Official catalogue : part VII. Transportation exhibits building, annex, special buildings and the lagoon : Department G. Transportation Exhibits : railways, vessels, vehicles : Williard A. Smith, Chief : Edited by The Department of Publicity and Promotion : M.P. Handy, Chief.* Chicago: W.B. Conkey co., Publishers to the World's Columbian Exposition, 1893 [ᶜ1893 by The World's Columbian Exposition].

21½x15. 2 *l* map, 1 *l* frontis, 60 p. Bright yellow wraps with black print and illus 4 modes of transportation. At head of title: "World's Columbian Exposition : 1893." C.t.: "Official catalogue of exhibits. World's Columbian Exposition : Department G. Transportation Building : Price, 15 cents." WCE red globe-seal lower left. Earlier edition than #1185. "Revised edition" is *not* on cover. ©(WM)

1184.2 World's Columbian Exposition. Department of Publicity and Promotion. ...*Official catalogue : part VII. Transportation exhibits building, annex, special buildings and the lagoon : Department G. Transportation Exhibits : railways, vessels, vehicles : Williard A. Smith, Chief : Edited by The Department of Publicity and Promotion : M.P. Handy, Chief.* Chicago: W.B. Conkey co., Publishers to the World's Columbian Exposition, 1893 [ᶜ1893 by The World's Columbian Exposition].

21½x15. 2 *l* map, 1 *l* frontis, 60 p. Bright yellow wraps with black print and illus 4 modes of transportation. At head of title: "World's Columbian Exposition : 1893." C.t.: "Revised edition. Official catalogue of exhibits. World's Columbian Exposition : Department G. Transportation Building : Price, 15 cents." WCE red globe-seal lower left. Earlier revision than #1185. ©(GLD,HML) $25 - 55

1185.   WCE. Dept Publicity. *Official Catalogue : part VII*: (FM,S,WM)   P➔
▸Add annotation: 1 *l* frontis of Trans Bldg, (6), 25-63 p. Bright yellow wraps. This is a revised ed published later than #1184.2.

1185.1 World's Columbian Exposition. Department of Publicity and Promotion. *Official Catalogue : of exhibits. World's : Columbian : Exposition : Departments G and J. Transportation and Electricity Buildings : parts VII and IX. Price, 15 cents : 1893.* Chicago: W.B. Conkey Co., Publishers to the Exposition, [1893].

22x15. 30 p (part VII), 38 p (part IX). Sepia wraps, black print. No seal and no illus on front wrap. Each part has its own t.p. The t.p. titles match exactly those of #1185 and #1191 respectively. The small page count in each section and the lack of "revised" on the front cover imply an early edition. ©. (FM,S)

Pt. 8. Department H: Manufactures and liberal arts building, leather and shoe trades, merchant tailors...

1186.1 World's Columbian Exposition. Department of Publicity and Promotion. *Official Catalogue : part VIII. Manufactures and Liberal Arts Building : Leather and Shoe Building : Department H. Manufactures :*

James Allison, Chief : Edited by The Department of Publicity and Promotion : M.P. Handy, Chief.
Chicago: W.B. Conkey, co., Publishers, 1893 [ᶜ1893 by World's Columbian Exposition.].

21½x15. 145 p. Orange-red wraps, black print. *No* globe seal or other cover design. At head of the
title: "World's Columbian Exposition : 1893." C.t.: "Official Catalogue of exhibits. World's Columbian
Exposition : Department H. Manufactures and Liberal Arts Building. Shoe and Leather Building. Part
VIII. Price, 25 cents." (FM,MSI)

1189.   WCE. Dept Publicity. *Official Catalogue : Dept. H & L:* (E,S)   P➔
  ▸Add cover annotation: Decorative vase. Red globe-seal in lower left
  corner.

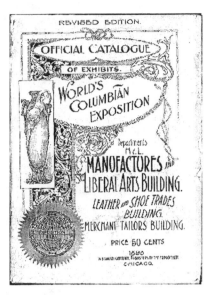

Pt. 9. Department J: Electricity building

1191.   WCE. Dept Publicity. *Official Catalogue : part IX:* (MIT,WM)

1192.   WCE. Dept Publicity. *Official Catalogue : part IX* [revised]: (FM,UIC)
  ▸Add annotation: 42, (6) p "memoranda." Lavender wraps. Tipped-in
  folding map after front cover.

Pt. 10. Department K: Fine arts

1192.1 World's Columbian Exposition. Department of Publicity and Promotion.
  ...Official catalogue : part X. Art galleries and annexes : Department K.
  Fine arts : Painting, Sculpture, Architecture, Decoration : Halsey C.
  Ives, Chief : Edited by The Department of Publicity and Promotion :
  M.P. Handy, Chief. Chicago: W.B. Conkey co., Publishers to the World's
  Columbian Exposition, 1893 [ᶜ1893 by The World's Columbian Exposition.]

22x15½. 108 p. White glossy coated wraps, brown print with pale green frond design, *no* seal logo.
Folded map after front cover. At head of title: "World's Columbian Exposition : 1893." C.t.: "Official
Catalogue : of exhibits : World's Columbian Exposition : Department K. Fine Arts : Part X. Price. 25
Cents." Probably the first issue of the fine arts catalogue. ☺ . (VtHx)

1193.   WCE. Dept Publicity. *Official Catalogue : part X* [141 p]: (E,GPL,HU,IHi,UCLA,UMD,WM)
  ▸Add publisher: Cambridge, MA: HULMS, 1983. Film Mas C 978.
  ---- Also found: 141 p, 1 *l*. No (8) p for memoranda.
  ---- Also found: 141 p. No 1 *l* and no (8) p for memoranda; otherwise exact.

1194.   WCE. Dept. Publicity. *Official Catalogue Part X* [196 p]:
  (GLD,Col,csuf,E,LBA,MSI,MSL,NPG,PSU,SHB,uiuc,UMD,UPa,WM)

$25 - 55

1195.   WCE. Dept Publicity. *Revised catalogue : Dept. Fine Arts* [506 p]: (CLP,HU,IHi,NLA,S,Stfd,UMD,Yale)
  ▸Add pub: New York: M. Knoedler, ᶜ1973. Microfiche. Six sheets.
  ---- Also found: Tan wraps, brown print with no seal on front cover. Red seal only on back cover. At
  bottom of front cover: "price one dollar." (S)

Pt. 11. Department L: Manufactures and liberal arts building

1195.1 World's Columbian Exposition. Department of Publicity and Promotion. *...Official catalogue : Part XI.*
  Manufactures and liberal arts building : Department L—Liberal arts : education, literature, medicine,
  surgery and dentistry, hygiene and sanitation, physical apparatus, photography, constructive architecture,
  commerce, religious organizations, charities and corrections, music. Selim H. Peabody, Chief. Edited by
  the department of publicity and promotion. M.P. Handy, Chief. Chicago: W.B. Conkey co. : publishers
  to the World's Columbian exposition : 1893.

21½x15½. 1 *l* frontis, (18), (15)-97, (3) p "memoranda." Maize wraps, black print, no cover illus.
"Price, 15 cents." This is a revised edition with the same cover words and seal location as later revised
edition, #1196; however, this seal is peach rather than red. At head of title: "World's Columbian
Exposition : 1893." ☺ . (WM)

Pt. 12. Department M: Anthropological building, Midway Plaisance and isolated exhibits

1196.1 World's Columbian Exposition. Department of Publicity and Promotion. ...*Official catalogue : part XII. Anthropology building : midway plaisance : and isolated exhibits : Department M. Ethnology : Archæology, Physical Anthropology, History, Natural History, Isolated and Collective Exhibits. F.W. Putnam, Chief : Edited by The Department of Publicity and Promotion : M.P. Handy, Chief.* Chicago: W.B. Conkey co., Publishers to the World's Columbian Exposition, 1893.

21½x14½. Folded map after front cover, 84 p. Pale blue wraps with black lettering. C.t.: "Revised Edition. Official Catalogue of exhibits and descriptive catalogue : World's Columbian Exposition : Department M. Anthropological Building : Midway Plaisance and Isolated Exhibits. Price, 15 cents." Red WCE globe-seal at left-center of front cover; no other cover design. ☺. (FM-Anthropology,NLA,WM)

1197. WCE. Dept Publicity. *Official catalogue. part XII* [90 p]: (FM)

Pt. 13. Department N: Forestry building

1198. WCE. Dept Publicity. *Official catalogue. Part XIII. Forestry*: (WM)
---- Also found: 39, (1) p "memoranda." Tipped-in folded grounds plan at front cover. *Has* red-globe seal (*with* underlying seal) in mid-left of cover and "Revised Edition" at top. Off-white wraps, black print with no other cover design, "price, 10 cents."

Pt. 14. Woman's building

1198.1 World's Columbian Exposition. Department of Publicity and Promotion. ...*Official catalogue : part XIV. Woman's building : Mrs. Bertha H. Palmer, President Board of Lady Managers. Edited by The Department of Publicity and Promotion : M.P. Handy, Chief.* Chicago: W.B. Conkey co. Publishers to the World's Columbian Exposition, 1893.

22x15½. 55 p. Lime-green wraps with red WCE globe-seal in upper left corner; no cover illus. Frontis is litho of Woman's Building. At head of title: "World's Columbian Exposition : 1893." C.t.: "Official Catalogue of exhibits. World's Columbian Exposition : Woman's Building : part XIV : Mrs. Bertha H. Palmer : President Board of Lady Managers : price, 15 cents."
---- Also found: 55 p. Yellow-tan wraps with *no* globe-seal logo. C.t. same as above except "price, 10 cents."
☺. (FM,UMD)

1198.2 World's Columbian Exposition. Department of Publicity and Promotion. ...*Official catalogue : part XIV. Woman's building : Mrs. Bertha H. Palmer, President Board of Lady Managers. Edited by The Department of Publicity and Promotion : M.P. Handy, Chief.* Chicago: W.B. Conkey co., Publishers to the World's Columbian Exposition, 1893; Cambridge, MA: HULMS, [1983]. Film Mas C 978.

22x15½. 86 p. Wraps with WCE globe-seal in upper left corner; no cover illus. At head of title: "World's Columbian Exposition : 1893." C.t.: "Official Catalogue of exhibits. World's Columbian Exposition : Woman's Building : part XIV : Mrs. Bertha H. Palmer : President Board of Lady Managers : price, 20 cents." ☺. (HU,IHi,WM)

1199. WCE. Dept Publicity. *Official catalogue : part XIV*: (csuf,FM,NJHx,S,WM)
▸Correct paging: 1 *l* fold map printed both sides, 1 *l* frontis of Woman's Bldg, 141 p.
---- Also found: Issued with "Price 25 cents" printed on cover, i.e., no blackout of former price.

Pt. 16. United States government building

1200. WCE. Dept Publicity. *Official catalogue : United State...part XVI*: (S,WM)
▸Correct paging: Folding ground plan after front cover. 1 *l* frontis of Govt Bldg, 156, (1) p index. *No* cover illus other than *upper* left red globe-seal.

1201. WCE. Dept Publicity. *Official catalogue : United State...part XVI*: (E,HU)
▸Correct paging: Folding map of grounds after front cover. 1 *l* frontis of Govt Bldg, 177 p. Cover illus with Govt Bldg and red globe-seal at *lower* left. P➔

Pt. 17. Group 176. Isolated exhibits, Midway Plaisance

1202.   WCE. Dept Publicity. *Official Catalogue...Dept. M*: (GLD,WM)
▶Add annotation: White wraps 22 p version does not have an illustrated front cover. Found with and without tipped-in folding map of "Buildings and Grounds" at front cover, "revised" is *not* on cover. Lists 41 exhibits. (GLD,WM)
---- Also found: Gray (or lime green) wraps with black print and red globe-seal slightly below mid left cover. Black print litho of Japanese lady holding parasol. The tipped-in folding map of fairgrounds at front cover is different from the white wraps version described above. "Revised" in *not* on cover; "Price, 10 cents." Text of 22 p is identical (41 exhibits listed). © (GLD,WM)

1204.   WCE. Dept Publicity. *Official Catalogue : part XVII* [36 p]: (csuf,S)

1204.1 World's Columbian Exposition. Department of Publicity and Promotion. *...Official Catalogue : part XVII. 1893 : of exhibits on the Midway Plaisance : isolated exhibits, midway plaisance. Group 176. Edited by The Department of Publicity and Promotion, M. P. Handy, Chief.* Chicago: W. B. Conkey co., Publishers to the World's Columbian Exposition, 1893 [°1893 by The World's Columbian Exposition].

21½x15. 36 p. Cream wraps, black print and WCE globe without underlying seal in bottom left corner. At top of cover: "Revised edition." Otherwise cover is same as #1204. "General index" in side front cover. On cover: "Price, 5 cents." At head of title: "World's Columbian Exposition." (ref) $90

Pt. 18. Department G: Collective exhibits of the Krupp cast-steel works, Essen, Germany

1205.   WCE. Dept Publicity. *Official Catalogue : Krupp*: Found bound together with #1206. (S,WM)

Pt. 19. Department M: Exhibits of the Columbus caravels (Santa Maria, Nina and Pinta)

1206.   WCE. Dept Publicity. *Official Catalogue : Caravels*: Found bound together with #1205. (S,WM)

End of *Official Catalog* section.

1207.   WCE. Dept Publicity. The o*fficial directory of the World's Columbian*:
(B,BCHx,CCA,Col,GPL,HML,ICRL,ISU,LHL,Merc,MSI,MSL,NLA,RU,UBO,UCB,UCI,UCLA,uiuc,Yale)

1208.   WCE. Dept Publicity. *Official guide to the grounds and buildings*: (ICRL,IStU,NAL,NDU,UIC,uiuc,UMC)
---- Also found: During construction, Aug 1892. Rust wraps, black print.

1208.1 World's Columbian Exposition. Department of Publicity and Promotion. *...Official : World's Fair guide : map and directory.* Chicago: Rand, McNally & co., printers, 1892?   P➔

20x13½. Green wraps, black print and design with illus of Columbus statue. Wraps hold one fold out map: 23x35 unfolded. C.t. At head of title in upper left corner: "Preliminary." Lower right: "Price ten Cents." Illus of Admin Bldg on outside back cover. Inside covers blank. © . (UMD)

1209.   WCE. Dept Publicity. *Plans and diagrams of all exhibit buildings*: (DC)
1210.   *The World's Columbian Exposition Hand Book souvenir*: (UCLA)

1210.1 *...World's fair city. Souvenir pocket guide.* Chicago: Willard & Brady, publishers, n.d.

15½x10½. (31) p. Salmon wraps. C.t. At head of title: "Price 10 Cents. Special Edition. Copyrighted." Guide with advertising material interspersed. © . (FM,IHi)
---- Compliments of Hotel Holland. Illus of the hotel (Lake Ave and 53rd St) on outside of back wrap.

1212.   *The World's Fair Maps and Guide*: (WM)

▸Add annotation: On back cover: "Robertson & Smith, printers." On first p: "1492 : The Columbian Exposition. 1893." String-tied. Tipped in maps are "Lake Shore" (front) and "Central Business District of Chicago" (back).   P↓

1213. *The Worlds Fair; some of its : Principal Sights and Exhibits..* New York: Columbia novelty publishing co., ᶜ1892 by the Columbia novelty publishing co.

20x14. 31 p. Self-wraps, black print. C.t. = caption title. Illus of Admin Bldg on front cover; ad for Clarks Thread on back cover. Illus of WCE bldgs with guide to the fair with snippets of other info. Article on the Bureau of Charities and Correction, pp 29 and 31. © (GLD)   P↓ $30 - 50

▸Improved and completed citation.

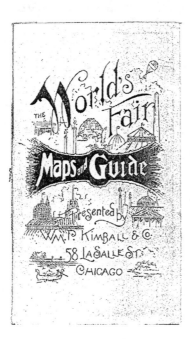

Chapter 7

MAGAZINES, NEWSPAPERS AND PERIODICALS

1217.1 *Aeronautics*. New York: American Engineer and Railroad Journal. 1 (1893-94).

"Proceedings of the conference of aerial navigation. Held in Chicago, August 1,2,3, and 4, 1893." 1.1 (1893): 3-. Listing of the important papers presented on such topics as balloons, gliding, propellers, motors for flying, and other aeronautical materials. The article includes a reprint of the World's Congress Auxiliary "Preliminary address of the World's congress committee on an international conference of aerial navigation." Dated December 1892, it was also a call for papers.

☞ Samuel Archer King, experienced aeronaut of 458 balloon ascensions from 1851 to 1908, made ascensions from the WCE grounds north of the Fine Arts Bldg in his "Eagle Eyrie." On September 22 (State Commissioners Day) he daringly took up a young girl, possessed with an insane desire to make the journey; they were caught in a counter-current and narrowly escaped drowning in Lake Michigan.

1217.2 *Aftenposten* [newspaper]. Oslo, Norway. (1993).

"Gokstadskipkopien 'Viking' på Oslo havn før seilasen over Atlanteren til verdensutstillingen i Chicago 1893. Verden jublet over ferden - unntatt Columbustilhengerne." 11 June 1993. Trans: The Gokstad-style long ship "Viking" sailed from Oslo harbor across the Atlantic to the WCE in Chicago; the World celebrates the trip—except for Columbus adherents. (UBO)

1219.1 *Albuquerque Democrat* [newspaper]. Albuquerque, NM. (1893).

"Pointers to World's Fair." 4 Apr. 1893: 2. [For another Albuquerque newspaper, see #1281.]

1219.2 *Allgemeine Zeitung* [German newspaper]. (1893).

"Das Kunstgewerbe auf der Weltausstellung zu Chicago." no. 263 (1893). 10 p. Trans: The art exhibit at the WCE.

1219.3 *American Agriculturist*. New York: Orange Judd Co. 51 (1892)

"The World's Fair at Chicago." 51.10 (1892): 577-78.

1219.4 *American Amateur Photographer*. F.C. Beach, ed. 4 (1892), 5 (1893).

◆Bain, Robert E.M. "Amateur Photography at the World's Fair." 4 (Mar. 1892): 108
◆"The Photographic Display at the World's Fair." 5 (Mar. 1893): 74.
◆"Congress of Photographers, Chicago, Illinois, July 31st to August 5th." 5 (Aug. 1893): 375-77.
◆Gould, Charles H. "The Photographic Exhibits at the World's fair." 5 (May 1893): 258-59.

☞ Beach was the outspoken critic of WCE official photographer, C.D. Arnold and his handling of the Photography Dept. Book #2348.3 contains a full description.

1222. *American Architect and Building News*: ▸Additional article: 41 (1893).
Olmsted, Frederick Law. "A report upon the landscape architecture of the Columbian Exposition to the American Institute of Architects." 41.924 (1893): 151-53.
▸See #1728.1 for a special World's Fair issue of *American Architect*.

1223.1 *American Catholic Quarterly Review*. (1895).

Eaton, John. "The Catholic educational exhibit at the Columbian exposition." (Jan. 1895).

1224.1 *American Florist : a weekly journal for the trade*. Chicago: The American Florist Company. 9 (1893).

"The World's Fair." 9.274 (1893): 83-4. B/w photo of NY State WCE floral display, p 83.

1224.2 *American Geologist*. 12 (1893), 13 (1894).

Frazer, Persifer. "Columbian exposition : a hasty glance taken in Aug. 1893, at the ores of the noble and the useful metals in the Mines and Mining building."

1225.　*American Heritage*: ▸Additional issue: 44 (1993).
　◆Miller, Donald L. "The White City." 44.4 (1993): 70-87. (A fine summary of the WCE and impact.)
　◆McClay, Wilfred M. "A tent on the porch." 44.4 (1993): 88-93. Centennial evaluation of Frederick Jackson Turner's famous paper on the West, which was first presented at the WCE World's Congress of Historians and Historical Students.

1226.　*American Historical Review*: ▸Additional issue: 55 (1950).
　Curti, Merle [Eugene]. "America at the World's Fairs, 1851-1893." 55 (July 1950): 833-56.

1226.1 *American History Illustrated*. 27 (1992).

"Alice Austen Goes to the Fair : The World's Columbian Exposition." 27.4 (1992): 20-21. See #1408.2. [The article title is the same as the Alice Austen House museum exhibit on Staten Island in Rosebank, NY. Austen took many photographs when she attended the WCE.]

1226.2 *American Industries* [journal]. Washington DC. (1893), (1894). 42x__. [Subject: US trade and tariffs].

1226.3 *American Institute of Architects*. *Proceedings of the Twenty-seventh Annual Convention, 1893*. (See #2236 in the original bibliography).

Olmsted, Frederick Law. "The landscape architecture of the World's Columbian Exposition." Pp 160-74.

1227.1 *American Journal of Photography*. 13 (1892), 14 (1893).

　◆Sachse, J.F. "The Photographic Congress Auxiliary." 13 (Nov. 1892): 484.
　◆"The World's Congress Auxiliary." 14 (Sept. 1893): 398-403.

1228.1 *American Monthly Magazine*. National Society of the Daughters of the American Revolution. Washington, DC. 2 (1893), 3 (1893), 4 (1894). [Issues found at the DAR archives, Washington, DC]

Columbian Liberty Bell Project:
◆Mickley, Minnie F. "Liberty bell chapter, Allentown, Pa." 2.2 (1893): 221-23. Promotion of the Columbian bell in the new Lehigh Chapter of NSDAR and suggested quotes to be put on the bell.
◆"Proposed Liberty Bell for the Columbus exhibition." 2.2 (1893): 228-29. Rpt of original correspondence from Nov 14–23, 1892, between M. Mickley and W.O. McDowell initiating the bell. Includes unpaged illus of the original Philadelphia Liberty Bell.
◆McGee, Howard Hawthorne. "The new Liberty bell." 2.4 (1893): 474-75. Poem and request for donations.
◆Desha, Mary. "The Columbian Liberty bell." 2.6 (1893): 659-61. Read before the Congress of Representative Women in the Memorial Art Palace, May 19, 1893. Contains reasons for the bell.
◆Gist, Mrs. George Washington. "The Columbian Liberty bell." 3.1 (1893): 65-8. Report on casting of the bell in Troy, NY.
◆Mickley, Minnie F. "Columbian bell of freedom; or bells and liberty." 3.5 (1893): 500-02. Paper of Feb 24, 1893, proposes permanent structure for the bell after the WCE.
◆"Chicago chapter, Chicago, Illinois." 3.5 (1893): 549-51. Announces "Columbus Day" festivities at the bell, Oct 30, 1893. Footnote to article states that the celebration was cancelled when Chicago's mayor was assassinated on Oct 28.

DAR Participation at the WCE:
◆"Meeting of the Daughters of the American Revolution to take part in the World's Congress of Representative Women at Chicago, May 19th, 1893." 2.4 (1893): 481-84. Rpt of letters urging participation at the DAR part of the World's Congress Auxiliary.
◆"World's Congress of Representative women. Meeting of the Daughters..." 2.6 (1893): 605-07. Summary report of the their congress on May 19, 1893.
◆Brown, Mary Spalding. "Department Congress : Of the National Society of the Daughters..." 3.1 (1893) 60-4. Full report of the activities of the May 19 meeting.

◆Shepard, Frances Welles. "Address of welcome." 3.2 (1893): 175-79. Rpt of the opening address given on May 19, 1893, lauds the women's contributions to the fair.
◆Cunningham, Floride. "Address of Miss Floride Cunningham. Lady Manager..." 3.2 (1893): 190. Announces gift of 1000 copies of "Miss Washington of Virginia" to the DAR at the WCE.
◆"Editor's note-book." 3.5 (1893): 578-79. Value of the fair to women and sad death of Mayor Carter.
◆McLean, Mrs. Donald. "A dissolving view of the White City." 3.6 (1893): 730-37. Nice description of her trip to the fair and visiting the Columbian Liberty Bell.
◆"Third continental congress of the National Society of the Daughters of the American Revolution." 4.5 (1894): 454-56. Contained in the report is the DAR at the WCE.

1229. *American Music*: ▶Specific article: (GLD,DC,UMA)
McKinley, Ann. "Music for the Dedication Ceremonies of the World's Columbian Exposition in Chicago, 1892." (Spring 1985): 42-51. Illus account of the ceremonies and music director Tomlins.

1230. *American Philatelist*: ▶Additional issues: 6 (1892), 7 (1893), 106 (1992), 111 (1997).
◆"Columbus post cards." 6.12 (1892): 212.
◆Wanamaker, John. "Columbian series of postage stamps and stamped envelopes." 7.2 (1893): 11-12. Wanamaker, US Postmaster-General, describes WCE issues.
◆"The Columbian stamps. (From the Congressional Record)." 7.3 (1893): 23-24. Senate debate on printing and selling the stamps. Some senators wanted *no* printing even though extra revenue would be generated; they felt a "Commemorative" would not circulate and thus would not be utilitarian.
◆"About the World's Fair Exhibit." 7.3 (1893): 36-9.
◆"Report of the treasurer : World's fair committee." 7.8 (1893): 119. The Club's expenses and credits to that time.
◆Sheppard, Stephen. "The Columbian Exposition." 106.5 (1992): 424-33.
◆---. "The World's Columbian Exposition Left Its Mark in U.S. History." 106.9 (1992): 832-36.
◆Stral, Harold M. and Kenneth C. Wukasch. "Cashing in on Columbus." 111.9 (1997): 848-54. Describes with color images how the colorful Goldsmith chromolith 1 cent postal cards, Scott UX10, were used for advertising. Excellent article on WCE postal history.

1232.1 *American Society of Civil Engineers : Transactions*. Advance Copy (1893), 30 (1893).

These *Transactions* contain papers prepared for the International Engineering Congress. See #1414.2 and #2194.4-6.

1236.1 *Anthony's Photographic Bulletin*. New York: E. & H. Anthony & Co. 24 (1893).

24.24 (1893) contains index for 1893; lists WCE photo items at pp 36, 38, 539-40, 601, and 665-66.

1236.2 *Antiques & Collecting Magazine*. Lightner Publishing Corp., Chicago. 103 (1998).

Harris, Moira F. "Is The Fair Over Yet?" 103.5 (1998): 26-30. Illustrated description of remainders from various fairs and impact of fairs.

1246.1 *Art Interchange : an illustrated guide for art amateurs and students, with hints on artistic decoration*. New York: The Art Interchange Co. Ed. Josephine Redding. 29 (1892).

37½x28½. Pale green wraps; black illus and print.
◆"Art Notes." Article about assembling a collection of American paintings for the WCE. Lists decorators and sculptors for the various bldgs of the WCE. 29.1 (1892): 7-8.

1248. *Art Quarterly*: ▶Add article:
Manson, Grant Carpenter. "Frank Lloyd Wright and the fair of '93." (Summer, 1993): 115-23.

1249.1 *Arthur's New Home Magazine*. Philadelphia: The Arthur publishing Co. (1892).

Dorr, R.E.A. "The exposition of 1893. Part VI." (Sept. 1892): 781-92.

1250. *Atlantic Monthly*: ▶Add article:
Van Brunt, Henry. "The Columbian Exposition and American civilization." 71 (May 1893): (577)-588.

1251.   *Ave Maria*: ▸Add article:
Spalding, J[ohn] Lancaster. "Views of education." (Paper read before the World's Congress of Representative Youth, July 18, 1893). [Spalding was President of the Catholic Educational Exhibit at the WCE; see #785.]

1252.   *B & O Field*: ▸Add issue details: "To the World's Fair via Washington." 3.1 (Mar. 1893): 11. Describes scenery along the route to Chicago. Explains that B&O lines terminated at the WCE. (WM)

1252.1 *Baltimore Sun*. Baltimore, MD. (1893).

"Art at the fair." Series of articles. Sept. 1893.

1252.2 *Belford's Monthly* [magazine]. Chicago. 10 (1893). (S)

"Belford's guide to Chicago and the fair." 10.6 (1893): 1-21. This article is appended after p 930 in the magazine. Blue-black wraps with white print.

1252.3 *Bethel Courier* [weekly newspaper]. Bethel, VT. (1893) (VtSSt)

"The World's Fair." 12 Oct. 1893: 1. Details horse races at the WCE.

1253.1 *Blue and Gray*. Philadelphia: Patriotic publishing co. 1 (1893).

"The Columbian exposition—will it pay?" 1.5 (1893): __.

1253.2 *Board of Trade Journal*. Providence, RI. 2 (1891). (S)

"World's Fair Notes." 2.8 (1891): 268-70. News notes on the WF and 2 p illus of fairgrounds.

1253.3 *Boonville Weekly Advertiser* [newspaper]. Boonville, MO. (1892) (MOHx)

"Missouri at the World's Fair." 25 Nov. 1892.

1256.1 *Bulletin of the American Museum of Natural History*. New York. 17 (1905).

Boas, Franz. "Anthropometry of central California." 17.4 (1905): 347-80.

1256.2 *Bulletin of the Essex Institute*. Salem, MA. 25 (1893).

"Report of Committee on Columbian Exposition." 25 (1893): 19-74. See #1923.3.

1256.3 *Bulletin of the National Association of Watch and Clock Collectors, Inc.* 25 (1983), 26 (1984), 28 (1986), 29 (1987), 30 (1988),31 (1989), 32 (1990).

◆Bullard, Geoffrey S., and Nahum H. Lewis. "The Waldorf-Astoria clock: Timing an America in Transition." 25.6 (1983): 675-85.
◆Lewis, N[ahum] H. "Horology of World's Columbian exposition : Chicago, 1893." 26.2 (1984): 191-200. Part 2. 26 (1984): 704-09. Parts continue to: Part 17. 32.3 (1990) 273-76.

☞ Clock and watch companies exhibited in the Manufactures Bldg. Goldsmiths' & Silversmiths' Company of London made the "Exposition Clock," which was exhibited at the WCE. It weighs two tons and is nine feet tall. It once stood in the Rose Room of the Waldorf-Astoria in New York City and now is in the hotel lobby. See #854.4 for the company's ad and illus of the clock.

1256.4 *Burlington Free Press and Times* [daily newspaper]. Burlington, VT. (1893). (VtSSt)

"It was Chicago Day." 11 Oct. 1893: 2.

1258.1 *Californian Illustrated Magazine*. Holder, Charles Frederick, ed. 4 (1893).

"California at the World's Fair." 4.1 (1893): --.

1259.   *California's Monthly Worlds*: . (S)   P↓

1260.1 *Capital-Journal* [newspaper]. Topeka, KS. (1993).

Ready, Catheryn. "Arch made of corn is portal to past at Kansas Museum of History." 26 Dec. 1993: D1. Article explains the WCE artifacts from Kansas collected for the centennial anniversary exhibition at the Kansas Museum 1992–93, in Topeka.

1260.2 *Carriage*. Philadelphia: Ware Brothers, publishers. (1893).

"Columbian Edition" published October 3–6, 1893. See #776.4.

1260.3 *Carriage Journal*. 30 (1993).

Wheeling, Ken. "Carriages in the White City : Chicago 1893." 30.4 (1993): 162-65. (SML)

1260.4 *Catholic Historical Review*. 55 (1970).

Cleary, James F. "Catholic participation in the World's Parliament of Religions, Chicago, 1893." 55.4 (1970): 585-609.

1263. *Century Magazine*: ▶Additional issue: (1902)
Burnham, Daniel H. "The White city and capital city." (1902). 2 pp.

1264. *Chautauquan*: ▶Additional issue: 38 (1903).
Zueblin, C. "White City and After." 38 (Dec. 1903): 373-84.

1268. *Chicago Herald*: ▶Special edition. (1893).
Chicago Day issue with WCE illus and articles throughout. 9 Oct. 1893.

1269. *Chicago History*: ▶Additional issues. 4 (1977), 16 (1987), 22 (1993), 23 (1994).
◆Weimann, Jeanne. "A Temple to Women's Genius : The Woman's Building of 1893." 4 (Spring 1977): 23-33.
◆Cassell, Frank A., and Marguerite E. Cassell. "The White City in Peril: Leadership and the World's Columbian Exposition." n.s. 12.3 (Fall 1983): 10-27. [The cover of this issue depicts the west entrance of Manufactures Bldg as painted by E.H. Blashfield, 1893—a gift to CHx.]
◆Lewis, Russell. "Everything Under One Roof: World's Fairs and Department Stores in Paris and Chicago." 12.3 (Fall 1983): 28-47.
◆Weimann, Jeanne. "Fashion and the Fair." 12.3 (Fall 1983): 48-56.
◆Anderson, Larry. "Yesterday's City : Steele MacKay's Grandiose Folly." 16.3-4 (1987): 104-14.
◆Shaw, Marian. "Yesterday's City : The Fair in Black and White." n.s. 22.2 (1993): 54-72. [This article is based upon *World's Fair Notes*, #2424.]
◆Savory, Jerold J. "Cartoon Commentary : At Chicago's World's Columbian Exposition, *Puck* and other magazines used cartoons to comment on everything from free admission fees to women's rights." n.s. 23.1 (Spring 1994): (32)-57.

1269.1 *Chicago Medicine*. Chicago: Chicago Medical Society. 96 (1993).

Beatty, William K. "Medicine at the World's Columbian Exposition." 96.14 (1993): 17-25. Excellent summary of medical activities at the WCE. Cover of issue is color illus of the Admin Bldg.

1269.2 *Chicago '93*. Chicago Department of Cultural Affairs. (1992–).

Newsletter format. Magazine features WCE centennial events in Chicago. See #2334.2.

1269.3 *Chicago Philatelist : A Monthly Journal Devoted to Philately*. Chicago: Oakley pub. co. 1 (1893).

26½x18½. Watermarked tan wraps with blue-black print and border. C.t. At top of cover: "Much in a Nutshell." "Price 5 Cents" per copy.
◆"How the World's fair will benefit philately." 1.4 (1893): 61. (S)
◆Entire issue devoted to the WCE. 1.6 (1893): (69)-75 + (1) p ad.

1271.1 *Chicago Skylines.* (1929).

Brown, A. Lawren. "A World's Fair Influence: Chicago Spared from Devastating Effects of Financial Depression of 1893." 5 Oct. 1929.

1273.1 *Christian at Work.* (1892).

Gill, Wilson L. "A Children's Palace at the World's Fair." 28 Apr. 1892. Reprinted as #853.1.

1273.2 *Christian Herald : and signs of our times.* New York: Bible House. De Witt Talamage, ed. 17 (1894).

35½x27. Black print on buff paper, illus. Price 5¢ each issue.
Large ad for Leonard Manufacturing Company WCE silver plated spoons on last page. Sales price for six spoons was 99¢; reduced from $9. 17.38 (1894): 608.

1273.3 *Christian Science Journal.* National Christian Scientists' Association. 11 (1893).

♦"Christian Science at the World's religious congress." 11.8 (1893): 337-46. Content and program listed. The founder of Christian Science, Rev. Mary Baker G. Eddy, was not in attendance.
♦Hanna, S.J. "'Not matter, but mind.'" 11.9 (1893): 409-12. A congratulations to the WCA.
♦Houk, Eliza P.T. "The World's parliament of religions." 11.10 (1893): 448-50.

1273.4 *Chronicles of Oklahoma.* Oklahoma Historical Society Quarterly. 53 (1975).

"Territorial Governors of Oklahoma." 53.1 (1975): 1-176. WCE content as it relates to Governors A.J. Seay and William C. Renfrow on pp 28, 39, 41, 43, 53.

1273.5 *Chronique : du journal général de l'imprimerie et de la librairie.* 81 (1892), 82 (1893).

All volumes are "2ᵉ Serie." All articles are in French and are titled "Exposition internationale de Chicago en 1893." 81.18: 97-104; 81.32: 155-58; 81.34: (163)-66; 81.51; 81.52; 82.7; 82.16; 82.22; 82.23.

1276.1 *Comfort.* Augusta, ME: Morse & Co. 4 (Jan. 1892).

1280. *Cosmopolitan:* ▸Additional issues and articles: 14 (1892).
♦Henrotin, Helen M. "The Great Congresses at the World's Fair." 14.5 (1893): 626-32.
♦"Impressions of the World's Fair, Chicago 1893." 16 (Dec. 1893): (129)-232.

1280.1 *Current Literature.* New York: Current Literature Publishing Co. 14 (1893). (S,UMD)　P⬇

"World's Fair Edition." 14.1 (1893): 1-30. Main entrance to Trans Bldg illus on front wrap.

1281. *Daily Citizen* [newspaper]. Albuquerque, NM. (1891), (1892). (GLD)
♦"Free Pass Restrictions. Free annual half-fare passes shall not be issued to world's fair commissioners..." 9 Jan. 1891: 1.
♦"H.B. No. 120, to provide...display of products of the territory of New Mexico at the World's Columbian Exposition of 1893." 27 Feb. 1891: 1. [Title given is first sentence of untitled article.]
♦"World's Fair." 26 Mar. 1891: 1.
♦"San Marcial Notes." "A World's Fair benefit ball was given here [San Marcial, NM]..." 29 Feb. 1892: 1.
♦"Mrs. Franc. L. Albright of Albuquerquer [sic]...in charge of the newspaper exhibit at the World's Fair." 18 Mar. 1892: 1. [Title given is first sentence of untitled article.]
♦"All together. The women of New Mexico should interest themselves in the World's fair work." 21 Mar. 1892: 2.

1282. *Daily Columbian:* Chicago: Department of Publicity and Promotion, 1893.
▸Example: Number 56, issued July 4, 1893. 8 p. Contains WCE contributions from other Chicago newspapers. Subscription rates were $1.00 per month.

1282.1 *Daily Leader* [newspaper]. Guthrie, OK. (1893).

> Paper advertised an upcoming "Columbian edition" to advertise Guthrie, Logan County, and local business interests at the WCE.
> ◆Barnes, Mollie E. "Features of the fair. An interesting and gossipy letter on the exposition. The Reception to the Infants—Opening Days—Delightful 'Teas'..." 27 June 1893: 3.
> ◆"Death's Carnival. ...Awful World's fair holocaust." 12 July 1893: 1. An example of articles about the Cold Storage Warehouse fire that appeared in the *Daily Leader* this week.
> ◆"Chicago day. Tremendous outpouring of people at the fair. ..." 11 Oct. 1893: 1.

1282.2 *Daily Oklahoma State Capital* [newspaper]. Guthrie, OK. (1893).

> ◆Illustrated WCE articles daily from June 1–Aug 14, 1893, by Robert Graves, Walter Wellman, and J.H. Beadle. Most are two full columns and appeared on p (3). Examples: "World on wheels : Infinite Variety of the Transportation Department" (June 1); "The woman's building : Mecca of the Fair Sex at the Exposition" (June 3); "State buildings : Nearly Two Score of the Beautiful Structures : to be seen at the world's fair" (June 5).
> ◆"Sunday Opening." 29 May 1893: 1.
> ◆Barnes, Mollie E. "How things look : A Letter from a Guthrie Woman on the World's Fair. The Oklahoma exhibit." 10 June 1893: 1.
> ◆"Open Sunday. The World's Fair Will Run Seven Days a Week. The chief-justice's order." 19 June 1893: 1.
> ◆Merrick, J.J. "How he saw it. Hon. J.J. Merrick tells of the Wonders of the World's Fair. Oklahoma's nice exhibit." 24 June 1893: 1.
> ◆Greer, Frank H. "The old man. An Interesting Chicago Letter From Editor Greer. His news of the trip." 27 July 1893: 1.
> ◆---. "Greer's knife. ...Another Interesting Letter from Chicago—Beneficial Instructions to Visitors--The Oklahoma Crowd and Their Doings—What it Costs to See the Fair." 31 July 1893: 1.
> ◆---. "Greer's quill. He Still Hangs Around the World's Fair. A fascinating letter. ...Everything Lovely in Chicago—The Fair Passeth Descriptions." 3 Aug. 1893: 1.

1283.1 *Delineator, A Journal of Fashion, Culture and Fine Arts* [monthly magazine]. New York: Butterick Publishing Company. 42 (1893).

> "Columbian Midsummer Number." 42.2 (Aug. 1893): 107-230 + ads before and after text. Brown wraps with black print, text on pulp paper, 28x20. B/w illus of fashions and sewing patterns, recipes. Contains 2 articles on the WCE and ads for companies at the fair.

1285.1 *Deseret Weekly* [magazine]. Salt Lake City, Utah. 47 (1893).

> Wells, Emmeline B. "Utah women in Chicago." 47.2 (1893): (33)-34. Description of Utah women's activities at the WCE, including Woman's Congresses, women's exhibits in the Utah Bldg, and records of those Utah women who provided musical entertainment, etc.

1285.2 *Deutsche Rundschau*. Berlin: Verlag von Gebrüder Paetel. Julius Rodenberg, ed. 21 (1895).

> Müller, F[riedrich] M[ax]. "Das Religions–Parlament in Chicago." 21.6 (Mar. 1895): 409-25. Rpt in English in his book, *Last Essays*, #2400.2. (LBA)

1287.1 *Doctor's factotum : A bi-monthly journal*. Yonkers, NY: The New York Pharmacal Assn. 1 (1894).

> "Special number : World's Fair souvenir." 1.6 (1894). Title of issue.

1287.2 *Doylestown Democrat* [newspaper]. Doylestown, PA. (1893).

> ◆WCE articles: 13 Apr. 1893: 1-2.
> ◆"May 1 Opening of Fair." 4 May 1893: 2.
> ◆"Pennsylvania at Chicago." 4 May 1893: 2.
> ◆"Bucks [County] at the Fair." 4 May 1893: 2.
> ◆Large illustration of Horticultural Bldg. 11 May 1893: 4.

1288.1 *ECHO* [Expo Collectors & Historians Organization]. Los Angeles. 10.4 n.s. (1981), 11.3 and 11.4 (1982), Nov. (1984). [Ed Orth, founder and president.]

☞ *Echo* ceased publication when Ed Orth died.

1290.1 *Electrical Industries*. Chicago. 1 (1893).   P➔

Sub-banner: "Devoted to the electrical and allied interests of the World's fair, its visitors and exhibitors." 1.13 (Sept. 7, 1893). 15 p. At head of title: "Weekly World's fair."

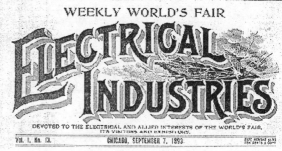

1291.1 *Electrotype Journal*. Chicago: A. Zeese & Co. 20 (1893). $30 - 60

World's fair number. 20 (Spring 1893). 33x26½. 16 p. Bird's-eye of WCE on front wrap. This issue presents A. Zeese illus found in many WCE publications. Tinted lithos on first 2 pages.

1291.2 *Elgin Daily Courier* [newspaper]. Elgin, IL. 33 (1893), 34 (1893).

1291.3 *Elgin Daily News* [newspaper]. Elgin, IL. (1893). [21st year, no vol numbers.]

1291.4 *Employee News*. Chicago?, Metropolitan Water Reclamation District. (1992).

King, Andrew. "Epidemics Endanger World's Fair." March 1992 ("MWRD History" insert). Premise is that filtered and pasteurized water from Waukesha, WI, was needed to dispel public health issues at the WCE. See #1050.16.

1298.   *Fair News*: ▶Add WCE articles: P➔
◆Dybwad, G.L. "New Mexico Territory at the World's Columbian exposition, 1893." 25.2 (1993): 21.

Volume 27 Number 2
March 1995

◆---. "Financial administration at the Columbian exposition, 1893." 26.1 (1994): 11.
◆---. "Interested in World's fairs? Interested in the information highway? Now you can have both!" 28.5 (1996): 2.
◆Dybwad, G.L., and Joy V. Bliss. "The Columbian Theatre : grand reopening, November 6, 1994 : Wamego, Kansas." 27.2 (1995): 10-11.
◆---, ---. "'Viking' til Verdensudstillingen." 28.3 (1996): 16-17.
◆---, ---. "Columbian Exposition Survivor Found At Muir Woods." 29.1 (1997): 14.
◆---, ---. "Columbian dolls." 30.5 (1998): 15-16.

1298.1 *Farm, Field & Fireside*. Chicago: Howard and Wilson Publishing Co. (1893). $22 - 55

◆"Chocolate at the world's fair." Easter No., 1 Apr. 1893: 311. 40x28. Pp 290-316. Blue wraps. (GLD)
◆"Worlds Fair Edition." 6 May 1893: 406-28. The entire illustrated issue is devoted to the opening of the Fair. Sepia illus cover showing Machinery Hall and 7 ethnic types from the Midway. (GLD)   P⬇

1298.2 *Feminist Studies*. 20 (1994).

Hutton, John. "Picking fruit: Mary Cassatt's Modern Woman and the Woman's Building of 1893." 20 (1994): 318-48. A review of the artist at the WCE.

1298.3 *Field Museum of Natural History Bulletin*. Chicago: Field Museum. 49 (1978).

Carter-De Vale, Sue. "The Gamelan." 49.1 (1978): 3-12. See #2342.4 for her thesis on this subject.

1301.   *Florida Home Seeker*: ▶Additional articles.
◆"Great World's Fair." 4.7 (July 1893): 2. Full page WF and Florida Bldg from a trip by the editor, O.M. Crosby.
◆"A sample day. At the World's Fair, Florida Department Horticultural Building." 4.8 (1893): 4. [Avon Park, Florida, had a WCE exhibit at which they handed out the town's newspaper.]

1301.1 *Folkebladet*. Hartvig Lasen, ed. Kristiania: Oscar Andersens Bogtrykkeri. 14 (1893). (UBO) P➔

31x23½. Norwegian language. Content similar to *Century*, *Review of Reviews*, or *Schribner's*.
◆"Viking." 14.12 (June 1893): 177-187. Many illus of Captain Magnus Andersen and his "Viking" ship, which sailed to the WCE from Oslo. Including Andersen, the 12 crew members are listed, such as Rasmussen from Bergen (see #2415 for Rasmussen's account of the trip).
◆"Amerikanske Columbus-Postmerker." 14.12 (1893): 189+. Description of WCE postage stamps.

1302.1 *Forest and Stream : Rod and Gun*. New York: Forest and Stream Publishing Co. 40 (1893), 41 (1893). P➔

41x28½. Contains many great ads for companies exhibiting at the WCE, including the Forest and Stream exhibit at the main hall entrance in the Fisheries Bldg.
◆"Forest and Stream in the World's Fair." 40.22 (1893): 472. Contains complete descriptions of gun exhibits at the WCE.
◆Buchanan, W.I. "World's Fair Show." 40.22 (1893): 478. Buchanan, Chief of the WCE Agriculture Dept, postponed kennel show at WF until Sept 19-22 due to construction delays.
◆"Chicago and the West." 41.7 (1893): 146. Article on the September Congress of Fisheries.
◆"Forest and Stream in the World's Fair." 41.7 (1893): 141.

1303. *Forum*: ▶Additional articles:
Van Rensselaer, M.G. "The artistic triumph of the fair-builders." Dec. 1892. Pp 527-40.

1305.1 *Gazette des beaux arts*. Paris. 10 (1893), 11 (1894). (LBA) P➔

◆[Hermant, Jacques]. "L'art à l'exposition de Chicago." 10.3 (Nov. 1893): (416)-25.
◆---. "L'art décoratif a l'exposition de Chicago." 11.3 (Feb. 1894): (149)-69.

1308. *Godey's*:
◆Greene, Herbert Wilber. "Music at the Columbian exposition." 127.758 (1893): 223-25.
◆Heydt, Geo. Frederic. "A glimpse of the tiffany exhibit." 127.758 (1893): 1-14 (following p 258).

1308.1 *Golden Rule : International Representative of the Young People's Societies of Christian Endeavor*. Boston: Christian Endeavor. 6 (1892).

[Untitled article] 6.39 (23 June, 1892): 673+. Article about and ad for the Hotel Endeavor. For other items on Christian Endeavor see #792.3 and #1127.

1308.2 *Goodform. An illustrated magazine for the people* [monthly]. Chicago: The Goodform co., Publishers. 3 (1892), 4 (1893), 5 (1893).

◆"World's Fair number." 3.5 (1892). Title of issue.
◆Giveen, Robert Fielding. "World's Columbian Exposition." 4.6 (1893): 351-55.
◆Marlow, Helen. "Hints for the World's Fair Visitor." 4.6 (1893): 337-41.

1308.3 *Granite Monthly : A New Hampshire magazine*. Granite Monthly Co. Pub., Concord, NH. 16 (1894). P➔

Metcalf, Henry H. "The first congregational church in Nashua, and its pastor." 16.1 (1893): 1-11. Ms. Mary Nutt gave 15 chimes exhibited at the WCE to the church. The bells were dedicated May 1894. See #2355.1.

1309. *Graphic*: 7 (1892).
"Dedication Souvenir. Oct. 21, 1892. World's Columbian Exposition." Extra Souvenir Number 7 (1892): 52 p, iv. Yellow and pumpkin illus wraps with WCE in background. Full issue devoted to WF and the administrators and commissioners. (WM)

1311.1 *Hardwood*. Chicago: Hardwood publishing co. 4 (1893). (FM)

♦Millspaugh, Charles F. "Hardwoods at the World's fair." 4.6 (1893): 186-89. See #2107.1.
♦Scattered articles about the WCE throughout. 4.6 (1893).

1312. *Hartford Courant* [newspaper]. Hartford, CT. (1995).

"Every postcard tells a story of bygone days." 8 June 1995. Describes first commercial postcard— introduced at the WCE.

1312.1 *Harper's Bazaar*. New York. 25 (1892), 26 (1893).

1313. *Harper's (Monthly) Magazine*: ▸Additional issues: 221 (1960).
Leighton, George R. "World's fairs: From Little Egypt to Robert Moses." 221.1322 (1960): (27)-37.
☞ Robert Moses, a prominent New Yorker, was involved in the 1939 and 1964 World's Fairs.

1314. *Harper's Weekly*: ▸Additional articles: **P➔**
♦"Present State of the Grounds and Buildings." 35.1822 (1891): 916. Title of Charles Graham b/w illus of WCE
♦Pickett, Montgomery Breckinridge. "The novel procession at the fair." 37.1906 (1893): 629-30. Illus. About the parade of the exhibitor-inhabitants of the Midway Plaisance.
♦S., J.G. "The Columbian Exposition." 37.1893 (1893): 310-11. WCE b/w illus p 308-09.
♦P., M.B. "The Chicago fire." 37: 1909 (1893): 700+. Burning of the WCE cold storage warehouse.
♦"An eight page World's Fair Supplement with this number." 37.1923 (1893). Issue of Oct 28, 1893; front illus of fairgoers on shore by the Manuf Bldg "waiting for the fireworks."

1315.1 *Harvard Graduates' Magazine*. W.R. Thayer, editor. Cambridge, Mass. 1 (1893).

"Harvard Clubs. Chicago." 1.2 (Jan. 1893): 318. In attendance was F.D. Millet, class of 1869, WCE Director of Decoration under Daniel Burnham. Prof. Frederick. W. Putnam, Chief of Ethnology and Archaeology spoke on the WF, stating he planned to start a museum in Chicago with exhibits from the fair (early beginnings of the Columbian Museum). Students discussed the Harvard exhibit at the upcoming WCE.

☞ As early as 1890, Frederick Putnum spoke of founding a Chicago museum at the close of the WCE.

1319. *Heresies*: ▸Additional article:
Grabenhorst-Randall, Terree. "The Woman's Building." 1 (1978): 44-__ .

1319.1 *Hertha* [magazine]. Stockholm, Sweden. 5 (1985).

Manns, Ulla. "Utestända kvinnor byggde eget hus..." 5 (1893): 34-36. Content: Women's pavilions built for World's fairs held in Chicago, 1893, and Philadelphia, 1876.

1319.2 *Historic Preservation*. 45 (1993).

Dean, A.O. "Revisiting the White City : (the lasting influences of the 1893 Chicago World's Columbian Exposition)." 45.2 (1993): 42-__ .

1320.1 *Home Magazine : A National Illustrated Journal.* Washington, DC: The Brodix Publishing Co. 4 (1892), 5 (1893).

"The World's Fair." 5.12 (Oct. 1893): 14. Contents include illus of the "Fine Arts building."

1320.2 *Home-Maker.* New York: J. Martin Miller, Pub. 10 (1893). P➔

Handy, Mrs. Moses P. "How to Live at the World's Fair." 10.2 (May 1893): 143-51. "World's Fair Edition" on front of brown wrap. The issue also contains an A. Zeese bird's-eye view of WCE on p (120). Extensive description of Woman's Dormitory (53rd and Ellis) and the Family Dormitory (75th and Electric El line) sponsored and run by the Board of Lady Managers.

1321.1 *Household.* [Boston magazine "Devoted to the interests of the American housewife."] 25 (1892), 26 (1893).

♦ "Rooms in Chicago." 26.3 (1893): 107. Room rates for WCE.
♦ "What to wear at the world's fair." 26.5 (1893): 163.
♦ "What Dolly found at the exposition." 26.10 (1893): 311-12.
♦ "What women have done." 26.11 (1893): 367. Article on W.C.T.U. and F.E. Willard fountain (see the Willard Memorial Library presentation book, #2446.WML).

1321.2 *Hub News* [weekly]. New York. For Carriage Makers, Vehicle Dealers and Manufacturers of supplies. 3 (1893).

20x13. 24 p. On cover: "Convention of the Carriage Builders' National Assoc'n,...You can visit the World's fair at same time." Carriage Builders met Oct 3-5, 1893. Mentions NY Day. Handout in the Trans Bldg. 3.20 (1893). . (Stfd-bound WCE Trans Dept Collection) P➔

1321.3 *Iliniwek.* 10 (1972). (IHi)

"Lorado Taft and the Utopian White City." 10.4 (1972): 26-32.

1321.4 *Illinois Historical Journal.* 84 (1991).

Sandweiss, Eric. "Around the World in a Day: International Participation in the World's Columbian Exposition." 84.1 (Spring 1991): 2-14. Issue cover illus of WCE "Street in Cairo."

1323.1 *Illustrated Buffalo Express.* Buffalo, NY: Geo. E. Matthews & Co. (1893).

Pictorial souvenir, 24 pp, issued on Dec 17, 1893. (CCA)

1324.1 *Image.* Rochester, NY: George Eastman House. 39 (1996).

Brown, Julie K. "'Seeing and Remembering': George Eastman and the World's Columbian Exposition, Chicago 1893." 39.1-2, (1996): 2-31. Article about Columbus Kodak cameras at the WCE, impact of roll film in promoting amateurs, and cameras invading privacy— "The Kodak Fiend." See her book on photography at the WCE, *Contesting Images, #2327.1.*

1325.1 *Indiana Magazine of History.* 80 (1984).

Cassell, Frank A. "Pride, Profits, and Politics: Indiana and the World's Columbian Exposition of 1893." 80.2 (1984): 92-121.

1328.1 *Inland printer : a technical journal devoted to the art of printing.* Chicago: The Inland Printer. 10 (Oct. 1892–Mar. 1893).

1328.2 *Inside collector*. 2 (1991).

Kaonis, Donna C. "1893 : The World's Columbian Exposition." 2.1 (1991): 37-47.

1331.1 *Irish National Federation of America: Home Rule bulletin*. New York: Irish National Federation of America. 1 (1893).

30x__. 12 p. 1.3 (Oct. 1893). National Library of Ireland catalogs under WCE.

1332. *Irrigator*: 1 (1893). ▸Add articles.
 ◆"World's Fair Buildings." 1.8 (1893): 163-68. Illus description of all the bldgs.
 ◆Rand, Geo. D. "Irrigation Apparatus at the World's Fair." 1.8 (1893): 173-74. Based on a 5-week visit, the author describes pumps and displays related to irrigation.

1332.1 *Jamestown Daily Alert* [daily newspaper]. Jamestown, ND. 19 (1893).

 ◆"Nearly a million : Attendance at the World's Fair on Chicago Day by Far the Largest Yet." 10 Oct. 1893: 1.
 ◆"North Dakota at the fair. The Flickertail State Has a Day at the World's Exposition." 19.230 (1893): 3.

1332.2 *Janesville Gazette* [daily newspaper]. Janesville, WI. 37 (1893).

 ◆"Can go to Chicago for $2.75 a round trip." 6 July 1893: 4. Discusses WF fare reductions.
 ◆"Special World's fair train." 7 Oct. 1893: 4. Local trains to head for Chicago Day, Oct 9, 1893.
 ◆"Chicago day crowd tax the whole city." 9 Oct. 1893: 1. The paper issued on Chicago Day.
 ◆"The fair has cost us at least $160,000." 9 Oct. 1893: 2. The paper's estimate of the money spent by citizens outside the community because of Chicago Day.

1332.3 *Jefferson City Daily Tribune* [newspaper]. Jefferson City, MO. (1890), (1891), (1892), (1893) (MOHx)

 ◆"Chicago Commissioners for World's Fair." 24 May 1890: 4-6.
 ◆"Comment on commissioners." 16 July 1891: 4.
 ◆"Sketch of Missouri Building for World's Fair." 21 Jan. 1892: 4-5.
 ◆"Missouri Day at World's Columbian Exposition." 1 Sept. 1893: 4-6.
 ◆"Disposal of Missouri Building following World's Fair of 1893." 3 Nov. 1893: 4-5.
 ◆"Sketch of awards won by Missouri at World's Fair." 21 Nov. 1893: 4.

1332.4 *Jewelers' Circular and Horological Review*. (1892), (1893), (1894).

Many articles on WCE watch and clock exhibits. See also #1256.3.

1333. *Journal of American Culture*: ▸Additional issue: 13 (1990).
Ziolkowski, E[ric] J. "Heavenly Visions and Worldly Intentions : Chicago Columbian Exposition and World's Parliament of Religions." 13.4 (1990): 9-15. See #2444.1 for another Ziolkowski publication.

1337.1 *Journal of the British dairy farmers' association*. London. (1893).

Cheesman, James. "The Columbian dairy cattle tests at the World's Fair, Chicago, 1893." See #277.c. and #718.1 for more on dairy tests.

1339. *Journal of the Illinois State Historical Society*: ▸Add articles. ▸Additional issues: 69 (1976), 79 (1986).
 ◆Weber, Jessie Palmer. "The Fine Arts building in Jackson Park, Chicago." 17 (1924): 417-27.
 ◆Parmet, Robert D. "Competition for the World's Columbian Exposition: The New York campaign." 65.4 (1972): 365-81.
 ◆Lederer, Francis L. "Competition for the World's Columbian Exposition: The Chicago campaign." 65.4 (1972): 382-94.
 ◆"Illinois and Illinoisans, 1876-1893." 69.4 (1976): 243-(249).
 ◆Downey, D.B. "The Congress of Labor at the 1893 World's Columbian Exposition." 76.2 (1983): 131-38.
 ◆Cassell, Frank A. "Welcoming the World: Illinois' Role in the World's Columbian Exposition." 79.4 (1986): 230-44.

1340.   *Journal of the Society of Arts*: 39 (1890), 40 (1891), 41 (1892), 42 (1893), 43 (1894).
▶Completed list of vols containing WCE info: Over 150 articles concerning the British bldg, exhibits, finances, visits, etc. for the WCE. A journal vol ran from Nov to Nov. (RSA)

1340.1 *Journal Star* [newspaper]. Peoria, IL. (1964), (1993).

◆Miller, Joy. "Society Queen Helped Run 1893 Chicago World's Fair." 15 Apr. 1964. A story of Mrs. Potter Palmer and the WCE.
◆Timm, Lori. "Wheel of time." 15 Aug. 1993. Describes the Ferris wheel and WCE.
◆D'Alessio, F.N. "Great Chicago fair of a century ago endures in society." 2 May 1993.

1341.   *Judge*: ▶Pub info and add issue: New York: The Judge Publishing Co.
"Suspense! Which one will get the fair?" C.t. for December issue 17.428 (1889) with color cartoon of 4 cities as children vying for fair and waiting for Uncle Sam to decide. Early coverage. (GLD) $25 - 50

1342.1 *Jul i Amerika 1917* [annual]. New York: Albert Bonnier publishing house. (UBO)

39½x27½. Unpaged. Norwegian language publication. Color cover of skier in the woods looking at a cozy Norwegian cottage.
◆Reymert, August. "Vikingefærden : Memoirer : 1. Vikingefærden. 2. Björnstjerne Björnson. 3. Ole Bull." First segment on Vikingefærden is (3) p. Illus. Subject: summary of humorous events that occurred while sailing the ship "Viking" to the WCE. Description of the skipper, Captain Andersen.

1343.1 *Kansas City Star* [daily newspaper]. 14 (1893).

"All fair records broken. Nothing Like Chicago Day known to Exposition Annals." 10 Oct. 1893: 1.

1343.2 *Kansas Heritage*. Topeka: Kansas State Historical Society. 1 (1993).

Marvin, Anne. " 'The spirit of Kansas' Goes to the Fair." 1.2 (1993): 18-22. Title refers to the oil painting by Mary Pillsbury Weston which was exhibited at the WCE and also shown for the centennial recreation of the WCE Kansas Exhibit at Topeka. [Marvin was curator for the excellent 1993 exhibit.]

1346.   *Keystone*: ▶Add article: (GLD)   P➜
"Keystone Watch Case Co.'s Exhibit." 14.10 (1893): 925-__ .

1347.   *Ladies' Home Journal*: ▶Add article:
Handy, Mrs. M[oses] P. "If you go to the fair." 10.7 (1893): 20.

1348.   *Ladies' World* [monthly]: New York: S.H Moore & Co.
▶Additional issue: 13 (1892).
41x28. Peach wraps, black print. Articles of fiction, fancy work, and many ads for WCE.

1353.1 *London Times*. (1892), (1893).

Research source: *Index to the Times newspaper, 1893*. 4 vol.
London: Samuel Palmer, 1894. Published in quarterly vols; WCE articles are listed in the last three vols of 1893.
◆"The Chicago World's fair." Oct. 12, 17, 20, 1892. A series of WCE articles; reprinted as #915.3.

1353.2 *Lumber Trade Journal*. Chicago. (1893). (FM)

Millspaugh, C[harles] F. "West Virginia's : forestry exhibit at the World's Columbian exposition." (15 Sept. 1893). See #2107.1 for more about Millspaugh.

1354.1 *Mail and Express* [newspaper]. New York. (1889).

"October the Twelfth AD 1492." 68x47. 12 Oct. 1889. 4 p. Contains an extensive illus summary of the Paris Exposition and promotes NYC as the site of a WF in 1892. (HU)

1356.1 *Mathematical Intelligencer.* 15 (1993).

> Parshall, Karen V.H., and David E. Rowe. "Embedded in the Culture : Mathematics at the World's Columbian Exposition of 1893." 15.2 (1993): 40-45.

1357. *Message and Deaconess World*: 9 (1893). ▸Add article.
"Bible Exhibit at the World's Fair." 9.9 (1893): 13-14. Describes American Bible Society exhibit. (WM)

1357.1 *Metropolitan Review Magazine.* (1993).

> Cassell, Frank A. "The World's Columbian Exposition." Supplement to Summer 1993 issue: 4-5.

1358. *Mid-America*: ▸Additional issue: 67 (1985).
Cassell, Frank A. "The Columbian Exposition of 1893 and United States Diplomacy in Latin America." 67.3 (1985): 109-24.

1359.1 *Milwaukee History.* 5 (1982).

> Cassell, Frank A. "Milwaukee and the Columbian Exposition of 1893." 5.4 (Winter 1982): 82-100.

1360. *Milwaukee Reader*: ▸Additional issue: 45 (1987).
Cassell, Frank A. "The English are Coming." 45.34 (Sept. 1987): 3-4.

1360.1 *Milwaukee Sentinel* [newspaper]. (1893).

1360.2 *Minerals. A monthly magazine.* New York: Wm. M. Goldthwaite. A. Chamberlain, ed. 3 (1893). (FM) **P➔**

> ♦C.M.S. "Biographical Sketches: IV. George Frederick Kunz." 3.7–8 (July–Aug. 1893): 121-24. Details Kunz's extensive WCE contributions.
> ♦Wilson, Harriet E. "World's Fair Notes. Part I." 3.7–8 (July–Aug. 1893): 131-33.

1360.3 *Minneapolis Tribune* [daily newspaper]. Minneapolis, MN. 27 (1893).

> "Tremendous. World's Fair Crowd on Chicago Day." 10 Oct. 1893: 1. Two column article about the festivities.

1360.4 *Minnesota History* [magazine]. 53 (1992).

> Becker, William M. "The Origin of the Minnesota State Flag." 53.1 (Spring 1992): 3-7. Minnesota's WCE Women's Auxiliary Board had a flag committee; they chose from 200 entries and displayed the new flag at the WF in Chicago.

1360.5 *Missouri Historical Review.* 80 (1986).

> Cassell, Frank A. "Missouri and the Columbian Exposition of 1893." 80.4 (1986): 369-94.

1360.6 *La Monde Illustre.* (1893)

> WCE articles in French language. May through Oct 1893 issues.

1365.1 *National Bulletin* [monthly]. Washington, DC: The Woman's Tribune. 2 (1893). (WM)

> Stanton, Elizabeth Cady. "Important Work to get Ready for the World's Fair." 2.4 (1893): (1)-(2).

1365.2 *National Geographic Magazine.* Washington, DC: National Geographic Society. 5 (1894).

> "Proceedings of the International Geographic Conference." 5 (31 Jan. 1894): 97-256. See #2200.

1365.3 *National Guard.* N.p.: The Guard Publishing Co. 2 (1893), 3 (1894).
♦Colby, Ella. "A Visit to the Fair." 2.10 (1893): 130+.

◆Searcy, Emmett [Coldwell]. "Our Experience at the Fair." 2.12 (1893): 159+.

◆"More World Fair Reminiscences." 3.2 (1894): 183+.

☞ Editor of the *National Guard,* Kate (Elizabeth) Warthen Brown Lee Sherwood, who later married Emmett Searcy, was president-general of the NTCC in 1893. At the same time, Emmett was NTCC commander and business manager. They attended the WCE; she took notes (#2445.OU) and collected souvenirs (see #2446.OU).   **P➜**

1365.4 *National Historical Magazine.* National Society of the Daughters of the American Revolution, Washington, DC. 78 (1944).

Williams, Josephine Tighe. "The Lost Liberty Bell, Second." 78.1 (1944): 26-8. Describes the Columbian Liberty Bell's history, and that it was first rung in front of the WCE Admin Bldg on Sept 11, 1893, and later disappearing while on display in Russia during WW II.

1365.5 *National League for Good Roads* [magazine]. 1 (1892).   **P➜**

"Proceedings of the Convention at Chicago : October 20–21, 1892..." 1.1 (1892): 1 *l*, 55 p+ unpaged plates. C.t. Pale blue wraps, blue print and design. Organizing issue. Many references to lobbying at upcoming WCE. Some members were from WCE depts and committees. ©.(WM)

1367.1 *New England journal of education.* (1893).

Gay, George E. "The earliest free public schools." (16 Feb. 1893).

1368.   *New England*: ▸Additional vol nos and articles: 7 (1892), 8 (1893), 10 (1894).
◆Upton, George P. "Music in Chicago." 7.4 (1892): 477-94. Includes music plans for WCE.
◆Downes, William Howe. "New England art at the World's Fair." 8 (1893): 352-77.
◆Wyman, J.C. "Rhode Island at the World's Columbian Exposition." 10 (June 1894): 427-40.
◆McIntyre, H.H. "Vermont at the World's Fair." 10.1 (Mar. 1894): 4-14. See #2088.1.

1368.1 *New Orleans Times Picayune* [daily newspaper]. 57 (1893).

"Chicago Day at the fair." 10 Oct. 1893: 4. Small article at back of paper because the big news locally was the Gulf storm of Oct 6, 1893, and relief efforts.

1370.   *New York Recorder* [newspaper]: ▸Add: New York: George W. Turner. 5 (1893).
"New York's banquet hall : Pride of World's Fair Managers, Joy of All the Critics." 5.770 (1893): 1-2.

1372.1 *Newtown Enterprise* [newspaper]. Newtown, PA.

◆"Sunday and the World's Fair." 10 June 1893: 1.
◆"A week at the Big Fair." 17 June 1893: 1.

1374.   *North American Review*: ▸Add articles:
◆"Europe at the World's fair." 155.432 (Nov. 1892): 623-30. Germany and Russian exhibits.
◆Chandler, W.E. "Shall immigration be suspended?" 156.434 (Jan. 1893): 1-8. Discusses effect of WCE on influx of foreigners and the associated costs.
◆"Foreign nations at the World's fair." 156.434 (Jan. 1893): 34-47. Japan and Italian exhibits.
◆"Europe at the World's fair." 156.435 (Feb. 1893): 236-46. British and French sections.
◆Royal Commissioner-General. "Spain at the World's fair." 156.436 (Mar. 1893): 332-37
◆Davis, George R., Dir. General. "Charges at the World's fair." 156.437 (Apr. 1893): 385-89. WCE efforts to promote fair housing prices.

◆"Foreign nations at the World's fair." 156.438 (May 1893): 611-17. Persian and Canadian exhibits.

◆M'Claughry, R.W., and John Bonfield. "Police protection at the World's fair." 156.439 (June 1893): 711-16. Chicago police and secret police activities to keep the WCE safe. Bonfield was a captain.

◆Countess of Aberdeen. "Ireland at the World's fair." 157.440 (July 1893): 18-24.

◆Duke of Veragua. "The family of Columbus." 157.440 (July 1893): 113-19.

◆"The women of to-day." 157.443 (Oct. 1893): 423-55. Various authors.

1375.1 *Den nye dialog* [magazine]. Denmark. (1993).

Ågård, Johannes. "Religionernes Verdensparlament 1893 : interview med Erik Håhr." No. 54 (1993): 4-9. Illus review of the WCE religious congresses held from Sept 11–27, 1893.

1375.2 *Oesterreichisch-Ungarische Zeitung : vormals Oesterreichisch-Amerikanische Zeitung.* [Chicago: Schober & Carqueville], 1893.   P↗

On illus cover: "Fest Schrift. 18 August 1893. Chicago." 13.26 (Aug. 1893). 80 p. Trans: Austrian-Hungarian Newspaper : formerly Austrian-American Newspaper. Special issue. WCE Admin Bldg illus on the front cover. ☺ . (ONB)

1375.3 *Ohio Propaganda* [monthly]. Cincinnati: Ohio Propaganda Co. 4 (1893).

4.10 (1893). 30½x22½. On cover: "The Natural Resources, Industrial Development and General Progress of the State of Ohio and the Chicago Exposition : Illustrated." Attractive cover with illus of the Americas laid over bird's-eye view of the WCE grounds. English and Portuguese. P→

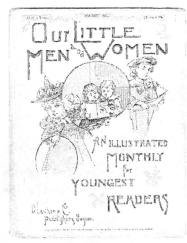

1375.4 *Open Court* [weekly journal]. Chicago: Open Court Publishing Co. 7 (1893).

◆Snell, Merwin-Marie. "The future of religion. A farewell address delivered before the parliament of religions at its last session." 7.319 (1893): 3823-25.

◆Koerner, G. "Programme of the catholic World's congress at Chicago." 7.319 (1893): 3825-27.

1376.1 *Our Little Men and Women. An Illustrated Monthly for Youngest Readers.* Boston: D. Lothrop Co. (1893).   P→

Bryar, Greta. "The Little Columbian Grandpa." One story about a boy and his neighbor friends going to the WCE and the sights they saw. Same title issued in 12 parts, one per month; this periodical has no vol or pt numbers. Ads.

1378. *Pacific Banner* [monthly newspaper]: Winthrop, ME (not NE): Dept of Peace & Arbitration National W.C.T.U. 4 (1893). ▶Add articles.

◆"The Boy's Brigade at the World's Fair." 4.11 (1893): 3. Denounces WCE boys military training camp.

◆"World's Peace Congress." 4.11 (1893): 3. Announces Aug Congress on Peace and Arbitration with a list of suggested subjects.

1379. *Plimpsest* [magazine]: Iowa City, IA. 74 (1993).

◆Davis, Merle. "Sundays at the Fair : Iowa and the Sunday Closing of the 1893 World's Columbian Exposition." 74.4 (1993): 156-59. (S)

◆Swain, Ginalie, et al. "Iowans at the 1893 World's Columbian Exposition: What They Took to the Fair, What They Did There, and What They Brought Back Home." 74.4 (1993): 160-87. Iowans at the WCE and current WCE remainders in Iowa. (S)

1380.1 *Past Times*. Chicago: Chicago Historical Society. (1993).

A calendar of events and newsletter of the Society. The June/July/August 1993 issue is devoted primarily to the Society's exhibit, "Grand Illusions," and city events remembering the WF.

1383.1 *Philatelic Journal of America* [monthly]. St. Louis: C[harles] H[aviland] Mekeel Stamp & Publishing Co. 9 (1893). (S) **P➜**

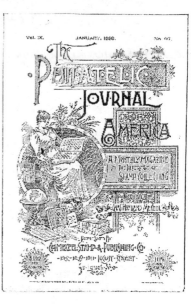

> ♦"Columbian adhesive postage stamps." 9.1 (1893): 5-6.
> ♦Rogers, Albert R. "A.P.A. exhibit of postage stamps : at the World's Columbian Exposition, Chicago, 1893." 9.3 (1893): 89-92.

1383.2 *Photo-American.* 3 (1892), 4 (1893), 5 (1893).

> Articles on WCE throughout vols 3, 4, and 5.
> Vidal, Léon. "Present and Future Possibilities of Photography, Read Before the Photographic Congress at Chicago." 4 (Oct. 1893): 341-47.

1383.3 *Photo Beacon* [magazine]. 5 (1893).

> ♦Nicol, John. "Photographs at the Fair: The American Exhibit." 5 (Aug. 1893): 257-58.
> ♦---. "Photographs at the Fair: The British Exhibit." 5 (Sept. 1893): 293.
> ♦"World's Fair Jottings." 5 (Apr. 1893): 116.

1383.4 *Photographic Times.* 23 (1893).

> ♦"Congress of Photographers, Programme." 23 (July 1893): 408.
> ♦Nicol, John. "A Plea for the National Recognition of Photography: Read at the World's Congress of Photography." 23 (Aug. 1893): 437-38.
> ♦Peabody, Selim H. "To photographers." 23.595 (1893): 71. Photographers urged to exhibit at WCE.
> ♦Ward, H. Snowden. "Photographers' Effort at Union: A Paper Read at the World's Congress of Photography." 23 (Nov. 1893): 644-46.

1385.1 *Post Office. A Monthly Journal for Stamp Collectors.* 2 (Apr. 1892–Mar. 1893), 3 (Apr. 1893–Mar. 1894), 4 (Apr. 1894–Mar. 1895). (GLD)

> Many short WCE articles and ads throughout; e.g., "Post Office at the World's Fair." 3.26 (1893).

1386.1 *Prairie School Review* [architecture magazine]. 9 (1972).

> Turak, Theodore. "A Celt Among Slavs: Louis Sullivan's Holy Trinity Cathedral." 9.4.(1972): 5-23. Contains description of the Russian exhibit at the WCE and two related illus.

1386.2 *Preservation.* Washington, DC: National Trust for Historic Preservation. 50 (1998).

> Young, Dwight. "At the birth of a new century, the White City inspired civic beauty. Why can't that happen again?" 50.5 (Sept./Oct. 1998): 112. Asks why there aren't more pretty places like the WCE.

1386.3 *Printers' Review.* Boston. (1893). (WM)

> "World's fair edition." n.s. no 13. 1 May 1893: 1-12. Yellowish tan wraps, brown print with illus of Golding & Co's Chicago storefront and 2 WCE Bldgs. Many printer's ads and lithos of presses. Exhibit located in Machinery Bldg, map on back. ☺. (WM) **P➜**

1386.4 *Proceeding of the Entomological Society* [journal]. Washington, DC. 4 (1896).

> Chittenden, Frank Hurlbut. "A pod-inhabiting longicorn found at the Columbian Exposition." 4 (1896): 42-3. (HU, Muse Comp. Zoo: E.D. Col.)

1386.5 *Professional Pointer. Issued in the interests of professional photographers.* New York: E. & H.T. Anthony & co. 1 (1893).

> WCE exhibit of Anthony Co and other WF articles. 1.1 (1893).

1386.6 *Progressive Architecture.* (Aug. 1974).

> Zimmerman, Lawrence G. "World of fairs: 1851–1976." No. 8 (Aug. 1974): 64-72.

1386.7 *Public Ledger* [daily newspaper]. Philadelphia. 116 (1893).

> "Chicago Day." 10 Oct. 1893: 1. One full column detailing the record attendance.

1387.   *Public Opinion*: ▶Add pub: Washington and New York: Public Opinion co. 15 (1893), 17 (189?).

1388.   *Puck*: ▶Add pub. New York: Keppler & Schwarzmann, Publishers.
WCE color cartoons front and back covers. 27.679 (12 Mar. 1890).

> ☞ *Puck* magazines, whether WCE related or not, are ephemera sought after for their color illus which are suitable for framing. The center folds are especially collectible. Hence the price for individual issues ranges from $30 - 75. The cartoons illustrated foibles of the day, especially political ones, thus it is much like *Judge* (#1341) or today's *National Lampoon.*

1390.1 *Queen Isabella Journal.* 2 (1891), 3 (1892).

1391.1 *Railway Review* [journal]. (1893)

> Walker, Aldace Freeman. "The effect of competition upon railway construction and operation : address before the Railway Congress Auxiliary of the World's Columbian Exposition, June 23, 1893." 26 pp.

1395.1 *Reporter* [weekly newspaper]. Springfield, VT. (1893). (VtSSt)

> ◆"A fair hospital." 4 Aug. 1893: 3.
> ◆"The livestock exhibit." 20 Oct. 1893: 2.

1396.   *Review of Reviews*: ▶Sample articles:
> ◆Barrett, J.P. "Engineer Ferris and his Wheel." 8.3 (1893): 269-76.
> ◆Cravath, J.R. "Electricity at the World's fair." 8.1 (1893): 35-39.
> ◆Knaufft, Ernest. "Art at the Columbian Exposition." 7.41 (1893): 551-63.
> ◆Meredith, Virginia. "Woman's part at the World's Fair. 1. The board of lady managers." 7.40 (1893): 417-19.
> ◆Stead, F. Herbert. "An Englishman's impressions at the fair." 8.1 (1893): 30-34.
> ◆Windsor, Henry Haven. "Transit facilities in Chicago and on the fair grounds." 7.41 (1893): 548-50.

> ☞ Herbert F. Stead was a brother to *Review of Reviews* Editor, W.T. Stead, who died with the Titanic.

1397.1 *Royale Forum.* (1973).

> Jailer, Mildred. "Everybody loved a fair." No. 143 (15 June 1973): 2-4.

1400.   *Scientific American*: ▶Add article:
"The Tiffany glass exhibit." 70.10 (1894): 146.

1401.1 *Scientific Machinist.* Cleveland, OH. 2 (1893).

> "World's fair number" [title of issue]. 2.21 (Nov. 1893).

1402.   *Scribner's*: ▶Additional issue: 20 (1896).
Andrews, E. Benjamin. "A History of the Last Quarter Century in the United States." 20.3 (March 1896): 268-95. A summary and illus of the WCE including the final fires. See #721.6.

1404. *Seaboard: Illustrated Marine Weekly*: 5 (1893). ▸Add article for listed issue: (WM)
"Awards to Marine exhibitors." 5.49 (1893): 976. Full page list of WCE maritime winners; navy print.

1406. *Smithsonian*: ▸Additional issue: 24 (1993).
Patton, Phil. "'Sell the cookstove if necessary, but come to the Fair.'" [sic] 24.3 (1993): 38-51.

1407.1 *Southwestern Historical Quarterly*. 98 (1994).

Meister, C. "The Texas-State Building, J. Riely Gordon contribution to the World's Columbian Exposition." 98.1 (1994): 1-_.

1407.2 *Springtown Weekly Times* [newspaper]. Springtown, PA. (1893).

♦"Emaus provides trout for Pennsylvania exhibit." 6 May 1893: 1.
♦"World's Fair opens." 13 May 1893: 2.

1407.3 *St. Johnsbury Caledonian* [weekly newspaper]. St. Johnsbury, VT. (1893). (VtSSt)

"Vermont's Building." 4 May 1893.

1407.4 *St. Louis Daily Globe-Democrat* [newspaper]. St. Louis, MO. (1893).

"The World's fair. A Mighty Display of the Progress of the Nations." 30 Apr. 1893: 40.

1408.1 *Stamp specialist*. (1948).

Ellis, F. "Dies of the Columbian stamped envelopes, commemorative of 1893." (1948).

1408.2 *Staten Island Advance* [newspaper]. Staten Island, NY. (1992).

"World's Fair Discovery Day at the Alice Austen House." 2 Oct. 1992: D2. See #1226.1.

1410.1 *Sun and Shade*. New York: Photo-gravure co. 6 (1893).

"The court of honor of the World's fair of Chicago." 32x26½. (2) p, 12 *l* plates of major WCE bldgs; plates are separated by tissue guards. The (2) p text describes each plate. Gray stiff wraps with illus of French's Statue of the Republic. 6.4 (Dec. 1893). A monthly artistic periodical.   P➔

1410.2 *Sun-Times* [newspaper]. Chicago. (1982).

Braden, William. "A fair to remember." 5 Dec. 1982: 72-73.

1412.1 *Sycamore True Republican* [newspaper]. Sycamore, IL. (1893).

♦"Illinois day. The State Building on the World's Fair Grounds Dedicated." 27 May 1893.
♦"Hastening the end. The Work of Demolition at the World's Fair Grounds Begins." 4 Nov, 1893.
♦Sibley, Lavinia Maud. "What a Little Girl Saw at the Fair." 15 Nov 1893. Lavinia was 10.
[Photocopies of many *True Republican* WCE articles are located in a 3-ring binder in the Sycamore Public Library History Room.]

1412.2 *T-Square* [drafting and architecture journal]. 1 (1931).

Watts, Harvey M. "The white city." 1 (May 1931): 24-27, 41-46.

1412.3 *Tampa Tribune* [newspaper]. Tampa, FL. (1993).

Hawes, Leland. "All she wanted was a Fair opportunity." 13 June 1993, sec. 4, Bay Life. Describes Mrs. Moseley's palmetto quilt exhibit at WCE, and Florida's failure to mount an effective presence at the WF due to politics and confusion.

1412.4 *Tansill's Punch* [monthly]. New York, Chicago and San Francisco: R.W. Tansill Co. 2 (1892).

> 28x22. Self-wraps, black print. Cartoon and humor magazine. (GLD)
> "The Fisheries building." 2.4 (1892): 14. Text and litho.

1412.5 *Technograph*. Champaign and Urbana, IL: U of Illinois Engineering Societies. 11 (1896-97).

> Peabody, Arthur. "The World's Columbian Exposition : a constructive problem and its value as a criterion." 11 (1896-97): 66-85. (HML)

1412.6 *Teknisk Ugeblad*. Kristiania: Foreningernes Forlag. 11 (1893). (UBO)

> 31½x24. Norwegian language. Trans: "Technical Weekly."
> ♦"Arkitektoniske arbeider til verdensudstillingen i Chicago." 11.8 (1893): 62. Architecture at WCE.
> ♦"Gasudstillingen i den norske håndværks- og industriforening." 11.12 (1893): 91. Norway's exhibits.
> ♦"Chicagoudstillingen." 11.13 (1893): 102. Scandinavian Engineering Society of Chicago's letter regarding their meeting at the WF.
> ♦"Chicago stipendierne." 11.13 (1893): 102. Expenses for Norwegian representatives to the WCE.
> ♦"'Det norske hus' på udstillingen i Chicago i 1893." 11.21 (1893): 167-68. Illus are architectural plan, front and side elevation, for the WCE Norway Bldg.
> ♦"Reise stipendier til Chicago udstillingen for anlaegsingteniører." 11.23 (1893): 175.
> ♦"Worthington kompagniets pumpstation på Chicago udstillingen." 11.30 (1893): 247-50. 3 lithos.
> ♦"Lehman tårnet." 11.32 (1893): 255 + fold out. Unrealized WCE ride planned by Karl H. Lehman. Fold out diagram showing the 10-turn downward spiral.
> ♦"Trinbane ved verdensudstillingen i Chicago." 11.34 (1893): 265-66. Describes three-track electrical transporter which would move 32,000 persons/hour. Unrealized.
> ♦"Lidt om Chicago udstillingens størrelse." 11.35 (1893): 267-69. Trans: A little bit about the size of the WCE. Compares size with previous World's fairs.
> ♦"Lehman tårnet i Chicago." 11.43 (1893): 317. Smaller two-turn ride, unrealized.
> ♦"Ferris hjul." 11.43 (1893): 318-19. Illus and description of the colossal wheel.

1412.7 *Temperance Publication Bureau*. (1893). (WM)

> Keane, J.J. "The Church is Against the Saloon." No. 6 (Feb. 1893): (3)-8. Pub was the work of The Catholic Total Abstinence Union of America. No WCE content; from intact collection.

1412.8 *Tin and Terne*. Pittsburgh, PA. 2 (1893). (WM)

> Patterson, B.S. "Tin and Tin Plate at the World's Fair." 2.11 (1893): 8. Rust wraps, black print. The plate exhibit was at the southern end of the Mining Bldg in a pavilion made of American tin. See #724.

1413. *To-day's Events*: ▶Additional issue. **P➜**
24 Oct. 1893. Below title: "Midway program." (8) p.

1414.1 *Tour du monde*. 65 (1894).

> Bruwaert, E. "Chicago et l'Exposition." 65 (1894).

1414.2 *Transactions of the American society of civil engineers*. New York: The Society. 29 (1893), 30 (1893).

> Complete set of papers given at the International Engineering Congress. See #1231.1 and #2194.4-6.

1417. *Union Signal* [newspaper]: Chicago. (1891), (1892), (1893).
A daily temperance W.C.T.U. paper with many articles about the WCE. ▶Add article:
"World's fair supplement" [title of issue]. No. 32. 11 Aug. 1892.

> ☞ Frances Elizabeth Willard was editor-in-chief of the *Union Signal* from 1892. National W.C.T.U. headquarters and the Willard Memorial Library (source "WML") are located in Evanston, Illinois.

1417.1 *United Opinion* [newspaper]. Bradford, VT. 12 (1893), 13 (1894). (GLD)

> ✦"From Queensland. South sea savages to visit the world's fair." 3 Mar. 1893: 2.
> ✦"Rooms for the millions. How World's Fair Authorities Will Take Care of Visitors." 10 Mar. 1893: 3. This "Inaugural Edition" has a 4 p supplement devoted to the WCE, pp 9-12.
> ✦"Men who make books. Member of the national typothetæ dine. Red Chamber of New York's Building at Jackson Park the Scene of a Brilliant Assemblage of Witty Men-Handsome Decorations." 29 Sept. 1893: 2. Poet Eugene Field was a member and guest at the dinner.
> ✦"The danse du ventre. Queer, Ugly and Belongs With the Museum Freaks, Says Kate Jordan." 5 Jan. 1894: 3. Describes dance and woman in the Street in Cairo, WCE.

1418. *United States trade mark association bulletin*: ▶Add article.
"Trade Mark Congress." 5.1 (1893): 5-7. Preliminary Address of the Committee on a Patent and Trade Mark Congress.

1419.1 *University School Record.* Cleveland, OH: Student publication of University School. 4 (1893). (GLD)

> ✦Darlington, C.L. "The Margles at the Fair." 4.1 (Oct. 1893): 3-5. Fictionalized account of his trip to the WCE.
> ✦"Locals." 4.2 (Nov. 1893): 9. Mr. H.P. McIntosh will donate ore specimens from the WCE exhibit of the Canadian Copper Co. to the school museum.   [Logo from cover] P➔

1420.1 *Utica Observer* [newspaper]. Utica, NY. 44 (1892).

1420.2 *Ventura County Historical Society Quarterly.* 4 (1959).

Pfiler, Robert. "Ventura County [California] at the Columbian Exposition." 4.4 (1959).

1420.3 *Vermont Watchman & State Journal* [newspaper]. (1894).

"The State Flower." 17 Oct. 1894: 4. Explains how women's committees at the WCE named the flower of the state for the first time. Vermont's flower is red clover. See #64.1. (VSA)

1420.4 *Wall Street Journal.* 5 (1893).

"At Chicago. Chicago special.–Paid attendance at World's Fair yesterday 713,646, and including..." 10 Oct. 1893: 1. This brief business article concerns Chicago Day and cancellation of the WCE debt.

1420.5 *Weekly Philatelist* [stamp news]. New Chester, PA. 1 (1893).   Per issue: $10 - 20

> ✦"The World's Fair City." 1.9 (1893): 1. S.B. Bratt Co. at 136 Wabash provided rooms for stamp societies during the WF. 23½x15. (GLD)
> ✦"The World's Fair City." 1.11 (1893): 1. (S)
> ✦"Report of the World's Fair Executive Committee." 1.19 (1893): 1. (S)
> ✦"The World's Fair City." 1.20 (1893): 1. (S)

1423.1 *Western School Journal.* Topeka, KS. 8 (1892).

> ✦"Next summer the World's Educational Congress..." 8.12 (1892): 278.
> ✦"Educational exhibit fund." 8.12 (1892): 291. Lists KS WCE educational exhibit expenditures by county to Nov 3, 1892.
> ✦Wooster, L. C. "The Columbian history of education in Kansas." 8.12 (1892): 291-92. Call for local school district history articles for inclusion in #1883, and rules for KS education displays at the WCE.

1423.2 *Wheelmen : Official Magazine of The Wheelmen* [semi-annual]. (1992).

Edwards, Karl. "Giddings' mounted infantry : Connecticut's first signal corps and the bicycle." No. 41 (Nov. 1992): 7-13. Article describes the Hartford Columbia Safety Bicycle, which was used by the First Signal Corp; the corps rode at the WCE (illus). A short biography of Albert A. Pope (see #980 to #982.1) whose co manufactured this bicycle. P⬇

1426.   *Woman's Home Missions*: 10 (1893). ▶Add article.
"Congress of Missions." 10.9 (1893): 134. Congress held Sept 28–Oct 5, 1893. Description of their exhibit in the Woman's Bldg.

1427.   *Woman's Tribune* [weekly newspaper]: Clara Bewick Colby, ed. (1893). ▶Add articles.
♦"World's Fair Notes." 10.16 (1893): 64. Describes Woman's Congress, 15–22 May. Illus of MA Bldg.
♦Randall, Sara E. "World's Fair Letter." 10.30 (1893): 120. Her view of women's activities at the WCE. Includes unhappy Indians from Albuquerque, NM, Indian School who did good work in industrial training.
♦"World's Fair Letter." 10.36 (1893): 144. Full page on Government Congress.
♦"A Glimpse of the fair." Harriet N. Ralston's trip through the WCE.
♦"Dental Congress." 10.38 (1893): 150. Lists woman dentists at the congress.
♦"Arbitration and Peace Congress." 10.38 (1893): 151. Women at the congress.

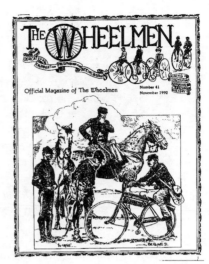

1428.   *World*: ▶Add annotation: "Columbian Exposition edition." 17 May 1891. Pp 29-36. Records the initial WF layout and personnel.

1429.   *World's Columbian Exposition Illustrated* [Campbell]:
[Untitled article]. 3.10: 276. Union News Company set up 50 newsstands on the WCE grounds designed around model railroad station concessions. Other vendors were allowed to apply to the Union News Company for space to sell related wares (gum/candy/smokes/etc.). See #1677 for a Union News sponsored publication.

1429.1 *World's Columbian Exposition News*. 2 (1893).

"Souvenir edition" [title of issue]. 2.52 (1893).

1431.   *World's Fair*: ▶Annotation: Published from 1981 to 1995.
Reinhardt, Richard. "She never saw the streets of Cairo." 1.2 (1981): 13-16.

1438.   *Young Crusader* [W.C.T.U. monthly magazine]: 7 (1893). ▶Add article:
Guernsey, Alice M. "The Children's Building." 7.8 (1893): 1-2. Illus article of activities and services in the Children's Bldg.

1440.1 *Zeitschrift für bildende Kunst*. 5 (1894). Trans: Newspaper for the visual arts.

Bode, W. "Eindrücke von einem Besuche der Weltausstellung." n.f.?, Bd. 5 (1894). Trans: Impression of a visit to the WF.

Chapter 8

MAGAZINES - BOUND

1441.1 *The Atlantic monthly : a magazine of Literature, Science, Art, and Politics.* Boston and New York: Houghton, Mifflin and Co., 1893 [c1892, c1893].

24½x17. Vol 71: iv, 860 p. Half leather and black cloth. See #1250. ☺ (GLD) $20 - 45

1442.   *The Century*: ▶Add bound issue: n.s. 21 (Nov. 1891–Apr. 1892).

1442.1 *Christian Science Journal.* National Christian Scientist's Association. 11 (Apr. 1893–Mar. 1894). (GLD)

1442.2 *The Cosmopolitan : a monthly illustrated magazine.* 14 (Nov. 1892–Apr. 1893). John Brisben Walker, ed.

24x18. 767, (1) p. Contains "The Great Congresses at the World's Fair" by Ellen Henrotin which is the only WCE article in vol 14. ☺ (GLD)   Volume 14: $20 - 40

1444.   *The Cosmopolitan* [Vol 16]: (B)

1446.1 *Demorest's family magazine.* New York: W. Jennings Demorest, Publisher, 1893.

28½x21½. Contains 12 issues for 1893: Vol 29, no 3-12 plus Vol 30, no 1-2. Half leather on marbled boards, red dyed edges. Sept. issue (no 11) is full WCE issue, but many articles and illus on WCE are scattered throughout. One pretty color litho per month (not WCE related). ☺ (GLD) $60 - 130

1447.   *Electrical Engineering*: (S)

1448.1 *Engineering News.* New York: Engineering news publishing co. 30 (July-Dec. 1893).

This railroad journal (35x27) has numerous articles and illustrations, some folding, relating to the WCE and the Transportation exhibits. Excellent source for WCE railroad info. (GLD) $140 - 280

1452.   *Harper's Weekly*: (GLD)   52 issues bound together: $250 - 450
---- Also found: Issues from 35.1818 (Oct. 1891) to 37.1930 (Dec. 1893) bound together.

1453.   *Harper's Young People*: (S)
1456.   *The Illustrated World's Fair* (Halligan): (CCA,CLP,HU,IStU,KS,RU)

1456.1 *The inland printer : a technical journal devoted to the art of printing.* Chicago: The Inland Printer Co., Publishers. 10 (Oct. 1892–Mar. 1893).

31x24½. v, (1), 560 p. Articles on WCE. ☺ (S)

1456.2 *Inter Ocean : illustrated supplement.* Chicago. Aug. 14, 1892–Jan. 14, 1894.

46x32. Blind stamped black cloth hc, gilt print. ☺ (MSI)

1456.3 *The Journal of the Franklin Institute, devoted to science and the mechanic arts.* Philadelphia: Published by the Institute. 133 (1892).

23x16. Vol 133, No 5, May 1892. In this vol, no 5 is the only number with WCE content. Pp 356-70 plus a fold out map of the grounds; no author listed. No WCE content in vol 134. (UPa)

1457.1 *The Post Office. A Monthly Journal for Stamp Collectors.* New York: Henry Gremmel, 2 (Apr. 1892–Mar. 1893), 3 (Apr. 1893–Mar. 1894), 4 (Apr. 1894–Mar. 1895).

23½x16. Vol 2: 108 p+ ads. Vol 3: 160 p+ ads. Vol 4: 180 p+ ads. Maroon cloth hc, gilt spine print. WCE articles are scattered throughout. [No WCE articles are found in Vol 1 (1891–92) or Vol 5 (1895–96).] ☺ (GLD)   Each: $20 - 55

1457.2 *The Review of Reviews*. New York. 4 (Aug. 1891–Jan. 1892), 6 (Aug. 1892–Jan. 1893), 7 (Feb.–June 1893), 8 (July–Dec. 1893). American edition. Albert Shaw, ed.

Vol 4: 24½x19. viii, 763, (1) p. Frontis illus of each issue is not included in pagination. Company binding: brown and tan cloth hc, brown and tan print and illus of globe and torch, gilt spine print. Brief WCE articles scattered throughout. **P→**

Vol 6: 24½x19½. viii, 776 p. Company binding: blood red cloth hc, gilt print. Numerous WCE articles and illus.

Vol 7: 25x20. 640 p. Not a company binding. Numerous WCE articles and illus.

Vol 8: 25x20. 752 p. Not a company binding. Numerous WCE articles and illus.

☺ (GLD)   Each: $20 - 40

☞ The English edition was edited by W.T. Stead. See #38 and #1396.

1459. *Scientific American*: (GPL)

1460. *Scientific American Supplement*: (CCA)

1461. *Scribner's Magazine*: ▶Additional issue. (1896). (GLD,S)
---- Also found: Bound in half leather.

1462. *World's Columbian Exposition Illustrated* (Campbell): (B,BrU,CCA,DC,GPL,HML,IHi,IStU,RU,UIC,WM)

1463. *World's Fair Puck*: (LBA,S,Stfd,Yale)

Chapter 9

MUSIC

1465.1 *American Day : July fourth : 1893 : at the : World's Columbian exposition : under the auspices of the : Municipality of Chicago.* Chicago: R.R. McCabe & co., printers, [1893?].

29½x18. 8 p. Buff wraps with litho of American flag; black print. Sheet music. Marten B. Madden was chairman of the committee. Mr. S.G. Pratt arranged the music. (ref)$165

☞ Mr. Pratt was also in charge of music at Chicago Day, October 9, 1893.

1466. *America's National Songs*: (E)
▸Add to blue wraps version: ᶜ1895 by Geo. M. Vickers. At top of cover: "Revised and enlarged : Columbian edition." At bottom of front cover: "With Compliments of Lit Brothers."
---- Also found: Philadelphia: Parkview Publishing Co., 1903? 15½x10. 46 p. Green wraps, chromolith of woman and eagle behind crossed flags. String tied. C.t. At head of title: "A.D. 1903 : Columbian Edition : Price 25¢..." Below cover illus: ᶜ1898 by Geo. M. Vickers.

1468. *The Auditorium*: (S) $20 - 45

☞ The Auditorium on Michigan Avenue in Chicago has been the home of Roosevelt University since the 1940s. The exterior is essentially identical to its 1893 appearance. The Auditorium's grand 9th floor banquet room with decorated semi-circular high ceilings is now the library. Frank A. Cassell is Dean and author of many WCE items (see index).

1468.1 *The auditorium : children's song festival : World's fair chorus : eleven hundred voices : Wednesday evening, April 6, 1892 : under the direction of Theodore Thomas and Wm. L. Tomlins.* Chicago?: [The Craig press], 1892?

18x15½. Sheet printed both sides in dark blue. C.t. Program on reverse. See #1537 for another Tomlins children's music item. ☺ (GLD) $18 - 40

1469.1 Beach, H.H.A. *Festival jubilate : composed for the dedication of the Woman's building, at the World's Columbian Exposition, Chicago, 1892.* Boston: Schmidt, ᶜ1892.

27x__. (43) p. Score for mixed voices with orchestra and piano. (HU)

1471. Blanchard. *Columbian Memorial*: (HU,IHi,UIC)
1472. Bloss. *The World's fair*: (UH)

1475. Brainard. *Sounds from St. John*: (WM)
▸Correction: (16) p with 16 music selections.

1475.1 Brigham, G.B. *African Patrol.* Chicago: National Music Co., ᶜ1893 by National Music Co.

35x26½. 6 p. Buff wraps, black print and illus of American and African Blacks. No lyrics. Embossed in red on cover "Souvenir of The A.C. Andrew Music Co. : Willimantic, Conn." [The National Music exhibit was in the Liberal Arts Bldg.] ☺ (S)

1476. Brooke. *Columbian Guards*: P➔
▸Correct paging: 6 p including b/w litho on cream front cover plus back cover ad. Internal pages are numbered 2–5. Song title: "Columbian guard march." (GLD) $40 - 80

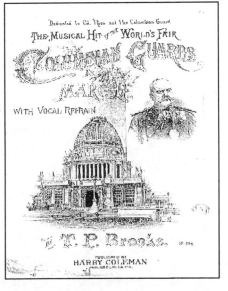

1478.   *Cairo Street Waltz*: (GLD,S)   P➜ $40 - 85
1481.   Chadwick. *Ode for the opening*: (GU,HU,Yale)

1482.1 *Clara Simond's popular songbook.* Chicago: Will Rossiter, ᶜ1893.

    26x17½. (14) p. Pink wraps with port illus of Simond, blue print.
C.t. "Price, 25¢." Contains songs such as "Naughty Doings on the
Midway Plaisance." ☺ (GLD) $20 - 45

1485.   *Columbus grand march* (Maywood): (S)
1486.   *Concert given in honor of Their Royal Highnesses*: (S)

1487.   Crist. *World's Fair Grand March*: (S)
    ---- Also found: Cover variant without port of Crist and with "50 Cts"
at bottom; black border.

1489.   DeMoss. *The Columbian souvenir songs*: (S)
    ---- Also found: 161, (2) p ads. Brown cloth spine over tan paper
boards; red and blue print and crossed US flags in color. Songs and music composed by DeMoss for each
state represented at the fair. Each state's building is pictured with its song.

1489.1 DeMoss, Henry S. *My Happy Little Home in Arkansas.* Chicago?: Compliments of W.G. Vincenheller,
Commissioner of Mines, Manufactures and Agriculture, ᶜ1893 by the DeMoss Family.

    18x13½. (2) p includes cover. Cover litho of Arkansas State Bldg by A. Zeese & Co. Words and music
by Henry S. DeMoss, as sung by the DeMoss family at the WCE. Also on cover: "Columbian Souvenir
Songs No. 14." For companion item, see #1489. ☺ (UoA)

    ☞ A set of kettle drums labeled for the World's Columbian Exposition, 1893, may be found at the Miles
Musical Museum in Eureka Springs, Arkansas.

1489.2 Ditson, Oliver, Co. *"World's fair." : "classic" "choice" : and "popular" : series.* [Boston: Oliver Ditson
co.], n.d.

    16½x14. (8) p includes self-wraps. Black print and design. Ads for 5 Ditson WCE music collections on
p (2). Ad similar to #1558. ☺ (WM)

1489.3 Ditson, Oliver, Co. *Oliver Ditson Company's : new and magnificent Music Books : 1893-4.* Boston: Oliver
Ditson Co. (The Sparrell print), n.d.

    13½x8. 49 p. Page 49 is the inside of the back cover. Blue flecked gray wraps, navy blue print and
design. Includes Ditson's World's fair music books. (S)

1493.   Everett. *World's fair musical souvenir*: (S)
1497.   Glazounow. *Triumphal March*: (HU,UCD)
1499.   *The Hand that Holds the Bread*: (Berk,DC,EvP,Heb,KCPL,Stfd,UMC,UMD,UVM,)

1499.1 Heins, Carl. *Worlds* [sic] *Columbian exhibition Gavot. Chicagoer weltausstellungs–Gavotte.* Op. 130. Berlin: Verlag von P. Thelen, [ᶜ1893].

    34x27. 1 *l* cover, 3-7, (1) p. Final page is a sample sheet from
"Zigeuner-Zug." Color litho cover entitled: "Chicago Exhibition Gavotte
: Chicagoer Weltausstellungs–Gavotte." ☺ . (ref)   P➜

1502.   *Hitchcock's Musical Pictorial and Descriptive*: (S)

1502.1 Holst, Eduard, and Anton Gill. *After the fair.* Milwaukee: Wm. Rohlfing & sons, [ᶜ1893 by Wm. Rohlfing
& Sons].

    35½x26½. 1 *l* cover, 3-6 p score, 1 *l* back cover with ad on outside. Title on cover printed in red;
remainder of cover print and border design are navy. C.t. = song title. At top of cover: "The hit of the
season." ☺ (GLD)   P⬇ $30 - 60

1503.   Holst. *World's Columbian Exposition March*:
▶Add to the "Also found" citation in the original book (i.e., English and
German title; no bird's-eye): 15 p. At head of c.t.: "1492 Eduard Holst
1892." For piano, four hands. (S)
---- Also found: 37½x27. 14 p. For piano solo. Cover facsimile of a
Sept 20, 1892, letter from Bertha Palmer to the publisher agreeing to have
this march dedicated to her. The facsimile is surrounded by a gilt floral
display and toped with a small port of Columbus. At top of cover is the
dedication to Mrs. Palmer. Title in blue on p 3; other pages with vignettes
of WCE bldgs in blue, all surrounded by stars and stripes, etc., in red. (S)

1505.1 Kingsley, W.B. *A memento of the great Chicago fair*. Cincinnati New
York Chicago: The John Church Co., [°1893 by The John Church Co.].

36x27½. 2-5 p. Self-wraps, black print. "Words by Jas. Greal." (S)

1506.   Kiralfy. *Imre Kiralfy's grand*: (DC,GLD,csuf,IHi,UMD)

☞ Kiralfy (1845–1919) was connected with the Earls Court Exhibition, London, from 1895–1903. He
was in charge of London's "Great White City" Franco-British Exhibition of 1908; the exhibition was the
site of the 1908 Olympic games.

1507.   Koelling. *World's Columbian Exposition Waltz*: (KS)
---- Flyer. (KS)

1507.1 Kranich & Bach Pianos. *The Leading Piano of the World : Kranich & Bach. Pianos : Before the public for
Thirty Years*. New York: Kranich & Bach (artwork ©Thos. Jay Gleason, NY), n.d.

13½x17½. (4) p. Folded sheet with chromolith illus front and back. Back cover bird's-eye view of the
WCE with caption: "World's Fair, Chicago. U.S.A. 1893." C.t. Ad. Sample music by Haslinger
entitled "Kosmos March" on p (3). ☺ (GLD,WM) $20 - 50

1507.2 Lamb, Henry. *The World's Fair. 2. English blonde, polka*. Boston: Oliver Ditson Co., °1892 by Oliver
Ditson Co.

35½x27½. 5 p. Buff wraps, black print with ports of six ladies in costume, one for each of the six pieces
in the set. Others pieces are: 1. "Fair Columbia, waltz," 3. "Italian girl, york," 4. "Scotch lassie,
galop," 5. "Chinese maiden, march," and 6. "Spanish belle, schottische." ☺ (S)

1509.1 LeBrunn, Geo[rge]. *HI-TIDDLEY-HI-TI, or I'm all right*. Baltimore, MD: Charles M. Stieff, n.d.

36x28. (4) p. Large folded buff sheet. Black print and illus with compliments of Stieff printed in red at top
and bottom. Also on front: "The Bromo-Seltzer collection of 54 Popular Songs, complete and unabridged,…
See The STIEFF PIANO at World's Exposition, Chicago, 1893, Department of Liberal Arts." Rpt of a song
in the Bromo-Seltzer collection; none of the collection has WF titles. Words by E.W. Rogers. WCE handout
for Emerson Drug Co. of Baltimore (see also #836.1). ☺ (GLD) $35 - 60

1510.   Little. *Chicago World's Exposition grand march*:
---- Also found: Little, C.E. …*Chicago : World's Exposition : Grand
March*. Chicago: F.S. Chandler & co., publishers, °1890 by F.S.
Chandler & co. 35x27. 1 *l* cover, (2)-6 p score, outside back cover with
ad. Satirical cover illus depicts "Uncle Sam" and globe flanked by 1492
and 1893 on pink background with beige border (illus is same as #1545).
C.t. same as #1545; song title and score are identical to Chicago Music
Co. version of #1510. C.t. At head of title: "Dedicated by the
publishers to all who believe in 'the eternal fitness of things.'" At bottom
of p (2): "Copyright 1890 by C.E. Little." [What was the business
connection was between the two different composers and publishers listed
for the same music, #1510 and #1545?] ☺ (GLD,KS,S)

1511.   Luders. *An Afternoon in Midway Plaisance*: (ref,S)   P↑ $40 – 95

1511.1 Luders, Gus[tav], and Arthur J. Lamb. *On The Lagoon.* Chicago:
Edward A. Saalfeld, ᶜ1893 by Edward A. Saalfeld.   P→

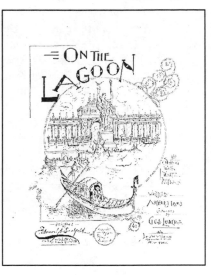

35½x26½. 1 *l* cover, 1-3 p score, outside back cover blank. Front
cover: very dark green print and illus of gondola on the Grand Basin
lagoon. ☺(GLD) $30 - 65

1512.   Mathewson. *Columbian Polka*: (GLD)   P↙ $30 - 60

1513.1 Maywood, Geo[rge]. *Ferris Wheel March.* Chicago: The S. Brainard's
Sons Co., ᶜ1893 by The S. Brainard's Sons Co.   P↓

35½x27½. 1 *l* cover, 3-5 p score, back cover ad. Front cover red
lettering, large b/w litho of the Ferris wheel, price: "40c." Song title
= c.t. See #1538, *Ferris Wheel March* sampler. ☺(GLD) $30 - 70

1514.   Maywood. *World's Exposition*: ☺(GLD) $30 - 65
▸Add cover description: Red lettering on beige wraps. There is no cover bird's-eye view, distinguishing
this version from those below.
---- Also found: "For Piano." 35x27. (1) p cover with WCE bird's-eye view, 2-5 p score, ads on outside
back cover include two dated 1898 and 1902. Bold red lettering on cream wraps; maize block over WCE
bird's-eye, which is "Copyrighted 1892 by A. Zeese & Co. Chicago." Front cover lists 4 versions: "For
Piano, 50c. Four Hands, 75c. Orchestra, 50c. Brass Band, 50c."
---- Also found: "Four Hands." 35½x27½. (1) p cover, 2-9 p score, ads on outside back cover are all
for World's fair music, undated. Bold red lettering on cream wraps; the WCE bird's-eye view is the same
as piano version's directly above. Printed under song title on pp
2 and 3 of this item: "Arranged for 4 Hands By F.A.G."

1518.1 Monroe, Karl. *Nations of all the Earth : a Thrilling Patriotic Song and chorus : Song of Welcome.*
Youngstown, OH: Published by D.O. Evans, ᶜ1893 by D.O. Evans.   P↗

35½x27½. 1 *l* cover, 3-5 p score; the outside back cover is blank. The cover has black print and litho of
the Admin Bldg on buff paper. C.t. The caption song title is: "Nations of all the earth. (Song of
welcome.)." ☺(GLD) $30 - 65

1518.2 Morgan, Bert. ...*Exposition waltz.* Chicago: Tryber & Sweetland, ᶜ1890 by Tryber & Sweetland.

34½x26. 3 p. Black print on cream paper. At top of cover: "Lakeside edition." Below title on p 1:
"Revised edition by the Author, 1891." The Lakeside organ is illus on back cover. (A)

1520.   *"Old Vienna"*: (S,UMD)

---- Also found: (4) p programme for "Wednesday, Sept. 27th, 1893." Otherwise the same.

1520.1 Ormsbee-Gregory, C. ...*Are You Going To The Fair At Chicago?* New York: B.W. Hitchcock, publisher, [ᶜ1893 by Benjamin W. Hitchcock].

36x27½. (3) p. Buff stock; black print. At top of cover: "Dedicated to the memory of Queen Isabella and Christopher Columbus." There are 4 verses. ☺ (GLD)   P➔ $30 - 65

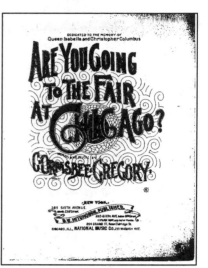

1522.   Paine. *Columbus March*: (HU)

---- Also found: Original manuscript of the *Columbus March and Hymn.* 36½x26. 78 p. (HU)

1522.1 Phelps, E.S. *Columbian fair march.* New York: Richard A. Saalfield, ᶜ1891 by J.H. Thomas.

34½x27. 5 p. Buff wraps with black print and ornate corner border design. No illus. No lyrics. ☺ (S)

1525.   Presto. *Musical instruments at the World's Columbian*: (RU)

1532.   Schleiffarth. *A trip through the Midway Plaisance*: (GLD,S) $35 - 60

---- Also found: 36x27½. 10 p includes front cover. Cream covers in matte finish, rust-red and chocolate print and design. C.t. with embossed "Midway Plaisance." At top of front cover (corrected): "Chicago Worlds [sic] Fair 1893." Original price was 75¢; the orchestra edition was $1.50.

1534.1 Smith, Eva Munson. *"Woman in Sacred Song." An address given in : assembly hall, woman's building, Columbian exposition, Chicago, Ill., Aug. 16, 1893.* Springfield, IL: [Eva M. Smith], 1893? P➔

17½x12½. 40 p. Frontis port of Smith. Beige wraps with brown print. C.t. Author also known by Mrs. George Clinton Smith. "It includes Poetry, Music, Biography and Portraits of Authors." ☺ . (IHi)

1536.   Steinert. *Catalogue of the M. Steinert*: (CUE,S,UPa)

▸Completed cite: Pale pink wraps, black print, string-tied. C.t. = t.p.

1536.1 Steinert, Morris. *The M. Steinert collection of keyed and stringed instruments. With various treatises on the history of these instruments, the method of playing them, and their influence on musical art.* New York: Charles F. Tretbar [Press of H.A. Rost], [ᶜ1893 by C.F. Tretbar].

26½x16. 7 *l*, (15)-170 p. Dark green cloth hc with embossed black floral band top and bottom, gilt spine print. Maize dj duplicates t.p. 1st *l* is t.p.; 5th *l* is half title which = #1536; 7th *l* is port of Steinert. Illus catalog of instruments he exhibited at WCE. ☺ (GLD,CU) $90 - 170

1536.2 Summy, Clayton F. *Catalogue of Weekes co.'s Musical Publication...* Chicago?: [Clayton F. Summy], n.d.

15x11½. 15 p. Self wraps of peach paper. Black print and design. No WCE content; from intact collection. Summy published *The Music Review*; ad on back cover. [Their exhibit was in Liberal Arts, Group 158, Section I, W-7.] (WM)

1536.3 Summy, Clayton F. *Clayton F. Summy's catalogue of Musical Publications.* Chicago?: Clayton F. Summy, n.d.

15x11. 11, (5) p ads+ ads inside covers. Gun-metal gray wraps, black print and design. C.t. Summy published *The Music Review*; ad on back cover. No WCE content; from intact collection. (WM)

1536.4 Swain, Frank. *The Last Day of the Fair. Waltz Brilliant.* [Chicago?]:
The Thompson music co., ᶜ1893 by Frank Swain.

35x26½. 1 *l* cover, (3)-7 p score, outside back cover ad. B/w cover
with litho of "I Will" lady shaking hands with people of various ethnic
extraction who are leaving the fairgrounds. C.t. At top of cover:
"Dedicated to George R. Davis, Director General, of the Worlds [sic]
Columbian exposition." © (GLD)   P➜ $30 - 65

1537.   Tomlins. *Children's Souvenir*: (GLD)   P↙ $30 - 65
---- Also found: Buff paper-covered hc boards, maize cloth spine;
same design as wraps ed. but all printed in black. Songs were sung by
the Exposition Children's Chorus, p 3. One song by poet Harriet
Monroe, p 8. (GLD)

1539.1 *Twelfth of the Regular Amateur Recitals. Thursday, October 26th,
1893...Assembly Hall, Woman's Building.* N.p.: n.p., n.d.

21½x14. Single leaf printed in maroon one side only. © (S)

1540.   Valisi. *Chicago Day Waltz*: (IHi)

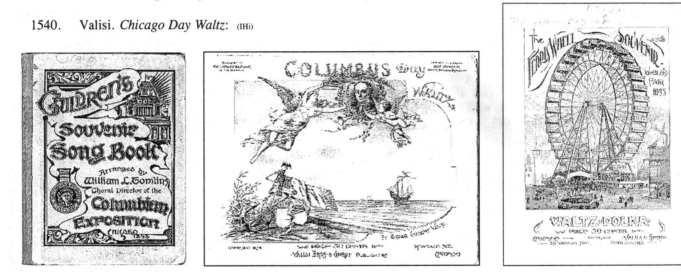

1540.1 Valisi, Giuseppe. *Columbus Day Waltz.* Chicago: Valisi Bros. & Giorgi, ᶜ1893.

28x36½. 4 p. Chromolith cover illus of angel and cherub surrounding port of Columbus all suspended
over the 3 caravels as they are about to land in the New World. Music and cover in landscape with cover
fold at top. "Dedicated to Mrs. Bertha Honore Palmer... President of Board of Lady Managers : World's
Columbian Exposition." © (GLD)   P↑ $45 - 90

1541.   Valisi. *The Ferris Wheel Waltz*: (GLD,UH)   P↗

1542.   Verner. *The Viking March*: © (GLD,S)   P➜
▸Corrections: 1 *l* cover, 3-5 p, back cover ad. C.t.: "The Viking March :
Captain Andersen's Viking Ship : From Norway to the World's Fair."
Page 3 title: *The viking march.*
---- Also found: Cover variants: White (or yellow) wraps, blue print.

1545.   Vogel. *Chicago World's Exposition Grand March*: (GLD)   P↓
---- Also found: Chicago: National. Rust background with beige border.

☞ See #1510 for different composer/publisher but same title and similar
cover design. Fairly common.

1547. *Weiner Musik erinnerung an old Vienna*: (LBA,WM) **P↗**

1547.1 Winteringer, J. Markus H., and Julius Falkner. *...Innes' march and two-step*. Pittsburg, PA: The Winteringer music co., [°1895 by Mrs. William Hyser].

   35x27½. 3 p. White folded sheet with red print and photo illus of Innes' large band in a band shell outside the WCE Admin Bldg. At head of title: "Dedicated to and especially written for F.N. Innes and His famous band." ☺ (S)

1547.2 *Women at an Exposition : Music composed by women and performed at the 1893 World's Fair in Chicago.* KOCH International Classics KOCH 70, °1991.

   12½x14 plastic case containing one compact disc. 19 songs. In addition to a bio of the performers, the descriptive pamphlet lists the music, including when and where it was performed at the Exposition. ☺ (RU,SPL)

1550. WCE. Bureau of Music. *[Programs of concerts.] Festival Hall Series*:
   ▸Add annotation: All programs have Columbus port logo at the top of page, followed by "World's Columbian Exposition. Chicago : May–October : 1893."
   ---- Festival Hall Series No. 1. *Wagner Programme.* May 22. 23x15. Folded *l*. ☺ . (ICRL,VtHx)

1551. WCE. Bureau of Music. *[Programs of concerts.] Music Hall Series*: ☺ (GLD) $25 - 50
   ---- Music Hall Series No. 26. *Ballad Concert.* June 29, 1893. 2 *l*.

1554. *World's fair ballad collection*: (HU,S)

1555. *The World's fair collection of Patriotic*: ☺ (GLD) $34 - 75
   ▸Correction: "Patriotic," "Songs," and "Airs" are capitalized on the t.p.; otherwise C.t. = t.p. Lists 5 other Ditson WF music collections which originally sold for $1 to $2 each depending on cover materials.

1560. *World's fair song and chorus collection*: (Fess,S)
   ▸Cover description: Brown (or tan) cloth hc, gilt design, black print.
   ▸Cover description: Padded leather, gilt print. (Fess)

Chapter 10

VIEW BOOKS

1562.1 *Album ___ : Worlds* [sic] *Columbian Exposition : 1893 : From Drawings By Special Artists.* Philadelphia: E.P. & Louis Restein, [ᶜ1892].

17x24½. (32) p. Gray wraps, raised gilt and dark gray print, string-tied. Chromolith plates of WCE views alternate with descriptions of each view. Similar to #1697. [Title torn.] (GLD) $20 - 40

1565.   American Biscuit. *The World's Fair reproduced with a Camera*: (KS)

1567.   *Architects Sketch of the World's Fair To be held at Chicago*: (Col,D,WM)
▶Add cover description: Red hc with rounded corners, floral and swallow design.

1567.1 *Art and Architecture at the World's Columbian Exposition : containing views of grounds, landscapes, main buildings, state buildings, foreign buildings, architectural details, interiors, exhibits, moonlight scenes,...: supplemented with : a collection of artotypes of the most famous paintings and statuary exhibited at the World's fair, Chicago, 1893.* Chicago: Rand, McNally & Co., 1894 [ᶜ1894 by Rand, McNally & Co.].

28½x33½. ca. (300) p. Forest green cloth spine on wheat colored cloth boards, gilt print. Similar to Rand, McNally's items #1580 and #1610. ☺ . (bgsu)

1569.   *Art and Artists of All Nations : Over Four Hundred Photographic Reproductions of Great Paintings embracing masterpieces of modern...art : including about One Hundred of the Greatest Paintings Exhibited in the Department of Fine Arts at the World's Columbian Exposition : descriptions of each painting prepared expressly for this work by well-known writers and art critics, among whom are commissioners of fine arts at the World's Columbian exposition : Angelo Del Nero...Henri Giudicelli...J.W. Beck,....*
▶Title capitalization corrections.
▶Additional library sources for publishers previously listed: (DU,UTA)
---- Also found: New York: Knight & Brown, 1898. (Col)
---- Also found: New York: Knight & Brown, 1901 [ᶜ1894 by Bryan, Taylor and Co.]. 28½x37. 400 p. Burgundy leather hc, gilt lettering with torch and wreath blind-stamped design, gilt edges (i.e., as pictured in original book). Format: caption below each photo. ☺ (GLD) $30 - 50
---- Also listed: 1899 publication date. (PSU)

1570.   *Art and Artists of all nations...including more than One Hundred Forty*: (GLD,HU,KSU,UCLA) $30 - 50
---- Also found: New York: Arkell Weekly co., 1894 [ᶜ1894 by Bryan, Taylor and Co.]. Full brown leather hc, gilt print and blind-stamp design same as illus in #1569. All three edges gilt.

1571.   *Art Folio of the World's Columbian Exposition*: (GLD,CU,HU,S,SML,UMD) $80 - 160
---- Also found: Cover variant. Folio: Half blue (or brown) cloth portfolio with embossed (cherubs and floral design) paper covered boards. Folding flaps, fore edge ribbon for tie closure. Gilt print. 14 *l.*
▶Title corrected by adding "the" after "of."

1572.   *Art Gems From the World's Columbian Exposition*: (B,CCA,HML,IHi,UoC)
1574.   *Art treasures from the World's fair*: (IHi,Stfd,URI)

1575.   *Beautiful scenes of the White City*: (GLD,CCA,Col,CU,FLP,HU,NSW,UBO,UIC) $25 - 45
▶Add bound volume cover description: Brown cloth hc; black print and gilt "Farewell Edition."

1575.1 Bee Hive Stores. *Worlds* [sic] *Fair. Bee hive stores : World's fair souvenir, Uhrichsville, O.* Uhrichsville, OH: [Bee Hive Stores, ᶜ1892 by A. Zeese & co.].

16x9. 11 *l* plates (no text). Accordion folded strip of glossy b/w illus of WCE bldgs (one side). Bold gilt print on gray card stock. C.t. Ad like #1606.1 except different advertiser. ☺ (GLD) $14 - 26

1577.   *Berühmte Kunstwerke. Eine Sammlung*:   (FM)

1577.1 Branca Brothers. …*Fernet-Branca : dei F^{lli} Branca : Milano : Chicago 1893.*
[Milan, It.: Branca Brothers (Lit. F^{ll} Tensi), n.d.   P→

16½x11½. (28) p includes panels on inside both covers. Accordion fold
illus of WCE bldgs with text on reverse of each panel. Unfolds downward
to 201½x11. Brown paper covered boards are cloth-hinged at top, dark
brown print and illus of eagle on globe holding Branca bottle in talons, WCE
scene in background. C.t. At head of title: "Souvenir World's Columbian
Exposition." Ad for their drinks. ☺ (GLD,B) $18 - 40

1577.2 Brown Mfg. Co. *The Great World's Fair at Chicago.* [Greenville, TN:
Brown Manufacturing Co.], n.d.

8x13½. (14) p includes insides of both wraps. Pulp wraps and text. Black
print and A. Zeese & Co lithos of WCE bldgs. Govt Bldg on front cover;
Illinois Bldg on outside back cover. Format: text on left page; illus on right
page. C.t. Ad for Brown's "Ramon Remedies"—e.g., Ramon's Nerve and Bone Oil, 25¢ and 50¢.
☺ (GLD) $15 - 35

1578.   Bucklen. *Souvenir portfolio of the World's Columbian*:   (csuf,DU,WM)

1579.   Buel. *Magic City*:   (B,BD,BPL,CCA,CLP,Col,CU,CWM,DC,DU,FLP,HML,HU,ICRL,IHi,IStU,IWU,KCPL,Knox,KS,LL,llpl,MCHx,MSI,MU,NPG,OHxS,
RCHx,SHB,Smth,SPL,Stfd,UAH,UBO,UCB,UCI,UCLA,UdM,UMA,UMD,UMN,UoA,UoC,UPa,URI,USFr,UWM,VAM,wsu,Yale)
▶Add publisher: Chicago: Library Resources Inc., 1970. Microfiche. LAC-13901.
---- Rpt ed: (Amh,bgsu,CCA,CU,FU,KSU,LACL,LU,MIT,NDU,sapl,sfpl,UAT,UBO,UCI,UI,UIC,uiuc,UMN,UPa,UTA,UVM,VCU,VT)

1580.   *Buildings and art at the World's fair*:   (DC,IHi,KCPL,llpl)

1581.   *The Buildings of the WCE*:   (DC,HML,NSW,Stfd,UMD,UoC,UVM)

1581.1 *Chicago.* N.p: n.p. (printed in Germany), n.d.

18x9½. 12 *l* accordion folded plates. Red paper
covered boards, no text. C.t. Plates include: "World's
fair globe Jackson Park," "Jackson Park from the
bridge," "Libby Prison," and "Auditorium." Post
fair? ☺ . (WM)

1582.   *Chicago Album*:   (GLD,IHi)   P→ $17 - 35
---- Also found: Bright red hc, black and gilt design,
gilt print.

1584.   *Chicago and the World's Columbian Exposition. Photo-Gravures from Recent Negatives*:   (UMA)

1585.   *Chicago and the World's Fair. Photo-gravures*:   (GLD,KBS) $25 - 50
▶Add description: 22½x28. Dark brown leatherette cover, gilt print, maroon string-tied.

1585.1 *Chicago and World's Columbian Exposition.* [Columbus, OH: Ward Brothers, 1893].

24x15½. 12 accordion fold leaves of illus. Black print and illus of Admin Bldg on dark sky blue (or gray)
boards. C.t. ☺ . (GLD,bgsu,IHi) $12 - 26

1588.1 Chicago Renting Agency. …*Album of the World's Columbian Exposition : Chicago.* Chicago: Chicago
Renting Agency, © by Whitehead & Lord Co.

8x14. (16) p. Green paper wraps, black print. C.t. Company name at head of title. Illus of WCE bldgs
with general visitor info. Agency's office was in the Masonic Temple. (S)

1588.2 *Chicago's Austellung in Word und Bild.* N.p: n.p., n.d.

28x34. (88) p of plates with captions in German language. Red cloth hc, bold silver print. C.t. Bound with no t.p.? Contains 10 p Midway section taken from the *Illustrated American* so we question whether this is a post-fair abbreviated version of #1602. Three title words are misspelled. ☺ (GLD) $25 - 55

1590.   *Chicago Times portfolio of the Midway types*: ☺ (GLD,B)   Each part: $10 - 20
▶Publisher correction: Chicago: The American Eng. Co. Publishers & Printers, ᶜ1893.

1591.   *The Chicago Tribune Art Supplements in two parts*: (B,CCA,Col,FM,ICRL,IHi,SPL,UIC)
---- Also found: Issued with a mailing envelope with red label.

1592.   *The Chicago Tribune. From Peristyle to Plaisance*: (IHi)
1593.   *Chicago Tribune Glimpses of the World's Fair*: (csuf,HU,IHi,Knox,NDU,NPG,UH,uiuc,UoC,UPa)

1593.1 *The Cincinnati Posts* [sic] *Portfolio Midway Types...* N.p.: Cincinnati Post, n.d.

20x27½. Textured leather, gilt print and "TYPES" illus as depicted in #1655. The Post's leather-bound version of #1590 and #1655. (S)

1594.   *The City of Palaces*: (bgsu,CCA,HU,SPL,UCLA,UMC,UWM,WM)
▶Covers: Brown (or blue) cloth hc, fancy floral design with two ovals in black and silver, gilt print.

1595.   *Columbian Album Containing Photographic Views of Buildings and Points of Interest*: (bgsu,CCA,HU,SPL)
▶Add publisher: Cambridge, MA: HULMS, 1983. Film Mas C 978.

1596.   *The Columbian Exposition Album Containing Views of the Grounds, Main and State Buildings*:
(bgsu,CCA,Col,CU,cul,CWM,HML,HU,ICRL,IHi,KSU,MOHx,MSL,NDU,NLA,nmsu,OU,S,Smth,UH,UI,UIC,UMD,UTA,Yale)
1597.   *Columbian exposition and Chicago's Wonders*: (S)

1598.1 *Columbian Gallery : a collection of : seventy-five photogravures and seventy-five : typogravures of celebrated paintings : by the most distinguished : artists of the age.* Remarque proof edition. Boston: Haskell publishing co. [Presswork by John Wilson and Son, University Press, Cambridge, ᶜ1893 By The Haskell Publishing Co.]

48½x34½. ca 150 p. Decorative wraps for each of the 17 parts. Also on t.p.: "with biographical, critical, and descriptive text by Clarence Lansing." Each part with a table of contents. ☺ . (GLD,ref)
---- Also found: Bound in 2 vol. Half leather over black cloth hc, gilt print and edges. (GLD)

1599.   *The Columbian gallery*: (GLD,CCA,CLP,Col,CU,DC,FLP,FM,ICRL,IHi,IStU,MOHx,sfpl,SPL,UCB,UMN,UNO,UoA,UPa,UTA,UWM) $30 - 70
---- Also found: Half leather hc over maroon cloth boards, gilt print and design.
---- Also listed: (260) p.

1600.   *The Columbian Portfolio of photographs of the World's fair*: (B,bgsu,CCA,CLP,GBP,HU,IStU,SHB,UCLA,UGa,UMD)

1601.   *The Columbian Souvenir Album A Memento of the World's Fair*: (Col,ICRL,S)
---- Also found: Cover variant: black glossy paper-covered boards with gilt print and design.

1603.   *Das Columbishe Weltausstellungs-album*: (GLD,Stfd) $20 - 50
---- Also found: Rand [ᶜ1893]: 2 *l* text, 112 *l* of plates printed both sides. Maroon cloth on beveled boards, gilt print and design on cover, gilt edges.

1604.   Crane. *Midway Plaisance sketches by W.H. Crane*: (Stfd)

1604.1 *Decalcomania. World's Columbian exhibition : 1893.* N.p.: n.p. (Made in Germany), n.d.

8½x13. 4 *l*. Accordion folded views tipped onto back cover; each is a color transfer decal of a different WCE bldg. Olive wraps, black print and illus of Admin Bldg and lagoon. C.t. ☺ (GLD) $25 - 60

1605.   *Dream city*: (B,bgsu,BrU,CCA,CLP,Col,CU,cul,CWM,D,DC,DU,ESU,FLP,GBP,GPL,HML,HPL,HU,ICRL,IHi,IStU,KBS,KCPL,Knox,KSU,LBA,LL,MCHx,
Merc,MH,MOHx,MSI,NAG,NDU,NPG,OHxS,sfpl,sfsu,SHB,slcl,slpl,SML,Smth,SPL,SStu,Stfd,UAT,UBO,UBW,UCI,UCB,UCLA,UdM,UGa,UI,UIC,uiuc,UMC,UMD,UN
O,UoA,UPa,UTA,UWM,VCU,VAM,Yale)

▸Correction: The dates 1893–94 listed in the pub info do not appear on the t.p. of the bound volume; this was the issue interval for the subscription set.

1606.1 Erie Preserving Co. *Worlds* [sic] *Fair Souvenir.* N.p.: n.p., n.d.

16x9. 10 *l* accordion fold glossy litho plates of WCE bldgs. Matte gray-green folded card wraps, gilt print; inside of card is ad for their goods. Last *l* is a litho of the Erie factory. Like #1575.1. (WM)

1607. *The Exposition publishing company's art folio (No. 1)*:
▸Add paging: 15 *l* of illus and text.

1609. *Famous paintings of the World : a collection of photographic reproductions*: (CWM,KCPL,sfpl,Stfd,UCLA)
▸New edition/new publisher: European Edition. New York: Bryan, Taylor, 1895.

1609.1 *Fifty Glimpses of the World's Fair : Chicago, 1893.* New York: William J. Kelly, [°1893 by William J. Kelly].

20x25. 1 *l* (t.p.), 2 *l* text (one side), 27 *l* with b/w lithos one side only, tissue guards. Green wraps with dark green print and design. C.t. = t.p. Tied with pink ribbon. Back wrap embossed with flower head designs. Bldgs and views of the WCE are illustrated. ☺ (GLD,HU)   P➔ $25 - 55

1610. *Fine arts at the World's Columbian*: (UIC,UMD,UMN,UWM)
1611. Flower. *Glimpses of the World's Fair*: (GLD) $20 - 45

1612. *Fotografiska vyer af Verldsutställningen*: (IHi,KBS,UMN)
▸Additional publisher: Chicago: N. Juul, 1894.

1614. *From peristyle to Plaisance or The White City Picturesque*: (Col,GPL,HU)
1615. *Gems of Modern Art : A collection of photographic reproductions of great modern*: (KCPL)

1616. *Gems of the World's fair and Midway Plaisance : With Accurate and*: (GLD,CCA,FLP,SStu,URI) $35 - 65
▸Expanded description: Brown cloth hc, black print and border with bird design. Plates from the California Midwinter Fair, 1894, are interspersed and not always identified as such.

1617. *Gems of the World's fair. Over 200 photographic views*: (SPL)

1617.1 *...Glimpses of the Rainbow City : Pan-American exposition, at Buffalo : 94 : original photographs, with full descriptions of buildings, monuments, statuary, promenades,... : also : Views of Paris Exposition, 1900, and of the White City, Chicago, 1893.* Chicago: Laird & Lee, publishers, °1901 by William H. Lee.

13x17½. (158) p. Frontis illus is "Temple of Music" where McKinley was assassinated. Illus wraps in shades of blue, red print. At head of title: "A Souvenir of the World's Most Magnificent Displays." On t.p.: "Three books in one." View book with same format as #1618. ☺. (bgsu,ICRL)

1618. *Glimpses of the World's Fair : A Selection of Gems of the White City*:
(B,bgsu,CCA,CLP,Col,CUA,D,DC,GPL,HML,HU,IHi,KSU,MOHx,NJHx,S,Smth,SStu,UAB,UCLA,UGa,UMA,UMC,UMD,UoA,Yale)
---- Also found: In original box with illus of Court of Honor.
---- Also found: Issued in a gray envelope, title and decoration in navy.

1619. *The Glories of the World's Fair : only the most magnificent views*: (B,MH)
1620. *The Government collection of original views of the World's Columbian Exposition secured by*: (RPL,UGa)
1621. Graham. *The World's Fair in Water Colors*: (CCA,CU,DU,FM,HU,IStU,LBA,UIC,UPa)

1622. *The Great White City: A Picture Gallery of the World's Fair and Midway*: (GLD,Col,HU) $ 30 - 70
▸Completed citation: Issued in 16 parts without t.p. Title is from the subscription covers. Text below each view. Found bound in purple cloth hc with gilt print, decorative end papers. (GLD)

1623. Halligan. *Halligan's illustrated world*: (CCA,GBP,IHi,MSI,UIC,uiuc)
---- Also found: 8, (320) p. Brown pebble-textured cloth over beveled boards. "Portfolio edition" is not printed on cover. One of the best of the view books: generous text and good illustrations.

1624. *Halligan's Illustrierte Welt*: (KCPL,UIC)

1624.1 Hancock, John, Mutual Life Insurance Co. *World's Fair : Souvenir Views : Chicago, 1893.* Boston: The John Hancock Mutual Life Insurance Co., n.d.

8x12. 9 *l*. Accordion folded strip of b/w views of WCE bldgs. Rust-brown wraps, black print. C.t. Handout at WCE. Hancock ad on back wrap. © (GLD) $14 - 28
---- Also Found: N.p.: n.p., n.d. Used as advertising by various manufacturers. (E)

1625. *The illustrated World's Columbian Exposition*: (csuf,IStU)
1626. *In Remembrance*: (GLD,B,CCA,Col,CU,IHi,RCHx,slpl,UTA,WM) P➡

1627. [Jackson]. *Jackson's Famous*: [White City, 1895]
(Col,CU,HML,HU,LBA,MSI,SStu,UIC,uiuc,UMN,VAM)
---- Also found: N.p.: n.p., n.d. 36x46. Bound horizontally, half leather over black cloth. C.t.: "World's fair : 1893." (GLD) $150 - 350

☞ The confusion with this book is that the t.p. and text of all copies are printed with the paper in a vertical (portrait) orientation with the 36 cm wide edge up; the illus lend themselves to binding in either direction. The result is that the book is found bound both vertically and horizontally. Since bound copies come from the subscription set, there can be variations in plate and text sequence.

1627.1 [Jackson, William Henry]. *Jackson's Famous Pictures of the World's Fair. "The White Flower of Perfect Architecture."* N.p.: n.p., n.d.

43x35. 1 *l* (t.p.), (39) plates of illus one side. Dark purple-gray glossy wraps, gilt print, purple cloth spine. No tissue guards between plates as in #1627. Gilt c.t., "The White City," is in exactly the same script as found on the cover of #1629. Appears to be a less expensive version of the other Jackson issues because of the limited number of plates and type of binding. Could be partial set (one of several volumes). [The Jackson plates were also used by advertisers; see #1587.] © (GLD,RU) $55 - 180

1627.2 [Jackson, William Henry]. *Die Weisse Stadt.* Chicago: The White Art Co., ᶜ1894.

36x45. 8 *l* German text and t.p., 80 *l* of plates with English titles. Introd by H.H. Coleman. (UWM)

1628. [Jackson]. *The White City : (As it Was)*:
(CCA,Col,CWM,EPL,FM,HU,ICRL,IHi,ISU,MIT,MSI,NDU,slpl,Stfd,UMD,UoA,UPa,WM,Yale) $150 - 350
▶Add binding: Blue pebble-textured folio with folding flaps, gilt print. 80 loose plates with no text.
▶New York City auction price May, 1993: $200.

1629. [Jackson]. *The White City (as it was) : the story of the World's* [Directors Edition]: (ICRL,FLP,UIC)
---- Also found: Same but without tissue denoting "Directors Edition." Issued without, or missing it?

1629.1 Key, John Ross. "World's Columbian exposition." Chicago: Orcutt Co., ᶜ1894.

45x64. 6 chromolithograph plates. No t.p. (uiuc)

1630. Martin. *Martin's World's fair album-atlas*: (B,CCA,cul,FLP,GPL,HML,ICRL,ISU,KBS,PSU,RU,UCD,UGa,UIC,uiuc,UMD,USFr,UTA,WM)
1631. Massey. *The World's fair through a camera and how I made my pictures*: (NLA)

1633. *The Midway plaisance of the World's Fair*: (CCA,E,UMD)
---- Also found: Cover variant for ᶜ1893 version: Maize speckled stiff wraps, embossed copper print, string-tied.

1634.   *Midway Types A Book of Illustrated*: (GLD,CU,IHi,uiuc) $30 - 60

1634.1 Mills, Knight & Co. ...*Columbian Year. 1892*. Boston:
Mills, Knight & Co., n.d.

15½x9. (32) p. Text on versos, illus on rectos. First (13)
p are ads; last (19) p are associated with WCE. String-tied
buff wraps with dark blue and red print and design. C.t.
At head of title: "1492." Mills made memoranda books,
leather goods, and ad specialties. Tipped-in undated map
of downtown Chicago at back cover by "A. Zeese & Co.,
Engraver's Chi." © (GLD) $18 - 45

1635.   *Moment-Aufnahmen der Weltausstellung*: (B,CCA,S)   P↗
▸Add cover description: Blue smooth wraps, red print.

1638.   *Official Photographs of the World's fair and Midway Plaisance with Accurate*: (HU)
1639.   *Official portfolio of the World's Columbian Exposition. Illustrated from water*: (GLD,CUE,PSU) $18 - 40
1642.   Orcutt. *Authentic portfolio of the World's Columbian exposition*: (B,CCA,FM,UPa)

1642.1 Orcutt Co. *Portfolio representing Water Color Sketches of views World's Fair Buildings*. Chicago: n.p., n.d.

21½x29½. Manila envelope with brown print and banner design. Contains 11 loose color plates of WCE
bldgs. "Price 50 cts" on upper right of envelope. (WM)

1643.   *Oriental and occidental northern and southern*: (A,CCA,FLP,FM,HU,ICRL,MCHx,MOHx,MSI,SPL,UCI,UCLA,UIC,UMD,UVM,Yale)

1643.1 *Panoramic Views : of : World's Fair : Chicago. 1893*.
Philadelphia?: Fred Veit, n.d.

10x13½. 9 WCE views in accordion fold out. Green wraps, navy
print and port of Columbus in upper left hand corner. C.t. White
paper with each b/w view on buff background; text on inside back
cover briefly describes each view. On cover: "Compliments of
Fred. Veit." Veit made trunks and bags; back cover ad for their
footwear. © . (E)   P→
---- Another ad publisher: Canton, OH: Hirschheimer Bros., 1893.
Clothing dealer. © (CCA)

1644.   Peterson. *Verdensudstillingen og Verdensudstillingen-Staden*: (UBO)
1645.   *The Photographic Panorama of the World's Fair*: (bgsu,uiuc,Stfd,UMD)

1646.   *Photographic views of the World's Columbian Exposition*: (GLD,IHi)   Each subscription section: $8 - 15
▸Correct orientation: 19x27.
---- Also found: Subscription set. Light blue wraps, black print. "With the compliments of Grand Rapids
Herald" follows c.t.

1647.   *The Photographic World's Fair and Midway Plaisance*: (FM)
---- Also found: Chicago: W.B. Conkey Co., Publishers, 1896 [©1894 W.B. Conkey Co.]. Red cloth hc,
not beveled; silver, gold, and black embossed cover design. T.p. in black and maroon.

1648.   *Photographien der Welt-Ausstellung und Midway Plaisance*: (A,UMD)
▸Title given in the original text is c.t. T.p. title: *Die photographirte Weltausstellung und Midway-
Plaisance : Die Haupt-Gebäude, die Eingänge, die ausläischen, Staats- und Territorial- Gebäude, die
reizenden Wasser- Ansichten, Stautuen und Gemälde und die anziehendsten Scenerien der Midway
Plaisance. Die reichhaltigste und beste bis jetzt...* [Chicago?: W.B. Conkey co, 1894].

15½x24. 226 p. Color litho frontis entitled: "Der Ehrenhof bei Mondschein." Red cloth beveled hc,
silver and black illus, gilt print. T.p. in red and black. Trans: Photographs of the World's exposition and
Midway Plaisance : The main buildings; entrance; foreign, states, and territorial buildings;... © (UMD)

1649. *Photographs of the World's fair an*: (B,bgsu,CCA,Col,HU,MA,MIT,NDU,PSU,sfpl,slpl,Stfd,UBO,UCB,UI,UIC,UMD,UMN,UTA)
▶Add publisher: Jersey City, NJ: Eureka pub. co., [ᶜ1894].

1650. *Photo-Gravures of the World's Columbian Exposition*: (ICRL,IHi,S,UTA)
▶Add info: 1 *l* (t.p.), 13 *l*. Gilt print c.t.: "Photo-Gravures of the World's Columbian Exposition at Chicago." Correct title capitalization: *Photo-Gravures*. Issued with a manila envelope with the same print and design as the cover.

1650.1 *Phototypes of the World's fair at Chicago : 1893*. Lynn, MA: Souvenir publishing co., ᶜ1892 [Souvenir publishing co., ᶜ1892].

12x15½. (32) p. B/w illus on both sides of sheets. Tan wraps, black print, string-tied. Cover is duplicate of t.p. On p (31) is an ad for Souvenir Calendars of the World's fair; on p (32) is an ad for "The Artist's Edition" of this book. ☺ . (E,MSL,WM)

1651. *Pictorial album and history World's fair and midway*: (FLP,RPL)
---- Also found: Black leather flexible cover.

1652. *Picturesque World's Fair. An Elaborate Collection of Colored*: (CCA,CLP,FLP,GPL,IHi,NDU,SML,SPL,UBO,UIC,UWM)

1652.1 Pittsburgh Chronicle Telegraph. *The White City. With Brush and Pen. Chronicle Telegraph's Souvenir of the World's Columbian Exposition Chicago, 1893*. [Chicago: Pittsburgh Chronicle Telegraph (The Winters Art Litho Co.)], n.d.

22x30. (28) p. Light brown wraps with gray/brown/red print and C. Graham illus. Graham color lithos printed by Winters Art Litho Co.; text in brown ink. C.t. String-tied. Ad with views similar to #1668 and #1697. ☺ (CCA,S)

1653. *Populäre Sammlung von Ansichten der Winters Kunst-Lithograph*: (GLD) $20 - 50

1654. *Portfolio of "Edition de Luxe" World's Fair Views*: (ref) $45 - 95
▶Add annotation: 30x22½. 60 *l* of loose plates. Maroon cloth folio hc with fold-in flaps, gilt title, also blind-stamped. C.t.

1655. *Portfolio of Midway types*: (B,Fess,IHi,S)
---- Also issued as *The Pioneer Press Portfolio of Midway types*. 12 parts.
---- Also found: Red cloth hc, blind stamped and gilt print. (Fess)

1656. *Portfolio of photographs of the World's fair*: (B,bgsu,CCA,CLP,CSL,HML,ICRL,MSI,NDU,sfpl,slcl,UIC,uiuc,UMD,UoC,UWM)
▶Add cover variant: Decorative light brown cloth boards making folding folio case with flaps that holds all 16 subscription issues. Black and light blue design, gilt print.
▶Add publisher: N.p.: n.p., n.d. That is, no publisher imprint on t.p. Cover title: "Photographs of the World's Fair." A post-fair reissue?

1656.1 *Portfolio of : Views : National Buildings. World's Columbian Exposition Chicago 1893*. N.p.: n.p., n.d.

16x24. (32) p. Peach glossy wraps, dark brown print, illus of Columbus and "Bird's-eye view of the Exposition Grounds." Color illus by C. Graham. C.t. Same format as #1656.2; similar to #1697. ☺ (S)

1656.2 *...Portfolio of : Views : State Buildings. Chicago*. N.p.: n.p., n.d.

17½x23½. (32) p. Pink wraps, black print and port of "Mrs. Potter Palmer." C.t. At head of title: "1492 1892 : World's Columbian Exposition." Graham color illus; same format as #1656.1. ☺ . (S)

1657. Ragan. *Art Photographs of the World and the Columbian Exposition*: (CLM,S,Yale)
---- Also found: Star, 1893: Black half leather over maroon cloth covered beveled boards, gilt print, marbled edges.
---- Also found: Black padded full leather with gilt print. All edges gilt. Satin end papers. (S)
▶Add publisher: San Francisco: The King publishing Co., 1893 [ᶜ1893 by Star Publishing Co.]. (CLM)

1658.   *Rand, McNally & Co's. pictorial Chicago and illustrated World's*: (B,bgsu,CCA,Col,HML,HU,MSI,NLA,slpl,UIC,UTA)
---- Also found: Green cloth hc, gilt print.

1659.   *Rand, McNally & Co's. Sketch Book*: (bgsu,CCA,D,E,ICRL,IHi,KS,NLI,SML,UIC,UTA,WM)
---- Also found: Blue-gray cloth embossed hc, red-brown design, gilt and black print. Same number of
pages as previously described (48), but text and illus vary.

1660.   *Reminiscences of the fair a portfolio of photographs*: (GLD) $35 - 75
▸Add annotation: 29x35. (4) p include t.p. and intro, (256) p of illus. Black half leather over brown
cloth boards, marbled edges. Format: each page has 1 illus with caption below.

1662.   [Ropp]. *The World's Fair Souvenir Album*: (GLD,CU) $30 - 60
---- Also found: Chicago: P.W. Rowe, 1894 [ᶜ1894 by C. Ropp & Sons]. 20x27. (256) p. Chiefly illus
of the fair and Chicago with interspersed text. Red cloth hc with gilt print and black border, beveled
boards, gilt edges. Note the corrected capitalization for the main title which is also the c.t. (GLD)

1662.1 Rose, Harold B. *Harold and Carlton : at the : Columbian Exposition : Chicago, 1893.* Hornellsville, NY:
The Times Association, printers and bookbinders, 1894.

13x18. 54, (158) p of plates printed both sides. Brown cloth hc, gilt print. Youthful glimpses of the
World's Fair. With Carlton C. Rose. ☺.(CCA)

1664.1 *St. Louis : through a camera.* St. Louis, MO: Woodward & Tiernan printing co., 1892.

17½x22½. (82) p. Cream wraps, gold print and design of photographer behind camera. On t.p.: "July,
1892." Text by James Cox; see #1676 and #1677 for other "through a camera" Woodward & Tiernan
view books. WCE handout. ☺.(LBA)

1665.   *Scenes and Gems of art from every land*: (GLD)
---- Also found: 1898 Reissue. C.t.: *Portfolio of one hundred Photographic Views.* On cover: New York,
Chicago [and] Springfield, OH: Mast, Crowell & Kirkpatrick, ᶜ1898. 26x35. (4) text on pulp, 5-36, 16, 20
p (WCE). Tan smooth wraps, brown print and floral leaf design. C.t. *Scenes and Gems* t.p. dated 1894
is behind front wrap; *The Photographic Panorama* t.p. dated 1894 is before final 20 p WCE section.
"Sunlight Series" at cover bottom. See #1645. ☺(GLD) $25 - 65

1667.   Shepp. *Shepp's World's Fair Photographed*: (B,bgsu,CCA,CLP,Col,CU,cul,DC,FLP,FM,FPL,HML,HU,ICRL,IHi,llpl,MSI,NSW,
RCHx,slpl,Smth,UBO,UCB,UCLA,UMD,UMN,UPa,UWM,Yale)

1668.   *Siegel, Cooper & Co.'s*: (GLD,csuf,S,UMD) $20 - 45
▸Add annotation: For another Siegel item, see their catalog for 1893, #1005.6

1668.1 Siegel, Cooper & Co. *Columbian Souvenir : with Compliments of Siegel Cooper & Co.* Chicago: Siegel,
Cooper & Co. (The Winters Art Litho Co.), n.d.

10½x16. (12) p. Chromolith front cover illus of Columbus standing
before two kneeling women (illus in portrait orientation); chromolith back
cover illus of their department store in Chicago. ☺.(E)   **P➔**

1669.1 *Souvenir of Chicago and the World's Columbian Exposition, 1893.*
Chicago: L. Shick, 1892.

16x24½. 15 plates folded accordion style + text inside back cover: "A
Descriptive Synopsis of the Columbian Exposition Buildings." Red paper
covered boards, gilt print. "A Louis Glaser Souvenir Album from
Leipzig, Germany." C.t. L. Shick, advertiser. (UMD)
---- Another advertiser: New York: R. Voigt, [1893]. (CCA)

1669.2 *Souvenir of the World's Columbian Exposition.* Chicago: Vandercook
engraving & pub. Company, n.d.

13½x8½. (18) panels accordion folded and tipped in tan (or gray) wraps, blue print and illus of Admin Bldg on front. Nine panels of views one side; nine text on the other. See original cite #1160 for illus of cover variants. Ad used by many companies; advertisers' info printed on outside back covers. ☺ . (GLD,E)   **P➔**

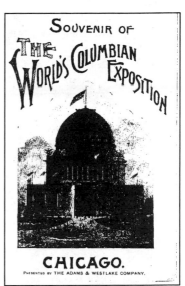

1669.3 *Souvenir of the World's Columbian Exposition. Chicago, Ill., 1893.* N.p.: n.p., 1893?

23½x15. 1 pink *l* ads, 16 p, 1 pink *l* ads. Tan wraps, red and black print and black ink vignette litho of Machinery Bldg. Caption title p 3: "The World's Columbian Exposition, Chicago, Ill., U.S.A. : To be open from May 1, 1893, to October 30, 1893." ☺ . (UMD)

1670.   *Souvenir of the World's Columbian Exposition in photo-*: (Amh,CCA,Col,HML,sfpl)

1670.1 *A Souvenir of the World's Columbian Fair : Chicago : 1893.* N.p.: n.p. (Printed in Germany), n.d.

11x14. 12 *l*. Accordion folded chromolith illus, one/ leaf. Tan textured paper on boards, gilt print. C.t. Outside back cover: "Compliments of Bragdon bros. dealers in Reliable Footwear," Westbrook, ME. ☺ . (GLD,E,S)   **P➔** $17 - 35
---- Also found: Ruppert Shoe Store, advertiser.
---- Also found: Without an advertiser.

1672.1 *Souvenir Portfolio of World's Fair Views.* N.p.: n.p, n.d.

30x23. Black (or dark brown) cloth folder containing 60 loose plates. C.t. Similar to #1654. ☺ (S,UIC)

1673.   *Souvenir World's Columbian Exposition. To be held*: (GLD,HU)
▶New publisher: Cambridge, MA: HULMS, 1983. Film Mas C 978.
---- Also found: 12½x17½. Ivory colored embossed wraps, gilt print. C.t.: "The World's Fair : Illustrated : Souvenir." T.p. publication date is 1892; otherwise the same. ☺ (GLD) $12 - 28

1675.   Stoddard. *Famous parks and public buildings of America*: (EPL,HU,UMC,UoC)

1675.1 Stoddard, John Lawson. *Portfolio of photographs of our country and our neighbors, prepared under the supervision of the distinguished lecturer and traveler, John L. Stoddard: containing a rare and elaborate collection of photographic views of the United States, Canada, Mexico, Central and South America.* Chicago: Werner, [1894?].

28x34. 2 *l*, (192) p of illus. Port. C.t.: "Portfolio of selected views." (Yale)

1676.   Todd. *World's Fair through a Camera. An interesting collection of views*: (B,HML,IHi,MH,S,UMD,UPa,VT,WM)
---- Also found: 2nd edition.

1677.   Todd. *World's Fair through a Camera. Snap shots by an*: (CCA,CLP,Col,HU,NPG,slu,UIC,uiuc,UMA,UMD,UTA,VAM,WM)
1678.   *A Trip through the Columbian exposition with a camera*: (DU,FLP,HML,HU,IHi,MCHx,slpl,Stfd,WM)
1680.   *The Vanished City : The World's Columbian Exposition in pen and picture*: (CU,UMD)
1681.   *The Vanishing City : A Photographic Encyclopedia of the WCE*: (CCA,HU,Knox,NDU,SPL)
1682.   *The vanishing White City, a superb collection of photographic views*: (slpl,UIC)

1682.1 *The Vanishing White City. 1492 1892.* N.p.: n.p., n.d.

28x34. Unpaged plates (both versos and rectos) with text captions. Half leather over textured brown cloth hc, gilt print with globe design in center. C.t. Issued without t.p. ☺ (GLD) $25 - 60

1683.   *The Vendome club*: ▶See #1045.3 for another Vendome Club item. (MSL)

1684. *Die Verschwundene Weisse Stadt*: (CLP,FM)
▸Further description: Subscription set in 20 parts with sepia wraps.

1685. *View Album of Chicago*: (CCA,FM,IHi,S,UPa)
---- Also found: Red paper covered boards, black print. String-tied, tasseled ends. (ref)
---- Also found: Blue paper covered boards. Bound with no t.p. (FM)

1687. *Views of the World's Columbian Exposition*: (csuf)
1688. *Views of the World's Fair*: (E)

1689. *Views of The World's Fair and Midway Plaisance : Comprising Rare Photographs of The Main Exposition Buildings...* Chicago: W.B. Conkey Co., 1894 [ᶜ1894 by W.B. Conkey Co.].
On cover: "Franklin series, v. 1, no. 5, March 1894." ☺ (GLD) $14 - 35
▸Title corrected and copyright info added. ▸Delete: 1904 and substitute 1894 in cover annotation.

1689.1 *Views of the World's Fair Chicago 1893.* N.p.: n.p., n.d.

9x14½. Accordion folded sheet with (8) panels of WCE views one side. Red and gilt stiff wraps, red and black print, red cloth spine. C.t. Eagle and shield in a central circle (back cover). (GLD,IHi) $12 - 25

1689.2 *Views : of the World's Fair : 1893 : Chicago. Eat "Scotch Oats."* Detroit, MI: Calven Lith Co., n.d.

9x15. 1 *l* (t.p.), 8 *l* color plates of WCE bldgs printed on one side of stiff stock. Yellow stiff wraps, brown print, string-tied. Ad? (GLD)   P➔ $25 - 50

1689.3 *Vistas of the fair in color. A book of familiar views of the World's Columbian Exposition.* Detroit: Williams, Davis, Brooks & Co., ᶜ1894 By Poole Bros.

35x40. 40 *l*. Black cloth pebbled hc, gilt print and design. Half of the colored plate set of #1690. Poole colored plates. Ad issue for D.A. Brooks' perfumes. ☺ (E) $130 - 300

1690. *Vistas of the fair in color. A portfolio of familiar views* [80 *l*]: (GLD,Col,FM,NSW) $250 - 600

1693. *Welcome in* [sic] *Chicago, 1893.* N.p.: n.p. (Made in Germany), n.d.
▸Corrected pub info and additional cover description: Stiff wraps in brown tones. ☺ (GLD) $15 - 35

1695. *The white city by Lake Michigan*: (CCA,Col,CU,E,HML,S,sfpl,UCLA,UIC,UMD)
---- Also found: 22½x14½. 12 *l*. Red stiff wraps.
---- Also found: 1 *l* (t.p.), 14 *l* of illus. Deep burnt orange flexible cloth covers, silver print, string-tied.

1695.1 *The White City, Chicago : 1893.* N.p.: n.p., n.d.

27½x34. (240) p of b/w plates with captions below each plate. Bound without a t.p. C.t. Brown cloth hc with bold gilt print. Similar in format to Buel's #1579 in that some pictures are identical and there is a bold title below the picture prefacing the explanatory note. However, dimensions of book, caption content, and number of pages do not match. Odd publication. ☺ (GLD) $27 - 60

1695.2 White Sewing Machine Co., comp. *The World's Columbian Exposition Views.* Cleveland, OH: White Sewing Machine co., n.d.

15x17½. (16) p. Flecked blue-gray wraps with navy print. Port of King Ferdinand? on back cover. Blue illus of WCE bldgs by A. Zeese, ᶜ1892, each with brief descriptive text in blue and co name inserted in picture. Includes illus of their sewing machine models. Invitation to visit their exhibit in Manufactures Bldg printed inside back cover. Bird's-eye on pp (8)-(9). ☺ (GLD) $20 - 45

1696. Wilde. *Chicago weltausstellung 1893 : 32 blatt*: (UMD)
---- Also found: Cover variant: 24x16½. Beautiful blue-gray cloth hc. Gilt and black print and design plus a bird's-eye of the ground in blues and greens. Content and format the same.

1697.   *The Winters Art Lithographing Company's popular portfolios of the World's*:
          (BCHx,bgsu,Col,CUE,HML,ICRL,IHi,KS,MIT,MOHx,NSW,Stfd,UH,UMD,UTA,VtHx,WM)

1697.1 *The Winters Art Lithographing Company's : portafólios populores de la exposition universal colombiana.*
          Chicago: Winters Art Lithographing Co., n.d.

    16x24. (32) p Includes 16 color plates by C. Graham. Tan wraps, black and gray-blue print, string-tied.
Ads in Portuguese for Sandwich Manufacturing Co in Uruguay are found on 15 text pages. Four different
booklets: (Num. 1) Sitios y edificios principales; (Num. 2) edificios de los estados; etc. Portuguese
version of #1697. (ref) $35

1697.2 *The Winters Art Lithographing Company's : Portefeuilles populaires : de : l'exposition universelle de
Chicago.* Chicago: The Winters Art Lithographing Co., n.d. [ᶜ1891 by the Winters Art Litho. Co. Chicago].

    16x24. (32) p. Gray stiff wraps, blue and black print, string-tied. Text description of bldgs alternating
with color illus of WCE bldgs. French version of #1697. ☺ . (SML)

1698.   *The wonders of the World's fair. A Portfolio of Views*: (UMN,UVM)

1700.   [Woolson Spice Co.] *Authentic World's Columbian
Exposition album*: ☺ . (CUE,ref)
---- Also found: Campbell, J[ames] B. Chicago:
J.B. Campbell, n.d. 14x21. 1 *l* (t.p.), 15 *l* color
litho plates with descriptive text. Buff wraps with
black, light brown, and red print and design; cover
port of Columbus. Center-fold is early bird's-eye
view of WCE grounds. (CUE)   **P→**
---- Also found: "Compliments of : The Enterprise
Carriage Manufacturing Co. : Miamisburg, Ohio."
Enterprise ads on last page and outside back cover.
No mention of publisher, Campbell. (ref) $50

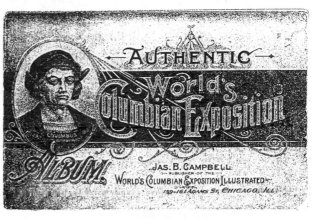

1702.   *World's Columbian Exposition*: (B,cul,D,E,IHi,ISU,PSU)
---- Also found: Compliments of A.B. Chase Co., Norwalk, Ohio.
---- Also found: Without an advertiser.

1702.1 *World's Columbian Exposition.* N.p.: Printed in Germany, n.d.   **P→**

    15x10½. 12 *l* of plates, folded; several plates open to reveal panoramic
views. Pink wraps with black print and front cover illus of woman on
winged wheel. C.t. Organ company advertiser: H. Lehr & co., Easton,
PA. Different from #1702. ☺ . (GLD,CCA,WM) $12 - 28
---- Also listed: Same cover. "Presented by Mertens, Yann & Garnett,
the largest and finest clothing store in Syracuse. ☺ . (CCA)

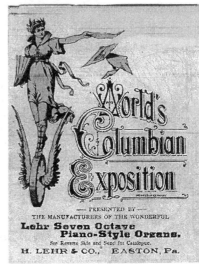

1703.   *World's Columbian Exposition art portfolio*: (DU,HML,ICRL)
---- Also found: [Chicago: J. Carqueville Lith. Co.], 1893?
"Compliments of Central Coal and Iron Co. Louisville, Kentucky."
Beige wraps. 15 full color plates (one double).
---- Also found: Without an advertiser.

1704.   *World's Columbian Exposition at Chicago : 1492–1893–1892*: (GLD,B,DU,GBP,HML,IHi,PSU,SStu)
1705.   *World's Columbian Exposition, Chicago*: (cul,D,MSI,S,sfpl,UIC,uiuc)

1705.1 *World's Columbian Exposition, Chicago. 1893.* [Columbus, OH: Ward Brothers, Publishers, 1892].

    15x13. 8 *l* folded accordion style. WCE bird's-eye view across first 2 *l*; remainder have 2 illus of WCE
bldgs each. C.t. Red stiff wraps, embossed black lettering and ornate border design. (ref,MOHx,S) $15

1706.   *World's Columbian Exposition : Chicago : 1893*:   (NJHx,S,UMD,Yale)

1706.1 *World's Columbian exposition, Chicago, 1893.* Chicago: Vandercook engraving and pub. co., n.d.

   11x15. (23) p includes inside back cover. Orange wraps with litho of Admin Bldg, black print. C.t.: "Souvenir of World's Columbian Exposition : Chicago, 1893 : Photograph Views. Compliments of (blank) ." Blank space intended for advertiser's name. ☺. (bgsu)

1707.   *World's Columbian Exposition : Chicago : North America*:   (AA,bgsu,CCA,UIC,UMD,WM)
   ---- Also found: 12 *l.* Ad for Gravely & Miller Tobacco Company, Danville, VA.
   ---- Also listed: 14 *l.* Red cloth hc, black and gilt print. "Compliments of Gray Bros."
   ---- Also listed: 14 *l.* Blue cloth hc, black and gilt print. "World's Fair route, CH&D Monon route."

1708.   WCE. Dept Photo. Arnold. *Portfolio of Views* [Woodward]:   (Col,csuf,FLP,FPL,HU,IHi,Knox,LBA,MH,NDU,OU,UMD,Yale)
1709.   WCE. Dept Photo. Arnold. *Portfolio of views* [National]:
   (Amh,B,bgsu,CCA,Col,CWM,FLP,HML,HU,llpl,NLA,NPG,Stfd,UCB,UCLA,uiuc,UMD,UTA)
1710.   WCE. Dept Photo. Arnold. *Official views* [50 plates]:   (CCA,Col,CU,cul,DC,DU,FM,HU,NLA,PSU,UCLA)
1711.   WCE. Dept Photo. Arnold. *Official views* [115 plates]:
   (CCA,CLP,Col,CWM,DU,FLP,HML,HU,ICRL,LBA,MSI,NPG,PSU,SML,SStu,Stfd,UCB,UCLA,UdM,uiuc,UMD,UMN,UPa,Yale)
1712.   WCE. Dept Photo. Arnold. *State Buildings portfolio of views*:   (CCA,Col,E)

1714.   WCE. Dept Photo. *Woman's building*:
   ▶Improved annotation: 18x25½. 1 *l* (t.p.), 12 *l* with one photo each. At bottom of each photo: ᶜ1893 by C.D. Arnold. On t.p.: C.D. Arnold, H.D. Higinbotham, Official Photographers. Two-tone gray (or white) wraps with illus of Woman's Bldg in center. At head of title: "World's Columbian Exposition."

1714.1 *World's Columbian Exposition : 1893 : Chicago.* [Columbus, OH: Ward Brothers, 1893].

   15½x13½. 6 *l* accordion folded strip. Two illus on one side of each *l* (12 illus total). Brick red textured boards with black print. C.t. ☺. (bgsu,UdM)

1715.   *World's Columbian Exposition. Jackson Park, Chicago, Illinois, U.S.A.* [vertical Chisholm]:
   (bgsu,CCA,cul,FM,ICRL,IHi,ISU,MCHx,MSI,RCHx,S,SPL,SStu,UMD,UTA)
1716.   *World's Columbian Exposition : Jackson Park, Chicago, Illinois, U.S.A.* [horizontal Chisholm]:   (B,Col)

1717.   *The World's Columbian Exposition : photo-gravures*:   (Col,CU,HU,ICRL,IHi,Knox,slu,Stfd,UGa)
   ---- Also found: Tan fancy embossed stiff wraps, silver print. No date on t.p. or copyright page.
   ---- Also found: Gray cloth hc with gilt print.
   ---- Also found: Pebble-textured maroon paper covered boards, gilt print.
   ---- Also found: Heavy parchment wraps with navy script. String-tied.

1717.1 *The World's Columbian Exposition : Photo-Gravures : From Negatives by the Albertype Company.* New York and Chicago: A. Wittemann, ᶜ1893 by A. Wittemann.

   22x27½. 1 *l* (t.p.), 16 *l* of plates printed one side. Maroon flexible cloth cover, gilt print, string-tied. Generally four illus per leaf. (S)

1718.   *World's Columbian exposition portfolio of Midway types*:   (UIC)
1719.   *The World's Columbian Exposition Reproduced*:   (BrU,Col,GPL,IHi)

1719.1 *World's Columbian exposition : souvenir.* Chicago: Theodore Reese, publisher [R.R. Donnelley & sons co., printers], [ᶜ1892 by Theodore Reese].

   12½x17½. (2) p, 12 *l.* Front wrap bird's-eye illus of fairgrounds. C.t. Below c.t.: "Presented by the Harvey land association." Back wrap has description of Harvey Land Ass'n located south of Chicago. First 2 pp describe the 12 views of bldgs which follow; all illus by A. Zeese & Co. ᶜ1892. ☺. (B,NHL)
   ---- Also found: No cover illus; on cover "Compliments of Julius C. Walk, Jeweler..." (B)

1719.2 *...World's Columbian Exposition : Souvenir : Compliments of (Blank)* Chicago: James P. Craig, Publisher, n.d.

13½x18. 1 *l* (t.p.), 16 *l* of photo repros of Chicago parks. White textured stiff wraps, scalloped edges on front, color litho of flowering plant in vase, Chicago WF logo in left upper corner, red and blue print, blue ribbon tied. At head of title: "1492. 1892." T.p. in blue and red. C.t.: "World's Columbian Exposition : Souvenir : In Chicago's Parks : 1893." Blank for advertiser. ©(GLD) P➜ $18 - 45

1720.   *World's Columbian Fair, Chicago*: (CCA,Col,DU,PPL,S,sfpl,UMD)
---- Also found: 14 *l* folded accordion style; first two are of Machinery Hall. Red cloth hc with gilt print and design of birds on tree branches.

1721.   *World's Columbian Fair : Chicago : 1893*: (HML,S)

1721.1 *World's Columbian Fair : 1893*. N.p.: n.p. (Printed in Germany), n.d.

17½x9½. 12 *l* of accordion folded illus from one continuous sheet 17x99. Pale blue card stock cover with dark blue print. C.t. Not the same as #1720; similar to #1702. ©. (CCA)
---- Also found: 12 *l*. White paper stiff wraps with red print and design. (S)

1723.   *The World's fair album : containing*: (CCA,CLP,E)

1724.   *World's Fair Album of Chicago*: (B,Col,csuf,D,GPL,S,UIC,WM)
---- Also found: Red paper covered boards, gilt print and illus of Admin Bldg. (S)
---- Also found: Landscape cover variant. Drab olive paper cover boards, gilt print, black and gilt design. (S)

1724.1 *World's Fair and Midway Scenes*. [Chicago]: Heath & Milligan Mfg. Co. Print, n.d.

9x14½. (32) p. Tan vellum wraps, maroon title. C.t. Glossy paper with sepia photo repros of fair scenes on each page, including Heath & Milligan Co's paint exhibit in the Manuf Bldg. Ad. The last illus shows bare-chested "Dahomy Village Beauties," [considered risqué in 1893]. ©(GLD)   P➜ $20 - 45

1725.   *World's fair : Chicago : 1893*: (GLD,S,UTA) $25 - 40
---- Also found: 1 *l* (t.p.), 46 *l* plates. Dark brown pebbled hc, gilt print, gilt edges. C.t.: "Chicago : Worlds Fair : 1893." Turquoise t.p. has elaborate litho of Columbus holding globe and pointing to proposed WCE bldgs in the distance. Illus are very early drawings of the WCE grounds and intended bldg designs.
---- Also found: Tan wraps with black print and litho.

1726.   *The World's Fair : Chicago, 1893 : Photo-gravures*: (Col,FLP,NUL,UMD)

1727.   *World's Fair : Chicago 1893 : Souvenir : Illustrated : Being a complete and concise*: (B,LHL,NHL,NLA,sfpl)
---- Also found: Gilt lettering on brown hc.

1728.   *World's fair, 1893. Photographs*: (CU)

1728.1 *World's fair extra of the American Architect*. [Boston: The heliotype printing co., 1893].

35x26. Loose and folded plates of photo repros of WCE bldgs. White glossy wraps, red print and design. Issue of Dec 23, 1893. Number 939. Original price was $3.50. ©(UMD)

1728.2 *World's Fair Route : Cincinnati to Chicago*. Cincinnati, OH: CH&D and Monon route, n.d.

22½x14. 14 *l*. Accordion folded black and turquoise-tinted illus on glossy paper. First illus is early bird's-eye of grounds on double leaf. Bright Prussian blue paper covered boards, black and gilt print and illus of woman sitting on winged wheel and Machinery Bldg, blue cloth spine. C.t. Ad for the Cincinnati, Hamilton & Dayton Railroad and Monon Route. ☺ (GLD) $15 - 30

1728.3 *World's Fair Views*. N.p.: n.p., 1894?

28x34½. (160) p. Dark red half leather over cloth hc, gilt print. C.t. Some illus with "W.B. Conkey Co."; others with "B.L. Snow" with copyright date 1894. Not related to #1599 variant with spine title "World's fair views." ☺ . (CCA)

1730.   *Worlds Masterpieces of Modern Painting*: (S)

1730.1 Yriarte, Charles. *The art of the world : illustrated in the masterpieces of modern English, American, French, German, Spanish, Dutch and Italian art as exhibited at the World's Columbian Exposition.* 2 vols. London: S. Low, Marston, [189-].

43x__. Illus as described in title. (SHB)

Chapter 11

SALESMEN'S SAMPLES

1730.2 *The Artistic Guide to Chicago and the World's Columbian Exposition.* [Philadelphia: J.H. Moore & co.], n.d.

35½x27. (4) p. Black print, b/w illus. "Bound in best English cloth, stamped in black and gold" and "retail price $1.50." Ad flyer for agents. Charles Banks' name is not on the flyer. ☺ . (E) ---- Also found: Chicago: National Publishing co., n.d. Contents same as Moore & co. above. ☺ . (csuf)   **P➔**

1730.3 Asher, A., & Co. ...*Ende April 1893...Die Deutschen Universitäten : für die Universitätsausstellung in Chicago 1893...* N.p.: n.p., n.d.

27½x20. (4) p. Folded sheet, black print. C.t. At head of title: co info. Flyer for #503 by Lexis in 2 vol. List of chapters; 1046 pp total. Dedicated to the Emperor for the University exhibits at WCE; in German. Price 24 marks (about $5.50). ☺ (WM)

1731.   Bancroft. *The Book of the Fair*: (GLD,csuf)
   ---- Also found: 28x21. (16) p of sample pages. Wraps with laid in ad. Ad letterhead: "Office of 'The Book of The Fair.'" Lists price of $1 each for the 25 parts. (csuf)
   ---- Also found: 1895 [ᶜ1894 by Hubert H. Bancroft]. 40½x31. Ca 50 p. Brown cloth hc, gilt print and design of the Admin Bldg. ☺ (GLD) $50 - 100

1731.1 Bancroft, Hubert Howell. *The book of the fair.* Chicago: The Bancroft company, n.d.

25x16½. (4) p. Folded glossy sheet, black and red print. Nicely illus prospectus for #733. ☺ . (S)

1732.   Banks. *The artistic Guide to Chicago and the World's Columbian*: (GLD,csuf) $25 - 50

1733.1 Blaine, James G[illespie], J[ames] W[illiam] Buel, John C[lark] Ridpath, and Benjamin Butterworth. *Columbus and Columbia : an authentic history of the man and the nation.* Philadelphia: Historical Pub. Co., n.d.

21½x13. (4) p. Folded yellow paper, black print. ☺ (GLD) $15 - 35

1734.   Blaine. *Columbus and Columbia*: ☺ (GLD,DU) $25 - 55
   ---- Also Found: Another Publisher: Chicago: National publishing co., n.d. [ᶜ1892 by H.S. Smith]. Embossed full leather front cover, half leather cloth back cover, illus cloth hc laid inside back cover. Many tipped-in yellow slips explaining aspects of the sample. Contains 6 chromoliths plus fold out chromolith bird's-eye view.

1736.1 [Cameron, William Evelyn.] *History of the World's Columbian.* N.p.: n.p., n.d.

26x32. 18 sample sheets with various page numbers, 48½x32, printed in blue and folded in half. Half leather front cover over brown cloth which has its hinge on the top so the pages fold down as you would view them in the actual book, #771; back cover has same c.t. but is the sample for the all brown cloth hc binding, blind stamped. The gilt cover titles are placed as they would be stamped on the actual book; and since the sample covers are the top half of the book, the lower part of the c.t. is missing. Bound with no t.p. or ruled pages for listing subscribers. Interesting way to sell a folio book. ☺ (GLD) $35 - 80

1737.1 Campbell, J[ames] B. *An authentic illustrated history : of the : Worlds* [sic] *Columbian Exposition : is the : Worlds* [sic] *Columbian Exposition Illustrated.* Chicago: J.B. Campbell Publisher, n.d.

20½x15. (4) p. Folded sheet, black print. Cover litho of Admin Bldg, Campbell's WCE headquarters. C.t. Lists single issues, 25 cents; bound volumes available in 3 styles. See #1429 and #1462. ☺ (GLD,WM)

1737.2 Campbell, J[ames] B. *Are You Going to the World's Fair? If so subscribe for the : World's Columbian Exposition Illustrated.* Chicago: n.p., n.d.

28x15½. (2) p. Flyer for their magazine (#1429), and other WCE publications. Black print. ☺ . (WM)

1738.1 Campbell, J[ames] B. *The Prize History : of the : World's Columbian Exposition. The "World's Columbian Exposition Illustrated. ..."* Chicago: J.B. Campbell, publisher, n.d.

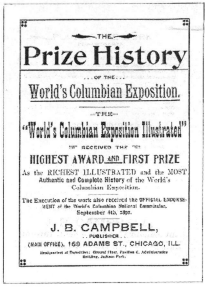

20½x14. (4) p. Folded sheet, black print. Illus. C.t. Bound 36 issue of the magazine, #1429, was $12 cloth; $15 half morocco, $18 Russian morocco. WCE office was "Ground Floor, Pavilion C, Administration Building, Jackson Park." ☺ . (WM)　　　　　P➔

1739. *Campbell's prize history*: (WM) ▸Add author: Campbell, J[ames] B.

1739.1 Century Co. *A Delightful Souvenir of the Fair. The Christmas book of 1893. The Century World's fair book for boys and girls,...* New York: The Century company, 1893?

25x19. (4) p. Folded glossy sheet, black print, illus of Ferris wheel. Cost $1.50. Illus ad and sample for #20 by Tudor Jenks. ☺ (S)

1739.2 *A colossal fraud!! Stop where you are : heed this warning : to our agents and the public...* N.p.: The publishers, n.d.

28x21½. (2) p. Sheet printed in red. Caption title. The publishers warn against *The World's Columbian Exposition* by White and Igleheart (#1057) as a fraud to their own publication by Major Ben. C. Truman— *The Pictorial History of the World's Fair* (#1042). [Note the difference between this intended Truman title and the published book, #1042.] See #1760.2, #1761.1, and #1769 for related items. ☺ (GLD)　　　$15 - 35

1741. *The Columbian decorative art*:
▸Add: Author is J.B. Young. This book is salesmen's sample of "Columbian Embroideries".

1741.1 *The Columbian Portfolio of Photographs of The World's Fair.* Rochester, NY: The Lyon Book co., n.d.

23x15. (4) p. Folded sheet. When open, front and back show a brilliant color illus of the ribbon-tied portfolio being advertised. Very showy prospectus. Caption title. See #1600 for full description of published portfolio. ☺ (S)

1741.2 Cutler, H[arry] G[ardner]. *The World's fair : its meaning and scope : Its Old-World Friends, Their Countries, Customs and Religions...* San Francisco: The King publishing co.; Chicago: Star publishing co., 1891 [ᶜ1891 by Star publishing co.].

25½x19. Full morocco with gilt print. Salesman's sample of #822. (ref)　　　$50

1742.1 *Dew drops and diamonds : of poetry and prose.* N.p.: Juvenile publishing co., 1892 [ᶜ1892 by E.E. Fowler].

26½x20½. Various sample pages. Red cloth hc with cherubs and vines in black and gilt print. Story of Columbus and the WCE with chromoliths of the WCE bldgs. Subscription sheets in back; see #8.1 for full book. Also bound with *The Young American Annual* at back; back cover is bright blue cloth hc with red design and silver print. ☺ (GLD)　　　$35 - 65

1742.2 Dibble Publishing Co. Kirkland, Joseph. *The Story of Chicago.* [Chicago]: n.p., n.d.

29x24½. (4) p. Folded cream coated sheet, black print and illus. C.t. Hc cloth was $3.50; half morocco, $5.00; full morocco, $7.00. Ad flyer for #901. ☺ (WM)

1744.   Eagle. *The Congress of Women*: (GLD) $25 - 65
---- Also found: Chicago and Philadelphia: International publishing co., [°1894 by W.B. Conkey co.].
Blind-stamped leather front cover with gilt print; dark olive green cloth back cover with gilt print. Hinged
leather spine replica with gilt print attached to front cover. Woman's Bldg frontis. See #71.

1744.1 Eagle, Mary K. Oldham. *The Congress of Women : held in the woman's building, World's Columbian
exposition,...sold for the benefit of the woman's memorial building fund.* N.p.: n.p., n.d.

28x20½. (4) p. Folded buff sheet. Ad flyer for the 824 p version of #71. Contains brief reviews and
excerpts of letters from women who participated in the congresses. (WM)

1744.2 Farmer, Lydia Hoyt, ed. *The national exposition souvenir. What America Owes to Women.* Introd. Julia
Ward Howe. N.p.: n.p., n.d.

14½x9. (4) p. Folded glossy sheet, navy print. C.t. At bottom of cover: "For sale in the Woman's
Building. World's Columbian Exposition, Chicago, Ill." Ad flyer for #841. © (WM)

1747.1 [Holley, Marietta]. *Samantha at the World's fair.* New York: Funk & Wagnalls co., 1893.

22½x16. Blue cloth hc, gilt print, silver design of Admin Bldg. Spine and board cover samples tipped-in;
blank ruled pages at end for subscriber's name and address. Salesman's sample of #18. © (S)

1747.2 Hyland, J.S., & Co. *1492 Columbian jubilee souvenir 1892.* Chicago: J.S. Hyland co., n.d.

18x27. (16) p. White stiff wraps, gilt print and border design, chromolith of Columbus landing. String-
tied. First (14) p are WCE illus and last (2) p are caption text explaining each plate. Inside both covers
are sales promotion for #804, "The Columbian Jubilee." © (S)

1750.1 Kühl, W.H., Pub. *Just published : Die Entdeckung Amerika's in ihrer bedeutung...* Berlin: n.p., n.d.

29½x22½. (4) p. Folded sheet, black print. Flyer for Konrad Kretschmer's Columbus book, 3£-15-0.
No WCE content; from intact collection; perhaps an exhibit handout. © (WM)

1751.1 Lothrop, D., Co. Ober, Frederick A. *In Press : The D. Lothrop Company will issue on or about May 1,
1893, In the Wake of Columbus...by Frederick A. Ober.* Boston: D. Lothrop co., n.d.

20½x11½. (4) p. Folded glossy sheet, orange and black print. Describes contents of Ober's book, #957.
"2.50 per volume." Ad flyer. © (S,WM)

1752.1 McKee, Oliver. *U.S. "snap shots" : An Independent, National, and Memorial Encyclopedia...* N.p.: The
Hub publishing co., 1892 [© by A.M. Thayer & Co., Boston].

21x15. 1½ cm thick; sample pages include color plates of WCE bldgs;
prospectus and subscriber signature pages at end. Red cloth hc, gilt print
same as book version, #925. "$2.00 per copy." © (GLD) P➔ $25 - 55

1754.1 Morgan, Horace H. *The historical World's Columbian Exposition and
Chicago Guide: authentic and reliable instructor...* St. Louis, MO and
San Francisco, CA: The Pacific publishing co., 1892.

23½x16½. Red leather front cover with spine sample inside front; half
leather over olive cloth back cover with blue cloth sample cover inside
back. Frontis is foldout chromolith bird's-eye. WCE chromoliths by C.
Graham and b/w illus in text. Ruled pages in back for buyer's orders.
Sample for #934. (GLD) $25 - 60

1755.   Moses. *The White City. The Historical, Biographical...Illinois*: (KCPL)
▸Add annotation: Prospectus for #940.

1756.   Northrop. *Pictorial history of the World's Columbian Exposition : being*: (WM)

1757.   Northrop. *Story of the new world*: (ref)

▸Add pub: Buffalo, NY: Callahan & Conneally, [ᶜ1892 by J.R. Jones].

1760.   *The Photographic World's Fair and Midway Plaisance*: (E)

1760.1 *Photographs of the World's fair : an elaborate collection of photographs of the buildings, grounds, and exhibits...* Chicago: The Werner co., [ᶜ1894 by The Werner co.].

29x33. Binding samples shown from leather (front cover), half-leather (back cover), brown cloth (inside back cover); gilt print covers and gilt top edge, marbled fore edge. Ruled sheets in back for subscriber's names and selected cover type. Sample for #1649. ☺ (GLD,MSI) $30 - 60

1760.2 *Pictorial history of the World's fair, Being a Complete Description of the World's Columbian Exposition from its Inception, by Major Ben. C. Truman,...* [Philadelphia: Mammoth Publishing Co.], n.d.

59½x42½. (2) p. B/w prospectus printed both sides. Illus. Caption title. Book costs were: cloth $2.75; half morocco $3.50; morocco $4.25. Note the title difference between this and the published book (#1042). Also see #1739.2, #1761.1, and #1769 for related Truman items. ☺ (GLD,S) $15 - 35
---- Also found: Philadelphia: Syndicate publishing co., n.d. 58½x42½. (2) p. B/w prospectus.

1761.1 *Private and Confidential letter to agents : who sell : The pictorial history of the World's fair by Major Ben. C. Truman,...* Philadelphia: Mammoth publishing co., n.d.

30½x15½. (2) p. Prospectus printed both sides. See #1042, #1739.2, #1760.2, and #1769 for related Ben. C. Truman items. ☺ (GLD) $15 - 35

1762.   *Proceedings : of : The International Congresses of Education of the World's Columbian exposition, held under charge of the National Educational Association, United States of America.* Winona, MN?: The Association?, 10 May 1894.
▸Improved citation: Author: National Educational Association. Dated form letter from the Secretary of the N.E.A. Caption title. Announces publication of the second ed of *Proceedings*, #2184. Contains an excellent reference list of the educational congresses held in 1893. . (UMD)

1762.1 *Proceedings of the World's Congress of Bankers and Financiers.* Chicago: Rand, McNally & co., 1893?.

26x15. 1 *l* flyer. "Bound in Cloth, price $3.00; Bound in Half Morocco, with Gilt Top, price $5.00." Includes attached stub. See citation #2238.
☺ . (GLD)   P➤ $14 - 30

1762.2 *Rand, McNally & Co.'s : universal atlas of the World.* Chicago: Rand, McNally & co., publishers, 1893 [ᶜ1888, 1890, 1891, 1892, by Rand, McNally & Co.].

36½x28½. Red cloth hc, gilt print front and back. Contains WCE descriptive text, pp (191)-(98), plus map of WF grounds. ☺ (E)

1762.3 Schulte Publishing Co. *...Special announcement. The International Congress of Anthropology.* Chicago: n.p., March 1894.

27½x21½. 1 *l*. Sales flyer, black print. $5/book, limited ed. Staniland Wake, ed. See #2177. ☺ (WM)

1763.   Shepp. *Shepp's World's Fair Photographed*: (DU,UMD)
1764.   *Shepp's World's Fair Photographed. A tornado of orders!*: (S)
1765.   Shuman. *Favorite dishes*: (S,WM)

1769.   Truman. *History of the World's fair : being A Complete and*: (GLD)
▸Delete: "---- Large b/w broadside prospectus printed both sides. (TD)" This is redefined in #1760.2.

1771.   White. *The World's Columbian Exposition, Chicago, 1893. A Complete History of the Enterprise*: (GLD)
---- Also found: Another publisher: St. Louis, MO [and] New York: N.D. Thompson publishing co.,

[ᶜ1893 by J.W. Ziegler]. Both covers are blue cloth with design in blue, brown, gold, and black. Illus front cover; replica of full book spine design on back. Spines of two leather editions are tipped-in inside front cover. Sales sample for #1057.

1771.1 White, Trumbull, and William Igleheart. *The World's Columbian Exposition.* Philadelphia: W.W. Houston & co., n.d.

46½x30½ unfolded. (4) p from folded sheet, black print and illus. Illus of book's front cover on p (4). Sales ad for #1057. ☺ (s)

1771.2 World's Columbian Exposition. Department of Publicity and Promotion. *The official directory of the World's Columbian Exposition.* Chicago: W.B. Conkey, Co., 1893 [ᶜ1892 by W.B. Conkey].

26x18½. Sample text with subscription pages at end. Blue cloth hc with gilt and black print (only this binding type is shown). Cloth ed priced at $2.50. Salesmen's sample for #1207. ☺ (s)

1773.1 World's Congress of Religions. Hanson, J[ohn] W[esley], ed. *The World's Congress of religions; the addresses and papers delivered before the Parliament, and abstract of the congresses held in the Art Institute, Chicago, Illinois, U.S.A., August 25 to October 15, 1893, Under the Auspices of the World's Columbian Exposition.* Philadelphia: W.W. Houston & co., 1894.

24x17½. Tooled morocco with elaborate floral blind stamp (front cover). Standard olive green cloth hc with black print (back cover). See illus of this cover at #2256 in the original bibliography. ☺ (E,ref,S) $30

1776. *Yankee doodle at the fair : The Best of Everything:* (s)

Chapter 12

STATES AND CITIES

-Arizona-

1779.   Arizona. *Arizona. World's Columbian Exposition*: (csuf,ICRL,UTA)

1779.1 Arizona (Territory). Humboldt. *"In Arizona : Will be Found the Wealth of the World."—Humboldt.* N.p.: n.p., n.d.

23x15½. (4) p. Folded cream glossy sheet, black print. Illus of Arizona's mineral exhibit on back. At top of p (2): "Arizona exhibit—World's Fair." List of contents of 27 cases and the "ore pyramids" on pp (2)-(3). [Humboldt is in the Mazatzal Mountains north of Phoenix and south of Flagstaff.] © (WM)

-Arkansas-

1781.   Arkansas. *Acts and resolutions of the General Assembly*:

☞ The women of Arkansas privately raised the necessary funds for a WCE exhibit.

1783.   Arkansas. *Arkansas. Eine genaue und zuverlässige*: (S)
1784.   Arkansas. AWFA. *Arkansas at the World's fair*: (UTA)

1784.1 Arkansas. Arkansas World's Fair Association? *The honor of your presence is requested at the opening exercises of the : Arkansas State Building : Thursday morning, June fifteenth, at eleven o'clock: World's Columbian Exposition...* N.p.: n.p., n.d.

20x15½. 1 *l*. Folded sheet, black print on front only. C.t. June 15 was the anniversary of Arkansas' admission to the Union. An invitation. © (S)

1785.   Arkansas. AWFD. *Arkansas in 1892–1893*: (Col,FM,MOHx,NAL,UTA,Yale)
1787.   Arkansas. *Fort Smith, Ark. Its History*: .(LBA,WM)   **P➔**

1788.   Arkansas. *Welcher Staat*:
▶Completed citation: [St. Louis: Woodward & Tiernan Printing Co.], n.d. (16) p.

-California-

1789.1 California. Alameda County World's Fair Association. *Alameda County : The garden spot of California : First in variety of products : Second in population and wealth.* Oakland: [Alameda County World's Fair Association] Oakland Tribune Print, n.d.

15x9. 8 p. Strip of buff paper unfolds to 15x36. Black print both sides. C.t. Facts and figures on many aspects of the area. © . (E,S)

1790.   [California]. Alameda County. *Columbian Exposition Souvenir*: (HU,LBA,S,SML,UCB,UCLA,UMD,Yale)
---- Also found: .Cover variant. 15x22. Gray wraps, red print, color view of the bay with sailboats on the water and city in the background. C.t.: "1893 : Alameda County California : Columbian Souvenir."

1791.   California. Brook. *The County and city of Los Angeles*: (GLD,HU,ICRL,LBA,S,SML,Stfd,UTA) $25 - 60
---- Also found: Buff wraps.

1791.1 California. Brook, Harry Ellington. *Irrigation : in : Southern California : issued for the use of the delegates : to the : International Irrigation Congress, : Los Angeles, California, : October 10-15, 1893, : by the : Publication Committee of the Congress.* Los Angeles?: Los Angeles Printing Co., July 1893.

19½x13½. 48 p. Pale blue-green glossy wraps with gilt and deep red print. Cover logo reads: "Irrigation. Science, not chance." On upper right of the cover: "World's Fair Edition. © . (SML)

1792.   California. Brook. *The Land of Sunshine*: (LBA,SML,UCB,UCLA,UMD)

1792.1 California. *By-Laws and official directory of the ___ County : World's Fair association : containing the Act of Congress inaugurating the World's Columbian Exposition and the act of the California legislature Creating the California World's Fair Commission : also Section of the County Government Bill Authorizing County Appropriations.* N.p.: n.p., 1891.

22½x8½. (4), 5-20 p. Wraps. C.t.= t.p. A blank is left on both cover and t.p. for the county's name. Similar to this example: #1823 (Delaware), #1864 (Indiana), and #1988 (New Mexico). ☺ . (UCLA)   **P➔**

1792.2 [California]: *California : big tree Joint Wine Exhibit...San Francisco. World's Columbian exposition. Chicago, 1893.* [Milwaukee: The American fine art co.], n.d.

18x10½. Tri-fold stiff leaf opens to 18x30½, three panels per side. C.t. When opened, the front panels are sepia text and back panels are multicolor and gilt with a litho of the wine exhibit housed in the stump of a hollow redwood "Big Tree." Wine statistics. A very attractive folding card. ☺ . (ref,UCB,WM) $95

1794.   California. CWFC. *Biennial report of the California World's fair*: (sfpl)

1795.   California. CWFC. Cummins (Mighels). *The story of the files : a review*:
(GLD,Col,csuf,HU,MH,NDU,OU,Stfd,UAH,UCI,UCLA,UIC,UMD,UMN,USFr) $70 - 135
▸Add pub: Louisville, KY: Lost Cost Press, 1973. Microfiche. Six sheets.
▸Add pub: Chicago: Library Resources Inc., 1970. Microfiche. LAC-11886.
---- Also found: Rpt. 1982. 470, (7) p ads. (ref) $35

1796.   California. CWFC. *Final report of the California World's fair commission*:
(Berk,CCA,Col,CU,ESU,HML,HU,LBA,Merc,MSL,NPG,OU,PSU,sfpl,Stfd,UCB,UCD,UCI,UCLA,UI,UMD,UTA,USFr,Yale)
---- Also found: Maroon cloth hc.

1796.1 California. California World's Fair Commission. *Report of the twenty-seventh Industrial Exposition of the mechanics' institute and preliminary World's fair exhibit of California. Held at the Mechanics' Pavilion from the 10th Day of January to the 18th Day of February, Inclusive.* N.p.: n.p., n.d.

21x15½. 2 *l*, (1)-140 p. Black cloth hc, gilt print. C.t.: "Report of the Twenty-seventh Industrial Exposition : Mechanics' Institute : San Francisco : 1893." The Mechanics' Institute exhibited at the request of the CA WF [WCE] Commission; the exhibit was then taken to the WCE. ☺ . (HML,UCLA)

1796.2 California. California World's Fair Commission. *Where to find : California Exhibits : in department buildings and grounds, World's Columbian Exposition, 1893.* New York: Max Stern & co., printers, 1893.

14½x11. 16 p. Tan wraps, black print. C.t.= t.p. Complete list of CA exhibits around the WCE grounds. List of CA commissioners inside front cover. ☺ (S)

1796.3 California. *The daily bulletin of the California Midwinter International Exposition.* Chicago: Department of publicity and promotion California state building, 1893.   **P➔**

52x21½. (4) p. Folded peach paper, black text and illus in newspaper format. "Issued daily" at the WCE California Bldg as a promotion for the Midwinter fair of 1894. Illus masthead of bldgs and California bruin symbol. Illustrated banner printed with Vol 1, No 45.
☺ (GLD) $100

1796.4 [California]. *Fanita Rancho : Santee, San Diego County, California. The sacred lotus. See Fanita Rancho exhibits at the World's fair.* [San Diego]: n.p., 1 July 1891.

14½x8. 8 p. Folded buff sheet, black print. C.t. [Located in the El Cajon area.] Dated. ☺ (S)

1797.1 [California]. Kern County World's Fair Association. *...Its location, soil, climate and resources. With Some Account of its Superior Advantages for Settlers.* Bakersfield: Kern County World's Fair Association (Dickman-Jones co., print, S.F.), [1892].

> 19½x10. Buff sheet unfolds to 33x81 with "Official Map of Kern County." Back side has 16 panels: 15 paged and 1 unpaged, all describing the county; black print. C.t. At head of title: "Kern County, California." © (WM)

1798.　[California]. Kern County. *Location, resources, attractions and*: . (ref,S,UCB)　　　　$40
> ►Add: C.t.: "The 'Kern-delta' : California." Wood-grain decorative wraps with stylized sun and wind.

1799.　California. *Literary and other exercises in : California State Building*: (csuf,Stfd,UCB,UMD)

1800.　California. Markham. *Resources of California*: (GLD,LBA,SML)　　　　$30 - 70
> ---- Also found: Hc bound in morocco leather, gilt print and border; red speckled edges. (GLD)

1800.1 [California]. Oakland. *The World's Columbian Exposition 1893 : Official Catalogue : Of all the Exhibits.* Ed. Department of Publicity and Promotion. Oakland: n.p., n.d.

> 23x15. 35, (5) p ads. Off-white wraps, black print and vignette of woman as part of design. C.t.: "Revised edition. Official Catalogue of exhibits. World's Columbian Exposition : price, 25 cents. 1893 : Oakland." On lower left cover: "Lou Wall." Cover and t.p. mimic the official WCE catalogs (see #1177-1206). Oakland women who participated in various WCE exhibits; includes CA ads. © . (UCB)

1800.2 [California]. Olympia Club of California. *Olympia Club : Concert and Athletic Entertainment : for the benefit of the California Room in the woman's building at the World's Columbian Exposition, Chicago : designed and furnished by Mrs. Frona Eunice Wait : Alternate Lady Manager for California.* [San Francisco]: n.p., [1893].

> 25x__ (microfilm). (4) p. A string-tied silk cloth program with the print on the cloth, scalloped edges. C.t. At bottom of cover: "San Francisco : Tuesday Evening, January 31st, 1893 : beginning at 8 o'clock precisely." Ad for Chickering Pianos on back. © (UCB)
> ---- 23x__ (microfilm). (4) p. Folded paper leaf. On bottom front cover January "23d" date is crossed out; corrected date "31st" is printed directly above. Ad for Chickering Pianos on back. © (UCB)

1800.3 [California]. *Picturesque Fresno : A Series of Twenty Photogravure Plates.* Vol. 1. World's Fair Edition. San Francisco: Printed and Published By W.B. Tyler, ᶜ1890 By W.B. Tyler.

> 28x36. (20) plates separated by guard sheets with descriptive letterpress. Buff stiff wraps, gilt lettering with tendrils; design of grapevines. C.t.: "Picturesque Fresno." © . (csuf)　　　　**P➜**

1800.4 [California]. *Picturesque San Jose and environments : An illustrated statement of the Progress, Prosperity and Resources of Santa Clara County, California. "The Garden of the World."* San Jose: H.S. Foote and C.A. Woolfolk [Press of Hurlbert Bros. & co.], [ᶜ1893 by H.S. Foote and C.A. Woolfolk].

> 17½x23. (82) p. Cream (or blue-green) wraps with bold decorative gilt print. WCE not mentioned but this item was found in two intact WCE collections. © . (LBA,SML)

1801.　[California]. SF Chronicle. *California at the World's Fair*: (S)

1801.1 [California]. San Francisco World's Fair Association. *San Francisco at the World's fair : Chicago, 1893.* N.p.: n.p., n.d.

> 15x11. (1)-(4), 5-7 p. Wraps. C.t. Pp (3)-(4) have a double page illus: "Relief Map and Panorama of San Francisco as it will appear at the World's Fair." On p 7: "Very respectfully : S.W. Bugbee, M.G. Bugbee, H.E. Wise, Committee of Ways and Means : S.F. World's Fair Ass'n." Written by the Board of Directors to develop interest in the importance of the City's representation at Chicago. © . (UCB)

1802.   California. SFWFA. SF Women's Literary Exhibit. *Catalogue of Californian writers*: (UCB,UCLA)
1803.   California. SFWFA. SF Women's Literary Exhibit. *A list of books by California*: (Col,sfpl,Stfd,UCB,UCLA)
1804.   California. Shasta County WF Committee. *Resources of Shasta County*: (UCB)

-Colorado-

1808.   Colorado. Ag Dept. *The Resources, Wealth and*: (FM,HU,LBA,MIT,MSL,NAL,NLI,OU,SML,UCB,uiuc,UMA,UPa,WM,Yale)

1809.   [Colorado]. *At the foot of Pike's Peak*: ☺(E,WM) $20 - 45
▸Completed citation: N.p.: [The Matthews-Northrup co., Buffalo, NY], n.d. (16) p includes covers. Buff self-wraps, green illus, brown print. Brown text print. Colorado Springs bird's-eye.

1812.   [Colorado]. *Colorado Gold Mining*: (KS,S)
1813.   [Colorado]. *The Colorado Mineral Palace casket*: (S)

1815.1 Colorado. *Location of Colorado State Exhibits, World's Columbian exposition.* N.p.: n.p., n.d.

8x13. Buff stiff card, black print both sides. Gives 8 locations at the WF and exhibit summaries. ☺(WM)

-Connecticut-

1817.   Connecticut. BLM. Knight. *History of the work*: (GLD,CCA,Col,CU,E,HML,HU,IHi, LBA,MOHx,MSI,MSL,NSW,SHB,Smth,Stfd,UIC,uiuc,UMC,UMD,UMN,UPa,UVM,VAM,VtSSt,WM,Yale) P➔

1818.   Connecticut. BLM. *Selections from the writings of Connecticut*: $45 - 90
(GLD,CU,HU,MH,SHB,Smth,Stfd,uiuc,UMN,UPa,UVM)
▸Completed citation: 29½x21. ix, 282 p. Beautiful blue and white cloth hc with fancy gilt design and print, gilt top edge.
---- Also found: New Haven, CT: RPI, 1976. "History of Women," reel 524, no 4012.

1819.   Connecticut. BWFM. *Connecticut at the World's*: (GLD,CLP,Col,CSL,CU,DU,E, HML,HPL,HU,LBA,MOHx,MSI,MSL,NSW,NUL,OHxS,SHB,Smth,Stfd,UCLA,UMC,UMN,UPa,UVM,WM,Yale)

1819.1 Connecticut. Connecticut Board of Agriculture. *...Twenty-Seventh Annual Report : of the : Secretary : of the : Connecticut Board of Agriculture, 1893.* Hartford: Press of The Fowler & Miller Co., 1893.

23x16. Variously paged. Black cloth hc, gilt coat of arms, gilt spine print. Frontis of CT Ag exhibit plus 11 articles and reports on their WF activities. CT aided the Columbian Commission by carrying out bomb calorimeter tests on food products at the WCE; results are reported here. ☺(GLD) $12 - 30

-Florida-

1824.1 Florida. Florida State Teachers' Association. *Florida School Exhibit. Circular no. 1.* Pensacola: n.p., 1892?

26½x20½. (8) p. Self wraps. Caption title. First page dated April 1892 and signed by W.F. Yocum, Committee Chairman. Contains: "Directions and Suggestions, relating to the preparation of an Educational Exhibit of the State of Florida for the Columbian Exposition..." ☺.(MSL)

1825.   Florida. *Fort Marion*: (S)

1825.1 [Florida]. Ingram, Mrs. H.K. *Florida: beauties of the east coast. A collection of Photographs, With Text by Mrs. H.K. Ingram.* St. Augustine: n.p., 1893.

15½x22. (56) p. Pale turquoise wraps with bold gold lettering and illus of plant, fountain, and building. C.t.: "Florida : Beauties of the East Coast." WCE handout.
☺ . (LBA)   P➔

1826. Florida. Pio. *The East Coast of Florida*: © (WM)
▶Completed citation: N.p.: n.p., n.d. Map after front cover, 48 p+ ads both sides back wrap. Beige stiff wraps with illus of fruit and palm tree. Author, Louis Pio was a land agent with an office in the "Florida Building, World's Fair, Chicago."

1827. Florida. *Regular session, 1893. Acts and resolutions*:

☞ Funds for Florida exhibits and the Florida Bldg—a miniature replica of old Fort Marion—were privately raised by the State's citizens.

-Georgia-

1828.1 Georgia. Cobb, Andrew Jackson. *The power of the General Assembly of the state of Georgia to appropriate money for a state exhibit at the World's Fair in Chicago...opinion of Andrew J. Cobb, delivered before the World's Fair Convention in Atlanta, May 6, 1891.* [Atlanta]: n.p., 1891?

22x__. 6 p. Microfilm: Cooperative Microfilming Project (NEH PS-20317). (UGa)

-Hawaii-

1829. [Hawaii]. *Hawaii : The burning crater of Kilauea*: (FM,S)

-Idaho-

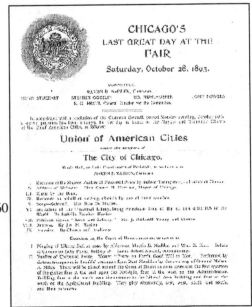

1832. Idaho. *Idaho at the Columbian exposition, 1893. Gem of the*: (WM)
▶Completed citation: N.p.: n.p., n.d. (14) p. Self-wraps, white string-tied. Photo illus of various Idaho exhibits at the WCE in several bldgs including the Idaho Bldg.

1833. Idaho. IWFC. Gregg. *Idaho Gem of the*: (Col,HU,ICRL,NAL,NSW,SML,UI,UTA,Yale)

1833.1 Idaho. *"Old Bingham" : the banner county of Idaho : at the : World's Columbian Exposition : 1893.* Chicago: S.D. Childs & co., printers, [1893]. P➔

22x15. 40 p. Light pink wraps, black print and illus. C.t. Statistics and illus of this Idaho county. Map on p 33. © . (FM,HU,S)

-Illinois-

1836. [Illinois]. Chicago. *Chicago's last great day at*: . (S)   P➔
▶Completed citation: (4) p. Folded buff sheet, black print. Caption title. For the Fair's last day, by resolution, Chicago arranged a day of honor—"Union of American Cities"—for the mayors and officials of chief cities.

1837.1 [Illinois]. Chicago. *Official programe. Chicago day : October 9, 1893. Souvenir. World's Columbian exposition. Chicago.* Chicago?: J.W. Aston, of Campbell Advertising Novelty Co., n.d.

25½x16. (4) p. Orange stiff card folded, black print. C.t. Bird's-eye of grounds on back cover. Condensed ed of #1838. © . (S) P↓

1838. [Illinois]. Chicago. *Official souvenir program*: (GLD,S) $25 - 60
▶Add: The front wrap of this Chicago Day program is reprinted on the cover of #2848.3 (see illus).

1839.1 [Illinois]. Chicago. The States' Association [of Chicago]. *States' Association to the World's Columbian Commission : Thursday, June twenty-sixth, 1890. Palmer House.* N.p.: n.p., n.d.

21½x16½. (4) p. Ribbon tied stiff wraps, steel engraving print of Santa Maria with Columbus portrait inset. Palmer House menu, program for the evening, and listing of Commissioners. (KS)

1840.1 [Illinois]. Harlev, William, & Son. "Letter to Dr. A. Brockenbrough." 19 Apr. 1890.

28x21½. One sheet printed in black. Front is letterhead; letter typed with purple ribbon, all caps. Written from Chicago, the letter begins: "My Dear Sir: We understand that you are one of the commissioners for the Virginia State Building..." Brockenbrough was from Chesapeake, VA. Back is very early plan of the WCE grounds in black with vignette of the IL Bldg to be built by Harlev; the architect was W.W. Boyington & Co. Harlev asks to bid on the VA Bldg through the Harlev Co. building committee, John Virgin, chairman. The "son" was "Alfred G.V. Harlev." ☺ (GLD) $22 - 50

☞ The Federal legislation establishing the WCE at Chicago was not formally signed by President Harrison until Apr 25, 1890, making this letter very formative material relating to the construction.

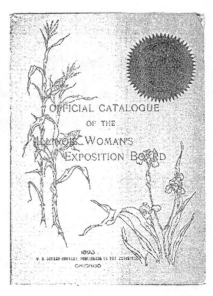

1841. Illinois. HBOC. Dunlap. *Report...Illinois Horticultural*: (CU,ICRL,IHi,uiuc,VT)
1842. Illinois. HBOC. *Facts, not fiction*: (S,uiuc)

1844. Illinois. Illinois Board. *The Illinois building and exhibits therein*: (CCA,HU,IHi,IStU,LL,MCHx,RPL,UIC,uiuc,UoA,Yale)
▶Add to 152 p version: Cover variant: Gray cloth hc.
▶Add to 156 p version: 23½x16. 156 p includes illus and interspersed plates, glossy paper. Plates on one side only, but verso counted in paging. Brown (or blue) cloth hc, gilt print, decorative end papers. C.t.: "Illinois State Building 1893." Contents different from the 152 p version.

1845. Illinois. Illinois Board. *Report*: (CLP,Col,CU,GBP,HU,IHi,Knox,LHL,MCHx,Merc,MOHx,MSL,NAL,NLA,Stfd,UAB,UCLA,UIC,UMC,UoA)

1845.1 Illinois. Illinois Board of World's Fair Commissioners. *...Yourself and ladies are respectfully invited to attend the Dedicatory Exercises of the Illinois State Building, on Thursday, May eighteenth next, at noon.* Chicago: n.p., 25 Apr. 1893.

20x12½. 1 *l*. Folded sheet printed one side, black print with litho of IL State Bldg. C.t. At head of title: "The World's Columbian Exposition..." Dated at Chicago. "La Fayette Funk, President." ☺ . (S)

1848. Illinois. IWEB. *Illinois Women's Work*: (CU,UIUC,WM)
---- Also found: 104 p. Light blue-green wraps, black print. Not bound with #1849.

1849. Illinois. IWEB. *Official Catalogue*: (CU,ICRL,IHi,WM)   P➔
---- Also found: 144 p. Light olive wraps, brown print. C.t. = t.p. Not bound with #1848.

1849.1 Illinois. Illinois Woman's Exposition Board. *Report : of the : Illinois Woman's Exposition Board, from 1891 to 1894.* N.p.: Published by the Illinois Woman's Exposition Board, 1895.

21½x15½. 40 p. Tan flecked wraps, black print. Their "History" starts on p 10 and is taken from the manuscript, #1847. Submitted by the President, M.L. Gould, to Governor Altgeld. ☺ (IHi)

1852. Illinois. *Souvenir of the Illinois Dairy Exhibit*: (IHi,NAL)

1853. Illinois. State Bureau. "Coal Mining exhibits...": ☺ . (MIT)
▶Correct paging: 3 *l*, (ix)-x, Lxxix, 162 p includes tables.

-Indiana-

1858. Indiana. BWFMI. Havens. *Indiana at the World's Columbian*: (Col,HU,NSW,S,SML,UBO,UCB)

1858.1 [Indiana]. Burford, W[illia]m B., Co. *Map of the city of Indianapolis*. Indianapolis: [Published by Wm. B. Burford, 1890].

11x6½. (8) p+ large folded map of city. Peach-orange stiff wraps, black print. Cover title: "City of Indianapolis." No WCE content; from intact collection. ☺ (WM)

1859.2 Indiana. Conner, John B. *Indiana Agriculture. Agricultural Resources and Development of the State. The struggles of pioneer life compared with present conditions*. Indianapolis: Wm. B. Burford, printer and binder, 1893.

22½x15. 24 p. Gray-green wraps, black print. C.t.= t.p. No WCE; from intact collection. ☺. (SML)

1859.3 Indiana. Dunn, J.P. *...The : Libraries : of : Indiana*. Indianapolis: Wm. B. Burford, lithographer, printer and binder, 1893.

22½x15. 35 p. No illus. At head of title: "Indiana World's Fair Monographs." Subject: facts and statistics of libraries in Indiana. ☺. (SML)

1860. Indiana. Harper. *The Associated Work of the Women of Indiana*: (MSL,SML)
---- Also found: Pale gray-green wraps, black print.

1862.1 Indiana. Meredith, Virginia C. *A monograph : on the : Live Stock of the State of Indiana*. Indianapolis, Wm. B. Burford, printer and binder, 1893.

22½x15. 12 p. No illus. Gray wraps with black print. C.t.= t.p. On t.p.: "Prepared by Mrs. Virginia C. Meredith, at the request of the Board of World's Fair Managers of Indiana." Brief description of the value to Indiana of various live stock breeds (horses, hogs, sheep, etc.). ☺. (Col,FM,SML)

1863. Indiana. *Souvenir of the Dedicatory Ceremonies of the Indiana State Building*: (HU,SML)
---- Also found: Pale lime-green wraps with green lettering.

1864. Indiana. *World's Columbian Exposition. Department of Indiana*: (MSL)

-Iowa-

1867. Iowa. ICC. Committee on Archæological. *A hand book of Iowa*:
(Col,CU,FM,HU,KSU,LBA,MSL,NLI,SML,Smth,Stfd,UCB,UCLA,UMC,Yale)
---- Also found: Rust cloth spine, gray stiff cardboard covers with black print as shown in the original bibliography. Rubber stamp at top of cover: "Compliments of the Iowa Columbian Commission."

1867.1 Iowa. Iowa Columbian Commission. Jarnagin, J.W. *To the Artists of Iowa, Greetings:*. Montezuma: Iowa Columbian Commission, 5 Dec. 1892.

28x21½. Single Commission letterhead sheet. Navy banner and litho of Iowa Bldg. Jarnagin was head of the Dept. of Ed and Fine Arts (red stamped in upper left). Announced pre-fair juried art exhibit at Cedar Rapids on Dec 27-29, 1892, with rules of the exhibit for Iowa artists only. ☺ (S)

1870. Iowa. ICC. *Report of the Iowa Columbian*:
(CU,HML,LU,NDU,S,SML,UVM,Yale)

1871. Iowa. ICC. *Souvenir of the Dedicatory*:
(GLD,ICRL,SML,WM)   P➔ $30 - 70
▶Additional annotation: String-tied.

1872. Iowa. ICC. *Souvenir Program. Iowa State Days*: (S)

-Kansas-

1875.   Kansas. BWFMK. *The board of managers, Kansas Exhibit. Proceedings*: . (ICRL,UTA)
▶Completed citation: 23½x15½. Khaki wraps, black print. C.t. Summary of WCE meetings, decisions, expenditures, and apportionment by county.

1876.   Kansas. BWFMK. *The Board of World's Fair Managers of Kansas invites you...Kansas Week*: (HU)

1877.   Kansas. BWFMK. *Report of the*: (Col,DU,E,ESU,HML,KCPL,KSU,Merc,MOHx,MSL,NAL,OHxS,RU,Stfd,UCLA,UMC,UPa,WM,Yale)
---- Also found: Brown (or maroon) cloth hc.

1877.1 Kansas. *Constitution and by-laws of the World's Columbian Club*. N.p.: n.p., n.d.

28x21½. Single sheet printed one side. Document seeks to form county "Ladies Columbian Clubs" to collect items, promote, and aid the Kansas exhibits at the WCE. See #1893.1 for related item. ☺ . (KsHx)

☞ The county Columbian Clubs helped to furnish the exhibits in the Kansas Bldg.

1877.2 Kansas. *Kansas building for the Worlds* [sic] *Columbian exposition submitted by 'utile dulci.'* N.p.: n.p., n.d.

33x21. Typescript. Caption title: "Specifications." A call for bids for erection of the Kansas Bldg at the WCE. Each specification was accompanied by a set of architect's bldg plans. ☺ . (KsHx)

☞ The building contract was awarded to Fellows and Vansant of Topeka for their lowest bid—$19,995.

1878.1 Kansas. *Kansas Educational Exhibit at the World's Fair, Chicago, 1893. Office of the board of directors. Educational exhibit notes*. Topeka: n.p., n.d.

28x21½. 1 *l*. Reminder to Kansas cities and counties regarding content and delivery of their exhibits to the WCE. See #1878 for related item. At bottom: "L.C. Wooster, Topeka, Kansas." ☺ . (OU)

1878.2 [Kansas]. Kansas Farmers' Alliance and Industrial Union. *...The World's Fair. How All Can Visit the Great Exposition. Read and ponder. The Kansas F.A. & I.U. World's fair information and protective association : Solves the Problem*. [Topeka: F.A. & I.U. (Douglass, printer), 189_].

15½x8. 8 p. Folded 15½x32 sheet, black print. C.t. Brochure from the Kansas contingent of the F.A. & I.U. describes their sponsored trips to the WCE. A week's visit without transportation: $11.10.
---- Two versions found, which differ at bottom of front cover: "Headquarters: 6825 May St., Chicago, Ill." or "Office: Room 39 Columbian Building, Topeka, Kansas." ☺ . (KsHx)

1882.   Kansas. KSHS. *A Directory of the Kansas Historical Exhibit*: (GLD,Col,Fess,FM,HU,ICRL,KSU,Merc,S,SML,UPa)

1883.   Kansas. KSHS. Kansas Educators. *Columbian History of Education*: (GLD,DC,ESU,HU,KCPL,KSU,MIT,UPa,WM) $22 - 42
---- Also found: Black shiny (or brown) cloth hc with gilt print.

1884.   Kansas. *Kansas Week at the World's Columbian Exposition...September 11th to 16th, 1893*.

☞ Captain John Brown was present at the Kansas Day ceremonies, Sept 12, 1893. He was one of five sons of John Brown, the Abolitionist, who was hung after his siege of Harper's Ferry. The elder Brown had followed his sons to Kansas Territory in 1855 to assist anti-slavery forces.

1887.   Kansas. *Mineral Resources of Kansas*: (SML)
1889.   Kansas. SBA. Hay. *Geology and mineral Resources of Kansas*: (HU,LU,NLI,SML.Stfd,UCLA,UMN)

1890.   Kansas. SBA. *World's Fair Report*: (GLD,HU,S,SML) $30 - 65
▶Corrected title capitalization: *...containing statistics*
---- Also found: Pale green wraps, black print, litho of capitol bldg on back cover.

1890.1 [Kansas]. State of Kansas Auxiliary [in Chicago]. *The World's exposition of 1892...Chicago,.* N.p.: n.p., n.d.

28x21½. 1 *l*. Caption title. Former Kansans living in Chicago issued this call to Kansans to support Chicago's bid for what would become the WCE. KsHx copy has a handwritten note from Auxiliary

Committee Chairman G.W. Burchard to Gov. L.U. Humphrey asking Humphrey to use his influence in favor of Chicago. ☺. (KsHx)   P➜

1892.   Kansas. *The University of Kansas*:   (WM)
▶Completed citation: [Topeka: Press of Hamilton printing co.], n.d. 14½x22½. 1 *l*, (26) p. Bone-white glossy wraps, black print. C.t. Prefatory note: "The State of Kansas wishes to give you...a glimpse of the University, as it exists in this Columbian Anniversary year." Many b/w photo-illus.

1893.   Kansas. Walters. *Columbian history of the Kansas state agricultural college*: (KSU)

1893.1 Kansas. *Women's Work at the Columbian Exposition.* N.p.: n.p., n.d.

21½x14. (3) p. Folded sheet (back blank). Caption title. A printed announcement by Mrs. Hanback and Mrs. Mitchell, organizers of the "Kansas Women's Columbian Club." Handout specifies women's exhibits to be collected for the WCE. See #1877.1 for related item. ☺. (KsHx)

1895.   Kansas. Wooster. "Letter issued to potential exhibitors...":
▶Add letterhead (author): Kansas educational exhibit at the World's fair. Chicago, 1893. Office of the board of directors.

1896.   Kansas. *You are most cordially welcomed by Kansas*: (S,WM)

-Kentucky-

1899.   Kentucky. KBM. *Kentucky Columbian Exhibit*: (S)
1900.   Kentucky. KBM. *Report of the Kentucky board of managers*: (GLD,MIT) $30 - 65

1900.1 Kentucky. Kentucky Board of Managers. *A short pamphlet devoted to the : Live Stock Interests of Kentucky. Prepared for Distribution at the World's Fair.* Danville: The Kentucky Advocate Printing Co., 1893.   P➜

18½x13½. 29, 1 *l*. Pale green wraps, maroon print with illus of horse head. C.t.: "Kentucky Live Stock. 1893." ☺. (FM)

-Louisiana-

1901.   Louisiana. *Acts passed by the general assembly of the state of Louisiana*:

☞ The Louisiana Building was partially furnished by the Creole Gallery of Art, New Orleans.

1901.1 [Louisiana]. *Louisiana Rice Exhibit : Rice Bran and Rice flour.* N.p.: n.p., n.d.

28x21½. 1 *l*. Buff sheet, black print. Table of analyses by the Sugar Experimental Station at New Orleans compares rice favorably with wheat as an animal feed. ☺ (WM)

1901.2 Louisiana. Louisiana State Board of Health. *The system : of : Maritime Sanitation : Inaugurated and brought to its present state of : perfection by the : Louisiana State Board of Health. Model exhibited at the World's Columbian Exposition,...* New Orleans: J.J. Hooper, Print, n.d.   P➜

15x9½. 8 p. Light brown wraps, black print. Handout in the Transportation Bldg. ☺. (Stfd—Bound WCE Trans Dept Collection)

1901.3 Louisiana. Neal, Della A. *Calcasieu Parish, Louisiana.* N.p.: n.p., n.d.

27½x20½. (4) p. Folded buff sheet, photo-illus of oranges. C.t. At bottom: "Headquarters : Louisiana building." Info about the area near the border with Texas. Neal was a delegate from the parish. ☺ . (WM)   P➔

1901.4 Louisiana. Poole, T.W. *Some late words about : Louisiana,...* New Orleans: Crescent steam print, 1891.

23½x15½. 135, (1) p. Salmon wraps, black print. Invitation to immigrate; state advantages and data. Poole was "Commissioner of Immigration" for Louisiana. Handout but no mention of WCE; from intact collection. ☺ (WM)

-Maine-

1901.5 [Maine]. *Addresses at the Dedication of Maine State Building as a library and art building at Poland Spring, Maine, July 1, 1895.* Lewiston: Printed at the Journal office, 1895.

23x15. 1 *l* (frontis), tissue guard, 1 *l* (t.p.), (3)-44 p. Rust wraps, black print. Frontis of Maine State Bldg. Text of the 11 addresses delivered at the dedication of the Maine Bldg as re-erected. C.t. = t.p. On t.p. below title: "Removed from the World's Columbian Exposition Grounds at Chicago and re-erected at Poland Spring by Hiram Ricker & Sons." See annotation to #1902 for more info. ☺ . (E)

1901.6 Maine. Board of World's Fair Managers of Maine. *...Committee on education, science, literature, and art.* N.p.: n.p., 1892.

28x20½. (4) p. Instruction for organizing the Maine exhibits in the designated areas. At head of title: "World's Columbian Exposition. Board of World's fair managers of Maine." ☺ (S)

1901.7 Maine. Board of World's Fair Managers [of Maine]. Mattocks, Charles P. "Letter to Board Members." 1892. Portland.

26½x20½. Printed form letter on Managers' letterhead with state seal. Illus of ME state bldg on back with list of committee members and exhibit divisions. Letter begins: "Dear Sir: If there are any Manufacturing Enterprises or Live Stock Interests in your section..." Mattocks, Executive Commissioner, requesting names of possible manufacturing exhibitors for the WCE. ☺ . (E)

1902. Maine. BWFMM. *Report of the Board of World's Fair Managers*: (GLD,S) $40 - 90
  ▶Correction: 23½x15. 1 *l* frontis, 36 p+ 17 unpaginated photos. (GLD)
  ---- Also found: Maroon stiff wraps. (S)

1903. Maine. Burleigh. *Inaugural address*: (E)
1904. Maine. Haynes. *The State of*: (GLD,LBA,S,UMD,WM) P➔$35 - 75

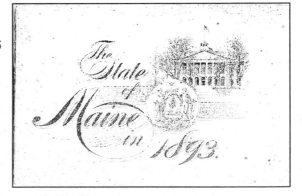

1904.1 Maine. *Inaugural address of Henry B. Cleaves to the Legislature of the State of Maine, January 5, 1893.* Augusta: Burleigh & Flynt, printers to the state, 1893.

23x14½. 1 *l* (t.p.), (3)-22 p. Pale green wraps, black print. C.t. = t.p. Speech discusses the future of Maine; refers to WCE as a mechanism for demonstrating Maine people and products to the nation and the world. ☺ . (E)

1905.1 Maine. Maine Board of Agriculture. Boardman, Samuel. L. *Agricultural Bibliography of Maine.* Augusta: Burleigh & Flynt, printers to the state, 1893.

23½x15½. 2 *l*, 117 p. Wraps. Portrait frontis. A catalogue of works by Maine writers displayed at the WCE. Publication of the WCE portion of the year's report, # 1905.2. (ref) $25

1905.2 Maine. Maine Board of Agriculture. ...*Thirty-fifth annual report of the secretary of the Maine Board of Agriculture for the year 1892*. Augusta: Burleigh & Flynt, printers to the state, 1893.

24x15½. 1 *l* (frontis), 240, 127, 127, (1) p, 2 *l*, 117, 19 p. B/w illus are not included in paging. Black cloth hc, gilt spine print. At head of title: "Agriculture of Maine." The 2 *l*, 117 p section by Samuel L. Boardman, under direction of B. Walker McKeen, Secretary, is entitled "Agricultural bibliography of Maine. A list of Maine writers on agriculture, with biographical sketches and a catalogue... A contribution to the agricultural literature section of the Columbian World's Fair." See rpt, #1905.1. ☺ (GLD) $15 - 30

1905.3 Maine. Maine Board of Agriculture. ...*Thirty-sixth annual report of the secretary of the board of agriculture, for the years 1893-94*. Augusta: Burleigh & Flynt, printers to the state, 1894.

24x15½. 1 *l* (frontis), 206, 180, 106 p. Contains numerous interspersed unpaged plates. Frontis fold map of Maine. Black cloth hc is blind-stamped, spine print. At head of title: "Agriculture of Maine." Complete reports of Maine exhibits and lectures at the WCE, also illus of the exhibits. ☺ (GLD) $20 - 30

1905.4 Maine. Maine Board of Agriculture. ...*Thirty-eighth annual report of the secretary of the board of agriculture for the year 1895*. Augusta: Burleigh & Flynt, printers to the state, 1896.

24x16. 1 *l* (frontis), 288, 146 p, 1 *l*, 122 p. Black cloth hc, gilt spine print. At head of title: "Agriculture of Maine." On p 115 of last section, the secretary of agriculture in May of 1896 describes receipt of Saint Gaudens bronze medal and award diploma for the apple exhibit. ☺ (GLD) $12 - 28

1905.5 Maine. *Maine register, state year-book and legislative manual from May 1, 1892 to May 1, 1893*. Portland: G.M. Donham, 1892 [°1892].

17½x12. Black cloth hc. Cover blind-stamped with state seal, gilt print on spine. Maine Board of World's Fair Managers listed on p 223. (ref) $12 - 28

1905.6 Maine. *Maine register, state year-book and legislative manual from May 1, 1893 to May 1, 1894*. Portland: G.M. Donham, 1893 [°1893].

17½x12. (12) p ads, (3)-854, (34) p ads. Black cloth hc. Cover blind-stamped with state seal, gilt print on spine. Maine Board of World's Fair Managers listed on p 223. ☺ (GLD) $12 - 28

1905.7 [Maine]. *Poland Spring : centennial : a souvenir*. South Poland: Hiram Ricker & sons (incorporated) [Press of Andrew H. Kellogg, New York], °1895.

18x22½. 1 *l* (frontis), (3)-88, (1) p. Frontis of Poland Spring House and Maine State Bldg. Good quality buff colored wraps that overhang text pages, multicolor emblem in lower right corner, string-tied. Brown text, green-toned illus. WCE Maine State Bldg described and illustrated in detail, including its transportation history and re-erection back in Poland Spring, ME. In addition, the Poland Water exhibit at the WCE is illus along with the award diploma the water received. See annotation to #1902 in the original bibliography for more about the Maine State Bldg. ☺ (GLD) $25 - 55

1906.1 Maine. Secretary of State. *Acts and resolves of the sixty-sixth legislature of the state of Maine. 1893*. Augusta: Burleigh & Flynt, printers to the state, 1893.

26x17. xxiii, 1 *l*, (165)-1059 p (acts),1 *l*, (131)-251 p (resolves and index). Tan paper-covered boards, black print, black cloth spine directly glued to signatures and boards. Act of Chapter 460 appropriates an additional $17,900 for the WCE Maine Bldg grounds, construction, exhibits and report (pp 712-13). Resolve of Chapter 230 appropriates $1000 for state representatives going to the opening of the Maine Bldg at the WCE (pp 167-68). ☺ (GLD) $16 - 40

1908.   [Maine]. Waldron. *The Summer State of Maine*: (GLD,E,S)
         ---- Found with and without the caption "Maine Building, World's Fair" for the illus on back cover.

-Maryland-

1908.1 [Maryland]. Abell, A.S., Co. *Maryland : its : Resources, Industries : and : Agricultural Condition : 1893*. Baltimore: The Sun (Press of The Sun Book and Job Printing Office), n.d.

16½x11½. 64 p+ unpaged plates, 1 fold map before back cover. Gold wraps, black print, illus of state seal. C.t. = t.p. Abell owned *The Sun* newspaper. ☺ . (S)   P➜

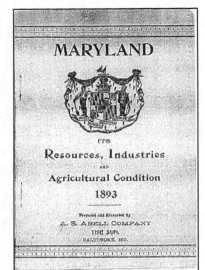

1908.2 Maryland. Board of World's Fair Managers of Maryland. *Maryland Day : World's Columbian Exposition : Chicago, Tuesday, September twelfth, Programme.* N.p.: n.p., n.d.

24½x15½. (4) p. Folded glossy sheet, black print, litho of Maryland State Bldg at top of cover. Francis Scott Key's (from Maryland) "Star Spangled Banner" reproduced on pp (2)-(3). On back: Frank Brown, Governor, reception at 6 p.m. ☺ (IHi)

1909.   Maryland. BWFMM. *Maryland : its resources*:   (FM,NAL,NLI,NSW,S,SML,WM,Yale)
---- Also found: Brown (or orange) cloth hc, gilt print and state shield design, marbled end papers.

1909.1 Maryland. Board of World's Fair Managers of Maryland. *The board : of : World's Fair Managers : for : Maryland, 1892-3.* [Baltimore: A. Hoen & co., n.d.].

16x10. 1 *l* (t.p.), (23) p. Ivory wraps, raised brown print. Title from a half title page. C.t.: "Maryland." The Maryland senate introduced a bill, No 9, for the appointment of a commission, arrangement of an exhibit, and appropriation for same; a defining document for MD at the WCE. ☺ . (E)

-Massachusetts-

1915.1 Massachusetts. *Acts and resolves : passed by the : Legislature of Massachusetts : during the : session of 1893. Published by the : Secretary of the Commonwealth.* Boston: Wright & Potter Printing Co., State Printer, n.d.

23x15½. 618 p. Under "Resolves," chapters 39, 88, and 111 have the same WCE content as described in #1914. ☺ (SML)

1915.2 [Massachusetts]. *Amesbury Mass. The Carriage Centre of the World. USA.* N.p.: [Amesbury Carriage Centre], n.d.   P➜

11x21. 39, (1) p+ text inside both covers. Tan wraps, black print; brown, light blue, and green design and port captioned "The Home of John G. Whittier : The Quaker-Poet." C.t. Caption title first p: "Amesbury and its Business." ☺ . (E)

1916.   Massachusetts. BWFMM. *Comparative statistics concerning the agriculture of Mass*:   (NAL)

1917.   Massachusetts. BWFMM. Joyce. *Outdoor Relief in the town of Brookline*:   (ref,S) $35
▶Add annotation: Capitalize "Relief." [Geo. H. Ellis, printer, Boston]. 23x15. 13, (1) p+ map tipped-in at back cover. Pink wraps with black print and line border. C.t. = t.p. Frontis illus of almshouse. Compares effectiveness and cost of distributing welfare to clients at their residences versus commitment to almshouses. Joyce was Secretary, Board of Overseers of the Poor.

1918.   Massachusetts. BWFMM. *Massachusetts' care of Dependent and Delinquent Children*:   (MSL)

1918.1 Massachusetts. Board of World's Fair Managers of Massachusetts. *Massachusetts Commission : World's Columbian exposition.* Boston: n.p., 10 Jan. 1893.

8½x14. 24 p. Maroon leather with gilt state seal. Caption title (no t.p. or c.t.). E.C. Hovey was Secretary; Francis A. Walker, Chairman. Prospectus for the celebration of a day during the Exposition to be known as Massachusetts Day. [Massachusetts Day at the WCE was June 17, 1893.] ☺ . (MSL)

1918.2 Massachusetts. Board of World's Fair Managers of Massachusetts. ...*Office of the advisory committee on fine arts for the state of Massachusetts.* Boston: n.p., 1892?

> 20½x13½. (4) p. Folded sheet, black print. At head of title: "World's Columbian Exposition." Announcement by Frederic P. Vinton, secretary, that art shown at the Massachusetts Charitable Mechanics' Association exhibit, Jan 2–7, 1893, would be used for Massachusetts art exhibits at the WCE; see #1925.10 for the Mechanics' catalog (date was changed to Jan 16–28, 1893). ☺ (WM)

1920.1 Massachusetts. Board of World's Fair Managers of Massachusetts. *Reception : to the : department chiefs : of the : World's Columbian Exposition. Monday, October 23, 1893. Massachusetts building.* N.p.: n.p., 1893.

> 13x9. 1 *l.* Card with brown print one side. "Programme of Music." C.t. Invitation. ☺ (S)

1921. Massachusetts. BWFMM. *Report of the Massachusetts board:*
> (Amh,BPL,CU,HML,HU,LBA,MIT,MSL,MU,NLA,UMA,UMD,UVM,VT,WM)
> ▸Add: Three-page report on Massachusetts Day at the World's Fair in back pocket.

1921.1 Massachusetts. Board of World's Fair Managers of Massachusetts. Rumford Kitchen Exhibit. *Guide to the Rumford kitchen. South door of the anthropological building. Leave the intramural railway at forestry station.* N.p.: n.p., n.d.

> 17½x13½. (4) p. Folded buff sheet, black print. Caption title. Explains the Rumford Kitchen's exhibits, operation, and contents. Based on Count Rumford's cooking inventions, the exhibit contained apparatus and literature from the New England Kitchen, Boston. The State Board invited this to be a part of the MA exhibit, Bureau of Hygiene and Sanitation. The Kitchen is also described and shown in the *Report*, #1921.
> ☺ (GLD,WM) $25 - 55

1921.2 Massachusetts. Board of World's Fair Managers of Massachusetts. Rumford Kitchen Exhibit. *Historical exhibit at Chicago. An Earnest Appeal from the Massachusetts Board of Managers.* Boston: n.p., 7 Dec. 1891.

> 28x21½. (1) p. Issued from the Sears Bldg at Boston, E.C. Hovey, Secretary; John W. Corcoran, Chairman. Request by the Board for historical articles for display at the MA Bldg, WCE. ☺ (MSL,WM)

1921.3 [Massachusetts. Board of World's Fair Managers of Massachusetts.] Rumford Kitchen Exhibit. *The Rumford kitchen leaflets. No. 1. Count Rumford.* N.p.: n.p., n.d.

> 17x13½. 4 p. Folded buff sheet, black print. Caption title. At bottom p 4: "The Life of Count Rumford, written by Rev. George E. Ellis ..." No WCE content; from intact collection. ☺ (WM)

1921.4 [Massachusetts. Board of World's Fair Managers of Massachusetts.] Rumford Kitchen Exhibit. *The Rumford kitchen leaflets. No. 2. Of the pleasures of eating, and of the means that may be employed for increasing it.* Rpt. N.p.: n.p., n.d.

> 17x13½. 3 p. Folded buff sheet, black print, blank back. Caption title. Under title: "An Essay by Count Rumford. Reprinted from The American Collection." No WCE content; intact collection. ☺ (WM)

1921.5 [Massachusetts. Board of World's Fair Managers of Massachusetts.] Rumford Kitchen Exhibit. Chittenden, R.H. *The Rumford kitchen leaflets. No. 3. The digestibility of proteid foods.* N.p.: n.p., n.d.

> 17x13½. 5 p. Buff self-wraps, black print, string-tied. Caption title. No WCE content; from an intact collection. ☺ (WM)

1921.6 Massachusetts. Board of World's Fair Managers of Massachusetts. Worcester, A. *Training Schools for Nurses in Small Cities.* Boston: Massachusetts' Board of Managers (George H. Ellis, printer), n.d.

> 23x15. 67 p. 2nd ed. Dr. Worcester was a Massachusetts obstetrician. ☺ (NSW)

1922.1 [Massachusetts]. Boston. Boston School Committee. ...*Schedule of pupil's work with directions as to its preparation for the educational exhibit of Boston, at the World's Columbian exposition.* Boston: Rockwell and Churchill, printers, 1892.

> 8°. 11 p. "Its Documents...1892. No. 11." (MSL-missing)

1923.   Massachusetts. *Catalogue of the Educational Exhibit*: (HU,MSL,SML,WM,Yale)

1923.1 Massachusetts. Department of Charities and Correction. *World's Columbian Exposition. ...Department of charities and correction.* N.p.: n.p., n.d.

27x20½. (3) p. Folded sheet, black print. Caption title. Request for exhibits and rules for submitting; to Joseph Lee, Secretary of the Dept, Boston. Refers to WCE Bureau of Charities and Correction. ☺ (WM)

1923.2 [Massachusetts]. Eldredge, D. *Massachusetts co-operative banks : or : building associations. A history of their growth from 1977 to 1893. Prepared for the World's Columbian Exposition. 1877—System Authorized. 1893—Assets over Fourteen Millions.* Boston: Press of Geo. H. Ellis, 1893.

22½x15. Tipped-in fold map, 2 *l*, (3)-44 p. Wraps. Rules and advantages of the co-op. ☺ (GLD) $20 - 45

1923.3 Massachusetts. Essex Institute. *Bulletin of the Essex institute, volume XXV. 1893.* Salem: [Essex Institute] Printed at the Salem Press, 1893.

23x16½. 2 *l* (t.p. and contents), 134 p. Bound with vol XXVI (1894): iii, 1-202, (4) p (notes and additions). Both vols have unpaged interspersed plates, some folded. Black cloth hc, gilt spine print. There is no WCE content in vol XXVI. Vol XXV contains the extensive illustrated report of the Essex committee on their WCE activities, pp 19-74. See #1923.4 and #1928 for other Essex Institute publications from the WCE. ☺ (GLD) $30 - 70

☞ Frederick W. Putnum, Chief of the WCE Department of Ethnology, was a member of the Essex Institute and a strong supporter of a grand Massachusetts presence at the WF. Mr. E.C. Hovey, Secretary of the MA Board of World's Fair Managers, gave the Institute full charge of furnishing rooms in the Massachusetts Bldg at the WCE.

1923.4 Massachusetts. Essex Institute. *Rooms of the Essex Institute, Jan. 20, 1893.* N.p.: n.p., n.d.

21½x14. 2 *l*. Sheet folded backwards, black print. A committee-of-12 call to members to furnish items for the Institute's decoration of the "Reception Rooms in the Massachusetts State Building, at the Columbian Exposition at Chicago,..." ☺ (WM)

1925.1 Massachusetts. Griffis, William Elliot. *Massachusetts: A typical American commonwealth.* Cambridge: John Wilson and son (University Press), 1893.

21½x18. 3 *l*, (5)-38 p. Illus. Glossy stiff text stock. This testimony to Massachusetts is described as a WCE handout on pp 32 and 37. ☺ . (Amh,SML,WM)

1925.2 [Massachusetts]. Housatonic Agricultural Society. *Souvenir Programme. 51st annual exhibition of the : Housatonic Agricultural Society, Great Barrington, Mass., September 28, 29 and 30, 1892.* [Great Barrington: Printed and Presented by Berkshire Courier co.], 1892.

19½x14. 32 p+ (8) p interspersed chromoliths of WCE bldgs. Tan wraps, black print. C.t. = t.p. Commemorates upcoming WCE but makes no mention that their show was a preparatory exhibit. ☺ (S)

1925.3 Massachusetts. Massachusetts Board of Education. *Abstract of the report of the state board of education : relating to : The Massachusetts School Exhibit at the World's Columbian exposition.* N.p.: n.p., 1893?

23½x15½. 34 p. Plates, plans, tables, diagrams. Tan wraps, black print. Half t.p. ☺ . (MSL)

1925.4 Massachusetts. Massachusetts Board of Education. Massachusetts Committee on Public Education. Dutton, Samuel T. *...Massachusetts Committee on Public Education. Public high school exhibit. Form of the exhibit, and general directions.* Boston: n.p., 20 Apr. 1892.

28½x21½. (4) p. No wraps, blue print. Caption title. At head of title: "World's Columbian exposition." Dutton was Secretary of the Committee; Edwin P. Seaver, Chairman. ☺ . (MSL,WM)

1925.5 Massachusetts. Massachusetts Board of Education. Massachusetts Committee on Public Education. Dutton, Samuel T. *...Massachusetts Committee on Public Education.* Boston: n.p., 25 Mar. 1892.

28½x21½. (3) p. No wraps. Caption title. At head of title: "World's Columbian exposition." This circular calls for participation in the State's WCE school exhibits. This is referred to as "Circular No. 2" in the text of *Circular No. 3* (#1925.6). ☺. (E,MSL)

1925.6 Massachusetts. Massachusetts Board of Education. Massachusetts Committee on Public Education. Dutton, Samuel T. *Circular No. 3. World's Columbian exposition. Massachusetts Committee on Public Education.* Boston: n.p., 28 Apr. 1892.

28½x21½. (3) p. No wraps, blue print. Caption title. Contains instructions for preparing educational exhibits for the WCE. ☺. (MSL,WM)

1925.7 Massachusetts. Massachusetts Board of Education. Massachusetts Committee on Public Education. Dutton, Samuel T. *Circular No. 5. World's Columbian exposition. Massachusetts Committee on Public Education. ...Department of art education.* Boston: n.p., 17 May 1892.

28½x21½. (3) p. No wraps. Caption title. Committee circular describing the requested content for the "State exhibit in drawing." ☺. (E,MSL)

1925.8 Massachusetts. Massachusetts Board of Education. Massachusetts Committee on Public Education. Dutton, Samuel T. *Circular No. 6. World's Columbian exposition. Massachusetts Committee on Public Education.* Boston: n.p., 19 May 1892.

28½x21½. (3) p. No wraps. Caption title. Kindergarten exhibit suggestions and directions. ☺. (MSL)

1925.9 Massachusetts. Massachusetts Board of Education. Massachusetts Committee on Public Education. Dutton, Samuel T. *Circular No. 7. World's Columbian exposition. Massachusetts Committee on Public Education.* Boston: n.p., 27 May 1892.

28½x21½. (1) p. Caption title. Contains corrections to *Circular No. 6*, #1925.8. ☺. (MSL)

1925.10 [Massachusetts]. Massachusetts Charitable Mechanics' Association. ...*Catalogue of the Massachusetts Fine Art Exhibit, at Massachusetts Charitable Mechanics' Association building, Huntington Avenue, Boston from January 16–28, inclusive.* N.p.: n.p., n.d.

26x20½. (7) p includes inside and outside back cover. Buff smooth self-wraps, black print. Caption title. At head of title: "World's Columbian Exposition." Held in Boston prior to WCE to determine art entries for the WF; 262 works listed. Daniel C. French was on the "Advisory Committee." (WM)

1927. [Massachusetts]. MIT. *Massachusetts Institute*: (HU,MIT)
▶Add: 24½x17½. 39 p. Yellow-tan wraps. Text and illus on glossy stock. Frontis: "Entrance Hall: Rogers Building." The MIT founder was Dr. William Barton Rogers; MIT was chartered in 1861.

1928. Massachusetts. *Salem at the*: (GLD,csuf,HU,ICRL,LBA,MSL,S,UTA,WM,Yale) P➡ $25 - 60
▶Clarification: Included are 2 unpaged plates on stiff stock. Catalog lists all of the exhibits shown by Salem that were found in various WCE bldgs. Many were contributed by the Essex Institute.

1929. Massachusetts. State Dept of Health. *A guide to its exhibit*: (HU)
1930. Massachusetts. State Dept of Inspection. *School-houses and public*: (HU,MSL)
1931. Massachusetts. Toomey. *Massachusetts of to-day*:
(Amh,BPL,DC,E,FM,HU,MH,MIT,MSL,Smth,SPL,UMA,UMC,UMD,VtHx)

1931.1 [Massachusetts]. Worcester. *A Tribute : to the : Columbian Year : by the : City of Worcester...* Worcester: Published for the Board of Trade By F.S. Blanchard & Co., 1893.

30x23½. 200 p. Charcoal gray wraps. Introduction mentions WCE. C.t.: "A Columbian Tribute : Worcester, Mass. : A Town June 14, 1722 – A City Feb.y 29. 1848." Illus promotional. ☺ (E,ref,S) $38

-Michigan-

1932.   Michigan. BWFMSM. Weston. *Report of the board*:   (Col,MSL)
1936.   Michigan. Fitch. *Catalogue of the Public School Exhibit*:   (HU)
1939.   Michigan. *Michigan and its resources*:   (LBA,NLI)
1940.   Michigan. MSBH. *Relative to the Michigan state*:   (csuf,HU,ICRL,MSL)

1944.   Michigan. *World's Columbian exposition. State of*:   (GLD,Col,UCB) $ 30 - 65
     ---- Also found: Tan wraps, black print.   P➔

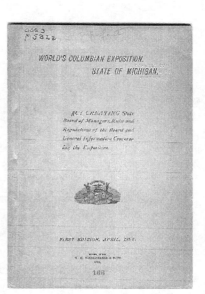

-Minnesota-

1945.   Minnesota. BWFMM. Barrett. *Minnesota and its flora*:   (WM)
1947.   Minnesota. BWFMM. *Minnesota: a brief*:   (Col,FLP,FM,MOHx,UMA,UMN,WM)
1948.   Minnesota. BWFMM. *Minnesota Day at the World's*:   (Col,S,UMN)
1949.   Minnesota. BWFMM. *Souvenir manual*:   (HU,MIT,NSW,UMD,UMN,WM)

1951.1 [Minnesota]. Minneapolis Chamber of Commerce. Sturtevant, C.C. *Tenth Annual Report of the : trade and commerce of Minneapolis : for the year ending December 31st, 1892.* [Minneapolis: Tribune job ptg. co. printers & binders], n.d.

     23½x15. 340 p+ unpaged folded maps of several railroad lines. Green wraps, black print. Includes reports from railroads servicing Minneapolis. Sturtevant was Chamber secretary; C.A. Pillsbury, its president. Mentions distribution of this publication at the WCE. ☺ (SML,WM)

1951.2 [Minnesota]. Minneapolis. *Pen and sunlight sketches : Minneapolis. Its Wonderful Development, Resources, Commerce, Manufactures, Financial Interests, Public Institutions and Prospects. Handsomely illustrated. Also Views of the Nation's Pride, the World's Columbian Exposition.* Minneapolis and Chicago: Phœnix publishing co., n.d.

     26½x21½. ii, (1) p (t.p.), pp 4-7, p numbered viii, 33-215, (1) p. Rebound. "Minneapolis at the World's Columbian exposition," pp (81)-(94). ☺. (UMN)

1951.3 [Minnesota]. *Saint Paul : The Queen City of the North-West. Its Wonderful Development, Resources, Commerce, Manufactures, Financial Interests, Public Institutions and Prospects. Handsomely illustrated. Also Views of the World's Columbian exposition.* St. Paul and Chicago: Phœnix publishing co., n.d.

     26½x21½. ii (ads), (1) (t.p.), 12-16 (index starting on back of t.p.), ?some pages missing, 33-216 p. Red cloth hc with bold gilt lettering, blind-stamp border design. ☺. (UMN)

1951.4 Minnesota. *Where Minnesota's Collective Exhibits can be found.* Mankato: Free Press Job Print, n.d.

     22x14. Single sheet, black print. Gives locations for 23 MN exhibits around the WCE grounds. ☺ (WM)

-Missouri-

     ☞ The Board in Missouri used several names: Board of World's Fair Managers of Missouri (BWFMM), Missouri World's Fair Commission, World's Fair Board of the State of Missouri, and World's Fair Commission of Missouri (WFCM). Joseph K. Gwynn was the Executive Commissioner.

     ☞ Gwynn's bequest helped build Gwynn Hall for Home Economics at the University of MO, Columbia.

1953.   Missouri. BWFMM. Gwynn. *Full-term report of the World's fair board*:   (MOHx)

1954.   Missouri. *A description of the Ozark Plateau in Southern Central Missouri*:   (WM)
     ▸Completed citation: Buffalo, NY: Matthews, Northrup & Co., Art Printing Works, 1889. Light green wraps with blue print and flower decoration. No mention of WCE; from an intact collection.

1955.   Missouri. Jones. *Reasons why The World's Fair of 1892 should be located at St. Louis*:   (S)
     ▸Add annotation for Darby imprint: 23x15. 36 p. Tan wraps with black print.

1957.1 Missouri. Missouri State Board of Agriculture. ...*Missouri at the fair : 1893.* Columbia: E.W. Stephens, Printer, 1894.

22x15. 38 p+ 9 plates of farm-animal illus, 1 folding. Pale green wraps, black print. At head of title: "Missouri State Board of Agriculture." Frontis port of Hon. J.K. Gwynn [executive commissioner of the World's Fair Managers of Missouri], C.t.; "Missouri at the World's fair." (MOHx)

1957.2 Missouri. Missouri World's Fair Commission. Gwynn, J[oseph] K. *Missouri at the Fair.* St. Louis: Missouri World's Fair Commission (Slawson Printing Co.), 1892.

26½x18. 50, (10) p+ text and ads inside wraps. Peach-tan wraps, black print and bird's-eye view of the Fair grounds. C.t. On cover: "Volume I June, 1892. Number I."- Intended to promote MO at the WF; no subsequent issues found. ☺. (MOHx)   **P➜**

1957.3 Missouri. Missouri World's Fair Commission. Gwynn, J[oseph] K. *Missouri at The Worlds* (sic) *Fair.* St. Louis: Missouri World's Fair Commission, n.d.

23x15½. 16 p. Gray wraps with black print and logo. C.t. Caption title: "World's Fair Information." Intended speech of Mar 24, 1892, before the MO House of Representatives. (MOHx)

1957.4 Missouri. *Programme for Missouri day. August 30th, 1893.* N.p.: n.p., n.d.

23x15. 1 *l.* For program to be held at the Missouri State Bldg starting at 2 p.m. ☺ (S)

1958. [Missouri]. St Louis Cong Committee. *An Appeal by Professor S. Waterhouse*: (HU,LBA,MOHx,UCB,uiuc)

1958.1 [Missouri]. Waterhouse, S[ylvester]. *The westward movement : of : capital, : And the Facilities which : St. Louis and Missouri : offer for : its investment.* 4th ed. [St. Louis: Published by the Merchants' Exchange of Saint Louis, 1890].

20x13½. 15 p includes front self-wrap. Buff paper, black print. C.t. Written by Waterhouse, Professor at Washington U, for the promotion of St. Louis as the site of the Columbian Expo. Includes article pp 11-15: "The Metropolitan Attractions of St. Louis" requested by the "St. Louis Congressional Committee on the World's Fair." See #1958. ☺ (GLD) $30 - 60

1958.2 Missouri. ...*World's Columbian Exposition. Department of Missouri. Containing : Act of Congress Creating World's Columbian Commission. Law Creating State Board of World's Fair Managers. By-laws of the board. Rules governing exhibits. Names and Addresses of : Officers, Committees, and Members of the Board. Issued October, 1891.* Brookfield: Press of the Brookfield Argus, 1891.

22½x14. 18 p. Tan wraps, black print. C.t. At head of title: "Dedication, Oct. 12, 1892. Formal opening, May 1, 1893." State law publication similar in format to #2063. (MOHx)

1959. Missouri. Winslow. *The Geology and Mineral Products of Missouri*: (WM)
▶Add cite info: (14) p including text on outside back wrap. Fold out geological map of the state after front wrap. Buff glossy self-wraps, black print. Caption title = c.t..

1960. Missouri. WFCM. Cox. *Missouri at the World's Fair*: (Col,FM,HU,KCPL,Merc,MIT,MOHx,MSL,NLA,NSW,SML,UMC,WM)
---- Also found: Pink wraps.

-Montana-

1961.1 Montana. Board of World's Fair Managers of the State of Montana. ...*Act of Congress Creating World's Columbian Commission : Law Creating Board of World's Fair Managers of Montana. Proceedings of board of World's fair managers. Rules and regulations for government of board : Reports of Executive*

Commissioner and Committees. Classification of exhibits. Names and addresses of Officers, Committees and Members of Board. [Helena: Independent Job Dept., 1892].　　　　　　　　　　　　　**P➔**

22x15.　46 p.　At head of title: "The World's Columbian Exposition, Chicago, Ill., 1893.　The board of World's Fair Managers of the State of Montana."　C.t.　Establishes the basic guidelines for state participation at the WCE; similar to #1816, #1864, #1944, #1988.　. (NSW,SML,UCLA)

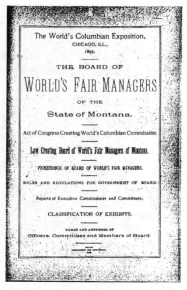

1961.2 Montana.　Board of World's Fair Managers of the State of Montana. *...The board of World's Fair Managers of the state of Montana. Proceedings of board of World's fair managers.　Reports of Officers and Committees.　Names and addresses of Officers, Committees and Members of Board.*　Helena: C.K. Wells Co., Printers and Binders, 1892.

22½x14½.　88 p.　Wraps.　C.t. = t.p.　At head of title: "World's Columbian Exposition, Chicago, Ill., 1893."　☺ . (ICRL,IHi,NSW)

1962.　Montana. BWFMSM. *Montana Exhibit*:　(csuf,ESU,HU,ICRL,LBA,MIT,MOHx,MSL,NSW,S,SML,UCB,UCLA,UI,UMC,UoA,UTA,Yale)
　▸Add publisher:　New Haven, CT: RPI, 1975 (Western Americana, Frontier History of the Trans-Mississippi West, 1550-1900; 3710).　(UoA)

-Nebraska-

1966.　Nebraska. Garneau. *Nebraska Her Resources, Advantages and Development*:　(csuf,E,MSL)
　---- Also found:　Yellow-gold wraps.

1968.　Nebraska. SBA. *Nebraska. Products and Resources*:　(S,WM)

-Nevada-

1969.　Nevada. *Nevada At the World's Fair*:　(ref,UCI)　　　　　　　　　　　　$135
1971.　Nevada. WFMN. *Report of Nevada State Board*:　(UCB,UCLA)

-New Hampshire-

1971.1 New Hampshire.　*The American alps, other summer haunts, and winter retreats.　With descriptions of the leading hotels and boarding houses, their accommodations and charges, and notices of leading tourists' hotels in large cities.　Distributed for the purpose of giving additional publicity to hotels and boarding-houses advertised in the White Mountain Echo.*　Bethlehem: Printed at the office of the White Mountain Echo, 1893.　　　　　　　　　　**P➔**

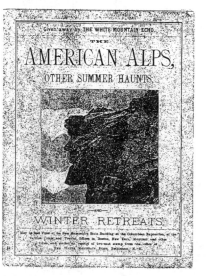

20x15.　40 p.　Illus.　Light green wraps, black print and illus of the "Great Stone Face."　On cover: "May be had free at the New Hampshire State Building at the Columbian Exposition,..."　☺ . (ICRL)

☞　Frederick Douglass spoke at the New Hampshire Bldg dedication ceremonies on June 27, 1893.

-New Jersey-

1976.　New Jersey. BWMESNJ. *Official Descriptive Catalogue*:　(CCA,Col,WM,Yale)
1977.　New Jersey. Dept Pub Instruct. Comm on Ed Exhibit. *Catalogue*:　(UPa)

1978.1 New Jersey.　Morris, S.R.　*World's Fair Photographs, Including Views of the New Jersey Educational Exhibit.　Chicago, 1893.*　N.p.: S.R. Morris, n.d.

ca 28x22. Photos. Columbia University's copy has laid in signed letter by Morris dated May 14, 1894. As noted on bottom of t.p., Morris was the Supt of the NJ Educational Exhibit. ☺. (Col)

1978.2 New Jersey. ...*New Jersey Agricultural Exhibit. List of woods : growing wild in New Jersey. Location : Agricultural Hall, E, 17 and 18.* [Trenton: John L. Murphy, Printer], n.d.

23½x15½. 8 p. Self-wraps, black print. C.t. At head of title: "International Exhibition." . (FM)   **P➔**

1979. New Jersey. *New Jersey Building*: (S,UMD)

1980. New Jersey. SBA. Dye. *New Jersey Hand-Book*: (FM,S)
---- Also found: Pale pink wraps.

1981. New Jersey. VanMeter. *Relics of ye Olden Days in Salem*: (FLP,WM)

1982. New Jersey. Yardley. *The New Jersey Scrapbook*: (GLD,E,HU,SHB,Smth,Stfd,uiuc,UMN,UVM) $110 -200
▶Completed citation: [°1893 by the Board of Women Managers for the State of New Jersey]. <u>Vol 1</u>: 1 *l* (frontis), xiii, 1 *l*, 423 p. Frontis is port of "Mrs. Richard Stockton" with tissue guard; pp (v)-viii are a "History of the Board of Women Managers for the State of New Jersey." <u>Vol 2</u>: 1 *l* (frontis), vii, 1 *l*, 446 p. Frontis is port of "Elizabeth Clementine Kinney" with tissue guard. Both vols contain b/w illus (with tissue guards) that are not included in paging. Gray cloth hc, gilt print and ribbon design, and state medallion in gilt/brown/blue. "Bindery of William Koch, Newark, N. J." 500 sets were printed.

-New Mexico-

1984.1 [New Mexico (Territory)]. Pecos Irrigation & Improvement Co. *The Pecos valley : The Fruit Belt : of : New Mexico.* Chicago: Rand, McNally & Co., Printers, n.d.   **P➔**

21x11. 17, (1) p. Folded sheet unfolds to 94½x50 of text and illus, black print. C.t. given is on the unnumbered panel. Back is a full sheet map of Chaves and Eddy Counties, which are located along the Pecos River. Water by irrigation. Advertising 1000s acres for sale. No WCE content; from an intact collection. ☺. (WM)

1984.2 [New Mexico (Territory)]. *The Pecos Valley : The Fruit Belt of New Mexico.* N.p.: n.p., n.d.   **P➘**

21½x15. 2 *l*, 3-40 p, 25 *l* of unpaged plates. Pale blue wraps, blue design of grape vines and fruit, gilt shield and white print. C.t. Frontis illus entitled "Source of the Rio Pecos." WCE handout to encourage immigration. Found in an intact collections of WCE ads. ☺. (GLD,LBA) $60-140

1985. New Mexico. *San Juan County*: (MSL,nmsu)

1988. New Mexico. *World's Columbian exposition*:
(GLD,nmsu,UTA) $80 - 140
---- Also found: 24 p. Greenish brown pulp wraps with black print and border. Laid in slip: "Compliments of W. H. Llewellyn, secretary."

-New York-

1990.1 New York. Board of General Managers. *The New York State Building, Jackson Park, Chicago, will be dedicated with appropriate ceremonies at noon, on Saturday, October 22nd, 1892.* Invitation. 12 Oct. 1892.

14½x20½. Stiff card printed one side with accompanying envelope. At the bottom of the card: "Albany, Oct. 12, 1892." © (IHi)

1991.   New York. BGM. *Report of the board of general managers*: (Amh,B,CCA,CLP,Col,CU,DC,E,FU,HML,HU,ISU,KS,KSU,LHL, MIT,MOHx,MSL,NLI,SHB,SML,SPL,Stfd,UAB,UCLA,UGa,UMC,UMD,UPa,UTA,UVM,VAM,Yale)
---- Also found: Presentation copy: Black leather over thick wood boards. On front cover: "Hon. Hugh Hastings, State Historian. Compliments of James B. Lyon." Gilt edges, red satin end papers. (S)

1992.1 New York. Board of General Managers. Wegmann, Edward. *Catalogue of the illustrations of the water-supply of the city of New York. Written for the Board of General Managers of the Exhibit of the State of New York at the World's Columbian Exposition.* New York: n.p., 1893; HU film Mas 8738.

18x12. 68 p. Light gray stiff wraps, black print. C.t. = t.p. No illus; this is text for their illus exhibit that described New York's three main aqueducts: Old Croton, New Croton, and Bronx River. (HU,LHL)

☞ In 1896, Edward Wegmann published an illustrated and expanded book on the New York water supply taken from these three aqueducts.

1992.2 New York. Board of General Managers. ...*World's Fair. Names of the general managers of the : Exhibit of the State of New York at the World's Columbian Exposition : to be held at Chicago, Illinois, May 1st to October 1st,* [sic] *1893.* Albany: The Argus co., printers, 1892.

24x15½. 47 p. Illus. Robin's-egg blue wraps, black print. At head of title: "1492—1892-3." Also on t.p.: "Executive and administrative departments of the state; officers of the board of general managers; district commissioners; board of women managers and officers; officers and heads of departments of the exposition; committees, etc.; national board of women managers; general information. The Laws of the State of New York in Relation to the State Exhibit Providing for the Commemoration of the 400th Anniversary of the Discovery of America, and Designating October 12, 1892, as a Public Holiday." C.t.: "State of New York. [State Seal illustration] World's Fair Manual." © . (ICRL)

1993.   New York. BOWM. *Board of Women Managers of the State of New York*: (HU,SHB,Stfd)
▸Add pub: New Haven, CT: RPI, 1977. History of Women. Reel 584, no 4594.

1993.1 New York. Board of Women Managers [of the State of New York]. Bureau of Applied Arts. *Catalogue of the preliminary exhibition of applied arts of New York under the auspices of the Bureau of applied arts of the New York state board of women managers to the World's Columbian exposition, at the American art galleries, from Friday, March 3, 1893, to Monday, March 13, 1893. ...* [New York: 1893].

19½x__. 30 p. (Col)

1993.2 New York. Board of Women Managers [of the State of New York]. Earle, Alice Morse, and Emily Ellsworth Ford, eds. *Early prose and verse.* New York: Harper & brothers pub., 1893.

16x10. __ p. Wraps. One of 6 titles by the Board reprinting items written by NY women. The booklets were placed in the Woman's Bldg library. See #1994, #1995, #2005.1. (ref)   each $30

1993.3 [New York. Board of Women Managers (of the State of New York)]. *Library of the Woman's Building.* N.p.: n.p., n.d.

23½x16. (4) p. Folded sheet. Caption title. Description of the library exhibit of the State of NY. Page (3) description of the library ceiling painted by Dora Wheeler Keith, NY. No author given. (WM)

1995.1 New York. Board of Women Managers [of the State of New York]. *Minutes of the meeting*[s] *of the Board of Women Managers of the State of New York at the World's Columbian Exposition* [and of the executive committee] *June 7, 1892* [to May 22, 1894]. [Albany: n.p., 1892–94]; New Haven, CT: RPI, 1977.

_x_. 1 vol (various paging). Microfilm: "History of women." Reel 584, no 4594. (HU,Smth,uiuc,UMN,UVM,)

1997.   New York. Board of Women Managers [of the State of New York]. *Report of the board of women managers for the exhibit of the state of New York at the World's Columbian exposition, 1893.* New York: Press of J.J. Little & co., n.d.

21½x15. 1 *l* (frontis), 107 p+ unpaged interspersed plates. Frontis depicts Pocahontas. Tan wraps with chocolate print. [Written by Florence C. Ives, Board of Women Managers for NY. See #2445.WM for her diary.] ☺ . (CU,SML)   ▸Completed and corrected citation.

1998.   New York. BOWM. *Statistical Report of the women*: (CU)

1998.1 [New York]. *Brooklyn Day : June 27, 1893 : Grounds of Columbian Exposition : Music hall.* N.p.: n.p., 1893.

15x11½. (3) p. Folded sheet, dark blue print, back blank. C.t. Chicago mayor Carter Harrison spoke "Address of Welcome." Special Chicago ed of the *Brooklyn Daily Eagle* was printed in Mach Hall. ☺ (S)

2001.   New York. *Chicago World : the Historical, Biographical and Philanthropical...New York*: (CCA,S)
▸Correction: This citation with its odd and various paging should have been placed in the "Salesmen's Sample" chapter. Also, this New York edition is similar to Chicago World Book pubs #940 and #1055.
---- Also listed: Paging: 72, (4) p, 43 *l* of plates.
---- Also found: 27x18½. Gray cloth hc, gilt print and cover design like #940 except this copy has "Chicago World" on banner and "New York" below. ☺(S)

2002.   New York. Davis. *Report on the exhibit of the workingman's model home*: (HU)
▸Additional citation info: (51) p. Plate and plans.

2003.1 New York.   *...Educational Exhibit of the State of New York...Circular I.* Albany: n.p., 26 Oct. 1892.

24x17½. 4 p. No wraps. Caption title. At head of title: "World's Columbian Exposition." Melvil Dewey, Director. Lists advisory board members in charge of NY's educational exhibit. ☺ . (MSL)

2003.2 New York.   *...Educational Exhibit of the State of New York...Circular 5 (Revision of circular 3).* Albany: n.p., 29 Nov. 1892.

24x17½. 18 p. No wraps, string-tied. Caption title. At head of title: "World's Columbian Exposition." Mevil Dewey, Director. Contains plan of the exhibit and suggestions for schools. ☺ . (MSL)

2005.   New York. *Exhibits of the state of New York at the World's Columbian Exposition*: (GLD,ICRL,S) $20 - 55
▸Spelling correction: Self-wraps with publisher printed on back: A.C. M'Clurg & Co.

2005.1 New York. Holden, Miriam Y., and Edward Hale Bierstadt. *A List of the Books Contained in the Library collected by the Board of Women Managers of New York for the World's Columbian Exposition of 1893, and afterwards given to the Library of the University of the State of New York.* N.p.: n.p., [1954?].

28½x21½. Typescript listing of the collection. The "Women's Library" was destroyed in the Capitol fire of 1911. This listing was taken from the State Library Bulletin for Sept 1894. Repository is the Schlesinger Library at Radcliff College— Vault 016.396 N54. ☺ . (HU)

2010.   [New York]. *New York and the World's fair*: (HU,ICRL,UCLA)

2010.1 [New York]. New York City. American Fine Arts Society (New York City). *Exhibition...of the pictures contributed by Sweden, Norway and Holland to the World's Columbian exposition; catalogue...* New York: [Knickerbocker], 1894?

8°. 41 p. (Col)

2011.1 [New York]. New York City. Committee for the International Exposition of 1892. Depew, Chauncey M[itchell], Bourke Cockran, Warner Miller, and James T. Wood. *...Arguments for the City of New York.* New York: The Committee of the International Exposition of 1892 Of the City of New York (Douglas Taylor, printer), 1890.

23x20½. 37 p. Tan wraps. C.t. At head of title: "Before the committee of the senate on the Quadri-Centennial Celebration of the Discovery of America, Washington, January 11th, 1890." See #249 for the federal issue of the arguments. ☺ . (HU,MSL)

2011.2 [New York]. New York City. Committee for the International Exposition of 1892. Depew, Chauncey
M[itchell], William C. Whitney and William E.D. Stokes. ...*Committee on legislation. To the People of
the United States of America:*... N.p.: n.p., 21 Nov. 1889.

23½x14. vii p. Buff self-wraps, black print. Caption title. At head of title: "Committee for the
International Exposition of 1892." Dated. Gives brief history of national meetings to determine the site of
the Fair and offers NYC as the best site. [Chicago won in April 1890.] ☺. (HU)

2012. New York. NYC. CIE–1892. *Letter of William E.D. Stokes...on the question of the location*: (Col,HU)
---- Also found: 26½x20½. 39 p. Buff self-wraps, black print. C.t. Also at head of title and a secondary
author: "Committee on legislation." (HU)

2013. [New York]. NYC. CIE–1892. *Names of the Members...International Exposition of 1892*: (S)
2014. New York. NYC. CIE–1892. *Official list of Committees...International Exposition of 1892*: (HU)

2019.1 New York. *New York Iroquois Exhibit. World's
Columbian Exposition 1893.* Buffalo: Gourier Light Co.,
1893.

8½x11½. Stiff card. Black print and litho of Indian
Village at Fairgrounds on one side. "John Wentworth
Sanborn, Director-in-Chief." [The various Native
American encampments were near the Ethnology Bldg on
the shore of South Pond.] ☺(GLD,S)   P➜ $16 - 32

2019.2 New York. New York State Library School. Dewey,
Melvil. ...*Comparative Library Exhibit of the American
Library Association : Circular 1.* Albany, NY: n.p., 1892.

25½x20. (2) p. Caption title is from upper left of front; hand-written at bottom: "5 Jan, 1893." At head
of title: "World's Columbian Exposition." On back: "Summary of plan of exhibit"; printed at bottom:
"13 Dec. 1892." Dewey's request to librarians to submit items for the Comparative Library. After the
WCE, the exhibit was to have been housed in the "fire proof capitol at Albany." [See A.L.A. in index for
related items.] [The Capitol burned in 1911; the exhibit was lost, see #2005.1.] ☺. (UMD,WM)

2019.3 New York. New York State Library School. Dewey, Melvil. ...*Comparative Library Exhibit of the
American Library Association : Circular 4.* Albany, NY: n.p., 1892.

25½x20. (4) p. Caption title is from upper left p (1); at head of title: "World's Columbian Exposition.
At head of text: "What should be sent." Dewey's name at end. Plan of the exhibit expanded from
"Circular 1" (#2019.2). ☺. (UMD,WM)

2019.4 New York. *N.Y. Columbian Celebration. Act of the Legislature : Providing for the : Celebration : In :
New York City : Of the : four Hundredth Anniversary : Of the : Discovery of America.* N.p.: n.p., n.d.

17x12½. 11 p. Tan pebbled-textured wraps, brown print, string-tied. C.t. = t.p. Brown print text on tan
paper. Committee members listed on pp 9-11. The act was promulgated on May 10, 1892; Frank Rice,
Secretary of State. ☺. (FM)

2020. [New York]. *Official Souvenir Programme of the New York Columbian*: (csuf,S)
▸Correction: Correct t.p. dates are "October 8th to 13th," however the cover dates are listed as "October
8th to 15th 1892." Also t.p. has "Copyrighted, 1892, by Rogers & Sherwood."
---- Also found: "Second edition" at head of title. 64 p. Tan wraps, blue print and illus. C.t. = t.p.

2020.1 [New York]. *Programme and Souvenir : Columbian Anniversary : with Illustrations and History. New
York, October 9, 10, 11, 12, 13, 1892.* New York: Phillips, n.d.

15x24. (56) p. Tan wraps, brown and green print. Text and ads. [This celebration delayed the
dedication of the buildings at the WCE.] ☺(S)

2020.2 New York. Shull, Josiah. ...*New York Dairy Exhibit.* [Ilion]: n.p., [1 May 1893].

20½x14. (3) p. Folded buff sheet, black print, no illus; back blank. Date and name at end. At head of title: "World's Columbian exposition." WCE Managers allotted to NY space and shelving for dairy products. ☺ (S)

2021.   New York. *Souvenir of the dedicatory ceremonies*: (CU)

-North Carolina-

2023.1 [North Carolina]. Committee on Colonial Exhibits. Kidder, Florence H. *Wilmington, North Carolina. As Chairman of the Committee...* N.p.: n.p., n.d.

21½x14. (3) p. Folded sheet, black print. Caption title. Suggestions for WCE exhibit of colonial artifacts from the 13 original colonies. Some states issued catalogs of items: e.g., NJ, #1976. ☺ (S)

2023.2 [North Carolina]. Cotton, Sallie (Southall). *The Virginia Dare Columbian Memorial Association to the people of North Carolina.* [Raleigh, n.d.]

10x21. 7 p. (UNC)

2026.   North Carolina. SBA. *Hand-book of North Carolina*: (FM,LBA)

-North Dakota-

2028.1 North Dakota. North Dakota Department of Public Instruction. Ogden, John. ...*Pertaining to the World's Columbian exposition, Chicago.* [Bismarck]: n.p., [7 Sept. 1891].

21½x14. (4) p. No wraps. Caption title. At head of title: "Circular No. 32. State of North Dakota. Department of Public Instruction." Instructions for preparing North Dakota's school exhibit. On p (4), Ogden is listed as the author of this circular. (ref)

2029.   North Dakota. SBWFMND. *North Dakota at the World's Columbian*: (LBA)

2029.1 North Dakota. State Board of World's Fair Managers for North Dakota. *North Dakota—The Golden Wheat State.* Chicago: Corbitt-Skidmore Co., Printers and Engravers, n.d.

11½x19½. (36) p+ folded map of ND before back cover. Pale green (or white) smooth wraps, maroon print with gilt wheat stalks. C.t.: "North Dakota." Illus and text promoting 160 free acres. The six-member Board is listed on p (1). ☺ . (S,WM)   **P➔**

-Ohio-

2030.   Ohio. BWFMO. Comm on Forestry. *The Ohio Forestry Exhibit consists of*: (WM)

2032.1 [Ohio]. Cincinnati. *Catalogue : Exhibit in Cincinnati Room, Columbian Exposition. 1492–1892.* N.p.: n.p., n.d.

20½x15½. 38 p. Tan wraps, chocolate print with circular logo, "juncta juvant." Brown text print. C.t. A complete list of 541 exhibited items in the Cincinnati Room. ☺ . (WM)

2032.2 Ohio. Clark, C. M. *Picturesque Ohio – A historical monograph.* Cincinnati: Cranston & Curts, 1892.

__x__ . __ p. Hc. "Columbian Edition." Special edition for the WCE from the 1887 work. (ref) $25

2033.1 [Ohio]. Woman's Columbian Exposition Association of Cincinnati and Suburbs. *Report of the woman's : Columbian Exposition : association of Cincinnati and Suburbs. 1892–1893.* N.p.: n.p., 1893.

20½x15. 40 p. Brown wraps, chocolate print. Text in chocolate print. C.t. = t.p. Complete report of the members, committees, activities before and during the WF. Dated "December 4th, 1893." Organization was started by Mary P. Hart, National Board of Lady Managers. ☺ (WM)

-Oklahoma-

2033.2 Oklahoma (Territory). *Governor's Message to Second Legislative Assembly of the Territory of Oklahoma, Delivered January 19, 1893.* Guthrie: State capital printing co., 1893.

22x15. 11 p. Bright red (or royal blue) wraps, black print. C.t. WCE activity of the territory summarized on p 11. Abraham J. Seay was territorial governor. (ODL)

2033.3 Oklahoma (Territory). *Governor's Message to Third Legislative Assembly of the Territory of Oklahoma, delivered January 8, 1895.* [Guthrie: n.p., 1895].

22x15. (3)-14 p. Deep royal blue wraps with black print. C.t. WCE message on p 9. William C. Renfrow, Territorial Governor. (ODL)

2033.4 Oklahoma (Territory). *Oklahoma Illustrated. A Book of Practical Information. Showing the Territory's Present Status and Future Prospects. Her Great Resources, Climate, Size, Inhabitants, Cities, Towns and Villages, and various other Valuable and Interesting Information. Fully Illustrated.* Guthrie: The Leader Printing co., ᶜ1894 by O.C. Seeley, Publisher.

24x16½. >225 p (some missing) + ads. Hc. Full page illus of Oklahoma's WCE Agricultural Exhibit on p 3. Brief report on pp 24-25. ☺ (OTM)

2033.5 Oklahoma (Territory). Renfrow, W[illiam] C. *Oklahoma and the Cherokee Strip : with map.* Chicago: Poole Bros. Printers, 1893.

17½x10. 16 p. Territorial map after front cover. Self-wraps, black print. C.t. On lower front cover: "...Oklahoma Building, Jackson park, Chicago." Renfrow was territorial governor. ☺ (WM)

2034. Oklahoma (Territory). *Report of Governor William C. Renfrow*: (ODL)
▶Completed citation: 22x15. 11 p. Mango colored wraps, black print.
C.t. = t.p. **P➔**

☞ By act of the OK legislative assembly, which took effect Dec 25, 1890, it was provided that the county commissioners should appoint a commissioner and one lady to assist him, who would cooperate with the Commissioner appointed by the US to make an OK exhibit. There was much difficulty securing commissioners, and it became apparent to the 2nd legislative assembly that a territorial appropriation was necessary and some officer be charged with execution of the trust. Therefore, the appropriations act of Mar 10, 1893 directed the treasurer to set apart $15K. The governor was given full power to make the exhibit a success.

2034.1 Oklahoma (Territory). *Report of the governor of Oklahoma Territory for the fiscal year ending June 30, 1893.* Washington: GPO, 1893.

23x15. 11 p. Salmon wraps with black print and border frame. C.t. = t.p. WCE appropriations and brief exhibit description on p 10. William C. Renfrow was Territorial Governor. ☺ (GLD) $50 - 110

2035. [Oklahoma Territory]. Santa Fe Railroad. *...Cherokee strip*:   **P➔** $50 - 100
☞ Oklahoma was opened in a series of land rushes beginning April 22, 1889, and ending with the Cherokee Strip in early 1893. Guthrie was the territorial capitol. See Oklahoma publications in the "States Chapter" and #2033.5 for another Cherokee strip item.

2035.1 Oklahoma (Territory). *Second biennial report of the Territorial Auditor, for the Two Years Beginning December 1, 1892, and Ending Nov. 30, 1894. Exhibit "F" of : governor's message to the third legislative assembly of the Territory of Oklahoma. January 8, 1895.* [Guthrie: Daily leader press, 1895].

22x15. 87 p. Pale blue wraps, black print. C.t. = t.p. The auditor, E.D. Cameron, reported proper disbursements to the "World's fair fund" on pp 15 and 17: $15,000 appropriation and total warrants redeemed of $10,698.57, leaving a balance of $4,301.43 which was returned to the General Fund. (ODL)

2035.2 Oklahoma (Territory). *Second biennial report of the territorial treasurer : For the two years beginning December 1, 1892, and ending November 30, 1894, Exhibit "G" of : governor's message to the Third Legislative Assembly of the Territory of Oklahoma. January 8, 1895.* [Guthrie: Daily leader press, 1895].

22x15. 9 p. Gray-tan wraps, black print. C.t. = t.p. Treasurer, M.L. Turner, reported WF warrant redemptions of $504.11 (p 4) and "World's fair fund" (p 7): $15,000 appropriation with total warrants redeemed of $10,698.57, leaving a balance of $4,301.43 which was returned to the General Fund. (ODL)

-Oregon-

2036.1 Oregon. Department of Public Instruction. *Oregon educational exhibit at the Columbian exposition 1893.* [Salem: Department of Public Instruction, 4 June 1892].

20½x13. 12 p. Self-wraps with black print and schematic of school rooms. C.t. Plans for their exhibit. Caption title: "Oregon's educational exhibit at the World's Columbian exposition, Chicago 1893. Announcement." © (S)

2037.1 Oregon. Oregon World's Fair Commission. *Catalogue of exhibits : Department of Mines, Mining and Metallurgy : of the : Oregon World's Fair Commission.* Portland: Press of Glass & Prudhomme, n.d. P➜

15x22½. 28 p. Dark blue print on light blue wraps. C.t. = t.p. "C.W. Ayers, Commissioner." © , (HML)

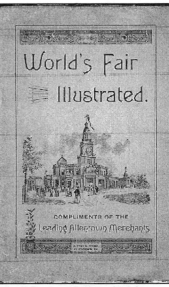

-Pennsylvania-

2040.1 [Pennsylvania]. Allentown Merchants. *World's Fair Illustrated. Compliments of the Leading Allentown Merchants.* Allentown: Ritter's print, n.d.

23½x15. (20) p+ text inside both wraps. Gray wraps, black print and illus of PA Bldg at WCE. C.t. Merchant ads interspersed with lithos of WCE bldgs with descriptive captions. © (GLD)

2041. Pennsylvania. BWFMP. Brownfield. *Pennsylvania Art Contributions*: (BCHx,HU,ICRL,MSL,NPG,SML,UBO,UPa)

2042. Pennsylvania. BWFMP. Farquhar. *Pennsylvania and the*: (BCHx,CLP,CU,HML,HU,LBA,LU,PSU,SML,UMD,UPa,WM,Yale)
▶Paging correction: 1 *l*, 191, (1) p. Colophon design in center of last page.

2043. Pennsylvania. BWFMP. Farquhar. *Catalogue* [218 p]: (CLP,Col,DU,FM,HU,MIT,NAL,NLI,NSW,PSU,SML,Stfd,UBO,UPa,UTA,WM,Yale)

2044. Pennsylvania. BWFMP. Farquhar. *Catalogue* [284 p]: (LU,HML,MSL)

2044.1 Pennsylvania. Board of World's Fair Managers of Pennsylvania. Farquhar, A[rthur] B. ..."*Pennsylvania Day," Thursday, September 7, 1893. Programme.* N.p.: n.p., n.d.

23x15. 1 *l*. Black print one side. At head of title: "Columbian Exposition." Program included 9 a.m. parade, 11 a.m. music and speeches, 3 p.m. balloon ascension, and evening reception with fireworks display at the Battleship Illinois. Farquhar was Executive Commissioner. © (GLD,S) $30 - 70

2045. Pennsylvania. BWFMP. *Minutes of the Board of World's Fair*: (CLP,S)
▶Add annotation: Minutes were also issued separately: e.g., "April 6, 1893." Pp 257-290. (S)

2045.1 [Pennsylvania]. Erie. ...*Souvenir : Of the Liberty Bell at Erie, April 26, Columbian Year, 1893.* Erie: Dispatch print, 1893.

14½x24. (16) p. Pale blue wraps, red and blue print, litho of the Liberty Bell, string-tied. C.t. At head of title: "Proclaim liberty throughout..." Illus of PA State Bldg at the WCE. The Bell was in Erie and on its way to the WCE. See #2050.3. ☺ (S)

2047.1 [Pennsylvania]. Pennsylvania Academy of the Fine Arts. ...*Catalogue of Works of Art : to be exhibited at the World's Columbian Exposition : Chicago, 1893 : Philadelphia : January 16th to February 4th : 1893.* [Philadelphia?: n.p., 1893?].

18x14½. 23 p. Wraps. C.t. At head of title: "Pennsylvania academy of the fine arts." . (FLP,HU)

2048. Pennsylvania. Penn Ad Comm Arts. *Department of fine arts. General Information For the Artists*: (HML,S) ▶Add annotation: This pamphlet contains blank forms. Artist were to list their artwork and send the forms to the committee in Philadelphia.

2049. Pennsylvania. Philadelphia. Beck. *The City of Philadelphia*: (UPa)

2049.1 [Pennsylvania]. Philadelphia. *Historical and Commercial : Philadelphia : Handsomely Illustrated : 1892 : With Supplement of the World's Columbian Exposition.* New York: A.F. Parson's publishing co., n.d.   P➔

26½x20. 1 *l*, iii-xi, (33)-295, (15) p supplement on WCE. No frontis. Light maize wraps, brown print, multi-color litho of Philadelphia City Hall. T.p. has ornate design of Liberty Bell and scroll work. Supplement has explanatory text and illus of main bldgs; illus ᶜ1892 by A. Zeese & Co. ---- Also listed: 2nd ed. 27x19½. 285, (8) p.
☺ . (BCHx,CCA,FLP,HML)

2050. [Pennsylvania]. Philadelphia. Joint Comm. Vickers. *Philadelphia : the story*: (CCA,cul,FM,HU,LBA,LU,SHB,slpl,SML)

2050.1 [Pennsylvania]. Philadelphia. Keyser, Charles S. *The Liberty Bell : Independence Hall : Philadelphia. A complete record of all the Great Events announced by the Ringing of the Bell from 1753 to 1835.* Philadelphia: Press of Dunlap Printing Co., 1895 [ᶜ1893 by Charles S. Keyser].

23½x15. 32 p. Tan wraps with black print and border. Frontis of Bell. Souvenir of its 1895 trip to Atlanta WF; the escort was Charles F. Warwick, Mayor. Describes the Bell's WCE travel itinerary and exhibit, p 31 (see #2050.3). On top of cover: "Presented by the City of Philadelphia." ☺ (GLD) $20 - 45

2050.2 [Pennsylvania]. Philadelphia. ...*Philadelphia and Its Environs. A guide to the city and surroundings.* Columbian ed. Philadelphia: J.B. Lippincott co., [ᶜ1893].

19x12½. 1 *l* fold color map of city, 240, (8) p ads on magenta paper. Gray glossy wraps, black print and design with city coat-of-arms, Wm. Penn statue, and Philadelphia harbor. No WCE content except "Columbian edition" at head of title on t.p. and cover. . (S)
---- Also found: Red cloth hc, gilt print. (ref) $50

2050.3 [Pennsylvania]. Philadelphia. *Philadelphia to World's Columbian Exposition, Chicago. Route and Schedule Time of the Special Train with the Official Escort of the "Old Liberty Bell."* N.p.: n.p., [1893].

14x9. (4) p. Folded card, black print and illus of Bell. C.t. The escort was Philadelphia mayor Edwin S. Stuart. "Leave Philadelphia, Tuesday, April 25th, 1893." [The Bell arrived in Chicago on Apr 28, 1893, in time for the May 1 Fair opening.] ☺ . (S)   P➔

2051.1 [Pennsylvania]. Pittsburgh. *Illustrative and descriptive : Of Some Things in and About : Pittsburgh : America's Industrial Centre. And the World's Columbian Exposition for 1893.* N.p.: n.p., n.d.

17x23½. (28) p. String-tied. Translucent wraps with no printing. Title from first underlying page (visible through cover). (S)

2053. Pennsylvania. State Comm Woman's Work. *A condensed statement of the work*: (BCHx,HU,UPa)

2054. Pennsylvania. State Fish. Meehan. *Fish, fishing and fisheries*: (HU,UMC,WM,Yale)
▸Completed citation: Pale blue wraps with black print and border. C.t. = t.p.

2054.1 Pennsylvania. State Fish Commissioners. *Report : of the : State Commissioners : of : fisheries, for the years 1892–93–94.* N.p: Clarence M. Busch, state printer of Pennsylvania, 1895.

24½x17. 3 *l*, 3-452 p. There are 12 *l* b/w plates (three fish per plate) between p 450 and the index to this volume, which begins on p 451. Also scattered and unpaged are 14 *l* of b/w lithos, 2 *l* (double leaf) map of Shad Fisheries locations, and 15 *l* chromoliths of fish (one fish per plate). First *l* is frontis: "Pennsylvania Fish Commission [Railroad] Car." Blind-stamped blue-black cloth hc, gilt spine print. Because of the great demand for copies of Meehan's publication (#2054), it was revised, elaborated, and printed in its entirety in this "Report," pp 257-450. It includes all 12 b/w and 15 color plates of fish described above. It is preceded by 4 photo-repros from their WCE exhibit and a 2-page article: "State fish exhibit at the World's fair." © (GLD) $60 - 130

-Rhode Island-

2061. Rhode Island. BWFMRI. Williams. *Rhode Island Day*: (GLD,HU,MIT,URI,Yale)   Wraps version: $40 - 65
▸Add to wraps version: Tan wraps, gilt print and illus of RI Bldg. Paging is the same as hc version.

-South Dakota-

2068.1 [South Dakota]. Illinois Roofing & Supply Co. *South Dakota State Building, World's Fair, Covered with "Gilbertson's Old Method Roofing Tin,...* Chicago: Illinois Roofing & Supply Co., n.d.

8½x16½. Single card of yellow blotter paper. Red and black print, black litho of South Dakota State Bldg. © (GLD)   P➔ $22 - 50

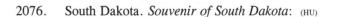

2076. South Dakota. *Souvenir of South Dakota*: (HU)

-Tennessee-

2077.1 Tennessee. Williams, Thos. L., and Lewis T. Baxter. *To the General Assembly of Tennessee.* Knoxville, n.p., 1891.

26½x20. (1) p. Open letter to the Tennessee General Assembly from the World's Fair Commissioners from Tennessee calling for an appropriation of $250,000 from a tax assessment for State representation at the WCE— "a burden so light that the people would not feel it." © . (KS,ref) $60

-Texas-

2079. Texas. Houston. *The City of Houston and Harris County*: (UTA)

2080. Texas. *San Antonio*: (WM)
▸Completed citation: N.p.: San Antonio Bureau of Information [Rubel Bros. printers, Chicago], n.d. 12 p. Light teal wraps, black print with bold "San Antonio" in center cover. C.t.

2080.1 Texas. Texas Board of Lady Managers. Tobin, Mrs. W.H. *To the Women of Texas.* N.p.: n.p., n.d.

21½x14½. (4) p. Caption title. Signed by Mrs. Tobin on p (4). As President of the State Board of Lady Managers, Tobin urges women to participate in Texas exhibits at the WCE. © . (UTA)

☞ Texas women's group raised funds from the citizens for Texas contributions at the WCE; the Texas Bldg was constructed for $30,000. The state itself made no official provision for the WCE; there is no reference to the Fair in *General Laws* from 1889 to 1893. For more about the difficulties of Texas, see #2340.6.

2080.2 Texas. *The Woman's World's Fair Exhibit Association of Texas invite you to be present at the Ceremonies of Texas Day, World's Columbian Exposition, Chicago, Saturday, September 16, 1893.* N.p.: n.p., 1893.

18½x12. 2 *l.* Folded sheet, black print and illus of TX Bldg at top. "Programm of Ceremonies at Texas Building, 2 o'clock p.m." is printed inside ☺ . (S)   P➔

-Utah-

2080.3 [Utah (Territory)]. Donan, P. *Utah : a peep into a mountain-walled treasury of the gods.* N.p.: n.p., [1891].

23½x17. 96 p. Turquoise wraps, red and gold print. C.t.= t.p. On t.p.: "Rhymes by Cy Warman." WCE handout. ☺ . (LBA)

2083. Utah. UBLM. *World's fair Ecclesiastical History of Utah*: (HU,UMD)
▶Add Publisher: Louisville, KY: Lost Cause Press, 1974. Microfiche. Five sheets.

2084. Utah. UWFC. *Utah at the*: (GLD,HU,MSL,OHxS,UMC,UMD)   P➔ $65 - 140
---- Also found: 172, L (i.e., 50 p), (1) p facsimile page from the Utah guest register.

-Vermont-

2086. Vermont. *Acts and resolves...1890*: (VSA)
2087. Vermont. *Acts and resolves...1892*: (VSA)

2088. Vermont. CCV. *Report of the World's Columbian*: (MSL,UVM,VtSSt)
▶Completed citation: Light salmon wraps, black print. State seal of VT on cover and t.p. C.t.= t.p. Illus of VT State Bldg on back. Includes descriptions of exhibits, exhibitors, and expenditures.

2088.1 Vermont. McIntyre, H.H. *Vermont : At the World's Fair.* [Boston]: n.p., [1894] © by H.H. McIntyre.

24x17. (5)-14 p. Self-wraps on glossy stock, black print, string-tied. Illus shows Fairbanks Scale exhibit (#840.3) and marble quarries. McIntyre was secretary for the World's Columbian Commission of VT. Rpt from the *New England Magazine*, March 1894 (#1368). ☺ . (UVM,VtHx)

2089. Vermont. State Board Ag. Spear. *Vermont, A glimpse of its Scenery and Industries*: (LBA,S)
▶Correction: "Glimpse" should be lower case.
---- Also found: Turquoise stiff wraps, gilt print and border.

2089.1 [Vermont]. Vermont Press Association. *Banquet to : The Vermont Press Association : by : The Illinois association of The Sons of Vermont at the Hotel Endeavor, Tuesday, May 9, 1893."* N.p.: n.p., 1893.

18x13. 2 *l.* Folded card. Gilt print cover. Inside menu in black ink. C.t. "Vermont sherbet" was served between courses. ☺ (S)

2089.2 [Vermont]. Vermont Press Association. *Issued by the Vermont Press Association : World's fair excursion : May 6 to 15, 1893 : coupon ticket book.* N.p.: n.p., n.d.

5½x13½. 19 *l* with tear-off stubs. "Issued by Central Vermont R.R. : Vermont Press Association." [VtHx has the ticket packet that belonged to S.R. Elliott, who was listed as an attendee (#2089.3) of the banquet above (#2089.1).] © . (VtHx)

2089.3 [Vermont]. Vermont Press Association. *Vermont Press Association. Summer Excursion to the World's Columbian Exposition, Chicago 1893.* N.p.: n.p., n.d.

16x10. 12 *l*. White stiff wraps, brown print and state seal. Brown-ink text. Ribbon tied at top; opens like vertical note pad. C.t. Includes the Press Association's itinerary from May 6–15, 1893; they traveled on the Central Vermont RR. On May 9, 1893, the Chicago "Sons of Vermont" gave a banquet (#2089.1) for them at the Hotel Endeavor (#1127). List of 188 press attendees. © (S,VtHx)

2089.4 Vermont. Vermont Senate. *Journal : of : the senate : of the state of Vermont. Biennial session, 1892.* Montpelier: Argus and Patriot Job Printing House, 1893.

22½x14½. 475 p. Black cloth spine, greenish-tan paper covered boards with black print. C.t. = t.p. State seal on t.p. Governor Fuller's inaugural speech of Oct 6, 1892, mentions WCE and VT participation, pp 375-76. © (VSA)

2089.5 Vermont. Vermont Senate. *Journal : of : the senate : of the State of Vermont. Biennial session, 1894.* St. Albans: Messenger Job Printing House, 1895.

22½x15½. 492 p. Half-calf over deep maroon marbled paper-covered boards. Spine titles are gilt on red and black labels. State seal on t.p. In his "Columbian Exposition," pp 413-15, Chauncey W. Brownell, Secretary of State, reports Governor Levi K. Fuller's farewell address in which he mentions the VT report on the WCE, #2088. © (VSA)

-Virginia-

2090. Virginia. *Acts and joint resolutions passed by the general assembly...1891–92*: (GMU)

☞ To raise funds, souvenirs were sold in the Virginia State Bldg. One of these souvenirs was a clear glass ax made by the Libbey Glass Company; it was a replica of George Washington's legendary cherry tree ax. Libbey filled in its name imprint and sold the molds after the Fair. Post Fair colored glass axes were made from these modified molds and do not bear the Libbey name.

2090.1 [Virginia]. *Bedford, the banner county of Piedmont : Virginia, offers homes to all.* Bedford: Bedford index print, 1892?

22½x14. 48 p+ large folded map of Bedford County at end. Tan wraps, chocolate print. C.t. Latest text date "Sept. 14th, 1892." Railroad ads inside both covers. Advantages of the area. No mention of WCE; from an intact collection. © (WM)

2091. Virginia. BWFMV. *Organization, by-laws, plan of work*: (Col,SML)
---- Also found: 55 p. (Listed as 54 p in the original bibliography; most likely missing its last page.)

2091.1 Virginia. Board of World's Fair Managers of Virginia. *World's Fair : Board of Managers : of Virginia. Proceedings of meeting : Held at Roanoke, Va., May 10, 11 and 12, 1892.* Richmond: Press of Andrews, Baptist & Marquess, 1892.

23x15. 12 p. Maize textured wraps, black print. C.t. Members of Board and standing committees listed, as well as resolutions including salaries. Meetings day and night. Lady members were put in charge of the replica of Mt. Vernon for the state bldg at the WCE. © (S)

2092.1 [Virginia]. Norfolk Chamber of Commerce. *The City by the Sea. Fact and figures about Norfolk : No. 2.* Norfolk: Green, Burke & Gregory, Printers, 1893.

21½x14. 1 *l* (map), xvi, 7-45, (7) p local ads. Map of the city and harbor. T.p. title. Buff wraps, blue print underlined in red. Back cover has circular city seal in red. From an intact WCE collection. . (WM)

2092.2 [Virginia]. Richmond Chamber of Commerce. Morrison, Andrew, ed. *The City on the James. Richmond, Virginia. The chamber of commerce book.* Richmond: George W. Engelhardt, Publisher [Andrews, Baptist & Marquess' Electric Press], 1893 [ᶜ1893 by George W. Engelhardt].

25½x17. 316 p. Teal stiff wraps with gilt and royal blue lettering and design. Ads inside both wraps are upside down. Frontis: "Officers of the Richmond chamber of commerce." C.t.: "The City on the James." WCE handout; from an intact collection. ☺. (SML)   **P➜**

2093.1 Virginia. State Board of Agriculture. Whitehead, Thomas. *Virginia: a hand-book : Giving its History, Climate, and Mineral Wealth; Its Educational, Agricultural and Industrial Advantages.* Richmond: Everett Waddey co., publishers and printers, 1893.

22x15. 1 *l*, vi, 9-341 p, folding color map at end. Frontis: "State board of agriculture." Green wraps, black and gold print and state logo. C.t. = t.p. From intact WCE collections. ☺. (FM,LBA,SML,WM)

2094. Virginia. *Works of Edward W. Valentine, sculptor, of Richmond*: (S)

-Washington-

2095. Washington. Hestwood. *The Evergreen State Souvenir : containing*: (GLD,Col,UCB) $32 - 75
2098. Washington. WWFC. *Biennial Report of the Washington World's Fair...1891 and 1892*: (SPL)

☞ Washington was the first state to apply for building space at the WCE. The flag pole in front of the state building was 238 feet tall and visible from many locations on the fairgrounds. Its height was slightly less than that of the Ferris wheel (264 feet).

2098.1 Washington. Washington (State) World's Fair Commission. *Circular of information. Women's department.* N.p.: O.C. White, state printer, n.d.

15x8½. 7 p. Tri-fold white paper, black print. Professional, domestic, and miscellaneous work of women. ☺ (UCB)

2099. Washington. WWFC. Evans. *The State of Washington : a brief history*: (HU,LBA,MSL,NSW,SPL,Stfd,UCB,UI,UMC,UPa)

2100. Washington. WWFC. *Final report...1894*: (MSL)

2100.1 Washington. Washington (State) World's Fair Commission. *Text of the law governing the Washington World's Fair Commission; rules and regulations adopted and officers elected at the meeting of the commission held at Olympia, August 21, 1891.* Olympia: n.p., 1891.

__x__. 19 p. (SPL)

-West Virginia-

2103. West Virginia. BWFMWV. Morgan. *Columbian History of Education in West Virginia*: (UPa,Yale)

2104. West Virginia. BWFMWV. Summers. *The Mountain State*: (FM,HU,NLI,S,SML,UPa,WM)
---- Also found: Folding map, 259, (1) p. Last page is a county information fold out.

2105. West Virginia. Elkins. *Speech of Hon. S.B. Elkins on West Virginia Day*: (WM)
▸Add: (4) p. Beige wraps, black print with no design.

2106. West Virginia. Harris. *Address of John W. Harris...on West Virginia Day*: (WM)
▸Add: 8 p. Light tan wraps.

2107. West Virginia. MacCorkle. *Address of Gov. Wm. A. MacCorkle...on West Virginia Day*: (WM)
▸Add: 12 p. Green wraps, black print.

2107.1 West Virginia. Millspaugh, C[harles] F. *West Virginia's : forestry exhibit at the World's Columbian exposition.* Chicago: The Lumber Trade Journal, 1893.

25x17½. 4 p. Self-wraps. Illustrations: portrait of Millspaugh and a litho of the WV exhibit in the Forestry Bldg. See #1311.1, #1353.2, and #2104 (chapter on timber) for other Millspaugh items. (FM)

☞ Millspaugh, from West Virginia, was leading authority of the time on lumber and woods. He was active at the WCE and gave many botanical items to the Field Columbian Museum, where he was Curator of Botany.

-Wisconsin-

2108. Wisconsin. *At The Head Of The Lakes*: (WM)
▶Completed citation: N.p.: [The Edward P. Allis. Co., 1893]. (16) p. Beige wraps, chocolate print and mill illus decoration. Text in green ink; illus in red. At head of title "Compliments of..." Centerfold is bird's-eye of a group of Superior, WI, flour mills. Ad.

2108.1 Wisconsin. Cunningham, Thomas J., comp. *The : blue book : of the : state of Wisconsin...1891.* N.p.: The Milwaukee Litho. & Engr. Co., n.d.

23x16. 2 double plates of the senate and assembly chambers, 1 *l* color frontis of capitol, 1 *l* (t.p.), v introd, (1) p, 1 *l*, 650 p, 1 *l* addenda, 4 double leaf colored maps. Bright blue cloth hc, gilt print and state seal. T.p. in blue and gilt. All World's Fair commissioners listed on pp 399-400. ☺ (GLD) $12 - 30

2108.2 Wisconsin. Kirkland, R.B. *Location of Wisconsin's Collective Exhibit.* N.p.; n.p., 1 June 1893.

23½x13½. 1 *l*. White sheet, blue print and border. Kirkland was Executive Commissioner for WI. Gives locations of major WI exhibits in 7 bldgs + exhibits by state citizens in other locations. ☺ (WM)

2111. Wisconsin. Peck. *"Ousconsin"*: (HU,LBA,NLI,WM,Yale)

2112.1 Wisconsin. *Proceedings of the State Historical Society of Wisconsin at its forty-first annual meeting held December 14, 1893.* Madison: Democrat printing co., state printer, 1894.

23x15. 1 *l* (frontis), 173 p. Frontis: WI Historical Society library. Half leather over marbled paper covered boards. "Exhibit at World's Fair," pp 65-67; they had spent $252.42 on several displays of books and artifacts. First? printing of Frederick Jackson Turner's famous WCE paper, *The Significance of the Frontier in American History.* He gave the paper before the Society on Dec 14, 1893, after the fair had closed. ☺ . (DC)

2112.2 Wisconsin. Richmond, Fred C. *Report : of the : mining industries : of the : state of Wisconsin, as exhibited at the : World's Columbian Exposition, Chicago, 1893.* Shullsburg: T.H. McElroy & son, printers, 1893.

21½x14½. 16 p. Pink wraps with black print. C.t.= t.p. Wisconsin's WCE mining exhibit list as reported to the State Board by Richmond. ☺ . (FM)

2115. Wisconsin. SHSL. *List of books by Wisconsin authors*: (DC,HU,LBA,MSL)
2116. Wisconsin. *World's Columbian Exposition. Department of Wisconsin*:
(GLD)   P➜ $34 - 75

Chapter 13

WORLD'S CONGRESSES

2117.1 Association for the Advancement of Women. ...*Historical account of the Association for the Advancement of Women. 1873-1893. Twenty-first women's congress. World's Columbian exposition, Chicago, 1893.* Dedham, MA: [Association for the Advancement of Women] Transcript Steam Job Print, 1893; New Haven, CT: RPI, 1976.

23x13½. 47 p. At head of title: "A.A.W. 'Truth, justice, and honor.'" Microfilm reel 501, no 3799.1. On t.p.: "Julia Ward Howe, President." ☺ . (HU,S,SHB,Smth,Stfd,UMA,UVM,VCU)

2118. Congress of Evolutionists. *Programme of The Congress of Evolutionists*: (S)

2118.1 Congress of Patents and Trademarks. Lee, Benjamin F[ranklin]. *What constitutes a patentable subject matter : an address delivered before the Congress of Patents and Trademarks of the World's Columbian Exposition of 1893.* New York: D. Taylor, 1894; Woodbridge, CT: RPI, 1988.

22x__. 35 p. RPI: 19th-century legal treatises—no 37350. (HU,NDU,OU,UCLA)

2118.2 [Congress of Philologists]. Association of Philologists. *Information for Visiting Members of the Congress of Philologists.* N.p.: n.p., n.d.

22x14. (1) p. Caption title. The Congress of Philology was held July 11–15, 1893; philology was a general division under the Dept of Literature. See #2144. This item was not generated by the WCA or the Dept, but rather is travel and lodging info from the Assn to members attending the WCA. ☺ . (UMD)

2119. Congress of Photographers. *Congress of Photographers*: (IHi)
---- Also found: Beige wraps. C.t.: "The World's Congress Auxiliary of the World's Columbian Exposition. Congress of photographers."

2120. Congress on Africa. *Official programme of the congress on Africa*: (MIT)

2121. Congress on Math and Astronomy. *Programme of a congress on mathematics*: ☺ . (MIT)
▶Add author, title correction, and paging: Department of Science and Philosophy. ...*Programme of a congress on mathematics and astronomy...* 21½x15. (6) p. Tri-fold. C.t.

2121.1 Department of Agriculture. General Committee on Agricultural Congresses. ...*Preliminary Address of the General Committee on Agricultural Congresses in Connection with the Exposition of 1893.* [Chicago?]: n.p., [1891?].

20½x15. (4) p. No wraps. Caption title. At head of title: Auxiliary information. Benjamin Butterworth, Chairman and date at end of text, July 4, 1891. ☺ . (MSL,SML,UMD)

2122. Dept of Ag. Gen Div Forestry. *Preliminary address...forestry*: (HU)
▶Add publisher and cite info: Cambridge, MA: HULMS, 1983. Film Mas C 978. Dated on p 4: "Chicago, June, 1893." Chairman was B.E. Fernow.

2122.1 Department of Agriculture. General Division of Horticulture. ...*Programme of the congress on horticulture, commencing August 16th, 1893, in the Memorial Art Palace,...* N.p.: n.p., n.d.

21x15. (4) p. Caption title. At head of title: Auxiliary boilerplate information. ☺ . (HU,MIT)

2123. Dept of Ag. *The Scope of this* [Agriculture] *department*: (MIT,WM)
▶Add date: Dated on p (6): "January 1892."
---- Also found: 20½x15. (12) p. Buff glossy self-wraps, string-tied. Dated on p (6): "January 1892"; dated on p (12): "July 4, 1891." (WM)

2123.1 Department of Art. General Division of Architecture. ...*Preliminary Address of the committee on a World's congress of architects.* N.p.: n.p., n.d.

21x15. (3) p. Caption title. Dated on p (3): "July 1892." At head of title: Auxiliary boilerplate. (MIT)

2124.1 Department of Art. General Division of Photographic Art. ...*Preliminary Address of the Committee of the World's Congress Auxiliary on a Congress of Photographers.* N.p.: n.p., n.d.

20½x15. (8) p. Self-wraps. Caption title. At head of title: Auxiliary boilerplate information. In red ink on p (8): "The Congresses of the Department of Art, including the Congress Of Photographers, will be held during the first week of August, 1893." See #2119 for related item. ☺. (SML)

2125.   Dept of Art. *[Preliminary publication.] The Scope of This* [Art] *Department*: (MIT,SML)
▸Add: (7) p. String-tied. Dated on p (4): "Chicago, December, 1891."

2126.1 Department of Commerce and Finance. General Division of Water Commerce. ...*Programme of the Water Commerce Congress to be held August 1, 2, 3, 4, 5, in the Memorial Art Palace...* N.p.: n.p., n.d.

21x15. (4) p. Caption title. At head of title: Auxiliary boilerplate. Chairman: John C. Dore. ☺. (MIT)

2129.   Dept of Commerce. *[Preliminary publication.] The Scope of this* [Commerce and Finance] *Dept*: (MIT,SML)
▸Add: Dated on p (9): "Chicago, October, 1891." String-tied.

2131.   Dept of Ed. *Official programme of the Department of Education*: (MIT)
---- Also found: 37 p. [Chicago: Press of Kindergarten Literature co.], n.d.

2132.   Dept of Ed. *The Scope of this* [Education] *Department*: (MIT,MSL,SML)
▸Add: Dated on p (10): "Chicago, September, 1891."
---- Also found: Same with the addition of a p (11) titled "World's fair authorities." String-tied.

2132.1 Department of Education. World's Educational Congress. ...*Preliminary Announcement.* N.p.: n.p., n.d.

24x15. 8 p. Buff self-wraps. Caption title. At head of title: "World's educational congress : Chicago, U.S.A. : July 25th to 28th, inclusive, 1893." The National Educational Association was in charge of organization. William T. Harris, Chairman. ☺. (ICRL)

2133.1 Department of Engineering. General Division of Aerial Navigation. *Preliminary address of the World's congress committee on an international conference of aerial navigation.* N.p.: n.p., n.d.

__x__. __ p. At head of title: Auxiliary boilerplate. Dated Dec 1892. O. Chanute, Chairman. The idea for this congress originated with Professor A.F. Zahm, of Notre Dame.
---- Also found: Rpt in *Aeronautics*. 1.1 (1893): 3-4. ☺. (Amh)

2134.   Dept of Engineering. *Official programme of The Department of Engineering*: (MIT)

2135.   Dept of Engineering. *[Preliminary publication.] The scope of this* [Engineering] *department*: (MIT,SML)
▸Add annotation and dates: A report of the Chairman of the General Committee, E.L. Corthell, starts on p (3) and is dated "Chicago, October 5, 1891. After Bonney's name on p (5) is the date: "Chicago, December, 1891." String-tied.

2135.1 Department of Engineering. ...*Preliminary Address of the General Committee on a World's Congress of Engineers, to be held in Connection with the Columbian Exposition of 1893.* N.p.: n.p., n.d.

20½x15. (6) p includes self-wraps. Caption title. At head of title: Auxiliary boilerplate info. Lists all of the engineering divisions and their subject contents. The chairman was E.L. Corthell. ☺. (SML)

2135.2 Department of Government. Committee on Civil Service Reform Congress. ...*Programme of the Civil Service Reform Congress to be held August 7, 1893, in the Memorial Art Palace,...* N.p.: n.p., n.d.

21x15. (3) p. C.t. At head of title: Auxiliary boilerplate. Sessions held on August 7-8, 1893. ☺. (MIT)

2135.3 Department of Government. General Division of Arbitration and Peace. ...*Programme of the congress on Arbitration and Peace. To be held in the Permanent Memorial Art Palace, Chicago, during the week beginning August 14th, 1893.* N.p.: n.p., n.d.

21x15. 6 p. Caption title. At head of title: Auxiliary boilerplate info. ☺. (MIT)

2135.4 Department of Government. General Division of City Government. ...*Programme of the Congress on City Government : August 9 and 10, 1893. In the Memorial Art Palace,...* N.p.: n.p., n.d.

21x15. (4) p. Caption title. At head of title: Auxiliary boilerplate information. Walter Q. Gresham, Chairman. ☺. (MIT)

2137. Dept of Govt. Gen Div of Political and Econ Reform. *Programme of the suffrage congress*: (MIT)
▶Add paging: (12) p.

2138. Dept of Govt. *General Opening of the congress of this Department, including Jurisprudence*: (MIT,S)
▶Add paging: (7) p includes front self-wrap.

2139. Dept of Govt. *[Preliminary publication.] The Scope of this* [Government] *Department*: (MIT,SML)
▶Add: String-tied. Dated on p (10) after Bonney's name: "Chicago, December, 1891." Rpt in #274.o.1.

2139.1 Department of Government. ...*Programme of the single tax congress : to be held during the Week of August 28, 1893, in the Memorial Art Palace...* N.p.: n.p., n.d.

21x15. (7) p. At head of title: Auxiliary boilerplate information. T. Ripley, Chairman. ☺. (MIT)

2139.2 Department of Labor. ...*Preliminary address of the general committee on labor congresses, including all germane industrial and economic problems.* N.p.: n.p., n.d.

20½x15. (4) p. Caption title. At head of title: Auxiliary boilerplate information. The preliminary address by Walter Thomas Mills, Chairman. Not dated. ☺. (SML,UMD)

2140. Dept of Labor. *[Preliminary publication.] The Scope of this* [Labor] *Department*: (MIT,SML)
▶Add paging and date: (8) p. Dated on p (6): "January 1892."
---- Also found: (16) p. String-tied. Contains two undated additional reports: Chairman Walter Thomas Mills and *Preliminary Address of Woman's Committee* (#2214), pp (13)-(16). (WM)

2141. Dept of Labor. *Programme of the labor congress*: (MIT,MSL)
▶Correct paging: (7) p including caption title page.

2143. Dept of Lit. Gen Div Libraries. *Preliminary address of the committee...congress of librarians*: (MIT,WM)
▶Add: Dated on p (2): "Chicago, January, 1893."

2144.1 Department of Literature. ...*Preliminary Address of the General Committee on Literary Congresses.* N.p.: n.p., 1891?

20x15. (4) p. Caption title. At head of title: Auxiliary information. William F. Poole, Chairman. Dated on p (4): "Exposition Headquarters, Chicago, July, 1891." ☺. (HU,SML,UMD)

2145. Dept of Lit. *[Preliminary publication.] The Scope of this* [Literature] *Department*: (HU,MIT,MSL,SML,WM)
▶Add pub info and date: N.p.: n.p., 1892? String-tied. Dated after Bonney's name on p (6): "Chicago, 1891"; dated on p (8): "Chicago, January, 1892." Includes Poole's #2144.1 as the last 4 pages.

2150.1 Department of Medicine. General Division of Dentistry. ...*Programme of The World's Columbian Dental Congress : to be held in the Memorial Art Palace,...August 14–19, 1893.* [Chicago: Press of Kindergarten Literature co.], n.d.

21x15. 11 p. Caption title. At head of title: Auxiliary boilerplate information. ☺. (MIT)

2152. Dept of Medicine. *The Scope of This* [Medicine] *Department*: (MIT)
▶Add: *[Preliminary publication.]* at head of title. Dated on p (7): "January 1892."

2152.1 Department of Moral and Social Reform. ...*The international congress of Charities, Correction and Philanthropy. Circular No. I. Chicago, Ill., U.S.A., July 25, 1892.* Chicago: n.p., 1892.

20½x15. (3) p. Folded sheet. Caption title. At head of title: "World's Columbian exposition. The World's congress auxiliary. Department of Moral and Social Reform Congresses." Announcement of Congress to be held June 12, 1893. Rutherford B. Hayes, ex-President, was asked to preside. ☺. (MIT,MSL)

2152.2 Department of Moral and Social Reform. ...*Preliminary Address of the Joint Committee on Moral and Social Reform Congresses.* N.p.: n.p., 1891?

20½x15. (4) p. Caption title. At head of title: Auxiliary boilerplate info. Dated Aug 1891. ☺ (SML,UMD)

2153. Department of Moral and Social Reform. *[Preliminary publication.]...The Scope of this* [Moral and Social Reform] *Department.* N.p.: n.p., n.d.

20½x15. (8) p. String-tied. Caption title from p (2). At the ellipse: Auxiliary boilerplate information. Dated p (5) after Bonney's name: "Chicago, January, 1892." (MIT,SML,WM)
▶Better and more uniform title than "To facilitate..." as it is given in the original bibliography.

2155. Dept of Music. *[Preliminary publication.] The Scope of This* [Music] *Department*: (MIT,SML)
▶Add: Dated after Bonney's name on p (5): "Chicago, August 1891." String-tied.

2156. Dept of Public Press. *[Preliminary publication.] The Scope of This* [Public Press] *Department*: (MIT,SML)
▶Add: Dated on p (4): "Chicago, December, 1891."
---- Also found: (8) p. String-tied. Dated after Bonney's name on p (4): "Chicago, December, 1891." On p (8): "When they [the congresses] will be held."

2157. Dept of Public Press. *Programme of the Public Press Congresses*: (UIC)

2157.1 Department of Religion. ...*Preliminary Address of the General Committee on Religious Congresses in connection with the Exposition of 1893.* [Chicago?]: n.p., [1891?].

20½x15. (4) p. Caption title. At head of title: Auxiliary boilerplate information. On p (4): "John Henry Barrows, Chairman General Committee on Religious Congresses, World's Congress Auxiliary, Chicago, Ills., U.S.A. Chicago, June 1, 1891." ☺. (UMD)

2158. Dept of Religion. Woman's Branch. *Preliminary address of the woman's general*: (WM)
▶Add: (4) p. Dated p (3): "Chicago, April, 1892." Augusta J. Chapin, chairman.

2160. Department of Religion. *[Preliminary publication.] ...The Scope of this* [Religion] *Department.* N.p.: n.p., n.d.

21x15. (18) p. String-tied. Title from p (2). Dated after Bonney's name on p (10): "Chicago, January, 1892." At the ellipse: Auxiliary boilerplate. Contains John Henry Barrows undated "Preliminary Address of the General Committee on Religious Congresses...," #2157.1, on pp (11)-(13). (MIT)
---- Also found: 20½x15. (16) p. String-tied. Title from p (2). Dated on p (10): "Chicago, January, 1892." (SML,WM)
▶Better and more uniform title than "To unite all religions..." as it is given in the original bibliography.
▶Completed citation.

2161. Dept of Religion. *Programme of The World's Religious Congresses*: (HU,SHB,UIC)
---- Also listed: 170 p. (SHB)

2162.1 Department of Science and Philosophy. Division of Psychical Research. ...*Department of science and philosophy. Division of psychical research. To* (blank). *Dear Sir: The Joint committee of Arrangements for the International Congress of Psychical Researchers, to be held in Chicago...* N.p.: n.p., n.d.

21x15. (4) p. Folded sheet. At head of title: Auxiliary boilerplate. An invitation (blank for name) to give an address on a specific subject at the Congress that began the week of Aug 21, 1893. ☺. (WML)

2163. Dept of Science. Gen Div of African Ethnology. *Preliminary address of the Auxiliary*: ☺. (HU,UMD)
2164. Dept of Science. Gen Div of African Ethnology. *Report in Behalf of the General*: (HU,MIT,MSL,S,Yale)

2164.1 Department of Science and Philosophy. General Division of Chemistry. Wiley, Harvey W[ashington]. *The World's congress auxiliary of the World's Columbian exposition.* N.p: n.p., 1893.

> 21½x15. (4) p. Folded sheet. Caption title. Dated July 1, 1893. Lists the 10 sections and temporary chairman for each. (HU)

2164.2 Department of Science and Philosophy. General Division of Geology. *...Preliminary Address of the Committee on a World's Congress of Geologists, to be held at Chicago...* N.p.: n.p., n.d.

> 20½x15. (7) p. String-tied. Caption title. At head of title: Auxiliary boilerplate info. Not dated. ☺ . (UMD) **P➜**

2164.3 Department of Science and Philosophy. General Division of Meteorology, Climatology and Terrestrial Magnetism. *...Preliminary Programme. Memorial Art Palace,...August 21st to 25th, 1893.* N.p.: n.p., n.d.

> 21x15. 12 p. C.t. At head of title: Auxiliary boilerplate. Full list of meetings ☺ . (MIT)

2164.4 Department of Science and Philosophy. General Division of Zoology. Forbes, S[tephen] A. *...Provisional program.* Champaign, IL: n.p., 1893.

> __x__. 4 p. See #268.1, Forbes Fish commission report. (HU)

2165.   Dept of Science and Phil. *Preliminary Address...Zoölogical Congresses*: (WM)
> ▶Add: (7) p. String-tied. Dated after names p (3): "Chicago, April, 1892." Stephen A. Forbes, Chair.

2166.   Dept of Science and Phil. *Programme of The World's Congress on Geology*: (MIT)
> ▶Add paging: (7) p.

2167.   Dept of Science and Phil. *[Revised preliminary publication.] The Scope of This* [Science...]: (MIT,SML,WM)
> ▶Add: (12) p. String-tied. No date p (9); dated after Bonney's name on p (12): "Chicago, September, 1891." (WM)
> ---- Also found: A (12) p version dated on p (9): "April, 1892." (SML)

2168.   Dept of Temperance. *[Preliminary publication.] The Scope of This* [Temperance] *Department*: (MIT,SML)
> ▶Add: (15) p. String-tied. "First Report of Secretary Sternes" pp (6)-(9). Dated p (9): "New York, December 15th, 1891." Dated after Bonney's name on p (11): "Chicago, January, 1892." Includes "Preliminary Address of the Woman's Committee on a World's Temperance Congress..." pp (12)-(15) by Frances E. Willard, Chairman, which is dated on p (15): "Chicago, July, 1891."

2172.   Historical Congress. Newton. *Colonial Virginia: a paper read before the historical*: (CWM,IHi)
2173.   Internat'l Christian Conf. *Christianity practically applied...Gen'l conferences*: (BU,ESU,HU,NSW,UMD,UMN)
2174.   Internat'l Christian Conf. *Christianity practically applied...Section conferences*: (BU,HU,UMD,UMN)

2174.1 International Congress of Anthropology. Executive Committee and Local Committee. Brinton, Daniel G., et al. Letter to Prospective Anthropology Congress Attendees. 15 June 1893. Chicago.

> 28x21½. Buff sheet on WCA (not anthropology) letterhead paper, printed one side in black. Letter begins "Sir: We beg to inform you that the International Congress of Anthropology..." Info about the Congress to begin Aug 28; five sections were organized. (WM)

2174.2 International Congress of Anthropology. Executive Committee and Local Committee. Brinton, Daniel G., et al. Letter to Prospective Anthropology Congress Attendees. 10 Aug. 1893. Chicago.

> 28x21½. Buff sheet on WCA anthropology letterhead paper, printed one side in black. Letter begins "Sir: We beg to inform you that the subjects to be brought before the International Congress." Info on the order of subjects for Aug 28–Sept 2. Proceedings subscription price given as $5.00. (WM)

2175.   Internat'l Cong of Anthro. Hale. *The Fall of Hochelaga*: (NLA)
2177.   Internat'l Cong of Anthro. Wake. *Memoirs of the International Congress*: (Amh,Col,FM,UMA,UMD,UPa,UVM)

2177.1 International Congress of Anthropology. Wake, C. Staniland. Letter to Prospective Anthropology Congress Speakers. 10 Aug. 1893. Chicago.

28x21½. (1) p. Printed letter on WCA, International Congress of Anthropology, Dept of Ethnology letterhead. Letter begins "Sir:--We beg to inform you that..." Calendar of events for the Anthropology Congress, Aug 28–Sept 2, 1893. Request for papers in preparation for printing the proceedings (#2177); subscription $5.00 per copy. ☺ . (FM)

☞ Wake was librarian for the WCE Department of Ethnology, and he was local secretary for the World's Congress of Anthropology. Wake worked at the Field Museum until his death. A trunk of his memorabilia was found in the museum and remained unclaimed by his daughter in England. See citation #2446.FM for more on Wake, including a WCE-library-list manuscript found in the trunk.

2177.2 International Congress of Charities, Correction and Philanthropy. Billings, John S., and Henry M. Hurd, eds. *Hospitals : dispensaries : and nursing : Papers and Discussions..., Section III, Chicago, June 12th to 17th, 1893.* Baltimore: Johns Hopkins Press (The Friedenwald co., printers); London: The Scientific Press, Limited, 1894 [ᶜ1894 by The Johns Hopkins Press].

3ʳᵈ Section. 25½x17. xiv, 719 p. Gray-blue cloth hc, gilt spine print. Editors were physicians. This section is also referenced as a part of the complete *Report of the proceedings*, #2180. ☺ . (CUA,UMD)

2177.3 International Congress of Charities, Correction and Philanthropy. *Care of children : sociology in institutions of learning : international congress of charities : Chicago : 1893.* Baltimore: The Johns Hopkins Press; London: The Scientific press, limited, 1894 [ᶜ1894 by the Johns Hopkins Press].

23½x16. Bound together. These two sections are also referenced individually as a part of the complete *Report of the proceedings*, #2180. 1 *l* half-title, 2ⁿᵈ Section: (4), (1)-163 p, 7ᵗʰ Section: (3) p, 1 *l*, (vii)-xx, 127 p. Navy cloth hc, gilt spine. Spine title. Half-title: "International Congress of Charities, Corrections, and Philanthropy. I. The care of dependent, neglected and wayward children. II. Sociology in institutions of learning."
2ⁿᵈ Section: Spencer, Anna Garlin, and Charles Wesley Birtwell, eds. *The Care of Dependent, Neglected and Wayward Children : being a report...* Seventeen papers that were presented the week of June 12, 1893, with proceedings interspersed. Friedenwald co., printers.
7ᵗʰ Section: Warner, Amos G., ed. *Sociology in Institutions of Learning : being a report of the seventh section...* Nine papers that were presented, 7 letters and communications plus proceedings. Also includes a reprint of a paper by Felix Adler ("American Education from a National Point of View") delivered at a general meeting of the congress but included here because its subject matter is closely related to that of the section. Warner was secretary of the section. ☺ (DC)

2178.   Internat'l Cong Charities. *Circular, no. _*: (HU)

2178.1 International Congress of Charities, Corrections and Philanthropy. Committee on the History of Child-Saving Work. *History of child saving in the United States: National Conference of Charities and Corrections; report of the Committee on the History of Child-Saving Work to the twentieth conference, Chicago, June, 1893.* Rpt. Montclair, NJ: Patterson Smith, 1971.

23x15½. xxvii, 347 p. Illus and ports. Patterson Smith reprint no 111. Introd by A. Platt. (ref)

2178.2 International Congress of Charities, Correction and Philanthropy. Gilman, Daniel C[olt], ed. *The organization of charities, being a report of the Sixth section of the International congress of charities : Chicago : 1893.* Baltimore: The Johns Hopkins Press [and] London: The Scientific press, limited, 1894 [ᶜ1894 by the Johns Hopkins Press].

6ᵗʰ Section: 23x15½. xxxii, 400 p includes diagrams. Also referenced in #2180. (DC,NYPL)

2178.3 International Congress of Charities, Correction and Philanthropy. *The insane : The feeble-minded : Criminals : International congress of charities : Chicago : 1893.* Baltimore: The Johns Hopkins Press [and] London: The Scientific press, limited, 1894 [ᶜ1894 by the Johns Hopkins Press].

23x15½. Bound together. These three sections are also referenced individually as a part of the complete *Report of the proceedings*, #2180. 1 *l* half-title, 4ᵗʰ Section: (3), (1)-193 p, 8ᵗʰ Section: (5), 6-22, (1) p index, 5ᵗʰ Section: (5), 6-107 p. Navy cloth hc, gilt spine. Spine title. Half-title: "International congress of charities, correction and philanthropy. I. Commitment, detention, care and treatment of the insane. II. Care and training of the feeble-minded. III. The prevention and repression of crime."
4ᵗʰ Section: Blumer, G. Adler, and A.B. Richardson, eds. *Commitment, Detention, Care and Treatment of the Insane : being a report of : the fourth section of the international congress of charities, correction and philanthropy*. Includes 14 papers presented plus the section's proceedings. The editors were physicians; Blumer was chairman of the section.
5ᵗʰ Section: Wines, Frederick H. *The Prevention and Repression of Crime : being a report of the fifth section...* Friedenwald co., printers. Opening address and 8 papers with interspersed proceedings. Wines was an L.L.D. ☺ (DC)
8ᵗʰ Section: Knight, George H, ed. *Care and Training of the Feeble-minded : being a report of the eighth section of the international congress of charities,...Chicago, June 1893*. Baltimore: Friedenwald co., printers. Three medical papers presented and report of their discussion. Lists the number of feeble-minded by state and reports a total of 95,571, based upon the 1890 census. Knight was a physician.

2179.   Internat'l Cong of Charities. *Programme, rules officers and members*: (DC,NYPL)
         ---- Also listed with title: *General Exercises of the International Congress of Charities,...Chicago, June 1893 : together with list of officers and members, programme and rules*. Baltimore: The Johns Hopkins press, 1894. 22½x15½. 47 p. Navy cloth hc with gilt lettering (bound with #2180, 1st section). (DC)

2179.1 International Congress of Charities, Correction and Philanthropy. Reitzenstein, Friedrich, Freiherr von. *Zur interntionale Behandlung der Armenfragen : ein Aufsatz für den im Juni 1893 in Chicago zusammentretenden internationalen Armenpflege-Kongress auf Anlass der betreffenden Sektionen*. Freiburg i.B.: F. Wagner, 1893.

         __x__. (4), 27 p. Trans: Towards international treatment of the poor. An essay in the section of the International Charities Congress gathered in Chicago in June 1893. (HU)

2180.   Internat'l Cong of Charities. *Report of the proceedings*: (DC)
         ▸The 8 sections were printed in vols either individually or in groups: see #2177.2-3, #2178.2-3.

2181.   Internat'l Cong of Ed. Bardeen. *The history of the educational journalism...New York*: ☺ . (HU,OU)
         ▸Add: Light blue wraps, black print. C.t. = t.p.

2182.   [Internat'l Cong of Ed]. Harris. *The World's Educational Congress. A paper read*: (MOHx)
2183.   Internat'l Cong of Ed. NEA. *Official programme of The International Congress of Education*: (S)
2184.   Internat'l Cong of Ed. NEA. *Proceedings of the International Congress*: (Amh,DC,ESU,HU,MIT,OU,UMC,UMA,UVM)

2185.1 International Congress of Education. *Supplement. Preliminary programme. World's Congress Auxiliary 1893. The International Congresses of Education of the World's Columbian exposition*. N.p.: n.p., n.d.

         21x9. 6 p. Tri-fold. Congresses to be held July 25–28, 1893. ☺ (S)

2188.   Internat'l Cong on Sunday Rest. *The Sunday problem*: (NSW)
2189.   Internat'l Cong on Water Transportation. *Water Commerce Congress*: (MIT,UPa)
2190.   Internat'l Eisteddfod Cong. *Eisteddfod Gydgenedlaethol*: (WM)

2191.   Internat'l Eisteddfod Cong. *Welshmen as Factors*: (CLP,UMA,UMD)
         ▸Add place of publication and cover description: Utica, NY. Black cloth hc, gilt print.
         ---- Also found: Publisher: Chicago: Library Resources Inc., 1971. Microfiche. One sheet. The Library of American Civilization, 15507.

2192.   Internat'l Eisteddfod Cong. *The WCE : internat'l eisteddvod...Cais a gwahoddiad*: (CCA,DU,HU,LBA,MSL,UMD)
         ---- Also found: Light gray wraps.

2193.   International Electrical Congress. *Proceedings : of the international electrical congress held in the city of Chicago. August 21st to 25th, 1893.* New York: American Institute of Electrical Engineers (Press of McIlroy & Emmet), 1894 [ᶜ1894 by the American Institute of Electrical Engineers].

24½x15½. xxiv, 488 p+ table of "Symbols of Physical Quantities and Abbreviations Units." Rose-red cloth hc. See #543.2 for another Electrical Congress item. ☺. (LHL,NYPL,UMD)   ▶Completed citation.

2194.   Internat'l Eng Cong. Div of Marine. Melville. *Proceedings of the International*: (DC,HU,LHL,LU,Stfd,UTA)

2194.1 International Engineering Congress. General Division of Aerial Navigation. *Proceedings of the conference on aerial navigation.* New York: American Engineer and Railroad Journal, 1893.

Proceedings are printed in vol 1, no 1 (October 1893) of *Aeronautics*, a monthly journal. (Amh, LHL)

2194.2 International Engineering Congress. General Division of Civil Engineering. Benzenberg, G[eorge] H[enry]. *...The sewerage system of Milwaukee and the Milwaukee river flushing works.* N.p.: American Society of Civil Engineers, 1893.

22½x14½. Pp 367-85. Tables and fold diagrams. Caption title. At head of title: "American society of civil engineers. ...Transactions. ...651. (Vol. XXX—November, 1893)." Congress paper. ☺. (MSL)

2194.3 International Engineering Congress. General Division of Civil Engineering. Mills, Hiram F[rancis]. *...Purification of sewage and of water by filtration.* N.p.: American Society of Civil Engineers, 1893.

22½x14½. 17 p. Caption title. At head of title: "Advance copy. Issued for purposes of Discussion. American society of civil engineers. ...Transactions. ...(Vol. , 1893.)." Congress paper. ☺. (MSL)

2194.4 International Engineering Congress. General Division of Civil Engineering. Salazar, L. *On the distribution of water in the City of Mexico.* [New York: n.p., 1893?].

23x__. 14 p. Translated from the Spanish by Alfred F. Sears. Prepared for the Congress. "Advance copy issued for purposes of discussion. American society of Civil Engineers. Transaction...1893." (CU)

2194.5 International Engineering Congress. General Division of Civil Engineering. *Transactions : of the American society of civil engineers.* Vol. 29. New York: Published by the Society, 1893.

23x15. 736 p+ many unpaged fold out illus, charts, and maps. Half cloth over marbled paper boards, red and black spine labels with gilt print. Vol 29 (July–Sept 1893); each paper prepared for the WCE. ☺. (UMD)

2194.6 International Engineering Congress. General Division of Civil Engineering. *Transactions : of the American society of civil engineers.* Vol. 30. New York: Published by the Society, 1894.

23x15. 722 p+ many unpaged fold out illus, charts, and maps. Half cloth over marbled paper boards, red and black spine labels with gilt print. Vol 30 (Oct–Dec 1893); every paper from Oct–Nov was presented at the WCE (no WCE in Dec). ☺. (UMD)

2194.7 International Engineering Congress. General Division of Civil Engineering. Violette, L. *...Notice on the Channel Bridge...July–August 1893.* Paris: Imp. Bastien et Georget, [ᶜ1893].

31x21½. 16 p. Buff wraps, black print. At head of title: "World's Columbian Exposition. International Engineering Congress. Civil Engineering Division." Early proposal for connecting France and England. Violette was a fellow of the French Society of Civil Engineers. ☺. (CCA)

2195.   Internat'l Eng Cong. Div of Military Eng. Comly. *Operations of the Division of military*: (HU,MIT)
---- Also listed: 53d Cong, 2d Sess. Senate. Ex. Doc. Vol vi. No 119.

2196.   International Engineering Congress. Divisions C and D Mining and Metallurgy. American Institute of Mining Engineers. *Transactions of the American Institute of Mining Engineers. ...Being Part I of the Proceedings, Papers and Discussions of the Chicago Meeting of 1893,...* 2 vol. New York City: Published by the Institute, at the office of secretary, 1894.

23½x16. Vol XXII: xx, 795 p. Vol XXIII: lxxxvii, 685 p. Half burgundy leather over burgundy cloth pebbled hc, gilt spine print. Red speckled edges. Complete text and illus for papers presented in this segment of the WCE Engineering Congress. ☺ (GLD,NYPL) Set $60 - 140
‣Completed citation.

2196.1 International Engineering Congress. *International Engineering Congress and Engineering Headquarters, World's Columbian Exposition, 1893. Proceedings of the General Committee of Engineering Societies, Meeting at Chicago, May 15, 1891.* Chicago?: n.p., 1891?

21x14. 12 p. Light brown wraps, black print. C.t. = t.p. Caption title: "Proceedings of Permanent Committee on International Engineering Congress and Engineering Headquarters, World's Columbian Exposition, 1893." A meeting to organize the WCE engineering congress. ☺ . (ICRL)

2196.2 International Engineering Congress. Society for the Promotion of Engineering Education. Wood, DeVolson, Ira O. Baker, and J.B. Johnson, eds. *Engineering Education : being the Proceedings of Section E of the World's Engineering Congress : held in Chicago, Ill. : July 31, to August 5, 1893.* Columbia, MO: Society for the Promotion of Engineering Education (E.W. Stephens, Printer), 1894.

23x15. viii, 342 p. No frontis. Dark blue cloth hc. Published as Vol I of their Proceedings. ☺ . (MIT,NSW)

2197. Internat'l Folk-Lore Cong. Bassett. *The International Folk-Lore Congress*: (Col,ESU,HU,IHi,slpl,UCD,UCLA,UIC,UPa)
‣Add annotation: Columbia University has "No. 62 of an edition of 600 copies."

Rpt edition: (uiuc,UMA,UWM)

2198. Internat'l Folk-Lore Cong. *Retrospect of the folk-lore of the Columbian Exposition*: (UPa)

2200. International Geographic Conference. National Geographic Society. *...Proceedings : of the : international geographic conference : in : Chicago : July 27–28, 1893.* Vol. 5. Washington, DC: Published by the National Geographic Society, 1894.

24½x15. Pp 97-256 are proceedings of the WCE conference. ☺ . (BM,csuf,UPa)
‣Completed and corrected citation.

2200.1 International Mathematical Congress. Klein, Felix. *The Evanston colloquium : Lectures on Mathematics delivered From Aug. 28 to Sept. 9, 1893 : before members of the congress of mathematics held in connection with the World's fair in Chicago : at Northwestern University, Evanston, Ill.* Rpt. New York: American Mathematical Society, 1911.

22½x15. xi, 109 p. Diagram. Rpt of the 1894 ed. See #2310.2 for a history of the Mathematical Congresses, including that held at the WCE, written in 1986. Klein was a German commissioner to the WCE from the University of Göttingen. ☺ . (LHL,UMA)

2201. Internat'l Math Cong. *Mathematical papers read at the international mathematical*:
(Amh,Col,CU,DC,HU,MIT,NDU,nmsu,OU,SHB,Smth,Stfd,UCD,UCLA,UMA,UMC,UoA,UMN,UPa,UTA,UVM)

2202. Internat'l Meteorological Cong. Fassig. *Report of the International Meteorological*: (HU,NSW,S)
‣Add cover description: Light tan wraps with black print.

2202.1 International Pharmaceutical Congress. American Pharmaceutical Association. Biroth, Henry. Letter to Members of the American Pharmaceutical Association. 1 Mar. 1893. Chicago.

28x22. (4) p. Folded buff sheet. Caption title: "Forty-First Annual Meeting at Chicago, Illinois, August 14 to 19, 1893." During the WCE. Pp (2)-(3) letter to members to change name to International Pharmaceutical Congress from World's Congress of Pharmacists and to start on Monday Aug 21. (WM)

2202.2 International Pharmaceutical Congress. American Pharmaceutical Association. *Forty First Annual Meeting of the American Pharmaceutical Association.* Chicago: Pictorial Printing Co., [1893].

19x13. (3) p. Folded stiff card wraps, gilt print and brown-toned illus; back cover illus of Admin Bldg. C.t. The (3) p dinner menu and program in dark blue print are ribbon-tied to inside of wraps. Held

Aug 16, 1893, in the Casino. This program includes the WCE speaker list. The Association's 1893 annual convention was part of its WCE congress. ☺ . (WM)   **P→**

2202.3 International Pharmaceutical Congress. American Pharmaceutical Association. *Program of the American Pharmaceutical Association : 41ˢᵗ annual meeting, August 14–19, 1893, Chicago.* Chicago: Pictorial printing co., n.d.

14x7½. 1 *l*, (6) p. Dark burgundy pebbled wraps, red string-tied, silver print. C.t Title from 1 *l* is: "Programme of The Meeting and Entertainment of the American Pharmaceutical Association." Includes visits to the WCE and to the Illinois Pharmaceutical Assn at the IL Bldg. On p (6): "Monday, August 21 10 ᴬ·ᴹ·—Opening of the Seventh International Pharmaceutical Congress in the Art Institute." (WM)

2205.1 National Prison Association. *Proceedings of the annual congress of the : National Prison Association : of the United States. Held at Chicago, June 7–10, 1893.* Chicago: Knight, Leonard & co., printers, 1893.

23x15½. 1 *l* (frontis), 134 p. Frontis: Rutherford B. Hayes. Blue-black cloth hc, gilt spine print. National meeting held at the Art Institute prior to a related session of the International Congress of Charities, Correction and Philanthropy also held at the Art Institute. Ex-president Hayes, a leader in prison reform, was eulogized. Members included Illinois governor John P. Altgeld and Chicago mayor Carter H. Harrison, both of whom were very active in improving correctional institutions. ☺ (GLD) $30 - 55

2206. Philosophical Congress. *Programme of philosophical congress*: (MIT)
▶Add: (4) p. Program listing events for six sessions covering two days, Aug. 21–22, 1893.

2208. Theosophical Congress. *The Theosophical Congress*: (UMD)
▶Add publisher: Chicago: Library Resources, 1970. Microfiche. One sheet. LAC-16458.

2209. Universal Peace Cong. Butterworth [Hezekiah]. *White city by the inland sea*: (Col)
2210. Universal Peace Cong. *Official report of the fifth universal peace congress*: (CU,HU,MSL,SHB,slu,UCD,UMN)

2210.1 Woman's Branch. *...Bulletin for the week commencing Monday, July 10.* N.p.: n.p., n.d.

23½x14. 1 *l*. White sheet printed one side. Caption title. Schedule of events, July 10–16. ☺ (WM)

2212. WB. Comm on Christian Missions. *Preliminary Address*: (WM)
▶Add: (4) p. Dated p (3): "Chicago, January, 1892." Chairman was Mrs. Franklin W. Fisk.

2213. Woman's Branch. Committee on Household Economics. *The Preliminary Address of the Woman's Committee on Household Economics, in the Woman's Branch of the World's Congress Auxiliary.* N.p.: n.p., [1892?].

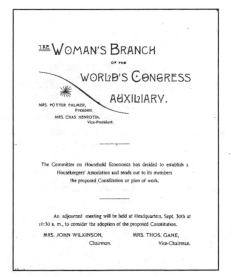

20½x14½. (4) p. Dated after Chairman Wilkinson's name on p (4): "Chicago, March, 1892." This committee was under the Depts of Agriculture and Labor. ☺ (WM)   ▶Corrected cite and added info.

2213.1 Woman's Branch. Committee on Household Economics. *Proposed constitution for the Illinois association of housekeepers and bureau of information.* N.p.: n.p., n.d.   **P→**

20½x15. (4) p includes front and back white self-wraps. Caption title on p (2). On front: "The Committee on Household Economics has decided to establish a Housekeepers' Association and sends out to its members the proposed Constitution or plan of work." Committee members listed on p (4). ☺ . (UMD)

2214.   WB. Comm on Labor. *Preliminary Address*: ☺. (MIT,SML,UMD)
▶Add: Undated. Mrs. J.D. Harvey, chairman.

2214.1 Woman's Branch. Committee on Municipal Order. ...*Preliminary address of the woman's committee on municipal order.* N.p.: n.p., [1891?].

20½x15. (4) p. Caption title. At head of title: Auxiliary boilerplate. Dated on p (4): "Exposition Headquarters, Chicago, July, 1891." Mrs. Henry Wade Rogers, Chairman. ☺. (UMD)

2214.2 Woman's Branch. Committee on Temperance. ...*Preliminary Address of the Woman's Committee on a World's Temperance Congress of Women in Connection with the World's Columbian Exposition of 1893.* N.p.: n.p., [1891?].

20½x15. (4) p. Caption title. At head of title: Auxiliary boilerplate. Date on p (4): "Chicago, July, 1891." Frances E. Willard, Chairman. ☺. (UMD)

2214.3 Woman's Branch. ...*The committees of the woman's branch of the auxiliary, for the World's congresses of 1893.* N.p.: n.p., [1891?].

20½x15. (4) p. Caption title. At head of title: Auxiliary boilerplate information. Dated on p (4): "Exposition Headquarters, Chicago, August, 1891." On top of p (2): "Special Committees of Women" —a complete listing of the various committees; chairmen noted. [Excellent reference.] * ☺. (UMD)

2214.4 Woman's Branch. ...*General announcement of the woman's branch of the auxiliary.* N.p.: n.p., n.d.

20½x15. (3) p. Caption title. At head of title: Auxiliary boilerplate. Not dated. This is the founding document for the Woman's Branch of the Auxiliary. ☺. (SML)

2215.   WB. *Programme of the World's Congress of Representative Women*: (ref,Smth)
---- Also listed: 7 edition of 10,000 each. 31 p. Self-wraps. (ref) $45
▶Add publisher: New Haven, CT: RPI, 1977. Microfiche. History of Women, reel 623, no 4975.

2215.1 Woman's Branch. ...*Special announcement in relation to the congress of representative women to be held during the week commencing May 15, 1893.* N.p.: n.p., n.d.

20½x15½. 2 *l.* Folded sheet with print on rectos. Announces opening of Congress on May 15. At head of title: Auxiliary boilerplate. At end: Bertha M.H. Palmer and Ellen M. Henrotin. ☺ (S)

2215.2 Woman's Branch. Young, Clarence E. *The World's Congress Auxiliary cordially invites you to attend the World's Congress of Representative Women,...* N.p.: n.p., n.d.

20x15½. 1 *l.* Folded sheet printed on front only. Congress/woman's branch letterhead. Invitation to the Congress meeting during the week of May 15, 1893. Subscribed by Young, Secretary of the World's Congress Auxiliary. Undated. ☺ (WM)

2216.   WB. World's Comm Women's Mission. *Program of Conference under the auspices...Women's*: (WM)
▶Completed citation: (4) p. Folded sheet. Printer info on back: [Boston: Beacon Press], n.d.

2217.   WCTU. *Program of the second World's and twentieth national*: (MSL)

2217.1 Woman's Christian Temperance Union. Willard, Frances E[lizabeth]. *Address : before the : second biennial convention of the World's Woman's Christian Temperance Union, and the twentieth annual convention of the national Woman's Christian Temperance Union. By their President,.... World's Columbian exposition, Chicago, Illinois, U.S.A. : Art Institute Building, October 16th to 21st, 1893.* Chicago: Woman's Temperance publishing association, n.d.; New Haven, CT: RPI, 1976.

__x__. 96 p. No illus. Wraps. C.t. Willard was president. See #2217 for the convention program.
---- Also found: RPI microfilm made from a NYPL copy. "Women in history." Reel 619, no 4932.
☺. (Stfd,UVM)

2219.   WCA. Bonney. Letter to Governors. 5 Mar. 1891:
▶This printed letter to Governor Prince of New Mexico was hand signed by Benjamin Butterworth.

---- Also found: Same printed form letter addressed to A.C. Mellette on 6 Mar. 1891. Mellette was Governor of South Dakota. ©. (MA)

2220.   WCA. Bonney. *World's Congress Addresses...Bonney*: (KSU)
2223.   WCA. *First Report of the Auxiliary to the directory*: (HU,UMD)

2224.   WCA. *General programme of the series*: (HU,MSL,SML)
---- Also found: (15) p with "[Corrected to January 1, 1893]" at top of p (1).

2225.   WCA. *The general programme of The World's*: (HU,MIT,UMD,WM)   P➔

2227.   WCA. *List of World's Congress Departments*: (Col,MIT,MSL)
▸Correct paging: (16) p. Delete both (10) p and 26 p in the original.
▸Add: String-tied self-wraps. Dated p (14): "Chicago, February, 1892."

2228.   WCA. *The Object of This* [World's Congress Auxiliary] *Org*: (SFe)

2228.1 World's Congress Auxiliary. *...Objects*. N.p.: n.p., [1892?].

20½x15. (2) p. Caption title. Info at head of title is the same as #2228.2 below, and the first page is identical. The general assignment of congress dates for the 16 primary departments as of June 1892 is given on p (2). © (HU,SML)

2228.2 World's Congress Auxiliary. *...Objects*. N.p.: n.p., n.d.

17½x15. (4) p. Caption title. At head of title: "Not matter, but mind. The World's Congress Auxiliary : Of the World's Columbian Exposition." Subtitles: objects, organization, places of meetings, suggestions for arrangement of congresses, explanatory. Unlike #2228, this item is undated. Rpt in #274.o.1. ©. (HU,MSL,SML)

2228.3 World's Congress Auxiliary. *...Opening of the World's Congresses of 1893*. Chicago: n.p., 1893.

22½x15½. 1 *l*. Folded sheet printed in black on front only. Dated : "Chicago, May 10, 1893." Invitation for the opening on "Monday morning, May 15th, at 10 o'clock." "By direction of the President. Clarence E. Young, Secretary." At top of caption title: "Not things, but Men." © (S)

2229.   WCA. *Original announcement* [1890]. (GLD,HU,MSL,SML) $22 - 45
▸Add cross-reference: Reprinted in #274.o.1.
---- Also found: No illus of Memorial Art Palace on last page and an extended title: *Original announcement of the object of this organization*.

2234.1 World's Congress Auxiliary. Young, Clarence E. *Not Things, But Men. Not Matter, But Mind. The World's Congresses of 1893. President, Charles C. Bonney*. N.p.: n.p., n.d.

11x16. Printed card, black ink one side only with facsimile of Young's signature. An otherwise blank card to be used for invitations and requests regarding the Congresses. (HU, WM)
---- Also found: On the above card, an invitation to the Dept of Literature to convene July 10, 1893. Purple typescript. © (WM)

2236.   WC of Architects. American Institute Architects. Stone. *Proceeding of the twenty-seventh annual*: (Col,KSU)

2237.   WC of Architects. Guastavino. *Lecture written for the congress of architects*: (CCA,UAH)
▸Add publisher: RPI. Reel 39, no 529. Subject: Architecture.

2238.   WC of Bankers. *World's Congress of Bankers and Financiers*: (GLD,Col,HML,NSW,Yale) $35 - 80
▸Add annotation: Addresses and papers given by such notables as Lyman J. Gage, William Jennings Bryan, and Mrs. Charles Henrotin. Henrotin spoke on "Women as Investors."

2241.1 World's Congress of Evolutionists. Skitton, James A. *Executive Committee of the World's Congress of Evolutionists*. New York: n.p., n.d.

28x20. Water-marked rag sheet, purple duplicating-ink typescript. Letter format stating that the Congress "is in contemplation and in course of active preliminary preparation, to be held in Chicago at a date not yet definitely determined..." Letterhead lists Dr. Lewis G. James, Chairman. ©(WM)

2242. WC of Homeopathic Physicians. Dudley. *Transactions of the World's Congress of homeopathic*: (CU,Stfd,Yale)

2244.1 World's Congress of Missions. Fisk, Mrs. Franklin W. Letter to members of mission societies. (Blank for date). Chicago.

28x21½. 1 *l*. Letter of invitation to members of all mission societies on a heavy white sheet with WCA/Woman's Branch letterhead. Pica typeset one side. Letter begins: "Dear (blank): The World's Congress of Missions, Auxiliary of the World's Columbian Exposition of 1893, is confidently expected to contribute." Mentions program content, plans to publish proceedings, and WCE meeting dates of Sept 29 to Oct 5. Fisk, Congress Chairman. (WM)

2245. World's Congress of Missions. Wherry, E.M., comp. *Missions at home and abroad. Papers and addresses presented at the World's congress of missions : October 2-4, 1893*. New York: American tract society, [ᶜ1895].

19x13. 486 p. Dark blue hc. E.M. Wherry was Corresponding Secretary of the Congress. ©. (NSW,NYPL)
▶Completed citation.

2248. WCR. Columbian Catholic Congress. Douglas. *Trade combinations and strikes*: (NDU)

2249. WCR. Columbian Catholic Congress. *Progress of the Catholic Church in America*: (CUA,MU)
---- Also found: 4th ed. 25½x18½. 2 vol in 1. Vol I: *l*, 467 p. + Vol II: 202 p.

2251. WCR. Columbian Catholic Congress. *The World's Columbian Catholic*: (GLD,CUA,E,MU,NDU,sfpl,slu) $24 - 60
---- Also found: Identical 3-vol-in-one version with: n.d.,[ᶜ1893 by J.S. Hyland & co.]. (GLD)

2253. WCR. Columbian Catholic Congress. *The World's Columbian Catholic Congresses*: (HU)
2254. WCR. *The Columbian Congress of the Universalist Church*: (HU,Yale)
2255. WCR. Hanson. *The Religions of the World*: (CU)

2254.1 World's Congress of Religions. Evangelical Alliance Congress. Taylor, Graham. *The sociological training of the ministry : Address delivered before The Evangelical Alliance Congress, at Chicago, October 13, 1893*. Chicago: n.p., 1893.

21x_. 20 p. Note that the Alliance Congress took place after the Association congress, #2254.2. (DC)

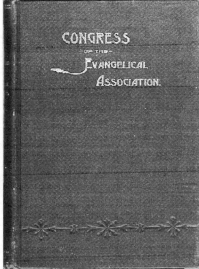

2254.2 World's Congress of Religions. Evangelical Association. Knobel, G.C., ed. *The congress of the Evangelical Association : A Complete Edition of the Papers Presented at its Sessions held at the art institute of Chicago : September 19–21, 1893*. Cleveland: Published by Thomas & Mattill, 1894 [ᶜ1894 by Thomas & Mattill].   P➔

21x15. (2)-333 p. Dark green cloth hc, gilt print and blind stamp design. Frontis of the 5 main organizers of the congress. An excellent history of the congress of religions and the Evangelical Assn are given pp 19-65. Port of Bonney on p (18). (GLD) $35 - 75

2256. WCR. Hanson. *The World's Congress of religions*:
(bgsu,CU,CUA,FM,HPL,HU,IWU,Knox,MOHx,NLA,OU,RU,slpl,slu,Stfd,UCD,UIC,UMD)
▶Add publisher: Grand Rapids, MI: P.D. Farrell, 1894.
▶Add publisher: Chicago: John W. Iliff & Co., 1894 [ᶜ1893 W.B. Conkey co.].

2257. WCR. McClure. *World's Fair Sermons by Eminent Divines*: (UIC)
2259. WCR. Mercer. *The New Jerusalem*: (HUL)
2260. WCR. Mercer. *Review of the World's Religious*: (HU,KCPL,NDU)

2262.   WCR. Savage. *The World's congress of religions*: (Yale)

2264.1 World's Congress of Representative Women. *...Department congress of the general federation of women's clubs...Thursday, May 18th, 1893.* Chicago: The Craig press, n.d.   P➔

  20½x15. (3) p. Folded sheet, back blank. C.t. At head of title: "World's congress of representative women under the auspices..." Program. Maud Howe Elliott spoke at the evening session. This Congress ran May 15 to 21, 1893. See #815.8 and #2442.1. ☺. (NHL)

2268.   WCRW. Sewall. *World's Congress of Representative Women*: (GBP,HML,MSL,NJHx,NSW,Smth,WML,Yale)
  ▸Add publisher: Beltsville, MD: NCR Corporation for the American Theological Library Association of Microtext, 1978. Microfiche. ATLA no F2106.

2268.1 World's Congress of Representative Women. *...Sunday evening concert.* N.p.: n.p., 1893?.

  20½x13. (4) p. Folded sheet. C.t. At head of title: "World's congress of Representative Women : May 15 to 21 inclusive, 1893. Memorial Art Palace, Michigan Ave., Foot of Adams St. : Chicago." Program of May 21, 1893, at the Memorial Art Palace's Hall of Columbus. ☺(GLD,S) $18 - 45

2269.   WCRW. *The World's congress of representative women*: (S)
  ▸Completed and corrected citation, including title capitalization: N.p.: n.p., n.d. 17½x12½. 1 *l* boilerplate, 5-30 p. Self-wraps, black print. C.t. Caption title on p 5: "The World's Congress of Representative Women, Chicago, May 15th to 21st, 1893. To the Representative Women of the World." Women's ports on 12 pages. Clarence E. Young's name subscribed on p 7.

2269.1 World's Congress of Representative Youth. Spalding, J[ohn] Lancaster. *Views of education. A paper read before the World's congress of representative youth in Chicago, July 18, 1893.* Rpt. from *Ave Maria*. Notre Dame, IN: Office of the "Ave Maria," n.d.

  21x14½. 18 p. Gray wraps with black print and border design. C.t. = t.p. ☺. (CUA)

2271.   World's Congress of the Deaf. *Proceedings of the World's congress of the deaf and the report of the fourth convention of the national association of the deaf, held at the memorial art palace. Chicago, Ill. : July 18th, 20th and 22nd, 1893.* N.p.: n.p., n.d.

  22x15. vii, (9)-282 p. ☺. (BM,UoC,Yale)   ▸Corrected and completed citation

2273.   WC on Ornithology. *Papers Presented to the World's Congress on Ornithology*: (CLP,CU,FM,UMN,UoA,Yale)

2275.1 World's Fisheries Congress. Smith, Hugh M., comp. *...The fisheries of Japan. By the Japanese bureau of agriculture.* Washington: GPO, 1894.

  29½x20. 1 *l* (t.p.), 419-38 p. Blue-flecked gray wraps with black print. C.t. = t.p. At head of title: "World's fisheries congress." Smith was US Fish Commissioner. Rpt of Article 45, Bulletin of the US Fish Commission. [See index under Fish Commission for related reports.] ☺(S)

2275.2 World's Fisheries Congress. Smith, Hugh M. *...Statistics of the fisheries of the United States.* Washington: GPO, 1894.

  29½x20. 1 *l* (t.p.), 389-417 p. Blue-flecked gray wraps with black print. C.t. = t.p. At head of title: "World's fisheries congress." Rpt of Article 44, Bulletin of the US Fish Commission. [See index under Fish Commission for related reports.] ☺(S)

2276.   World's Hort Cong. *Selection in seed growing, comprising papers read*: (HML)

2277. World's Lib Cong. ALA. Dewey. *Papers Prepared*: <small>Amh,CU,DC,HU,KCPL,MSU,NLA,S,SHB,Stfd,UCLA,UMA,UMC,UMN,UPa,UTA)</small>
▸Add cross-reference: See #718.3 for ALA papers and proceedings from this congress.

2279. WPR. Barrows. *Christianity the world-religion*: <small>(Amh,UMC)</small>

2281. WPR. Barrows. *The World's parliament of religions : An illustrated*: <small>(Amh,BRA,BU,CLP,CU,DC,ESU,FM,FPL,GU,HPL,
HU,IHi,IWU,Knox,LBA,LU,MIT,MU,NLA,NSW,SHB,slu,Smth,SPL,Stfd,UAB,UAH,UBO,UCD,UCLA,UI,UIC,UMA,UMC,UMD,UoA,UoC,USFr,UVM,VT,WML)</small>
▸Add publisher: Chicago: Library Resources Inc., 1970. Microfiche. LAC-20341 and LAC-20342.
▸Add publisher: Ann Arbor: UMI, 1976. "Religion in America." Reels 6:7 to 7:1.
▸Add publisher: Toronto: Hunter, Rose & Co., [ᶜ1893].

☞ The World's Parliament of Religions held a centennial meeting in Chicago in 1993. The Parliament papers are published in: *A Global Ethic : The Declaration of the Parliament of the World's Religions*. New York: Continuum, 1993. See #2382.3.

2284. WPR. Barrows. *The Parliament of Religions at*: ☺. (ICRL)   **P➔**
▸Corrected pub info and add size: New York London and Toronto: Funk & Wagnalls co., [1892?]. 23½x16.

2285. WPR. Barrows. *The religious possibilities of the World's Fair*: <small>(ICRL)</small>

2287. World's Parliament of Religions. Barrows, John Henry. *The World's first parliament of religions : Its Christian Spirit, Historic, Greatness and Manifold Results. A brief summary of testimonies gathered from many lands, indication what the world has said of this memorable...* Ed. George S. Goodspeed. Chicago: Hill & Shuman, Successors to the Parliament Publishing Co., [ᶜ1895 by Hill & Shuman]; Chicago: Library Resources Inc., 1970. Microfiche. LAC-40046.

19½x13½. 1 *l* (frontis port of Barrows), 62 p. ☺ (CUA,UAH,UoC)
▸Completed citation.

The Parliament of Religions
at the World's Fair

BY
Rev. JOHN HENRY BARROWS, D.D.
*Pastor of the First Presbyterian Church of Chicago and Chairman of the
General Committee on Religious Congresses*

REPRINTED FROM
THE MISSIONARY REVIEW OF THE WORLD,
JUNE, 1893

New York
FUNK & WAGNALLS COMPANY
London and Toronto

2289.1 World's Parliament of Religions. Brodbeck, Adolf. *Ein Tag im Religion-Parlament zu Chicago. Enthaltend die Reden des Hauptages nebst Kommentaren.* Bamberg: Druck und Verlag der Handels-Druckerei, [1895].

20x13. 124, (1) p. Ivory wraps, blue and silver ink, illus of globe on angel's back. Trans: "A day in the Parliament of Religions at Chicago. Containing the [eight] speeches from the important days with commentary." Brodbeck wrote one speech and provided commentary on the remainder. ☺. (HU)

2289.2 World's Parliament of Religions. Brown, Olympia. *Crime and the Remedy. An Address delivered before the Parliament of Religions at the Hall of Columbus, Art Institute, Chicago, September 22, 1893.* N.p.: n.p., n.d.; HULMS microfilm N.S. 1508 no. 7931.

__x__. (3) p. Folded sheet. Caption title. Discusses inherited tendencies for wrong doing. Remedy is women's emancipation to vote and make laws concerning families. Brown was a member of the Universalist Church. Original is at Radcliffe College. (Stfd)

2289.3 World's Parliament of Religions. Byrne, Tho[ma]s S[ebastian]. *Man : from a Christian point of view. Read before the Parliament of Religions in Chicago, September 13, 1893.* Cincinnati, OH: [Press of Robert Clarke & Co., ᶜ1893 by The very Rev. Thomas Sebastian Byrne, D.D.].

22½x15. 32 p. Sand colored wraps, black print. C.t. = t.p. ☺. (CUA)

2289.4 World's Parliament of Religions. Carus, Paul. *The dawn of a new era and other essays.* Chicago: The open court publishing co.; London: K. Paul, Trench, Trüber & co., ltd., 1899.

__x__. 50 p. Subject World's Parliament of Religions. Contains: "The dawn of a new religious era," "The new orthodoxy," and the late Professor [George John] Romanes's "Thoughts on religion."
---- Also found: *The dawn of a new religious era and other essays.* Rev and enlarged ed. Chicago [and] London: The Open Court publishing co., 1916 [ᶜ1916 by The Open Court publishing co.]. 20½x14½.

128, (3) p index. Brown cloth hc, gilt top edge, gilt cover and small rising sun design, gilt spine print. Description and impact of the Parliament of Religions. [Carus owned Open Court Publishing.] © (UoC)

2289.5 World's Parliament of Religions. Carus, Paul. *The World's Parliament of Religions.* __: __, 1896.

Folio. (HU)

2291. WPR. *The Gospel in pagan religions*: (UoC)

2293. WPR. Houghton. *Neely's history*: (GLD,BRA,BU,CU,HU,IHi,IWU,KCPL,MOHx,MU,NDU,NLA,OU,sfpl,slpl,UCD,UIC,UMD,UMN,UWM)
---- Also found: 5th ed. Chicago [and] New York: F. Tennyson Neely, Publisher, 1894. 22½x16½. 1 *l* frontis of Art Institute, (2) p, 1 *l* (port of Houghton), (2), 1001 p. Navy blue cloth hc, gilt print and blind stamped, marbled end papers. © (GLD) $40 - 75

2294. WPR. Jewish Denominational Cong. *Judaism at the World's*: (DC,LBA,Stfd)

2295. WPR. Jewish Women's Cong. *Papers of the Jewish*: (GLD,D,UMD)
▶Correct publisher: The Jewish publication society of America.
---- Also found: 268, (2) contents, (10) p book ads.

2296. WPR. Kuroda S[hinto]. *Outlines of the Mahâyâna*: (LBA,WM)   **P➜**

2297. WPR. Lorimer. *The Baptists in history : with an introduction*: © (UMN)
▶Completed citation: Printer is [Norwood Press, Boston]. 20x13. Maroon cloth hc, gilt spine. C.t.: "The Baptists in History."

2298. WPR. Mansfield. *Adventual essays delivered*: © (GLD) $30 - 65
▶Completed and corrected citation: 19x14. 1 *l* (frontis), iv, 1 *l* contents, (7)-154 p+ unpaged ports with tissue guards before each essay. Frontis: port with tissue guard of Rev. D.R. Mansfield, husband of the editor. Essays were given on Adventist Day at the Parliament, Sept 14, 1893. Dark brown cloth hc with gilt print. Gives history of the WCE Congresses, World's Parliament of Religions, and the Advent Christian Church, which believes in the prophetic second advent of Christ.

2300. WPR. Religious Congress for Friends. *Friends presentation of their faith*: (HUL)

2301.1 World's Parliament of Religions. Tomlins, William L. *Souvenir 1893 : World's Parliament of Religions.* N.p.: n.p., n.d.

8½x16. (24) p. Wraps, black print and illus of Art Institute where Congresses were held. C.t. Musical program given by Tomlins, head of WCE music, on Sept 27, 1893. © (Fess)

2303. WPR. United Brethren. *The church of the United Brethren in Christ*: (S)
---- Also found: 14½x9½. 50 p+ Shuey publishing ads inside both covers and outside back. Buff wraps, black print. (S)

2304. World's Railway Commerce Cong. *Addresses delivered before the*: (FPL,HML,HU,UAH,uiuc,UMN,UPa,UVM,VT,Yale)
▶Completed citation: Brown cloth hc, gilt spine print. No frontis. Terminal *l* is printed both sides.

2304.1 World's Railway Commerce Congress. Nimmo, Joseph, Jr. *The evolution of the American railroad system : an address by Joseph Nimmo, Jr., before the World's Congress Auxiliary of the World's Columbian Exposition of 1893 : delivered at Chicago, Ill., June 22, 1893.* [Washington, DC: n.p., ᶜ1893]; Woodbridge, CT: RPI, [1987?].

25x__. 41, (1) p. Dated on p (42): July 12, 1893. Part of "19th-century legal treatises," number 26116 in RPI. (HU,NDU,OU,UCLA,UH)

2304.2 World's Railway Commerce Congress. Walker, Aldace Freeman. See *Railway Review*, #1391.1, for her address before the Railway Congress.

2305.   World's Religious Parliament Extension. *The World's parliament of religions...a memorial*: (CU,NPG,UoC)

2306.   World's Religious Parliament Extension. *The World's Parliament of Religions*: (CU)

2308.   World's Temperance Cong. Stearns. *Temperance in all nations*: (WML)
▶Completed annotation: 24x16½. Vol 1: 475, 108 p. Vol 2: 434 p. Burgundy cloth hc, black print and design. The Society resolved on Sept 24, 1889, to have a Temperance Congress even before Chicago was chosen as the fair site.

2309.1 Żmigrodzki, Michal, comp. *Auxiliary : czyli : to kilkadziesiat kongresów odbytych w czasie kolumbijskiej wystawy w chicago 1893 roku.* Krakow [Poland]: Ksiegarnia Spolki Wydawniczey Polskiej, 1895.

24½x15½. (3), (5)-105 p. Light tan-flecked wraps. Black print on pulp paper. C.t. = t.p. Title trans: "An auxiliary : or : over one hundred congresses that took place during the Columbian Exposition in Chicago in 1893." Publication info: "Krakow: Association of Polish publishers, 1895." On p (3), the author thanks several people for taking him into their homes during the Congresses, primarily Fletcher Basset, Chairman of the International Congress of Folklorists. ©. (HU)

Chapter 14

RECENT BOOKS ABOUT THE WORLD'S COLUMBIAN EXPOSITION

There are several reasons why this is a much expanded chapter from the original 1992 bibliography. First, many of the general histories of Chicago and Illinois were reviewed for WCE content. Most described and commented on the fair. Not all histories are listed, so the citations given here should be considered examples. Second, many people are still writing about the WCE or describing some facet of its impact. And third, centennial celebrations of the Columbian Exposition and the centenary of the World's Parliament of Religions were held in Chicago in 1993; they produced a wealth of written comparisons, reports, and analyses.

In this chapter, sources listed are only a sample listing, and the number of source locators listed for a citation may not reflect the relative scarcity of an item; not all of our old sources were checked for recent book acquisitions, especially for books cataloged under subjects other than World's Columbian Exposition.

For this chapter only, shortened forms of publishers' names (see *MLA Handbook*) are used when it should not impair locating a publication in one of the resources, for example, *Books in Print*.

2309.2 Adams, Henry. *The education of Henry Adams : An Autobiography.* Boston and New York: Houghton Mifflin co., [°1918 by the Massachusetts Historical Society].

24x17½. x, 519, (1) p. Historian who reminisces about his visit to the WCE, chap 22, pp 339-43.
---- 1927 rpt: 20x14. x, 517 p. Royal blue cloth blind stamped hc, gilt spine print.
---- 1931 rpt: New York: Modern Library, [°1931]. 17x__. x, (v)-x, 517 p.
---- 1942 rpt: Boston: Printed for the members of the Limited editions club at the Merrymount press, 1942. 27x__. xvii, 485, (1) p. 1500 copies
---- 1945 rpt: [New York]: Editions for the Armed Services, Inc., [1945]. 12x17. 510 p.
---- 1973 rpt: Ed. and introd. Ernest Samuels. xxx, 705 p. Gray cloth hc with gray, burgundy, blue print and black design.
☺ (sfsu,Stfd,USFr)

☞ This is considered by many to be one of the finest autobiographies of Western literature. It details the author's varied and influential career and has been reprinted many times.

2310.   Adamms. *Twenty Years at Hull-House*: (GMU,NPG,UMA,UTA)
---- Also found: New York: Penguin, °1981. Signet Classic paperback. 18x10½. xviii, 19-320 p.

2310.1 Aimone, Linda, and Carlo Olmo. *Le esposizioni universali 1851–1900 : il progresso in scena.* [Torino, Italy]: Umberto Allemandi & C., [°1990].

30½x22½. 3 *l*, (9)-232 p, 2 *l*. Light teal blue paper cover boards, black spine print. Light teal blue dj. Italian text. Series half title: "Archivi di Arti Decorative." Architecture of the various fairs during this period is compared. WCE bibliography pp 218-19. Also a complete chronological listing and summary description of international and industrial fairs from 1756 to 1915. [Prior to 1851, there were industrial fairs only.] ☺ (SML)   [about $60] 90,000 Lire

2310.2 Albers, Donald J., G[erald] L. Alexanderson, and Constance Reid. *International Mathematical Congresses : an illustrated history : 1893–1986.* Rev. ed. [New York]: Springer-Verlag, [°1987 by Springer-Verlag].

28x21½. 64 p. Illus, ports. The first mathematical congresses were held at the WCE, pp 2-3. ☺ . (LHL)

2311.1 Allwood, John. *The Great Exhibitions.* London: Studio Vista, [°1977 Allwood].

28x23. 192 p. B/w and color illus. Gray-green paper covered boards. Frontis cartoon illus from *Puck* is the magazine's humorous idea of how the Chicago WF would look. Chap 6, pp 75-94, is entitled "Eiffel's Tower and Chicago's White City." ☺ (SML,VAM)

2311.2 *The American renaissance : 1876–1917.* New York: Brooklyn Museum (Distributed by Pantheon Book), [°1979 Brooklyn Museum].

31x24. 232 p. Illus, four folding, some colored. Cream cloth spine and paper covered boards, gilt print. C.t. = t.p. References to the influence of WCE on art and architecture are scattered throughout. A folding panorama plate of the Court of Honor on p 17. © (UNM)

2312.1 American Society of Mechanical Engineers. *Chapin Mine pumping engine : National Historic Mechanical Engineering Landmark, June 6, 1987, Iron Mountain, Michigan.* [New York: ASME?, 1987].

28x__. (6) p. Fold sheet. Illus and ports. Mentions Edwin Reynold's design of the Reynolds-Corliss horizontal quadruple expansion engine which lit thousands of 16-candle power lamps at the WCE. (HML)

2312.2 *The American Urban Experience.* Videocassette. Rotch Visual Collections, Massachusetts Institute of Technology, 1983. 27 min.

Series "Understanding Cities." Includes WCE impact on layout and architecture of American cities. (ref)

2313.   Andersen. *70 år tilbakeblikk*: (UBO)

2313.1 Anderson, H. Allen. *The Chief : Ernest Thompson Seton and the Changing West.* College Station: Texas A&M UP, [ᶜ1986].

23x16. xii, 363 p. Black cloth hc, silver spine print; black dj, red and white print, Seton port. Frontis port of Seton. Impact on Seton of his one day trip to WCE and Wild West Congress, pp 44-48. (ref)

☞ Seton, founder of the American Boy Scouts, was an artist of western life, illustrator, lecturer, and author of beloved wild life stories.

2314.   Anderson and Brown. *Ferris wheels*: (KCPL,PPL,slpl,VT)

2314.1 Anderson, Norman D. *Ferris Wheels : An Illustrated History.* Bowling Green, OH: Bowling Green State U Popular P, [ᶜ1992].

28x24. ii, 407 p. Illus. Beige glossy wraps, brown and red print, illus of the Ferris wheel. (ESU,EvP,GPL,HML,HU,Knox,S)

2314.2 Anderson, Philip J., and Dag Blanck, eds. *Swedish-American life in Chicago : cultural and urban aspects of an immigrant people, 1850–1930.* Urbana, IL: U of Illinois P, ᶜ1992.

24x__. xii, 394 p. Illus. Hc. Articles by many authors. Swedish WCE contributions described. (Knox)

2315.   Applebaum: (APL,bgsu,CCA,CLP,Col,CUA,CU,CUE,cul,CWM,DC,EPL,EvP,FLP,FM,GBP,GPL,HML,HU,IHi,ISU,KSU,LL,LU,MH,MIT,MSI,NDU,NPG, NSW,NUL,PPL,RPL,sapl,sfsu,slcl,Smth,Stfd,UAB,UAT,UCB,UCLA,UdM,UH,UIC,uiuc,UMA,UMD,UMN,UoA,UPa,UTA,VCU,VT,Yale)

2315.1 Atmananda [P.M.]. *Cicago prashnottari; or Questions and answers on Jainism for the Parliament of religions held at Chicago, U.S.A. in 1893.* ___: ___, 1905.

24x__. 8, 110, (1) p. Port. Subject: Jainism Congresses at the World's Parliament of Religions, Chicago 1893. Text in Sanskrit; introd in English and Sanskrit. Atmananda lived 1836–96.
---- Also found: Agra: Printed by Pt. Khayali Ram, 1918. (2), vi, 214, (4) p. Ports, plates. (UoC,UPa)

2315.2 Babst, Earl D., and Lewis G. Vander Velde, eds. *Michigan and the Cleveland era : Sketches of University of Michigan Staff Members and Alumni Who Served the Cleveland Administrations : 1885–89, 1893–97.* Ann Arbor: U of Michigan P, 1948 [ᶜ1948 U of Michigan P].

23½x16. xi, (2) p, 1 *l* (port of Cleveland), (3)-372 p. Blind-stamped navy blue cloth hc, gilt spine print. Illus end papers. Biography no 9 is of Thomas W. Palmer, class of 1849, president of the WCC. No 14 is of Edwin Willits, class of 1855, head of the WCE govt exhibits. © (GLD)

2316.   Badger. *The Great American Fair*: (Amh,APL,bgsu,BPL,CC,CCA,Col,CSL,CU,CUA,cul,CWM,DC,EPL,ESU,EvP,FLP,FM,FU,GBP,GU,HML, HPL,HU,IHi,IStU,ISU,IWU,KCPL,Knox,KSU,LL,LU,MH,MIT,MOHx,MSI,NDU,NLA,NPG,OU,PPL,RPL,RU,sapl,sfpl,sfsu,slcl,slpl,slu,Smth,SPL,Stfd,UAH,UAT, UCB,UCD,UCI,UCLA,UdM,UGa,UH,UIC,uiuc,UMA,UMC,UMD,UMN,UNO,UoA,UPa,USFr,UTA,UVM,UWM,VCU,WM,Yale)

2317.   Badger. *The World's Columbian Exposition: patterns of change*: (HML,UCLA)

2317.1 Baedeker, Karl, ed. *The United States : With an Excursion into Mexico : A Handbook for Travelers : 1893.* Rpt. New York: Da Capo, 1971.

__x__. cvlii, 516 p. Blue cloth hc, gilt print, color dj. Folding color map of Chicago showing Jackson Park and WCE, but it contains no other WCE content. (ref,S)
---- Also found: Original 1893 edition in its red cloth flexible cover. (ref) $150 - 270

2318. Baker, C. *Life and character of William Taylor Baker*: (CU,DC,HU,IHi,S,Stfd,UCLA,UIC,UMN,UoA)

2318.1 Baker, Paul R. *Richard Morris Hunt.* Cambridge, MA [and] London: MIT Press, [c1980, 1986].

Paperback [First paperback ed 1986]: 25½x17½. xvi, 588 p. Tan glossy wraps, illus of Victorian house. Hunt was designer of the Admin Bldg; his involvement with WCE is scattered throughout. (ref)

2319.1 Bay, J. Christian. *History* [of the Field Museum]. Chicago: John Crerar Library, 1929.

28x21½. 5, 7, 16, 7, 16, 11, 47 p, 3 *l* appendix. Typescript copy. Describes other museums and WCE influence on saving exhibits and documents. F.W. Putnum, chief of the WCE Dept of Ethnology, suggested a Chicago museum, which was then funded by Marshall Field, retail magnate. Also describes some of the early exhibits obtained from the WCE. ☺ (FM)

2320. Beachboard. *United States Postal Card Catalog*: (GLD,S)
---- Also found 1980 ed: "35th Anniversary Edition." White wraps, purple and yellow print. Special appendix of exposition postal cards.
---- Also found 1970 ed: "25th Anniversary Edition." White wraps, blue and yellow print. Special appendix of exposition postal cards.

2321. Beer. *The mauve decade : American life*: ☺ (GLD,Stfd) $10 - 25
▶Add original publisher: New York: Alfred A. Knopf, 1926 [c1926 by Knopf]. 268, (1) p printer's info. Mauve paper covered boards, tan cloth spine. Title labels on spine and cover. (GLD)
---- Also found: New York: Vintage Books, [1961, c1926 by Knopf, renewed 1954 by Alice Beer, c1960 by Random House]. Introd. Frank Freidel. 18½x11. xxii, 1 *l*, 193 p, vi index, (1) p bio. Orange and mauve wraps with b/w print. (GLD)
---- Also found: Armed Services ed. 10x14. 256 p. (Stfd)

☞ Knopf published the first edition; Garden City published the reprint. The book describes WCE personalities and their impact on the period. The "Mauve Decade" is a reference to heavy use of purple and lavender hues in Impressionist paintings in the "Gay '90s."

2321.1 Beloit College. *Treasures of Beloit College : A 100 Works from the Logan Museum of Anthropology and the Wright Museum of Art.* Beloit, WI: Beloit College P, [c1995 Board of Trustees of Beloit College].

21x27. 99 p. Color glossy stiff wraps, photo repro of engraved limestone rock. Logan Museum is named for Frank G. Logan, Chicago businessman, who outbid other Chicago men for the Horatio N. Rust collection of American Indian artifacts exhibited at the WCE. Lucius Fisher, Jr., son of one of the College's founders, outbid museums for the collection of accurate casts of famous Greek statues made by the Greek government for exhibit at the WCE and now housed in the Wright Museum. The book is a catalog of the best items from these two collections. ☺ (BCL)

2321.2 Benedict, Burton. *The anthropology of : World's fairs : San Francisco's Panama Pacific : international exposition of 1915.* London and Berkeley: The Lowie museum of anthropology, [c1983 by the Regents of the U of California].

35x23. xv, 175, (1) p. Illus, some colored. White cloth hc, gilt spine print, dj. Although the major emphasis is on the 1915 fair, there are anthropological references to many WFs, including scattered WCE references and comparisons. ☺ (GLD,MSI) $35 - 70

2321.3 Berger, Miles L. *They built Chicago : Entrepreneurs Who Shaped a Great City's Architecture.* Chicago: Bonus Books, [c1992 Bonus Books].

28½x23. 2 *l*, (v)-xxxii, 459 p. No frontis. Black paper covered boards, silver spine print; glossy dj with color panoramic photo of downtown Chicago. End papers with Pierson Graphics Corp. bird's-eye panorama of downtown Chicago. Segments on various businesses with biographies of entrepreneurs; mention of WCE developers is scattered throughout. © (ref)

2321.4 Berghoff Restaurant. *Berghoff* [menu]. Chicago?: Berghoff, 1995?

34x19. Folded stiff leaf with repro of the R. Mark Melnick painting of the restaurant at 17 West Adams in Chicago. Melnick also painted a large triptych of the WCE Court of Honor, which is prominently displayed along with other WCE murals and photos on both the main floor and basement. Berghoff beer was introduced to Chicago at the WCE in 1893; the popular restaurant opened in 1898. © (GLD)

2321.5 Beversluis, Joel D[iederik], ed. *A SourceBook for the Community of Religions*. Chicago: Council for a Parliament of the World's Religions, 1993 [ᶜ1993 Council for a Parliament of the World's Religions].

28x21½. xii, 240 p. No frontis. Yellow and gray glossy stiff wraps, black print. Includes plans for the 1993 Centennial Parliament to be held in Chicago. History of the 1893 Parliament. Includes papers submitted by religious leaders. © (EvP,PPL)

2322.   Bigler, Brian J., and Lynn Martinson Mudrey. *The Norway building of the 1893 Chicago World's fair : A Buildings Journey From Norway to America: An Architectural Legacy*. [Blue Mounds, WI: Little Norway, ᶜ1992].

28x21½. 88 p. Glossy green stiff wraps, illus of Norway Bldg. Includes many illus and bibliographic index. See Norway, #624. © (GLD)   ▶Completed post-publication citation.

2322.1 Billington, Ray Allen. *Frederick Jackson Turner : historian, scholar, teacher*. New York: Oxford UP, 1973 [ᶜ1973 by Billington].

23½x16½. 3 *l*, v-x, (2) p, 1 *l*, 3-599. Tan cloth hc, royal blue and rust spine print. Dark gray dj with port of Turner in blue ink, cream and gray lettering. Turner gave his landmark paper, "Significance of the Frontier in American History," at the Historical Congress. Book describes the events leading up to Turner's presentation (pp 124-31). See #1225 of this supplement. (OU,ref)

2322.2 Blaser, Werner, ed. *Chicago Architecture : Holabird & Root : 1880–1992*. Basel-Boston-Berlin: Birkhäuser Verlag, [ᶜ1992 Birkhäuser Verlag Basel].

23½x25. 192 p. Gray cloth hc, red print, no design. Text in English and German. Chap 3 is entitled: "The World's Columbian Exposition: Use of Eclectic Themes." © . (KSU)

2322.3 Blaugrund, Annette. *Paris 1889 : American Artists at the Universal Exposition*. New York: Henry N. Abrams, [ᶜ1989 Pennsylvania Academy of the Fine Arts].

29x23½. 304 p. Blind-stamped blue cloth hc, silver spine print; glossy color illus dj with black print. Several comparisons to the WCE with WCE illus. © (S)

2322.4 Bloch, Robert. *American Gothic*. New York: Simon & Schuster, 1974.

21½x14½. 222 p. Orange cloth hc, white spine print. Dj. A mystery novel set at the WCE. (ref)

2323.   Bloom, Sol. *The autobiography of Sol Bloom*. New York: G.P. Putnam's Sons, [ᶜ1948].

22x15. 4 *l*, 345 p. Frontis port of Bloom. Red-brown cloth hc, gilt print and facsimile of Bloom's autograph. His WCE activities scattered throughout. See #1083. © (CHx,Stfd,UTA)   ▶Completed citation.

2323.1 Boas, Franz. *Anthropometry of central California*. Rpt. New York: American Museum of Natural History, 1905.

25x16. 347-80 p + 9 unpaged plates on glossy stock. Gray-flecked wraps, black print. Caption title. C.t.: "The Huntington California Expedition. Anthropometry of Central California." Rpt from the *Bulletin of the American Museum of Natural History*, vol 17 pt 4, 1905. Boas writes about the anthropometrical investigation of V.K. Chestnut in 1892 and 1893, which was carried out for Professor F.W. Putnam, WCE Anthropological Dept. Huntington appears in the c.t. because, in the same article, Boas also writes about that expedition of 1899 and 1900. © (OU)

2323.2 Boland, Charles Michael. *Ring in the jubilee : The Epic of America's Liberty Bell.* Riverside, CT: Chatham press, [°1973 by Boland].

23x15½. 3 *l*, 7-128 p with b/w illus. Frontis of Independence Hall. Red, white, and blue glossy wraps; illus of Liberty Bell. Describes the Liberty Bell in the Pennsylvania Bldg of the WCE and at other fairs, as well as the 1893 Columbian Liberty Bell (replica). See #828. © (GLD,NDU)

☞ The new Columbian Liberty Bell was rung in front of the Administration Building on Chicago Day, October 9, 1893, and for many other special occasions. See #1228.1.

2323.3 Bolotin, Norman, and Christine Laing. *The Chicago World's fair of 1893 : The World's Columbian exposition.* Washington, DC: Preservation Press, [°1992].

29x22½. x, 166 p. Red cloth hc, gilt print; illustrated glossy dj. Nostalgic journey through the WCE with many illus. © (GLD,BPL,CCA,csuf,CU,DC,FM,GBP,HU,IHi,LL,MH,MIT,MOHx,MSI,OU,S,sfsu,slpl,StLa,TD,UGa,UIC,uiuc,UMC,UMD,UMN)

2324.   Bolton. *A model*: (Amh,BU,DC,HU,Smth,UVM)
▶Additional info: Olive-green cloth hc, white print and black design. His visit to WCE pp 129-97.

2324.1 Bomar, William J. *Postal Markings of U.S. Expositions.* ___: David G. Phillips Publishing Co., 1986?

25½x18. 224 p. Hc and softbound editions. (ref)
---- Also found: Rev. ed. Tampa, FL: BJB Publishing, 1996? 28x21½. 278 p. An illustrated price guide. Furnished unbound.

2325.1 *The Books of the fairs : Materials about World's Fairs, 1834–1916, in the Smithsonian Institution Libraries.* Chicago and London: American Library Association, 1992.

28x21½. (4), v-xx, 268 p. Blue linen hc, silver print. Introd essay by Robert W. Rydell, who wrote #2419 and #2420. Includes their extensive WCE collection. © (csuf,CU,HML,S,SI,Stfd,WM)

2325.2 Bordaz, Robert, et. al., comp. *Le livre des expositions universelles : 1851–1989.* [Paris: Musée des arts décoratifs, °1983 - Union Centrale des Arts Décoratifs].

30x22½. 351 p. Illus. Cobalt shading into light blue cover. Trans: The book of World's expositions 1851–1989. In addition to fair histories, including the WCE (pp 93-98), this book proposes a centennial of the 1889 Paris Expo (starting p 330). See #2355 and #2421.4 for other WF anthologies. (BRA,WM)

2325.3 Boyer, Paul. *Urban Masses and Moral Order in America, 1820–1920.* Cambridge, MA and London: Harvard UP, [°1978].

23½x15½. xvi, 1 *l*, 387 p. Paperback wraps with white print and illus of city tenements. C.t. = t.p. WCE references throughout. Boyer's thesis is that the WCE atmosphere and purity were the hopeful moral bright spots at the end of the 19th century; interest and unity generated by the WCE resulted in moral utopia separate from highlights such as the architecture and invention of the midway. (ref)

2325.4 Brandon, Ruth. *The Life and many deaths of Harry Houdini.* New York: Random, [°1993 by Brandon].

24x16½. x, 355, (2) p. Maize paper covered hc, red cloth spine. Red and caramel dj with red, black, white print and b/w port of Houdini in locked chains. At age 19, Houdini (born Ehrich Weiss) "booked at Kohl and Middleton's dime museum on the Midway at the" WCE. He performed 20 shows a day for $12/week with his brother Theodore (p 37). See #2427.1 [Kohl's was in downtown Chicago.] © (ref)

2327.   Broun. *American Painting and Sculpture in the Fine Arts Building*: (DU,NAG,NPG,SAL)

2327.1 Brown, Julie K. *Contesting images : Photography and the World's Columbian Exposition.* Tucson & London: U of Arizona P, [°1994 by Arizona Board of Regents].

28½x22. xvi, 1 *l*, 3-185, (1) p author bio. Illus and maps. Brown cloth hc, gilt spine print. Cream glossy dj, brown and black print; positive and negative image of WCE building in lavender tones. WCE photography other than the official C.D. Arnold photography concession. Also, social aspects of US history, 19th century.

---- Also found: Wraps version. Same paging. Same cover design and color as hc dj. $10 - 35

☺ . (GLD,Amh,APL,BPL,BU,CCA,CU,CWM,DC,EvP,FM,HML,HU,IHi,IStU,KCPL,KSU,MH,MIT,OU,PPL,RPL,RU,sapl,SHB,slcl,Smth,SPL,Stfd,UCD,UIC,uiuc, UMA,UMC,UMD,UMN,UoC,UVM,VCU)

2328.   Brown. *Altgeld of Illinois*: (Smth,Stfd)

2328.1 Buffalo Bill Memorial Museum. *Buffalo Bill's Wild West.* [Lookout Mountain, CO: Buffalo Bill Memorial Museum], n.d.

27½x20½. (12) p. Illus. Muted color wraps depicting Buffalo Bill riding the prairie on his horse. The full program for "Buffalo Bill's Wild West and congress of rough riders of the world. Chicago Columbian exposition 1893" is found on p (12). A museum informational handout. [See index under Buffalo Bill for related Cody items.] ☺ (GLD)

2328.2 Bullard, Thomas R. *The Columbian intramural railroad: A Pioneer Elevated Line.* Oak Park, IL: [Thomas R. Bullard], 1987.

21½x14. 19 p. Illus by author. Pistachio green wraps with black print. Bullard was a noted railroad aficionado who wrote many publications. Excellent description of the intramural railroad construction and exhibit. [See also Intramural RR in index.]. ☺ (GLD,FM,UIC,uiuc) $6 - 12

2329.   Burg. *Chicago's white city of 1893*: (Amh,APL,bgsu,BPL,BrU,CCA,Col,CU,CUA,CUE,CWM,DC,DU,ESU,EvP,FLP,FM,FU,GBP,GU,HML, HU,IStU,ISU,KSU,Knox,LL,LU,MH,MIT,MOHx,MSI,MSU,MU,NDU,NLA,nmsu,NPG,PPL,RPL,RU,sapl,sfsu,SHB,slcl,slu,Smth,SPL,Stfd,StLa,UAH,UAT,UCB,UCI, UCLA,UdM,UH,UIC,uiuc,UMA,UMC,UMD,UMN,UNO,UoA,UPa,URI,USFr,UTA,UWM,UVM,VT,WMwsu,Yale)

2330.   Burnham. *Final Official Report*: (Amh,CCA,CUA,CU,CUE,cul,CWM,FLP,FM,HML,HU,IHi,KSU,LU,MH,MIT,MSI,NDU,NUL,OU,PSU,SHB, Stfd,UBO,UCB,UCLA,UGa,UIC,uiuc,UMD,UMN,UoC,UPa,UTA,UWM,VT) $275

☞ A facsimile copy of the original 8 vol report deposited in the library of the Art Institute of Chicago.

2330.1 Burnham, Daniel H., and Edward H. Bennett. *Plan of Chicago : prepared under the direction of : the commercial club : during the years MCMVI, MCMVII, MCMVIII.* Chicago: The Commercial Club, 1909 [ᶜ1908 by the Commercial Club of Chicago.] Rpt. as *Plan of Chicago.* Ed. Charles Moore. Introd. William R. Hasbrouck. New York: Da Capo press, 1970 [ᶜ1970 Da Capo Press].

Rpt: 32x24½. i-viii (new t.p. plus intro), i-xviii, 1*l*, 164, (1) p. Hc. T.p. in red and black. Color plates and architectural plans, some folding. WCE content scattered pp 4-120. ☺ (WM)

2332.1 Carlton, Donna. *Looking for Little Egypt.* Bloomington, IN: IDD Books, ᶜ1994.

28x__. 103 p. History of the belly dance in US history; includes WCE description. (UoC)

2332.2 Carter, Robin Borglum. *Gutzon Borglum : his life and work.* [Austin, TX: Eakin Press, ᶜ1998]

28x21½. (3)-95 p. Stiff card wraps, red and black print and illus of Borglum and head of Lincoln from Mt. Rushmore, SD. C.t. = t.p. Illus bio of sculptor Borglum whose most famous work is the 4 Presidents at Mt. Rushmore. He exhibited a bronze, "Indian Scouts," illus on p (18), at the WCE Fine Arts Palace, Group 139. Carter is Borglum's granddaughter. ☺ (GLD)

☞ The Borglum Historical Center in Keystone, South Dakota, in the Black Hills contains many of Borglum's studies and works including the WCE "Indian Scouts" bronze in the lobby. He won a gold medal at the St. Louis 1904 World's Fair for the sculpture "Return of the Boer."

2332.3 Cassell, Frank A. *A confusion of voices : reform movements and the World's Columbian Exposition of 1893.* [Milwaukee: Golda Meir Library, U of Wisconsin, 1984?].

28x21½. 30 *l*. Fromkin Memorial Lecture of Nov 7, 1984. Subject: Social movements—U.S. See #2337.1. (MU)

2332.4 Caughey, John Walton. *Hubert Howe : Bancroft : Historian of the West.* Berkeley and Los Angeles: U of California, 1946 [ᶜ1946 by the regents of the U of California].

23x16. ix, 2 *l*, 422 p. Blue cloth hc, gilt print and design of prospectors. Yellow/blue/brown dj, brown print. Frontis port of Bancroft. Pp 326-29, describes Bancroft's his deep interest in the WCE, his *The Book of the Fair* (#733), and its folio editions. Also discusses F. Turner (#1225, #2322.1). (ref)

2332.5 Çelik, Zeynep. *Displaying the orient : architecture of Islam at nineteenth-century world's fairs.* Berkeley, Los Angeles, Oxford: U of California P, [ᶜ1992 by Regents of the U of California].

26x18½. xv, (1), 245 p, 1 *l*. Glossy dj with b/w illus of 1878 Paris Expo Algerian Palace on buff background; white print on blue block upper left. Light tan cloth hc, black spine print. Islamic cultures at WFs, focusing on architecture of their pavilions. WCE scattered pp 4-174 with many illus. Series: Comparative Studies on Muslim Societies, 12. ☺ (WM)

2332.6 *The centennial history of Illinois.* 5 vol. Springfield: Illinois centennial commission, 1920 [ᶜ1920 by Illinois centennial commission].

ca 23x17. All vols: maroon cloth hc, gilt design and spine lettering. The social and political impact of the WCE is described in vols 4 and 5. ☺ (CU,Heb,Knox,LU)
Vol. 4: Bogart, Ernest Ludlow, and Charles Manfred Thompson. *The industrial state 1870–1893.* 3 *l*, (7) p, 1 *l*, 553 p. Frontis: Court of Honor at the WCE.
Vol. 5: Bogart, Ernest Ludlow, and John Mabry Mathews. *The modern commonwealth 1893–1918.* 3 *l*, (6) p, 1 *l*, 544 p.

2332.7 *A Challenge to Civic Pride : a plea for the preservation and rehabilitation of : the fine arts building : of the World's Columbian exposition.* Chicago?: n.p., [1922].

21x15½. 15 p. Beige wraps, black print. Illus copyrighted by Riel Studio, Chicago. A booklet distributed by a group of Chicago organizations in response to a movement by the board of South Park Commissioners to destroy the Fine Arts Bldg. ☺ . (IHi)

2332.8 Chandler, Daniel Ross. *Toward Universal Religion : Voices of American and Indian Spirituality.* Westport, CT [and] London: Greenwood Press, [ᶜ1996 by Chandler].

23x16½. xxxiii, 1 *l*, 240 p, 1 *l*. Dark blue cloth hc, gilt print. Extensive description of spiritual leaders from India who presented papers at the Parliament of Religions, WCE, 1893. ☺ (sfsu,UoC)

2333. Chappell. *The Chicago World's Fair* [filmstrip]: (CCA,CU,Knox,UIC)
▶Add: This work is in 2 parts: A 35 mm filmstrip and an audiocassette. Filmstrip originally made at De Paul U by Chappell; commercially available from George W. Colburn Laboratory, Chicago, 1977. The cassette is the accompanying soundtrack for the film.
---- Also found: Reissued in a 16½-minute videocassette on the occasion of the WCE centennial.

2333.1 Chatfield-Taylor, H[obart] C. *Chicago.* Boston and New York: Houghton Mifflin, 1917 [ᶜ1917 by Hobart C. Chatfield-Taylor and Lester G. Hornby].

26x18. viii, 2 *l*, 3-128, (2) p. Many interspersed unpaged plates of illus, each has a tissue guard with letterpress. Tan paper covered boards, ornate gilt design and print, black vignette of Chicago city street, gilt top edge, rough-cut fore and bottom edges. One of 1000 copies. GLD copy inscribed by the author. Tipped-in color frontis of Rush Street. T.p. printed in red and black inks. WCE and its aftermath are described in chap 4, "The South Side." Author's reminiscences of life in Chicago. ☺ (GLD,BPL,FPL,Knox)

2333.2 Cheney, Margaret. *Tesla : Man : Out of Time.* [New York]: Laurel (Dell), [1983, ᶜ1981 by Cheney].

17½x10½. xvi, 320 p + (8) p of glossy photo illus at center book. Glossy black stiff paperback with white print and illus of Tesla. The original publisher was Prentice-Hall. Detailed account of Nikola Tesla's amazing career as inventor of radio and 60 cycle polyphase electrical power and motors. He is also depicted as a philosopher, visionary, and Serbian poet. He gave high voltage demonstrations at the WCE, exhibited models there of his electrical inventions, and spoke at the Electrical Congress on April 25, 1893 (pp 72-75). His WF models are on exhibit in the Tesla Museum in Belgrade (p 279). ☺ (GLD)
----Also found: Rpt. New York: Barnes and Noble, [ᶜ1981 by Cheney : 1993 Barnes and Noble].
21½x15. xvi, 320 p. Blue paper-covered boards with black cloth spine, gilt spine print. Blue dj with white and yellow print and port of Tesla in his laboratory. (ref)

2334.   *Chicago and its two fairs*:   (CCA,EvP,GBP,HML,HU,IHi,S)

2334.1 Chicago Daily News. Pike, Claude O., ed. ...*The Chicago Daily News almanac and year book for 1933 : with World's Fair Guide and : Buyer's Classified Directory*. Chicago: Chicago Daily News, ᶜ1932.

19x13. lxvi ads, 891 p, lxvii-lxxxi ads, (2) p ads + ads printed inside both wraps. Blue-green stiff wraps, illus of WF bldg, black print. At head of title: "[Forty-ninth year]." Pulp text except pp 29-92 printed on pink stock; illus description of Century of Progress and WCE on these pages. ☺ (GLD) $16 - 38

2334.2 Chicago Department of Cultural Affairs. *Chicago '93 : Celebrating the Past : Creating the Future*. Chicago: Department of Cultural Affairs, 1993?

30½x20½. 16 p. Colorful stiff wraps with stylized graphic image of the Statue of the Republic. C.t. Issued for Chicago schools as a children's activity book commemorating the WCE. Stylized map of the WCE grounds on the back cover. Mayor Richard Daley's message on p 1. One of many centennial activities advertised under the logo "Chicago '93." See #1269.2 for their magazine. ☺ (GLD,S,UIC)

2334.3 Chicago Historical Society. *The World's Columbian Exposition : A Nostalgic Exhibit*. Rpt. N.p: [Chicago Historical Society], 1953.

18½x11½. Pp 193-224. Tan glossy wraps, brown print, illus of Mayor Harrison opening the Fair. From *Chicago History*, 3.7 (1953). Issued to celebrate the 60ᵗʰ anniversary of the WCE. (MSI)

2334.4 Chicago Public Library. *Seven Days at the Fair: A Celebration of the World's Columbian Exposition*. Chicago: Chicago Public Library, n.d.

21½x28. 36 p. White stiff wraps with black print and color illus of the Court of Honor by Nichols. Illus catalog of their centennial exhibit in Special Collections from May 1 to Dec 31, 1993. ☺ (GLD,CPL)

2334.5 *Chicago Symphony Orchestra : 1992–93 Season*. [Chicago]: n.p., [1992?].

22½x14. 90 p. Color glossy wraps with illus of current Symphony Hall. "Spring 1993." "Music At The 1893 World's Columbian Exposition" by Ezra Schabos, pp 52, 54, 90, with illus of the interior of the WCE Music Hall. ☺ (S)

2334.6 Chicago Tribune. *A century of tribune editorials*. N.p.: Chicago Tribune, [ᶜ1947 by Tribune company].

21½x15½. (14), 156 p. Maroon stiff wraps, gray print on buff block. C.t. = t.p. Issued for the centennial of the founding of the newspaper, this book reprints 100 of its top editorials including "The opening of the fair : May 2, 1893" (pp 63-64). ☺ (GLD) $8 - 24
---- Also found: Rpt. of 1970. 156 p. (GPL)

2334.7 Chicago Tribune. *Pictured encyclopedia of the World's greatest newspaper; a handbook of the newspaper as exemplified by the Chicago tribune—issued to commemorate its eightieth birthday*. Chicago: Chicago Tribune, [ᶜ1928].

19x11. 2 *l*, 790 p. Illus. (ICRL)

2334.8 ...*Chicago's century of progress*. Chicago: Rand McNally, ᶜ1933 by Rand McNally.

32x25. 32 p. Illus are b/w and color. Tan wraps, cover blocked in blue and orange, deco style horse and rider. At head of title: "1833–1933." WCE Court of Honor text and illus p 20. ☺ (GLD)

2334.9 Cinkovich, Brenda Dianne. "The gallery of honor in the woman's building at the 1893 Columbian exposition: successes and failures." MA diss. Illinois State U, 1994.

28x21½. 2 *l* (purpose), 2 *l* (t.p. and approval p), i-iii, 1-147 p numbered one side. Tipped-in b/w glossy photographs pp 115-30. The Gallery of Honor was intended to present to the world the artistic achievements of women. Comparison is made between public opinion on this exhibit and that displayed in the Fine Arts Bldg--primarily by men. Author concludes: Critic bias played an important role in the lessened status of the Gallery of Honor works; also ineffective selection process, inadequate display space, general exhibition status of the Woman's Bldg. She feels successes were from talent of artists, Bertha Palmer, and the Board of Lady Managers. ☺ . (IStU)

2334.10 Claitor, Diana. *100 Years Ago : The Glorious 1890s*. New York: Gallery, [ᶜ1990 by M&M Books].

4°. 192 p. Dark gray cloth hc. Multicolor dj with illus of pair on a tandem bicycle. WCE pp 88-89: three illus and brief but fine summary of fair and its impact. (ref)

2334.11 Cohen, Jean-Louis. *Scènes de la vie future : l'architecture européenne et la tentation de l'Amérique, 1893-1960*. Paris: Flammarion, [ᶜ1995].

28x21½. 223 p. Illus. Catalog issued for exhibit at Centre de Cultura Contemporania, Barcelona, Spain, Feb–Apr 1996. US architecture including the WCE. French language ed of #2334.12. (CCA,Stfd)

2334.12 Cohen, Jean-Louis. *Scenes of the world to come : European architecture and the American challenge, 1893-1960*. Montreal: Canadian Centre for Architecture, [ᶜ1995].

28x21½. 223 p. Illus. English language ed of #2334.11 and 2334.13. (CCA,CU,DC,Stfd)

2334.13 Cohen, Jean-Louis. *La temptació d'Amèrica : ciutat I arquitectura a Europa 1893-1960*. [Barcelona, Spain]: Centre de Cultura Contemporania : Institut d'Edicions, [ᶜ1996].

28x21½. 223 p. Illus. Spanish language ed of #2334.12. (CCA)

2334.14 Collins, David R. and Evelyn Witter. *Notable Illinois women*. Rock Island, IL: Quest publishing, [ᶜ1982 by Quest].

23x15. 152 p. Stiff blue wraps with dark blue print. Includes bios of WCE notables such as Bertha Palmer, Francis Willard, Harriet Monroe, and Jane Addams. ☺ (GLD)

Joy V. Bliss and a Restored Painting from the WCE, Columbian Theatre, Wamego, KS

2335.1 Columbian Theatre Foundation. *The campaign for the Columbian : The Columbian : 1994*. [Wamego, KS: The Foundation], n.d.

28x22. 1 *l*, (19) p. Tan wraps, black print and design; plastic binder. C.t. Architectural plans and b/w illus of paintings. WCE murals from the Govt Bldg that were purchased by J.C. Rogers after the Fair closed are described, as well as restoration of the paintings and the old Wamego theater that housed them for 100 years. Dedication ceremonies announced for Oct 1994. ☺ (GLD) P➔

☞ The Columbian Theatre is partially comprised of architectural elements from the WCE. In addition, the park in Wamego, Kansas, contains WCE statues purchased by Rogers. See annotation to #523 and #2110 for more about Rogers and his other WCE purchases.

2335.2 *The Columbian Theatre Museum and Art Center : Grand Opening Commemorative Guide : October - November 1994*. [Wamego, KS: The Columbian Theatre Foundation, 1994].

28x21½. 40 p. Illus, some colored. White glossy wraps, red and black print on tan background, photo illus of the WCE paintings. C.t. Description of the restoration and opening of "The Columbian." The dedication ceremonies were held Nov 6, 1994. ☺ (GLD)

2335.3 *Come to the fairs*. Videocassette. With Bill Moyers. PBS, 1984, ᶜ1983. 58 min.

Part of series: "A walk through the 20th century with Bill Moyers." A survey of America's World's Fairs beginning with the WCE. (UMD)

2335.4 Condit, Carl W. *The Chicago school of architecture : A History of Commercial and Public Building in the Chicago Area, 1875-1925*. Chicago and London: U of Chicago P, [ᶜ1964 by U of Chicago].

24½x17½. xviii, 238 p+ unpaged plates. Blue cloth hc, silver spine print. Detailed descriptions of the impact of Sullivan, Adler, Root, and Burnham on turn-of-the-century Chicago architecture; e.g., Sullivan's "Golden Door" for the WCE Transportation Bldg was a copy of his vaulted ceiling in the Schiller Bldg auditorium, 1891–92 (plates 89, 94). WCE architecture described throughout. ☺ . (BU,KSU)

2336.   Cooley and Traczyk. *Ho-o Den*: (UoC)

2337.   Cordato. *Representing the expansion of women's sphere*: (HML,WM)

2337.1 Corré, Alan D., ed. *The Quest for Social Justice II : The Morris Fromkin Memorial Lectures : 1981–1990*. Milwaukee: Golda Meir Library : U of Wisconsin, 1992 [ᶜ1992 by Board of Regents of the U of Wisconsin].

23½x16. 217 p. Cloth hc. Dj with port of Fromkin. Contains "A Confusion of Voices: Reform Movements and the World's Columbian Exposition of 1893." Pp 59-76. See #2332.3. (ref)

2337.2 Cronon, William. *Nature's metropolis : Chicago and the Great West*. New York [and] London: Norton, [ᶜ1991 by Cronon].

23½x16. xxiii, 2 *l*, (5)-530 p+ unpaged illus. Royal blue paper boards, maroon cloth spine with gilt print. Chap 8 (pp 341-69): "White City Pilgrimage." Unpaged b/w WCE-related photos between pp 328-29. Exceptionally well documented: appendix, notes, bibliography, and index (pp 387-530). ☺ . (FM)

2338.   Crook. *Louis Sullivan, The World's Columbian Exposition, and American Life*: (csuf,HU,MU,UTA)
▶Add size: 28x21½.

2340.   Cunningham. *The image of the artist in Chicago fiction*: (bgsu)
▶Correct paging: 279 *l*.

2340.1 Currey, J. Seymour. *Chicago: Its History and Its Builders : A century of marvelous growth*. Vol. III. Chicago: S.J. Clarke publishing co., 1912.

Vol III. 26½x18½. xii, 407 p+ unpaged b/w illus. Rebound. "I Will" lady on t.p. Detailed WCE content from chap 41 to 46 (pp 1-105 + unpaged b/w illus). ☺ (DC,UIC)

2340.2 Currey, J. Seymour. *Manufacturing and Wholesale Industries of Chicago*. Chicago: Thomas B. Poole co., 1918.

27½x21. xvi, 473 p. Frontis port of Currey. WCE described, as well as its impact on manufacturing and sales, chapters 13-15. ☺ (IHi)

2340.3 Curry, Jane, ed. *Marietta Holley : Samantha Rastles the Woman Question*. Urbana and Chicago: U of Illinois P, [ᶜ1983 by Board of Trustees of U of Illinois].

23x15. xvi, 1 *l* (port of Holley), 235 p, 1 *l*. Two-tone blue wraps, b/w print. Includes bibliography. Describes women and their status at the turn of the century through Holley's writings. Excerpts and commentary from *Samantha at the World's Fair* (see #18). ☺ (OU,ref)

2340.4 Curti, Merle [Eugene]. *Probing Our Past*. New York: Harper & brothers, [1955].

21½x14. Chap 10 (pp 246-77): "America at the World's Fairs, 1851–1893." This chapter was previously printed in *American Historical Review* in 1950. See #1226. (UMD)

2340.5 Cutler, Irving. *The Jews of Chicago : From Shtetl to Suburb*. Urbana & Chicago: U of Illinois P, [ᶜ1996].

28x21½. xii, 1 *l*, 315 p, (2) p. Maroon cloth hc, gilt spine print; white dj with red and blue print and illus of Jewish market interior. WCE, pp 103-05, and Parliament of Religions. See #2395.6. (GPL,Knox)

2340.6 Cutrer, Emily Fourmy. *The Art of the Woman : The Life and Work of Elisabet Ney*. Lincoln and London: U of Nebraska P, [ᶜ1988, U of Nebraska P].

24x15. xv, 270 p, 1 *l*. Frontis illus of the colorful and controversial sculptor Ney (1833–1907) in her Austin, TX, studio. Black cloth hc, silver spine print. Chap 6-7 have WCE content. Illus of her statue of Sam Houston exhibited and acclaimed at WCE. Describes how the Texas legislature would not and could not legally grant funds for exhibits. Describes the disorganized TX volunteer committees trying to establish a WCE exhibit; they finally formed the Women's World's Fair Association. Best of the Ney biographies; see Jan Fortune and Lorado Taft citations. ☺ (ENM,UNM)

☞ The Elisabet Ney Museum, 304 E. 44ᵗʰ St., Austin, Texas, holds the original plaster statue of Sam Houston sculpted by Ney and exhibited in the Texas Bldg at the WCE. The Museum has original correspondence between Ney and Mrs. Benedette Tobin, President of the Texas Bldg. A bust of Tobin was exhibited in the Assembly room of the WCE Woman's Bldg and is now shown at the Ney Museum. Ney later created statues of other Texas heroes.

2340.7 D'Andrea, Christian Francis. "Millionaires, palaces, and civic vision: the arts of money and memory at the World's Columbian Exposition." Harvard U Hoopes Prize, 1994.

28x21½. 64 *l*. Illus, some color. (Harvard Archives: HU 92.94)

2340.8 Daniel, Pete. *A talent for detail. The photographs of Miss Frances Benjamin Johnston, 1889–1910.* New York: Harmony Books, [1974].

Oblong 4°. ix, 182 p. Cloth hc. Highlights her fine photos of the WCE and St. Louis fair. (ref) $100

2341. Darnall. *From the Chicago fair to Walter Gropius*: (CU)
2342. Darney. *Women and World's Fairs*: (CCA)

2342.1 Dedmon, Emmett. *Fabulous Chicago.* New York: Random, [ᶜ1953 by Dedmon].

24x16½. 5 *l*, xi-xxi, 359 p+ 1 *l* author biography. Many b/w illus. Black, white, and wine illus cloth hc, spine print, dj. Blue dyed top edge. End papers are maps of Chicago. Chapter 18 (pp 220-37) is entitled "The Glories of the White City." See the book's index: "Columbian Exposition" for further reference to the WCE. © (GLD,BCPL,BPL,CU,DC,FM,GBP,GPL,Knox,LL,Smth,UIC,UTA)
---- Enlarged Ed: New York: Atheneum, 1981. xxii, 447 p. Red-brown cloth spine over blue blind-stamped paper boards. Top edge dyed red. (UIC)

2342.2 The Delphian Society. *The World's progress : with illustrative text from masterpieces of Egyptian, Hebrew, Greek, Latin, modern European and American literature : fully illustrated.* Vol. X of 10 vols. [Chicago]: The Delphian Society (W.B. Conkey co., printing and binding, Hammond, IN), [ᶜ1913 by the Delphian Society].

25x18. 1 *l* frontis, viii, 2 *l* colored US map, ix-xiv, (1)-550 p. Hunter green textured cloth hc, gilt spine design and print. Gilt top edge; other edges untrimmed. First *l* is colorized frontis entitled "Oxen ploughing," tissue guard. Harriet Monroe's "Columbian Ode" on pp 100-02. Chapter 11 (pp 103-10) is titled "The Columbian Exposition"; chapter 12 (pp 111-51) titled "The World's Fair Congresses" has 13 articles on women's contributions. All World's fairs to 1913, chap 9–18. © (GLD) set $30 -70
---- Also found: Rpt as *The Delphian course : a systematic plan of education, embracing the world's progress and development of the liberal arts.* Vol. X of 10 vols. [Chicago]: The Delphian society (W.B. Conkey co., printing and binding, Hammond, IN), [ᶜ1913 by The Delphian society, revised 1916, 1919, 1922]. Same size, paging, and cover.

2342.3 Desjardins, Anne Louise. "American landscape legacies : Mount Auburn Cemetery, the Columbian Exposition and Disneyland." MA diss. Cornell U, 1993.

28½x21½. v, 122 p. Typescript with illus. Impact of WCE landscape, WCE illus. © (CU)

2342.4 De Vale, Sue Carole. *A Sudanese gamelan: a gestalt approach to organology.* PhD diss. Northwestern U, 1977; Ann Arbor: UMI, 1977. 7805248.

28x21½. v, 278 p. Typescript. The gamelan, an arrangement of various percussion instruments, is from the western part of Java and was obtained by the Field Museum directly from the WCE Java Village. See #1298.3 for the author's subsequent article on this topic. © . (RU)

2344. Doolin. *1893 Columbian Exposition Admissions and Concessions*: (B,csuf,UIC)
2346. Downey. *Rite of passage*: (MU,NPG,UIC)

2346.1 Drury, John. *Old Chicago Houses.* New York: Bonanza Books, [1976, ᶜ1941 by the U of Chicago P].

23½x16½. xix, 518 p. Hunter green paper covered boards, gilt spine print. Tan dj, black print, b/w illus of Victorian home. Many references to WCE throughout as many of the homes depicted were owned by WCE dignitaries. Gives history of each house and owner. © (GLD,Knox,UIC,WM)

2347.   Druyvesteyn. "The World's Parliament of Religions": (UoC)

2347.1 Duell, Marshall. "Frank Miller and the international expositions." MA diss. U of California, Riverside, 1987.

28x__. 106 *l*. Illus. Map. Plan. (HML)

2348.   Duis. *Chicago : Creating New Traditions*: (UMA,USFr,UTA,WM)

2348.1 Dunlap, Leslie Kathrin. "Red and Black in the White City." BA thesis. Carlton College, Northfield, MN, 1989.

28x21½. ___ p. Thesis in American Studies. (ref)

2348.2 Dybwad, G.L., and Joy V. Bliss. *Annotated Bibliography: World's Columbian Exposition, Chicago 1893 : With Illustrations and Price Guide...* Albuquerque, NM: The Book Stops Here, 1992 [ᶜ1992 by Dybwad and Bliss].

28x22. 1 *l* frontis, xii, 444, (2) p+ tipped-in fold map/chart at inside back cover. Frontis is a repro of steel engraved invitation to dedicatory ceremonies. New Mexico sky blue wraps with gilt Statue of the Republic and blood red print. Over 2700 distinct entries categorized in chapters. Index. (B,bgsu,BPL,CCA,CU, CUE,CHx,Col,CoU,csuf,DU,Fess, FM,GBP,GPL,HL,HU,IaHx,IHi,InHx,IStU,JHU, Knox,KU,KyU,LC,LMi,LU,MCHx,MPL,NAG,ncsu,NDU,NJSt,NL,nmsu,NYPL,OC, PU,PSU,RPB,RU,SHB,SI,slu,Stfd,SU,TU,UCD,UDe,UGa,UIC,uiuc,UMD,UMi,UMN,UNM,UoC,UPa,USD, UTA,UTn,UWa,VAM,VCU,WiHx,WM,wusl)

2348.3 Dybwad, G.L., and Joy V. Bliss. *Chicago Day : at the : World's Columbian Exposition: Illustrated With Candid Photographs*. Albuquerque, NM: The Book Stops Here, 1997 [ᶜ1997 by Dybwad and Bliss].

28½x22. 140 p. Illus color hc. First 4 pages are color plates; 225 total illus. Laid-in large folded map with red overlay showing camera angles. Based on newspaper accounts, describes planning (Alderman Kerr) the grand WCE event that commemorated the 22ⁿᵈ anniversary of the 1871 Chicago fire and the tells what happened on Oct 9, 1893. Includes 43 reproductions of platinum candid photos from Chicago Day. Record attendance was over ¾ million people. Includes recipes from Columbian cookbooks.

(A,B,CPL,CU,E,F,Fess,FM,GPL,IHi,KCPL,MPL,NYPL,S,TD,ULC,UoC,UVM,VCU,WiHx,WM) **P→**

2348.4 Eberhardt, Joseph Peter. "Financing the World's Columbian exposition." Chicago State U, 1978.

28x21½. 25 p. Yellow wraps, black print. Ring-bound typescript. Paper in the History Dept for fulfillment of course in historic research. ☺ (MSI)

2348.5 Edelstein, T.J., ed. *Imagining an Irish past : the Celtic revival, 1840-1940*. Chicago: David and Alfred Smart Museum of Art, distributed by U of Chicago P, ᶜ1991.

25x__. xvii, (4) p plates, __ p. Illus, some colored. Catalog of exhibition held Feb 5-16, 1992. Includes: "Selling national culture : Ireland at the World's Columbian Exposition" by Neil Harris. (MH,ref)

2348.6 Edwards, Hywel Teifi. *Eisteddfod Ffair y Byd : Chicago, 1893*. [Llandysul]: Gwasg Gomer, 1990.

21½x14. xx, 196 p. Pink, red, and pale blue wraps with dark blue and white lettering. Well illus with contemporary photos and prints. Trans: Eisteddfod at the World's Fair : Chicago, 1893. Welsh festival or gathering—specifically for music and verse. See #2190-92 for other Welsh WCE pubs. ☺. (CUE)

2349.   Eglit. *Columbiana : The Medallic History of Christopher*: (B,H,ref,S,SPL,UMD)   [1965] edition: $120+

2350.1 Ellsworth, Frank L. *Law on the Midway : The Founding of the University of Chicago Law School*. Chicago: Law School of the U of Chicago, [ᶜ1977 by U of Chicago].

30x22½. viii, 191 p. No frontis. Tan cloth hc, gilt cover design, gilt spine print. Brief description of WCE, especially the Congresses on reform and on law. Describes the start of the U of Chicago north of the Midway just before the fair opened. Mentioned in this book: the law school was started by William R. Harper, Charles Bonney of the congresses was a member of the Chicago Bar, and Mayor Harrison was murdered by a distraught lawyer on Oct 28, 1893. ☺ (ref)

2351. Emple. *The Maine State Building from Chicago to Poland Spring*:
▶Corrected spelling: *Poland Spring* [not Springs].

2351.1 *The Encyclopedia of : Collectibles : Typewriters to World War Memorabilia*. Alexandria, VA: Time-Life books, [ᶜ1980 Time-Life Books].

29x23½. 176 p. Illus. Brown glossy paper covered boards, colored illus of watches. Last vol in a set on collectibles. Chap "World's Fair Souvenirs," pp 120-(33), written by Larry Zim, includes WCE. (ref)

2352.1 Essid, Joe. *No god but electricity : American literature and technological enthusiasm in the electric age, 1893-1939*. PhD diss. Indiana U, 1993; Ann Arbor: UMI, ᶜ1994.

28x22. ix, 326 *l*, illus. (HML)

2352.2 Fabos, Julius Gy., et. al. *Frederick Law Olmsted, Sr. : Founder of Landscape Architecture in America*. [Boston]: U of Massachusetts P, 1968 [ᶜ1968 U of Massachusetts P].

26x26. 8 *l*, 113 p+ unpaged fold out of Central Park after p 24. Illus. Tan cloth hc, black facsimile of Olmsted's signature. Olmsted's preliminary "super block" sketch of WCE grounds on p 94; WCE illus pp 93-98. Olmsted's young partner and aid on the WCE plan, Harry Codmen, died unexpectedly in 1893. [See Olmsted in index for related citations.] ☺ (OU)

2352.3 *The fair view : representations of the World's Columbian exposition of 1893*. [Ann Arbor: U of Michigan College of Literature, Science, and the Arts], 1993?

21½x14. 31, (1) p. Dark brown print and illus on cream stock. Glossy wraps with color facsimile typogravure by J.A. Castaigne showing an aerial view of WCE grounds and a balloon basket. The WCE and its illus are described in four categories of the exhibit, which was held in Chicago at the Terra Museum, Aug–Oct 1993, and in Ann Arbor at the U of Michigan Museum, Oct–Dec 1993. Text and design by Diane Kirkpatrick, U of Michigan. ☺ (GLD,DC,Fess,MH)

2352.4 Farr, Finis. *Chicago : a personal history of America's most American city*. New Rochelle, NY: Arlington house, [ᶜ1973 by Arlington House].

23x16. 428 p. Olive-green paper covered boards, black print "A" in box. Illus glossy dj, b/w print. Chap 8, "The World's Fair," pp 168-98, plus scattered references and impact discussions. ☺ (GLD,CU,Knox,USFr)

2352.5 Fauster, Carl U., comp. *Libbey glass : Since 1818 : Pictorial History & Collector's Guide*. Toledo, OH: Len Beach Press, [ᶜ1979].

29x24½. xi, 415 p. Pumpkin colored cloth hc, brown print; glossy illus dj, red print. References to Libbey at the WCE scattered throughout. ☺ (S)

2352.6 *The Ferris wheel : at the : Louisiana purchase exposition, St. Louis, 1904*. N.p.: n.p., n.d.

16x8. (12) panels. Buff sheet unfolds to 31½x24. C.t. One side (including cover) is in black print and describes the wheel, its Columbian debut on June 21, 1893, and how it was moved to St. Louis. Across the back 6 panels is a map of the Louisiana expo in b/w, blue-green, and red; at top in red "The best place to see the Fair is from the top of the FERRIS WHEEL." ☺ (GLD) P➡

2354.1 Field, Eugene. *The clink of the ice : and other poems worth reading*. Chicago: M.A. Donohue & Co., [ᶜ1905 by M.A. Donohue & Co.].

19x12½. 1 *l* (frontis port), 1 *l* (t.p.), 3-142 p. Yellow-green cloth hc, gilt print, boy waiter in red, b/w ice bucket. "The Midway," pp 137-38, refers to Adlai Stevenson (then Vice Pres of the US) at the WF. [His grandson (same name) was an IL politician during the Eisenhower admin.] See #1060.3 for more about Field. ☺ (GLD)

2354.2 Field Museum. Dillenburg, Eugene. "Centennial Objects : Final Report." [Chicago: Field Museum], 1 Feb. 1994.

28x21½. Loose leaf booklet. 145 p+ 33 p titled "A Brief History of exhibits at the Field Museum : 1924–1994 : Fifth edition October 18, 1994." Topics by FM depts: Anthropology, Botany, Geology, Zoology, Photography. "Objects" are listed for all depts; in addition, the anthropology listing includes accessions (other depts have their accession records kept by the Museum Archives in the library). Anthropology accessions are listed for 1893–94 plus any subsequent accessions (gift, purchase, or collections from the field) that could be clearly traced to the WCE. Dillenburg was Coordinator of Special Projects for Program Development. ☺ (FM)

2354.3 Fifer, J. Valerie. *American progress : the growth of the transport, tourist, and information industries in the nineteenth-century west : seen through : The Life and Times of George A. Crofutt : Pioneer and Publicist of the Transcontinental Age.* Chester, CT: Globe Pequot Press, [°1988 by Fifer].

25x17½. x, 472 p. Red-orange cloth hc, gilt spine print; yellow and white glossy dj with red and blue print and illus of old locomotive leaving Omaha depot, 1878. Frontis repro of allegorical painting designed by Crofutt. WCE on pp 347 and 388. Describes Crofutt travel guides to the west. ☺ (GLD)

2354.4 Findling, John E. *Chicago's great World's fairs.* Manchester, Eng. [and] New York: Manchester UP, [°1994 by Findling].

British ed. 23½x15½. x, 173 p. Blue cloth hc, gilt spine lettering. Glossy dj with illus of Century of Progress Travel and Trans Bldg. Series: "Studies in design and material culture." Comparisons are made to show the evolution of architecture and exhibition displays between the 1893 and 1933 World's fairs held in Chicago. ☺ (CU,DC,HU,Knox,MH,sfsu,SML,Stfd,uiuc,UMN,UoC,VAM)   £ 35
---- Also listed: US ed. New York: St. Martins Press, 1995. 208 p. 25 illus. Hc. (ref)

2355.   Findling and Pelle. *Historical Dictionary of World's Fairs*: (bgsu,GBP,HML,MOHx,slu,SML,UBO,UoC,WM)
▶Correct copyright date: [°1988].

☞ See #2325.2 and #2421.4 for other World's fair anthologies.

2355.1 First Church of Nashua. *The First Church Tricentennial : 1685–1985 : The First Church of Nashua, N.H. Congregational – U.C.C.* [Nashua, NH: Puritan Press], 1985?

23x15½. 1 *l* (t.p.), (2), 80 p. Off-white stiff wraps, black and red print, church and cross illus. On p 40 "The First Church Chime" is explained: A set of 10 bells founded by the W.E. Vanduzen Co of Cincinnati, were displayed and rung at the WCE and then moved to the church with five more bells after the fair closed. Inaugurated June 28, 1894, refurbished and rededicated in Sept 1998. See #1308.3. (ref)

☞ The Vanduzen & Tift Company of Cincinnati had their exhibit in the Liberal Arts Bldg, and the chimes were hung and rung from the southeast tower of Machinery Hall.

A Columbian bell in the First Church tower, Nashua, NH

2355.2 Foner, Philip S. *The Life and Writings of Frederick Douglass : Reconstruction and After.* Vol. IV. New York: International publishers, [°1955 by International].

21x14½. 574 p. Black cloth hc, gilt spine print. Reprints Douglass's writings regarding the WCE (pp 469-90): his introd to Ida Well's book (#1053) and his lecture on Haiti as Commissioner in charge of exhibit from Haiti at the WCE on occasion of dedication of Haitian Pavilion, Jan 2, 1893. ☺ (GLD,MIT)

2355.3 Fortune, Jan, and Jean Burton. *Elisabet Ney.* New York: Alfred A. Knopf, 1943 [°1943 by Knopf].

22x15½. 7 *l*, 3-300 p, v (index), 1 *l*. Frontis self-port bust of Ney. Teal cloth hc, black print cover and spine. German sculptor living in Austin commissioned to execute plaster statues of TX heroes for the TX Bldg. WCE content in Chapter 10, pp 235-40. See #2340.6. ☺ (ENM,UNM)

2355.4 Fowler, Allan. *World's fairs and expos.* Chicago: Childrens press, [°1991 by Childrens].

22x19. 44, (4) p. Illus. Durable glossy paper illus hc. WCE mentioned on scattered pages. Juvenile book of the series "A New True Book." (ref)

2356. French. *Memories of a sculptor's wife*: (Stfd)

2356.1 Freund, Edith. *Chicago Girls*. New York: Poseidon, [ᶜ1985 by Freund].

24x16½. 427 p, 1 *l* author bio. Paper covered boards with maroon cloth spine, gilt spine print; dj with brown photo illus of Victorian clothing on chair, white print. Novel set at the WCE, no illus. ☺ (GPL)

2357. Friebe, [Wolfgang]. *Buildings of the World exhibitions*. Trans. Jenny Vowles and Paul Roper. [German Democratic Republic: Printed by Druckerei Volksstimme Magdeburg, ᶜ1985 Edition Leipzig].

28x25. 224 p. Blue cloth hc, silver print; dj photo of the Atomium symbol from the 1958 Brussels WF. Includes b/w lithos and photo-illus, some colored. Friebe, a German architect, emphasizes 1851–1970 WF structures. WCE on pp 109-14. See #2357.1 for the German language version. ☺ (GLD,S.Stdf,WM)
▶Completed citation.

2357.1 Friebe, Wolfgang. *Vom Kristallpalast zum sonnenturm*. [Leipzig: Druckerei Volksstimme Magdeburg, ᶜ1983 by Edition Leipzig].

28x25. 224 p. Blue cloth hc, silver print; glossy dj with photo of 1970 Osaka World's Fair grounds. Original German language version of #2357. WCE on pp 109-14. ☺ (SML)

2358. Friz. *The Official Price Guide to World's Fair memorabilia*: (BCPL)

2358.1 Gage, Emma Abbott. *Western wanderings and summer saunterings through picturesque Colorado*. Baltimore: Lord Baltimore Press, 1900.

ca 17x14. Illus with 28 plates. Frontis port of Gage. Description of remaining WCE bldgs at Jackson Park at the turn of the century, pp 248-50. ☺ . (csuf)

2358.2 Gamble, Russell. *Beaux Arts Academicism In Milwaukee And The Midwest After The World's Columbian Exposition 1893, Using The Milwaukee Public Library And Its Competition As the Focus*. [Milwaukee: ___, 1977?].

28x21½. 1 *l*, (1)-3 outline, 1-20 p text, 2 *l* bibliography. Photocopy of typescript. On t.p.: "By Russell Gamble : April 26, 1977 : Professor D. Stillman Art History Seminar." Based upon competitive architectural entries for the 1893 Milwaukee Public Library—Museum, the seminar concluded that Beaux Art preceded the WCE. (MPL)

2358.3 Garland, Hamlin. *A son of the middle border*. New York: Macmillan, 1917 [ᶜ1914 and 1917 by P.F. Collier & son, ᶜ1917 by Garland].

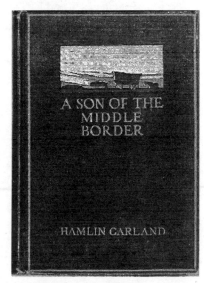

21x14½. 3 *l*, v-vii, 1 *l*, 467 p, 3 *l* (Macmillan ads). Black cloth hc; red print and border; vignette of wagon train stamped in gilt, gray, black, and red; gilt spine. Garland's WCE visit described, pp 456-61. [1917 version found signed by Garland and listed at $125]. P➔
---- Also found: New York: Macmillan, 1924 [ᶜ1914 and 1917 P.F. Collier & son; ᶜ1917 Garland]. vii, 1 *l*, 467 p. Same cover as 1917 version. B/w frontis litho by Alice Barber Stephens.
---- Also found: Paperback ed. Lincoln and London: U of Nebraska P, [ᶜ1917, ᶜ1979 by U of Nebraska P]. xxiv, 1 *l*, 467 p. No frontis. Black wraps with white print and vignette of rural village, man and child at water pump. ☺ (GLD,Berk,csuf,LPL,OU)

☞ This book contains Garland's famous statement upon witnessing the grandeur of the White City: "Sell the cook stove if necessary and come. You *must* see this fair." Page 458.

2359. Gilbert. *Perfect Cities : Chicago's Utopias of 1893*: (GLD,BPL,CCA,GMU,S,UCI,UMA,UMD,UTA,WM)
---- Also found: Paperback ed. Chicago and London: U of Chicago P, [1993]. 23x15. xiv, 279 p.

Frontis: map of Chicago showing WCE grounds. Green and pale yellow glossy wraps, sepia illus of Moody Church and Machinery Hall.

2359.1 Ginger, Ray. *Altgeld's America : the Lincoln ideal versus changing realities.* New York: Funk, 1958.

Hc: 21½x14½. Chap I: "White City in the Muck." Many WCE details scattered throughout, e.g., Louis Sullivan, Union League Club, Bertha Palmer. Altgeld was the Gov of IL during the WCE.
---- Wraps: Chicago: Quadrangle Books, [1965 by Quadrangle, ᶜ1958 by Funk]. 21½x14½. 4 *l*, 376 p. Red, white, and blue flag-type design with b/w ports of six important Chicago men. Chap I: "White City in the Muck."
---- Wraps: xii, 378 p. Red glossy stiff wraps, b/w print, illus of part of the Court of Honor.
(BPL,BU,csuf,CU,DC,FPL,GPL,Heb,LU,NUL,UIC,UMA,UTA)

2359.2 Glibota, Ante, and Frédéric Edelmann. *Chicago 150 years of architecture : 1833 - 1983.* Paris: Musée-Galerie de la Seita, [1985].

31x31. 383 p. Blue cloth hc, white print; colored glossy dj. Text in French and English. Contains brief section on the WCE with French illus—e.g., map of fairgrounds with bldg names in French. The architectural illus were displayed in Chicago from Oct 1, 1985–Jan 15, 1986, by the Chicago Tribune and Carson Pirie Scott & Co. See #2361.2. (KSU,MSI,WM)

2360.   Goldstein. "Art in Chicago: ☺. (NPG)
▶Capitalization correction: "Art in Chicago and the World's Columbian exposition of 1893."

2360.1 Gonzalez, Cristina. "The Columbian exposition grounds : Chicago 1892." Paper. Harvard U, 1992.

28x21½. (29) p. Typescript of class paper.—(Loeb Design Library SB469.6.G66x 1992). ☺. (HU)

2360.2 Goodspeed, Thomas Wakefield. *A history of the university of Chicago : Founded by John D. Rockefeller : the first quarter-century.* Chicago: U of Chicago P, [ᶜ1916 U of Chicago].

23½x16½. xvi, 522 p. Maroon cloth hc with gilt school crest, gilt spine print. Many WCE dignitaries, e.g., Marshall Field, gave money to expand the school and secure land north of the Midway Plaisance and surrounding the Union Theological Seminary; this became an integral part of UoC. Located in the center of the campus, the Seminary bldg is now a popular bookstore. Scattered references to WCE. On p 391: the doors opened autumn quarter of 1892; no summer quarter of 1893 because the fair was not conducive to study and the school could make money renting its rooms to fair attendees. ☺ (DC)

2360.3 Grant, Bruce. *Fight for a City : The Story of the Union League Club of Chicago and Its Times 1880–1955.* Chicago, New York [and] San Francisco: Rand McNally, [ᶜ1955 by The Union League Club]. P➔

21½x15½. 352 p. B/w illus. Frontis illus on p 2 of the "Clubhouse of the Union League Club of Chicago." Blue cloth hc, gilt design and spine print; color illus dj, black print. Foreword by Herbert Hoover. Issued to commemorate the 75th anniversary of the Club. Member interaction with the WCE scattered throughout. Chap 10: "The World's fair lives on." Presentation copies signed by author and the president of ULC, Alex Bailey. ☺ (GLD,GPL,UTA,ULC)

2361.   Greenhalgh. *Ephemeral Vistas*: (bgsu,FM,LHL,SML,VAM,WM)
---- Also found: British ed. *Ephemeral vistas : the exposition universelles, great exhibitions and World's fairs, 1851-1939.* Manchester: Manchester UP, [ᶜ1988 Greenhalgh]. 24x17. xii, 245 p. Red cloth hc, gilt spine print, glossy dj with illus of 1851 Crystal Palace. Series: "Studies in Imperialism." The expositions are set in their social and political context. Greenhalgh was a tutor in History of Design, which was run jointly by the V&A Museum and the Royal College of Art, London.

2361.1 Grossman, James R., ed. *The frontier in American culture. An Exhibition at the Newberry Library...* Chicago: Newberry Library, [ᶜ1994 Newberry Library].

25½x17½. xiii, (1), 116 p+ color plates not included in pagination. Color wraps, illus of Buffalo Bill's Rough Rider Congress. Two topics: Turner and Buffalo Bill at the WCE. Essays by Richard White and Patricia Nelson Limerick. Also available in hc. [See index under Buffalo Bill for related Cody items.] (OU,ref)

2361.2 *A guide to 150 years of Chicago architecture.* [Chicago]: Chicago Review Press, [ᶜ1985 by Museum of Science and Industry].

21½x22½. 151 p. WCE from pp 30-33. Companion to #2359.2. There is a note from curator, Ante Glibota, on p 4. Alternate author: Robert Bruegmann. ☺. (KSU,UMA,WM)

2361.3 *The Guinness Book of Records 1492 : The World 500 Years Ago.* ___: Facts on File, 1992.

__x__. 192 p. Lists new advances during the life and times of Christopher Columbus. (ref)

2361.4 Hales, Peter B[acon]. *Constructing the Fair : Platinum Photographs by C.D. Arnold of the World's Columbian Exposition.* [Chicago]: Art Institute of Chicago, [ᶜ1993 Art Institute].

25½x31. (6), 50 p. Illus. Frontis of Trans Bldg under construction. B/w illus glossy cover; b/w illus translucent dj. Issued for the Art Institute's centennial exhibit. ☺ (DC,NAG,ref,S,SAL,SHB,Stfd,UIC,VAM,WM) $35

2361.5 Hales, Peter B[acon]. *Silver cities : the photography of American urbanization, 1839–1915.* Philadelphia: Temple UP, [ᶜ1984 by Temple U].

26x18½. x, 315 p. Illus, chiefly photographs. Gray cloth hc, white spine print. Chap 3: "At Its Peak: Grand-Style Photography and the World's Columbian Exposition, 1892–1895," pp 131-59. ☺(sapl,UNM)

2361.6 Halper, Albert, ed. *This is Chicago : An Anthology.* New York: Henry Holt, [ᶜ1952 by Halper].

22x15. (i)-xiii, 1 *l*, 487 p. Bright yellow cloth hc, red spine print. A collection of previously published fiction and non-fiction articles about Chicago. "The Columbian Exposition of 1893," by Lloyd Lewis and Henry Justin Smith is found pp 279-91. See #2389.1. ☺(GLD,OU)

2361.7 Hannon, Daniel Leroy. *The MacKaye spectatorium : a reconstruction and analysis of a theatrical spectacle planned for the World's Columbian exposition of 1893 : with a history of the producing organizations.* PhD diss. Tulane U, 1970; Ann Arbor: UMI, ᶜ1971.

UMI: 22x17. x, 320 *l*. Illus. Doctorate thesis in Theater and Speech. ☺. (DC,UTA)

☞ The spectatorium was located just outside the north end of the exposition grounds. Before any stage performances were held, it failed financially in the economic panic of 1893.

2361.8 Hardin, Sandra. "The World's Columbian Exposition of 1893 : American women's door to opportunity." Paper. Duke U, 1980.

28x22. i, 102 *l*, 3 *l* of plates : illus and ports. Honors paper in history. (DU)

2361.9 Harris, Neil. *Chicago's dream, a world's treasure : the Art Institute.* [Chicago?]: Art Institute, 1993.

22x__. 64 p. Illus analysis of the Art Institute. Issued for their WCE centennial celebration. (NAG)

2361.10 Harris, Neil. *Cultural excursions : marketing appetites and cultural tastes in modern America.* Chicago and London: U of Chicago P, [ᶜ1990 by U of Chicago].

26x18½. viii, 453 p. Illus. Dark gray cloth hc with gold lettering. Selected essays. Section on American cities and American fairs, including the WCE. ☺. (BU,HML,OU,UoA,USFr)

2362. Harris. *The land of contrasts: 1880–1901*: (OU,UBO,USFr)

2362.1 Harris, Neil, Wim de Wit, James Gilbert, and Robert W. Rydell. *Grand illusions : Chicago's World's fair of 1893.* [Chicago]: Chicago Historical Society, [ᶜ1993 by Chicago Historical Society].

21½x26½. xvi, 170 p. Colored glossy stiff wraps. Illus of painting of Ag Bldg on front cover. Issued in conjunction with the Society's 100th anniversary display by the same name; held in Chicago May 1, 1993–July 17, 1994. ☺ (CCA,CU,EvP,FM,GBP,HU,MH,MSI,S,Smth,Stfd,uiuc,UMD,UMN,UoC,VAM,VCU,WM)

2362.2 Harrison, Carter H., [Jr.]. *Growing up with Chicago : Sequel to "Stormy Years."* Chicago: Ralph Fletcher Seymour Publisher, [ᶜ1944 by Harrison].

23½x16½. 6 *l*, 11-375 p includes illus. Sky blue cloth hc, gilt print. First *l* is frontis: b/w photo of crowd in attendance when Carter H. Harrison, Sr., popular mayor of Chicago, spoke for American Cities Day, WCE, Oct 28, 1893. At home in the evening after this speech, the senior Harrison was assassinated by a distraught lawyer. Describes his father's WCE activities. See #709. © (GLD,BU,CU,UIC)

2362.3 Harrison, Carter H. [Jr.] *Stormy years : the autobiography of Carter H. Harrison : five times mayor of Chicago.* Indianapolis [and] New York: Bobbs-Merrill, [ᶜ1935 by Bobbs-Merrill].

23½x17. 8 *l*, 15-361 p. Dark blue cloth hc; gilt print. Gray dj with black print and sepia port of Harrison on the telephone. Frontis same port as dj illus. In this autobiography, Harrison, also describes his father's WCE activities and assassination. See #709. © (GLD,BU,CU,FPL,OU,UIC,UMA,UTA)

2363.1 Harry, Alison M. "Representations of Women at International Exhibitions 1893-1908." MA diss. Royal College of Art [Great Britain], 1994.

30x21. 2 *l*, 61 p printed one side only, 8 *l* bibliography, 24 *l* of plates with illus laid in. Red cloth hc, black spine label with gilt print. Typescript. Examines role and portrayal of women in the WCE and Franco-British Exhibition of 1908. © (VAM)

2363.2 Harry Ransom Humanities Research Center. Flukinger, Roy. *For all the world to see: The world's fairs of London, Chicago, & New York.* Austin, TX: U of Texas, 1992.

61x46 sheet printed both sides and folded to 15½x23. Title printed in black and copper. Ad for a lecture tour and exhibit at the U of TX at Austin. Dr. Julie K. Brown (#2327.1) gave the WCE lecture on Oct 28, 1992. The exhibit took place Oct 12, 1992–Feb 26, 1993. © (UVM)

2364.   Hartman. *Fairground fiction*: (bgsu,csuf,CU,FM,IHi,MSI,NDU,slpl,UCLA,UIC,UTA,WM)

2364.1 Hatch, Alden. *American Express : A Century of Service.* Garden City, NY: Doubleday, 1950 [ᶜ1950 by Harlan Logan].

22x15. 287 p. Blue cloth hc, silver print, illus end papers; blue glossy dj, red and white print. No frontis. Chap 7 description of American Express at WCE; William Swift Dalliba was in charge at the fair for the company. He had over 300 wagons for hauling freight. © (GLD)

2364.2 Hauger, Torill Thorstad, and Odd S. Lovall. *Den store chicagoreisen.* [Oslo, Norway]: Universitetsforlaget, [ᶜ1988 Universitetsforlaget].

25x17½. 95 p. Color illus glossy paper hc; red, blue, and black print. Fictional story for young people about the Fritjof Fredriksen family in Chicago in 1893. Even pages are unpaged and contain non-fictional facts on Chicago life. "Peders Kapittel," pp (82)-91, contains trip to WCE. In Norwegian. (ref)

2364.3 Hayes, Dorsha B. *Chicago : crossroads of American enterprise : A Cities of America Biography.* New York: Julian Messner, publishers, [ᶜ1944 by Hayes].

23x16½. 5 *l*, xi-xxi, 1 *l*, 3-316 p. Brown cloth hc, black print. Double t.p. in brown and black inks. Chicago history with WCE on pp 218-27, 250, 294. Issued for the series "The Cities of America Biographies" edited by Leo Lerman. © (GLD,UIC)

2364.4 Heise, Kenan, and Ed[ward] Baumann. *Chicago originals : a cast of the city's colorful characters : expanded and updated.* [Chicago]: Bonus Books, [ᶜ1995].

23x15. xii, 307 p. Light blue glossy stiff wraps, red and black print and cartoons of five Chicagoans. Includes descriptions of several WCE dignitaries and their roles at the fair. (GLD)

2364.5 Heise, Kenan, and Michael Edgerton. *Chicago : center for enterprise : an illustrated history...* 2 vol. Woodland Hills, CA: Windsor publications, [ᶜ1982 by Windsor].

28½x22. Vol 1: 271, (1) p. Illus (b/w and color). Vol 2: (273)-567, (1) p. Illus (b/w and color). Light blue cloth hc, silver spine print. Navy blue cloth slipcase with tipped-in city graphics (front) and explanation sheet (back). Chap 9, "The white city and the black city : the 1890s," pp 161-99. Many other scattered references describe the WCE and its impact. ☺ (GLD) $75

2364.6 Heller, Alfred. *World's Fairs and the End of Progress, An Insider's View.* Corte Madera, CA: World's Fair, Inc., 1998.

__x__. 259 p. Illus. White wraps, yellow print, scenes from fairs. Contains 8 chapters on WF's from 1851 to "2015," including WCE. Predicts from his long experience with world's fair what would occur at a 2015 centennial Pan-Pacific fair in San Francisco. Heller was editor of *World's Fair*, #1431. (ref)

2364.7 Hernon, Peter, and Terry Ganey. *Under the Influence : The Unauthorized Story of the Anheuser-Busch Dynasty.* New York: Simon & Schuster, 1991.

24x15½. __ p. Hc with dj photo-illus of family wedding and Mr. Busch. Chap 8 description of the rancorous competition between Adolphus Busch and Captain Pabst of Milwaukee's Pabst Brewing Co. for the 1893 WCE prestigious "America's best" beer award. (ref)

2364.8 Herrick, Mary J. *The Chicago schools : A Social and Political History.* Beverly Hills [CA]/London: Sage publications, [ᶜ1971 by Sage].

24½x16½. 464 p. Navy blue cloth hc, gilt print. No frontis. Impact of the Gay 90s on Chicago schools and changing tax structures for school support; descriptions of the WCE and its effect on the schools, pp 71, 76–79. Interaction of Gov. Altgeld, Mayor Harrison, and the schools. ☺ (DC)

2364.9 Hibler, Harold E., and Charles V. Kappen. *So-called dollars. An Illustrated Standard Catalog with Valuations.* New York: Coin and Currency Institute, [ᶜ1963].

29x22. xi, 156 p. Yellow cloth hc, black spine print. Yellow and blue dj with yellow, white, and black print and illus of coins. Important reference for WCE commemoratives and medals, pp 20-31, 144. See #2349 for another Columbian coin reference. ☺ (OU,ref) $60

2364.10 Hill, John, and Beverly Carren Payne. *World's Fairs and Expos: The Modern Era: A Select Bibliography.* Belconnen, A.C.T., Australia: Canberra College of Advanced Education, 1982.

_x_. 54 p. Library Bibliographic Series, no 7. (ref)

2365. Hilton. *Here today and gone tomorrow*: (BCPL,S)
▶Add: 24x16. Magenta and white glossy paper covered boards, black print and illus.

2366. Hines. *Burnham of Chicago*: (BPL,csuf,MSI,NPG,Smth,Stfd,UAH,UTA)
---- Also found: xxiii, 445 p. Paperback with glossy red cover. (ref)

2366.1 Hirsch, Susan E., and Robert I. Goler. *A city comes of age : Chicago in the 1890s.* [Chicago: Chicago Historical Society (Pride in Graphics), [ᶜ1990 by Chicago Historical Society].

21½x25½. 1 *l* half title, (4), 170 p. Black stiff wraps, white print, collage of ports from the time. C.t. = t.p. WCE scattered throughout. "Visions of a Better Chicago" by Goler, includes Ida B. Wells, WCE World's Congress Auxiliary, and White City Amusement Park modeled after the Midway. (WM)

2368. Hoffmann. *The Architecture of John Wellborn Root*: (CCA,HML,UoC)
▶Note: Correct spelling of author's name is Hoffmann, not Hoffman.

2368.1 Holberg, Ruth Langland. *Not So Long Ago.* New York: Thomas Y. Crowell co., 1939 [ᶜ1939].

22½x16½. (4) p, 1 *l*, 131, (1) p of author comments. Illus, some color. Frontis drawing of family on the Midway. Gray cloth hc, blue illus of family on phone. Juvenile novel of kids' trip to the WCE from Milwaukee with their parents. Nice descriptions of the sights and events at the Fair. ☺ (GLD) $35

2369.1 Homsher, Jane Elizabeth Romano. "The genius of liberty, cultural motherhood at the World's Columbian Exposition, Chicago, 1893." MA thesis. San Francisco State U, 1994.

28x21½. vi, 87 p typescript printed one side. Presents classical feminine iconography and 19th century social and cultural assumptions about the roll of women in a democratic society. This construct created a sense of national unity that reaffirmed fundamental beliefs about the promise of American political and economic institutions and attempted to balance the forces of economic resolution, social displacement, and ethnic diversity which were present during the WCE. ☺ (sfsu)

2369.2 Hoobler, Thomas, Dorothy Hoobler, and Carey-Greenberg Associates. *The Summer of Dreams : The Story of a World's Fair Girl.* [Morristown, NJ]: Silver Burdett Press, [ᶜ1993 by Carey-Greenberg].

22x14½. 3 *l*, 1-63, (1) p ad. Glossy color hc shows girl and Ferris Wheel. Frontis charcoal drawing of girl. Rénee Graef illustrations. C.t. = t.p. Fictional account of "Cristina" at the WCE. ☺ (GLD,BPL,RPL,uiuc)

2369.3 Hopkins, Doreen Willa Mae. "A modern analysis of the world's fairs as a marketing vehicle of socio-economic change." MA thesis. San Francisco State U, 1969.

28x21½. vii, 200 p typescript printed one side. Contains copies of correspondence with officials of the 1964–65 NY WF about marketing intent. Brief history of major fairs including the WCE. Describes how world's fairs evolved from earlier trade fairs and their attempts to market new products. ☺ (sfsu)

2370.   Horowitz. *Culture & The City*: ☺ (GLD,FM,WM)
---- Also found: Chicago and London: U of Chicago P, [ᶜ1976, 1989]. 21½x13½. xv, 288 p. Blue glossy wraps, b/w print, illus of the Chicago Art Institute. Republication of her 1976 thesis.

2372.   Howells. *Letters of an Altrurian Traveler*: (Amh,bgsu,BPL,Col,CU,CUA,CWM,DC,DU,FLP,FU,GU,HU,ISU,KCPL,KSU,MH,MSU,MU, NDU,nmsu,SHB,Smth,Stfd,UCB,UCI,UCLA,UI,UIC,uiuc,UMC,UMD,UMN,UoA,UPa,UWM,wsu)
---- Also found: Paperback rpt.

2372.1 Hunt, Gaillard. *The Department of State of the United States : its history and functions.* New Haven: Yale UP; London: Humphrey Milford Oxford UP, 1914 [ᶜ1914 By Yale UP].

22x15. viii, 2 *l*, 459 p. No frontis. Red cloth hc, gilt spine print and top edge. Hunt prepared part of the State Dept exhibit at the WCE and two succeeding fairs (described in the preface). ☺ . (DC,UMA)

2372.2 Hunter, Stanley K. *Footsteps at the American World's fairs : The International Exhibitions of Chicago, New York & Philadelphia, 1853 - 1965 : Revisited in 1993.* Glasgow: Exhibition Study Group, ᶜ1996.

30x21½. 87 p. Spiral bound book, yellow covers, black print, illus of the Chicago Day poster from Oct 9, 1893. B/w illus. C.t. Exhibition Study Group No 3. Description of the author's trips to US WF sites; he attended the Columbian centennial celebrations in Chicago. ☺ (GLD,S)   **P↗**

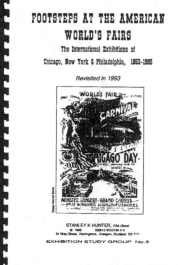

2372.3 *Illinois Theatre : Chicago.* Chicago: Illinois Theatre, 1904.

19x13½. (68) p. Gray wraps, light-gray print, illus of the facade of the Illinois Theatre. C.t. Theater program for Victor Herbert's *Babette*, Mar 28, 1904. Program pages have borders and vignettes of Chicago scenes in red; illus include WCE views: Court of Honor, Field Museum (Fine Arts Palace), and the Art Institute where the World's Congresses were held. ☺ (GLD) $14 - 30

2372.4 *Images de villes idéales: Les expositions universelles : Civic Visions, World's Fairs.* Montreal: Centre Canadien d'Architecture, [1993].

24x20½. 35 p. White wraps, colored map of NYC and Queens. French and English on each page. Illus pamphlet for a CCA exhibit on WFs. One article by Neil Harris. Display list and text on several fairs, including WCE, pp 20-23. ☺ . (GLD,CCA)   **P→**

2373.1 Iriye, Akira, ed. *Mutual Images : Essays in American-Japanese Relations*. Cambridge, MA and London: Harvard UP, 1975 [ᶜ1975 by the President and Fellows of Harvard College].

24½x16. x, 1 *l*, 304, (1) p. White cloth hc, black spine print. WCE explained in Chap 2 by Neil Harris (see #2361.9-2362.1); US–Japan interaction at WFs, including WCE, is described. Brief bibliography of fairs from pp 272-76. ☺ (UNM)

2374.1 Japan. Asakawa, K[anichi]. *Japan, from the Japanese government history...* Memorial ed. New York: P.F. Collier & son co., [ᶜ1928].

23x__. xxiii, 361 p. Frontis. 7 port, illus, maps, 1 color plate. Series: The history of nations, vol VII. Rev ed of *History of the empire* (#569), which was compiled in 1893 for the WCE. (DC, UVM)

2375.   Japan. [*Fukushima-ken*]: (HU,UCLA,Yale)
▶Add annotation: The 1973 ed listed in the original bibliography is a rpt of the 1902 ed published by Fukushima-ken Naimubu Dai 4-ka and of the 1895 ed by Rinji Hakurankai Jimukyoku.

2375.1 Japan. *Naikoku Kangyō Hakurankai shinsa hyōgo*. 9 vol. Tōkyō: Meiji Bunken Shiryō Kankōkai, Shōwa 50 [1975].

22x__. 9 vol. Subject: Japanese exhibition awards. Other name: "Japan. Rinji Hakurankai Jimukyoku (Chicago Exposition, 1893) Rinji Hakurankai Jimukyoku hokoku. 1975." Rpt of the 1877 ed, 1894 ed, and 1901–02 ed. Series: Meiji zenki sangyō hattatsushi shiryō : Kangyō hakurankai shiryō. (HU,UCLA)

2375.2 Jensen, Oliver. *The American Heritage History of : railroads in America*. New York: American Heritage : Bonanza books,[ᶜ1975 by American Heritage, 1981 Bonanza].

30½x24. 320 p. Illus. Brown cloth hc, gilt spine print. Glossy dj with illus of locomotive, red and orange print. Illus references to cars and trains shown at the WCE, pp 77, 222-23, 232-33. (ref)

2376.   Johnson, Diane Chalmers. *American art nouveau*: (NAG)
▶Add annotation: Black cloth hc, black spine print, blind stamped nouveau design. Color frontis. WCE impact and explanations throughout.

2377.   Jones. *The Ferris wheel*: (GPL,IHi)

2377.1 Kalfus, Melvin. *Frederick Law Olmsted : The Passion of a Public Artist*. New York and London: New York UP, 1990 [ᶜ1990 by New York U].

23½x15½. xiii, 1 *l*, 415 p. Brown cloth hc, gilt spine print. WCE, including Olmsted's differences with Burnham, are discussed in chap 14: "Defending the vision." Other scattered ref. Vol 18 of "The American Social Experience Series." [See index under Olmsted for related citations.] ☺ . (OU)

2378.   Karlowicz. *The architecture of the World's Columbian Exposition*: (Col,FU,KSU,NDU,NPG,slpl,uiuc,UPa,UTA,UWM)
---- Also listed: University Microfilms. One reel. (uiuc)

2378.1 Karp, Ivan, and Steven D. Lavine, eds. *Exhibiting cultures : the poetics and politics of museum display*. Washington, DC: Smithsonian Institution Press, ᶜ1991.

23x__. x, 468 p. Illus. Based on papers given at a 1988 Smithsonian conference. (Amh,Knox,MH,OU,slu,Smth)

2378.2 Kasson, John F. *Amusing the millions : Coney Island at the Turn of the Century*. New York: Hill & Wang, [ᶜ1978 by Kasson].

22½x18½. 5 *l*, 3-119, (1) p. Orange cloth hc. Illus brown and orange glossy dj. Extensive description of WCE midway as a precursor to amusement parks. ☺ (S)

2378.3 Kelly, Regina Z. *Chicago: Big-Shouldered City*. Chicago: Reilly & Lee, 1962 [ᶜ1962 by Reilly & Lee].

21x14½. vi, 2 *l*, 158 p. Pale blue cloth hc, black spine print. Color dj illus represents old and new Chicago, black print. Chap 5 (pp 125-46) describes the WCE. Docunovel. ☺ (GLD)

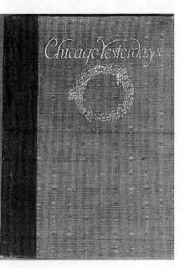

2379.   Kirkland. *Chicago yesterdays*: (GLD,CU,Smth,Stfd,UIC,UTA)   P→

2380.1 Kjær, Iver. *Runes and immigrants in America : the Kensington Stone : the World's Columbian Exposition in Chicago and Nordic identity.* Minneapolis, MN: Center for Nordic Studies, 1994.

__x__. 31 p. Illus. (UBO,UMN)

2381.   Knutson. *The White City*: (Col,HML,UIC,UTA)

2382.   Kogan. *A continuing marvel : The Story of the Museum of Science*: (FM)
▶Corrected paging and added annotation: [ᶜ1973 by Herman Kogan]. (5) p, 1 *l*, (1)-233 p+ unpaged b/w and color illus. Museum's origins from WCE, pp 3-6. Color frontis of Lenox R. Lohr, president of the museum. See #2390.1 for Lohr's book.

2382.1 Kogan, Herman, and Lloyd Wendt. *Chicago a : pictorial history.* New York: Bonanza Books, [ᶜ1958].

27½x20½. 4 *l*, (9)-224 p. Light tan linen hc, brown spine print, color illus dj. End papers are bird's-eye views of Chicago. Heavily illustrated (b/w). WCE primarily found pp 152-70. © (GLD,UTA)

2382.2 Kogan, Herman, and Rick Kogan. *Yesterday's Chicago.* Miami, FL: E.A. Seemann Publishing, [© by H. Kogan and R. Kogan, 1976?].

26x18½. 204 p. Red vinyl hc, gilt spine print. Chicago history in pictures with scattered brief references to the WCE. "Seemann's Historic Cities Series No. 22." (WM)

2382.3 Küng, Hans, and Karl-Josef Kuschel, eds. *A Global Ethic : The Declaration of the Parliament of the World's Religions.* New York: Continuum, [ᶜ1993 R. Piper GmbH & Co KG, Munich].

21x14. 1 *l*, 124 p. White glossy stiff wraps, red and black bold print and design. "Special edition" at upper right corner of cover. Translation by John Bowden of German texts from the centenary World's Parliament of Religions. The Parliament was held in Chicago in 1993. © (DC,EvP,sapl,sfsu,UMN,UoC,USFr)

2382.4 Küng, Hans, ed. *Yes to a global ethic.* New York: Continuum, 1996.

22x__. xi, 239 p. Content based on the 1993 World's Parliament of Religions held in Chicago. (Stfd,USFr)

2382.5 Kyriazi, Gary. *The great American amusement parks a pictorial history.* [Secaucus, NJ]: Castle books, [1978 ᶜ1976].

25½x22. 256 p. Blue paper covered boards, red spine. Color illus glossy dj depicts carnival Ferris wheel. Frontis depicts roller coaster. Briefly describes the WCE midway and concessions. © (ref)

2383.   Lancaster. *The incredible World's parliament of religions*: (HU,sfsu,UAT,UCD,UIC,UMA)

2383.1 Lancaster, Clay. *The Japanese influence in America.* New York: Walton H. Rawls, [ᶜ1963].

31x24. xix, 1 *l*, 292, (1) p. Heavy brocade black cloth hc, gilt print spine. 1 *l* is color folded print of Commodore Perry landing in Japan, 1854. Excellent detailed description of the Japanese pavilion (Ho-o-den) at the WCE, as well as Japanese pavilions at other US World's fairs. © (GLD,MIT,OU,Stfd,UBO,USFr)

2385.   Lauzon. *The United States Columbian issue*: (S)

2386.   Lawson. *The Great Wheel*: (GLD,APL,bgsu,BPL,CU,CUA,cul,DU,EPL,ESU,EvP,FLP,GMU,IStU,KCPL,KSU,LL,MH,MSU,OU,PPL,RPL,S,sfsu, slpl,Smth,UAT,UCLA,uiuc,UMC,UMN,UTA,UVM,wsu,Yale)
▶Rpt ed: New York: Walker, 1993. Series: Newberry Honor Roll. (IStU,RPL)

☞ Juvenile story of immigrant boy working on the "Wheel" at the Fair. Contains a few errors of fact.

2387. Lederer. "The Genesis of the World's Columbian Exposition": (IHi)
---- Also listed: 28x21½. ii, 82 *l*.

2387.1 Lee, Robert. *Fort Meade & the Black Hills*. Lincoln & London: U of Nebraska P, [ᶜ1991 by the U of Nebraska P].

23½x15½. xi, 321 p. Illus. Black cloth hc, silver spine print. Indian Troop L from Fort Meade was selected to attend the WCE from Oct 15–25, 1893, as described on p 151. ☺ (MA,OU,Stfd)

2387.2 Leffingwell, Albert. *The vivisection question*. New Haven, CT: Tuttle, Morehouse & Taylor, 1901.

22½x14½. viii, 267 p. A series of reprinted articles on vivisection. Includes Leffingwell's paper "An Ethical Basis for Humanity," pp (73)-84, which was read before the Humane Congress of the WCE on Oct 12, 1893. ☺ . (HU,KCPL,SHB,UMN)

2387.3 Lewis, Arnold. *An Early Encounter with Tomorrow : Europeans, Chicago's Loop, and the World's Columbian Exposition*. Urbana: U of Illinois P, [ᶜ1997].

27x__. xv, 353, (1) p bio. Blue cloth hc, silver spine print. No frontis. Chap 8: "The World's Columbian Exposition"; also extensive WCE references and illus throughout. Book contains writings, including those occasioned by the WCE, about "The Loop" by English, German, and French visitors. Theme is Chicago, a crucible for the future. ☺ (CU,DC,HU,Knox,Stfd,UVM)

2389.1 Lewis, Lloyd, and Henry Justin Smith. *Chicago : the history of its reputation*. New York: Harcourt, Brace and co., [ᶜ1929 by Harcourt, Brace].

22½x16. xii, 508 p. Blood red cloth hc, silver print, red dyed top edge. 1st ed. No frontis. WCE info scattered pp 177 to 493. Halper's #2361.6 contains a chap from this book. See "Centennial edition," #2389.2 ☺ (GLD,CU,DC,FPL,GPL,Knox,OU,Smth,UIC,UMA,USFr,UTA)
---- Also found: Rpt as *Chicago : the history of its reputation : 1833 – Centennial Edition – 1933*. New York: Blue Ribbon books, [ᶜ1929 by Harcourt, Brace]; New York: Harcourt, Brace, [ᶜ1929]. 21½x15. xii, 518 p. Dull red cloth hc, black print. Frontis of 1933 Century of Progress [centennial of the founding of Chicago]. Red and black illus glossy dj; black, red, and white print. (ref)

2389.2 Lindsey, Bessie M. *American historical glass : historical association adds distinction to glassware*. Rutland, VT: Charles E. Tuttle, ᶜ1967, 1980 by Walter Risley.

5th Printing: 23½x16. xxviii, 541 p. Blue cloth hc, gilt print; gold dj, red and black print, illus of glass plates and trays. Items are numbered and include WCE glassware. ☺ (S)

2390.1 Lohr, Lenox R. *...Fair management : The Story of A Century of Progress Exposition*. Chicago: Cuneo Press, 1952 [ᶜ1952 by Cuneo].

24x16. 4 *l*, (5), 7-300 p+ unpaged illus. Blue cloth hc, gilt print. Tan, blue, and black dj; white and black print. At head of title: "A Guide For Future Fairs." Description of the 1933 fair; comparisons with the WCE are scattered throughout. (ref)

☞ Lohr was General Manager under Rufus Dawes of the 1933 fair.

2390.2 Longstreet, Stephen. *Chicago : 1860–1919*. New York: David McKay co., [ᶜ1973 by Longstreet].

23½x16. xxiii, 547 p. Magenta cloth hc with gilt spine print. WCE scattered throughout, especially chap 38, "The big fair," and chap 39, "The nearly white city." Foibles of Chicago including WCE. (CU)

2390.3 Loring, John. *Tiffany's 150 years*. Garden City, NY: Doubleday, 1987.

31½x23½. 191 p. Blind-stamped red cloth hc. Illus glossy dj. History of Tiffany's and some of the Tiffany items at WCE. ☺ (S,Stfd)

2390.4 Love, Richard H. *Louis Ritman : from Chicago to Giverny: How Louis Ritman Was Influenced by Lawton Parker and Other Midwestern Impressionists*. Chicago: Haase-Mumm, [ᶜ1989 by Love].

28½x23. 1 *l* (color illus of Ritman painting "Sunlight"), (i)-xv, 279 p. Interspersed b/w and unpaged color plates. Tipped-in color frontis is p (ii). Blue-black cloth hc, white spine print. Color glossy dj has illus of Ritman painting "Woman Gardening." Scattered WCE references. Chap 4: "The Impact of the World's Columbian Exposition and of Hamlin Garland on Impressionism," pp 41-56. © (GLD)

2390.5 Lowe, David. *Lost Chicago*. Boston: Houghton Mifflin, 1975 [°1975 by Lowe].

28½x23½. xii, 1 *l*, 241 p. Chap VIII (p 148-70), "Dreams of Empire," is WCE chap; b/w illus.
---- New York [and] Avenel, NJ: Wings, [°1975 by Lowe]. 28½x23½. xii, 1 *l*, 1-239 p. Charcoal paper covered boards, gray cloth spine with gilt print. B/w glossy dj.
---- New York: American legacy press, [°1975 by Lowe : 1985 ed by American legacy, distributed by Crown Publishers]. xii, 1 *l*, 241 p. Charcoal paper covered boards, gray cloth spine with gilt print. B/w glossy dj with illus of Marshall Field Wholesale Store, 1885.
© . (BPL,KSU,NUL)

2391.   Luckhurst. *The Story of Exhibitions*: (Knox,SML,VAM,WM)

2391.1 Manchester, William. *The Arms of Krupp : 1587–1968*. Boston [and] Toronto: Little, [°1968].

24x16½. xvi, 976 p. Black cloth hc, gilt print. Dj. Description of the WCE Krupp pavilion pp 219-20. For other Krupp items, see #318.1 and #903.1-#906. (ref,USFr)

2391.2 Mark, Grace. *The dream seekers : A Novel*. New York: William Morrow, [°1992 by Mark].

24x17. 5 *l*, 11-412 p. No frontis. Yellow paper covered boards, red cloth spine; glossy illus dj depicting the Admin Bldg. Fiction. Tale of two women and a brother, the WCE, and labor conditions in 1893.
© (APL,BCPL,Berk,BPL,DC,EPL,EvP,GBP,GPL,IStU,LL,Merc,NLA,RPL,sapl,slcl,slpl,UPa,UTA)

2392.   Marshall. *Notes on Talcott's method of determining terrestrial latitudes*: (BU,LHL,HU,MH,Stfd,UMD,UMN)

2392.1 Mathews, Nancy Mowll. *Mary Cassatt : A Life*. New York: Villard Books, 1994 [°1994 by Mathews].

24x17½. ix, 2 *l*, (3)-383 p, 1 *l*. Black paper covered boards, black spine cloth with silver print. Black glossy dj, white print with port of Cassatt. WCE pp 202-17. Cassatt was commissioned to paint in the Woman's Bldg. She also exhibited works at other fairs. (ref)

2392.2 Matthews, Clifford N., and Roy Abraham Varghese. *Cosmic beginnings and human ends : Where Science and Religion Meet*. Chicago and LaSalle, IL: Open Court, [°1995 by Open Court].

23x15½. ix, 433 p. Illus. Black glossy wraps with magenta, green, white, and blue print; illus of moon shining on water. Symposium papers. A symposium by the same name as this book's title was part of the centennial Parliament of Religions held in Chicago (see #2382.3, #2422.1, #2423.1, #2444.1). © (DC)

2392.3 Mattie, Erik. *World's Fairs*. New York: Princeton Architectural Press, 1998.

30½x23. 260 p. Black cloth hc, gilt print. Dj illus with 1964 US Steel world globe, yellow print. C.t.= t.p. Fairs since 1851. Chap entitled "World's Columbian Exposition, Chicago," pp 86-99. (ref)

2392.4 Mayer, Harold M., and Richard C. Wade. *Chicago: Growth of a Metropolis*. Chicago and London: U of Chicago P, [°1969 by U of Chicago].

24x21½. ix, 1 *l*, 3-510, (1) p. Fold illus. Black cloth spine over off-white cloth boards, silver print. Chap 4: "The White City and the Gray, 1893–1917," pp 193-205, plus scattered WCE references throughout. © (Heb,Knox,MSI,UIC,WM)

2394.   McCullough. *World's fair midways*: (bgsu)
---- Rpt: New York: Arno Press, 1976 [°1976] 190 p, 4 *l* plates. (UIC)

2394.1 McCutcheon, John T. *Drawn from memory by...Containing Many of the Author's Famous Cartoons and Sketches*. Indianapolis [and] New York: Bobbs-Merrill, [°1950 by Evelyn Shaw McCutcheon].

22½x15½. 1 *l* half-title, 1 *l* port, (3)-459 p+ unpaged plates, (1) p acknowledgment. Green cloth hc with gilt facsimile of his signature and cartoon design. McCutcheon was a long-time Chicago resident and Pulitzer Prize winning newspaper cartoonist and writer who visited the WCE often and drew illus of it (pp 70-77). He also worked at the 1894 Mid-Winter Fair in CA. He died in 1949. © (GLD) $16 - 40

2394.2 McFeely, William S. *Frederick Douglass.* New York [and] London: Norton, [ᶜ1991 by McFeely].

22x15. xiii, 465 p. Tan and brown illus glossy stiff wraps. Includes a description of Douglass's WCE involvement. ☺ (OU,S)

2395.   McGlothlin. *World's fair spoons:* (S)   ▶See #2413.1 for another spoon book.

2395.1 McGovern, James J. *The life and letters of Eliza Allen Starr.* Chicago: Printed at Lakeside Press, 1905.

24½x16½. 7 *l*, 13-452 p. Dark blue cloth hc, gilt spine print. Frontis port of Starr with tissue guard. Repro of letter pp 430-31 mentions her paper "Woman's Work in Art" given at the Woman's Congress at the Art Institute. An active artist and promoter of catholic education, Starr received a gold medal for art education at the WCE. ☺ (IHi)

2395.2 McShane, Linda. *"When I Wanted the Sun to Shine" : Kilburn and Other Littleton, New Hampshire Stereographers.* [Littleton, NH: Linda McShane, ᶜ1993 by McShane].

26½x20½. vi, 121 p. Illus. Blue wraps, sepia colored photo repro, white print. Describes Kilburn's company as the authorized stereocard company for the WCE. Gray card mounts were sold on the WCE grounds; tan card mounts were sold elsewhere. The stereocard business failed with the advent of the color picture postcard and popular amateur photography. Extensive archives of WCE stereocards can be found in Littleton. See #2439.3 for another stereo card book. ☺ (GLD)   P➔

☞ The title derives from an interview quote of Benjamin Kilburn, originator and owner of Kilburn Brothers stereoptic view business. Outdoor sunlight was used to individually expose stereo card pairs on photographic paper. The stereo factory was equipped with long rows of south-facing windows and ledges for the operators to perform the sun-generated imaging process.

2395.3 Mears, Helen Farnsworth. *Helen Farnsworth Mears : An exhibition of sculpture.* Oshkosh, WI: Paine art center, 1970.

23x15½. Brochure. Mears (1872–1916) was a student of Lorado Taft (#1045). She sculpted a 9-ft statue, "The Genius of Wisconsin," which was exhibited in the Wisconsin Bldg at the WCE. (RCHx)

2395.4 Meeker, Arthur. *Chicago, with love.* New York: Alfred A. Knopf, 1955 [ᶜ1955 by Meeker].

22x14½. xiv, 293, ix, (1) p. Black cloth spine over red paper blind-stamped boards. Bio sketches of Bertha Palmer and Caroline Kirkland; brief description of WCE (pp 142-46). ☺ (UIC)

2395.5 Megson, Frederic H., and Mary S. Megson. *American Exposition Postcards : 1870–1920 : a catalog and price guide.* Martinsville, NJ: The postcard lovers, [ᶜ1992].

21½x14. 287 p. Illus. Frontis. Wraps. . (ref)

2395.6 Mendelsohn, Felix. *Chicago : Yesterday and Today.* Chicago: Felix Mendelsohn, 1932 ᶜ1932 Mendelsohn.

31x23½. 159 p. Chiefly illus. Dark red "watered" cloth hc, gilt print. Describes and illustrates the WCE and the magnificent structures being built for the coming Century of Progress fair. A condensed version of a 1929 volume entitled *Chicago and its makers.* ☺ . (CCA)

2396.   Meites. *History of the Jews:* (Knox)
---- Also found. Rpt. Chicago: Wellington publishing, [ᶜ1990]. 28x21½. xxxiv, 1 *l*, 36-854, pp (337)-354 supplement, 1 *l*, pp 673-701 supplement. Black cloth hc, gilt spine print. Chap 8: "The World's Fair, and After, 1892-1900," pp 175-200. (Knox)

2396.1 Miami-Dade Community College. *The great World's fairs and expositions : the Mitchell Jr. collection of decorative and propaganda arts.* Miami, FL: Miami-Dade community college, [ᶜ1986 Mitchell Wolfson Jr. Collection].

31½x31. (5), 1-80 p, *2 l.* B/w and color illus. White embossed stiff wraps with black spine print. WFs 1851–1970. Exhibit of Wolfson's collection includes 27 WCE items. Accompanied by 46 p typescript "Addenda" that contains 34 additional WCE items. ☺ (S,WM)

2396.2 Miller, Donald L. *City of the Century: The Epic of Chicago and the Making of America.* New York: Simon & Schuster, [ᶜ1996 by Miller].

24x16½. 704 p. Illus. Pink paper covered boards, black spine cloth with copper print. Silvery-pink and black glossy dj, Court of Honor illus; b/w print. WCE content chap 12, 14, and 15. ☺ (GLD,ref,USFr)
---- Also found: Softbound ed: [New York]: Touchstone, [1997]. 23½x15½. 704 p. Stiff blue wraps with brown and white print and illus of Court of Honor. Extensive ref lists, pp (553) – 704. (GLD)

2396.3 Miller, George, and Dorothy Miller. *Picture postcards in the United States 1893–1918.* ___: Crown Publishers, ᶜ1975.

__x__. __ p. Includes Scott UX10 US postal WCE issue, the first picture postcard. (ref)

2396.4 Moffat, Bruce G. *The "L" : The Development of Chicago's Rapid Transit System, 1888–1932.* Chicago: Central Electric Railfans' Association, [ᶜ1995].

28½x21½. 305, (1) p+ 2 loose reprinted maps. Hc. Multi-color glossy dj with illus of the "L." The Columbian Intramural railway is described thoroughly. [See also Intramural RR in index.] (ref)

2396.5 Mogensen, Margit. *Eventyrets tid : Danmarks deltagelse i Verdensudstillingerne 1851–1900.* Kerteminde: Landbohistorisk Selskab, 1993.

__x__. 419 p. Illus. Includes WCE in 1893. In Danish. Trans: Fantastic times : Denmark's participation in the World's Fairs 1851–1900. (ref)

2396.6 *A monograph of the works of McKim Mead & White 1870–1915 : new edition four vols. in one with essay...* New York: Arno Press, 1977.

34x26½. 73, (4) p, 1 *l,* 1-399A plates, (4) p index. Maize paper covered boards. Red glossy dj with white print and illus. Contains plans and views of McKim, Mead, and White bldgs, including their WCE Agricultural Bldg and bldgs from other fairs. (ref,Stfd)
---- Also found: New Edition. New York: B. Blom, 1973.

2398.　Monroe. *Harlow Niles Higinbotham : a memoir*: (UoC)

2398.1 Moore, Andy, and Susan Moore. *The penny bank book : Collecting Still Banks through the penny door.* Exton, PA: Schiffer Publishing, [ᶜ1984 by Andy and Susan Moore].

31½x23½. viii, (9)-190 p. Catalog with b/w and color plates. Blue glossy paper covered boards, illus of bank on front. WCE banks scattered from ref numbers 779-1250. ☺ (S)

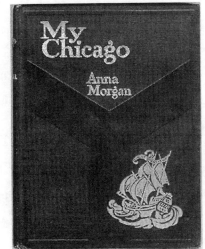

2399.　Moore. *Daniel H. Burnham: Architect, Planner of Cities*:
(GMU,HML,MSI,Smth,Stfd,UAH,UMA)
▶Add publisher: Chicago: Library Resources Inc., 1970. Microfiche. LAC-21426.

2399.1 Morgan, Anna. *My Chicago.* Chicago: Ralph Fletcher Seymour Publisher, [ᶜ1918 By Morgan].

21x16. 8 *l,* 11-201 p. Blue cloth blind-stamped hc, gilt print and yellow embossed vignette of old sailing ship at lower right. Rough-cut fore edge. Frontis port of Morgan. She describes the literary and artistic elite of Chicago and her interaction with influential people at the WCE. GLD copy inscribed to a friend by the author. ☺ (GLD,Knox,UTA)　　P➔

2400.   Morrison, Hugh. *Louis Sullivan : prophet of modern architecture.* New York: Museum of modern art and W.W. Norton, [^c1935 by Norton]; New York, Peter Smith, 1952. ☺ . (GLD,Heb,NPG,OU,Stfd)
---- Also found: Reissued ed. New York: Norton, ^c1998. 25x__. xxxvii, 362 p. Revised list of Sullivan bldgs by Timothy J. Samuelson.
‣Corrected title and publisher.

2400.1 Muccigrosso, Robert. *Celebrating the new world : Chicago's Columbian Exposition of 1893.* Chicago: Ivan R. Dee, [^c1993 by Muccigrosso].

21½x14. xii, 2 *l*, (3)-209, (1) p. Scattered b/w illus. Turquoise paper covered boards, blue cloth spine with gilt print. From the set: The American Way series. Includes bibliographical references and index.
☺ (GLD,Amh,CU,CWM,DC,EvP,GBP,GPL,HU,IStU,KCPL,Knox,MH,MIT,RPL,RU,S,sapl,sfsu,slcl,slpl,slu,Stfd,UCD,UGa,UIC,uiuc,UMA,UMD,UMN,UoC,UVM)

2400.2 Müller, F[riedrich] Max. *Last essays.* London, New York and Bombay: Longmans, Green and co., 1901.

19x13. vi, (2), 375, 40 p. Blue cloth hc, gilt spine print. Müller's essay on the WCE Parliament of Religions, pp (324)-45. Essays on the science of religion; second series. See original German language magazine article #1285.2. ☺ . (DC,FPL,LBA)

2401.   Neufeld. "The Contribution of the World's Columbian Exposition of 1893 to the idea: (CU,UMC,UPa,UTA)
‣Dissertation published on microfilm in 1981. (UTA film #15,465.)

2401.1 Nikhilananda, (Swami). *Vivekananda : A Biography.* Calcutta, India: Advaita ashrama (printed in India By P.C. Rayat Sri Gouranga Press Private), [^c1953 by Swami Nikhilananda, English edition 1953, Indian edition 1964].

19x13. xii, 1 *l*, 350 p. Port of Swami Vivekananda after the WCE on the 1 *l*. Beige cloth spine over tan paper covered boards. Born in 1863, Vivekananda leapt into prominence representing Hinduism at the 1893 Parliament of Religions in Chicago. The keynote of his address was universal toleration and acceptance; he became a strong and vocal advocate for harmony of religions. Vivekananda at the Parliament is described in two chap, pp 97-137. ☺ (GLD) $18 - 40

2401.2 *The nineties : Glimpses of a lost but lively world, by....* New York: American Heritage, ^c1967.

28½x22. 144 p. Illus. Matte paper covered boards, red print, color illus of "Gay '90s" lady dressed in finery. T.p. spans pp 2-(3). On front cover: "An American Heritage extra." Scattered ref to WCE throughout. Chapters by various authors; the chap, "Chicago," by Robert S. Gallagher contains illus, description, and impact of the WCE, pp (12)-(29). ☺ (GLD) $8-16

2402.1 *One Sky Above Us.* Videotape. By Geoffrey C. Ward and Dayton Duncan. The West Film Project / Greater Washington Educational Telecommunications Assn, ^c1996. 65 min.

Series: *The West.* Episode 9. Co-production of Insignia Films and WETA-TV, Washington, DC. This segment celebrates the Columbian Exposition which signaled the close of the old west and the start of US industrial power. Broadcast on the Public Broadcasting System (PBS). (HPL,PPL)

2402.2 Orvis Co. *Mary Orvis Marbury : The Columbian Exposition Display Panels (1893).* N.p.: Orvis, n.d.

26x15. Plaque at the American Museum of Fly Fishing, Manchester, VT. Marbury was a leading tier of fishing flies and author on the subject. The museum's floor and ceiling mounted cases have the flies shown at the WCE as well as photos of lakes and streams where the flies were used to advantage. Orvis remains a leading manufacturer of fishing flies. A WCE remainder. . (ref)

2402.3 Osborne, Georgia L., and Emma B. Scott, comps. *Brief Biographies of the figurines on display in the Illinois state historical library.* Springfield, IL: Printed by authority of the State of Illinois, 1932.

23x15½. 148 p. Brown wraps, black print. No frontis; port of Minna Schmidt on p (4). Schmidt made and gave 129 figurines of deceased but important women to Illinois State Historical Society. This booklet lists biographies of each woman depicted by figurine. Chap 5 is women from "The World's Columbian Exposition Period to 1929" and includes Henrotin and Palmer. (BU,DC,EvP,HU)

2402.4 O'Sullivan, Thomas. *North Star Statehouse : An Armchair Guide to the Minnesota State Capitol.* [St. Paul, MN]: Pogo Press, [ᶜ1994 by Pogo].

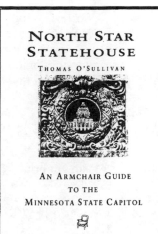

23x15. xiii, 110 p. Pale lavender wraps, purple print, illus of the capitol set in an ornamental panel found on the bldg. The architect, Cass Gilbert, was strongly influenced by the WCE, and the Minnesota capitol reflects that unity, design, and grandeur. Gilbert had friends and WCE participants add to the decoration: paintings by Francis D. Millet, Chief of Decoration, and several mammoth sculptures by Daniel C. French. French was asked to reproduce his Quadriga, which sat atop the Peristyle at the Fair, for the top front of the capitol; he did so substituting a male figure for Columbus, the chariot driver figure in 1893. The capitol was commissioned in 1893 and completed in 1905. ☺ (GLD,H)   **P→**

2403.   Otis. *The Chicago Symphony Orchestra: Its Organization*:   (UTA)

2403.1 Ottlik, Iván. *Nagyméltóságu gróf Bethlen András földmivelésügyi M. K. o excellentiájához tiszteletteljes jelentése : Ott folyamán tett amerikai tanulmányutjáról.* Budapest: n.p., 19__.

26x__. 73 p. Description of trip to the USA and the WCE. (UoC)

2405.   Packer, E.E. *The White City : being an account of a trip to the World's Columbian exposition at Chicago in 1893.* San Diego, CA: n.p., 1933.

22x14½. 1 *l*, 61 p. Portrait of the author tipped-in. Textured hc. C.t.: "The White City." ☺ . (Yale)
▸Completed and corrected citation.

2405.1 Pangborn, J.P. *The World's Railway.* New York: Bramhall House, 1974.

30½x23. 164 p. Hc, dj. Illus. Contains B&O RR at the WCE. (ref)

2406.1 Pease, Theodore Calvin. *The story of Illinois.* Chicago and London: U of Chicago P, [ᶜ1925, 1949, 1965].

3rd ed: 21x14. xvi, 331 p. Green cloth hc, dark blue spine print. Chap 13: WCE pp 186-208. (USFr)
---- Also found: 1975 paperback of the third edition. (Heb)

2407.   Peterson. *Diplomat of the Americas : a biography of William I. Buchanan*: ☺ (S,UNM)
▸Completed citation: 24½x16½. xvi, 458 p, 4 *l* plates. Frontis port of Buchanan. Dark gray-green paper-covered boards (or charcoal cloth), gilt spine print. WCE in Chap 4, "Homage to America's Discoverer." Buchanan was Chief of the Ag Dept. On verso of t.p.: [ᶜ1977 State U of New York P].

2408.1 Pettit, William A. *The resurrection of the first Columbian half dollars.* ___: ___, 1967.

27½x20½. __ p. C.t. For special exhibit at the Professional Numismatist Guild and Chicago Coin Club Convention at the Palmer House, Chicago, Oct 19–22, 1967. (H)

2408.2 Pierce, Bessie Louise. *As others see Chicago : impressions of visitors, 1673–1933.* Chicago: U of Chicago P, [ᶜ1933].

23x16½. xiii, 540 p. Green linen hc, gilt spine print. Written for Century of Progress fair in Chicago. Contains many reminiscences and personal accounts of WCE scattered throughout. ☺ (Knox)

2408.3 Pierce, Bessie Louise. *A history of Chicago.* Vol. III. New York: Knopf, 1957 [ᶜ1957 U of Chicago].

24½x17. 4 *l*, ix-xii, 3 *l*, (3)-575, xxxvi, 1 *l*. Blue cloth hc, gilt spine print. Vol III of 3-vol set is entitled "The rise of a modern city : 1871-1893." WCE ref scattered throughout. Final chap is "The White City," one b/w illus. Contents: WCE organization, architecture, congresses, educational demonstrations, music and arts, effect of the WCE on money market and real estate prices, and women's activities. ☺ . (CU,DC,OU,Smth,UIC,USFr,UTA,VAM)

2408.4 Plum, Werner. *...Les expositions universelles au 19ème siècle, spectacles du changement socio-culturel.* Bonn – Bad Godesberg: Friedrich-Ebert-Stiftung, [1977].

18x11. 176 p. Vermilion wraps with Lissajous figure. At head of title: "Aspects sociaux et culturels de l'industrialisation." Translation to French from the German original. Trans: (see below). ☺ . (BRA)

---- English ed: *World exhibitions in the nineteenth century : pageants of social and cultural change.* (sfsu)

2410. *Poetisas Mexicanas*: (CU,UCI)

2410.1 Pratt, Richard Henry. *Battlefield and classroom : Four Decades with the American Indian, 1867–1904.* New Haven & London: Yale UP, 1964 [ᶜ1964 by Yale U].

25½x18½. xiii, 1 *l* (port), (ix)-xix, 337 p, 1 *l*, 33 plates, (339)-358 p. No frontis. Brown cloth hc, gilt print on spine. Part of "Yale Western Americana series, 6." Contents: Large amount of info about Pratt's trip to the WCE with 500 Indian students from the Carlisle Indian School, Carlisle, PA. Pratt was a Brigadier General, retired. ☺ (MA,OU,Stfd,UNM,USFr)

☞ Indian schools, like Carlisle, were started by reformers called "Friends of the Indians." The intent was to take young Indians away from the reservation and teach them the ways of the whites. Thus, in time, the deplorable treatment of the Indians during the settlement of the West would be erased and the Indian assimilated into American society. It only worked for a few because when students graduated their new skills meant little back on the reservation.

2412.1 Pridmore, Jay. *Museum of Science and Industry, Chicago.* Chicago: Abrams, [ᶜ1997].

29x24. 160 p. Illus, some color. Dark blue cloth hc, blind stamped, green spine print. Color matte dj, white and blue print. Several ref to its founding at WCE as the Fine Arts Bldg in Jackson Park. Most dramatic is illus on p 20 of the abandoned and dilapidated Field Museum (Fine Arts) in 1920. (ref)

2413. *The Quest for Unity : American Art Between World's Fairs*: (GLD,CCA,Col,CU,HU,NAG,SAL,sfpl,UCB,UCI) $12 - 28

2413.1 Rainwater, Dorothy T., and Donna H. Felger. *American Spoons : Souvenir and Historical.* [Hanover, PA]: Everybodys Press, [ᶜ1968, ᶜ1977 by Rainwater and Felger].

25½x17½. 416 p+(14) p price guide. Pebbled wraps, illus of spoons on blue background, title in white. WCE spoons scattered throughout. B/w illus. Index. See #2395 for another spoon book. ☺ (S)

2415.1 *Recollections of life & doings in Chicago : from the Haymarket Riot to the end of World War I By An Old Timer.* Chicago: Normandie House, 1945 [ᶜ1945 by Charles H. Hermann].

23½x16½. 4 *l*, 11-273, (1) p. No frontis. Maroon cloth hc, gilt print and design. Red, white, and black dj. Includes reminiscences of several visits to the WCE. (ref)

2415.2 Regnery, Henry. *The cliff dwellers : The History of a Chicago Cultural Institution.* N.p.: Chicago Historical Bookworks, 1990.

24½x15. viii, 64 p. Tan paper covered boards over red cloth spine, gilt cover design and spine print. Sheet laid in acknowledging Donald Amadei, photographer. Club was founded by Hamlin Garland (frontis), and named after the Henry Fuller book of same title. Chap 1, pp 3-6, on WCE impetus. (GLD)

2415.3 Renner, Doris. "The World's Columbian fair in Chicago 1893 : Weltausstellung Chicago 1893." Thesis (Diplomarbeit). Salzburg U, 1987.

29½x21. 104 *l*. Text in German. ☺ . (ONB)

2415.4 *...Reports on the New York Exhibition of 1853 : and the : World's Columbian Exposition : of 1893 : 1854–94.* Vol. 42. Shannon, Ire.: Irish UP, [ᶜ1991 Irish UP].

34½x21. 3 *l*, 9-534 p. Illus, part folded. Red cloth hc, gilt print. At head of title: "Irish University press area studies series : British parliamentary papers : United States of America : 42." Rpt of select documents from the 19ᵗʰ century British House of Commons sessional and command papers. ☺ . (HML)

2415.5 *Revisiting the white city : American art at the 1893 World's fair.* [Washington, DC: National museum of American art and national portrait gallery Smithsonian institution, 1993 ᶜ1993 by Smithsonian].

28x21½. 408 p. Blue and green illus glossy wraps, white and red print. B/w and color illus. Published by the Gallery on the occasion of their Columbian centennial exhibition of WCE artwork, Apr 16–Aug 15, 1993. Essays by Robert W. Rydell and Carolyn Kinder Carr.
---- Also found: Hc with glossy dj.
☺ (Amh,CU,CWM,DC,GLD,HML,HU,IStU,Knox,KSU,MH,MIT,MSI,NAG,NDU,RU,S,SHB,slu,Smth,Stfd,UIC,uiuc,UMA,UMC,UMD,UMN,UoC,UVM,VAM,WM)

2415.6 Richards, Laura E., and Maud Howe Elliott. *Julia Ward Howe : 1819–1910.* 2 vols. Boston and New York: Houghton Mifflin co., 1916 [ᶜ1915 by Richards and Elliott].

22½x16. Vol 1: 8 *l*, (3)-392 p. Vol 2: 6 *l*, (3)-434 p, 1 *l*. Interspersed plates not included in paging. Blue-black cloth hc, gilt signature facsimile, gilt spine print, gilt top edges. Frontis port of Julia Ward Howe in each vol. Authors were assisted by Florence Howe Hall. Indexed. Howe's women's rights activities at the WCE are described. ☺ (GLD,Stfd,UMN,UoC)

☞ This publication won the Pulitzer Prize for biography in 1917. All three authors (Laura, Maud, and Florence) were Howe's daughters; Maud Elliott edited #835.

2415.7 Ridpath, John Clark. *Ridpath's history of the United States.* Philadelphia: Historical publishing co., [ᶜ1902, 1906 by E.J. Stanley].

25½x20. (2)-656 p. Illus. Red cloth hc with nice black and gilt design. Chap 31 has 17 pp on WCE and chap 32 has 12 pp. (ref) $18

2415.8 Riedy, James L. *Chicago sculpture.* Urbana, Chicago [and] London: U of Illinois P, [ᶜ1981 by Riedy].

25½x18. xii, 339, (1) p. Glossy stiff wraps, black print, illus of Picasso sculpture in Daley Plaza. WCE scattered throughout, especially Chap 1: "Sculpture and the Columbian Exposition," pp 23-40. Impact of WCE sculpture on existing sculpture in the city. See #1269 for mag article by Riedy. ☺ (WM)

2416.   Roesch. *World's Fairs : Yesterday, Today, Tomorrow*: (GLD,CU,MOHx)
▶Later ed: *World's fairs : Yesterday, Today, Tomorrow.* New York: John Day, [ᶜ1962, 1964, 1967].

1967 ed: 21½x16. 127 p. Black and gold cloth hc, red and yellow print. WCE described in chap 5, pp 29-34. World's fair book for young people. Data in this edition brought up to date, 1967. ☺ (GLD)

2416.1 Roper, Laura Wood. *FLO, A Biography of Frederick Law Olmsted.* Baltimore and London: Johns Hopkins UP, [ᶜ1973 by Roper].

24x17. xvii, 1 *l*, 555 p. Maroon cloth hc, silver spine print. Frontis port of Olmsted. Includes Olmsted's activities and impact at the Chicago fair; chap 33 and 34. [See index under Olmsted for related citations.] ☺ (csuf,HPL,OU,Smth,UoC,USFr)

2417.   Ross. *Silhouette in diamonds : The Life of Mrs. Potter Palmer*: (GLD)
▶Add dj description: Rust and white dj, white and black print; full-length port of Mrs. Palmer.

2418.   Rossen. *Columbian World's Fair Collectibles*: (B,Col,EPL,FLP,IHi,IStU,MSI,NPG,slcl,StLa,UAH,UIC,uiuc,VAM,WM) $15 - 32

2418.1 Russell, Don. *The lives and legends of Buffalo Bill.* Norman and London: U of Oklahoma P, [ᶜ1960 (6th printing 1988) by the U of Oklahoma P].

23x16. x, 1 *l*, 3-514 p. Wraps are two-tone brown, b/w print, image of a bucking bronco sculpture. Frontis of William Cody. Describes Cody's Wild West and Congress of Rough Riders of the World: "hit its high point at the World's Columbian Exposition in Chicago in 1893." [See index under Buffalo Bill for related Cody items.] ☺ . (BBM,OU,Stfd)

2419.   Rydell. *All the world's a fair* [thesis]: (HML)
2420.   Rydell. *All the World's a fair* [book]: (bgsu,FM,HML,Knox,MSI,slu,UBO,VtHx)

2420.1 Rydell, Robert W[illiam, II], and Nancy Gwinn, eds. *Fair representations : World's Fairs and the Modern World.* Amsterdam: VU UP, 1994 [ᶜ1994 Amerika Instituut].

24x17. (5), (1)-253 p. B/w illus. White glossy wraps, blue and red print and design. Eleven contributors in addition to the editors. Attempt to answer the question, what makes the social reality of the WFs believable for the millions of visitors to them? Includes the WCE. Series: "European contributions to American studies." ☺ . (SML)

2421. Saint-Gaudens. *The reminiscences*: ☺ . (BPL,DC,MIT,NPG,RPL,Smth,UBO,UCB,UMN,USFr,UTA,UoC,VAM)

▶Corrected capitalization: *The reminiscences of Augustus Saint-Gaudens*.

☞ Saint-Gaudens wrote a 70-page condensation, same title, for *Century* magazine, vol 77, 1909.

2421.1 Saurino, Mary Ann. "The white city: urban space and social order at the Columbian exposition." MA diss. U of Minnesota, 1985.

28x21½. 137 p. Typescript. Thesis: The socioeconomic elite saw it as their responsibility to define the American city through WCE construction, aesthetics, and activities. Perception of the socioeconomic value of the WCE changed from 1893–1903, as judged by books published during that period (p 102). Bibliography from pp (129)-37. ☺ (UMN)

2421.2 Schaaf, Barbara C. *Mr. Dooley's Chicago*. Garden City, NY: Anchor/Doubleday, 1977 [ᶜ1977 Schaaf].

21½x15. 4 *l*, 399, (1) p author bio + unpaged illus. Black cloth spine over black paper covered boards, gilt facsimile signature; multicolor illus glossy dj, b/w print. "Mr. Dooley" was a Chicago *Evening Post* popular cartoon character and political satire column created by Finnley Peter Dunne in the 1890's. This book reprints selected articles, including several related to the WCE. ☺ (GLD)

2421.3 Schlereth, Thomas J. *Victorian America : Transformations in Everyday Life, 1876–1915*. [New York]: HarperCollins*Publishers*, [ᶜ1991 by Schlereth].

21½x14½. xvi, 363 p. Illus. Brown and buff hc. WCE pp 169-76. Other scattered references and analysis of World's fairs' impact on "moving, working, housing, consuming, communicating, playing, striving, living and dying." ☺ . (HML)

2421.4 Schroeder-Gudehus, Brigitte, and Anne Rasmussen. *Les fastes du progrès : Le guide des Expositions universelles : 1851–1992*. Paris: Flammarion, 1992 [ᶜ1992 – Flammarion].

24x17½. 255 p. Illus wraps, white lettering, original colors of the painting "Le Dôme central à l'Exposition universelle de 1889." C.t. Individual summaries of WFs, including the WCE with its bibliography pp 121-27. Includes glossary and essays on classification systems and international regulations. Text in French. Title trans: The Displays of Progress : The Guide to Universal Expositions : 1851–1992. See #2325.2 and #2355 for other recent WF anthologies. (SML)

2422.1 Seager, Richard Hughes, ed. *The Dawn of Religious Pluralism : Voices from the World's Parliament of Religions, 1893*. La Salle, IL: Open Court, [ᶜ1993 by Open Court].

23x15½. xvii, 502, (16) p of plates. Includes contemporary photos. Burnt-orange cloth hc with gilt design and spine print. Dj. Sepia text and illus. Sixty addresses given to the Parliament in 1893. See Seager's PhD diss at #2423. ☺ . (DC,UMA,UMD)

☞ The World's Parliament of Religions met in Chicago in August 1993 for the 100th anniversary of the first Parliament, which was held at the WCE in 1893.

2423. Seager. *The World's Parliament of Religions*: (UoC)

2423.1 Seager, Richard Hughes. *The World's parliament of religions : The East/West Encounter, Chicago, 1893*. Bloomington and Indianapolis: Indiana UP, [ᶜ1995 by Seager].

23½x15½. xxxi, 208 p includes b/w illus. Maroon cloth hc, gilt spine print. A brief history of the WCE with major emphasis on the parliament of religions. Also describes the aftermath and influence of the parliaments. ☺ . (BrU,DC,GBP,Heb,OU,sfsu,Stfd,UIC,UMC,UoC)

2423.2 Seto City Folk Historical Material Museum. *Beauty in the Japanese modern pottery : Mainly The Exhibit of International Exposition in Chicago*. Japan: Seino graphic arts, ᶜ1997.

30x21. (6), 112, (2) p. Multicolor matte stiff wraps, black Kana title print. Title from last page. English and Japanese text describes their WCE exhibits. Beautiful color plates of pottery, many from WCE. A few plates are the same as those in #2435.3. © (GLD,Fess,S) $45 - 70

2423.3 Shackleton, Robert. *The book of Chicago.* Philadelphia: Penn publishing co., 1920 [°1920 by Penn].

19½x14½. 4 *l*, 354 p. Green cloth hc, gilt print. WCE pp 227-38 plus scattered references. © . (UIC)

2424.   Shaw, Marian. *World's Fair Notes : A Woman Journalist Views Chicago's 1893 Columbian Exposition.* St. Paul, MN: Pogo Press, [°1992].   P➔

25x18. 108 p. Glossy stiff wraps, color illus of Ferris wheel. Reprints 20 articles Shaw wrote for the *Argus* (newspaper), Fargo, North Dakota.
© (GLD,csuf,CU,D,F,FM,GBP,GPL,HML,HU,IHi,KCPL,MSI,PPL,RPL,S,SHB,slpl,Stfd,StLa,UCI,UCLA,UIC,uiuc,UMN,WM)
▶Post-publication completed citation.

2427.   Siegal. *Chicago's Famous Buildings*: (NUL)
▶Completed citation: 20½x12. xiv, 271 p. Glossy b/w stiff wraps, red and white spine. Describes downtown bldg around the time of the WCE but no direct mention of the Fair.

2427.1 Silverman, Kenneth. *Houdini!!! : the career of Ehrich Weiss.* [New York]: Harper Collins, [°1996 by Silverman].

24½x17½. xi, 1 *l*, (3)-465 p, 1 *l* author info. Blue paper covered boards, black cloth spine with silver print; white dj, blue and red print, illus of Houdini in chains. Nineteen years old and not-yet-famous, Houdini, with friend Jacob Hyman, had the "Houdini Brothers" act on the Midway in 1893 and played the Kohl & Middleton show at Chicago's "State Street Globe Dime Museum near Van Buren Street" during the week of Oct 23, 1893 (pp 8-9 and illus). (ref)

2428.   Simkin. *Fairs Past and Present*: (MIT)

2428.1 Slabaugh, Arlie R. *United States commemorative coinage.* Racine, WI: Whitman publishing, [1963].

2nd Printing: 20x14. 144 p. Gray textured paper covered hc, copper print. Excellent descriptions with illus of the first US commemorative coins: Columbian half (pp 11-15) and Isabella 25¢ (pp 16-17). Also coinage from other WFs. [The Isabella quarter is the only US coin depicting a foreign ruler.] © (GLD)

2428.2 Smith, Carl S. *Chicago and the American Literary Imagination : 1880–1920.* Chicago and London: U of Chicago P, [°1984 by U of Chicago].

23x15½. 3 *l*, vii-xiv, 232 p. B/w illus. Brown, blue, and white glossy wraps; blue print. Description of WCE and its influence on literature scattered throughout. © (GLD,BPL,UMA,USFr,UTA,UoC)

2428.3 Smith, George W. *History of Illinois and her people.* Vol. III. Chicago and New York: American historical society, 1927 [°1927 by American Historical Society].

28x20½. 441 p. Black cloth pebbled hc, gilt spine print. Frontis port of Smith. Vol 3 of 6-vol set. Chap 10: "Illinois in World's fairs." WCE and World's congresses on pp 232-67. © . (Smth,UIC)

2428.4 Smith, Henry Justin. *Chicago's great century : 1833 : 1933.* Chicago: Consolidated Publishers for A Century of Progress 1933, ___.

22x15. 4 *l*, 198 p+ b/w illus not included in paging. First *l* is frontis port of William B. Ogden, Chicago's first mayor. Blue cloth hc, silver print. Chap 13, pp 102-13, entitled "Hail Columbus," contains WCE info. See #2389.1 and #2389.2 for other H.J. Smith Chicago histories. . (FPL,OU,UTA)

2428.5 *Some facts concerning "The Pioneer."* N.p.: n.p., n.d.

27x20½. 1 *l* card illus of Pioneer "Courtesy Republic Steel Corp.", 2 *l* typescript, 1 *l* photo repro of "Pioneer." Description of the 1831 railroad engine built by Matthias W. Baldwin, founder of Baldwin Locomotive in PA. Mentions the WCE "Pioneer" exhibit. © (FM)

2428.6 *Souvenir of Chicago. In Colors.* Chicago: V.O. Hammon Publishing, ᶜ1915 V.O. Hammon. **P→**

16x20½. (100) p. Color lithos on both sides of pages with descriptive text beneath each. String-tied brown stiff wraps with light brown embossed border. C.t,: "Chicago." Cover image of "I Will" (see #1588). In addition to showing the continued usage of "I Will" to personify Chicago, the whale-back boat ("Christopher Columbus") is shown as still in service, as well as La Rabida, Field Columbian Museum (Fine Arts Bldg), German Bldg, Auditorium Theatre, and Art Institute. ☺ (GLD)

☞ The "I Will" motto is still used. It was used on Chicago's 1976 Bicentennial flag and appears on the sides of some of the Chicago Transit Authority subway cars.

2429.   Sparks. *The Dream City : A story of the World's fair*: (B,ICRL)

2431.   Spillman. *Glass from World's fairs*: (GLD,HML,S,WM)
---- Also found: Glossy stiff wraps, same multicolor litho rpt from 1889 Paris Expo as the hc.

2431.1 Stevenson, Elizabeth. *Park Maker: A Life of Frederick Law Olmsted.* New York: Macmillan; London: Collier Macmillan, [ᶜ1977 by Stevenson].

24x16½. xxv, 1 *l*, 484 p+ 8 *l* plates between pp 228-29 not included in paging. Green cloth hc, gilt spine print. Green and brown dj with port of Olmsted. Includes his important landscape architectural contributions to the WCE. [See index under Olmsted for related citations.] ☺ (GLD,DC,IHi,Stfd,OU,UoC)

2431.2 Stritch, Thomas. *The Kawneer Story.* Niles, MI: Kawneer company, 1956.

20½x14½. 223 p. Cloth spine, paper covered boards with etching of man in a shop bending aluminum frame. C.t. = t.p. Illus by Philip Reed. A biography of founder Francis Plym. Inspired by a trip to the WCE (pp 1-2) and educated in architecture at the U of Illinois, he started Kawneer, manufacturer of commercial aluminum extrusions for architectural curtain walls and windows. ☺ . (ref) $18

2431.3 Strout, Richard Lee, ed. *Maud.* New York: Macmillan, 1939 [ᶜ1939 by Macmillan].

24x16½. xii, 1 *l*, 593 p. No frontis. Gray-blue cloth hc, gilt cover and spine print. Publication of the six vol (1881–95) diary of Isabella Maud Rittenhouse, an artist who wrote for *Godey's Ladies' Book.* Maud summarizes her 15 days at the WCE and the grand beauty of the event, pp 564-65. ☺ (GLD.Stfd)

2431.4 Sullivan, Louis H. *The autobiography of an idea.* New York: Press of the American Institute of Architects, 1924.

21x14. 330 p. Contains Sullivan's denunciation of WCE architecture after his fortunes had declined.
---- New York: Press of the American Institute of Architects, 1926.
---- New York: Dover Publications, 1955.
(csuf,DC,Heb,MIT,NUL,Smth,UBO,UMN,UTA)

2432.   Swift. *The World's Columbian Exposition and the University of Chicago : Radio*: (HU,IHi,Smth)

2432.1 Szuberla, Guy Alan. "Urban vistas and pastoral garden: studies in the literature and architecture of Chicago : (1893 - 1909)." PhD diss. U of Minnesota, 1971.

28x21½. 3, (3), 249 numbered *l*. Includes segments on Burnham and Sullivan (WCE architects); and WCE authors, Fuller, Herrick, and Dreiser. ☺ . (csuf)

2432.2 Taft, Lorado. *The history of American sculpture.* New York: Macmillan, 1903 [ᶜ1903 Macmillan].

26x19. 1 *l*, xiii, 544 p, 1 *l* ads. Frontis of Lincoln statue. Deep red cloth hc, gilt print and design of statue by Warner, gilt top edge. All major sculptors at the WCE described; includes illus of MacMonnies

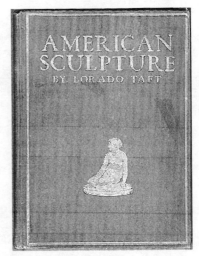

Fountain, p (337). Taft criticizes E. Ney's statue of Sam Houston in the Texas Bldg (see #2340.6) as effeminate. ☺ (GLD,Stfd,UoC)   **P➔**
---- Also found: New York: Macmillan, 1924. Series: The History of American Art. Edited by John C. Van Dyke.

2433.   Tallmadge. *The Story of architecture in America*: (Stfd)
---- Also listed: 1927 1st ed.

2434.1 Teasdale, Wayne, and George F. Cairns, eds. *The community of religions : voices and images of the Parliament of the World's Religions.* New York: Continuum, 1996.

23x__. 259 p. Description of the 1993 centennial Parliament of Religions held in Chicago. Dr. David Ramage, Jr., was chair of the Council for a Parliament of the World's Religions. (EvP,GBP,UoC,USFr)

2434.2 Tenorio-Trillo, Mauricio. *Mexico at the : World's Fairs : Crafting a Modern Nation.* Berkeley Los Angeles London: U of CA Press, [°1996].

23½x16. xiv, 373 p. Dark green paper covered boards with maroon cloth spine and gilt spine print. Red and black dj, white print and illus of 1889 souvenirs in b/w. C.t. =t.p. Scattered references to WCE plus pp 184-86. Excellent appendix and index with list of Mexican delegates to WCE. ☺ (GLD)

2434.3 Tharp, Louise Hall. *Saint-Gaudens and the gilded era.* Boston [and] Toronto: Little, [°1969 by Tharp].

24x16½. xii, 419 p. Illus. Tan cloth hc, gilt spine print; pale yellow dj, black and red print, illus of a Saint-Gaudens' sculpture. Text and illus of Saint-Gaudens' WCE work are scattered throughout. Also extensive discussion of Stanford White, joint architect of the Ag Bldg and a womanizer, who was killed by a jealous husband—Harry K. Thaw. ☺ . (GLD,Berk,NAG,NPG,OU,UBO,UCB,UMA,UoC,USFr)

2434.4 Thomas, Rose Fay. *Memoirs of Theodore Thomas.* New York: Moffat, Yard and co., 1911 [°1911 by Moffat, Yard].

23x16. xviii, 569 p. Navy blue cloth hc, gilt emblem, gilt spine print, gilt top edge. Biography written by his wife. Chap 17 and 18 detail the WCE Director of Music activities of Thomas. He received one of the inaugural ceremony metals to "Artists who Designed the World's Columbian Exposition." See #1486 in the original bibliography for more about Thomas. (ref,Stfd,UoC)

2435.1 Tobias, Michael, Jane Morrison, and Bettina Gray, ed. *A Parliament of Souls : in search of global spirituality.* San Francisco: KQED Books, [°1995 by KQED, Inc.]

23x18½. viii, 291, (3) p. Color wraps. Text accompanying the PBS series of conversations with 28 spiritual leaders. Introd mentions the 1893 and 1993 Parliaments as antecedents to the TV version. ☺ (sapl)

2435.2 Todd, John Emerson. *Frederick Law Olmsted.* Boston: Twayne, [°1982 by G.K. Hall & Co.].

21x15. 212 p. Frontis port of Olmsted. Orange cloth hc, gilt spine print. Chap 7: "The Heights: Biltmore and the World's Columbian Exposition of 1893." Other scattered ref to Olmsted's WCE design. Twayne's World Leaders Series. [See Olmsted in index for related citations.] ☺ . (OU,USFr)

2435.3 Tokyo National Museum. *Umi o wattata Meiji no bijutsu.*[front cover title] : *World's Columbian Exposition of 1893 Revisited : 19ᵗʰ century Japanese art shown in Chicago, U.S.A.* [back cover title]. Tokyo: Tokyo National Museum, [°1997].

30x21. 131, (2), xi p. Color glossy stiff wraps, white and maize print. Illus of Japan exhibits at WCE on both covers. Contains Japan exhibit text of Bancroft (#733) in Japanese. Plan and elevation of the Ho-o-den on the Wooded Island. Many beautiful color plates of exhibited art and cloisonné, b/w illus of their WCE pavilions. Anglicized c.t. from front; English title on back. Part English text. ☺ . (GLD,Fess,S,Stfd)

2436.   Tozer. *American attitudes toward machine technology*: (Amh,CU,HML,LU,slu,UMN)

2436.1 Trachtenberg, Alan. *The incorporation of America : Culture and Society in the Gilded Age.* New York: Hill and Wang, [ᶜ1982 by Trachtenberg].

21½x14½. 3 *l*, vii-viii, 2 *l*, 3-260, (1) p. Royal blue cloth hc, silver spine print. Chap 7: "White City" describes the WCE. Other scattered ref to the WCE and the Congresses throughout. A bibliographical essay (pp 249-50) based upon recent books analyzes the WCE in the context of modern times. ☺ (OU,UNM)

2437. Treseder. *A visitor's trip to Chicago in 1893*: (IHi)

2437.1 Turner, Frederick Jackson. *The significance of the frontier in American history.* Ithaca, NY: Cornell UP, [ᶜ1956].

28x21½. 37 p. Dark green paper covered boards, green cloth spine with gilt print. Woodcuts by Elfriede Abbe. Rpt of Turner's essay first read at the American Historical Assn (WCE congresses) meeting held in Chicago July 11–13, 1893 (see #230.2 for the original). Limited ed—275 copies. DC copy no 121 signed by Abbe. ☺ (DC)

2437.2 [Turner, Frederick Jackson]. *Rereading Frederick Jackson Turner: The significance of the frontier in American history.* New York: Holt, 1994.

24x16. Hc. Rpt and descriptive analysis of Turner's WCE paper (see #230.2). (ref)

2437.3 Twombly, Robert. *Louis Sullivan: His Life and Work.* New York: Viking, [1986].

24x16. x, 2 *l*, 530 p. Blue paper boards, navy cloth spine. Tan illus dj. Several references and comments on WCE and its architecture, including Sullivan's Transportation Bldg. (ref)

2437.4 Union League Club of Chicago. *The spirit of the Union League Club : 1879–1926 : "Welcome to Loyal Hearts : We join ourselves to no party which does not carry the flag and keep step to the music of the Union."* N.p.: n.p., [ᶜ1926 by Union League Club of Chicago].

25x16½. 4 *l*, 142 p+ 1 *l* limited edition presentation page. Gray-blue paper covered boards with gilt design and embossed name of recipient, linen spine with gilt label. Blue vignettes at the bottom of most pages. Chapters by various authors. Chap 4 describes the Club's interaction with the WCE. Seven of 12 members of the WCE Company executive committee were Union League members. Other club members included Director-General George R. Davis and Daniel H. Burnham, Director of Works. GLD copy number 469; total number not specified. ☺ (GLD,ULC)

2437.5 United Federation of Doll Collectors. *World's Columbian Exposition Revisited : Chicago 1893–1993. UFDC 44ᵗʰ Annual Convention.* [Kansas City, MO: UFDC (Coplin Printing, Youngstown, OH), ᶜ1993 by the UFDC].

28x22. 2-103 p. Tan stiff wraps, brown print and design. Color and b/w illus. Dedicated to centennial of WCE. WCE collectibles, Columbian stuffed doll info, excellent descriptions. ☺ (GLD,B,Fess,S) P➔

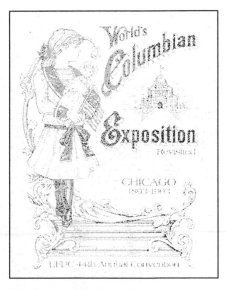

2437.6 United Federation of Doll Collectors. *World's Columbian Exposition Revisited : Chicago 1893-1993. UFDC 44th Annual Convention. 10th Annual Paper Doll Luncheon* [Kansas City, MO: UFDC (Coplin Printing, Youngstown, OH), ᶜ1993 by the UFDC]

30½x22½. 6 *l* white glossy stiff stock + back cover paper dolls, making 7 *l*. Tan stiff wraps, brown print and design as in #2437.5. Colorful Columbian paper dolls and illus. Pretty commemorative from the Columbian centennial doll convention. ☺ (GLD,Fess,S)

2437.7 University of Michigan Library. *The White City : World's Columbian Exposition : Chicago 1893. February 1, 1993–April 2, 1993.* Ann Arbor: U of Michigan Library, [ᶜ1993].

22x14. 15, (1) p. Light gray wraps, black print, illus of plan for WCE grounds. A Columbian centennial exhibit catalog listing and describing WCE prints and other items. ☺ . (GLD,UMi,UVM)

2438.   Upton. *Theodore Thomas, a musical autobiography*:   (Stfd)

2439.1 Wade, Louise Carroll. *Chicago's pride : The Stockyards, Packingtown, and Environs in the Nineteenth Century*. Urbana and Chicago: U of Illinois P, [ᶜ1987 by the Board of Trustees of the U of Illinois].

24x16½. xvi, 423, (1) p. Blue cloth hc, silver spine print. Dj with red with white "Chicago" and an aerial view of Chicago. Ten interspersed pages on the WCE.   (UTA)

2439.2 Wagenknecht, Edward. *Chicago*. Norman: U of Oklahoma P, [ᶜ1964 by U of Oklahoma P].

20x14. ix, 182 p. Orange cloth hc, gilt spine print, yellow dyed top edge. No frontis. Red and black t.p. Chap 1 (pp 3-24), "The White City," details the WCE's importance in the development of American culture; other scattered WCE ref. The Centers of Civilization Series. © (GLD,BPL,FPL,OHxS,Smth,UMA,USFr,UTA)

2439.3 Waldsmith, John S. *Stereo : views : an illustrated history and price guide*. Radnor, PA: Wallace-Homestead, ᶜ1991 by Waldsmith.

25x18. ix, 1 *l*, 271 p. Colored stiff wraps, photo illus of stereo cards and view master reels. C.t. = t.p. WCE-related stereo cards described pp 100-05, 136, and 149. See #2395.2 for related item. (ref)

☞ Obtain more information on stereo cards from the National Stereoscopic Association (NSA), PO Box 14801, Columbus, OH 43214. NSA publishes *Stereo World* and has established the Oliver Wendell Holmes Stereoscopic Research Library, which is located at Eastern College in St. David's, PA.

2439.4 Walter, Dave, comp. *Today Then : America's Best Minds Look 100 Years into the Future on the Occasion of the 1893 World's Columbian Exposition*. [Helena, MT]: American & World Geographic Publishing, [ᶜ1992 American & World].

23x15½. 3 *l*, 7-226 p, 1 *l*. No frontis. Ports and illus. Blue and red glossy stiff wraps, blue and white print. Rpts of 74 American Press Association syndicated articles from 1892–93. Each author was asked to predict the world situation in 100 years, i.e., 1993, from his/her perspective. Each article is accompanied by a bio of the author, usually with port. © (GLD,BPL,CU,CWM,DU,HU,IHi,NJHx,slcl,slpl,SPL,UCD,uiuc,UMD)

2439.5 Wanamaker, John. *Golden book of the Wanamaker stores : Jubilee year 1861–1911*. N.p.: n.p., [ᶜ1911 by Wanamaker].

23x15½. x, 1 *l*, 318 p+ many unpaged plates, fold map in back. Maroon cloth hc, gilt print, gilt top edge. Frontis port of Wanamaker. Mentions their 1876 Centennial and 1893 Columbian displays. (ref)

2439.6 Waterman, A.N. *Historical review of Chicago and Cook County : and selected biography*. Vol. I. Chicago [and] New York: Louis publishing, 1908.

27x18½. Vol I: 3 *l*, (1)-495 p. Hc, gilt edges. Frontis: steel engraved port of Waterman with tissue guard. WCE, pp 67-72, includes Chicago Day and the Parliament of Religions. A 3-vol set. © . (UIC)

2439.7 Weigel, John C[onrad]. *A remarkable man and the Columbian Exposition; Lombard's Harlow Higinbotham, the Exposition's administrative genius*. [Galesburg, IL: Knox College], 1973.

28x21½. 5 p. Illus. Rpt from *Knox Alumnus*, Nov 1973. (IHi)

2441.   Weimann. *The Fair Women*: (GLD,Amh,APL,BCPL,Berk,bgsu,BPL,CC,CCA,Col,CU,CUA,cul,DC,DU,E,EPL,EvP,FLP,FM,GPL,GU,HML,HU,IHi, ISU,IWU, KCPL,Knox,KSU,LACL,LBA,LU,MCHx,MH,MIT,MSI,MSU,NDU,NPG,OU,PPL,PSU,RPL,RU,S,sapl,sfpl,sfsu,SHB,slcl,slu,Smth,SPL,Stfd,UCB,UCD, UCI,UCLA,UIC,uiuc,UMA,UMC,UMD,UMN,UoA,UPa,URI,USFr,UTA,UWM,VCU,VT,WM,wsu,Yale)

2441.1 Wells-Barnett, Ida. B. *Selected works of Ida B. Wells-Barnett*. Comp and introd. Trudier Harris. New York [and] Oxford: Oxford UP, 1991 [ᶜ1991 by Oxford UP].

17x13. xxxi, 322 p. Illus. Frontis port of Ida B. Wells-Barnett. Navy blue hc, gilt print. From the series: Schomburg library of nineteenth-century Black women writers. © . (Berk,bgsu,HU,Knox,MU,SHB,UMA,UMD)

2441.2 Wendt, Lloyd. *Chicago Tribune : The rise of a great American newspaper*. Chicago, New York [and] San Francisco: Rand McNally, [ᶜ1979 by Rand McNally].

25x17½. 5 *l*, 11-861 p, 1 *l*. Black cloth hc, silver print; black; white and red glossy dj. Frontis litho of top of Tribune bldg. Tribune's WCE involvement scattered pp 284-558. See Wendt, #2382.1. (USFr,UTA)

2441.3 Wendt, Lloyd, and Herman Kogan. *Give the Lady What She Wants!* South Bend, IN: And Books, 1981 [ᶜ1952 by Marshall Field & Co.].

20½x14. 383 p. Hunter green and pink wraps, white and red print. The story of the Marshall Field department store in Chicago, including its destruction in the great fire of 1871 and how Harry Selfridge masterminded promotions. WCE on pp 217-20 and 223-25. See #2382, #2382.1, and # 2441.2. ☺ (GLD)

2441.4 Whiteman, John, Jeffrey Kipnis, and Richard Burdett, eds. *Strategies in architectural thinking.* [Chicago]: Chicago Institute for Architecture and Urbanism, ᶜ1992.

28x__. 256 p. Illus. A selection of conference papers that includes "Frank Lloyd Wright at the Midway : Chicago, 1893" by Mark Rakatansky. (UMD)

2441.5 Williams, Kenny J. *In the city of men : Another Story of Chicago.* Nashville, TN: Townsend press, [ᶜ1974 by Williams].

22x15. xvii, 1 *l*, 3-483 p. Blue cloth hc, gilt print. C.t. = t.p. Extensive discussion of WCE and its personalities scattered throughout. Comprehensive Chicago bibliography, pp 435-68. ☺ (GLD,UIC)

2441.6 Wilson, William H[enry]. *The City Beautiful Movement.* Baltimore and London: Johns Hopkins UP, [ᶜ1989 by Johns Hopkins UP].

26x18½. x, 1 *l*, 365, (2) p. Illus. Burgundy cloth spine over black cloth hc, gilt spine print. Series: "Creating the North American Landscape." Olmsted and his influence upon the WCE, pp 53-74. Theses: Olmstedian landscape architecture was the taproot for the City Beautiful Movement; contrary to other writers, the WCE was neither the inspiration for the movement nor the beginning of comprehensive city planning. [See index under Olmsted for related citations.] (Knox,OU,slu,UAH,USFr)

2441.7 Wojtowicz, James W. *The W.F. Cody Buffalo Bill collector's guide with values.* Paducah, KY: Collector Books, [ᶜ1998 by Wojtowicz].

28½x22. 271, (1) p ad for Shroeder's books. Glossy hc with illus of tickets to Chicago summer 1893 show. B/w and color illus. Includes WCE Congress of Rough Riders items. [See Buffalo Bill in index for more Cody citations.] ☺ (S)

2442.1 Wood, Mary I. *The history : of : the general federation : of women's clubs : for the first twenty-two years of its organization.* New York: The history department : general federation of women's clubs, [ᶜ1912 by General Federation of women's clubs].

21x15. 1 *l* frontis, x, 445 p. Frontis port of Mrs. "Jennie June" Croly. Green cloth hc, gilt spine print. Description of the federated clubs' meeting at the WCE on May 18, 1893, (pp 53-58). Also their first meeting in Chicago in 1892 to plan for the WF. See #815.8 and #2264.1. ☺ (LPL,Stfd,UoC,WML)

2443. *The World's Columbian*: ▶Original citation was pre-pub info; publication info below:

Bertuca, David J., Donald K. Hartman, and Susan M. Neumeister, comps. *The World's Columbian Exposition : a centennial bibliographic guide.* Westport, CT.: Greenwood, 1996.

25x16. xxix, 440 p. Illus, map. Green cloth hc, silver print on black rectangular background. Number 26 in "Bibliographies and Indexes in American History." Excellent reference, especially regarding WCE articles from major periodicals of the time. WCE remainders chap by collector Charles E. Gregersen, Chicago. Not all citations indexed; e.g., cite A31 is our original bibliography, #2348.2. Source listings for unpublished items only. ☺ (BU,CU,DC,HML,HU,IHi,Knox,NAG,OU,S,Stfd,UMN,UVM)

2443.1 Yates, JoAnne. *Control through Communication : The Rise of System in American Management.* Baltimore and London: Johns Hopkins UP, [ᶜ1989 by Yates].

23½x15½. xx, 339 p. Sepia cloth hc, black spine print; glossy sepia dj, black and sepia print. How the Library Bureau devised the first vertical files and cases in 1892 and exhibited them at the WCE, winning a gold medal is described pp 56-57. Her thesis is that vertical files revolutionized office communication and productivity. © . (VSA)

2443.2 Yost, Nellie Snyder. *Buffalo Bill : His Family, Friends, Fame, Failures, and Fortunes*. Chicago: Swallow, [ᶜ1979, 1980].

23x17½. 5 *l*, 500 p. Illus. Brown cloth hc, white spine print; light tan dj, chocolate print and illus. Map end papers. Chap 24, pp 236-54, includes the WCE and Cody congress. The show opened Apr 3, 1893, in Chicago—before the WCE opened. The cast numbered 500 to 600. [See index under Buffalo Bill for more Cody citations.] © (OU,Stfd,UoC)

2444.   Ziff. *The American 1890s: The Life & Times of a Lost Generation*: (Stfd)
▶Add info: 22x__. viii, 376 p.

2444.1 Ziolkowski, Eric J., ed. *A museum of faiths : histories and legacies of the 1893 World's Parliament of Religions*. Atlanta, GA: Scholars, 1993.

24x__. xiii, 366 p. Series: Classics in religious studies; no 9. See #1333 for a Ziolkowski article.
(DC,IWU,RU,UoC)

2444.2 Zukowsky, John, ed. *Chicago Architecture : 1872-1922 : Birth of a Metropolis*. Munich: Prestel-Verlag with The Art Institute of Chicago, [ᶜ1987 Prestel-Verlag].

30½x23½. 480 p. B/w and color illus. Gray cloth hc, royal blue spine print. Dj illus with Wrigley Bldg. Frontis is an aerial view of Chicago downtown about 1930. WCE scattered throughout. French perspective of the Fair and Chicago architecture by Henri Loyrette. Essays by Sally Chappell, Neil Harris, and others. English language ed of #2444.3. © . (KSU,NUL,OU,Stfd,WM)
---- Also listed: Available in soft cover.
---- Also listed: Published in German language.

2444.3 Zukowsky, John. ...*Chicago : Naissance d'une métropole, 1872-1922*. Paris: Prestel-Verlag, [ᶜ1987 Prestel Verlag.]

30x27½. 480 p. Glossy stiff wraps, b/w print, illus is overhead view of Chicago "L" and street scene below. At head of title: "Musée d'Orsay : 2 octobre 1987–3 janvier 1988." French language edition of #2444.2. © . (NUL)

Chapter 15

UNPUBLISHED UNIQUE WORKS

2445. DIARIES:

2445. **csuf**: Wilson, Emily. Diary at WCE, May 29–June 10, 1893. 73 p.

2445. **Fess**: 1) Diary with wraps entitled "Notes," no author. (11) p handwritten list of sights and events seen at WCE from Oct 8–13, 1893. 2) Japanese folding fan printed at the Ho-o-den and carefully handwritten in ink with notes on the owner's visits to the many WCE exhibits. Unique.

2445. **GLD**: ▶Correction: 1) Chase, Mary E. An account of visits to WCE bldgs just *after* the fair opened.

2445. **IaHx**: [see original bibliography—2445.a].

2445. **InHx**: [see original bibliography—2445.b].

2445. **LL**. Humphry, Grace. "Notes from the World's Fair." No date; Springfield, IL. (39) p hand written in pen in a red "Capitol Composition" booklet, 21x17½. She visited all of the major bldgs, state bldgs, Midway, foreign bldgs, and saw one of the evening illuminations.

2445. **MCHx**: 1) Wilson, Edward. 24½x19½. A five vol set of hand printed and illustrated journals entitled "Daleite" dating from 1885–1902. Bound in half leather. Wilson was Editor of the *Daily Pantagraph* (Bloomington, IL) before moving to Chicago in 1896 to work for the *Chicago Record*. This marvelous artfully crafted set is done in magazine format, including two column print. His account of the WCE entitled "Adventures at the fair" was written in May–June 1893.—(Box 2). 2) Lewis, E.J. Diaries 1889–1907, including 1893 WF.—(Box 3).

2445. **OU**: Searcy, Kate Warthen. 2 diaries of her WCE observations of buildings and people which were used for articles she later wrote for the *National Guard*, #1365.2—(Western History Archives Collection # 574).

2445. **RSA**: 2 diaries.

2445. **S**: 1) Ruled (140) p copy book with check cloth cover entitled "Exercises" contains handwritten notations of exhibits seen and bldgs visited, some prices. 2) Pitt, Sophie R. "Our trip to Chicago...June 1893." 12½x8. Unpaged black leather bound and ruled notebook with hinge at top. Detailed diary in pencil of WCE visit, June 13–23, 1893. 3) Gay, Daniel J., Worcester, Mass. 26½x21½. Hinged at top. Full leather, blind stamped black and gilt border, glued on WCE Admission ticket in center. 65 p typed diary with interleaved photos taken by the author and labeled on tissue guards. Beautiful book with detailed descriptions of the Fair. 4) Baker, Horace. Half morocco leather over green cloth hc. 144 p. June 19–July 29, 1893. Handwritten with tipped-in extra folded notes. Detailed account of buildings and exhibits by an observant visitor.

2445. **SStu**: Donner-Hill Family Papers. 18½x11½ note book used as diary. Hill family's 14 p diary segment describes 11 days at the WCE: June 26–July 7, 1893.—(Special Collections MC 18).

2445. **UMi**: [see original bibliography—2445.d].

2445. **UMN**: Freeman, A.F. "Min Amerikafärd." 210 p diary of his trip to America, including the WCE on pp 136–93. Handwritten in Swedish; beautiful script.—(Special Collections F548.5.F74x 1893a).

2445. **UNC**: 1) Allensworth, Emma H. Detailed record of her visit to the WCE by a young woman from Nashville, TN.—(SHC #3214). 2) Cotton, Sallie. 56 p journal of her trip to the WCE.—(FCCB C8471c). 3) Ker, Mary Susan. 39 vol diary spanning 1886–1923. Entries from July and Sept 1893 at the WCE. She describes the crowded conditions, sights, high costs, and the unhappiness of vendors.—(SHC #1467).

2445. **UVM**: Benedict, Katherine A. Pease. 54 small diaries from 1867–1918, including the one for 1893 in which she describes her trip to the WCE. Attending from May 28–June 5, she wrote about the weather and many exhibits she saw.—(Benedict Family Papers, Carton 11).

2445. **whmc**: Fike, Henry C. Diaries of trip to the WCE.—(C2215-vol 14, 16, 17).

2445. **WM**: Ives, Florence C., member of the NY Board of Lady Managers. Diary, 1892–94. 21½x18. 241 p ruled book, "Record" on cover. Cloth textured hc, ½ morocco, green dyed edges. Describes her official WCE visit for NY and the extensive aggravations getting exhibits back home. Reports theft of (NY?) Colored Women's exhibit, Oct 2, 1893; WCE agreed to pay full value of exhibit. She met many influential WCE dignitaries. Mentions her writing draft for #1997.—(Archives Doc. 128, Joseph Downs Collection).

2445.1 **Yale**: [see original bibliography—2445.e].

2446. MISCELLANEOUS:

2446. **AIC**: [see original bibliography—2446.a].

2446. **ASL**: The record groups at the Archives are tabulated in Dixon, Alan J., *Descriptive inventory of the archives of the state of Illinois. Index*. 1978. WCE material is listed on p 22: 1) Correspondence of John Peter Altgeld [IL Governor during the fair]. 4 cubic feet.—(Record Group 101.22). 2) Warrant Ledger for the WCE: Dec 8 1891–Sept 30, 1895. 1 vol. Chronological list of warrants and disbursements issued by the IL Auditor for the Illinois Board of World's Fair Commissioners and the Illinois Woman's Exposition Board. Includes construction of IL Bldg, per diems, and salaries.—(Record Group 105.25). 3) Illinois Woman's Exposition Board. Expense Book. Sept 19, 1891–May 17, 1895. 1 vol. Invoices, names, officers, salaries, kitchen expenses, etc. The State Board of Commissioners could spend 10% of total state WCE appropriations on promoting woman's industries at the WCE.—(Record Group 506).

2446. **BBM**: 1) WCE admission tickets.

2446. **CCA**: 1) Paper 3-D pop-up model of the site of the WCE printed "Made in Germany." 32x49x12 cm high. Accompanied by 1 sheet illus bird's-eye view, 25x32. 2) Woven bookmark showing Machinery Hall. 3) Invitation card to the Centennial celebration of the WCE, Art Institute, Chicago, May 1, 1993. 4) Four 3-D pop-up cards showing WCE bldgs. 5) spoon. 6) ticket. 7) Metal souvenir.

Centre Canadien d'Architecture pop-up 3-D model of WCE

2446. **CHx**: [see original bibliography—2446.b].

2446. **Col**: 1) "Massachusetts State building, World's Columbian Exposition. Chicago 1893." 28x36. C.t. for vol with 20 mounted photos.—(Avery AA 730 M3 C4). 2) 4 vol of WCE pamphlets [1889–1893]: vol 1, Metallurgy and miscellaneous; vol 2, Metallurgy; vol 3, American miscellaneous; vol 4, Foreign miscellaneous.—(Mines Reading Room D 669 C43). 3) Vol of Arkansas WCE pamphlets.—(974.8 Z).

2446. **CPL**: Ellsworth, James W., Collection. 12 linear feet. 18 boxes. Ellsworth was a member of the WCE Board of Directors. The collection is divided into 3 parts: Incoming and outgoing correspondence, departmental records, and ephemera.

2446. **CSA**: [see original bibliography—2446.c].
2446. **csuf**: [see original bibliography—2446.d].

2446. **CU**: [see original bibliography—2446.e]. 2) Grevatt family postcards. Collection includes 12 (full set) Koehler WCE postcards sent to various family members.—(Kroch Lib Rare & Mss #2534). 3) A 31x27 ledger containing copies of letters of the "Columbian Exposition Office : Fifth Judicial District : State of New York – Syracuse, N.Y." June 18, 1892, to Apr 4, 1893. Extensive collection of letters by Lena P. Bennett secretary to Chief Clerk, W.H. Cole, who died in July 1892, regarding the commission's exhibits (never realized) up to the time the furniture was sold and the commission disbanded.—(Kroch Lib Rare & Mss #1508). 4) "The Libbey Glass co.'s World's Fair Factory" 31½x31½ map of grounds.—(Kroch Lib Rare & Mss #1508). "Souvenir of the Columbian Exposition, Chicago, 1893." [n.p., 1893] 25 p illus mounted in an 18x26 album.—(Annex library).

2446.   **CVHx:** [see original bibliography—2446.f].

2446.   **DelHx:** [see original bibliography—2446.g and h].

2446.   **DU:** 1) Papers of: Chambers Baird, Sr. and Jr., Flavius Josephus Cook, Robert Lee Flowers, Ann Henshaw Gardiner, Hemphill Family, Sir Ivor John Caradoc Herbert, Anna P. Knight, Marshall McDonald, Joseph A. Miller (388 items from 1891–1905), John Quincy Adams Nadenbousch, Cornelius Miller Pickens, James Edward Stagg, Jesse Turner. 2) Badge Collection. 3) Currency Collection. 4) Photographs shown at WCE from the 1891 survey of the Columbia River.—(For details see: Davis, Richard C., and Linda Angle Miller, eds. *Guide to the Cataloged Collections : Manuscript Department of the William R. Perkins Library : Duke University.* Santa Barbara, CA [and] Oxford, England: Clio Books, 1980).

2446.   **E:** 1) Large framed certificate hand drawn and signed by the WCE Russian delegation. 2) Tickets. 3) Real photo of the ME State Bldg. 4) Tokens and medals. 5) WCE trade cards.

2446.   **ENM:** 1) Correspondence between sculptor Elisabet Ney and Benedette Tobin, President of the WCE Texas Bldg. 2) Ney's statue of Sam Houston that was displayed in Texas Bldg. 3) Bust of Tobin that was displayed in Woman's Bldg.

2446.   **Fess:** 1) Candid photo album from the WCE. 2) WCE Trade cards. 3) China collection. 4) Medal collection. 5) 4 different WCE pop-ups from Germany. 6) Libbey Glass collection. 7) Paper weight collection. 8) Silk ribbon collection. 9) WCE Satsuma pottery collection. 10) WCE Mauchline ware collection. 11) Large spoon collection.

2446.   **FM:** An extensive guide to WCE related material in the Field Museum (FM) is "Centennial Objects : Final Report" (see #2354.1).

☞ As we researched in libraries for our original bibliography, we found many deaccessioned books from the FM in other Chicago libraries and assumed that the Museum contained little of interest concerning the WCE. How wrong we were! The library contains many books and materials of primary importance concerning the fair. The Museum displays a portion of its original acquisitions from the WCE on the main floors, and the librarians are enthusiastic supporters of maintaining WCE documents.

A. **Field Museum Library:**

1) "Catalogue of Books, Pamphlets and Journals forming the Library of the Department of Ethnology, World's Columbian Exposition, Chicago, 1893 lent for the use of the Department or presented to the Columbian Museum, Chicago" (working title). C. Staniland Wake's unpublished handwritten manuscript in ink on typewriter paper and versos of official WCE stationery is an alphabetical listing of 1310 numbered citations. Wake was a FM Anthropology Dept clerk.

2) "Railroad Memorabilia Collection." A box with 27 folders; contains a printed list of contents. Railroad tickets, passes, timetables dated before the WCE opened; part of the WCE Dept of Transportation exhibit.

3) "Correspondence from 1893–1979" contains:

a. Clement E. Stretton's list of the "Stretton Collection" of British railroad items exhibited at the WCE and a NY Central & Hudson RR *Health and Pleasure* railroad catalog for 1893;

b. letters concerning disposition of Trans Dept exhibit from J.G. Pangborn, B&O WCE Railroad Commissioner; Willard A. Smith, chief Dept of Trans; C.K. Lord, B&O Railroad; and E.E. Ayer;

c. letters by Marshall Field about the WCE;

d. letters from the WCE President, H.N. Higinbotham;

e. World's Columbian Commission itinerary for Jan 26, 1894;

f. contract between B&O RR and Columbian Museum, (4) p, and inventory list of the B&O collection transferred to the museum, (94) p, typed.

4) Three ledger vols, each listing 5000 books, that were used by the FM to list its initial accessions; all libraries listed came from WCE exhibits. The blank ledger books were developed by Melvil Dewey and published by Library Bureau, Boston. Examples of WCE libraries:

a. Dept of Anthropology, b. Dept of Mines, c. Office of the Director and Chief, d. B&O Railroad

ACCESSION No.– 54
Date Feb 16 1894
FIELD COLUMBIAN MUSEUM
OF CHICAGO.

Report—Department **T**
Accession From
Address Philadelphia and Reading R.R. Co.

GIFT, EXCHANGE, LOAN, DEPOSIT, FOR EXAMINATION.

Catalogue No.

Description of Objects

Engine Rocket.

THIS CARD IS ACCOMPANIED BY
Detailed report by
Catalog of
Correspondence of
Memoranda
(Signed) J.G. Pangborn

FM accession record for the "Rocket" displayed in the WCE Transportation Department

Collection, e. Russian Commission, f. Imperial Japanese Commission, g. Kansas Board of WF Managers, h. New South Wales Commissioners, i. F.J.V. Skiff Transportation Exhibit, and j. Conkey Publishing Co's publications on the WCE.

5) Five file folders with typescript copies of 23 signed letters concerning WCE exhibits, chiefly the Dept of Ag, W.I. Buchanan, Chief of Dept.

6) Massive leather bound hc ledger book, 60x96½x10 cm thick. 800 p. Printed for the WCE Company by P.F. Pettibone & Co, Chicago; each of the 53 columns are printed with a WCE dept, bureau, admin office, or congress heading. The ledger is divided into many handwritten categories and financial figures and dates are neatly entered below them; the last entry is dated Apr 30, 1896. A most impressive financial document defining the WCE.   **P→**

M. Trombley, B. Williams, and G. Dybwad with WCE Ledger Open, FM

7) "Illuminated Spanish Missal." Written on parchment from the 15th century and found in Peru. Leather bound with studded cover and thick wood boards. Tagged with Dept of State exhibit, Dept A; FM accession no 17118 (WCE).

8) "Manuscript Ptolemaeus Cosmographia 1504." C.t. Handwritten. Tag states that it was transferred from exhibit in Dept A; FM accession no 17117 (WCE).

9) "Accession I-139 : Original Catalog : Collection of Gems & Semi Precious Stones Bought of Tiffany & Co." 36x23. 360 p. Half morocco leather over black cloth hc ledger, marbled edges, ruled pages. Handwritten entries for each gem from nos 1–1026, ending on p 48; rest of pages blank. Original listing of the collection from WCE Tiffany Exhibit bought by H.N. Higinbotham and given to the Field Museum. The gems are still at FM.

G. Dybwad and M. Trombley with WCE Financial Ledger, FM

10) 18-cm diameter embossed metal dish, silver plated, centered Columbus with "World's Columbian Exposition" underneath. Six WF bldgs depicted on circumference.

11) Thirteen original hardened steel die for stamping commemorative WCE coins. **P↘**

12) Columbian Guard sword number 2438 with scabbard and black tassel. **P↓**

13) Set of Columbian entrance tickets.

14) 9.2 cm diameter bronze medal: bird's-eye view obverse, Columbus and G. Washington busts reverse.

15) WCE stock subscription ledger from treasurer Seeberger's office. No title. 35x21. (48) p. Alphabetically tabbed fore edge, marbled boards, and ruled pages. Complete list of names, including many notable companies and personages (see #206).

16) Illinois charter of "Columbian Museum Chicago." 35½x21½ legal format. (5) p. Sept 16, 1893.

17) Letter from D.N. Bertolette, US Navy, from Buenos Aires, Feb 24, 1892, to Herman Strecker, Reading, PA, a leading US entomologist. Light yellow high rag paper with

Commemorative WCE Coin Die and Columbian Guard Sword number 2438, FM Library

letterhead: "World's Columbian Exposition : Surgeon D.N. Bertolette, US Navy : Special Commissioner to : Argentine Republic, Paraguay and Uruguay." Discusses exhibits for WCE.

18) Folder with 3 photos of H.N. Higinbotham, WCE President. Two candid photos 11x6½ and 1 studio port 24x16½ dated "Sept. 26-1911."

19) Papers and documents related to founding of the FM.

B. **Field Museum Archives**: [NB: The Archives are now part of the Main Library, 3rd floor. Cataloging in progress; inquire at the main desk.]

1) Esai, Armand, comp. "Archives Index." 28x21½ by 3 cm thick loose-leaf finders list for Board of Trustee meetings, documents, historical info that has been removed from files, deceased trustees and research associates, closed bequests, contracts, documents-early funds, and obsolete accessions (1893–).

2) Meeting minutes for the formation of the Columbian Museum. 24½x20. 123 p. Morocco leather spine over marbled paper boards, marbled edges. Handwritten meeting entries, Aug 17–28, 1893. Sidney C. Eastman, Secy. A museum for WCE exhibit material was proposed at the first meeting (see #208.5).

3) "Record of Minutes of the Executive Committee of the Field Columbian Museum." 41½x30. 501 p. Massive leather bound ledger book, green dyed edges. Handwritten meeting minutes May 22, 1894–Jan 8, 1912. Topics include acquisition of WCE exhibits and their display. Ed E. Ayer, founder, was present at all meetings. Spine: "Record. Executive Com : Field Columbian Museum."

4) "Records : Field Columbian Museum." 42x30. Unpaged index + 500 p. Gray cloth heavy ledger book, marbled edges. Handwritten meeting minutes Sept 30, 1893–Dec 16, 1912. Beautifully handwritten documents of incorporation and list of staff. Resolve of Nov 25, 1893, to change name from "Columbian Museum" to "Field Columbian Museum." Discussion about running the museum and WCE acquisitions and displays. On June 2, 1894, the Museum opened in the Fine Arts Bldg, Jackson Park; after renovation, that bldg became the home of the Museum of Science and Industry in 1933.

5) Large framed bird's-eye view of WCE grounds painted by Childe Hassam.

6) Obsolete and miscellaneous accessions are found in nine document cases; file folders contain letters, other paperwork, and pamphlets (some published) relating to the acquisition of items FM no longer owns.

Document Case 1 (files #1-65): Letters regarding donation of items to FM unless otherwise indicated:

a. H.F. Mackern letter directing Argentine exhibit be divided between FM and U of Pennsylvania.—(#4);

b. E.C. Pace letters directing tender of Illinois Forestry exhibit—(#12);

c. Russian Commissioner General's letter directing tender of Russian Liberal Arts Exhibit—(#15);

d. Jos. W. Collins, Dept of Fish and Fisheries, letters regarding donating Russian Cement Co and the J.W. Marston and Co exhibits—(#18, #51);

e. Austrian Section's notices to the collector of customs of intent to abandon their exhibit—(#24);

f. Lyster Nash letter donating Columbian Ceramic Society's booth and cases along with a photo of the display and a detailed blueprint for its construction—(#37);

g. E.A. Parsons letters about donating national commissioners' portraits that hung in Admin Bldg—(#38);

h. E.W. Peabody letters listing items donated by the Pennsylvania RR—(#44);

i. F.W. Brewer, Bureau of Sanitation, letter about sanitation items donated—(#48);

j. Max Richter, acting German Imperial Commissioner, letter about donating workman's safety outfits—(#52);

k. Selim H. Peabody letter about donation of Japanese instrument box—(#_);

l. John W. Woodside five letters about donation of John the Baptist ports—(#_); and

m. letter from head of Chilean mining exhibit.—(#_).

Document Case 2 (files #66-137):

a. Form letter for exhibit donations (see #846.1);

b. letters on WCE stationery directing transfer of exhibits to FM; and

c. inventory lists of items donated by companies [FM "Archives Index" has a list of companies; use index to find particular file folder].

Document Case 3 (files #138-186):

The FM had storage facilities at the Pennsylvania RR Bldg warehouse, 64th St–Jackson Park, and 55th and Jefferson. Many items were soaked by water and destroyed. June 25, 1894.—(#139).

Document Case 4:

a. Many letters from Wm. E. Curtis and others about the La Rabida exhibits, especially requests for return or sale of objects loaned by Pope Leo and the Vatican.—(Misc correspondence);

b. Lafayette Funk letter about donating a "Souvenir Album of the Illinois Exhibit."—(#16);

c. four typewritten sheets by the Dept of Mines and Mining listing the number of articles to be removed from their bldg along with list of permits to universities, colleges, etc. (e.g., Columbia College: 15 packages with specimens from MO);

d. 3-page list of textiles accessions from WCE.—(General Correspondence);

e. Wm. E. Curtis letter notifying E.E. Ayer, FM President, that he had taken pictures of all items loaned to La Rabida and had placed the negatives at the disposal of the Columbian Museum; also a 24 p handwritten list of the negatives.—(#46);

f. Jos. W. Collins letter about Baroness Burdett-Coutts's wish to give the exhibit of the fishery school, Baltimore, Ireland.—(#51);

g. John S. Neligh, Nebraska Bldg, correspondence about a missing donated corn table valued at $300 and made by the women of Cuming County; the reply confirmed disposal because of damage, then vermin.—(#52);

h. correspondence between N. Yamataka, Japanese Imperial Commission, and Putnam about the donation of the Imperial Quarantine Station.—(#53);

i. Jos. W. Collins letter about donating William F. Nyes' WCE watch, clock, and chronometer in oils exhibit.—(#66).

Document Case 5 (mixed file numbers):

a. Correspondence, estimates evaluating exhibit articles, inventory of La Rabida donated by US State Dept (well over 1000 items);

b. letters regarding a donated venetian gondolier's suit from "The World's Fair Venetian Gondola Co.";

c. letters regarding donating a silver filigree Horticulture Bldg model after it toured US cities to pay for its cost (a plan of A.M. Endweiss of Monterey, Mexico).—(General Correspondence).

Document Case 6 (mixed file numbers):

a. Dept E collection of Economic Minerals inventory list;

b. Dept of Industrial Arts artifacts (e.g., Rockwood Pottery);

c. Royal Norwegian Commission inventory of donated items from Norway Bldg.

Document Case 7:

a. List of articles donated from the Transportation Bldg;

b. Wales articles donated;

c. trains and boats donated from the Transportation Bldg;

d. inquiries about whether items donated had shown up in the FM inventory;

e. B&O collection list;

f. Baldwin Locomotive Works models and photographs.

Document Case 8:

a. *There She Blows* booklet (see #722.11);

b. list of artifacts from the Norwegian Transportation exhibit;

c. letter about purchase from the British Guiana Commission;

d. letters regarding the storage by the FM of items from US Dept of State, Bureau of American Republics.

Document Case 9:

H.W. Thorp, General Manager Goodrich Transportation Co, letter of May 9, 1900, offering "a correct model of the Chinese War Junk" exhibited at the WF.—(#133).

C. **Field Museum Anthropology Accession Files:** [Files in active use]:

1) Remenyi collection of South African antiques sold to FM after the WCE for $1500; complete correspondence.—(Acc 1).

2). Complete accession records for all components of the Javanese gamelan (see #2342.3), a 3½ octave xylophone, which was sold to FM by the Java Chicago Syndicate for $1500, including all the performers' costumes.—(Acc 3).

3) The Putnam-FM purchase of South Sea artifacts and photography from the WCE Ethnology Dept for $3500 from J.G. Peace of New Caledonia; file includes Peace's printed catalog of the sale items.—(Acc 9).

4) British Guiana folder contains the original list of exhibits, "Ethnology of British Guiana," and J.J. Quelch's 11 p handwritten list of 206 items.—(Acc 14).

5) Rev. E.F. Wilson collection for the WCE Dept of Ethnology. Typewritten list of Assinaboin items collected plus various related slips and notes.—(Acc 23).

6) Lt Robert Peary, Smith Sound, Greenland, original accession records for WCE Eskimo material—(Acc 25).

7) Correspondence for the purchase of the following:

a. G.M. West collection of ethnology specimens from the Micmac Indians, Nova Scotia—(Acc 26);

b. J.M. McLean expedition material from Blackfeet Indians, Alberta, Canada—(Acc 28);

c. W.K. Moorhead artifacts from the Hopewell Mound expedition, Ross County, OH—(Acc 30); and

d. G.P. Scriven, Salamanca Indians, Costa Rica, collection purchased by FM for $500.40.—(Acc 32).

8) Roger Welles, Jr., collector, typescript of 110 Venezuelan articles exhibited at the WCE.—(Acc 35).

9) A.L. Knight, C.L. Metz, and Harlan I. Smith, collectors and exhibitors' 3-p typescript of articles from OH and KY.—(Acc 39).

10) Harlan I. Smith's typescripts of WCE expedition, Little Miami Valley, OH.—(Acc 40).

11) Harlan I. Smith's typescripts of WCE expedition, Saginaw Valley, MI.—(Acc 41).

12) Copy of F.A. Ober's 4-p typescript catalog of Puerto Rico, West Indies, 1892, WCE articles.—(Acc 42).

13) Arthur W. Fairbanks' interesting 6-p letter to F.W. Putnam introducing a collection of Ree Indian items being shipped from Berthold, ND.—(Acc 55).

14) WCE ethnology collection from the Tsimshian (Skeena River, British Columbia).—(Acc 60).

15) George Hunt, WCE ethnology collection from Kwakiutl, Northern Vancouver Islands.—(Acc 61).

16) Marcus O. Cherry, WCE ethnology collection from the Yukon Valley.—(Acc 62).

17) Jas. B. Swan, WCE ethnology collection from Cape Flattery/Neah Bay.—(Acc 63).

18) Carl Hagenbeck's correspondence with the FM concerning the purchase of the WCE-Hagenbeck Zoological Arena collection; also a purchase order for $6000.—(Acc 81).

19) Wyman Brothers, Mississippi Valley archeology material, also beadwork, costumes, misc articles from the Sioux Indians.—(Acc 97).

D. **Field Museum Anthropology Archives**: [Archival records include original Field Notes (FN) and Collection Records (CR) that supplement the information in the Anthropology Accession Files. The contents are either too bulky or fragile or are not regularly used.] Examples of archival records (no finding guide):

J. Klein, Registrar, FM Anthropology Department

1) George Dorsey's (58) p handwritten description of graves and mummies from his WCE expedition to Ancon, Peru.—(FN).

2) Ernest Volk's 113 p typescript, "Report of Explorations in the Delaware Valley," Mar 1891–Mar 1893, for the WCE under F.W. Putnam's direction.—(FN).

3) James Deans, WCE ethnology collection from Haida Indians, North Pacific Coast.—(CR Acc-21).

4) Warren K. Moorhead expeditions for the WCE:

a. Little Miami Valley, OH, field notebook; b. Southern Ohio, Fort Ancient, 57 p typescript report to the WCE; and c. account of exploration of Hopewell Mounds.—(FN).

E. **Field Museum Photography Department**:

1) Half of the photographs taken during Moorhead's Hopewell Mounds expedition to southern Ohio, Apr 1891–Jan 1892. The expedition was undertaken at F.W. Putnam's request with the purpose of obtaining WCE exhibit materials. [The other half of the collection went to Ohio University.]

2) Two hundred and twenty glass lantern slides of WCE views.

2446. **FSA**: [see original bibliography—2446.i].

2446. **GLD**: [see original bibliography—2446.j]. 3) Fifty-eight 10x13 cm candid photographs taken during Chicago Day and mounted on blind-stamped beveled 20x25 cm boards; published in #2348.3. 4) Matthew Griswold, US House of Representatives, hand-written letter to Mr. B.W. Austin of Oak Cliff, Texas, dated July 27, 1892, announcing the $5 million dollar WCE appropriation passed in the House. 5) Tickets for workmen, admission, rides. 6) WCE stationery. 7) Chicago World's Fair—1992 Authority stationery.

2446. **GPL**: [see original bibliography—2446.k]. 2) "Map of Jackson Park : Showing Proposed Improvements for World's Columbian exposition. 1893." Chicago: Benedict & Co., Engr's, n.d. 39x30½ b/w early map of WCE mounted on hardboard.—(T500 C1 J13). 3) "Side elevation of machinery hall and annex : Ground-plan of machinery hall and annex." N.p.: n.p., n.d. 43x70 b/w printed map on mounted on hardboard.—(T500 C1 M18). 4) "World's Columbian Exposition Electricity Building. Van Brunt & Howe Architects." 58x48 b/w print on buff sheet mounted on 2 folding hardboards.—(T500 C1 E1). 5) 58x42 b/w print on buff of elevation of Manufactures and Liberal Arts Bldg by E. Elwood Deane on top and ground and gallery floor plans printed below. Mounted on 2 folding hardboards.—(T500 C1 M1).

2446. **H**: 1) "Ferris Wheel Data." Typescript of financial data including construction and salvage information for the Ferris wheel at the St. Louis World's Fair, 1904. 2) Marion Shaw WCE notebook.

2446. **HL**: [see original bibliography—2446.l].

2446. **HML**: 1) Pennsylvania RR Co, Office of Secretary. Board Files, 1843–1950 [microform]. 94 reels. Series I: Board file (1843–1906). Among the many important papers are files on the WCE. Correspondence regarding transporting the Krupp cannon to the WCE and about construction of the exhibit building.—(Finding Aid p 378; Acc 1807). 2) Cushman, Helen Baker. Business papers, 1853–1992. 3) Remington Rand Division of Sperry Rand Corp. Records 1830–1975. 4) 6 WCE candid photos—(Acc No 75.2002.280). 5) 8 mounted WCE photos. 6) Photo of Krupp gun loaded at Maryland Steel Co on its way to WCE. 7) DuPont, Henry Balin. 7 candid photos from trip to WCE. 8) DuPont, Pierre S. 17 candid photos he took at the WF and 12 C.D. Arnold WCE mounted photos. 9) DuPont, Pierre S. Roll of 4x5 inch nitrate film, approximately 100 frames, taken at the WCE. [The photo archives staff has duplicated

78 of these in negative and contact print.] 10) Tallman, Frank (E.I. DuPont executive). 137 candid photos from his WCE visit; many unique views including the failed Spectatorium. 11) Microfilm copies of the 1144 WCE Official Award diplomas. 12) St. Gaudens WCE official award medal. 13) Ad cards and a deck of boxed WCE playing cards. 14) WCE admission tickets. 15) 45 chromolithographs of the WCE. 16) Chromolith pop-up.—(Items 4-16 are from Pictorial Collections).

2446. **HU**: 1) WCE charts and award, 1892.—(Harvard Archives UAI 20.892 pf). 2) Visitors' book, 1892.—(Harvard Archives UAI20.892.36.3). 3) Contracts and records, 1892.—(Harvard Archives UAI 20.892.36.2). 4) Correspondence regarding exhibit of writings, 1893.—(Harvard Archives UAI 20.892.34). 5) Photo-negative copies of portraits sent to WCE, 1893.—(Harvard Archives UAI20.892.2 p/gN). 6) Beecher, James C. Papers.—(Schlesinger: A-123). 7) Henrotin, Ellen Martin. Papers.—(Schlesinger: A-142). 8) Ormsby, Edna Reed. Papers.—(Schlesinger: A/O735). 9) Beals, Jesse Tarbox. Papers.—(Schlesinger: M-124). 10) Baker, Adelaide Nichols. Papers.—(Schlesinger: A/B167; A/B167a). 11) Putnam, Frederick Ward. Papers.—(Harvard Archives HUG1717.xx). 12) Agassiz, Elizabeth Cabot Cary. Papers.—(Schlesinger: A-3; A/A262; A/A262a-g). 13) Facsimile charts for WCE, 1892.—(Harvard Archives UAI20.892.36.4). 14) Records relating to expositions. Harvard College Observatory.—(Harvard Archives UAV 630.392 hd). 15) Villard, Henry. Business papers.—(Baker Business: Mss Div Mss: 8993 1862-1900). 16) Bound vol of WCA pamphlets.—(Widener: Econ 5958.93.54).

2446. **IaHx**: [see original bibliography—2446.m].

2446. **IdHx**: [see original bibliography—2446.n].

2446. **IHi**: Manuscripts Department: 1) Garland, (Solomon?). Letter of Nov 2, 1893. 2 p. Briefly describes the dismantling of the WCE.—(SC544). 2) 8 handwritten remembrances by Illinois pioneer women of Crawford, Pike, and Sangamon counties. Includes WCE comments. Written on "Illinois Woman's Exposition Board" letter head paper for the Board.—(SC794). 3) "Stories of pioneer mothers of Illinois." C.t. of a leather bound vol of about 150 p. Handwritten accounts of Illinois pioneer life written for the Illinois Woman's Exposition Board (WCE) for display in the Woman's Bldg.—(SC794). 4) "Sangamon County Columbian Exposition Club. Secretary's report." Black cloth covered boards, handwritten on 95 pp. C.t. Report covers the club's aid to IL and the WCE Feb 4, 1892–Feb 6, 1893.—(SC1331). 5) "History of the Columbian Exposition Club of Sangamon County : Auxiliary to the Woman's Exposition Board of the State of Illinois." 28x21½ typing paper. 8 *l* handwritten title and report + 7 *l* report handwritten by Lydice R. Hyle to Mrs Charles Ridgby, President of the Club, Dec 26, 1893. This double folder also contains 8 *l* loose leaves of correspondence regarding the WCE.—(SC1331). 6) Garrand, Wilson Coburn. Illinois Board of World's Fair Commissioners Secretary. Vols 26-31. Vols include: a) "Record of Proceedings : Illinois Board of World's Fair Commissioners" with black leather covered heavy boards, 46x26x5, beautifully dated by hand from July 1, 1891–Dec 1, 1893; b) "Visitors (sic) Register : Illinois : state building : World's Columbian Exposition : 1893," a set of two half-morocco leather volumes, 46x27x6, vol 1 from May 8–Sept 4, 1893, and vol 2 from Sept 5–Oct 31, 1893; c) "Register of Illinois Soldiers and Sailors Visiting the Illinois State Building, 1893," measuring 53x28x6 cm. 7) A wonderful collection of unused letterhead stationery and envelopes from many of the state bldgs and WCE commissions.—(IHi vertical file). 8) WCE stock certificate.

2446. **InHx**: [see original bibliography—2446.o and p].

2446. **KsHx**: [see original bibliography—2245.q]. 3) "Script for Columbian exposition exhibit by Anne Marvin : June 9, 1993." 41 p script of the centennial recreation of the WCE Kansas Exhibit at the Kansas Museum of Natural History, Topeka.

2446. **KSU**: 1) 36 mounted WCE photographs.

2446. **LaMus**: [see original bibliography—2446.s].

2446. **MA**: 1) Passbook with tickets issued to Mrs. A.C. Mellette, wife of South Dakota Governor and Chairman of SD hostesses at the WCE. 2) A.C. Mellette's invitation to dinner in honor of the U.S. President following the WCE dedicatory ceremonies. 3) A.C. Mellette's invitation to a reception at the Auditorium for US and foreign governors.

2446. **MaHx**: [see original bibliography—2446.t].

2446. **MCHx**: 1) Hutton Family: a) six letters mentioning 1893 WF—(Box 1); b) two paper WCE napkins—(Box 3); c) advertising cards—(Box 3). 2) Six Columbian Exhibition admittance tickets.

2446. **MPA**: [see original bibliography— 2446.u].

2446. **MPL**: [see original bibliography— 2446.v].

2446. **MSI**: 1) Actual locomotives from the WCE Transportation Bldg, such as NY Central's "999." P➔ 2) Electrical generator. 3) Gilt and painted wooden prow and stern decorations from the Viking Ship exhibit from Norway. P⬇ 4) Satin glass slipper. 5) Several pieces of original "staff" covering used on the temporary buildings. 6) Pin tray. 7) Employee concessions pass with photo ID. 8) Colored and decorated silk scarf. 9) Diploma of Honorable Mention issued by the Board of Lady Managers. 10) 12 3-ft x

G. Dybwad and "999" Exhibited at the WCE, MSI

6-ft magnificently painted canvases from the Royal Doulton Pottery Co exhibit at the WCE. They depict the history of pottery. 11) Campbell, Frank Thomas. Unpublished typed manuscript: "The White City : Recollections of the World (sic) Columbian Exposition of 1893." ix, 66 p. Campbell, a southeast Iowa farm boy, describes how he saved money in advance of the opening to go to the WCE and what the WF was like when he got there. Probably written in preparation of the 1933 fair in Chicago; gift to MSI for its WCE Centennial display. 12) 27x15 wooden box containing a unique set of hand carved wooden miniature replicas of statuary and architectural details destined for implementation at the WCE. Includes the caryatids used on the facade of the Fine Arts Bldg, now the Museum of Science and Industry. P➔ 13) Admission tickets. 14) Photos of the WCE. 15) Loose collection of W.H. Jackson prints from various

Sample Box of WCE Architectural Elements, MSI Archives

subscription editions (copies of some of these are sold in the Museum Gift Store). 16) Box of over 200 WCE stereo-view cards, 22 cm in total length. 17) 2 tickets to dedication ceremonies. 18) Bronze Columbus plaque. 19) Shell purse. 20) 4 metal trays. 21) China plates from Germany. 22) Clear glass tumbler. 23) Salt and pepper shakers. 24) Shell and metal napkin rings. 25) Letter opener. 26) Pin box. 27) Ladies leather purse. 28) Stamp safe. 29) Glass plaque of Admin Bldg. 30) 7 paperweights. 31) Milk glass lamp with Columbus landing scene.

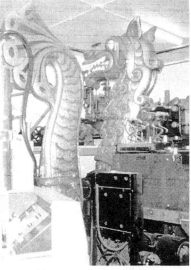

2446. **MSL**: 1) A vol of 39 photographs of the Massachusetts State Bldg at the WCE.—(606:1893 M31b). 2) Several awards certificates.—(Drawer 50 Misc. 606:1893 U58u1-3). 3) Pocket memorandum and dedication ceremonies issued by the Massachusetts Board of WF Managers. 32 p.—(Pam 606:1893 M41p).

M. Woodward, G. Dybwad, and L. Graedel, MSI Archives

Viking Ship Prow and Stern, and WCE Generator, MSI Archives

2446. **NAC**: [see original bibliography— 2446.w].

2446. **NDU**: Edwards, James F. Papers. 15.5 linear feet. Records of the WCE. Edwards was Notre Dame history professor and librarian for 52 years and a collector of artifacts and manuscripts.—(HESB Archives CEDW GEDW). 2) Onahan, William James, Chicago banker and civic leader. 4.75 linear feet. Speeches, papers, programs from the Columbian Catholic Congress which he organized.—(HESB Archives CONA MONA). 3) Collection of the Archdiocese of Chicago. Pamphlets, clippings, and material from WCE Catholic events.—(HESB Archives CACH). 4) Satolli, Francesco. Papers, 1893-95. 2.5 linear inches. Program of a WCE play.—(HESB Archives CSAT). 5) Catholic Educational Exhibit records, 1892-94. Letters from Bishop Spalding and Brother Maurelian about the Catholic Educational Exhibit.—(HESB Archives CCEE).

2446. **NeHx**: [see original bibliography—2446.x].

2446. **NHSt**: [see original bibliography—2446.y].

2446. **NJHx**: 1) Morris, George Perry. Papers. 4 linear feet. Includes letters to Frederick Perry Noble, Secretary for the African Ethnological Congress (AEC), Chicago, August 1893.—(From: *Guide to the Manuscript Collections of the New Jersey Historical Society.* ᶜ1979). 2) Two letters to C.C. Bonney, President World's Congress Auxiliary, June 15 and July 22, 1892; 72 letters to Frederick Perry Noble on the AEC, Oct 15, 1891–Jan 25, 1893; 14 letters to Joseph E. Roy on the AEC, June 11–July 19, 1893; 12 letters to Clarence E. Young on the AEC, July 8, 1892–Jan 6, 1895.—(Data file MG843).

2446. **NL**: [see original bibliography—2446.z]

2446. **NPG**: Kurtz, Charles M. Papers. In the Archives of American Art.

2446. **OC**: [see original bibliography—2446.aa].

2446. **OhHx**: [see original bibliography—2446.ab].

2446. **OHxS**: "Register : Oklahoma building : 1893." 36x23. 2 vol. Half burgundy leather over black cloth covered pebbled boards, gilt print on front covers of both vols. Signed registers of visitors to the Oklahoma (joint Territorial) Bldg; guests from June 7–Oct 30, 1893.—(Archives).

2446. **OU**: Searcy, Emmett Coldwell (1832–1934). Papers contain: 1) "The Columbian Transportation & Hotel Railway Co ticket. 2) Brotherhood Wine Co pamphlet. 3) 1904 WF items. 4) WCE trade cards. 5) Used Chicago Day ticket. 6) Pamphlets #764.1, #1813, and #1878.1. 7) Pamphlet #1050.12 (2 copies). 8) *National Guard* mag, #1365.2 (several issues).—(Western History Archives Collection # 574).

2446. **PI**: [see original bibliography—2446.ac].

2446. **PU**: [see original bibliography—2446.ad]

2446. **RPB**: [see original bibliography—2446.ae]

2446. **RSA**: 1) Four letter books. 2) Five minute books. 3) Twelve ledgers. 4) One box file receipts. 5) Cellar book. 6) Visitors' book. 7) Parcel marked "Colonies, Sir Henry Wood's letters," Mar 11–Oct 19, 1893. 8) Parcel marked "Chicago Executive Transit." 9) Parcel marked "Fine Arts Regulation & Information for Exhibitors." 10) Parcel marked "Photographs & Plans." 11) Parcel marked "Foreign Office Correspondence April 1891-November 1893."

2446. **S**: 1) Album of about 50 letters either on Montana Board of WF Managers stationery or to the Board. 2) Kurtz, Charles M. Extensive album of correspondence. 3) Extensive collection of WCE tickets. 4) Very large collection of WCE trade cards. 5) Paper and board games from the WF. 6) Posters and maps from the WCE. 7) Many magazines from the Fair. 8) "Fresno County, California State Building : register of visitors at the World's Columbian exposition, 1893." 46x31½. (250) p. Half morocco over black cloth pebbled heavy boards. Dated June 27–Sept 22, 1893, plus undated pages; ca 16,000 total signatures. 9) "Album" of autographs of WCE/WCC officials. 22½x18½. Navy leather with fine gilt border and gilt all edges. C.t. 45 signatures on Royal Irish linen paper. **P➜**

Dr. Sheppard with a small part of his WCE collection; G. Dybwad at right

2446. **SDHx**: [see original bibliography—2446.af].

2446. **SDSHx**: [see original bibliography—2446.ag].

2446. **SFe** (New Mexico): [see original bibliography—2446.ah].

2446. **TD**: [see original bibliography—2446.ai].

2446. **UBO**: 1 folded sheet. Handwritten in Norwegian. Artists' protest against the proposed jury for the Chicago exhibition competition; May 10, 1892. Signed by Edvard Munch and 22 other painters plus 3 sculptors.—(Ms.fol.3578 Skougaard).

2446.   **UCB**: 1) Turrill, Charles B. Papers: A box plus 3 vols of newspaper clippings, line drawings of WCE bldgs, Sunday closing letter and petition, *World's Fair Tickets Are Works of Art* prospectus to sell WF tickets. Many published items glued into the vols.—(Turrill, Charles B. papers: Box II and Vol 10-13: BANC MSS C-B 545). 2) Schewitzer, Jeffery. WCE postcard collection.—(BANC MSS 70/196 C).

2446.   **UCLA**: 1) Newspaper clippings. 2) Postcards, correspondence, and ephemera. 3) "Chicago Concessions," a carbon typescript accounting of concessions, 14 p, and concessionaires, 12 p, and percentages of sales due the WCE by each. For example, Adams chewing gum remitted 70% of sales to the WCE; C.D. Arnold, head of photography, remitted 0%.—(Collection 344 in Special Collections).

2446.   **UFl**: [see original bibliography—2446.aj].

2446.   **UIC**: 1) Special Collections contains extensive WCE material (largely gifts) listed only in its own catalog. This includes books and pamphlets (#768, 880, 1271.1, 1390.1, 1575, 1621, 1627, 1652, 1682, and 2333), photos, programs, magazines, tickets.—(Special Collections, cataloged by year of acquisition). 2) In addition, the Lawrence J. Gutter collection contains the following: photo of Ferris wheel, pamphlets (#24, 25, 382, 578, 767.1, 820, 862, 1000, 1061, 1089, 1108, 1168, 1192, 1591, 2157), silk ribbon, stock share certificate, and tickets.—(Special Collections, Gutter Collection.)

   ☞ The Gutter Collection of Chicago items is listed in the booklet: *In search of a city*. [Chicago, 1983].

2446.   **ULC**: 1) Painting by Elizebeth Nourse (1873-1938) entitled "Good Friday," winner of art contest in the WCE Woman's Building. 2) About 25 mounted photographs of WCE bldgs by C. D. Arnold.

2446.   **UMC**: Holds a collection of 7 published but uncataloged pamphlets.—(Annex 606 C432z9).

2446.   **UMD**: WCE misc: maps of WCE and Chicago, toys, postal cards and WCE stamps, tickets, photographs, invitations, trade cards, stereo cards.—(Uncataloged in Special Collections/Architecture Lib.)

2446.   **UMi**: [see original bibliography—2446.ak].

2446.   **UNC**: 1) Cotten family papers. 4 boxes. Cotton, Mrs. Sallie S. Materials relating to her WCE activities. She served on a national committee as a representative of North Carolina women.—(SHC #3589). 2) Ker, Mary Susan (1838–1923). Papers and correspondence. 11.5 linear feet.—(SHC #1467).

2446.   **UoA**: Purdue, Albert Homer. Papers. 3 linear feet. Only WCE item: "Diploma of Honorable Mention to Purdue for his assistance to John C. Branner in producing and exhibiting a relief map of Arkansas, The World's Columbian Exposition, Sept 13, 1894 [sic, should be 1893]."—(MC 205).

   ☞ Purdue was the first student of geology at Stanford U (1890–93); while at Stanford he worked under John Casper Branner, former State Geologist for Arkansas.

2446.   **UoC**: 1) Starr, Frederick. Papers. 2) Jones, Jenkin Lloyd. Papers. 6.5 linear ft. A Unitarian minister; includes his 1893 World's Parliament of Religions documents. 3) Arnold, C.D. Photographs.

2446.   **UPa**: Exhibit of games in the Columbian exposition. N.p.: n.p., n.d.—(394.3 C89.6 - Museum).

2446.   **USD**: [see original bibliography—2446.al].

2446.   **UTA**: Photographs of the Western Electric Company exhibit at the WCE.—(OCLC# 20941619).

2446.   **UVa**: [see original bibliography—2446.am].
2446.   **UWy**: [see original bibliography—2446.an].
2446.   **VaHx**: [see original bibliography—2446.ao].
2446.   **WaSt**: [see original bibliography—2446.ap].

2446.   **whmc**: 1) Pohlman, George. Collection.—(C3476-folder #82). 2) Reeves, Charles Monroe. Papers. Journalist and organizer for the WCE and St. Louis fair.—(C3356-10 folders). 3) Blair, Henry William. Papers. Senator from NH.—(C2224-folder #30). 4) Breckenridge, William Clark. Papers. Saint Louis business man and historian.—(C1035-folder #55). 5) Duncan-Lowman Family papers. Correspondence.—(C487-folder #6). 6) Oliver Family papers. Folders #1960 and #1715.—(C3731-folders #1048,#1049). 7) Benecke Family papers. Correspondence evaluating electrical generators at the WCE for Capt. Louis Benecke, lawyer, Brunswick, MO.—(C3825-4 folders).

2446.   **WiHx**: [see original bibliography—2446.aq].

2446.   **WM**: 1) Forty mounted photos from C.D. Arnold's Dept of Photography.—(Archives Collection 46, Box 6). 2) Eight Dept of Photography photos mounted, plus 37 mounted candid photos of WCE by Isabel Tapley.—(Archives Collection 46, Box 7). 3) Two decks of WCE playing cards. 4) Full set with envelope of the 10 WCE US postal cards. 5) Two silk bookmarks of Admin Bldg by Grant Co. 6) Two WCE silks. 7) Silk bookmark of Bertha Palmer by John Best & Co, mounted on paper. 8) Authorization for Barrie to photograph fine art works of Childe Hassam.

2446.   **WML**: 1) "Contributors to Willard fountain, Presented to Chicago. Columbian Ex. Year 1893." Chicago: Geo. E. Marshall & Co., n.d. 25x34. 4½ cm thick. 334 hand-numbered pages. Full tooled leather on heavy wood boards, multi-layered heavy spine binding, gilt design and gilt spine print, marbled edges. Spine title. Caption title at top of each ledger styled pages: "contributors to Willard fountain." One-of-a-kind presentation copy to Francis E. Willard, President of the Women's Christian Temperance Union, Evanston, IL. Handwritten list of contributors by state. 2) Letter to Phoebe Couzins from Willard, June 5, 1892 disclaiming any "unfriendliness" and alluding to the report of the Board of Lady Managers (#48). 3) Letter to A. Gordon, private secretary to Willard, from E.A. Wheeler, Grand Rapids WCTU secretary, requesting her to speak on the Children's Bldg at the WF, 21 Apr 1892. 4) Typed letter from B. Palmer, President Board of Lady Mgrs, to Willard, Apr 5, 1892, asking her to give the prayer at their "white elephant" fund raiser (#795). 5) letter from B. Palmer to Willard regarding speaking at the Federation of Women's Clubs, Mar 25, 1892 (see #2264.1, #2442.1). 6) Correspondence regarding the fair. 7) WCE official pass book with photo of Anna Gordon, private secretary to Willard. 8) Letters to the WCTU on WCE and WCA letterhead stationery. 9) Invitation (#54.5) to Willard to attend the dedication of bldgs ceremony.

2446.   **Yale**: [see original bibliography—2446.as].

2447.   SCRAPBOOKS:

2447.   **A**: [see original bibliography—2447.a].

2447.   **BPL**: [see original bibliography—2447.b].

2447.   **CCA**: 1) Album of (28) p. 14 pages contain 4 Kodak photographs each.—(QMCA87-B13214). 2) Album, 18x26, containing 27 photographs.—(QMCA89-F191).

2447.   **CHx**: [see original bibliography—2447.c].

2447.   **CLP**: 1) Bier, C.W., comp. Scrapbook of World's Fair views.—(qr 725.9 C43).

2447.   **Col**: Scrapbook of blanks and forms used in the executive depts US libraries in 1893 and mounted by the NY State Library School for the ALA. Used at the WCE Comparative Library Exhibit.—(New York State Library. School. Records, 1887–1957).

The Fesses with their Columbian furniture and silverware. G. Dybwad in the center.

2447.   **F**: [see original bibliography—2447.d].

2447.   **Fess**: Two WCE scrapbooks   **P↗**

2447.   **FM**: Newspaper clippings pasted in book entitled "The Bankers' Directory of the United States and Canada." 21x16. Ca (200) p. Some of the original book pages have been cut out to prevent the scrapbook from swelling its binding. Includes "Chicago Day" (Oct 9, 1893) and "Colored Folk's Day" (Aug 25, 1893).—(Main Library "Archives").

2447.   **GLD**: [see original bibliography—2447.e]. 3) Scrapbook. 22½x29½. 2 cm thick. Half leather over black cloth boards. 40 *l* of WCE illus neatly arranged and pasted on both sides of sheets. Some hand written notes accompany illus. Illus are from newspapers and disbound view books. Ticket, Pennsylvania Day ribbon and programme, signature from World's Congress on Africa. $150 - 250

2447.   **GPL**: [see original bibliography—2447.f].

2447. **HL**: [see original bibliography—2447.g].

2447. **HU**: Scrapbook entitled "Harvard historians exhibited at the Chicago Exhibition, 1893."—(Harvard Archives UAI20.892.36 p/as #170).

2447. **InHx**: [see original bibliography—2447.h].

2447. **KsHx**: [see original bibliography—2447.i].

2447. **LBA**: 1) Greenough, C.P. World's Fair folio scrapbook of C.P. and Mrs. M.D. Greenough, travelers to the WCE on a Whitcomb excursion (Boston, 1893).—($N45C//PZG85). 2) Album of mounted photographs with handwritten captions. 30½x39.—($45C//P).

2447. **MSI**: Lunneen, John. Columbian Exposition Souvenir Book. 18x14½. 1 cm thick. A lined ledger book. Contains tickets and ad cards from an Oct trip to the WCE.

2447. **NL**: [see original bibliography—2447.j].

2447. **NYPL**: [see original bibliography—2447.k].

2447. **PU**: [see original bibliography—2447.l].

2447. **S**: [see original bibliography—2447.m]. 5) Sheppard, Stephen. Photo scrapbook from the opening day of the "Grand Illusions," WCE centennial retrospective exhibit of the Chicago Historical Society, 1993. Also exhibits and tours at the Museum of Science and Industry, Chicago Symphony Hall, the Art Institute's "Constructing the Fair," and City Hall. 6) Hand printed scrapbook. 38x30. (54) p. "Columbia" (3-act play), poems, and music; illus with 1890s die-cuts—(Log #3856). 7) Auchincloss, Charles Crook. 48x32. Red cloth hc, gilt "Columbian Souvenir." Nautical clippings and illus include Apr 1893 Columbian Naval Parade in NY harbor.—(Log #496B). 8) Bidwell, Geo. H. 35x29. Red cloth hc album, c.t.: "Columbian souvenir," illus Columbus "medal" and US shield. 27 *l* about ½ full of WCE clippings and hand written text including Opening Day. Bidwell used "World's Fair Accommodation Co., Utica, NY."—(Log #423A). 9) Orange hc, gilt and black "Columbian Souvenir." Contains complete sets of 36 WCE Singer Sewing cards (#1005.10), 12 WCE Quaker Oats cards, and WCE ads and handouts.—(Log #273B). 10) Echert, Sallie L., Avondale, Cincinnati, Ohio. Gray-blue cloth hc, gilt and black "Columbian Souvenir," Columbus bust "medal" and US flag shield. Many WCE souvenirs decoratively tipped-in; Sallie and her sister stayed at the Fair for 2 months. Great scrapbook.—(Log #363B). 11) Brown and black paper covered boards, tipped on litho of 5 people in a row boat. 30x25. 8 *l* covered both sides with WCE ads and handouts primarily from the Manufactures Bldg and Machinery Hall.—(Log #192G). 12) Brown cloth hc, "Columbian Souvenir," illus Columbus "medal" and US flag shield. 43x36½. (68) p+ inside back cover. Filled with hundreds of chromolith cards, ads, and illus from the WCE.—(Log #6198).

2447. **SI**: [see original bibliography—2447.n].

2447. **SPL**: 1) 32x__. (38)p. Scrapbook of mounted Chicago newspapers clippings. Feb 4–Sept 1, 1893.

2447. **SStU**: [see original bibliography—2447.o].

2447. **UMD**: Gruel, Léon. Scrapbook. Masterfully and meticulously assembled by Gruel, master book binder. 32x24. 2½ cm thick. One-fourth morocco over red marbled paper covered boards, marbled end papers. This is a treasure of beautifully preserved pamphlets, news articles, invitations received by Gruel, form letters, magazine and periodical articles, and copies of #426, #385.1, #448.1, #441.1, and #1273.5. For Gruel item, see #412.—(Special Collections, Architecture Library).

2447. **UoC**: [see original bibliography—2447.q]. 4) Scrapbook on the World's Columbian Exposition.

2447. **WM**: 1) Cogneson, Charles. 20x15½x1 cm thick. Half of pages used. Consists mostly of tickets carefully glued down: railroad, Chicago transit, Chicago Day and Manhattan Day admission, and WCE exhibits; also railroad menu.—(Archives). 2) Glaenzer, Georges. One 28x36 *l* from scrapbook. Includes tintype souvenir "on the midway." French news clipping about Glaenzer's trip to Chicago, invitation from City of NY in 1892 for foreign and US officers escorting the 3 replicas of Columbus's caravels from Spain.—(Archives).

2447. **Yale**: 23x__. Scrapbook of clippings about Thomas B. Bryan, particularly while he was a resident of Chicago and active in promotion of the World's Fair in 1890, 1891, 1892.—(Zeta Uah C43 L1 S3).

Chapter 16

BEFORE AND AFTER THE WORLD'S COLUMBIAN EXPOSITION

THE MADRID EXPOSITION OF 1892

2447.1 Colombia. ...*Catálogo especial : de la : república de colombia.*
Madrid: Est. tipográfico «sucesores de rivadeneyra», 1892.   **P➔**

> 22x15. 136 p. Tan wraps, black print. At head of title: "Cuarto
> centenario del descubrimiento de américa : exposición : histórico-
> americana." C.t. Trans: Special catalog of the Republic of
> Colombia. Colombia exhibited first in Madrid, then at the WCE.
> ☺ . (FM-Anthropology archives A-13)

2447.2 Colombia. *Las piedras grabadas : de : chinauta y anacutá : informe :
del : auxiliar de la sub-comision 3.ª De las : exposiciones de madrid
y chicago : 1892.* Bogatá: Imprenta de Antonio M. Silvestre, [1892].

> 25x17. 7 p+ 2 fold outs at back cover. Lavender wraps, black
> print. C.t. At end of text: "Lazaro M. Giron [and] Abril de 1892."
> Trans: The engraved stones of Chinauta and Anacutá.
> ☺ . (FM-Anthropology archives A-13)

2449.1 *Exposición internacionel de Madrid : 1893.* ___: ___, [1892].

> 41½x33. (4) p ads in orange and blue, 28 p, (4) p ads in orange and blue. Colored glossy wraps. Text
> has elaborately decorated and colored borders. Ports. Plan of the exposition bldg. Text is in several
> languages, not English. Text covers the history of Columbus. Lists rules and regulations. Alternate title:
> "IV° Centenario del Descubrimiento de América." (UMD-cover missing)

2451.1 Luce, Stephen Bleecker. *History of the participation of the U.S. in the Columbian historical exposition at
Madrid.* Washington: GPO, 1895.

> 23x__. 1 *l*, 7-89 p. Plate, plan. (HU)

2451.2 U.S. Commission to the Madrid Exposition. Brinton, Daniel G[arrison]. ...*Report upon the collections
exhibited at the Columbian Historical Exposition.* Washington: GPO, 1895.

> 23x__. 3 *l*, 23-89 p. At head of title: "Commemoration of the fourth centenary of the discovery of
> America. Columbian Historical Exposition, Madrid." Rpt of part of #2456. (HU,UCLA)

2453.1 U.S. Commission to the Madrid Exposition. Curtis, William Eleroy. ...*Report of Wm. E. Curtis, assistant
to Commissioner-General, in charge of the Historical Section, exhibit of the United States at the
Columbian Historical Exposition, Madrid, Spain, 1892.* Washington: GPO, 1895.

> 24½x15. 215-278 p. Illus, ports, and 13 plates are not included in paging. At head of title:
> "Commemoration of the fourth centenary of the discovery of America, Columbian Historical Exhibition,
> Madrid." Descriptive list of 136 Columbus exhibits in Madrid; includes list numbered 150-310 of exhibits
> at the WCE, pp 275-78. Rpt of part of #2456. (HU,KCPL)

2454.1 U.S. Commission to the Madrid Exposition. Hough, Walter. *The ancient Central and South American
pottery in the Columbian Historical Exposition at Madrid in 1892.* Washington: GPO, 1895.

> 25x__. 1 *l*, 339-365 p+ 4 plates. Illus. Rpt of part of #2456. (HU)

2455. US. Comm. *Iconographia colombino. Catálogo*: (CU)

2455.1 U.S. Commission to the Madrid Exposition. Mercer, Henry Chapman. *Chipped stone implements in the
Columbian Historical Exposition at Madrid.* Washington: GPO, 1895.

> 25x__. 1 *l*, 367-397 p+ 3 plates. Illus. Rpt of part of #2456. (HU)

2455.2 U.S. Commission to the Madrid Exposition. Nuttall, Zelia. *Ancient Mexican feather work at the Columbian historical exposition at Madrid.* Washington: GPO, 1895.

25x__. (329)-37 p. Plates. Rpt of part of #2456. (HU)

2456. US. Comm. *Report of the United States Commission to the Columbian Historical exposition*: (csuf,CU,HU,slpl) ---- Also listed: [Selected reports of the United States Commission to the Columbian Historical Exposition at Madrid, 1892–1893, and special papers.] Washington: GPO, 1895. Pp 19-89, (213)-78, (5)-17. (IHi)

THE CALIFORNIA MID-WINTER EXPOSITION

2457.1 Chandler, Arthur, and Marvin Nathan. *The Fantastic Fair : The Story of the California Midwinter International Exposition : Golden Gate Park, San Francisco, 1894.* [St. Paul, MN]: Pogo Press, [°1993 Pogo] **P➔**

21½x22. ix, (1), 82 p. Tan glossy wraps with brown print and color litho of the Admin Bldg. Color plates included in paging. A history of the Fair based upon a set of Charles Graham color lithographs published by the Winters Art Lithographing Company of Chicago, 1894. The organization and concepts of the Fair show their WCE antecedent. ☺ (GLD,H)

2457.2 Nathan, Marvin. *San Francisco's international expositions : a bibliography : including listings for the mechanics' institute exhibitions.* San Francisco: Marvin R. Nathan, °1990 by Nathan.

21½x14. 2 *l*, 43 p. Light blue wraps with black print and design. Bibliography of items from the California Mid-winter Fair pp 9-15. The Mechanics' Institute had an exhibition in California in early 1893 for the purpose of sending exhibits to the WCE by May 1893 (see #1796.1). ☺ (GLD)

THE PROPOSED CHICAGO WORLD'S FAIR OF 1992

☞ Note: The Illinois State Historical Library (IHi) in Springfield, IL, has a large file (several cubic feet) of 1992 World's Fair committee meeting minutes, publications, stationery etc. The original plan for the fair covered 575 acres but was then reduced to 105 acres of landfill south of Meigs Field. The consulting architects were Skidmore, Owings & Merrill. The fair was canceled in 1985 and planning ceased.

Letterhead and Logo for the Proposed Columbian Centennial Fair

2457.3 Braden, William. "Our fair bid periled by the...Falklands?" *Sun-Times* 18 July 1982, sec. 2: 1+.

This Chicago newspaper segment describes the current status of the Chicago proposal to the Bureau of International Expositions (BIE) for the 100 year Columbian Exposition anniversary in 1992. The Chicago fair organizers were led by Thomas G. Ayers. The 1992 fair was to occupy a 575-acre site along the lake front. The article shows a scale model of the proposed fair grounds. ☺ (GLD)

☞ Later, the Chicago proposal to the Bureau of International Expositions (BIE) to host the 1992 centennial fair was approved. Later still, after Chicago did not gain approval from the citizens, ethnic groups, and the mayor, the BIE granted the 1992 fair to Seville, Spain.

2457.4 Chicago. Bryne, Jane M. *Chicago 1992 : Executive Summary.* Chicago?: City of Chicago, 1982.

21x26. 11, (1) p. Gray stiff wraps, black print, string-tied. Plain white wrap paper covers the wraps. Early promotion for the 1992 fair with illus of 3-D model of planned grounds and buildings. Bryne was mayor until 1983 when Harold Washington became mayor until his death in 1987. ☺ (IHi)

2457.5 Currie, Barbara Flynn. Papers. Currie was chair of 1992 World's Fair Committee, 1983–86. Correspondence and reports, some published. A copy of World's Fair House Bill 2313, "Chicago World's Fair-1992 Authority Act": approved Feb. 11, 1983. (IHi—Box 6 and Box 13)

2458. *1992 World's Fair Forum papers*: ▶Add new volume titles.
Vol I: *Legacies from Chicago's World's fairs*: (IHi,NDU,uiuc)

Vol II. *Women's participation in Chicago's World's fairs : past and future.* ᶜ1984.

28x22. 62 p (variously paged). Contents: Marilyn Domer, "The Role of women in Chicago's World's fairs: from the sublime to the sensuous." Jean S. Hunt, "The Women's congresses." Susan Kmetty Catania, "Women's Committee 1992 Chicago World's Fair: a 1984 report." (IHi,uiuc)

Vol III. *Visions of the 1992 fair : creative proposals for planners.*

28x22. 56 p (variously paged). Contents: Stanley J. Hallett, "Visions of the future." Willard L. Boyd, "Visions of the 1992 Fair." Stephen and Donna Toulmin, "New attitudes to technology: proposals for the 1992 World's Fair." (IHi,llpl)

☞ Willard L. ("Sandy") Boyd, proponent of the Chicago 1992 Fair, was President of the Field Museum, retiring in 1996. He aided the unification of Chicago's museums and parks along the lake shore, a project which resulted in the present museum campus.

Vol IV: ▶Correct publication date is February 1985. (IHi,llpl,uiuc)

Vol V: *Managing and financing the fair.* ᶜ1985

28x22. 52 p (variously paged). Contents: John D. Kramer, "An approach to fair planning." Barbara Flynn Currie, "The state perspective." Bernard L. Stone, "A Councilman's view: It's not too late for change." Plus comments from the panelists. (IHi,llpl)

Vol VI: *After the fair : benefits for the future.* ᶜ1985.

28x22. 90 p (variously paged). Contents: E. James Peters, "What expositions have left their cities." Lee Botts, "The last chance for an open lakefront." Elizabeth Hollander, "What can a World's fair do for Chicago." Plus comments from the panelists. (IHi,uiuc)

2458.1 Chicago. World's Fair Advisory Committee. *Age of Discovery : a theme catalog.* Vol. I. April 1985.

28x21½. 105 p. Silver wraps, white and royal blue print and trim. Describes how the theme was developed, why a Fair was needed, what was to be gained, suggestions for exhibits and events. © (IHi)

2458.2 Chicago. World's Fair Advisory Committee. *Age of discovery News : 1992 Chicago World's Fair.*

43x28½. Newspaper format on coated stock. Vol 1, No 1, 1984. (4) p. See #1218. (IHi)
---- Also found: Newspaper format on coated stock. Vol 1, No 2. (6) p. (PPL)

2458.3 Chicago. World's Fair Advisory Committee. Arthur D. Little, Inc. *Report to the Chicago World's Fair 1992 Authority. Feasibility and Benefits of the Chicago 1992 World's Fair.* N.p: n.p., 1985?

28x21½. vii, 15 chapters each paged separately. Typescript. Yellow wraps, black print and design of city skyline. This analysis by Arthur D. Little, Inc., covered all aspects of the proposed fair. © (IHi)

2459.1 Chicago. World's Fair Advisory Committee. *Draft : World's fair financial outlook: Detailed Nine-Year Projections of Fair Revenues, Costs & Benefits.* 9 May 1985.

28x21½. 1 *l* table of contents, 62 numbered leaves printed one side. C.t. © (IHi)

2464.1 Chicago World's Fair – 1992 Authority. [Stationery].

Address and telephone number printed at the bottom of each piece of stationery: "One First National Plaza, Chicago, Illinois 60603 : 312/444 1992."
Letter paper and No. 10 Envelopes: 28x21½. Two letterheads, both with blue, white, and gray logo: 1) "Chicago 92 : Age of Discovery." Full list of directors down left margin. Same return address and logo on the matching envelope, but printed in b/w.

2) "1992 World's Fair." No list of directors. Matching envelope in blue and gray. © (GLD)
Notepad: 21½x14. Same letterhead as #1 letter above (no directors) but printed in b/w. © (GLD)
Bookmark: 27x7. Same logo and colors as #1 letter (no directors). © (GLD)

2464.2 Chicago World's Fair – 1992 Authority. Environmental Science and Engineering, Inc. *Interim report on environmental mitigation measures and significant cost considerations.* N.p.: Prepared for 1992 World's Fair Authority, June 1985.

28x21½. 1 *l*, ii, 57 p. Glossy wraps, navy print and globe overlay. Bibliography. © (IHi)

2465.1 Longworth, R.C. "A Postmortem on the Fair." *Chicago Tribune.* 27 June 1985, sec. 1: 11.

2466.   McClory. *The Fall of the Fair : Communities Struggle for Fairness*: (IHi,S)

2467.1 Nedza, Edward A. Papers, 1979–86. Illinois State Senator (Democrat from Chicago). His involvement with the 1992 Fair Authority. (IHi—Box 5)

2467.2 Tuerk, Fred James. Papers, 1971–1988. Republican representative from Peoria, IL. Includes his involvement with the 1992 Fair Authority. (IHi—Box 2)

MASTER INDEX

Titles and authors are intermixed and arranged alphabetically. There are at least two index entries for those books that have both title and author. Shortened titles end in ellipses but include at least the first unique word. Official authors: "WCA" (World's Congress Auxiliary), "WCC" (World's Columbian Commission), and "WCE" (World's Columbian Exposition) are given where this information is deemed helpful—as are country names and state abbreviations.

Titles which begin with English or foreign definite articles are alphabetized by the word following this initial article; e.g., English "A, An, The"; French "L', La, Le, Les"; German "Die, Der, Das, Ein"; and Spanish "El, La." In this index accents over letters have no effect alphabetically.

Hyphenated words are alphabetized as though the hyphen is not present and the words are separate. Numbers in titles are entered as though the number is written out (e.g., 1893 is indexed under eighteen). Titles beginning with initials (*A.E. Cannon*) or letters (*ALA*) are found before words beginning with the first letter (*Aborigine*). Abbreviations "Dr.," "Mr.," "Mrs.," and "St." are alphabetized in the order of the printed letters.

Because of their frequent occurrence at head of title, the words "World's Columbian Exposition" or their foreign equivalents, dates "1492"and "1893," and "World's Congress Auxiliary" boilerplate information are not always treated as beginning the title, especially if the lettering is small compared to other parts of the title. If a title begins with one of these antecedents, try these words in the index first; if you don't find the item, go to phrases that follow these or to the author's name.

The format for Chapter 15, Unpublished Unique Works, has been simplified: the source locator follows the citation number.